GLEIM® | Aviation

2019 EDITION

FUNDAMENTALS OF INSTRUCTING

FAA Knowledge Test Prep

for the FAA Computer-Based Pilot Knowledge Test

by
Irvin N. Gleim, Ph.D., CFII, and Garrett W. Gleim, CFII

Gleim Publications, Inc.
PO Box 12848 · University Station
Gainesville, Florida 32604
(352) 375-0772
(800) 87-GLEIM or (800) 874-5346
Website: www.GleimAviation.com
Email: admin@gleim.com

For updates to the first printing of the 2019 edition of
Fundamentals of Instructing
FAA Knowledge Test Prep

Go To: www.GleimAviation.com/updates

Or: Email update@gleim.com with **FOI 2019-1** in the subject line. You will receive our current update as a reply.

Updates are available until the next edition is published.

ISSN 1553-6890
ISBN 978-1-61854-188-8

First Printing: June 2018

YOU CAN HELP

This 2019 edition is designed specifically for pilots who aspire to obtain the flight instructor certificate and/or ground instructor certificate. Please send any corrections and suggestions for subsequent editions to us via the feedback links within the online components or using the form at www.GleimAviation.com/questions.

A companion volume, ***Flight/Ground Instructor FAA Knowledge Test Prep***, is available, as is ***Flight Instructor Flight Maneuvers and Practical Test Prep***, which focuses on the FAA practical test, just as this book focuses on the FAA knowledge test. Save time, money, and frustration--order online at www.GleimAviation.com today! Please bring these books to the attention of flight instructors, fixed-base operators, and others with a potential interest in acquiring their flight instructor certificates. Wide distribution of these books and increased interest in flying depend on your assistance and good word. Thank you.

Environmental Statement -- This book is printed on recyclable, environmentally friendly groundwood paper, sourced from certified sustainable forests and produced either TCF (totally chlorine-free) or ECF (elementally chlorine-free).

Our answers have been carefully researched and reviewed. Inevitably, there will be differences with competitors' books and even the FAA. If necessary, we will develop an UPDATE for ***Fundamentals of Instructing FAA Knowledge Test Prep***. Visit our website or email update@gleim.com for the latest updates. Updates for this 2019 edition will be available until the next edition is published. To continue providing our customers with first-rate service, we request that technical questions about our materials be sent to us via the feedback links within the online components. We will give each question thorough consideration and a prompt response. Questions concerning orders, prices, shipments, or payments will be handled via telephone by our competent and courteous customer service staff.

ABOUT THE AUTHORS

Irvin N. Gleim earned his private pilot certificate in 1965 from the Institute of Aviation at the University of Illinois, where he subsequently received his Ph.D. He is a commercial pilot and flight instructor (instrument) with multi-engine and seaplane ratings and is a member of the Aircraft Owners and Pilots Association, American Bonanza Society, Civil Air Patrol, Experimental Aircraft Association, National Association of Flight Instructors, and Seaplane Pilots Association. He is the author of flight maneuvers and practical test prep books for the remote, sport, private, instrument, commercial, and flight instructor certificates/ratings and the author of study guides for the remote, sport, private/recreational, instrument, commercial, flight/ground instructor, fundamentals of instructing, airline transport pilot, and flight engineer FAA knowledge tests. Three additional pilot training books are *Pilot Handbook*, *Aviation Weather and Weather Services*, and *FAR/AIM*.

Dr. Gleim has also written articles for professional accounting and business law journals and is the author of widely used review manuals for the CIA (Certified Internal Auditor) exam, the CMA (Certified Management Accountant) exam, the CPA (Certified Public Accountant) exam, and the EA (IRS Enrolled Agent) exam. He is Professor Emeritus, Fisher School of Accounting, University of Florida, and is a CFM, CIA, CMA, and CPA.

Garrett W. Gleim earned his private pilot certificate in 1997 in a Piper Super Cub. He is a commercial pilot (single- and multi-engine), ground instructor (advanced and instrument), and flight instructor (instrument and multi-engine), and he is a member of the Aircraft Owners and Pilots Association and the National Association of Flight Instructors. He is the author of study guides for the remote, sport, private/recreational, instrument, commercial, flight/ground instructor, fundamentals of instructing, and airline transport pilot FAA knowledge tests. He received a Bachelor of Science in Economics from The Wharton School, University of Pennsylvania. Mr. Gleim is also a CPA (not in public practice).

REVIEWERS AND CONTRIBUTORS

Paul Duty, CFII, MEI, AGI, Remote Pilot, is a graduate of Embry-Riddle Aeronautical University with a Master of Business Administration-Aviation degree. He is our aviation product manager and the Gleim Part 141 Chief Ground Instructor. Mr. Duty is an active flight instructor, commercial pilot, and remote pilot. He researched questions, wrote and edited answer explanations, and incorporated revisions into the text.

Bill Nesbitt, CFII, AGI, IGI, is a former USAF pilot and graduate of Emory University and the University of Florida. He holds type ratings in the Boeing 707 and 720. As an aviation editor, he researched questions, wrote and edited answer explanations, and incorporated revisions into the text.

Karl Winters, CFI, AGI, Remote Pilot, is a graduate of Purdue University and is one of our aviation editors. He researched questions, wrote and edited answer explanations, and incorporated revisions into the text.

The CFIs who have worked with us throughout the years to develop and improve our pilot training materials.

The many FAA employees who helped, in person or by telephone, primarily in Gainesville; Orlando; Oklahoma City; and Washington, DC.

The many pilots who have provided comments and suggestions about *Fundamentals of Instructing FAA Knowledge Test Prep* during the past several decades.

A PERSONAL THANKS

This manual would not have been possible without the extraordinary effort and dedication of Jacob Bennett, Julie Cutlip, Ethan Good, Blaine Hatton, Kelsey Hughes, Fernanda Martinez, Bree Rodriguez, Teresa Soard, Justin Stephenson, Joanne Strong, Elmer Tucker, and Candace Van Doren, who typed the entire manuscript and all revisions and drafted and laid out the diagrams, illustrations, and cover for this book.

The authors also appreciate the production and editorial assistance of Sirene Dagher, Jessica Hatker, Kristen Hennen, Belea Keeney, Katie Larson, Diana León, Bryce Owen, Jake Pettifor, Shane Rapp, Drew Sheppard, and Alyssa Thomas.

Finally, we appreciate the encouragement, support, and tolerance of our families throughout this project.

Returns of books purchased from bookstores and other resellers should be made to the respective bookstore or reseller. For more information regarding the Gleim Return Policy, please contact our offices at (800) 874-5346 or visit www.GleimAviation.com/returnpolicy.

TABLE OF CONTENTS

NOTE: The FAA does not release its complete database of test questions to the public. Instead, sample questions are released on the Airman Testing page of the FAA website on a quarterly basis. These questions are similar to the actual test questions, but they are not exact matches.

Gleim utilizes customer feedback and FAA publications to create additional sample questions that closely represent the topical coverage of each FAA knowledge test. In order to do well on the knowledge test, you must study the Gleim outlines in this book, answer all the questions under exam conditions (i.e., without looking at the answers first), and develop an understanding of the topics addressed. You should not simply memorize questions and answers. This will not prepare you for your FAA knowledge test, and it will not help you develop the knowledge you need to competently teach someone how to fly.

Always refer to the Gleim update service (www.GleimAviation.com/updates) to ensure you have the latest information that is available. If you see topics covered on your FAA knowledge test that are not contained in this book, please contact us at www.GleimAviation.com/questions to report your experience and help us fine-tune our test preparation materials.

Thank you!

PREFACE

This book has three purposes:

1. To provide you with the easiest and fastest means of passing the Fundamentals of Instructing (FOI) Knowledge Test
2. To help experienced and inexperienced aviation instructors improve instruction techniques
3. To assist flight and/or ground instructors in organizing and presenting aviation ground schools that prepare individuals to pass the FAA pilot knowledge tests

FOI Knowledge Test

Successful completion of the FOI knowledge test is required by the FAA for those seeking the flight instructor or ground instructor certificates. The introduction of this book (beginning on the next page) contains a discussion of the requirements to obtain the flight instructor and ground instructor certificates and a description of the FOI knowledge test, how to prepare for it and take it, and how to maximize your score with minimum effort. Study Units 1 through 6 contain outlines of what you need to know to answer the FAA knowledge test questions, as well as all of the previously released FAA test questions and our own similar questions, each accompanied by a comprehensive explanation.

NOTE: Appendix A contains a practice test, consisting of 50 questions from this book, that reflects the subject matter composition of the FAA knowledge test.

Improving Instruction Methods

The FAA has published *Aviation Instructor's Handbook* (FAA-H-8083-9A), which explains the basic principles and processes of teaching and learning. This is the subject matter of the FOI knowledge test. This material is more easily presented and studied in outline format, as it appears in Study Units 1 through 6 of this book. Both experienced and inexperienced aviation instructors will find the study of these outlines very useful in improving their instruction methods.

Appendix B of this book (162 pages in length) is a reprint of the main text of *Aviation Instructor's Handbook*, which specifically concerns flight instruction. It is useful reading and a valuable periodic review for CFIs; thus, we include it in this Gleim book. We do not reproduce the six appendixes found in the FAA text because they are beyond the scope of preparing for the knowledge test. However, they are important and reference practical content that you will need to be familiar with as you begin working as a CFI. You should certainly reference the appendixes and learn from them. Our reproduction of the FAA text consists of nine chapters:

1. Human Behavior
2. The Learning Process
3. Effective Communication
4. The Teaching Process
5. Assessment
6. Planning Instructional Activity
7. Instructor Responsibilities and Professionalism
8. Techniques of Flight Instruction
9. Risk Management

Ground School Course Suggestions

Many aviation instructors would like to increase the general public's interest in learning to fly. These instructors also enjoy teaching. Appendix C of this book consists of suggestions on how to find (or become) a sponsor for a "ground school." It also contains suggestions on course organization, lecture outlines, and class presentation.

Enjoy Flying Safely!
Irvin N. Gleim
Garrett W. Gleim
June 2018

INTRODUCTION: THE FAA PILOT KNOWLEDGE TEST

This introduction explains how to obtain a flight instructor certificate, including a sport pilot rating. The ground instructor certificate is also addressed. It explains the content and procedures of the relevant Federal Aviation Administration (FAA) knowledge tests, including how to take a test at a computer testing center. The remainder of this introduction discusses and illustrates the Gleim **Online Ground School** and **FAA Test Prep Online**. Achieving an instructor certificate is fun. Begin today!

Fundamentals of Instructing FAA Knowledge Test Prep is one of four related books for obtaining your flight and/or ground instructor certificate. The other three books are

1. ***Flight/Ground Instructor FAA Knowledge Test Prep***
2. ***Flight Instructor Flight Maneuvers and Practical Test Prep***
3. ***Pilot Handbook***

Flight/Ground Instructor FAA Knowledge Test Prep prepares you to pass the FAA's flight and/or ground instructor knowledge test. If you are planning to obtain both the flight and ground instructor certificates, you only need to pass the Fundamentals of Instructing (FOI) test once.

Flight Instructor Flight Maneuvers and Practical Test Prep is a comprehensive, carefully organized presentation of everything you need to know to prepare for your flight training and for your flight instructor practical (flight) test. It integrates material from FAA publications and other sources.

Pilot Handbook is a complete pilot reference book that combines over 100 FAA books and documents, including *AIM*, Federal Aviation Regulations, ACs, and much more. Aerodynamics, airplane systems, airspace, and navigation are among the topics explained in ***Pilot Handbook***.

While the following books are not included in the list above, you may want to purchase them if you do not already have them:

FAR/AIM is an essential part of every instructor's library. The Gleim ***FAR/AIM*** is an easy-to-read reference book containing all of the Federal Aviation Regulations applicable to general aviation flying, plus the full text of the FAA's *Aeronautical Information Manual (AIM)*.

The Gleim ***Aviation Weather and Weather Services*** book combines all of the information from the FAA's *Aviation Weather* (AC 00-6), *Aviation Weather Services* (AC 00-45), and numerous FAA publications into one easy-to-understand reference book.

WHAT IS A FLIGHT INSTRUCTOR CERTIFICATE?

A flight instructor certificate is similar in appearance to your commercial pilot certificate and will allow you to give flight and ground instruction. The certificate is sent to you by the FAA upon satisfactory completion of your training program, two knowledge tests, and a practical test. It expires at the end of the 24th month after issue. A new certificate is sent to you by the FAA upon renewal. A sample flight instructor certificate is reproduced below.

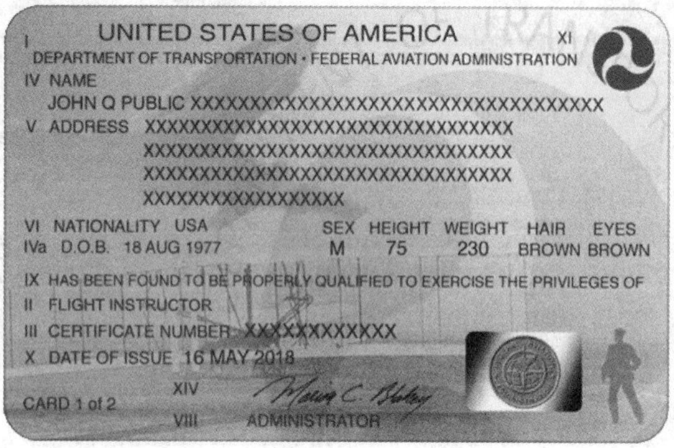

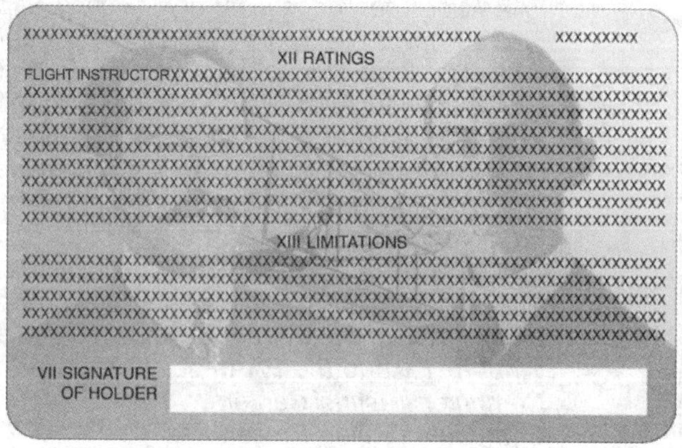

REQUIREMENTS TO OBTAIN A FLIGHT INSTRUCTOR CERTIFICATE

1. Be at least 18 years of age.
2. Be able to read, write, and understand English (certificates with operating limitations may be available for medically related deficiencies).
3. Hold a commercial or airline transport pilot (ATP) certificate with an aircraft rating appropriate to the flight instructor rating sought (e.g., airplane, glider).
   a. You must also hold an instrument rating to be a flight instructor in an airplane.
4. Study this book, ***Flight/Ground Instructor FAA Knowledge Test Prep***, ***Flight Instructor Flight Maneuvers and Practical Test Prep***, ***FAR/AIM***, ***Aviation Weather and Weather Services***, and ***Pilot Handbook*** or use the Gleim Online Ground School to learn
   a. Fundamentals of instructing
   b. All other subject areas in which ground training is required for recreational, private, and commercial pilot certificates
5. Pass both the FOI and the flight instructor knowledge tests with scores of 70% or better.
   a. All FAA knowledge tests are administered at FAA-designated computer testing centers.
      1) Page 11 contains additional details.
   b. The FOI and flight instructor tests consist of 50 and 100 multiple-choice questions, respectively, selected from the airplane-related questions in the FAA's flight and ground instructor knowledge test bank.
   c. Questions similar to those you will see on the knowledge test are reproduced in this book with complete explanations.
   d. You are not required to take the FOI knowledge test if you
      1) Hold an FAA flight or ground instructor certificate,
      2) Hold a current teacher's certificate authorizing you to teach at an educational level of the 7th grade or higher, or
      3) Are employed as a teacher at an accredited college or university.

6. Demonstrate flight proficiency (14 CFR 61.187).
   a. You must receive and log flight and ground training and obtain a logbook endorsement from an authorized instructor on the following areas of operations for an airplane category rating with a single-engine or multi-engine class rating:
      1) Fundamentals of instructing
      2) Technical subject areas
      3) Preflight preparation
      4) Preflight lesson on a maneuver to be performed in flight
      5) Preflight procedures
      6) Airport and seaplane base operations
      7) Takeoffs, landings, and go-arounds
      8) Fundamentals of flight
      9) Performance maneuvers
      10) Ground reference maneuvers
      11) Slow flight, stalls, and spins (single-engine only)
         a) Slow flight and stalls (multi-engine only)
      12) Basic instrument maneuvers
      13) Emergency operations
      14) Multi-engine operations (multi-engine only)
      15) Postflight procedures
   b. A CFI who provides training to an initial applicant for a flight instructor certificate must have held a flight instructor certificate for at least 24 months and have given at least 200 hr. of flight training as a CFI.
   c. You must also obtain a logbook endorsement by an appropriately certificated and rated flight instructor who has provided you with spin entry, spin, and spin recovery training in an airplane that is certificated for spins and who has found you instructionally competent and proficient in those training areas, i.e., so you can teach spin recovery.
7. Alternatively, enroll in an FAA-certificated pilot school that has an approved flight instructor certification course (airplane).
   a. These are known as Part 141 schools or Part 142 training centers because they are authorized by Part 141 or Part 142 of the Federal Aviation Regulations.
      1) All other regulations concerning the certification of pilots are found in Part 61 of the Federal Aviation Regulations.
   b. The Part 141 course must consist of at least 40 hr. of ground instruction and 25 hr. of flight instructor training.
8. Successfully complete a practical (flight) test, which will be given as a final exam by an FAA inspector or designated pilot examiner. The practical test will be conducted as specified in the FAA's Flight Instructor Practical Test Standards (FAA-S-8081-6).
   a. FAA inspectors are FAA employees and do not charge for their services.
   b. FAA-designated pilot examiners are proficient, experienced flight instructors and pilots who are authorized by the FAA to conduct flight tests. They do charge a fee.

GLEIM SUCCESS TIPS

The FAA's Flight Instructor Practical Test Standards are outlined and reprinted in the Gleim ***Flight/Ground Instructor Flight Maneuvers and Practical Test Prep*** book.

REQUIREMENTS TO OBTAIN A GROUND INSTRUCTOR CERTIFICATE

1. To be eligible for a ground instructor certificate, you must
   a. Be at least 18 years of age.
   b. Be able to read, write, and understand English (certificates with operating limitations may be available for medically related deficiencies).
   c. Exhibit practical and theoretical knowledge by passing the FOI and the appropriate ground instructor knowledge tests.
      1) Item 5.d. on page 2 discusses when the FOI knowledge test is not required.
2. Ground instructor certificates cover three levels of certification:
   a. Basic ground instructor (BGI) may provide
      1) Ground training in the aeronautical knowledge areas required for a sport, recreational, or private pilot certificate
      2) Ground training required for a sport, recreational, or private pilot flight review
      3) A recommendation for the sport, recreational, or private pilot knowledge test
   b. Advanced ground instructor (AGI) may provide
      1) Ground training in the aeronautical knowledge areas required for any certificate or rating (except for an instrument rating) issued under Part 61
      2) Ground training required for any flight review, but not for an instrument proficiency check (IPC)
      3) A recommendation for a knowledge test required for any certificate issued under Part 61 except for the instrument rating knowledge test
   c. Instrument ground instructor (IGI) may provide
      1) Ground training in the aeronautical knowledge areas required for an instrument rating to a pilot or instructor certificate
      2) Ground training required for an instrument proficiency check
      3) A recommendation for the instrument rating knowledge test for a pilot or instructor certificate

      NOTE: The Gleim ***Instrument Pilot FAA Knowledge Test Prep*** covers the IGI knowledge test, which consists of 50 questions with a 2.5 hr. time limit.
3. If you are not a CFI, the Federal Aviation Regulations require you to have a ground instructor certificate to teach ground school or to sign off applicants for the appropriate pilot knowledge test.

> Your BGI or AGI knowledge test may have a few non-airplane questions. We have excluded all non-airplane questions from this book. Take your best guess at these questions without worry. It is not worth the few points to study all of the extra questions unless you are going to teach subjects related to rotorcraft, gliders, or lighter-than-air aircraft. Recall that this book has its primary focus on Flight Instructor – Airplane, and that is why non-airplane questions are excluded.

REQUIREMENTS TO OBTAIN A FLIGHT INSTRUCTOR CERTIFICATE WITH A SPORT PILOT RATING

1. To obtain a flight instructor certificate with a sport pilot rating, you must pass both practical and knowledge tests.
   a. To take the knowledge tests for both the fundamentals of instructing and the aeronautical knowledge areas for a sport pilot certificate, you must receive a logbook endorsement from an authorized instructor who trained you or evaluated your home-study course on the materials. This certifies that you are prepared for the tests.
2. For your convenience, a standard authorization form for the flight instructor sport pilot rating knowledge test is reproduced on page 325. It can be easily completed, signed by a flight or ground instructor, torn out, and taken to the computer testing site.

FAA PILOT KNOWLEDGE TEST AND TESTING SUPPLEMENT

1. This book is designed to help you prepare for and pass the FAA FOI knowledge test for the flight and/or ground instructor certificate, which consists of 50 questions and has a time limit of 1.5 hours.
   a. The remainder of this introduction explains the FAA test procedures.
2. The FAA has one FOI figure contained in a book titled *Airman Knowledge Testing Supplement for Flight Instructor, Ground Instructor, and Sport Pilot Instructor*, which you will be given to use at the time of your test.
   a. For the purpose of test preparation, we have reproduced the figure on page 115 in this book.
3. In an effort to develop better questions, the FAA frequently **pretests** questions on knowledge tests by adding up to five "pretest" questions. The pretest questions will not be graded.
   a. You will NOT know which questions are real and which are pretest, so you must attempt to answer all questions correctly.
   b. When you notice a question NOT covered by Gleim, it might be a pretest question.
      1) We want to know about each pretest question you see.
      2) Please contact us at www.GleimAviation.com/questions or call 800-874-5346 with your recollection of any possible pretest questions so we may improve our efforts to prepare future instructors.

FAA'S KNOWLEDGE TESTS: CHEATING OR UNAUTHORIZED CONDUCT POLICY

The following is taken verbatim from an FAA knowledge test. It is reproduced here to remind all test takers about the FAA's policy against cheating and unauthorized conduct, a policy that Gleim consistently supports and upholds. Test takers must click "Yes" to proceed from this page into the actual knowledge test.

14 CFR part 61, section 61.37 Knowledge tests: Cheating or other unauthorized conduct

(a) An applicant for a knowledge test may not:
(1) Copy or intentionally remove any knowledge test;
(2) Give to another applicant or receive from another applicant any part or copy of a knowledge test;
(3) Give assistance on, or receive assistance on, a knowledge test during the period that test is being given;
(4) Take any part of a knowledge test on behalf of another person;
(5) Be represented by, or represent, another person for a knowledge test;
(6) Use any material or aid during the period that the test is being given, unless specifically authorized to do so by the Administrator; and
(7) Intentionally cause, assist, or participate in any act prohibited by this paragraph.

(b) An applicant who the Administrator finds has committed an act prohibited by paragraph (a) of this section is prohibited, for 1 year after the date of committing that act, from:
(1) Applying for any certificate, rating, or authorization issued under this chapter; and
(2) Applying for and taking any test under this chapter.

(c) Any certificate or rating held by an applicant may be suspended or revoked if the Administrator finds that person has committed an act prohibited by paragraph (a) of this section.

FAA PILOT KNOWLEDGE TEST QUESTION BANK

In an effort to keep applicants from simply memorizing test questions, the FAA does not currently disclose all the questions you might see on your FAA knowledge test. We encourage you to take the time to fully learn and understand the concepts explained in the knowledge transfer outlines contained in this book. **Using this book or other Gleim test preparation material to merely memorize the questions and answers is unwise and unproductive, and it will not ensure your success on your FAA knowledge test.** Memorization also greatly reduces the amount of information you will actually learn during your study.

The questions and answers provided in this book include all previously released FAA questions in addition to questions developed from current FAA reference materials that closely approximate the types of questions you should see on your knowledge test. We are confident that by studying our knowledge transfer outlines, answering our questions under exam conditions, and not relying on rote memorization, you will be able to successfully pass your FAA knowledge test and begin learning to become a safe and competent instructor.

FAA QUESTIONS WITH TYPOGRAPHICAL ERRORS

Occasionally, FAA test questions contain typographical errors such that there is no correct answer. The FAA test development process involves many steps and people and, as you would expect, glitches occur in the system that are beyond the control of any one person. We indicate "best" rather than correct answers for some questions. Use these best answers for the indicated questions.

Note that the FAA corrects (rewrites) defective questions as they are discovered; these changes are explained in our updates (discussed on page ii). However, problems due to faulty or out-of-date figures printed in the FAA Airman Knowledge Testing Supplements are expensive to correct. Thus, it is important to carefully study questions that are noted to have a best answer in this book. Even though the best answer may not be completely correct, you should select it when taking your test.

REORGANIZATION OF FAA QUESTIONS

1. Questions previously released by the FAA were **not** grouped together by topic; i.e., they appeared to be presented randomly.
   a. We have reorganized and renumbered the questions into study units and subunits.
2. Pages 319 through 322 contain a list of all the questions in FAA learning statement code order, with cross-references to the study units and question numbers in this book.
   a. For example, question 3-18 is assigned the code PLT230, which means it is found in Study Unit 3 as question 18 in this book and is covered under the FAA learning statement, "Recall FOI techniques - responsibilities."

HOW TO PREPARE FOR THE FAA PILOT KNOWLEDGE TEST

1. Begin by carefully reading the rest of this introduction. You need to have a complete understanding of the examination process prior to initiating your study. This knowledge will make your studying more efficient.
2. After you have spent an hour analyzing this introduction, set up a study schedule, including a target date for taking your knowledge test.
   a. Do not let the study process drag on and become discouraging; i.e., the quicker, the better.
   b. Consider enrolling in an organized ground school course, like the Gleim **Online Ground School**, or one held at your local FBO, community college, etc.
   c. Determine where and when you are going to take your knowledge test.

3. Work through Study Units 1 through 6.
   a. All previously released questions in the FAA's flight and ground instructor knowledge test question bank that are applicable to fundamentals of instructing have been grouped into the following six categories, which are the titles of Study Units 1 through 6:

      Study Unit 1 -- The Learning Process
      Study Unit 2 -- Barriers to Learning
      Study Unit 3 -- Factors Affecting Learning
      Study Unit 4 -- Teaching Methods
      Study Unit 5 -- Planning Instructional Activity
      Study Unit 6 -- Critique and Evaluation

   b. Within each of the study units listed, questions relating to the same subtopic are grouped together to facilitate your study program. Each subtopic is called a subunit.
   c. To the right of each question, we present
      1) The correct answer
      2) The appropriate source document for the answer explanation (e.g., *FAA-H-8083-9A Chap 1* means *Aviation Instructor's Handbook*, Chapter 1)
      3) A comprehensive answer explanation, including
         a) A discussion of the correct answer or concept
         b) An explanation of why the other two answer choices are incorrect
4. Each study unit begins with a list of its subunit titles. The number after each title is the number of questions that cover the information in that subunit. The two numbers following the number of questions are the page numbers on which the outline and the questions for that particular subunit begin, respectively.
5. Begin by studying the outlines slowly and carefully. The outlines in this part of the book are very brief and have only one purpose: to help you pass the FAA knowledge test.
   a. **CAUTION:** The **sole purpose** of this book is to expedite your passing the FAA knowledge test for the fundamentals of instructing certificate. Accordingly, all extraneous material (i.e., topics or regulations not directly tested on the FAA knowledge test) is omitted, even though much more knowledge is necessary to be an instructor. This additional material is presented in three related Gleim books: ***Flight/Ground Instructor FAA Knowledge Test Prep***, ***Flight Instructor Flight Maneuvers and Practical Test Prep***, and ***Pilot Handbook***.
6. Next, answer the questions under exam conditions. Cover the answer explanations on the right side of each page with a piece of paper while you answer the questions.

> GLEIM SUCCESS TIPS®
>
> Remember, it is very important to the learning (and understanding) process that you honestly commit yourself to an answer. If you are wrong, your memory will be reinforced by having discovered your error. Therefore, it is crucial to cover up the answer and make an honest attempt to answer the question before reading the answer.

   a. Study the answer explanation for each question that you answer incorrectly, do not understand, or have difficulty with.
   b. Use our **Online Ground School** or **FAA Test Prep Online** to ensure that you do not refer to answers before committing to one AND to simulate actual computer testing center exam conditions.
7. Note that this test book contains questions grouped by topic. Thus, some questions may appear repetitive, while others may be duplicates or near-duplicates. Accordingly, do not work question after question (i.e., waste time and effort) if you are already conversant with a topic and the type of questions asked.

8. As you move through study units, you may need further explanation or clarification of certain topics. You may wish to obtain and use the following Gleim books described on page 1:
   a. ***Flight Instructor Flight Maneuvers and Practical Test Prep***
   b. ***Pilot Handbook***
   c. ***Aviation Weather and Weather Services***
9. Keep track of your work. As you complete a subunit, grade yourself with an A, B, C, or ? (use a ? if you need help on the subject) next to the subunit title at the front of the respective study unit.
   a. The A, B, C, or ? is your self-evaluation of your comprehension of the material in that subunit and your ability to answer the questions.
      A means a good understanding.
      B means a fair understanding.
      C means a shaky understanding.
      ? means to ask your CFI or others about the material and/or questions, and read the pertinent sections in ***Flight Instructor Flight Maneuvers and Practical Test Prep*** and/or ***Pilot Handbook***.
   b. This procedure will provide you with the ability to quickly see (by looking at the first page of each study unit) how much studying you have done (and how much remains) and how well you have done.
   c. This procedure will also facilitate review. You can spend more time on the subunits that were more difficult for you.
   d. **FAA Test Prep Online** provides you with your historical performance data.

Follow the suggestions given throughout this introduction and you will have no trouble passing the FAA knowledge test the first time you take it.

With this overview of exam requirements, you are ready to begin the easy-to-study outlines and rearranged questions with answers to build your knowledge and confidence and PASS THE FAA's FUNDAMENTALS OF INSTRUCTING KNOWLEDGE TEST.

The feedback we receive from users indicates that our materials reduce anxiety, improve FAA test scores, and build knowledge. Studying for each test becomes a useful step toward advanced certificates and ratings.

MULTIPLE-CHOICE QUESTION-ANSWERING TECHNIQUE

Because the FOI knowledge test has a set number of questions (50) and a set time limit (1.5 hours), you can plan your test-taking session to ensure that you leave yourself enough time to answer each question with relative certainty. The following steps will help you move through the knowledge test efficiently and produce better test results.

1. **Budget your time.** We make this point with emphasis. Just as you would fill up your gas tank prior to reaching empty, so too should you finish your exam before time expires.
   a. If you utilize the entire time limit for the test, you will have about 1.8 minutes per question.
   b. If you are adequately prepared for the test, you should finish it well within the time limit.
      1) Use any extra time you have to review questions that you are not sure about and similar questions in your exam that may help you answer other questions.
   c. Time yourself when completing study sessions in this book and/or review your time investment reports from the Gleim **FAA Test Prep Online** to track your progress and adherence to the time limit and your own personal time allocation budget.

2. **Answer the questions in consecutive order.**
    a. Do **not** agonize over any one item. Stay within your time budget.
    b. Mark any questions you are unsure of and return to them later as time allows.
        1) Once you initiate test grading, you will no longer be able to review/change any answers.
    c. Never leave a multiple-choice question unanswered. Make your best educated guess in the time allowed. Remember, your score is based on the number of correct responses. You will not be penalized for guessing incorrectly.
3. **For each multiple-choice question,**
    a. **Try to ignore the answer choices.** Do not allow the answer choices to affect your reading of the question.
        1) If three answer choices are presented, two of them are incorrect. These choices are called **distractors** for good reason. Often, distractors are written to appear correct at first glance until further analysis.
        2) In computational items, the distractors are carefully calculated such that they are the result of making common mistakes. Be careful, and double-check your computations if time permits.
    b. **Read the question carefully** to determine the precise requirement.
        1) Focusing on what is required enables you to ignore extraneous information, to focus on the relevant facts, and to proceed directly to determining the correct answer.
            a) Be especially careful to note when the requirement is an **exception**; e.g., "Which of the following is **not** a type of hypoxia?"
    c. **Determine the correct answer** before looking at the answer choices.
    d. **Read the answer choices carefully.**
        1) Even if the first answer appears to be the correct choice, do **not** skip the remaining answer choices. Questions often require the "best" answer of the choices provided. Thus, each choice requires your consideration.
        2) Treat each answer choice as a true/false question as you analyze it.
    e. **Click on the best answer.**
        1) You have a 33% chance of answering the question correctly by blindly guessing; improve your odds with educated guessing.
        2) For many multiple-choice questions, at least one answer choice can be eliminated with minimal effort, thereby increasing your educated guess to a 50-50 proposition.
4. After you have been through all the questions in the test, consult the question status list to determine which questions are unanswered and which are marked for review.
    a. Go back to the marked questions and finalize your answer choices.
    b. Verify that all questions have been answered.

EDUCATED GUESSING

> GLEIM SUCCESS TIPS
>
> The FAA knowledge test sometimes includes questions that are poorly worded or confusing. Expect the unexpected and move forward. Do not let confusing questions affect your concentration or take up too much time; make your best guess and move on.

1. If you don't know the answer, make an educated guess as follows:
   a. Rule out answers that you think are incorrect.
   b. Speculate on what the FAA is looking for and/or the rationale behind the question.
   c. Select the best answer or guess between equally appealing answers. Your first guess is usually the most intuitive. If you cannot make an educated guess, re-read the stem and each answer choice and pick the most intuitive answer. It's just a guess!
2. Avoid lingering on any question for too long. Remember your time budget and the overall test time limit.

SIMULATED FAA PRACTICE TEST

Appendix A, "Fundamentals of Instructing Practice Test," beginning on page 141, allows you to practice taking the FAA knowledge test without the answers next to the questions. This test has 50 questions randomly selected from the questions in our fundamentals of instructing knowledge test bank. Topical coverage in the practice test is similar to that of the FAA knowledge test.

It is very important that you answer all 50 questions in one sitting. You should not consult the answers, especially when being referred to figures (charts, tables, etc.) throughout this book where the questions are answered and explained. Analyze your performance based on the answer key that follows the practice test.

It is even better to practice with Test Sessions in the Gleim **FAA Test Prep Online**. These simulate actual computer testing conditions, including the screen layouts, instructions, etc., for PSI.

More information on the Gleim **FAA Test Prep Online** is available on pages 15 and 16.

AUTHORIZATION TO TAKE THE FAA PILOT KNOWLEDGE TEST

The FAA does not require an instructor endorsement for your initial attempt of the FOI or any other instructor knowledge test, except for sport pilot instructor applicants. If you fail the knowledge test, you will need an instructor endorsement before you can retake the exam.

WHEN TO TAKE THE FAA PILOT KNOWLEDGE TEST

1. You must be at least 16 years of age to take the FOI knowledge test.
2. Take the FAA knowledge test within 30 days of beginning your study.
   a. Get the knowledge test behind you.
3. You must obtain your flight or ground instructor certificate within 24 months.
   a. Otherwise, you will have to retake your knowledge test.

WHAT TO TAKE TO THE FAA PILOT KNOWLEDGE TEST

1. Picture identification of yourself (e.g., valid driver's license)
2. Proof of age

COMPUTER TESTING CENTERS

The FAA has contracted with a computer testing service (PSI) to administer FAA knowledge tests. PSI has testing centers throughout the country. To register for the knowledge test, call (800) 947-4228. More information can be found at www.GleimAviation.com/testingcenters.

COMPUTER TESTING PROCEDURES

When you arrive at the testing center, you will be required to provide positive proof of identification and documentary evidence of your age. The identification must include your photograph, signature, and actual residential address if different from the mailing address. This information may be presented in more than one form of identification. Next, you will sign in on the testing center's daily log. Your signature on the logsheet certifies that, if this is a retest, you meet the applicable requirements (discussed in "Failure on the FAA Pilot Knowledge Test" on page 13) and that you have not passed this test in the past 2 years.

Next, you will be taken into the testing room and seated at a computer terminal. A person from the testing center will assist you in logging onto the system, and you will be asked to confirm your personal data (e.g., name, Social Security number, etc.). Then you will be given an online introduction to the computer testing system, and you will take a sample test. If you have used our **FAA Test Prep Online**, you will be conversant with the computer testing methodology and environment and will breeze through the sample test. When you have completed your test, an Airman Knowledge Test Report will be printed out, validated (usually with an embossed seal), and given to you by a person from the testing center. Before you leave, you will be required to sign out on the testing center's daily log.

YOUR FAA PILOT KNOWLEDGE TEST REPORT

1. You will receive your FAA Pilot Knowledge Test Report upon completion of the test. An example test report is reproduced on the next page.
   a. Note that you will receive only one grade as illustrated.
   b. The expiration date is the date by which you must take your FAA practical test.
   c. The report lists the FAA learning statement codes of the questions you missed so you can review the topics you missed prior to your practical test.
2. Use the FAA Listing of Learning Statement Codes listed below to determine which topics you had difficulty with.

PLT022 Define Aeronautical Decision Making (ADM)
PLT103 Recall Aeronautical Decision Making (ADM) - hazardous attitudes
PLT204 Recall effective communication - basic elements
PLT211 Recall evaluation testing characteristics
PLT227 Recall FOI techniques - integrated flight instruction
PLT228 Recall FOI techniques - lesson plans
PLT229 Recall FOI techniques - professionalism
PLT230 Recall FOI techniques - responsibilities
PLT231 Recall FOI techniques / human behavior - anxiety / fear / stress
PLT232 Recall FOI techniques / human behavior - dangerous tendencies
PLT233 Recall FOI techniques / human behavior - defense mechanisms
PLT270 Recall human behavior - social / self-fulfillment / physical
PLT271 Recall human factors (ADM) - judgment
PLT272 Recall human factors - stress management
PLT295 Recall instructor techniques - obstacles / planning / activities / outcome
PLT306 Recall learning process - levels of learning / transfer of learning / incidental learning
PLT307 Recall learning process - memory / fact / recall
PLT308 Recall learning process - laws of learning elements
PLT481 Recall student evaluation - learning process
PLT482 Recall student evaluation - written tests / oral quiz / critiques
PLT487 Recall teaching methods - demonstration / performance
PLT488 Recall teaching methods - group / guided discussion / lecture
PLT489 Recall teaching methods - known to unknown
PLT490 Recall teaching methods - motivation / student feelings of insecurity
PLT491 Recall teaching methods - organizing material / course of training
PLT504 Recall use of training aids - types / function / purpose
PLT505 Recall use of training aids - usefulness / simplicity / compatibility

   a. Look them over and review them with your CFI so (s)he can certify that (s)he reviewed the deficient areas and found you competent in them when you take your practical test. Have your CFI sign off your deficiencies on the FAA Pilot Knowledge Test Report.
3. Keep your FAA Pilot Knowledge Test Report in a safe place because you must submit it to the FAA evaluator when you take your practical test.

APPLYING FOR YOUR GROUND INSTRUCTOR CERTIFICATE

Flight instructor applicants will take their FAA Pilot Knowledge Test Reports to their FAA practical tests. A ground instructor applicant (BGI, AGI, or IGI) does not, however, have to take an FAA practical test.

You must take your FAA Pilot Knowledge Test Report and a completed Airman Certificate and/or Rating Application (FAA Form 8710-1) to your local Flight Standards office where you will be issued an appropriate temporary ground instructor certificate. An FAA-designated examiner cannot issue a ground instructor certificate. Also, on FAA Form 8710-1, the Instructor's Recommendation block does not require an instructor's signature.

Your permanent ground instructor certificate will be mailed to you from the FAA in Oklahoma City.

Computer Test Report

U.S. DEPARTMENT OF TRANSPORTATION
Federal Aviation Administration
Airman Knowledge Test Report

NAME:

APPLICANT ID: EXAM ID:

EXAM: Fundamentals of Instructing (FOI)

EXAM DATE: 10/08/2018 EXAM SITE:

SCORE: 96 GRADE: PASS TAKE: 1

Learning statement codes listed below represent incorrectly answered questions. Learning statement codes and their associated statements can be found at **www.faa.gov/training_testing/testing/airmen**.

Reference material associated with the learning statement codes can be found in the appropriate knowledge test guide at **www.faa.gov/training_testing/testing/airmen/test_guides**.

A single code may represent more than one incorrect response.

PLT229 PLT306

EXPIRATION DATE: 10/31/2020 CTD's Embossed Seal

DO NOT LOSE THIS REPORT

AUTHORIZED INSTRUCTOR'S STATEMENT: (If applicable)

On ____________ (date) I gave the above named applicant ___ hours of additional instruction, covering each subject area shown to be deficient, and consider the applicant competent to pass the test.

Name ____________________ Initial____ Cert. No.________ Type______
(Print clearly)

Signature ______________________________________

FRAUDULENT ALTERATION OF THIS FORM BY ANY PERSON IS A BASIS FOR SUSPENSION OR REVOCATION OF ANY CERTIFICATES OR RATINGS HELD BY THAT PERSON. THIS INFORMATION IS PROTECTED BY THE PRIVACY ACT. FOR OFFICIAL USE ONLY.

FAILURE ON THE FAA PILOT KNOWLEDGE TEST

1. If you fail (score less than 70%) the knowledge test (which is virtually impossible if you follow the Gleim system), you may retake it after your instructor endorses the bottom of your FAA Pilot Knowledge Test Report certifying that you have received the necessary ground training to retake the test.
2. Upon retaking the test, you will find that the procedure is the same except that you must also submit your FAA Pilot Knowledge Test Report indicating the previous failure to the computer testing center.

3. Note that the pass rate on the FOI knowledge test is about 95%; i.e., fewer than 1 out of 10 fail the test initially. Reasons for failure include
   a. Failure to study the material tested and mere memorization of correct answers. (Relevant study material is contained in the outlines at the beginning of Study Units 1 through 6 of this book.)
   b. Failure to practice working through the questions under test conditions. (All of the previously released FAA questions appear in Study Units 1 through 6 of this book.)
   c. Poor examination technique, such as misreading questions and not understanding the requirements.

GLEIM ONLINE GROUND SCHOOL

1. Gleim **Online Ground School (OGS)** course content is based on the Gleim Knowledge Test Prep books, **FAA Test Prep Online**, FAA publications, and Gleim reference books. The delivery system is modeled on the Gleim FAA-approved online **Flight Instructor Refresher Course**.
   a. Online Ground School courses are available for
      1) Sport Pilot
      2) Private Pilot
      3) Instrument Pilot
      4) Commercial Pilot
      5) Flight/Ground Instructor
      6) Fundamentals of Instructing
      7) Airline Transport Pilot
      8) Flight Engineer
      9) Canadian Certificate Conversion
   b. OGS courses are airplane-only and have lessons that correspond to the study units in the Gleim FAA Knowledge Test Prep books.
   c. Each course contains study outlines that automatically reference current FAA publications, the appropriate knowledge test questions, FAA figures, and Gleim answer explanations.
   d. OGS is always up to date.
   e. Users achieve very high knowledge test scores and a near-100% pass rate.
   f. **Gleim Online Ground School is the most flexible course available!** Access your OGS personal classroom from any computer with Internet access 24 hours a day, 7 days a week. Your virtual classroom is never closed!
   g. **Save time and study only the material you need to know!** Gleim **Online Ground School** Certificate Selection will provide you with a customized study plan. You save time because unnecessary questions will be automatically eliminated.
   h. **We are truly interactive. We help you focus on any weaker areas.** Answer explanations for wrong choices help you learn from your mistakes.

GLEIM FAA TEST PREP ONLINE

Computer testing is consistent with aviation's use of computers (e.g., flight simulators, computerized flight decks, etc.). All FAA knowledge tests are administered by computer.

Computer testing is natural after computer study and computer-assisted instruction is a very efficient and effective method of study. The Gleim **FAA Test Prep Online** is designed to prepare you for computer testing because our software simulates PSI. We make you comfortable with computer testing!

FAA Test Prep Online contains all of the questions in this book, context-sensitive outline material, and on-screen charts and figures. It allows you to choose either Study Mode or Test Mode.

In Study Mode, the software provides you with an explanation of each answer you choose (correct or incorrect). You design each Study Session:

- Topic(s) and/or FAA learning statement codes you wish to cover
- Number of questions
- Order of questions -- FAA, Gleim, or random
- Order of answers to each question -- Gleim or random
- Questions marked and/or missed from last session -- test, study, or both
- Questions marked and/or missed from all sessions -- test, study, or both
- Questions never seen, answered, or answered correctly

In Test Mode, the software emulates the operation of the FAA-approved PSI computer testing centers. When you finish your test, you can and should study the questions missed and access answer explanations. Thus, you have a complete understanding of how to take an FAA knowledge test and know exactly what to expect before you go to a computer testing center.

The Gleim **FAA Test Prep Online** is an all-in-one program designed to help anyone with a computer, Internet access, and an interest in flying pass the FAA knowledge tests.

Study Sessions and Test Sessions

Study Sessions give you immediate feedback on why your answer selection for a particular question is correct or incorrect and allow you to access the context-sensitive outline material that helps to explain concepts related to the question. Choose from several different question sources: all questions available for that library; questions from a certain topic (Gleim study units and subunits); questions that you missed or marked in the last sessions you created; questions that you have never seen, answered, or answered correctly; questions from certain FAA learning statement codes; etc. You can mix up the questions by selecting to randomize the question and/or answer order so that you do not memorize answer letters.

You may then grade your study sessions and track your study progress using the performance analysis charts and graphs. The Performance Analysis information helps you to focus on areas where you need the most improvement, saving you time in the overall study process. You may then want to go back and study questions that you missed in a previous session, or you may want to create a Study Session of questions that you marked in the previous session. All of these options are made easy with **FAA Test Prep Online**'s Study Sessions.

After studying the outlines and questions in a Study Session, you can further test your skills with a Test Session. These sessions allow you to answer questions under actual testing conditions. In a Test Session, you will not know which questions you have answered correctly until the session is graded.

Recommended Study Program

1. Start with Study Unit 1 and proceed through study units in chronological order. Follow the three-step process below.
   a. First, carefully study the Gleim Outline.
   b. Second, create a Study Session of all questions in the study unit. Answer and study all questions in the Study Session.
   c. Third, create a Test Session of all questions in the study unit. Answer all questions in the Test Session.
2. After each Study Session and Test Session, create a new Study Session from questions answered incorrectly. This is of critical importance to allow you to learn from your mistakes.

Practice Test

Take an exam in the actual testing environment of the PSI testing centers. **FAA Test Prep Online** simulates the testing formats of these testing centers, making it easy for you to study questions under actual exam conditions. After studying with **FAA Test Prep Online**, you will know exactly what to expect when you go in to take your pilot knowledge test.

On-Screen Charts and Figures

One of the most convenient features of **FAA Test Prep Online** is the easily accessible on-screen charts and figures. Several of the questions refer to drawings, maps, charts, and other pictures that provide information to help answer the question. In **FAA Test Prep Online**, you can pull up any of these figures with the click of a button. You can increase or decrease the size of the images, and you may also use our drawing feature to calculate the true course between two given points (required only on the private pilot knowledge test).

Free Updates and Technical Support

Gleim offers FREE technical support to all users of the current versions. Call (800) 874-5346, send an email to support@gleim.com, or fill out the technical support request form online (www.GleimAviation.com/contact). Additionally, Gleim **FAA Test Prep Online** is always up to date. The program is automatically updated when any changes are made, so you can be confident that Gleim will prepare you for your knowledge test. More information on our email update service for books is on page ii.

STUDY UNIT ONE
THE LEARNING PROCESS

(7 pages of outline)

1.1 CHARACTERISTICS OF LEARNING

1. Learning can be defined as a change in behavior as a result of experience.
   a. The behavior change can be physical and overt (a better glide path, for instance), or psychological and attitudinal (better motivation, more acute perceptions, insights).
2. The learning process may include any (or all) of the following elements: verbal, conceptual, perceptual, motor skills, emotional, and problem solving.
3. While learning the subject at hand, the student may be learning other useful things as well. This learning is called incidental and can have a significant impact on the student's total development.

1.2 THE PRINCIPLES OF LEARNING

1. Educational psychology professor Edward L. Thorndike has suggested several "principles of learning" that apply to the learning process. While these principles are not absolute, they do give important insight into effective teaching.
2. The **principle of readiness** states that ~~if a student is~~ ready to learn, and has a strong purpose, clear objective, and well-fixed reason for learning, (s)he will make more progress than if (s)he lacks motivation. Readiness implies single-mindedness.
3. The **principle of exercise** states that those things most often repeated are best remembered or performed.
   a. The basis of the principle is to provide opportunities for a student to practice and then direct this process towards a goal.
4. The **principle of effect** relates to the emotional reaction of the learner:
   a. Learning is strengthened when accompanied by a pleasant or satisfying feeling.
   b. Learning is weakened when associated with an unpleasant feeling.
5. The **principle of primacy** states that those things learned first often create a strong, almost unshakable impression.
   a. This principle means that bad habits learned early are hard to break. Instructors must thus insist on correct performance from the outset of maneuvers.
6. The **principle of intensity** states that a vivid, dramatic, or exciting experience teaches more than a routine or boring experience.
   a. The principle of intensity thus implies that a student will learn more from the real thing than from a substitute.
7. The **principle of recency** states that the things most recently learned are best remembered.
   a. Instructors recognize the principle of recency when they determine the sequence of lectures within a course of instruction.

1.3 PERCEPTION AND INSIGHT

1. Perceiving involves more than the reception of stimuli from the five senses. Perceptions result when the person gives meaning to sensations being experienced.
   a. Thus, perceptions are the basis of all learning.
2. It takes time and opportunity to perceive.
   a. A properly planned training syllabus allows sufficient time and opportunity for key perceptions to occur.
3. A person's basic need is to maintain, enhance, preserve, and perpetuate the organized self.
   a. Thus, all perceptions are affected by this basic need.
4. Self-concept, or self-image, has a great influence on the total perceptual process.
5. Fear or the element of threat narrows the student's perceptual field.
   a. The resulting anxiety may limit a person's ability to learn from perceptions.
6. Insight occurs when associated perceptions are grouped into meaningful wholes, i.e., when one "gets the whole picture."
   a. Evoking insights is the instructor's major responsibility.
   b. Instruction speeds the learning process by teaching the relationship of perceptions as they occur, thus promoting the development of insights by students.
   c. An instructor can help develop student insights by providing a secure and nonthreatening environment in which to learn.

1.4 MEMORY

1. Memory is an integral part of the learning process. It includes three parts: the sensory register, the short-term or working memory, and the long-term memory.
   a. The **sensory register** receives input from the environment and quickly processes it according to the individual's preconceived concept of what is important. This occurs on a subconscious level.
      1) **Precoding** is the selective process by which the sensory register recognizes certain stimuli and immediately transmits them to the working memory for action.
         a) Irrelevant stimuli are discarded by the sensory register.
   b. The **short-term memory** (or working memory) is the receptacle of the information deemed important by the sensory register.
      1) The information may temporarily remain in the short-term memory, or it may rapidly fade.
         a) Retention of information by the short-term memory is aided when the information is initially categorized into systematic chunks in a process known as **coding**.
         b) Retention is also aided by repetition or rehearsal of the information (rote learning).
      2) Information remains in the short-term memory for longer periods when it can be related to an individual's previous knowledge or experiences through a process known as recoding.
         a) **Recoding** may be described as a process of relating incoming information to concepts or knowledge already in memory.

b) Methods of recoding vary with the subject matter, but they typically involve some type of association, such as mnemonics.

i) Mnemonics include, but are not limited to, acronyms, acrostics, rhymes, and chaining.

ii) A mnemonic uses a pattern of letters, ideas, images, or associations to assist in remembering information.

iii) The use of associations such as rhymes and mnemonics is best suited to the short-term memory

c) Short-term memory is the part of the memory system where information is stored for roughly 30 seconds, after which it may rapidly fade or be consolidated into long-term memory, depending on the individual's priorities. Several common steps help retention in short-term memory. These include rehearsal or repetition of the information and sorting or categorization into systematic chunks.

i) The short-term memory is not only time limited; it also has limited capacity, usually about seven bits or chunks of information at a time. A seven-digit telephone number is an example.

d) The ability to retrieve knowledge or skills from memory is primarily related to two things: (1) how often that knowledge has been used in the past and (2) how recently the knowledge has been used.

i) These two factors are called frequency and recency of use. Frequency and recency can be present individually or in combination.

c. The **long-term memory** is where information is stored for future use.

1) For the stored information to be useful, some special effort must have been expended during the recoding process.

2) It should be noted that the long-term memory is a reconstruction, not a pure recall of information or events.

1.5 FORGETTING AND RETENTION

1. The following are three theories of forgetting:

a. The **theory of fading** states that a person forgets information that is not used for an extended period of time. Students are saddened by the small amount of actual data retained several years after graduation.

b. The **theory of interference** suggests that people forget something because a certain experience has overshadowed it or the learning of similar things has intervened. This theory might explain how the range of experiences after graduation from school causes a person to forget or lose knowledge. In other words, new events displace many things that had been learned. From experiments, at least two conclusions about interference may be drawn. First, similar material seems to interfere with memory more than dissimilar material; second, material not well learned suffers most from interference.

c. The **theory of repression or suppression** states that memories are pushed out of reach because the individual does not want to remember the feelings associated with them. Unpleasant or anxiety-producing material is forgotten by the individual.

1) **Repression** is an unconscious form of forgetting and is unintentional.

2) **Suppression** is conscious and intentional.

2. Responses that produce a pleasurable return are called praise.

a. Praise stimulates remembering because responses that give a pleasurable return tend to be repeated.

1.6 TRANSFER OF LEARNING

1. The student may be either aided or hindered by things learned previously. This process is called transfer of learning.
   a. Positive transfer occurs when the learning of one maneuver aids in learning another.
      1) EXAMPLE: Flying rectangular patterns to aid in flying traffic patterns.
   b. Negative transfer occurs when a performance of a maneuver interferes with the learning of another maneuver.
      1) EXAMPLE: Trying to steer a taxiing plane with the control yoke the way one drives a car.
      2) Negative transfer thus agrees with the interference theory of forgetting.
2. By making certain the student understands that what is learned can be applied to other situations, the instructor helps facilitate a positive transfer of learning.
   a. This is the basic reason for the building-block technique of instruction in which each simple task is performed acceptably and correctly before the next learning task is introduced.
   b. The introduction of instruction in more advanced and complex operations before the initial instruction has been mastered leads to the development of poor habit patterns in the elements of performance.

1.7 LEVELS OF LEARNING

1. Learning may be accomplished at any of four levels.
   a. The lowest level, **rote learning**, is the ability to repeat back what one has been taught without necessarily understanding or being able to apply what has been learned.
      1) EXAMPLE: Being able to cite the design maneuvering speed of an airplane.
      2) Many students use commercially-developed training material to memorize FAA testing concepts, which is another example of rote learning.
         a) While test preparation materials may be effective in preparing students for FAA tests, the danger is that students may learn to pass a given test but fail to learn other critical information essential to safe piloting and maintenance practices.
         b) FAA inspectors and designated examiners have found that student applicants often exhibit a lack of knowledge during oral questioning, even though many have easily passed the FAA knowledge test.
         c) Because test preparation materials emphasize rote learning, instructors should stress that these materials are not designed as stand-alone learning tools. They should be considered as a supplement to instructor-led training.
   b. At the **understanding** level, the student not only can repeat what has been taught but also comprehends the principles and theory behind the knowledge.
      1) EXAMPLE: Being able to explain how gross weight affects design maneuvering speed.
      2) Being able to explain (not demonstrate) is the understanding level.

c. At the **application** level, the student not only understands the theory but also can apply what has been learned and perform in accordance with that knowledge.

1) The student understands the procedure, has had the procedure demonstrated, and has practiced the procedure to a point that it can be performed with consistency.

2) This is the level of learning at which most instructors stop teaching.

d. At the **correlation** level, the student is able to associate various learned elements with other segments or blocks of learning or accomplishment.

1) EXAMPLE: Know what to do if, during the flight portion of the practical test, the examiner closes the throttle and announces "simulated engine failure."

1.8 DOMAINS OF LEARNING

1. In addition to the four basic levels of learning discussed in Subunit 1.7, learning can be categorized in other ways.

2. Three **domains of learning** have been identified based on what is learned:

   a. The **cognitive domain** deals with knowledge (e.g., facts, concepts, or relationships).

   b. The **affective domain** relates to attitudes, beliefs, and values.

   c. The **psychomotor domain** concerns physical skills. These skills involve physical movement, coordination, and the use of motor skills.

3. Each of the domains of learning has a hierarchy of educational objectives.

   a. A listing of the hierarchy of objectives is often referred to as a taxonomy.

      1) A **taxonomy of educational objectives** is a systematic classification scheme for sorting possible learning outcomes into the three domains of learning and ranking them in a developmental hierarchy from least complex to most complex.

         a) Each of the three domains of learning has several distinct learning outcomes. These outcomes are equivalent to the educational objective levels.

      2) The following are hierarchical taxonomies for the three domains of learning:

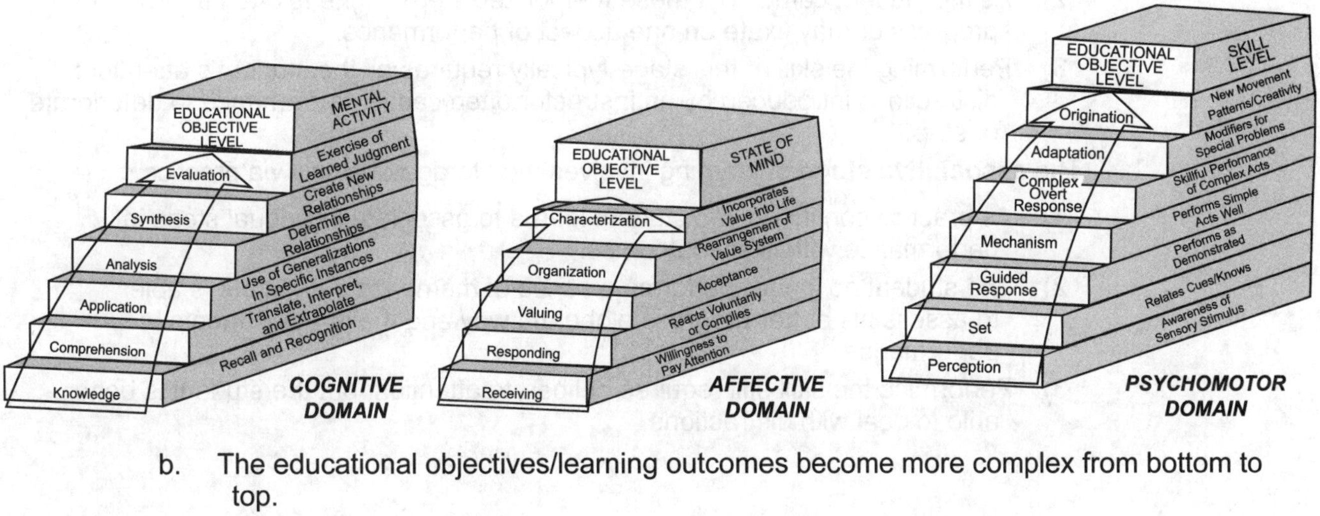

   b. The educational objectives/learning outcomes become more complex from bottom to top.

1.9 LEARNING SKILLS AND THE LEARNING CURVE

1. The best way to prepare a student to perform a task is to provide a clear, step-by-step example. Students need a clear picture of what they are to do and how they are to do it.
2. Learning typically follows a pattern that, if shown on a graph, would be called the learning curve. The first part of the curve indicates rapid early improvement. Then the curve levels off. This leveling-off of an individual's learning rate is called a **learning plateau**.
   a. Learning plateaus are a normal part of the learning process and tend to be temporary, but instructors and students should be prepared for them.
      1) Keep in mind that the apparent lack of increasing proficiency does not necessarily mean that learning has ceased.
   b. A learning plateau may signify any number of conditions. For example, the student may
      1) Have reached capability limits.
      2) Be consolidating levels of skill.
      3) Have lost interest.
      4) Need a more efficient method for increasing progress.
   c. Instructors themselves can bring on a learning plateau by overpractice.
      1) After repeating any task three or four times, give it a break to avoid causing a learning plateau.
   d. The instructor should prepare the student for the likelihood of learning plateaus during training to avert discouragement.
   e. Instructors can help students who fall into a learning plateau by moving them to a different place in the curriculum and giving the plateaued task a break.
3. The development of any skill acquisition has three characteristic stages: cognitive, associative, and automaticity. An instructor must learn to recognize each stage in student performance in order to assess student progress.
   a. The **cognitive stage** of learning has a basis in factual knowledge. Since the student has no prior knowledge of flying, the instructor first introduces him or her to a basic skill.
      1) The student memorizes the steps required to perform the skill.
      2) As the student carries out these memorized steps, (s)he is often unaware of progress or may fixate on one aspect of performance.
      3) Performing the skill at this stage typically requires all the student's attention; distractions introduced by an instructor often cause performance to deteriorate or stop.
   b. The **associative stage** of learning involves the storage of a skill via practice.
      1) As practice continues, the student learns to associate individual steps in performance with likely outcomes.
      2) The student no longer performs a series of memorized steps but is able to assess his or her progress along the way and make adjustments in performance.
      3) Performing the skill still requires deliberate attention, but the student is better able to deal with distractions.

c. The **automatic response stage** of learning produces automaticity, which is one of the by-products of continued practice.

 1) As procedures become automatic, less attention is required to carry them out, so it is possible to do other things simultaneously, or at least do other things more comfortably.
 2) By this stage, student performance of the skill is rapid and smooth. The student devotes much less deliberate attention to performance and may be able to carry on a conversation or perform other tasks while performing the skill.
 3) The student makes far fewer adjustments during his or her performance, and these adjustments tend to be small.
 4) The student may no longer be able to remember the individual steps in the procedure or explain how to perform the skill.
 5) An example of a student who has reached the automatic response stage is a student who can fly an ILS approach while simultaneously handling the radio communications.

4. There are three types of practice, each of which yields particular results in acquiring skills.

a. During **deliberate practice**, the student practices specific areas for improvement and receives specific feedback after practice.

 1) Studies of skill learning suggest a student achieves better results if distractions are avoided during deliberate practice.
 2) When feedback is needed to correct student performance, it should be brief and explicit.

b. **Blocked practice** is practicing the same drill until the movement becomes automatic.

 1) Doing the same task over and over leads to better short-term performance but poorer long-term learning.
 2) It tends to fool not only the student but also the instructor into thinking the skills have been well learned.

c. **Random practice** mixes the skills to be acquired throughout the practice session.

 1) This type of practice leads to better retention because, by performing a series of separate skills in a random order, the student starts to recognize the similarities and differences of each skill, which makes the practice more meaningful.
 2) The learner also is able to store the skill more effectively in the long-term memory.

QUESTIONS AND ANSWER EXPLANATIONS: All of the Fundamentals of Instructing knowledge test questions chosen by the FAA for release as well as additional questions selected by Gleim relating to the material in the previous outlines are provided on the following pages. These questions have been organized into the same subunits as the outlines. To the immediate right of each question are the correct answer and answer explanations. You should cover these answers and answer explanations while responding to the questions. Refer to the general discussion in the Introduction on how to take the FAA knowledge test.

Remember that the questions from the FAA knowledge test bank have been reordered by topic and organized into a meaningful sequence. Also, the first line of the answer explanation gives the citation of the authoritative source for the answer.

QUESTIONS

1.1 Characteristics of Learning

1. A change in behavior as a result of experience can be defined as

A. learning.

B. knowledge.

C. understanding.

Answer (A) is correct. *(FAA-H-8083-9A Chap 2)*
DISCUSSION: Learning can be defined as a change in behavior as a result of experience.
Answer (B) is incorrect. Knowledge is awareness as a result of experience but not necessarily a change in behavior. Answer (C) is incorrect. Understanding is only one of the four levels of learning.

2. The learning process may include some elements such as verbal, conceptual, and

A. habitual.

B. experiential.

C. problem solving.

Answer (C) is correct. *(FAA-H-8083-9A Chap 2)*
DISCUSSION: The learning process involves many elements. Verbal, conceptual, perceptual, motor skill, problem solving, and emotional elements may be used at the same time.
Answer (A) is incorrect. Habits are the customary or usual way of doing things and can be changed by the learning process. Answer (B) is incorrect. All learning is by experience, but it takes place in different forms in different people.

3. While learning the material being taught, students may be learning other things as well. This additional learning is called

A. residual.

B. conceptual.

C. incidental.

Answer (C) is correct. *(FAA-H-8083-9A Chap 2)*
DISCUSSION: While learning the subject at hand, students may be learning other things as well. They may be developing attitudes (good or bad) about aviation depending on what they experience. This learning is called incidental, but it may have a great impact on the total development of the student.
Answer (A) is incorrect. Residual is not a term used to define any type of learning. Answer (B) is incorrect. Conceptual learning is an element of learning the subject at hand, not other incidental things.

1.2 The Principles of Learning

4. Individuals make more progress learning if they have a clear objective. This is one feature of the principle of

A. primacy.

B. readiness.

C. willingness.

Answer (B) is correct. *(FAA-H-8083-9A Chap 2)*
DISCUSSION: One feature of the principle of readiness is that when a student has a strong purpose, a clear objective, and a well-fixed reason to learn something, (s)he will make more progress than if (s)he lacks motivation.
Answer (A) is incorrect. The principle of primacy states that first experiences create a strong, almost unshakable impression. Answer (C) is incorrect. There is no principle of willingness.

5. Things most often repeated are best remembered because of which principle of learning?

A. Principle of effect.

B. Principle of recency.

C. Principle of exercise.

Answer (C) is correct. *(FAA-H-8083-9A Chap 2)*
DISCUSSION: The principle of exercise states that those things most often repeated are best remembered. This is the basis of practice and drill.
Answer (A) is incorrect. The principle of effect relates to the learner's emotional reaction to the learning experience. Answer (B) is incorrect. The principle of recency states that things most recently learned are best remembered.

6. Providing opportunities for a student to practice and then directing this process towards a goal is the basis of the principle of

A. exercise.

B. learning.

C. readiness.

Answer (A) is correct. *(FAA-H-8083-9A Chap 2)*
DISCUSSION: The principle of exercise states that those things most often repeated are best remembered. You must provide opportunities for your student to practice and then direct this process towards a goal.
Answer (B) is incorrect. Learning is a change in behavior as a result of experience. The principle of exercise is part of the learning process. Answer (C) is incorrect. The principle of readiness states that individuals learn best when they are ready to learn, not practicing a task.

7. The principle that is based on the emotional reaction of the learner is the principle of

A. effect.

B. primacy.

C. intensity.

Answer (A) is correct. *(FAA-H-8083-9A Chap 2)*

DISCUSSION: The principle of effect is the one which directly relates to the learner's emotional reaction. Pleasant experiences strengthen the learning process, whereas unpleasant experiences tend to weaken it.

Answer (B) is incorrect. The principle of primacy states that a strong, almost unshakable impression is created by first experiences. Answer (C) is incorrect. The principle of intensity states that dramatic or exciting experiences teach more than routine experiences.

8. Which principle of learning often creates a strong impression?

A. Principle of primacy.

B. Principle of intensity.

C. Principle of readiness.

Answer (A) is correct. *(FAA-H-8083-9A Chap 2)*

DISCUSSION: Primacy, the state of being first, often creates a strong, almost unshakable impression. For the instructor, this means that what is taught must be right the first time. The first experience should be positive and functional and should lay the foundation for all that is to follow.

Answer (B) is incorrect. The principle of intensity means that a student will learn more from the real thing than from a substitute. Answer (C) is incorrect. The principle of readiness means that a student must be willing and eager to learn.

9. Which principle of learning implies that a student will learn more from the real thing than from a substitute?

A. Principle of effect.

B. Principle of primacy.

C. Principle of intensity.

Answer (C) is correct. *(FAA-H-8083-9A Chap 2)*

DISCUSSION: The principle of intensity states that a vivid, dramatic, or exciting learning experience teaches more than a routine or boring experience. Thus, the principle of intensity implies that a student will learn more from a real thing than from a substitute.

Answer (A) is incorrect. The principle of effect is based on the emotional reaction of the student. Thus, pleasant experiences strengthen the learning, while unpleasant experiences weaken the learning. These may be experienced by learning from either the real thing or a substitute. Answer (B) is incorrect. The principle of primacy states that a strong, almost unshakable impression is created by first experiences. These experiences may be from either a real thing or a substitute.

10. Which principle of learning often determines the sequence of lectures within a course of instruction?

A. Principle of primacy.

B. Principle of recency.

C. Principle of intensity.

Answer (B) is correct. *(FAA-H-8083-9A Chap 2)*

DISCUSSION: The principle of recency states that the things most recently learned are best remembered. The farther a student is removed time-wise from a new fact or understanding, the more difficult it is to remember it. The principle of recency often determines the sequence of lectures within a course of instruction.

Answer (A) is incorrect. The principle of primacy means to the instructor that what is taught must be right the first time. Answer (C) is incorrect. The principle of intensity means that a student will learn more from the real experience than a substitute.

1.3 Perception and Insight

11. What is the basis of all learning?

A. Perception.

B. Motivation.

C. Positive self-concept.

Answer (A) is correct. *(FAA-H-8083-9A Chap 2)*

DISCUSSION: Initially, all learning comes from perceptions that are directed to the brain by one or more of the five senses. Perceptions result when a person gives meaning to sensations.

Answer (B) is incorrect. Motivation is the dominant force that governs a student's progress and ability to learn, not the basis for all learning. Answer (C) is incorrect. Positive self-concept is a factor that affects an individual's ability to learn, not the basis of all learning.

12. Perceptions result when a person

A. gives meaning to sensations being experienced.

B. is able to discern items of useful information.

C. responds to visual cues first, then aural cues, and relates these cues to ones previously learned.

Answer (A) is correct. *(FAA-H-8083-9A Chap 2)*
DISCUSSION: Perceptions occur when a person gives meaning to sensations being experienced. This is the difference between just seeing something and understanding what is seen.
Answer (B) is incorrect. A person who is able to discern items of useful information has learned, not just perceived. Answer (C) is incorrect. It describes the rote level of learning, i.e., memorization without concern for meaning.

13. A basic need that affects all of a person's perceptions is the need to

A. maintain and enhance the organized self.

B. accomplish a higher level of satisfaction.

C. avoid areas that pose a threat to success.

Answer (A) is correct. *(FAA-H-8083-9A Chap 2)*
DISCUSSION: A person's basic need is to maintain and enhance the organized self. The self is a person's past, present, and future and is both physical and psychological. A person's most fundamental need is to preserve and perpetuate this self. Thus, all perceptions are affected by this need.
Answer (B) is incorrect. Accomplishing a higher level of satisfaction is a goal, not a basic need. Answer (C) is incorrect. Avoiding areas that are a threat to success is a defense mechanism, not a basic need that affects perceptions.

14. Which factor affecting perception has a great influence on the total perceptual process?

A. Self-concept.

B. Goals and values.

C. Time and opportunity.

Answer (A) is correct. *(FAA-H-8083-9A Chap 2)*
DISCUSSION: A student's self-concept (or self-image) has a great influence on the total perceptual process. Negative self-concepts inhibit the perceptual process by introducing psychological barriers, which tend to keep a student from perceiving. Positive self-concepts allow the student to be less defensive and more ready to digest experiences by assimilating all of the instructions and demonstrations offered.
Answer (B) is incorrect. Perceptions depend on one's goals and values in that every experience is colored by the individual's own beliefs and value structures, but they do not have a great influence on the total perceptual process. Answer (C) is incorrect. It takes time and opportunity to perceive, but it is not a great influence on the total perceptual process.

15. Which factor affecting perceptions is based on the effectiveness of the use of a properly planned training syllabus?

A. Basic need.

B. Time and opportunity.

C. Goals and values.

Answer (B) is correct. *(FAA-H-8083-9A Chap 2)*
DISCUSSION: It takes time and opportunity to perceive. Learning some things depends on other perceptions that have preceded these learnings and on the availability of time to sense and relate these new things to the earlier perceptions. Thus, sequence and time are necessary to learn; a properly planned training syllabus facilitates sequencing and timing. The effectiveness of using a properly planned training syllabus is proportional to the consideration given by the instructor to the need for sufficient time and opportunity for perception to occur.
Answer (A) is incorrect. A person's basic need is to maintain and enhance the organized self, which does not relate to a properly planned training syllabus. Answer (C) is incorrect. Goals and values are the basis for perceptions. Every experience and sensation that gets funneled into one's central nervous system is colored by the individual's beliefs and value structures, which do not relate to a properly planned training syllabus.

16. In the learning process, fear or the element of threat will

A. narrow the student's perceptual field.

B. decrease the rate of associative reactions.

C. cause a student to focus on several areas of perception.

Answer (A) is correct. *(FAA-H-8083-9A Chap 2)*
DISCUSSION: Fear or the element of threat will impair the student's perceptual field. This is because one tends to limit attention to the threatening object or condition rather than to what should be learned.
Answer (B) is incorrect. The element of threat causes stress and anxiety; the mind tends to race, often irrationally, thereby increasing, not decreasing, the rate of associative reactions. Answer (C) is incorrect. Fear or the element of threat will cause a student to focus only on the threatening object or condition, not on several areas of perception.

17. Which is one of the ways in which anxiety will affect a student?

A. Anxiety may limit the student's ability to learn from perceptions.

B. Anxiety will speed up the learning process for the student if properly controlled and directed by the instructor.

C. Anxiety causes dispersal of the student's attention over such a wide range of matters as to interfere with normal reactions.

Answer (A) is correct. *(FAA-H-8083-9A Chap 8)*

DISCUSSION: Anxiety is a state of mental uneasiness arising from fear of anything, real or imagined, which threatens the person who experiences it. Anxiety may have a potent effect on actions and on the ability to learn from perceptions.

Answer (B) is incorrect. Perceptions blocked by anxiety will tend to slow, not speed up, the learning process. Answer (C) is incorrect. Anxiety narrows, not disperses, a student's attention.

18. The mental grouping of affiliated perceptions is called

A. insights.

B. association.

C. conceptualization.

Answer (A) is correct. *(FAA-H-8083-9A Chap 2)*

DISCUSSION: Many principles, theories, and learned tasks can be treated as pieces relating to other pieces in the overall pattern of the task to be learned. This mental relating or grouping of associated perceptions is called insight.

Answer (B) is incorrect. Association is not the final, completed mental picture, although it is a necessary process to connect the affiliated perceptions. Answer (C) is incorrect. It refers only to the formation of individual ideas.

19. Insights, as applied to learning, involve a person's

A. association of learning with change.

B. grouping of associated perceptions into meaningful wholes.

C. ability to recognize the reason for learning a procedure.

Answer (B) is correct. *(FAA-H-8083-9A Chap 2)*

DISCUSSION: Insights, as applied to learning, involve a person's grouping of associated perceptions into meaningful wholes. As perceptions increase in number and are grouped to become insights by the student, learning becomes more meaningful and permanent.

Answer (A) is incorrect. Insights involve the grouping of perceptions into meaningful wholes, not the association of learning with change. Answer (C) is incorrect. The ability to recognize the reason for learning a procedure is a feature of the principle of readiness, not insight.

20. Instruction, as opposed to the trial and error method of learning, is desirable because competent instruction speeds the learning process by

A. motivating the student to a better performance.

B. emphasizing only the important points of training.

C. teaching the relationship of perceptions as they occur.

Answer (C) is correct. *(FAA-H-8083-9A Chap 2)*

DISCUSSION: Competent instruction speeds the learning process by teaching the relationship of perceptions as they occur, thus promoting the development of insights by the student.

Answer (A) is incorrect. Motivating a student to a better performance is just one element of instruction. Answer (B) is incorrect. Instructors must emphasize all points of training, not just the major, important points.

21. Name one way an instructor can help develop student insights.

A. Provide a secure and nonthreatening environment in which to learn.

B. Point out various items to avoid during the learning process.

C. Keep learning blocks small so they are easier to understand.

Answer (A) is correct. *(FAA-H-8083-9A Chap 2)*

DISCUSSION: Pointing out the relationships of perceptions as they occur, providing a secure and nonthreatening environment in which to learn, and helping the student acquire and maintain a favorable self-concept are most important in fostering the development of insights.

Answer (B) is incorrect. The instructor should point out the relationships of perceptions as they occur, not point out various items to avoid during the learning process. Answer (C) is incorrect. Insights develop when a student's perceptions increase in number and are assembled into larger, not smaller, blocks of learning.

1.4 Memory

22. The use or association of rhymes or word patterns to aid in remembering is called

A. acronyms.

B. mnemonics.

C. coding.

Answer (B) is correct. *(FAA-H-8083-9A Chap 2)*

DISCUSSION: A mnemonic uses a pattern of letters, ideas, images, or associations to assist in remembering information. It is a memory-enhancing strategy that involves teaching learners to link new information to information they already know.

Answer (A) is incorrect. Mnemonics may include acronyms but are not necessarily acronyms themselves. Answer (C) is incorrect. Coding is a sorting process. It is not designed for remembering information.

23. Which memory system processes input from the environment?

A. Working.

B. Long-term.

C. Sensory register.

Answer (C) is correct. *(FAA-H-8083-9A Chap 2)*

DISCUSSION: The sensory register receives input from the environment and quickly processes it according to the individual's preconceived concept of what is important (i.e., it recognizes certain stimuli as significant). The sensory register processes inputs or stimuli from the environment within seconds, discards what is considered extraneous, and processes what is considered by the individual to be relevant.

Answer (A) is incorrect. The working, or short-term, memory is the receptacle for the information determined to be relevant by the sensory register. Once in the short-term memory, the information may temporarily remain for immediate use, or it may fade rapidly. Answer (B) is incorrect. The long-term memory is where information is stored for future use.

24. While short-term memory is time-limited, it also has a capacity limit of

A. usually 5 bits or chunks of information.

B. usually 7 bits or chunks of information.

C. usually 9 bits or chunks of information.

Answer (B) is correct. *(FAA-H-8083-9A Chap 2)*

DISCUSSION: The short-term memory is not only time limited; it also has limited capacity, usually about seven bits or chunks of information at a time. A seven-digit telephone number is an example.

Answer (A) is incorrect. The short-term memory is not only time limited; it also has limited capacity, usually about seven, not five, bits or chunks of information at a time. Answer (C) is incorrect. The short-term memory is not only time limited; it also has limited capacity, usually about seven, not nine, bits or chunks of information at a time.

25. The use of some type of association, such as rhymes or mnemonics is best suited to which memory system?

A. Short-term.

B. Sensory.

C. Long-term.

Answer (A) is correct. *(FAA-H-8083-9A Chap 2)*

DISCUSSION: For information to remain in the short-term memory for a significant amount of time, it must be categorized in some way. The information is initially grouped into systematic chunks in a process called coding. It must then be related to concepts or knowledge already in memory in a process called recoding. The use of some type of association, such as rhymes or mnemonic devices, is well suited to this task.

Answer (B) is incorrect. The sensory register detects and processes stimuli on a subconscious level. They are then discarded or transferred to the short-term memory according the individual's preconceived concept of what is important. Answer (C) is incorrect. In order for information stored in long-term memory to be useful, some special effort must have been expended during the recoding process while the information was in short-term memory.

26. How can recoding be described?

A. The relating of incoming information to concepts or knowledge already in memory.

B. The initial storage of information in short-term memory.

C. The selective process where the sensory register is set to recognize certain stimuli.

Answer (A) is correct. *(FAA-H-8083-9A Chap 2)*

DISCUSSION: Recoding takes place in the short-term memory, when new information is adjusted to individual experiences. Recoding may be described as a process of relating incoming information to concepts or knowledge already in memory.

Answer (B) is incorrect. The initial storage of information in short-term memory is coding, not recoding. Answer (C) is incorrect. The selective process where the sensory register is set to recognize certain stimuli is precoding, not recoding.

27. Which of the following memory systems would be enhanced with practice and repetition?

A. Long-term.

B. Short-term.

C. Perception.

Answer (B) is correct. *(FAA-H-8083-9A Chap 2)*

DISCUSSION: Short-term memory is the part of the memory system where information is stored for roughly 30 seconds, after which it may rapidly fade or be consolidated into long-term memory, depending on the individual's priorities. Several common steps help retention in short-term memory. These include rehearsal or repetition of the information and sorting or categorization into systematic chunks. The sorting process is usually called coding or chunking.

Answer (A) is incorrect. Practice and repetition enhance short-term memory, with the hope that these memories will become long-term memories. Answer (C) is incorrect. Student perceptions are unrelated to short-term memory.

28. Which of the following statements about long-term memory is true?

A. Long-term memory is a reconstruction, not a pure recall of information or events.

B. Long-term memory is not subject to limitations such as time, biases, and, in many cases, personal inaccuracies.

C. Initial encoding is not related to long-term memory.

Answer (A) is correct. *(FAA-H-8083-9A Chap 4)*

DISCUSSION: Long-term memory is a reconstruction, not a pure recall of information or events.

Answer (B) is incorrect. Long-term memory is in fact subject to limitations, such as time, biases, and, in many cases, personal inaccuracies. Answer (C) is incorrect. If initial encoding is not properly accomplished, recall is distorted and may be impossible.

29. Where is information for future use stored?

A. Short-term memory.

B. Sensory register.

C. Long-term memory.

Answer (C) is correct. *(FAA-H-8083-9A Chap 2)*

DISCUSSION: Information for future use is stored in the long-term memory.

Answer (A) is incorrect. Short-term memory is where information is temporarily stored, not stored for future use, after the sensory register deems it to be significant. Answer (B) is incorrect. The sensory register processes stimuli from the environment according to the individual's preconception of what is important. Significant information is sent to the short-term memory for immediate, not future, use.

30. The selective process by which the sensory register discards and transmits certain stimuli to the working memory is called

A. recoding.

B. coding.

C. precoding.

Answer (C) is correct. *(FAA-H-8083-9A Chap 2)*

DISCUSSION: Precoding is the selective process by which the sensory register recognizes certain stimuli and immediately transmits them to the working memory for action.

Answer (A) is incorrect. Recoding is the process of relating incoming information to concepts already in memory. Answer (B) is incorrect. Coding is the initial sorting or categorization of information into systematic chunks in the short-term memory to aid in retention.

31. The ability to retrieve knowledge or skills from memory is primarily related to

A. absence of interference.

B. how often that knowledge has been used in the past.

C. the practice of "information chunking."

Answer (B) is correct. *(FAA-H-8083-9A Chap 2)*

DISCUSSION: The ability to retrieve knowledge or skills from memory is primarily related to how often and how recently the knowledge has been used in the past. These two factors are called frequency and recency of use. Frequency and recency can be present individually or in combination.

Answer (A) is incorrect. The absence of interference is not the primary factor in the ability to retrieve knowledge. Answer (C) is incorrect. Chunking is one of the steps that help retention of short-term memory. After rehearsal or repetition of the information, it is sorted or categorized into systematic chunks. The sorting process is usually called coding or chunking.

1.5 Forgetting and Retention

32. The phenomenon of information not used for an extended period of time becoming harder to recall is termed

A. fading.

B. forgetting.

C. retrieval failure.

Answer (A) is correct. *(FAA-H-8083-9A Chap 2)*

DISCUSSION: The theory of fading, or decay, suggests that a person forgets information that is not used for an extended period of time. It has been suggested that humans are physiologically pre-programmed to eventually erase data that no longer appears pertinent.

Answer (B) is incorrect. Forgetting typically involves a failure in memory retrieval. Answer (C) is incorrect. Retrieval failure is simply the inability to retrieve information, for example, the "tip-of-the-tongue" phenomenon when a person knows the meaning of a word or the answer to a question but cannot retrieve it.

33. When a person has difficulty recalling facts after several years, this is known as

A. repression.

B. fading.

C. retrieval failure.

Answer (B) is correct. *(FAA-H-8083-9A Chap 2)*

DISCUSSION: The theory of fading or decay suggests that a person forgets information that is not used for an extended period of time.

Answer (A) is incorrect. Repression is the practice of submerging an unpleasant experience into the subconscious. Answer (C) is incorrect. Retrieval failure is simply the inability to retrieve information. Some would call it the "tip-of-the-tongue" phenomenon when a person knows the answer to a question but cannot retrieve it.

34. When the learning of similar things overshadows other learning experiences, it is called

A. suppression.

B. correlation.

C. interference.

Answer (C) is correct. *(FAA-H-8083-9A Chap 2)*

DISCUSSION: The theory of interference states that new or similar events can often replace previously learned facts. Most susceptible to this replacement by interference are closely similar materials and materials not well learned to begin with.

Answer (A) is incorrect. Suppression is not a consideration (or theory) as to why a person forgets. Answer (B) is incorrect. Correlation is the highest level of learning, which means that it is resistant to forgetting.

35. According to one theory, some forgetting is due to the unconscious practice of submerging an unpleasant experience into the subconscious. This is called

A. suppression.

B. immersion.

C. repression.

Answer (C) is correct. *(FAA-H-8083-9A Chap 2)*

DISCUSSION: Repression is the unconscious form of forgetting where memories are pushed out of reach because the individual does not want to remember the feelings associated with them.

Answer (A) is incorrect. Suppression is a conscious, not unconscious, form of forgetting. Answer (B) is incorrect. Immersion is not discussed in the *Aviation Instructor's Handbook* and is a nonsense answer in this context.

36. Responses that produce a pleasurable return are called

A. reward.

B. praise.

C. positive feedback.

Answer (B) is correct. *(FAA-H-8083-9A Chap 2)*

DISCUSSION: Responses that give a pleasurable return, called praise, tend to be repeated, thus stimulating and encouraging retention.

Answer (A) is incorrect. Rewards are motivators and are not usually responses (e.g., praise); that is, they are normally financial, self-interest, or public recognition. Answer (C) is incorrect. Positive feedback (e.g., constructive criticism) is part of the learning, not retention, process. Positive feedback teaches a student how to capitalize on things done well and to use them to compensate for lesser accomplishments.

37. The act of consciously pushing a memory out of reach due to feelings associated with remembering it is

A. avoidance.

B. suppression.

C. repression.

Answer (B) is correct. *(FAA-H-8083-9A Chap 2)*

DISCUSSION: Suppression is a conscious form of forgetting where the student intentionally forces memories that are unpleasant or anxiety-producing into the subconscious.

Answer (A) is incorrect. Avoidance is not a theory of forgetting and is not discussed in the *Aviation Instructor's Handbook*. Answer (C) is incorrect. Repression is an unconscious, not conscious, form of forgetting.

38. When a new experience displaces memories or information that had been previously learned, it is called

A. fading.

B. retrieval failure.

C. interference.

Answer (C) is correct. *(FAA-H-8083-9A Chap 2)*

DISCUSSION: Interference theory suggests that people forget something because a certain experience has overshadowed it or the learning of similar things has intervened. In other words, new events displace many things that had been learned.

Answer (A) is incorrect. The theory of fading suggests that a person forgets information that is not used for an extended period of time. Answer (B) is incorrect. Retrieval failure is simply the inability to retrieve information, for example, the "tip-of-the-tongue" phenomenon when a person knows the meaning of a word or the answer to a question but cannot retrieve it.

1.6 Transfer of Learning

39. The performance of rectangular patterns helps a student fly traffic patterns. What type transfer of learning is this?

A. Lateral.

B. Positive.

C. Deliberate.

Answer (B) is correct. *(FAA-H-8083-9A Chap 2)*

DISCUSSION: Transfers of learning can be negative or positive. Since the learning of Task A (flying rectangular patterns) helps in the learning of Task B (flying traffic patterns), it is advantageous and therefore a positive transfer of learning.

Answer (A) is incorrect. There is no lateral transfer of learning, only positive or negative. Answer (C) is incorrect. There is no deliberate transfer of learning, only positive or negative.

40. Which transfer of learning occurs when the performance of a maneuver interferes with the learning of another maneuver?

A. Adverse.

B. Positive.

C. Negative.

Answer (C) is correct. *(FAA-H-8083-9A Chap 2)*

DISCUSSION: Transfers of learning can be negative or positive. If the learning of Task A helps in the learning of Task B, the transfer of learning is deemed to be positive. If, on the other hand, Task A interferes with Task B, the transfer is a hindrance to learning and is thus negative.

Answer (A) is incorrect. There is no adverse transfer of learning, only positive or negative. Answer (B) is incorrect. The transfer of learning is a hindrance and is thus negative.

41. To ensure proper habits and correct techniques during training, an instructor should

A. use the building block technique of instruction.

B. repeat subject matter the student has already learned.

C. introduce challenging material to continually motivate the student.

Answer (A) is correct. *(FAA-H-8083-9A Chap 2)*

DISCUSSION: The building-block technique of teaching insists that each simple task be performed correctly before the next is introduced. This technique fosters thorough and meaningful performance and good habits, which will be carried over into future learning.

Answer (B) is incorrect. Too much repetition can lead to boredom. The instructor must mix teaching methods to sustain interest and promote learning. Answer (C) is incorrect. Complex or difficult tasks introduced before simpler ones are mastered can be frustrating, not motivating, for the student. This approach will not ensure proper habits; the student will likely develop bad habits from trying to perform tasks not completely understood.

1.7 Levels of Learning

42. What level of knowledge is being tested if asked, "What is the maneuvering speed of the aircraft listed in the owner's manual?"

A. Rote.

B. Application.

C. Understanding.

Answer (A) is correct. *(FAA-H-8083-9A Chap 2)*

DISCUSSION: The lowest level, rote learning, is the ability to repeat something back that one has been taught without understanding or being able to apply what has been learned. An example of rote learning is to be able to cite the maneuvering speed of the aircraft listed in the owner's manual.

Answer (B) is incorrect. Application is the ability of a student to apply what has been taught. This is the third level of learning and is achieved after the student understands, has practiced, and can consistently perform a task. Answer (C) is incorrect. The second level of learning is understanding, which has been achieved when a student can put together a block of learning and develop an insight into the performance of a task.

43. Once a student understands a procedure, has had the procedure demonstrated, and has practiced the procedure until it can be performed with consistency, the student has demonstrated what level of learning?

A. Application.

B. Rote.

C. Duplication.

Answer (A) is correct. *(FAA-H-8083-9A Chap 2)*

DISCUSSION: Application is a basic level of learning at which the student puts something to use that has been learned and understood.

Answer (B) is incorrect. Rote learning is simple memorization without necessarily gaining an understanding of what has been memorized. Answer (C) is incorrect. Duplication is not a level of learning.

44. Commercially-developed test preparation material

A. teaches higher-order thinking skills.

B. replaces instructor-led training.

C. places emphasis on rote learning rather than more advanced learning levels.

Answer (C) is correct. *(FAA-H-8083-9A Chap 4)*

DISCUSSION: While commercially-developed training material is a great study aid, it emphasizes rote learning rather than higher levels of learning that promote increased understanding. Commercially-developed training material should be used as a supplement to instructor-led, comprehensive training, not as a replacement for it. Gleim supports and encourages the view that students should strive for a level of understanding beyond rote memorization. That is why, for 30+ years, all of our knowledge test preparation books have included both multiple-choice questions and Knowledge Transfer Outlines. These detailed outlines help students conceptualize why the correct answers are correct and the incorrect answers are incorrect. We also provide additional outline material for students' practical training in our Flight Maneuvers series of books. These texts, which are actually three books in one [the Practical Test Standards (PTS) or Airman Certification Standards (ACS), where appropriate, the Flight Maneuvers portion, plus the Oral Exam Guide], prepare Gleim students for the higher-level thinking demanded of these future pilots.

Answer (A) is incorrect. Higher-order thinking skills involve decision-making principles. Commercially-developed training material emphasizes rote learning rather than higher levels of learning that promote increased understanding. For this reason, instructor-led training is essential for the student to develop higher-order thinking skills. Answer (B) is incorrect. While commercially-developed training material is a great study aid, it cannot be used as a replacement to instructor-led training because it focuses on rote learning rather than higher levels of learning.

45. A disadvantage of using commercially-developed test preparation material is that

A. the emphasis is on correlation learning.

B. students may learn to pass a given test.

C. students often exhibit a lack of knowledge during oral questioning.

Answer (C) is correct. *(FAA-H-8083-9A Chap 4)*

DISCUSSION: FAA inspectors and designated examiners have found that student applicants often exhibit a lack of knowledge during oral questioning, even though many have easily passed the FAA knowledge test. This is most often the result of student memorization rather than true concept understanding. The emphasis of test preparation materials is on rote learning rather than higher levels of learning that promote increased understanding. Gleim supports and encourages the view that students should strive for a level of understanding beyond rote memorization. That is why, for 30+ years, all of our knowledge test preparation books have included both multiple-choice questions and Knowledge Transfer Outlines. These detailed outlines help students conceptualize why the correct answers are correct and the incorrect answers are incorrect. We also provide additional outline material for students' practical training in our Flight Maneuvers series of books. These texts, which are actually three books in one [the Practical Test Standards (PTS) or Airman Certification Standards (ACS), where appropriate, the Flight Maneuvers portion, plus the Oral Exam Guide], prepare Gleim students for the higher-level thinking demanded of these future pilots.

Answer (A) is incorrect. While commercially-developed training material is a great study aid, it emphasizes rote learning rather than higher levels of learning, such as correlation, that promote increased understanding. Answer (B) is incorrect. Commercially-developed training material is incredibly useful at helping students pass FAA tests. This is only a disadvantage if the student memorizes the material and fails to develop understanding of the covered topics.

46. During the flight portion of a practical test, the examiner simulates complete loss of engine power by closing the throttle and announcing "simulated engine failure." What level of learning is being tested?

A. Application.

B. Correlation.

C. Understanding.

Answer (B) is correct. *(FAA-H-8083-9A Chap 2)*

DISCUSSION: When the examiner simulates complete loss of engine power by closing the throttle and announcing "simulated engine failure," the examiner is testing at the correlation level of learning. The applicant must be able to correlate (associate) the engine failure with the requirements to perform the elements of an emergency approach and landing; e.g., establish best-glide speed, select a field, perform restart checklist, plan a flight pattern to the selected field, complete all appropriate checklists, etc.

Answer (A) is incorrect. The application level of learning is tested when the examiner closes the throttle and tells the applicant to perform an emergency approach and landing. Answer (C) is incorrect. The understanding level of learning is tested when the examiner asks the applicant to explain the elements of an emergency approach and landing.

47. At which level of learning do most instructors stop teaching?

A. Application.

B. Correlation.

C. Understanding.

Answer (A) is correct. *(FAA-H-8083-9A Chap 2)*

DISCUSSION: Most instructors stop teaching at the application level of learning. Discontinuing instruction on an element at this point and directing subsequent instruction exclusively to other elements is characteristic of piecemeal instruction, which is usually inefficient. It violates the building block concept of instruction by failing to apply what has been learned to future learning tasks.

Answer (B) is incorrect. Correlation is the highest level of learning and should be the goal of each instructor. Instructors all too often stop at the application level. Answer (C) is incorrect. Understanding is the second level of learning, and at this point, a student understands a task but may not be able to do it. Instructors will usually continue teaching to the next level, which is application.

48. When asking a student to explain how gross weight affects maneuvering speed, what level of learning is being tested?

A. Application.

B. Correlation.

C. Understanding.

Answer (C) is correct. *(FAA-H-8083-9A Chap 2)*

DISCUSSION: At the understanding level of learning, a student will be able to explain how gross weight affects maneuvering speed (V_A). Understanding is the next level after rote memorization and the level before acquiring the skill to apply knowledge, which is application (correlation is the fourth and highest level of learning). Being able to explain (not demonstrate) is the understanding level of learning, not the application or correlation level.

Answer (A) is incorrect. At the application level, a student will be able to apply the knowledge that gross weight affects maneuvering speed when determining the appropriate airspeed for entering turbulent air or maneuvers that require an airspeed at or below V_A. Answer (B) is incorrect. At the correlation level, a student has developed the ability to correlate the elements of maneuvering speed with other concepts, such as gust loads, accelerated stalls, load factors, acceleration forces in the aircraft, etc.

49. Students who use test preparation materials in preparing for FAA tests may commit which of the following adverse actions?

A. Focusing on test-taking skills rather than critical information essential for safe piloting.

B. Excelling in the oral exam portion of practical tests.

C. Focusing on correlation level learning.

Answer (A) is correct. *(FAA-H-8083-9A Chap 4)*

DISCUSSION: By relying on test preparation materials as a source of learning, students may learn to pass a given test but fail to learn other critical information essential to safe piloting and maintenance practices.

Answer (B) is incorrect. FAA inspectors and designated examiners have found that student applicants often exhibit a lack of knowledge during oral questioning, even though many have easily passed the FAA knowledge test. Answer (C) is incorrect. Test preparation materials often encourage rote-level learning, not correlation.

1.8 Domains of Learning

50. Which domain of learning deals with knowledge?

A. Affective.

B. Cognitive.

C. Psychomotor.

Answer (B) is correct. *(FAA-H-8083-9A Chap 2)*

DISCUSSION: Domains of learning are classified based on what is to be learned. The cognitive domain of learning deals with knowledge (e.g., facts, concepts, or relationships).

Answer (A) is incorrect. The affective domain deals with attitudes, beliefs, and values, not knowledge. Answer (C) is incorrect. The psychomotor domain deals with physical skills, not knowledge.

51. Affective domain relates to

A. physical skills.

B. knowledge.

C. attitudes, beliefs, and values.

Answer (C) is correct. *(FAA-H-8083-9A Chap 2)*

DISCUSSION: Domains of learning are classified based on what is to be learned. The affective domain relates to attitudes, beliefs, and values.

Answer (A) is incorrect. The psychomotor domain, not the affective domain, relates to physical skills. Answer (B) is incorrect. The cognitive domain, not the affective domain, relates to knowledge.

52. The educational objective levels for the cognitive domain are

A. receiving, responding, valuing, organization, and characterization.

B. perception, set, guided response mechanism, complex overt response, adaptation, and origination.

C. knowledge, comprehension, application, analysis, synthesis, and evaluation.

Answer (C) is correct. *(FAA-H-8083-9A Chap 2)*

DISCUSSION: Each domain of learning has multiple educational objective levels. The six educational objective levels of the cognitive domain are knowledge, comprehension, application, analysis, synthesis, and evaluation.

Answer (A) is incorrect. Receiving, responding, valuing, organization, and characterization are the five educational objective levels of the affective, not cognitive, domain. Answer (B) is incorrect. Perception, set, guided response mechanism, complex overt response, adaptation, and origination are the seven educational objective levels of the psychomotor, not cognitive, domain.

53. The listing of the hierarchy of objectives is often referred to as a

A. taxonomy.

B. skill.

C. domain.

Answer (A) is correct. *(FAA-H-8083-9A Chap 2)*

DISCUSSION: Each of the domains of learning has a hierarchy of educational objectives. The listing of the hierarchy of objectives is often called a taxonomy.

Answer (B) is incorrect. A skill is what is learned in the psychomotor domain of learning. It is not a hierarchy of educational objectives. Answer (C) is incorrect. Domains of learning contain, but are not, hierarchies of educational objectives.

54. The most complex outcome in the affective domain is

A. organization.

B. characterization.

C. valuing.

Answer (B) is correct. *(FAA-H-8083-9A Chap 2)*

DISCUSSION: A taxonomy of educational objectives is a systematic classification scheme for sorting learning outcomes into the three domains of learning (cognitive, affective, and psychomotor) and ranking the desired outcomes in a developmental hierarchy from least complex to most complex. The most complex learning outcome in the affective domain is characterization in which the learner incorporates a value or attitude into his or her life.

Answer (A) is incorrect. Organization (in which the learner rearranges his or her value system to accommodate a new value or attitude) is the second-most-complex, not the most complex, learning outcome in the affective domain. Answer (C) is incorrect. Valuing (in which the learner accepts a new value or attitude) is the third-most-complex, not the most complex, learning outcome in the affective domain.

55. Learning objectives can be sorted in a system known as a

A. taxonomy.

B. database.

C. schema.

Answer (A) is correct. *(FAA-H-8083-9A Chap 1)*

DISCUSSION: The hierarchy of learning objectives is known as a taxonomy. Taxonomy is the systematic classification of learning outcomes into one of the three broad categories or domains of learning (cognitive, affective, and psychomotor).

Answer (B) is incorrect. A database is an interconnected group of data elements. Answer (C) is incorrect. "Schema" is a term used in information technology to refer to the layout of a database.

56. The least complex outcome in the psychomotor domain is

A. adaptation.

B. mechanism.

C. perception.

Answer (C) is correct. *(FAA-H-8083-9A Chap 2)*

DISCUSSION: A taxonomy of educational objectives is a systematic classification scheme for sorting learning outcomes into the three domains of learning (cognitive, affective, and psychomotor) and ranking the desired outcomes in a developmental hierarchy from least complex to most complex. The least complex learning outcome in the psychomotor domain is perception in which the learner has awareness of sensory stimuli.

Answer (A) is incorrect. Adaptation (in which the learner modifies his or her performance of a skill for special problems) is the second-most-complex, not the least complex, learning outcome in the psychomotor domain. Answer (B) is incorrect. Mechanism (in which the learner performs simple acts well) is the fourth-least-complex, not the least complex, learning outcome in the psychomotor domain.

57. Which of the following domains relates a grouping of levels of learning associated with a person's attitudes?

A. Affective.

B. Cognitive.

C. Psychomotor.

Answer (A) is correct. *(FAA-H-8083-9A Chap 2)*

DISCUSSION: The affective domain is a grouping of levels of learning associated with a person's attitudes, personal beliefs, and values, which range from receiving through responding, valuing, and organization to characterization.

Answer (B) is incorrect. The cognitive domain is a grouping of levels of learning associated with mental activity. In order of increasing complexity, the domains are knowledge, comprehension, application, analysis, synthesis, and evaluation. Answer (C) is incorrect. The psychomotor domain is a grouping of levels of learning associated with physical skill levels, which range from perception through set, guided response, mechanism, complex overt response, and adaptation to origination.

58. An example of a skill involving the cognitive domain would be

A. Understanding how the flight controls should be positioned during a turn.

B. A positive reception for learning new skills.

C. Performing a short-field approach and landing to Practical Test Standards/Airman Certification.

Answer (A) is correct. *(FAA-H-8083-9A Chap 2)*

DISCUSSION: The cognitive domain includes remembering specific facts (content knowledge) and concepts that help develop intellectual abilities and skills, such as understanding how and why the flight controls should be positioned in a certain way.

Answer (B) is incorrect. This answer choice best describes the affective domain. The affective domain addresses a learner's emotions toward the learning experience. It includes feelings, values, enthusiasms, motivations, and attitudes. Answer (C) is incorrect. This answer choice best describes the psychomotor domain. The psychomotor domain is skill-based and includes physical movement, coordination, and use of the motor-skill areas.

59. An example of a skill involving the psychomotor domain would be

A. Responsiveness to an instructor's demonstration of steep turns.

B. Applying back pressure to maintain altitude during a steep turn.

C. Correlating pitch control inputs during a medium-bank with those of a steep turn.

Answer (B) is correct. *(FAA-H-8083-9A Chap 2)*

DISCUSSION: The psychomotor domain is skill-based and includes physical movement, coordination, and use of the motor-skill areas, such as physically manipulating the flight controls during a steep turn.

Answer (A) is incorrect. This answer choice best describes the affective domain. The affective domain addresses a learner's emotions toward the learning experience. It includes feelings, values, enthusiasms, motivations, and attitudes. Answer (C) is incorrect. This answer choice best describes the cognitive domain. The cognitive domain includes remembering specific facts (content knowledge) and concepts that help develop intellectual abilities and skills.

60. Which of the following would be an example of a skill involving the psychomotor domain?

A. Memorizing aircraft V-speeds.

B. Computing takeoff distance over a 50 foot obstacle.

C. Programming a Global Positioning System (GPS) receiver.

Answer (C) is correct. *(FAA-H-8083-9A Chap 2)*

DISCUSSION: The psychomotor domain is skill-based and includes physical movement, coordination, and use of the motor-skill areas. Development of these skills requires repetitive practice and is measured in terms of speed, precision, distance, and techniques. Skills involving the psychomotor domain include learning to fly a precision instrument approach procedure, programming a global positioning system (GPS) receiver, or using sophisticated maintenance equipment.

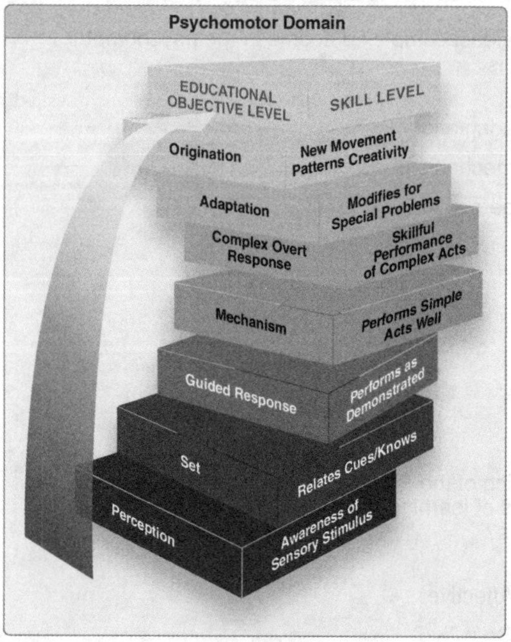

Figure 2-12.

Answer (A) is incorrect. Skills in the psychomotor domain involve physical movement, coordination, and use of the motor-skill areas. Memorization is only the cognitive domain and does not encompass all seven educational objective levels.

Answer (B) is incorrect. Skills in the psychomotor domain involve physical movement, coordination, and use of the motor-skill areas. Computing a takeoff distance does not require physical movement or coordination and, therefore, does not require all seven education objective levels.

61. An example of a skill involving the affective domain would be

A. Responding to an instructor's question.

B. Recalling the information needed to answer an instructor's question.

C. Practicing the conditions of an instructor's question to determine an answer.

Answer (A) is correct. *(FAA-H-8083-9A Chap 2)*

DISCUSSION: The affective domain addresses a learner's emotions toward the learning experience. It includes feelings, values, enthusiasms, motivations, and attitudes, including responsiveness to instructor inquiries.

Answer (B) is incorrect. This answer choice best describes the cognitive domain. The cognitive domain includes remembering specific facts (content knowledge) and concepts that help develop intellectual abilities and skills. Answer (C) is incorrect. This answer choice best describes the psychomotor domain. The psychomotor domain is skill-based and includes physical movement, coordination, and use of the motor-skill areas.

62. Which domain of learning includes physical movement and coordination?

A. Affective.

B. Cognitive.

C. Psychomotor.

Answer (C) is correct. *(FAA-H-8083-9A Chap 2)*

DISCUSSION: Domains of learning are classified based on what is to be learned. The psychomotor domain concerns physical skills (e.g., movement and coordination).

Answer (A) is incorrect. The affective domain relates to attitudes, beliefs, and values, not physical skills. Answer (B) is incorrect. The cognitive domain deals with knowledge (e.g., facts, concepts, or relationships), not physical skills.

63. The educational objective levels; receiving, responding, valuing, organization, and characterization; are a part of which domain of learning?

A. Psychomotor.

B. Affective.

C. Cognitive.

Answer (B) is correct. *(FAA-H-8083-9A Chap 2)*

DISCUSSION: Each domain of learning has multiple educational objective levels that start with the least complex and end with the most complex. Receiving, responding, valuing, organization, and characterization are the five educational objective levels of the affective domain.

Answer (A) is incorrect. The educational objective levels of the psychomotor domain are perception, set, guided response, mechanism, complex overt response, adaptation, and origination. Answer (C) is incorrect. The educational objective levels of the cognitive domain are knowledge, comprehension, application, analysis, synthesis, and evaluation.

64. The educational objective level of the psychomotor domain at which a student's skill demonstrates new movement patterns and creativity is

A. origination.

B. complex overt response.

C. adaptation.

Answer (A) is correct. *(FAA-H-8083-9A Chap 2)*

DISCUSSION: Each educational objective level of the domains of learning has a distinct learning outcome. The learning outcome where a student's skill demonstrates new movement patterns and creativity is equivalent to the origination educational objective level of the psychomotor domain.

Answer (B) is incorrect. At the complex overt response educational objective level, the student would demonstrate skillful performance of complex acts, not new movement patterns and creativity. Answer (C) is incorrect. At the adaptation educational objective level, the student would demonstrate modifiers for special problems, not new movement patterns and creativity.

65. The least complex outcome in the cognitive domain is

A. synthesis.

B. knowledge.

C. comprehension.

Answer (B) is correct. *(FAA-H-8083-9A Chap 2)*

DISCUSSION: A taxonomy of educational objectives is a systematic classification scheme for sorting learning outcomes into three domains of learning (cognitive, affective, and psychomotor) and ranking the desired outcomes in a developmental hierarchy from least complex to most complex. The least complex learning outcome in the cognitive domain is knowledge where the learner has the capacity to recall and recognize facts, concepts, or relationships.

Answer (A) is incorrect. Synthesis (in which the learner has the capacity to create new relationships) is the fifth most complex, not the least complex, learning outcome in the cognitive domain. Answer (C) is incorrect. Comprehension (in which the learner has the capacity to translate, interpret, and extrapolate) is the second most complex, not the least complex, learning outcome in the cognitive domain.

1.9 Learning Skills and the Learning Curve

66. The best way to prepare a student to perform a task is to

A. explain the purpose of the task.

B. provide a clear, step-by-step example.

C. give the student an outline of the task.

Answer (B) is correct. *(FAA-H-8083-9A Chap 2)*

DISCUSSION: The best way to prepare a student to perform a task is to provide a clear, step-by-step example. Having a model to follow permits a student to get a clear picture of each step in the sequence (e.g., what it is, how to do it).

Answer (A) is incorrect. While a student should know the purpose of a task, (s)he must be provided with a clear, step-by-step example showing how to perform the task. Answer (C) is incorrect. An outline is not as useful as a clear, step-by-step example.

67. During learning, a leveling-off process or plateau is

A. normal and should be expected after an initial period of rapid improvement.

B. normal and can be overcome with more practice.

C. not normal and requires that the instructor reteach the lesson in a different format to ensure student learning and retention.

Answer (A) is correct. *(FAA-H-8083-9A Chap 2)*

DISCUSSION: Learning plateaus are normal and should be expected after an initial period of rapid improvement.

Answer (B) is incorrect. Instructors should also be aware that they can bring on a learning plateau by over-practice. After repeating any task three or four times, give it a break to avoid causing a learning plateau. Answer (C) is incorrect. Learning plateaus are normal and can sometimes be alleviated by the instructor better explaining the lesson, the reason for the lesson, and how it applies to the student. Reteaching lesson content is not necessary in the event of a learning plateau.

68. A learning plateau may be defined as the

A. leveling-off in learning at the point which a student has reached the highest competence of a particular subject.

B. gradual decrease in learning almost to the point where it appears to have ceased before it resumes and proficiency increases.

C. point in the learning curve at which skill proficiency retrogresses.

Answer (B) is correct. *(FAA-H-8083-9A Chap 2)*

DISCUSSION: A learning plateau may be defined as the gradual decrease in learning rate. This is normal and should be expected by the instructor and student after an initial period of rapid improvement. Note that the apparent lack of increasing proficiency does not necessarily mean that learning has ceased.

Answer (A) is incorrect. A learning plateau is the leveling-off of an individual's rate of learning, usually after a period of rapid improvement, not after reaching the highest competence of a particular subject. Answer (C) is incorrect. A learning plateau is a gradual decrease in learning rate almost to the point where it appears to have ceased before it resumes and proficiency increases, not retrogresses.

69. Which is true concerning "learning plateaus"?

A. Learning plateaus are the direct result of poor instruction.

B. Learning plateaus are a normal part of the learning process and tend to be temporary.

C. Learning plateaus are caused by under-practice.

Answer (B) is correct. *(FAA-H-8083-9A Chap 2)*

DISCUSSION: Learning plateaus are a normal part of the learning process and tend to be temporary, but instructors and students should be prepared for them to avoid discouragement.

Answer (A) is incorrect. Learning plateaus are normal, even in quality instruction. They often occur after a period of rapid improvement on the part of the student. Answer (C) is incorrect. Learning plateaus can be caused by over-practice, not under-practice. After repeating any task three or four times, give it a break to avoid causing a learning plateau. Keep in mind that the apparent lack of increasing proficiency does not necessarily mean that learning has ceased.

70. Instructors can help students who arrive at a learning plateau by

A. Continuing practice to help the student move past it.

B. Assuming that the plateau represents the student's maximum skill achievement.

C. Moving the student to a different place in the curriculum.

Answer (C) is correct. *(FAA-H-8083-9A Chap 2)*

DISCUSSION: Instructors can help students who fall into a learning plateau by moving them to a different place in the curriculum and giving the current task a break. Learning plateau problems can sometimes also be alleviated by the instructor better explaining the lesson, the reason for the lesson, and how it applies to the student.

Answer (A) is incorrect. Rather than treating a learning plateau, overpractice can actually create one. After repeating any task three or four times, give it a break to avoid causing a learning plateau. Answer (B) is incorrect. Keep in mind that the apparent lack of increasing proficiency does not necessarily mean that learning has ceased. The point is that, in learning motor skills, a leveling-off process, or plateau, is normal and should be expected after an initial period of rapid improvement.

71. The three stages of skill acquisition are

A. cognitive, associative, and automatic.

B. cognitive, understanding, and automatic.

C. cognitive, additional, and automatic.

Answer (A) is correct. *(FAA-H-8083-9A Chap 2)*

DISCUSSION: The three stages of skill acquisition are cognitive, associative, and automatic.

Answer (B) is incorrect. Understanding is not one of the three stages of skill acquisition. Answer (C) is incorrect. The three stages of skill acquisition are cognitive, associative, and automatic.

72. Which stage of skill acquisition is characterized by the ability to perform a procedure rapidly and smoothly while devoting little deliberate attention to performance and simultaneously performing other tasks?

A. Cognitive stage.

B. Associative stage.

C. Automatic response stage.

Answer (C) is correct. *(FAA-H-8083-9A Chap 2)*

DISCUSSION: By the automatic response stage, student performance of the skill is rapid and smooth. The student devotes much less deliberate attention to performance and may be able to carry on a conversation or perform other tasks while performing the skill.

Answer (A) is incorrect. There is a lack of understanding of the skill in the cognitive stage; thus, there can be no automatic performance of the skill by the student. Answer (B) is incorrect. At the associative stage, the student no longer performs a series of memorized steps but is able to assess his or her progress along the way and make adjustments in performance. There is, however, no smooth or rapid skill performance associated with this stage.

73. Which stage of skill acquisition may be characterized by student ability to assess personal progress and make adjustments in performance?

A. Cognitive stage.

B. Associative stage.

C. Automatic response stage.

Answer (B) is correct. *(FAA-H-8083-9A Chap 2)*

DISCUSSION: As the storage of a skill continues due to practice, the student learns to associate individual steps in performance with likely outcomes. The student no longer performs a series of memorized steps but is able to assess his or her progress along the way and make adjustments in performance.

Answer (A) is incorrect. Cognitive learning has a basis in factual knowledge. Since the student has no prior knowledge of flying, the instructor first introduces him or her to a basic skill. The student then memorizes the steps required to perform the skill. As the student carries out these memorized steps, (s)he is often unaware of progress or may fixate on one aspect of performance. Answer (C) is incorrect. While student performance assessment certainly exists in the automatic response stage, it is not the characterizing trait of the stage. Rather, the characterizing trait of the automatic response stage is that a student performs automatically, even instinctively, to flight tasks. The student devotes far less deliberate attention to performing the task.

74. Distractions can be used as a valuable learning tool, but they should be avoided during

A. deliberate practice.

B. blocked practice.

C. random practice.

Answer (A) is correct. *(FAA-H-8083-9A Chap 2)*

DISCUSSION: In order for a student to gain skill knowledge and learn how to perform the skill on the automatic level, a student must engage in deliberate practice. Studies of skill learning suggest a student achieves better results if distractions are avoided during deliberate practice. When feedback is needed to correct student performance, it should be brief and explicit.

Answer (B) is incorrect. Blocked practice is practicing the same drill until the movement becomes automatic. The *Aviation Instructor's Handbook* does not specifically state distractions should be avoided during blocked practice. Answer (C) is incorrect. Random practice mixes up the skills to be acquired throughout the practice session. The *Aviation Instructor's Handbook* does not specifically state distractions should be avoided during random practice.

75. If a student can fly an ILS while communicating with ATC at the same time, (s)he has reached which stage of skill acquisition?

A. Associative stage.

B. Automatic response stage.

C. Psychomotor stage.

Answer (B) is correct. *(FAA-H-8083-9A Chap 2)*

DISCUSSION: As procedures become automatic, less attention is required to carry them out, so it is possible to do other things simultaneously, or at least do other things more comfortably. By the automatic response stage, student performance of the skill is rapid and smooth.

Answer (A) is incorrect. Even demonstrating how to do something does not result in the student learning the skill. Practice is necessary in order for the student to learn how to coordinate muscles with visual and tactile senses. Learning to perform various aircraft maintenance skills or flight maneuvers requires practice. Another benefit of practice is that as the student gains proficiency in a skill, verbal instructions become more meaningful. A long, detailed explanation is confusing before the student begins performing, whereas specific comments are more meaningful and useful after the skill has been partially mastered. Answer (C) is incorrect. As the storage of a skill via practice continues, the student learns to associate individual steps in performance with likely outcomes. The student no longer performs a series of memorized steps but is able to assess his or her progress along the way and make adjustments in performance. Performing the skill still requires deliberate attention, but the student is better able to deal with distractions.

76. Studies of skill learning suggest that a student achieves better results if distractions are avoided during what type of practice?

A. Deliberate practice.

B. Blocked practice.

C. Random practice.

Answer (A) is correct. *(FAA-H-8083-9A Chap 2)*

DISCUSSION: During deliberate practice, the student practices specific areas for improvement and receives specific feedback after practice. Studies of skill learning suggest a student achieves better results if distractions are avoided during deliberate practice. When feedback is needed to correct student performance, it should be brief and explicit.

Answer (B) is incorrect. Using distractions during blocked practice can actually be helpful in preventing student and instructor from falsely determining that repeated skills have been well learned. Answer (C) is incorrect. Random practice relies heavily on the incorporation of distractions to mix up the skills to be acquired throughout the practice session. This type of practice leads to better retention because performing a series of separate skills in a random order helps the student recognize the similarities and differences of each skill.

77. What type of practice is repeating the same drill or doing the same task again and again until the movement becomes automatic?

A. Deliberate.

B. Blocked.

C. Random.

Answer (B) is correct. *(FAA-H-8083-9A Chap 2)*

DISCUSSION: Blocked practice is practicing the same drill until the movement becomes automatic. Doing the same task over and over leads to better short-term performance but poorer long-term learning.

Answer (A) is incorrect. In order for a student to gain skill knowledge and learn how to perform the skill on the automatic level, a student must engage in deliberate practice. However, this type of practice in and of itself does not produce the ability to perform skills automatically. Answer (C) is incorrect. Random practice mixes up the skills to be acquired throughout the practice session to increase long-term skill retention. This practice type is not effective at producing automatic responses, but rather more meaningful ones.

78. Which stage of skill acquisition may be characterized by performing memorized steps unaware of progress?

A. Cognitive stage.

B. Associative stage.

C. Automatic response stage.

Answer (A) is correct. *(FAA-H-8083-9A Chap 2)*

DISCUSSION: In the cognitive stage, learning has a basis in factual knowledge. Since the student has no prior knowledge of flying, the instructor first introduces him or her to a basic skill. The student then memorizes the steps required to perform the skill. As the student carries out these memorized steps, (s)he is often unaware of progress or may fixate on one aspect of performance. Performance is deliberate and often characterized by the student making many abrupt control inputs.

Answer (B) is incorrect. At the associative stage, the student no longer performs a series of memorized steps but is able to assess his or her progress along the way and make adjustments in performance. Answer (C) is incorrect. By the automatic response stage, student performance of the skill is rapid and smooth. The student devotes much less deliberate attention to performance and may be able to carry on a conversation or perform other tasks while performing a skill.

79. Distractions interjected by instructors during training may help

A. students learn to ignore distractions.

B. students determine whether or not a distraction warrants further attention or action on their part.

C. students learn more effective multitasking techniques.

Answer (B) is correct. *(FAA-H-8083-9A Chap 8)*

DISCUSSION: A distraction is an unexpected event that causes the student's attention to be momentarily diverted. Students must learn to decide whether or not a distraction warrants further attention or action on their part. Once this has been decided, the students must either turn their attention back to what they were doing or act on the distraction.

Answer (A) is incorrect. Not all in-flight distractions should be ignored. Some require immediate action on the part of the pilot. Answer (C) is incorrect. Multitasking is not a strategy for identifying and prioritizing distractions during flight.

STUDY UNIT TWO
BARRIERS TO LEARNING

(4 pages of outline)

2.1 SELF-CONCEPT

1. Self-concept is how one pictures oneself.
   a. Self-concept or self-image can be described in terms such as "confident" or "insecure."
      1) "Confident" denotes a favorable view of self, or positive self-concept.
      2) "Insecure" denotes an unfavorable view of self, or negative self-concept.
   b. This is a powerful determinant in learning.
   c. Self-concept has a great influence on the total perceptual process.
2. If a student's experiences tend to support a favorable self-image, the student tends to remain receptive to subsequent experiences. These students are less defensive and more receptive to new experiences, instructions, and demonstrations.
3. Negative self-concept contributes most to a student's failure to remain receptive to new experiences and creates a tendency to reject additional training.
4. Instructors must be able to detect negative self-image in their students and strive to prevent these feelings from undermining the instructional process.
   a. An instructor can foster the development of insights by helping the student acquire and maintain a favorable self-concept.
      1) The way instructors conduct themselves, their own positive attitudes, and the manner in which they instruct can help their students achieve this positive view.
         a) EXAMPLE: During an introductory flight with a potential flight student, the instructor does not focus on emergency procedures or potential hazards to flight, but instead emphasizes how smooth, efficient, and enjoyable the flight was.

2.2 DEFENSE MECHANISMS

1. Certain behavior patterns are called defense mechanisms because they are subconscious defenses against the reality of unpleasant situations. People use these defenses to soften feelings of failure, alleviate feelings of guilt, and protect feelings of personal worth and adequacy.
2. Although defense mechanisms can serve a useful purpose, they can involve some degree of self-deception and distortion of reality.
   a. They alleviate symptoms, not causes.

3. Common defense mechanisms:
    a. **Repression** – A person places uncomfortable thoughts into inaccessible areas of the unconscious mind. For example, a student pilot may have a repressed fear of flying that inhibits his or her ability to learn how to fly.
        1) Things a person is unable to cope with at present are pushed away to be dealt with at another time, or hopefully never to be dealt with because they faded away on their own accord.
        2) The level of repression can vary from temporarily forgetting an uncomfortable thought to amnesia, where the events that triggered the anxiety are deeply buried.
        3) Repressed memories do not disappear and may reappear in dreams or slips of the tongue ("Freudian slips").
    b. **Denial** – Refusal to accept external reality because it is too threatening. It is the refusal to acknowledge what has happened, is happening, or will happen.
        1) Denial is a form of repression through which stressful thoughts are banned from memory.
        2) Related to denial is minimization. When a person minimizes something, (s)he accepts what happened, but in a diluted form, usually justifying the event because "nothing bad happened."
    c. **Compensation** – Process of psychologically counterbalancing perceived weaknesses by emphasizing strength in other areas.
        1) Students often attempt to disguise the presence of a weak or undesirable quality by emphasizing a more positive one.
        2) Compensation involves substituting success in a realm of life other than the realm in which the person suffers a weakness.
    d. **Projection** – An individual places his or her own unacceptable impulses onto someone else. A person relegates the blame for personal shortcomings, mistakes, and transgressions to others.
        1) A student pilot who fails a flight exam and says, "I failed because I had a poor examiner" believes the failure was not due to a lack of personal skill or knowledge.
        2) This student projects blame onto an "unfair" examiner.
    e. **Rationalization** – When a person cannot accept the real reasons for his or her own behavior, this device permits the substitution of excuses for reasons. Rationalization is a subconscious technique for justifying actions that otherwise would be unacceptable.
    f. **Reaction formation** – A person fakes a belief opposite to his or her true belief because the true belief causes anxiety. The person feels an urge to do or say something and then actually does or says something that is the opposite of what (s)he really wants.
    g. **Fantasy** – Occurs when a student engages in daydreams about how things should be rather than doing anything about how things are. The student uses his or her imagination to escape from reality into a fictitious world–a world of success or pleasure.
        1) Fantasy provides a simple and satisfying escape from problems, but if a student gets sufficient satisfaction from daydreaming, (s)he may stop trying to achieve goals altogether.
        2) Lost in the fantasy, the student spends more time dreaming about being a successful pilot than working toward the goal.
        3) When carried to extremes, the worlds of fantasy and reality can become so confused that the dreamer cannot distinguish one from the other.
    h. **Displacement** – Results in an unconscious shift of emotion, affect, or desire from the original object to a more acceptable, less threatening substitute.
        1) Displacement avoids the risk associated with feeling unpleasant emotions and puts them somewhere other than where they belong, similar to repression.

2.3 STRESS, ANXIETY, AND FATIGUE

1. Normal individuals react to stress by responding rapidly and exactly, often automatically, within their experience and training.
   a. This underlines the need for proper training prior to emergency situations.
   b. The effective individual thinks rapidly, acts rapidly, and is extremely sensitive to his or her surroundings.
2. Abnormal reactions to stress may result in inadequate, illogical, or random responses. These may include
   a. Inappropriate reactions, such as extreme overcooperation, painstaking self-control, inappropriate laughter or singing, and very rapid changes in emotion
   b. Marked changes in mood (e.g., high spirits followed by deep depression)
   c. Severe, unreasonable anger toward the flight instructor, service personnel, or others
3. Anxiety is probably the most significant psychological barrier affecting flight instruction. It is the extreme worry brought on by stressful situations (e.g., an emergency, an exam, etc.). Anxiety can be countered by
   a. Treating fears as a normal reaction rather than ignoring them,
   b. Reinforcing the student's enjoyment of flying, and
   c. Teaching students to cope with fears.
4. Fatigue is one of the most treacherous hazards to flight safety as it may not be apparent to a pilot until serious errors are made. Fatigue can be either acute (short-term) or chronic (long-term).
   a. **Acute fatigue**, a normal occurrence of everyday living, is the tiredness felt after long periods of physical and mental strain, including strenuous muscular effort, immobility, heavy mental workload, strong emotional pressure, monotony, and lack of sleep.
      1) A CFI who is familiar with the signs indicative of acute fatigue will be more aware if the student is experiencing them as the signs of acute fatigue are often apparent to others before the individual notices any signs of fatigue.
      2) Acute fatigue is characterized by
         a) Inattention
         b) Distractibility
         c) Errors in timing
         d) Neglect of secondary tasks
         e) Loss of accuracy and control
         f) Lack of awareness of error accumulation
         g) Irritability
   b. **Chronic fatigue** is a combination of both physiological problems and psychological issues and occurs when there is not enough time for a full recovery from repeated episodes of acute fatigue.
      1) Without resolution, human performance continues to fall off, judgment becomes impaired, and unwarranted risks may be taken.
      2) Recovery from chronic fatigue requires a prolonged and deliberate solution.
         a) Chronic fatigue's underlying cause is generally not "rest-related" and may have deeper points of origin. Therefore, rest alone may not resolve chronic fatigue.
            i) Chronic fatigue is a combination of both physiological problems and psychological issues. Psychological problems such as financial, home life, or job-related stresses cause a lack of quality rest that is only solved by mitigating the underlying problems before the fatigue is solved.

2.4 THE OVERCONFIDENT OR IMPATIENT STUDENT

1. Because they make few mistakes, students who are fast learners may assume that the correction of errors is unimportant.
   a. This overconfidence soon results in faulty performance.
   b. For apt students, a good instructor will constantly raise the standard of performance for each lesson, demanding greater effort.
2. Impatience is a greater deterrent to learning pilot skills than is generally recognized. For example: a strong desire to make an early solo flight.
   a. The impatient student fails to understand the need for preliminary training. (S)he seeks only the final objective without considering the means necessary to reach it.
   b. Instructors can correct impatience by presenting the necessary preliminary training one step at a time, with clearly stated goals for each step.
      1) Instructors should emphasize that it is necessary to master the basics if the entire task is to be performed competently and safely.
   c. Impatience can result from instruction set at the pace of a slow learner when it is applied to a motivated, fast learner.
      1) It is important that an instructor analyze each student's ability and adapt lessons accordingly to counteract this trait.

QUESTIONS AND ANSWER EXPLANATIONS: All of the Fundamentals of Instructing knowledge test questions chosen by the FAA for release as well as additional questions selected by Gleim relating to the material in the previous outlines are provided on the following pages. These questions have been organized into the same subunits as the outlines. To the immediate right of each question are the correct answer and answer explanations. You should cover these answers and answer explanations while responding to the questions. Refer to the general discussion in the Introduction on how to take the FAA knowledge test.

Remember that the questions from the FAA knowledge test bank have been reordered by topic and organized into a meaningful sequence. Also, the first line of the answer explanation gives the citation of the authoritative source for the answer.

QUESTIONS

2.1 Self-Concept

1. The factor which contributes most to a student's failure to remain receptive to new experiences and which creates a tendency to reject additional training is

A. basic needs.

B. element of threat.

C. negative self-concept.

Answer (C) is correct. *(FAA-H-8083-9A Chap 2)*

DISCUSSION: A student with a negative self-concept is resistant to new experiences and may reject additional training. People tend to avoid experiences that contradict their self-concept.

Answer (A) is incorrect. A student's basic needs can be used by the instructor to promote learning. For instance, personal safety is one of the most important basic needs, and aviation training heavily emphasizes this need. Answer (B) is incorrect. An element of threat will cause a student to limit his or her attention to the threatening object or condition. Once this is removed, the student will be able to learn.

2. An instructor may foster the development of insights by

A. helping the student acquire and maintain a favorable self-concept.

B. pointing out the attractive features of the activity to be learned.

C. keeping the rate of learning consistent so that it is predictable.

Answer (A) is correct. *(FAA-H-8083-9A Chap 2)*

DISCUSSION: Especially in a field such as aviation training, the instructor can foster the development of insights by helping the student acquire and maintain a favorable self-concept. The student who feels sure of his or her knowledge, skills, and judgments learned in class will also feel better about actual performance and his or her own ability to fly.

Answer (B) is incorrect. The attractive features in a learning situation tend to increase motivation rather than insight. Answer (C) is incorrect. Learning rates will vary, not stay constant, with each training lesson.

3. What is an outcome of a student showing a favorable self-concept?

A. A more receptive attitude to experiences.

B. Failure to remain open to new learning experiences.

C. A positive attitude on the part of the flight instructor.

Answer (A) is correct. *(FAA-H-8083-9A Chap 7)*

DISCUSSION: Students with a favorable self-concept will be more receptive to subsequent experiences. Students who show favorable self-concept are less defensive and more receptive to new experiences, instructions, and demonstrations.

Answer (B) is incorrect. Failure to remain open to new learning experiences is a result of an unfavorable view of self, or negative self-concept. Answer (C) is incorrect. An outcome of a student's favorable self-concept will not guarantee that a positive attitude will be shown by the instructor. However, the way in which instructors conduct themselves, and their own positive attitudes, can help their students achieve this same positive view.

4. Which term denotes a favorable view of self?

A. Insecure.

B. Unassured.

C. Confident.

Answer (C) is correct. *(FAA-H-8083-9A Chap 7)*

DISCUSSION: Being confident denotes a favorable view of self, or positive self-concept.

Answer (A) is incorrect. The term "insecure" denotes an unfavorable view of self, or negative self-concept. Answer (B) is incorrect. The term "unassured" is similar to the term "insecure" and portrays a negative view of self.

2.2 Defense Mechanisms

5. Defense mechanisms

A. are subject to the student's normal behavioral processes.

B. are related to the conscious domain.

C. involve some degree of self-deception and distortion of reality.

Answer (C) is correct. *(FAA-H-8083-9A Chap 1)*

DISCUSSION: Defense mechanisms involve some degree of self-deception and distortion of reality. They alleviate the symptoms but not the causes. Defense mechanisms do not solve problems. Moreover, because defense mechanisms operate on an unconscious level, they are not subject to normal conscious checks and balances.

Answer (A) is incorrect. Defense mechanisms occur on a subconscious level, and are thus not subject to the student's normal behavioral processes. Answer (B) is incorrect. Defense mechanisms are not related to the conscious domain.

6. Although defense mechanisms can serve a useful purpose, they can

A. provide feelings of adequacy.

B. alleviate the cause of problems.

C. involve some degree of self-deception and distortion of reality.

Answer (C) is correct. *(FAA-H-8083-9A Chap 1)*

DISCUSSION: Although defense mechanisms can serve a useful purpose, they can also be hindrances. Because they involve some self-deception and distortion of reality, defense mechanisms do not solve problems.

Answer (A) is incorrect. Defense mechanisms mask and protect feelings of adequacy rather than provide them. Answer (B) is incorrect. Defense mechanisms alleviate symptoms, not causes, of problems.

7. If an instructor has a student with a hidden fear of flying that inhibits learning, the student is most likely displaying which defense mechanism?

A. Reaction formation.

B. Repression.

C. Projection.

Answer (B) is correct. *(FAA-H-8083-9A Chap 1)*

DISCUSSION: Repression is the defense mechanism whereby a person places uncomfortable thoughts into inaccessible areas of the unconscious mind.

Answer (A) is incorrect. In reaction formation, a person fakes a belief opposite to the true belief because the true belief causes anxiety. Answer (C) is incorrect. Through projection, an individual places his or her own unacceptable impulses onto someone else.

8. When a student uses excuses to justify inadequate performance, it is an indication of the defense mechanism known as

A. fantasy.

B. displacement.

C. rationalization.

Answer (C) is correct. *(FAA-H-8083-9A Chap 1)*

DISCUSSION: Rationalization is a subconscious technique for justifying unacceptable actions or performance. This allows a student to substitute excuses for reasons and make those excuses plausible and acceptable to themselves.

Answer (A) is incorrect. Fantasy is the defense mechanism in which the student escapes (either physically or mentally) from a frustrating experience. Answer (B) is incorrect. Displacement is the defense mechanism in which the student shifts emotion, affect, or desire from the original object to a more acceptable, less threatening substitute.

9. Fantasy is a defense mechanism students use when they

A. want to escape from frustrating situations.

B. cannot accept the real reasons for their behavior.

C. place blame on someone or something other than themselves.

Answer (A) is correct. *(FAA-H-8083-9A Chap 1)*

DISCUSSION: The defense mechanism of flight allows a student to escape from a frustrating situation. This escape can be physical flight (absenteeism, illness, etc.) or mental flight (daydreaming).

Answer (B) is incorrect. If a student cannot accept the real reasons for his or her behavior, (s)he may rationalize, not take flight. Answer (C) is incorrect. Students who place blame on someone or something other than themselves are displaying the defense mechanism of projection.

10. Students may display the defense mechanism called denial, which is revealed by the student's

A. hostility.

B. attempts to minimize the situation.

C. attempts at rationalization.

Answer (B) is correct. *(FAA-H-8083-9A Chap 1)*

DISCUSSION: Minimization is related to denial. When a person minimizes something, (s)he accepts what happened but in a diluted form.

Answer (A) is incorrect. Aggression is not associated with the defense mechanism of denial. Answer (C) is incorrect. Rationalization is the process of justifying a course of action, not denying it.

11. When students subconsciously use the defense mechanism called rationalization, they

A. use excuses to justify acceptable behavior.

B. cannot accept the real reasons for their behavior.

C. fake a belief opposite to their true belief because the true belief causes anxiety.

Answer (B) is correct. *(FAA-H-8083-9A Chap 1)*

DISCUSSION: Rationalization is a subconscious technique for justifying unacceptable actions or performance. This allows a student to substitute excuses for reasons and make those excuses plausible and acceptable to themselves.

Answer (A) is incorrect. In rationalization, excuses are used to justify unacceptable, not acceptable, behavior. Answer (C) is incorrect. When students fake a belief opposite to their true belief, they are displaying the defense mechanism of reaction formation. This is done because their true belief causes them anxiety.

12. When a student engages in daydreaming, it is the defense mechanism of

A. compensation.

B. fantasy.

C. denial.

Answer (B) is correct. *(FAA-H-8083-9A Chap 1)*

DISCUSSION: A student engaging in daydreaming is an example of fantasy or mental escape.

Answer (A) is incorrect. Through compensation, students often attempt to disguise the presence of a weak or undesirable quality by emphasizing a more positive one. Answer (C) is incorrect. Denial is a refusal to accept external reality because it is too threatening. It is the refusal to acknowledge what has happened, is happening, or will happen.

13. When students display the defense mechanism called repression, they

A. refuse to accept reality.

B. place uncomfortable thoughts into inaccessible areas of the unconscious mind.

C. attempt to justify actions by asking numerous questions.

Answer (B) is correct. *(FAA-H-8083-9A Chap 1)*

DISCUSSION: In repression, things a person is unable to cope with in the present are pushed away to be dealt with at another time, or hopefully never to be dealt with at all because they faded away on their own accord.

Answer (A) is incorrect. When students refuse to accept reality, they are exhibiting the defense mechanism of denial. Answer (C) is incorrect. Attempting to justify actions is an example of rationalization.

14. When a student presents a belief opposite to what (s)he truly believes, it usually is an indication of the defense mechanism known as

A. fantasy.

B. reaction formation.

C. displacement.

Answer (B) is correct. *(FAA-H-8083-9A Chap 1)*

DISCUSSION: In reaction formation, a person fakes a belief opposite to his or her true belief because the true belief causes anxiety.

Answer (A) is incorrect. Fantasy is the defense mechanism when a person mentally removes himself or herself from a frustrating situation. Answer (C) is incorrect. Displacement is the defense mechanism in which the student shifts emotion, affect, or desire from the original object to a more acceptable, less threatening substitute.

15. When a student attempts to disguise the presence of a weak or undesirable quality by emphasizing a more positive one, the defense mechanism is usually in the form of

A. projection.

B. compensation.

C. rationalization.

Answer (B) is correct. *(FAA-H-8083-9A Chap 1)*
DISCUSSION: Compensation is a process of psychologically counterbalancing perceived weaknesses by emphasizing strength in other areas.
Answer (A) is incorrect. Through projection, an individual places blame for his or her own unacceptable impulses onto someone else. Answer (C) is incorrect. Rationalization is a process of making excuses for unacceptable behavior.

16. A student pilot who fails a practical test and attributes the failure to an "unfair" evaluation by the examiner may be demonstrating a defense mechanism known as

A. Rationalization.

B. Projection.

C. Denial.

Answer (B) is correct. *(FAA-H-8083-9A Chap 1)*
DISCUSSION: Through projection, an individual places his or her own unacceptable impulses onto someone else. A person relegates the blame for personal shortcomings, mistakes, and transgressions to others.
Answer (A) is incorrect. Rationalization is a subconscious technique for justifying actions that otherwise would be unacceptable. It does not involve the placement of blame on any other party. Answer (C) is incorrect. Denial is a refusal to accept external reality because it is too threatening. It does not involve the placement of blame on any other party.

2.3 Stress, Anxiety, and Fatigue

17. When under stress, normal individuals usually react

A. by showing excellent morale followed by deep depression.

B. by responding rapidly and exactly, often automatically, within the limits of their experience and training.

C. inappropriately such as extreme overcooperation, painstaking self-control, and inappropriate laughing or singing.

Answer (B) is correct. *(FAA-H-8083-9A Chap 1)*
DISCUSSION: When under stress, normal individuals begin to respond rapidly and exactly, within the limits of their experience and training. Many responses are automatic, which indicates the need for proper training in emergency operations prior to an actual emergency.
Answer (A) is incorrect. Marked changes in mood, e.g., excellent morale followed by deep depression is an abnormal, not a normal, reaction to stress. Answer (C) is incorrect. Inappropriate reactions, such as extreme overcooperation, painstaking self-control, and inappropriate laughter or singing, are abnormal, not normal, reactions to stress.

18. A student reacting abnormally to stress is most likely to display which of the following indications?

A. The student is using automatic responses.

B. The student has a rapid and exacting response.

C. The student is using inadequate, illogical, random responses or no response at all.

Answer (C) is correct. *(FAA-H-8083-9A Chap 1)*
DISCUSSION: The following student reactions are indicative of abnormal reactions to stress. None of them provides an absolute indication, but the presence of any of them under conditions of stress is reason for careful instructor evaluation. Instructors should look for inappropriate reactions, such as extreme over-cooperation, painstaking self-control, inappropriate laughter or singing, and very rapid changes in emotions. Marked changes in mood on different lessons, such as excellent morale followed by deep depression and severe anger directed toward the flight instructor, service personnel, and others are warning signs of unusual reactions to stress.
Answer (A) is incorrect. A student using automatic responses is a normal reaction to stress. Answer (B) is incorrect. A rapid and exacting response is a normal reaction to stress.

19. Which would most likely be an indication that a student is reacting abnormally to stress?

A. Slow learning.

B. Inappropriate laughter or singing.

C. Automatic response to a given situation.

Answer (B) is correct. *(FAA-H-8083-9A Chap 1)*
DISCUSSION: Inappropriate laughter or singing is an abnormal reaction to stress. The instructor should be alert for other inappropriate (and possibly dangerous) reactions.
Answer (A) is incorrect. Slow learning is a normal, not an abnormal, reaction to stress. Answer (C) is incorrect. Automatic response to a given situation is a normal, not an abnormal, reaction to stress.

20. One possible indication of a student's abnormal reaction to stress would be

A. a hesitancy to act.

B. extreme overcooperation.

C. a noticeable lack of self-control.

Answer (B) is correct. *(FAA-H-8083-9A Chap 1)*

DISCUSSION: Extreme overcooperation is an indication that a student is reacting abnormally to stress. The abnormally tense or anxious student may be noticeably over-agreeable.

Answer (A) is incorrect. A hesitancy to act is an indication of anxiety, not an abnormal reaction to stress. Answer (C) is incorrect. Painstaking self-control, not a lack thereof, is an indication of an abnormal reaction to stress.

21. The instructor can counteract anxiety in a student by

A. treating the student's fears as a normal reaction.

B. discontinuing instruction in tasks that cause anxiety.

C. allowing the student to decide when he or she is ready for a new maneuver to be introduced.

Answer (A) is correct. *(FAA-H-8083-9A Chap 1)*

DISCUSSION: Psychologists tell us that a student's fear is a normal reaction and should be treated as such by an instructor. Treating fear as normal will help in counteracting anxiety.

Answer (B) is incorrect. Discontinuing instruction in stressful tasks will not help the student to overcome the anxiety. Perhaps a different approach to the task is necessary. Answer (C) is incorrect. It describes an example of negative motivation, which would tend to contribute to the student's anxiety.

22. Which of the following is required to recover from chronic fatigue?

A. Mitigating the underlying physiological and psychological causes.

B. A break in instruction and practice.

C. Proper rest and time to "clear your thoughts."

Answer (A) is correct. *(FAA-H-8083-9A Chap 8)*

DISCUSSION: The underlying cause of chronic fatigue is generally not rest-related and may have deeper points of origin. Psychological problems such as financial, home life, or job-related stresses are some examples. Mitigating the underlying problems is essential before the fatigue issue can be solved.

Answer (B) is incorrect. Chronic fatigue is only solved by mitigating the underlying problems that are causing the fatigue. Answer (C) is incorrect. Chronic fatigue is only solved by mitigating the underlying problems that are causing the fatigue.

23. The principal reason why fatigue is one of the most treacherous hazards to flight safety is that

A. fatigue can overtake even a physically robust person.

B. it is usually impossible for a CFI to detect student fatigue early in a lesson.

C. it may not be apparent to a pilot until serious errors are made.

Answer (C) is correct. *(FAA-H-8083-9A Chap 8)*

DISCUSSION: Fatigue is one of the most treacherous hazards to flight safety because it may not be apparent to a pilot until serious errors are made.

Answer (A) is incorrect. Although it is true that fatigue can overtake even a physically robust person, this is not the principal reason why it is such a treacherous hazard. Answer (B) is incorrect. It is important for a CFI to be able to detect fatigue, both in assessing a student's substandard performance early in a lesson and in recognizing the deterioration of performance.

24. Chronic fatigue

A. Occurs when there is not enough time for a full recovery from repeated episodes of acute fatigue.

B. Is the tiredness felt after long periods of physical and mental strain and lack of sleep.

C. Impairs personal performance and ability but not pilot judgment.

Answer (A) is correct. *(FAA-H-8083-9A Chap 8)*

DISCUSSION: Prolonged exposure to acute fatigue without adequate time for recovery can result in chronic fatigue.

Answer (B) is incorrect. This describes acute, not chronic, fatigue. Chronic fatigue's underlying cause is generally not "rest-related" and may have deeper points of origin. Answer (C) is incorrect. Unless preventive measures are taken, chronic fatigue will certainly impact both personal performance and pilot judgment.

25. Chronic fatigue may best be described as a

A. combination of both physiological problems and psychological issues.

B. cluster of specific symptoms such as errors in timing and neglect of secondary tasks.

C. result of over-application of a learning task.

Answer (A) is correct. *(FAA-H-8083-9A Chap 8)*

DISCUSSION: Chronic fatigue is a combination of both physiological problems and psychological issues.

Answer (B) is incorrect. Errors in timing and neglect of secondary tasks are symptoms of acute, not chronic, fatigue. Answer (C) is incorrect. Acute fatigue occurs as a result of the over-application of a learning task. To prevent this, the student should be given a break in instruction and practice.

26. Chronic fatigue as a result of physiological problems and/or psychological issues may be evidenced by a student pilot's apparent

A. Increase in knowledge and skill retention.

B. Need for sleep.

C. Acceptance of unwarranted risks.

Answer (C) is correct. *(FAA-H-8083-9A Chap 8)*

DISCUSSION: Without resolving the underlying causes of chronic fatigue, human performance gradually falls off, judgment becomes impaired, and unwarranted risks may be taken.

Answer (A) is incorrect. Chronic fatigue brings about a decrease, not an increase, in a student's knowledge and skill retention. Answer (B) is incorrect. Chronic fatigue's underlying cause is generally not "rest-related" and may have deeper points of origin. Therefore, rest alone may not resolve chronic fatigue.

27. Acute fatigue symptoms may include

A. error accumulation, inattention, and distractibility.

B. dizziness, weakness, nausea, tingling of hands and feet, abdominal cramps, and extreme thirst.

C. unwarranted risk taking.

Answer (A) is correct. *(FAA-H-8083-9A Chap 8)*

DISCUSSION: Acute fatigue is characterized by, among other things, inattention, distractibility, and errors in timing.

Answer (B) is incorrect. Dizziness, weakness, nausea, tingling of hands and feet, abdominal cramps, and extreme thirst are symptoms of dehydration, not acute fatigue. Answer (C) is incorrect. Unwarranted risk taking is a symptom of chronic fatigue, not acute fatigue.

28. A sign that a student may be experiencing acute fatigue is

A. Acceptance of unwarranted risks.

B. Neglect of secondary tasks.

C. Increased attention to detail.

Answer (B) is correct. *(FAA-H-8083-9A Chap 8)*

DISCUSSION: A CFI who is familiar with the signs indicative of acute fatigue will be more aware if the student is experiencing them. One common sign of acute fatigue is the neglect of secondary tasks. Because the mind's resources are limited, secondary or non-essential tasks are often overlooked.

Answer (A) is incorrect. Acceptance of unwarranted risks is a common indicator of chronic, not acute, fatigue. Pilot judgment as it relates to safety decisions is not typically compromised in acute fatigue, but this would be a common deficiency in someone suffering from chronic fatigue. Answer (C) is incorrect. Inattention, not increased attention, to detail is a common sign of acute fatigue.

29. Acute fatigue is

A. a function of physical robustness or mental acuity.

B. a combination of both physiological problems and psychological issues.

C. observable by performance deficiencies that are apparent to others before the individual notices any physical signs of fatigue.

Answer (C) is correct. *(FAA-H-8083-9A Chap 8)*

DISCUSSION: Acute fatigue may be observed by performance deficiencies that are apparent to others before the individual notices any physical signs of fatigue. One of the main characteristics of acute fatigue is lack of awareness of error accumulation. Third parties can, therefore, notice errors before you.

Answer (A) is incorrect. Acute fatigue is not necessarily a function of physical robustness or mental acuity. Answer (B) is incorrect. Chronic fatigue, not acute fatigue, is a combination of both physiological problems and psychological issues.

30. Which of the following is a sign of acute fatigue?

A. Error accumulation.

B. Nausea.

C. Acuteness of vision.

Answer (A) is correct. *(FAA-H-8083-9A Chap 8)*

DISCUSSION: Acute fatigue is characterized by such symptoms as inattention, distractibility, errors in timing, and neglect of secondary tasks. Error accumulation is a result of these types of symptoms.

Answer (B) is incorrect. Nausea is a symptom of dehydration, not acute fatigue. Answer (C) is incorrect. Acuteness of vision is a possible symptom of a minor illness, such as a cold, not acute fatigue.

31. Acute fatigue may be evident by a student's apparent

A. desire to take unwarranted risks.

B. dizziness, weakness, and nausea.

C. errors in timing.

Answer (C) is correct. *(FAA-H-8083-9A Chap 8)*

DISCUSSION: Acute fatigue is characterized by such symptoms as inattention, distractibility, and errors in timing.

Answer (A) is incorrect. The desire to take unwarranted risks is a symptom of chronic, not acute, fatigue. Answer (B) is incorrect. Dizziness, weakness, and nausea are symptoms of dehydration and heat stroke.

32. Which would most likely be an indication that a student is reacting normally to stress?

A. Slow learning.

B. Inappropriate laughter or singing.

C. Automatic response to a given situation.

Answer (C) is correct. *(FAA-H-8083-9A Chap 1)*

DISCUSSION: When under stress, normal individuals begin to respond rapidly and exactly, within the limits of their experience and training. Many responses are automatic, which indicates the need for proper training in emergency operations prior to an actual emergency.

Answer (A) is incorrect. While slow learning can be a normal reaction to stress, it could also be the result of a learning plateau. This choice is not the best answer to the question because it could just as likely be the result of something else as the result of an abnormal reaction to stress. Answer (B) is incorrect. Inappropriate laughter or singing is an abnormal, not a normal, reaction to stress.

2.4 The Overconfident or Impatient Student

33. Students who grow impatient when learning the basic elements of a task are those who

A. are less easily discouraged than the unaggressive students.

B. should have the preliminary training presented one step at a time with clearly stated goals for each step.

C. should be advanced to the next higher level of learning and not held back by insisting that the immediate goal be reached before they proceed to the next level.

Answer (B) is correct. *(FAA-H-8083-9A Chap 8)*

DISCUSSION: Impatient students fail to see why they must learn one step thoroughly before they move to the next. Presenting the preliminary training with clearly stated goals for each step will minimize student impatience.

Answer (A) is incorrect. Impatient students are often aggressive and more easily discouraged than unaggressive students. Answer (C) is incorrect. It is necessary to hold a student until (s)he masters the basics if the whole task is to be performed competently and safely. This is the basis of the building block technique of instruction.

34. Which obstacle to learning is a greater deterrent to learning pilot skills than is generally recognized?

A. Anxiety.

B. Impatience.

C. Physical discomfort.

Answer (B) is correct. *(FAA-H-8083-9A Chap 8)*

DISCUSSION: Failing to understand the need for preliminary training, the impatient student can only see the ultimate objective of flying an airplane. This impatience can be detrimental to the usual, careful acquisition of pilot skills.

Answer (A) is incorrect. Although anxiety may be detrimental to the learning process, it is generally recognized as such, whereas impatience has an equal effect and is not widely recognized. Answer (C) is incorrect. Although physical discomfort may be detrimental to the learning process, it is generally recognized as such, whereas impatience has an equal effect and is not widely recognized.

35. Should an instructor be concerned about an apt student who makes very few mistakes?

A. No. Some students have an innate, natural aptitude for flight.

B. Yes. The student may assume that the correction of errors is unimportant.

C. Yes. The student will lose confidence in the instructor if the instructor does not invent deficiencies in the student's performance.

Answer (B) is correct. *(FAA-H-8083-9A Chap 7)*

DISCUSSION: Because apt students make few mistakes, they may assume that the correction of errors is not important. Such overconfidence soon results in faulty performance. For such students, a good instructor will constantly raise the standard of performance for each lesson, demanding greater effort.

Answer (A) is incorrect. Regardless of natural gift, apt students may assume that the correction of errors is not important. Such overconfidence soon results in faulty performance. Answer (C) is incorrect. The instructor should not invent deficiencies in order to diminish a student's confidence. On the contrary, a good instructor will constantly raise the standard of performance for each lesson, demanding greater effort.

36. What should an instructor do with a student who assumes that correction of errors is not important?

A. Divide complex flight maneuvers into elements.

B. Try to reduce the student's overconfidence to reduce the chance of an accident.

C. Raise the standard of performance for each lesson, demanding greater effort.

Answer (C) is correct. *(FAA-H-8083-9A Chap 7)*

DISCUSSION: Because apt students make few mistakes, they may assume that the correction of errors is not important. Such overconfidence soon results in faulty performance. For such students, a good instructor will constantly raise the standard of performance for each lesson, demanding greater effort.

Answer (A) is incorrect. Dividing complex tasks into simpler elements should be done with students whose slow progress is due to a lack of confidence, not apt students. Answer (B) is incorrect. Reducing students' overconfidence would be inefficient for properly motivating the apt student. After realizing the impatience of such students comes only from improperly paced instruction, instructors should give them challenges fitting their abilities.

37. The overconfidence of fast learners should be corrected by

A. high praise when no errors are made.

B. raising the standard of performance for each lesson.

C. providing strong, negative evaluation at the end of each lesson.

Answer (B) is correct. *(FAA-H-8083-9A Chap 7)*

DISCUSSION: Because apt students make few mistakes, they may assume that the correction of errors is not important. Such overconfidence soon results in faulty performance. For such students, a good instructor will constantly raise the standard of performance for each lesson, demanding greater effort.

Answer (A) is incorrect. High praise will only lead the student to become more overconfident. Answer (C) is incorrect. A strong, negative evaluation should not be used to diminish a student's confidence. On the contrary, a good instructor will constantly raise the standard of performance for each lesson, demanding greater effort.

38. Faulty performance due to student overconfidence should be corrected by

A. increasing the standard of performance for each lesson.

B. praising the student only when the performance is perfect.

C. providing strong, negative evaluation at the end of each lesson.

Answer (A) is correct. *(FAA-H-8083-9A Chap 7)*

DISCUSSION: Because apt students make few mistakes, they may assume that the correction of errors is not important. Such overconfidence soon results in faulty performance. For such students, a good instructor will constantly raise the standard of performance for each lesson, demanding greater effort.

Answer (B) is incorrect. Students need consistent, fair critique of every performance, perfect or not. Overly high standards also frustrate students by making them work too hard without reward (and for an unrealistic goal). Answer (C) is incorrect. The principle of effect states that learning is weakened when associated with an unpleasant feeling. Aside from being unfair, the continual negative evaluations will also increasingly frustrate students.

39. A method for correcting student impatience is for the instructor to

A. Present the necessary preliminary training one step at a time, with clearly stated goals for each step.

B. Key the instruction to utilize the interests and enthusiasm students bring with them.

C. Avoid assigning impossible or unreasonable goals for the student to accomplish.

Answer (A) is correct. *(FAA-H-8083-9A Chap 8)*

DISCUSSION: With every complex human endeavor, it is necessary to master the basics if the whole task is to be performed competently and safely. The instructor can correct student impatience by presenting the necessary preliminary training one step at a time, with clearly stated goals for each step.

Answer (B) is incorrect. This solution is appropriate for combating worry or lack of interest on the part of the student, not impatience. Answer (C) is incorrect. This solution is appropriate for combating a student's feelings of unfair treatment during flight instruction, not impatience.

40. What is an example of a student showing impatience?

A. A student not wanting to fly without an instructor on board.

B. A student desiring to conduct a cross-country flight before the basic elements of flight have been learned.

C. A student wishing to solo an aircraft.

Answer (B) is correct. *(FAA-H-8083-9A Chap 8)*

DISCUSSION: An impatient student wants to undertake tasks before (s)he is ready or competent. An impatient student seeks only the final objective without considering the means necessary to reach it.

Answer (A) is incorrect. An example of a student not wanting to fly solo would show worry, not impatience. Answer (C) is incorrect. There is nothing wrong with a student desiring to accomplish a task such as flying an aircraft solo. An impatient student, however, would want to solo before (s)he is properly prepared and competent.

STUDY UNIT THREE
FACTORS AFFECTING LEARNING

(11 pages of outline)

Study Units 1 and 2 cover the learning process and barriers to learning, respectively. This study unit discusses human behavior, communication skills, and instructor professionalism. Understanding all three of these topics will help you become an exemplary instructor.

1) You need to understand human behavior and how to guide your students to be safe and responsible pilots. The subunit on Aeronautical Decision Making and Risk Management will help you correct the negative behaviors your students may have.
2) Possessing knowledge of what it takes to be a safe and proficient pilot is but one important element of being a competent instructor. You must also have effective communication skills so you can pass this knowledge to your students.
3) Being an instructor is a significant responsibility. Pilots and others in the aviation community hold Flight Instructors and Ground Instructors in the highest esteem, and your daily actions must reflect professionalism. It is imperative that you model your behavior as a standard-setter and be professional at all times.

3.1 HUMAN NEEDS

1. Human needs can be organized into a series of levels. The "pyramid of human needs" has been suggested by Abraham Maslow. For instance, physical needs must be satisfied before so-called "higher" needs can be used as motivators. He suggests that needs must be satisfied in the following ascending order.
2. **Physiological needs** are biological needs.
   a. They consist of the need for air, food, water, and maintenance of the human body.
   b. Unless the biological needs are met, a person cannot concentrate fully on learning, self-expression, or any other tasks.
   c. Instructors should monitor their students to make sure that their basic physical needs have been met. A hungry or tired student may not be able to perform as expected.
3. **Safety and security needs** become essential after the basic biological needs are met.
   a. Security needs are about keeping oneself from harm.
   b. The aviation instructor who stresses flight safety during training mitigates feelings of insecurity.
4. **Love and belonging needs** are social needs that people pursue to overcome feelings of loneliness and alienation.
   a. Aviation students are usually out of their normal surroundings during training, and their need for association and belonging is more pronounced.
   b. Instructors should make every effort to help new students feel at ease and to reinforce their decision to pursue a career or hobby in aviation.

5. **Esteem needs** are about feeling good about oneself.
   a. Humans have a need for a stable, firmly based, high level of self-respect and respect from others.
   b. Humans get esteem in two ways: internally or externally.
      1) Internally, a person judges himself or herself worthy by personally defined standards.
         a) High self-esteem results in self-confidence, independence, achievement, competence, and knowledge.
      2) Most people, however, seek external esteem through social approval and esteem from other people, judging themselves by what others think of them.
         a) External self-esteem relates to one's reputation, such as status, recognition, appreciation, and respect of associates.
   c. When esteem needs are satisfied, a person feels self-confident and valuable as a person in the world.
      1) When these needs are frustrated, the person feels inferior, weak, helpless, and worthless.
      2) Esteem needs not only have a strong influence on the student-instructor relationship but also may be the main reason for a student's interest in aviation training.
6. **Cognitive and aesthetic needs** include the need to know and understand and the emotional results of achievement.
   a. Humans have a deep need to understand what is going on around them. If a person understands what is going on, (s)he can either control the situation or make informed choices about what steps might be taken next.
   b. The brain even reinforces this need by giving humans a rush of dopamine whenever something is learned, which accounts for that satisfying "eureka!" moment, such as when a student pilot completes his or her first solo flight.
   c. Aesthetic needs (e.g., how well something is liked) can factor into the student-instructor relationship. If an instructor does not "like" a student, this subtle feeling may affect the instructor's ability to teach that student, and vice versa.
7. **Self-actualization needs** include a person's need to be and do what the person was "born to do."
   a. These needs are only triggered when all underlying needs are met.
   b. Self-actualized people realize their potential, seek to develop themselves further, and think creatively.
   c. Self-actualized people are characterized by
      1) Being problem-focused
      2) Incorporating an ongoing freshness of appreciation of life
      3) A concern about personal growth
      4) The ability to have peak experiences
   d. Helping a student achieve his or her individual potential in aviation training offers the greatest challenge as well as the greatest reward to the instructor.

3.2 MOTIVATION

1. Motivation is the reason one acts or behaves in a certain way and lies at the heart of goals.
   a. Motivation is probably the dominant force governing the student's progress and ability to learn.
   b. Slumps in learning are often due to declining motivation.
2. **Positive motivation** is essential to true learning, is provided by the promise or achievement of rewards, and is generally the more effective way to properly motivate students.
   a. Such rewards may involve financial gain, satisfaction of the self-concept, personal gain, or public recognition.
      1) Intangible positive motivations may include the desire for personal comfort and security, group approval, and the achievement of a favorable self image.
      2) Tangible positive motivation may include rewards that involve financial gain or public recognition.
3. **Negative motivations** are those that cause a student to react with fear and anxiety.
   a. Negative motivations in the form of reproof and threats should be avoided with all but the most overconfident and impulsive students.
4. Motivations may be
   a. Positive or negative
   b. Tangible or intangible
   c. Obvious or subtle and difficult to identify
5. Sources of motivation vary, but all offer some type of reward in exchange for performing work. It is important for an instructor to make the student aware that a particular lesson can help him or her reach an important goal.
   a. When students are unable to see the benefits or purpose of a lesson, they will be less motivated.
   b. Confusion, disinterest, and uneasiness on the part of the student could happen as a result of not knowing the objective of each period of instruction.
   c. If motivation is to be effective, students must believe that their efforts will be suitably rewarded in a definite, tangible manner.
6. To maintain motivation, an instructor must reward success by frequently presenting positive feedback.
   a. EXAMPLE: Praising incremental successes during training, relating daily accomplishments to lesson objectives, and commenting favorably on student progress.
7. Student anxiety can be minimized throughout training by emphasizing the benefits and pleasurable experiences that can be derived from flying, rather than by continuously citing the unhappy consequences of faulty performances.
8. Both drops in motivation and learning plateaus, which are a common source of frustration, are normal and can be overcome by reminding students of their own goals and reassuring them that there will be rewards for their continued efforts.

3.3 AERONAUTICAL DECISION MAKING AND RISK MANAGEMENT

1. **Aeronautical decision making (ADM)** can be defined as a systematic approach to the mental process used by pilots to consistently determine the best course of action in response to a given set of circumstances.
2. One step in the ADM process for good decision making is to identify personal attitudes hazardous to safe flight.
   a. Examples of classical behavioral traps that experienced pilots may fall into are the compulsion to complete a flight as planned, the desire to please passengers, the pressure to meet schedules, and the determination to get the job done.
   b. At some time, many experienced pilots have fallen prey to dangerous tendencies or behavior problems that must be identified and eliminated, including
      1) Peer pressure
      2) Scud running
      3) Loss of positional or situational awareness
      4) Operating without adequate fuel reserves
   c. In order to gain a realistic perspective on your attitude toward flying, you should take a Self-Assessment Hazardous Attitude Inventory Test.
   d. ADM addresses the following five hazardous attitudes:
      1) **Antiauthority** – "Do not tell me what to do!"
         a) EXAMPLE: During a stall recovery, the CFI allows the student to exceed maneuvering speed. An antiauthority attitude expressed by the CFI would be "The aircraft can handle a lot more than the maneuvering speed."
      2) **Impulsivity** – "Do something quickly!"
         a) EXAMPLE: On short final, the CFI realizes his student has forgotten to lower the flaps and immediately adds full flaps. The impulsivity attitude expressed by the CFI would be "I have to extend the flaps to get this aircraft down."
      3) **Invulnerability** – "It will not happen to me."
         a) EXAMPLE: Before a flight, the CFI does not check to verify a student has completed a pre-flight inspection. The invulnerability attitude expressed by the CFI would be "Nothing bad will happen on this flight."
      4) **Macho** – "I can do it."
         a) EXAMPLE: A pilot is on an instrument approach in which the aircraft in front of him have had to go around yet continues instead of diverting to an alternate. The macho attitude expressed by the pilot would be "I am better than others and can make it."
      5) **Resignation** – "What is the use?"
         a) EXAMPLE: A non-instrument-rated pilot continues into an area of known low visibility. The resignation attitude expressed by the pilot would be "What can I do about the weather conditions?"
3. In the ADM process, the first step in neutralizing a hazardous attitude is recognizing it.
   a. When you recognize a hazardous thought, you should label it as hazardous; then correct the attitude by stating the corresponding antidote.
   b. Hazardous attitudes, which contribute to poor pilot judgment, can be effectively counteracted by the appropriate antidote, as listed below.
      1) Antiauthority -- "Follow the rules. They are usually right."
      2) Impulsivity -- "Not so fast. Think first."
      3) Invulnerability -- "It could happen to me."
      4) Macho -- "Taking chances is foolish."
      5) Resignation -- "I am not helpless. I can make a difference."

4. **Stress** describes the body's response to a set of circumstances that induces a change in an individual's current physiological and/or psychological patterns of functioning, forcing the individual to adapt to these changes.
   a. Success in reducing stress associated with crisis management on the flight deck begins by making a personal assessment of stress in all areas of your life.
   b. To help manage flight deck stress, you should try to relax and think rationally at the first sign of stress.
5. The DECIDE process consists of six elements to help provide a pilot a logical way of approaching ADM. These elements are to
   a. **D**etect
   b. **E**stimate
   c. **C**hoose
   d. **I**dentify
   e. **D**o
   f. **E**valuate

   These elements represent a continuous loop decision process that can be used to assist a pilot in the decision-making process when faced with a change in a situation that requires a judgment.
6. A flight instructor should begin teaching ADM when the student has the ability to control the airplane confidently during the most basic maneuvers.
7. **Risk management** is a decision-making process designed to systematically identify hazards, assess the degree of risk, and determine the best course of action associated with each flight. This process relies on situational awareness, problem identification, and good judgment to reduce the risks associated with each flight.
   a. **Situational awareness** is defined as the accurate perception and understanding of all the factors and conditions within the four fundamental risk elements that affect safety before, during, and after the flight.
   b. The four fundamental risk elements in the ADM process that comprise any given aviation situation are the
      1) **Pilot (PIC)** – The pilot's fitness to fly must be evaluated, including competency in the aircraft, currency, and flight experience.
      2) **Aircraft** – The aircraft performance, limitations, equipment, and airworthiness must be determined.
      3) **Environment** – Factors such as weather and airport conditions must be examined.
      4) **External pressures** – The purpose of the flight is a factor that influences the pilot's decision to begin or continue the flight.
   c. Risk management involves two broad steps: risk assessment and risk mitigation.
      1) Every flight has hazards and some level of risk associated with it. It is critical that pilots and especially students are able to differentiate in advance between a low-risk flight and a high-risk flight and then establish a review process and develop risk mitigation strategies to address flights throughout that range.
      2) All identified risks should be addressed in proper risk management. Risks must be either accepted or mitigated in some way.
         a) Common mitigation strategies include taking along a more experienced pilot or flight instructor, delaying the flight, or canceling the flight altogether.

3.4 EFFECTIVE COMMUNICATION

1. The process of communication is composed of three dynamically interrelated elements:
   a. A source (instructor)
   b. The symbols used in composing and transmitting the message (e.g., words)
   c. The receiver (student)
2. Communication takes place when one person transmits ideas or feelings to another person or to a group of people.
   a. The effectiveness of communication is measured by the similarity between the idea transmitted and the idea received.
   b. Effective communication has taken place when, and only when, the receivers react with understanding and change their behavior accordingly.
   c. Instruction has taken place when a procedure has been explained and the desired student response has occurred.
3. The effectiveness of persons acting in the role of communicators is related to at least three basic factors.
   a. First, their ability to select symbols that are meaningful to the listener.
   b. Second, communicators consciously or unconsciously reveal attitudes toward themselves, toward the ideas they are trying to transmit, and toward their receivers.
      1) Thus, to communicate effectively, instructors must reveal a positive attitude while delivering their message.
   c. Third, to be more likely to communicate effectively, communicators should speak or write from a broad background of accurate, up-to-date, stimulating material.
4. **Symbols** are oral and visual codes used to communicate.
   a. Ideas are communicated only when symbols are combined into meaningful wholes (e.g., sentences, paragraphs, chapters, etc.).
   b. Symbols are perceived through three sensory channels: visual, auditory, or kinesthetic (touching, doing, etc.).
      1) Instructors will be more successful in gaining and retaining student attention by using a variety of these channels.
   c. The feedback an instructor gets from a student needs to be monitored constantly in order to modify the symbols, as required, to optimize communication.
5. To understand the process of communication, at least three characteristics of receivers must be understood.
   a. First, they exercise their ability to question and comprehend the ideas that have been transmitted.
   b. Second, the receiver's attitude may be one of resistance, willingness, or of passive neutrality. Communicators must gain the receiver's attention and then retain it.
      1) The communicator will be more successful in this area by using a varied communicative approach.
   c. Third, the receiver's background, experience, and education frame the target at which communications must aim.

3.5 BARRIERS TO EFFECTIVE COMMUNICATION

1. Probably the greatest single barrier to effective communication is the lack of a common core of experience between communicator and receiver.
   a. A receiver's past experience with the words and things to which they refer determine how the receiver responds to what the communicator says.
   b. A communicator's words cannot communicate the desired meaning to another person unless the listener or reader has had some experience with the objects or concepts to which these words refer.
   c. In order for communication to be effective, the students' understanding of the meaning of the words needs to be the same as the instructor's understanding and desired thought.
2. Confusion between the symbol (word or sign) and the symbolized object results when a word is confused with what it is meant to represent.
   a. Words and symbols do not always represent the same thing to each person.
   b. To communicate effectively, speakers and instructors should be aware of these differences and choose words or symbols that represent what is intended.
3. Overuse of abstractions should be avoided.
   a. **Concrete words** refer to objects that human beings can experience directly.
   b. **Abstract words** stand for ideas that cannot be directly experienced or things that do not call forth specific mental images.
      1) Abstractions thus serve as shorthand symbols that sum up large areas of experience.
   c. The danger with using abstract words is that they may not evoke in the listener's mind the specific items of experience the communicator intends.
   d. By using concrete words, the communicator narrows (and gains better control of) the image produced in the minds of the listeners and readers.
4. **Interference**, or the prevention of a process or activity from being carried out properly, is composed of factors outside the control of the instructor yet may be overcome.
   a. **Physiological interference** is any biological problem that may inhibit reception.
      1) EXAMPLE: Hearing loss, injury, or physical illness.
   b. **Environmental interference** is caused by external physical conditions.
      1) EXAMPLE: Aircraft noise or vibration or lighting conditions.
   c. **Psychological interference** is a product of how the instructor and student feel at the time the communication process is occurring.
      1) EXAMPLE: If either the instructor or student is not committed to the communication process, communication is impaired.
   d. The instructor must recognize when interference occurs and adapt the presentation to allow the student to be more receptive to new ideas.

3.6 INSTRUCTOR RESPONSIBILITIES

1. Flight instructors are responsible for producing the safest pilots possible with the overall focus on education and learning. There are five main responsibilities of aviation instructors.
   a. Helping Students Learn
      1) The use of standards, and measurement against standards, is key to helping students learn.
      2) Knowing the objective of each period of instruction gives meaning and provides interest to student and instructor.
   b. Providing Adequate Instruction
      1) Flight instructors should analyze the student's personality, thinking, and ability to tailor their teaching technique to the student.
   c. Demanding Adequate Standards of Performance
      1) Evaluation of demonstrated ability during flight instruction must be based upon established standards of performance, suitably modified to apply to the student's experience and stage of development as a pilot.
      2) In evaluating student demonstrations of piloting ability, it is important for the flight instructor to keep the student informed of his or her progress.
         a) EXAMPLE: This may be done as each procedure/maneuver is completed or summarized during postflight critiques.
   d. Emphasizing the Positive
      1) Emphasize the positive because positive instruction results in positive learning.
   e. Ensuring Aviation Safety
      1) The safety practices aviation instructors emphasize have a long-lasting effect on students.
      2) Emphasizing safety by example is one of the best actions an instructor can take to ensure aviation safety.
2. Additional responsibilities of flight instructors include
   a. Evaluation of student piloting ability
      1) In evaluating student demonstrations of ability, it is important for the aviation instructor to keep the student informed of progress. This may be done as each procedure or maneuver is completed or summarized during a postflight or class critique.
   b. Pilot supervision
   c. Practical test recommendations
   d. Flight instructor endorsements
      1) Examples of all common endorsements can be found in the current issue of AC 61-65, Appendix A.
   e. Additional training and endorsements
   f. Pilot proficiency
   g. See and avoid responsibility
   h. Student's pre-solo flight thought process
3. It is a flight instructor's responsibility to teach the student how to take charge during a flight. A pilot in command (PIC) must know when to tell any passengers, even a designated pilot examiner (DPE), when the PIC finds actions in the aircraft that distract and interfere with the safe conduct of the flight.
   a. Instructor responsibilities include teaching the student to divide his or her attention between the distracting task and maintaining control of the aircraft.
   b. Properly interjected distractions may help students learn to determine whether a distraction warrants further attention or action on their part.

4. Flight instructors have a particular responsibility to provide guidance and restraint regarding the solo operations of their students.
   a. Before receiving an instructor endorsement for solo flight, a student should be required to demonstrate the consistent ability to perform all of the fundamental maneuvers without the need of instructor assistance.
   b. The student should also be capable of handling ordinary problems that might occur, such as traffic pattern congestion, a change in the active runway, or unexpected crosswinds.
5. **Minimizing Student Frustrations**
   a. Motivate Students
      1) More can be gained from wanting to learn than from being forced to learn.
      2) Too often, students do not realize how a particular lesson or course can help them reach an important goal.
      3) When students can see the benefits and purpose of the lesson or course, their enjoyment and efforts increase.
   b. Keep Students Informed
      1) Students feel insecure when they do not know what is expected of them or what is going to happen to them.
      2) Instructors can minimize feelings of insecurity by telling students what is expected of them and what they can expect in return.
      3) Instructors keep students informed in various ways, including giving them an overview of the course, keeping them posted on their progress, and giving them adequate notice of examinations, assignments, or other requirements.
   c. Approach Students as Individuals
      1) When instructors limit their thinking to a group mentality without considering the individuals who make up that group, their efforts are directed at an average personality that really fits no one.
      2) Each student group has its own personality that stems from the characteristics and interactions of its members, but each individual within the group has a unique personality to constantly be considered.
   d. Give Credit When Due
      1) When students do something extremely well, they normally expect their abilities and efforts to be noticed. Otherwise, they may become frustrated.
      2) Praise or credit from the instructor is usually ample reward and provides an incentive to do even better. Praise pays dividends in student effort and achievement when deserved, but when given too freely, it becomes valueless.
   e. Criticize Constructively
      1) Although it is important to give praise and credit when deserved, it is equally important to identify mistakes and failures. It does not help to tell students they have made errors and not provide explanations.
      2) If a student has made an earnest effort but is told that the work is unsatisfactory, with no other explanation, frustration occurs.
      3) Errors cannot be corrected if they are not identified, and if they are not identified, they will probably be perpetuated through faulty practice. On the other hand, if the student is briefed on the errors and is told how to correct them, progress can be made.

f. Be Consistent

1) Students want to please their instructor–the same desire that influences much of the behavior of subordinates toward their superiors in industry and business.
2) Naturally, students have a keen interest in knowing what is required to please the instructor. If the same thing is acceptable one day and unacceptable the next, the student becomes confused. The instructor's philosophy and actions must be consistent.

g. Admit Errors

1) No one, including students, expects an instructor to be perfect. The instructor can win the respect of students by honestly acknowledging mistakes.
2) If the instructor tries to cover up or bluff, students are quick to sense it. Such behavior tends to destroy student confidence in the instructor.
3) If in doubt about some point, the instructor should admit it.

h. Assignment Goals

1) Goals the student considers difficult but possible usually provide a challenge and promote learning.
2) In a typical flight lesson, reasonable goals are listed in the lesson objectives and the desired levels of proficiency for the goals are included in statements that contain completion standards.

i. Students will remain engaged if they are aware of the progress they are making.

1) One way to make students aware of their progress is to repeat a demonstration or example and to show them the standards their performance must ultimately meet.

3.7 INSTRUCTOR PROFESSIONALISM

1. Although the term professionalism is widely used, it is rarely defined. In fact, no single definition can encompass all of the qualifications and considerations of true professionalism. The following are some of the major considerations:

   a. Professionals must be able to reason logically and accurately.
   b. Professionalism requires good decision-making ability.

      1) Professionals cannot limit actions and decisions to standard patterns and practice.
      2) Professionals commit themselves to continuous learning and development.

   c. Professionalism demands a code of ethics.

2. The professional flight instructor should be straightforward and honest.

   a. Anything less than a sincere performance is quickly detected and immediately destroys instructor effectiveness.
   b. Student confidence tends to be destroyed if instructors bluff when in doubt.
   c. The well-prepared instructor instills not only confidence but good habits, since preparing well for a flight is a basic requirement for safe flying. Students quickly become apathetic when they recognize that the flight instructor is inadequately prepared.

3. The attitude, movements, and general demeanor of the flight instructor contribute a great deal to his or her professional image.

   a. The instructor should avoid erratic movements, distracting speech habits, and capricious changes in mood. The professional image requires development of a calm, pleasant, thoughtful manner that puts the student at ease.

4. The professional relationship between the instructor and the student should be based on a mutual acknowledgment that both the student and the instructor are important to each other and that both are working toward the same objective.
   a. Accepting lower-than-normal standards to please a student will **NOT** help the student/instructor relationship.
   b. Reasonable standards strictly enforced are not resented by an earnest student.
   c. Students must be treated with respect, regardless of whether they are quick to learn or require more time to absorb certain concepts.
5. The professional flight instructor should accept students as they are with all of their faults and problems.
   a. However, (s)he should also build student self-confidence, set challenges, and generally create an atmosphere for learning.
6. A flight instructor who is not completely familiar with current pilot certification and rating requirements cannot do a competent job of flight instruction.
   a. Flight instructors must strive to maintain the highest level of knowledge, training, and currency in their field.
   b. For a professional performance as a flight instructor, it is essential that the instructor maintain current copies of
      1) The Federal Aviation Regulations, especially Parts 1, 61, and 91;
      2) The *Aeronautical Information Manual*;
      3) Practical Test Standards or Airman Certification Standards; and
      4) Appropriate pilot training manuals.
   c. True performance as a professional is based on study and research.
7. Flight instructors fail to provide competent instruction when they permit students to partially learn an important item of knowledge or skill.
   a. More importantly, such deficiencies may in themselves allow hazardous inadequacies to develop in the student's ongoing piloting performance.
8. Aviation instructors should be constantly alert for ways to improve the services they provide to their students, their effectiveness, and their qualifications.

QUESTIONS AND ANSWER EXPLANATIONS: All of the Fundamentals of Instructing knowledge test questions chosen by the FAA for release as well as additional questions selected by Gleim relating to the material in the previous outlines are provided on the following pages. These questions have been organized into the same subunits as the outlines. To the immediate right of each question are the correct answer and answer explanations. You should cover these answers and answer explanations while responding to the questions. Refer to the general discussion in the Introduction on how to take the FAA knowledge test.

Remember that the questions from the FAA knowledge test bank have been reordered by topic and organized into a meaningful sequence. Also, the first line of the answer explanation gives the citation of the authoritative source for the answer.

QUESTIONS

3.1 Human Needs

1. Before a student can concentrate on learning, which human needs must be satisfied?

A. Security.

B. Biological.

C. Psychological.

Answer (B) is correct. *(FAA-H-8083-9A Chap 1)*

DISCUSSION: Physiological, or biological, needs consist of the need for air, food, water, and maintenance of the human body. Unless the biological needs are met, a person cannot concentrate fully on learning, self-expression, or any other tasks.

Answer (A) is incorrect. The need for security is only a driving force once all of the physiological needs are met. Answer (C) is incorrect. Psychological needs, such as belonging and esteem, are only important after the basic biological and security needs are met.

2. After individuals are physically comfortable and have no fear for their safety, which human needs become the prime influence on their behavior?

A. Esteem.

B. Self-Actualization.

C. Belonging.

Answer (C) is correct. *(FAA-H-8083-9A Chap 1)*

DISCUSSION: When individuals are physically comfortable and do not feel threatened, they seek to satisfy their social needs of belonging, that is, to overcome feelings of loneliness and alienation.

Answer (A) is incorrect. The need of esteem follows after the need of belonging. Generally speaking, a person must feel accepted by peers to develop stable, positive self-esteem. Answer (B) is incorrect. The needs of self-actualization are only applicable after all other human needs have been met.

3. Which of the student's human needs offer the greatest challenge to an instructor?

A. Physiological.

B. Psychological.

C. Self-Actualization.

Answer (C) is correct. *(FAA-H-8083-9A Chap 1)*

DISCUSSION: When all of the foregoing needs are satisfied, the needs for self-actualization are activated. Self-actualization is a person's need to be and do what the person was "born to do." Helping a student achieve his or her individual potential in aviation training offers the greatest challenge as well as reward to the instructor.

Answer (A) is incorrect. Physiological needs are needs that the instructor has no direct impact on. These basic biological needs include the need for air, food, water, and maintenance of the human body. Answer (B) is incorrect. Psychological needs include the student's need to belong, have positive self-esteem, cognitively know and understand, and emotionally be drawn to learning. While difficult to develop, these needs are not as difficult to encourage as self-actualization.

4. The need for realizing one's own potentialities, for continued development, and for being creative is defined as a(n)

A. esteem need.

B. social need.

C. self-actualization need.

Answer (C) is correct. *(FAA-H-8083-9A Chap 1)*

DISCUSSION: Self-actualization needs are the needs for realizing one's own potentialities, for continued development, and for being creative.

Answer (A) is incorrect. Esteem needs relate to feeling good about one's self. Answer (B) is incorrect. Social needs are the needs to belong and to associate with other people.

3.2 Motivation

5. Which is generally the more effective way for an instructor to properly motivate students?

A. Maintain pleasant personal relationships with students.

B. Provide positive motivations by the promise or achievement of rewards.

C. Reinforce their self-confidence by requiring no tasks beyond their ability to perform.

Answer (B) is correct. *(FAA-H-8083-9A Chap 2)*

DISCUSSION: Providing positive motivation is generally considered the most effective way to properly motivate people. Positive motivations are provided by the promise or achievement of rewards.

Answer (A) is incorrect. Maintaining pleasant personal relationships with students (while desirable) is not the more effective way for an instructor to properly motivate students. Answer (C) is incorrect. A student who is not required to perform a task beyond present abilities will neither be motivated nor make any progress.

6. Motivations that cause a student to react with fear and anxiety are

A. tangible.
B. negative.
C. difficult to identify.

Answer (B) is correct. *(FAA-H-8083-9A Chap 2)*
DISCUSSION: Negative motivations may produce fears and may thus be seen by the student as threats. Negative motivation generally intimidates students and should be avoided.
Answer (A) is incorrect. Motivations, whether tangible or intangible, can be either positive or negative. Answer (C) is incorrect. Motivations, whether very subtle or difficult to identify, can be either positive or negative.

7. How can an instructor help a student cope with fear and anxiety?

A. By emphasizing the benefits and pleasurable experiences from flying.
B. By minimizing fear by teaching the student advanced maneuvers.
C. By keeping the student focused on achieving Practical Test Standards (PTS).

Answer (A) is correct. *(FAA-H-8083-9A Chap 1)*
DISCUSSION: Student anxiety can be minimized throughout training by emphasizing the benefits and pleasurable experiences that can be derived from flying, rather than by continuously citing the unhappy consequences of faulty performances.
Answer (B) is incorrect. Anxiety for student pilots is usually associated with certain types of flight operations and maneuvers. Instructors should introduce these maneuvers with care so that students know what to expect and what their reactions should be. Answer (C) is incorrect. The PTS should not be introduced to the student prior to the last 3 hours of training prior to the practical test.

8. Motivations in the form of reproof and threats should be avoided with all but the student who is

A. overconfident and impulsive.
B. avidly seeking group approval.
C. experiencing a learning plateau.

Answer (A) is correct. *(FAA-H-8083-9A Chap 2)*
DISCUSSION: Educational experts have shown that negative motivation is useful only for a student who is overconfident and impulsive. Otherwise, negative motivation in the form of reproof and threats tends to discourage student behavior.
Answer (B) is incorrect. Group approval is a strong motivating force. Use of reproofs and threats with a student seeking group approval would only alienate him or her from the group. Answer (C) is incorrect. One of the reasons a student has reached a learning plateau is due to a lack of motivation. Use of reproofs and threats would only cause a student to remain at the plateau longer.

9. When students are unable to see the benefits or purpose of a lesson, they will

A. be less motivated.
B. not learn as quickly.
C. be expected to increase their efforts.

Answer (A) is correct. *(FAA-H-8083-9A Chap 2)*
DISCUSSION: Students will be less motivated if they are unable to see the benefits or purpose of a lesson. It is important for the instructor to make the student aware that a particular lesson can help him or her reach an important goal.
Answer (B) is incorrect. While a student may not learn as quickly when (s)he is unable to see the benefits or purpose of a lesson, (s)he will become less motivated. Answer (C) is incorrect. The frustration of working without a known goal will likely decrease, not increase, their efforts.

10. Confusion, disinterest, and uneasiness on the part of the student could happen as a result of not knowing the

A. importance of each period of instruction.
B. objective of each period of instruction.
C. subject of each period of instruction.

Answer (B) is correct. *(FAA-H-8083-9A Chap 7)*
DISCUSSION: Knowing the objective of each period of instruction gives meaning and interest to the student as well as the instructor. Not knowing the objective of the lesson often leads to confusion, disinterest, and uneasiness on the part of the student.
Answer (A) is incorrect. Confusion, disinterest, and uneasiness on the part of the student could happen as a result of not knowing the objective of each period of instruction, not its importance. Answer (C) is incorrect. Confusion, disinterest, and uneasiness on the part of the student could happen as a result of not knowing the objective of each period of instruction, not its subject. The subject of the instructional period will be obvious if it has been planned appropriately.

11. Which statement is true concerning motivations?

A. Motivations must be tangible to be effective.

B. Motivations may be very subtle and difficult to identify.

C. Negative motivations often are as effective as positive motivations.

Answer (B) is correct. *(FAA-H-8083-9A Chap 2)*

DISCUSSION: Motivations may be subtle, subconscious, and difficult to identify. A student may be motivated without even being aware (s)he is being influenced.

Answer (A) is incorrect. Intangible motivations can be as effective (or even more effective) than tangible motivations. Rewards such as accomplishment, fame, and peer acceptance are intangible, but they are among the best positive motivators. Answer (C) is incorrect. Negative motivation tends to discourage the student.

12. For a motivation to be effective, students must believe their efforts will be rewarded in a definite manner. This type of motivation is

A. subtle.

B. negative.

C. tangible.

Answer (C) is correct. *(FAA-H-8083-9A Chap 2)*

DISCUSSION: Students, like any worker, need and want tangible returns for their efforts. These rewards must be constantly apparent to the student during instruction.

Answer (A) is incorrect. The student is often unaware of the application of subtle motivation and thus feels unrewarded for his or her effort. Answer (B) is incorrect. Negative motivations are not as effective as positive motivations, as they tend to intimidate students and cause unpleasant experiences.

13. An instructor can most effectively maintain a high level of student motivation by

A. making each lesson a pleasurable experience.

B. relaxing the standards of performance required during the early phase of training.

C. continually challenging the student to meet the highest objectives of training that can be established.

Answer (A) is correct. *(FAA-H-8083-9A Chap 2)*

DISCUSSION: An instructor can most effectively maintain a high level of motivation by making each lesson a pleasant experience for a student. People avoid negative experiences, but they will seek out and want to repeat positive experiences.

Answer (B) is incorrect. Relaxing the standards of performance required during the early phase of training may actually reduce a student's motivation. Reasonable standards strictly enforced are not resented by an earnest student. Answer (C) is incorrect. Performance standards should be set to the student's potential and not his or her current ability or to unrealistically high objectives. Improvement must be fostered.

14. Examples of tangible positive motivation may include

A. rewards such as accomplishment, personal comfort, and peer acceptance.

B. penalties in the form of reproof and threats.

C. rewards that involve financial gain or public recognition.

Answer (C) is correct. *(FAA-H-8083-9A Chap 2)*

DISCUSSION: Examples of positive motivations that are tangible may involve financial gain or public recognition.

Answer (A) is incorrect. Rewards such as accomplishment, personal comfort, and peer acceptance, while positive, are types of intangible motivators. Answer (B) is incorrect. Motivations in the form of reproof and threats are defined as negative motivations.

15. Which statement is true regarding sources of motivation?

A. A desire for monetary gain is the main source of motivation for each individual.

B. All sources of motivation offer some type of reward in exchange for performing work.

C. Sources of motivation are normal and can be overcome by reminding students of their own goals.

Answer (B) is correct. *(FAA-H-8083-9A Chap 2)*

DISCUSSION: Sources of motivation vary, but all offer some type of reward in exchange for performing work.

Answer (A) is incorrect. While the desire for monetary gain is a source of motivation to some, there are many different sources of motivation, and each individual may have a different one. Sources of motivation all offer some type of reward in exchange for performing work. Answer (C) is incorrect. Drops in motivation, not sources of motivation, can be overcome by reminding students of their own goals. Sources of motivation all offer some type of reward in exchange for performing work.

16. How can drops in motivation be overcome?

A. By reminding students of their own goals and reassuring them there will be rewards for their continued efforts.

B. By praising incremental successes during training, relating daily accomplishments to lesson objectives, and commenting favorably on student progress.

C. By making each lesson a pleasurable experience.

Answer (A) is correct. *(FAA-H-8083-9A Chap 2)*

DISCUSSION: Drops in motivation, which are a common source of frustration, are normal and can be overcome by reminding students of their own goals and reassuring them that there will be rewards for their continued efforts.

Answer (B) is incorrect. Praising incremental successes during training, relating daily accomplishments to lesson objectives, and commenting favorably on student progress are ways to maintain motivation, not to overcome a drop in motivation. Answer (C) is incorrect. While an instructor should strive to to make each lesson a pleasurable experience, this will not guarantee that students will not experience a drop in motivation.

3.3 Aeronautical Decision Making and Risk Management

17. What is the systematic approach to the mental process used by pilots to determine the best course of action in response to a given set of circumstances?

A. Pilot Judgment Chain.

B. Aeronautical Decision Making.

C. Crew Resource Management.

Answer (B) is correct. *(FAA-H-8083-9A Chap 8)*

DISCUSSION: Aeronautical Decision Making is defined as the systematic approach to the mental process used by pilots to determine the best course of action in response to a given set of circumstances.

Answer (A) is incorrect. The sentence presented is the definition of Aeronautical Decision Making, not the Pilot Judgment Chain. Answer (C) is incorrect. Crew Resource Management pertains to team management concepts on the flight deck, as well as those that affect flight attendants, maintenance personnel, and others. The sentence that makes up this question describes Aeronautical Decision Making.

18. Which of the following identifies accurate perception of the aircraft and environmental factors that affect the aircraft and passengers during a specific period of time?

A. CRM.

B. Situational Awareness.

C. ADM.

Answer (B) is correct. *(FAA-H-8083-9A Chap 8)*

DISCUSSION: Situation awareness is defined as an accurate perception and understanding of all the factors and conditions within the four fundamental risk elements that affect safety before, during, and after the flight.

Answer (A) is incorrect. Crew Resource Management (CRM) refers to the application of team management concepts on the flight deck environment, including cabin crew, maintenance personnel, and others. It is situational awareness that involves the accurate perception and understanding of all the factors and conditions within the four fundamental risk elements that affect safety before, during, and after the flight. Answer (C) is incorrect. Aeronautical Decision Making (ADM) is defined as the systematic approach to the mental process used by pilots to determine the best course of action in response to a given set of circumstances. It is situational awareness that involves the accurate perception and understanding of all the factors and conditions within the four fundamental risk elements that affect safety before, during, and after the flight.

19. One of the risk elements in the Aeronautical Decision Making process is?

A. Fuel on board.

B. Passengers.

C. Aircraft.

Answer (C) is correct. *(FAA-H-8083-9A Chap 8)*

DISCUSSION: The four fundamental risk elements incorporated into aeronautical decision making are the pilot, the aircraft, the environment, and the type of operation that comprises any given aviation situation.

Answer (A) is incorrect. Fuel on board is not one of the risk elements included in the aeronautical decision making process. The pilot, the aircraft, the environment, and the type of operation are the four fundamental risk elements included in ADM. Answer (B) is incorrect. The passengers are not considered to be one of the risk elements included in aeronautical decision making. The pilot, the aircraft, the environment, and the type of operation are the four fundamental risk elements included in ADM.

20. Risk management, as part of the aeronautical decision making (ADM) process, relies on which features to reduce the risks associated with each flight?

A. Application of stress management and risk element procedures.

B. The mental process of analyzing all information in a particular situation and making a timely decision on what action to take.

C. Situational awareness, problem recognition, and good judgment.

Answer (C) is correct. *(AC 60-22)*

DISCUSSION: Risk management is that part of the ADM process which relies on situational awareness, problem recognition, and good judgment to reduce risks associated with each flight.

Answer (A) is incorrect. Risk management relies on situational awareness, problem recognition, and good judgment, not the application of stress management and risk-element procedures, to reduce the risks associated with each flight. Answer (B) is incorrect. Judgment, not risk management, is the mental process of analyzing all information in a particular situation and making a timely decision on what action to take.

21. The aeronautical decision making (ADM) process identifies several steps involved in good decision making. One of these steps is

A. making a rational evaluation of the required actions.

B. identifying personal attitudes hazardous to safe flight.

C. developing a "can do" attitude.

Answer (B) is correct. *(AC 60-22)*

DISCUSSION: The ADM process addresses all aspects of decision making on the flight deck and identifies several steps involved in good decision making. One of these steps is to identify personal attitudes hazardous to safe flight.

Answer (A) is incorrect. Making a rational evaluation of the required actions is a step in good judgment, not a step in good decision making. Answer (C) is incorrect. The "can do," or macho, attitude is one of the personal hazardous attitudes to identify in the steps involved in good decision making.

22. Examples of classic behavioral traps that experienced pilots may fall into are to

A. promote situational awareness and then necessary changes in behavior.

B. complete a flight as planned, please passengers, meet schedules, and "get the job done."

C. assume additional responsibilities and assert PIC authority.

Answer (B) is correct. *(AC 60-22)*

DISCUSSION: Pilots have been known to fall into a number of classic behavioral traps. Pilots, particularly those with considerable experience, as a rule always try to complete a flight as planned, please passengers, meet schedules, and do what it takes to "get the job done."

Answer (A) is incorrect. To promote situational awareness and then to make necessary changes in behavior are part of learning good decision making, not classical behavioral traps. Answer (C) is incorrect. Assuming additional responsibilities and asserting PIC authority are not examples of classical behavioral traps.

23. Hazardous attitudes occur to every pilot to some degree at some time. What are some of these hazardous attitudes?

A. Antiauthority, impulsivity, macho, resignation, and invulnerability.

B. Poor situational awareness, snap judgments, and lack of a decision making process.

C. Poor risk management and lack of stress management.

Answer (A) is correct. *(AC 60-22)*

DISCUSSION: The five hazardous attitudes addressed in the ADM process are antiauthority, impulsivity, invulnerability, macho, and resignation.

Answer (B) is incorrect. Poor situational awareness and snap judgments are indications of the lack of a decision-making process, not hazardous attitudes. Answer (C) is incorrect. Poor risk management and lack of stress management lead to poor ADM and are not considered hazardous attitudes.

24. In the aeronautical decision making (ADM) process, what is the first step in neutralizing a hazardous attitude?

A. Recognizing hazardous thoughts.

B. Recognizing the invulnerability of the situation.

C. Making a rational judgment.

Answer (A) is correct. *(AC 60-22)*

DISCUSSION: Hazardous attitudes, which contribute to poor pilot judgment, can be effectively counteracted by redirecting that hazardous attitude so that appropriate action can be taken. Recognition of hazardous thoughts is the first step in neutralizing them in the ADM process.

Answer (B) is incorrect. Invulnerability is a hazardous attitude. The first step in neutralizing a hazardous attitude is to recognize it. Answer (C) is incorrect. Before a rational judgment can be made, the hazardous attitude must be recognized then redirected so that appropriate action can be taken.

25. Success in reducing stress associated with a crisis on the flight deck begins with

A. eliminating the more serious life and flight deck stress issues.

B. knowing the exact cause of the stress.

C. assessing stress areas in one's personal life.

Answer (C) is correct. *(AC 60-22)*

DISCUSSION: If you hope to succeed in reducing stress associated with crisis management on the flight deck, it is essential to begin by making a personal assessment of stress in all areas of your life.

Answer (A) is incorrect. In order to eliminate the more serious life and flight deck stress issues, you must first make an assessment of stress in all areas of your life to identify those stressors. Answer (B) is incorrect. In order to know the exact cause of the stress, you must first make an assessment of stress in all areas of your life to identify stressors and the causes of them.

26. The DECIDE process consists of six elements to help provide a pilot a logical way of approaching aeronautical decision making. These elements are to

A. estimate, determine, choose, identify, detect, and evaluate.

B. determine, evaluate, choose, identify, do, and eliminate.

C. detect, estimate, choose, identify, do, and evaluate.

Answer (C) is correct. *(AC 60-22)*

DISCUSSION: The DECIDE model, comprised of six elements, is intended to provide a pilot with a logical way of approaching decision making. These six elements, using the acronym DECIDE, are detect, estimate, choose, identify, do, and evaluate.

Answer (A) is incorrect. One of the elements of the DECIDE process is "do," not "determine." Answer (B) is incorrect. Two of the elements of the DECIDE process are "detect," not "determine," and "estimate," not "eliminate."

27. If a pilot wanted to mitigate risk during a cross-country flight in MVFR conditions, the pilot could

A. Take a pilot who is IFR-rated.

B. Continue the flight as planned.

C. Stay out of controlled airspace.

Answer (A) is correct. *(FAA-H-8083-9A Chap 9)*

DISCUSSION: Risk assessment is only part of the risk management equation. After determining the level of risk, the pilot needs to mitigate, or reduce, the risk. In this example, the pilot could reduce the risk by taking a qualified IFR-rated pilot along on the trip in case the weather deteriorated below VFR minimums.

Answer (B) is incorrect. Continuing the flight as planned is acceptance, not mitigation, of the risk of flying in MVFR conditions. Answer (C) is incorrect. Deciding to stay out of controlled airspace should be an immediate red flag, as it signals that the pilot may try to push his or her limits and continue into weather that could present additional hazards. Risk mitigation is about reducing total risk, not adding additional potential risks to the planned flight.

28. A pilot's inexperience in direct crosswinds greater than 10 knots is an example of which of the fundamental risk elements?

A. The pilot in command.

B. The aircraft.

C. The external pressures.

Answer (A) is correct. *(FAA-H-8083-9A Chap 9)*

DISCUSSION: The pilot is one of the risk factors in a flight. The pilot must ask, "Am I ready for this trip?" in terms of experience, currency, and physical and emotional condition. If the pilot has experience with 10 knots of direct crosswind, it could be unsafe to exceed a 10-knot crosswind component without additional training. Therefore, the crosswind experience level is that pilot's personal limitation until additional training with a CFI provides the pilot with additional experience for flying in crosswinds that exceed 10 knots.

Answer (B) is incorrect. The pilot's lack of experience level in crosswinds that exceed 10 knots is a personal limitation and risk factor, not one having to do with the aircraft itself. Answer (C) is incorrect. The pilot's lack of experience level in crosswinds that exceed 10 knots is a personal limitation and risk factor, not one having to do with external pressures associated with a planned flight.

29. Which of the following aircraft risks can be mitigated during the preflight inspection?

A. Urgency of completing the flight.

B. Weather en-route.

C. Fuel quantity.

Answer (C) is correct. *(FAA-H-8083-9A Chap 9)*

DISCUSSION: As part of a preflight inspection, the pilot in command should check the fuel quantity to ensure that the amount is accurate compared with what was ordered and what was planned for during the preflight planning phase.

Answer (A) is incorrect. The urgency of completing the flight is a risk factor associated with external pressures, not the aircraft. This risk factor should be dealt with during the pilot's evaluation of the planned flight, not during the preflight inspection. Answer (B) is incorrect. The weather en-route for a planned flight is an environmental risk factor, not one associated with the aircraft. This risk factor should be dealt with during the preflight planning phase rather than during the preflight inspection.

30. The antidote for the antiauthority hazardous attitude is

A. "Follow the rules. They are usually right."

B. "It could happen to me."

C. "I am not helpless. I can make a difference."

Answer (A) is correct. *(FAA-H-8083-9A Chap 8)*

DISCUSSION: The antidote for the antiauthority hazardous attitude is "Follow the rules. They are usually right."

Answer (B) is incorrect. "It could happen to me" is the antidote for the invulnerability hazardous attitude. Answer (C) is incorrect. "I am not helpless. I can make a difference" is the antidote for the resignation hazardous attitude.

31. The macho attitude can be described by which of the following statements?

A. "Do something quickly!"

B. "I can do it."

C. "Do not tell me what to do!"

Answer (B) is correct. *(AC 60-22)*

DISCUSSION: "I can do it" is an example of a macho attitude. It is characteristic of an individual who thinks (s)he is superior to others.

Answer (A) is incorrect. The impulsivity attitude is expressed by taking action quickly with little thought for the consequences. A macho attitude is displayed by someone who thinks "I can do it." Answer (C) is incorrect. "Do not tell me what to do!" is the thought had by one who displays the antiauthority attitude. A macho attitude is displayed by someone who thinks "I can do it."

32. During a stall recovery, the instructor allows the student to exceed maneuvering speed. Which best illustrates an 'anti-authority' reaction by the instructor?

A. There has not been a problem doing this in the past.

B. The aircraft can handle a lot more than the maneuvering speed.

C. The student should know how to recover from a stall by this time.

Answer (B) is correct. *(AC 60-22)*

DISCUSSION: An example of the antiauthority ("Don't tell me what to do!") attitude would be an instructor allowing a student to exceed maneuvering speed during a stall recovery. The specific antiauthority attitude expressed by the instructor is "The aircraft can handle a lot more than the maneuvering speed."

Answer (A) is incorrect. This attitude falls closer to the hazardous attitude of invulnerability ("It won't happen to me"). There might not have been a problem in the past, but it could happen. Answer (C) is incorrect. The hazardous attitude in this answer selection is resignation ("What's the use?"). The instructor in this case should instead ask himself or herself "How can I teach this student how and when to recover from a stall?"

33. The body's response to a set of circumstances that induces a change in an individual's current physiological and/or psychological patterns of functioning forcing the individual to adapt to these changes is

A. risk management.

B. aeronautical decision making.

C. stress.

Answer (C) is correct. *(AC 60-22)*

DISCUSSION: Stress describes the body's response to a set of circumstances that induces a change in an individual's current physiological and/or psychological patterns of functioning, forcing the individual to adapt to these changes.

Answer (A) is incorrect. Risk management is the part of the decision-making process that relies on situational awareness, problem recognition, and good judgment to reduce risks associated with each flight, not stress. Answer (B) is incorrect. Aeronautical decision making is a systematic approach to the mental process used by pilots to consistently determine the best course of action in response to a given set of circumstances. Stress describes the body's response to a set of circumstances that induces a change in an individual's current physiological and/or psychological patterns of functioning, forcing the individual to adapt to these changes.

34. What is the antidote to the hazardous attitude of invulnerability?

A. "It could happen to me."

B. "Not so fast. Think first."

C. "Taking chances is foolish."

Answer (A) is correct. *(AC 60-22)*

DISCUSSION: To properly counteract the attitude of invulnerability, the antidote is thinking or saying "It could happen to me."

Answer (B) is incorrect. "Not so fast. Think first." describes the antidote to the hazardous attitude of impulsivity. Answer (C) is incorrect. A macho attitude can be neutralized by thinking "Taking chances is foolish."

35. To help manage flight deck stress, you should

A. evaluate the effect(s) of the action taken to counter the change.

B. recall the antidote "I am not helpless. I can make a difference."

C. try to relax and think rationally at the first sign of stress.

Answer (C) is correct. *(AC 60-22)*

DISCUSSION: To help manage flight deck stress, you should try to relax and think rationally at the first sign of stress.

Answer (A) is incorrect. Evaluating the effect(s) of the action taken to counter the change describes the sixth element of the DECIDE model, evaluate. Answer (B) is incorrect. The antidote "I am not helpless. I can make a difference" will not help reduce stress, but instead will help counteract the tendency to display an attitude of resignation.

3.4 Effective Communication

36. The effectiveness of communication between instructor and student is measured by the

A. degree of dynamic, interrelated elements.

B. similarity between the idea transmitted and the idea received.

C. relationship between communicative and dynamic elements.

Answer (B) is correct. *(FAA-H-8083-9A Chap 3)*

DISCUSSION: Communication takes place when one person transmits ideas or feelings to another person or group of people. Its effectiveness is measured by the similarity between the idea transmitted and the idea received.

Answer (A) is incorrect. The process, not the effectiveness, of communication is composed of three dynamic, interrelated elements -- the source, the symbols, and the receiver. Answer (C) is incorrect. The relationship between the communicative elements (source, symbols, and receiver) is dynamic. There are no dynamic elements.

37. Effective communication has taken place when, and only when, the

A. information is transmitted and received.

B. receivers react with understanding and change their behavior accordingly.

C. receivers have the ability to question and comprehend ideas that have been transmitted.

Answer (B) is correct. *(FAA-H-8083-9A Chap 3)*

DISCUSSION: The rule of thumb among communicators is that communication succeeds only in relation to the reaction of the receiver. Effective communication has taken place only when the receivers react with understanding and change their behavior.

Answer (A) is incorrect. Information may be transmitted and received without effective communication. Only when the receiver reacts to the information being transmitted and received with understanding, and changes his or her behavior accordingly, has effective communication taken place. Answer (C) is incorrect. The ability to question and comprehend ideas that have been transmitted is only one characteristic of a receiver.

38. When has instruction taken place?

A. When a procedure has been explained, and the desired student response has occurred.

B. When the student hears what is presented.

C. When all the required material has been presented.

Answer (A) is correct. *(FAA-H-8083-9A Chap 3)*

DISCUSSION: Instruction has taken place when the instructor has explained a particular procedure and subsequently determined that the desired student response has occurred.

Answer (B) is incorrect. Instruction has taken place when the instructor has explained a particular procedure and subsequently determined that the desired student response has occurred, not only when the student hears what is presented. Answer (C) is incorrect. Instruction has taken place when the instructor has explained a particular procedure and subsequently determined that the desired student response has occurred, not only when all the required material has been presented.

39. To communicate effectively, instructors must

A. recognize the level of comprehension.

B. provide an atmosphere which encourages questioning.

C. reveal a positive attitude while delivering their message.

Answer (C) is correct. *(FAA-H-8083-9A Chap 3)*

DISCUSSION: Communicators consciously or unconsciously reveal attitudes toward themselves, the ideas they are trying to transmit, and their receivers. These attitudes must be positive if the communicators are to communicate effectively.

Answer (A) is incorrect. An instructor can recognize the level of a student's comprehension in the application step of the teaching process, not during the communication process. Answer (B) is incorrect. While an instructor should provide an atmosphere that encourages questioning, the student must exercise his or her ability to ask questions to communicate effectively.

40. To be more likely to communicate effectively, an instructor should speak or write from a background of

A. technical expertise.

B. knowing the ideas presented.

C. up-to-date, stimulating material.

Answer (C) is correct. *(FAA-H-8083-9A Chap 3)*

DISCUSSION: A basic factor of a communicator's effectiveness is the ability to speak or write from a broad background of accurate, up-to-date, and stimulating material.

Answer (A) is incorrect. A speaker or writer with technical expertise may depend on technical jargon. Reliance on technical language can impede effective communication, especially when the receiver lacks a similar background. Answer (B) is incorrect. Just knowing the ideas presented does not ensure that effective communication will take place. A communicator must be able to make the receiver react with understanding and change his or her behavior accordingly.

41. In the communication process, the communicator will be more successful in gaining and retaining the receiver's attention by

A. being friendly and informative.

B. using a varied communicative approach.

C. using a variety of audiovisual aids in class.

Answer (B) is correct. *(FAA-H-8083-9A Chap 3)*

DISCUSSION: The most successful communicator will use the variety of channels that best communicates the necessary ideas and techniques, i.e., a varied communicative approach.

Answer (A) is incorrect. Effective, engaging communication is more complex than merely being friendly. The source, the symbols, and the receiver are all interrelated in the communication process. Answer (C) is incorrect. Audiovisual aids can often further the learning, not the communication, process by supporting, supplementing, or reinforcing important ideas. By presenting the material in a new manner, instructional aids can even improve communication between instructor and student.

42. Communication takes place when

A. one person transmits ideas or feelings to another person or to a group of people.

B. symbols are used to transmit messages.

C. the instructor takes into account the student's background, experience, and education.

Answer (A) is correct. *(FAA-H-8083-9A Chap 3)*

DISCUSSION: Communication takes place when one person transmits ideas or feelings to another person or to a group of people.

Answer (B) is incorrect. While symbols are used to transmit messages, the receiver has to have the same understanding of the symbol as the communicator for communication to take place. Answer (C) is incorrect. Knowledge of the student's background does not guarantee communication will take place. Communication takes place when one person transmits ideas or feelings to another person or to a group of people.

43. The three dynamically interrelated elements that compose the process of communication are

A. Visual, auditory, and kinesthetic.

B. Source, symbol, and receiver.

C. Background, experience, and education.

Answer (B) is correct. *(FAA-H-8083-9A Chap 3)*

DISCUSSION: The process of communication is composed of a source, the symbols used in transmitting the message, and the receiver.

Answer (A) is incorrect. The three sensory channels through which symbols are perceived are the visual, auditory, and kinesthetic channels. The process of communication, however, is composed of a source, the symbols used in transmitting the message, and the receiver. Answer (C) is incorrect. The process of communication is composed of a source, the symbols used in transmitting the message, and the receiver.

44. What is true of symbols?

A. Ideas can be communicated by presenting individual symbols.

B. The three sensory channels that symbols are perceived through are words, signs, visual aids.

C. Instructors should use a variety of sensory channels to be more successful in gaining and retaining student attention.

Answer (C) is correct. *(FAA-H-8083-9A Chap 3)*

DISCUSSION: Instructors will be more successful in gaining and retaining student attention by using a variety of sensory channels.

Answer (A) is incorrect. Ideas are communicated only when symbols are combined into meaningful wholes (e.g., sentences, paragraphs, chapters, etc.). Instructors will be more successful in gaining and retaining student attention by using a variety of sensory channels. Answer (B) is incorrect. Symbols are perceived through three sensory channels: visual, auditory, or kinesthetic, not words, signs, or visual aids.

45. Oral and visual codes used to communicate are called what?

A. Signals.

B. Sensory channels.

C. Symbols.

Answer (C) is correct. *(FAA-H-8083-9A Chap 3)*

DISCUSSION: Symbols are defined as oral and visual codes used to communicate.

Answer (A) is incorrect. Symbols, not signals, are defined as oral and visual codes used to communicate. Answer (B) is incorrect. Sensory channels are ways through which symbols are perceived. Oral and visual codes used to communicate are symbols.

3.5 Barriers to Effective Communication

46. Probably the greatest single barrier to effective communication in the teaching process is a lack of

A. respect for the instructor.

B. personality harmony between instructor and student.

C. a common experience level between instructor and student.

Answer (C) is correct. *(FAA-H-8083-9A Chap 3)*

DISCUSSION: The greatest single barrier to effective communication is the lack of common experience between the communicator and the receiver. Those with the least in common usually find it difficult to communicate.

Answer (A) is incorrect. While lack of respect for the instructor is a barrier to communication, it is not as great and as prevalent as a lack of common experience between the communicator and the receiver. Answer (B) is incorrect. While lack of personality harmony is a barrier to communication, it is not as great and as prevalent as a lack of common experience between the communicator and the receiver.

47. A communicator's words cannot communicate the desired meaning to another person unless the

A. words have meaningful referents.

B. words give the meaning that is in the mind of the receiver.

C. listener or reader has had some experience with the objects or concepts to which these words refer.

Answer (C) is correct. *(FAA-H-8083-9A Chap 3)*

DISCUSSION: Since a common core of experience is basic to effective communication, a communicator's words cannot communicate the desired meaning to another person unless the listener or the reader has had some experience with the objects or concepts to which these words refer.

Answer (A) is incorrect. The words must have not only meaningful referents, but the exact same meaningful referents in order for the communicator and the receiver to share a desired meaning. Answer (B) is incorrect. Words only arouse desired meanings if the communicator generates the desired response in the mind of the receiver. The nature of this response is determined by the receiver's past experiences with the words and the concepts to which they refer.

48. Which of the following is an example of a problem with using abstract words?

A. They may stand for ideas that cannot be directly experienced by the learner.

B. They tend to confuse the listener between the symbol and the symbolized object.

C. They reduce the effectiveness of role-playing methods.

Answer (A) is correct. *(FAA-H-8083-9A Chap 3)*

DISCUSSION: Abstract words stand for ideas that cannot be directly experienced; i.e., they do not call forth the specific mental image in the mind of the student that the instructor intends. The word "aircraft" is an abstract word. It does not call to mind a specific aircraft in the imaginations of various students.

Answer (B) is incorrect. Confusion between the symbol and the symbolized object is a barrier to communication separate and distinct from the use of abstract words. Answer (C) is incorrect. Reducing the effectiveness of role-playing methods is not among the problems of using abstract words.

49. The danger in using abstract words is that they

A. sum up vast areas of experience.

B. call forth different mental images in the minds of the receivers.

C. will not evoke the specific items of experience in the listener's mind that the communicator intends.

Answer (C) is correct. *(FAA-H-8083-9A Chap 3)*

DISCUSSION: The purpose of abstract words is not to bring forth specific ideas in the mind of the receiver but to serve as shorthand symbols that sum up vast areas of experience. The danger in using abstract words is that they will not evoke the specific items in the listener's mind that the communicator intends.

Answer (A) is incorrect. The purpose, not the danger, of using abstract words is to use them as shorthand symbols that sum up vast areas of experience. Answer (B) is incorrect. Abstract words do not call forth mental images; on the contrary, they stand for ideas that cannot be directly experienced.

50. By using abstractions in the communication process, the communicator will

A. bring forth specific items of experience in the minds of the receivers.

B. be using words which refer to objects or ideas that human beings can experience directly.

C. not evoke in the listener's or reader's mind the specific items of experience the communicator intends.

Answer (C) is correct. *(FAA-H-8083-9A Chap 3)*

DISCUSSION: Abstract words are necessary and useful. Their purpose is not to bring forth specific items of experience in the minds of receivers but to serve as shorthand symbols that refer to thoughts or ideas. The danger is that an abstract term might not evoke in the listener's mind the specific item of experience the communicator intended.

Answer (A) is incorrect. Abstract words are not used to bring forth specific items of experience in the minds of the receivers. Answer (B) is incorrect. Concrete, not abstract, words refer to objects or ideas that human beings can experience directly.

51. What is required for communication to be effective?

A. The student's past experience needs to be the same as the instructor's.

B. The student's understanding of the meaning of symbols needs to be the same as the instructor's intended meaning.

C. The instructor should explain technical terms that he uses in speech.

Answer (B) is correct. *(FAA-H-8083-9A Chap 3)*

DISCUSSION: A student's understanding of the meaning of words and symbols needs to be the same as the instructor's understanding of the words and symbols. This requires the instructor to spend time making sure the students understand that terminology and the correct or intended use.

Answer (A) is incorrect. A student and instructor will never have exactly the same experiences in life. Because past experience varies greatly among each individual, the student's understanding of the meaning of the words needs to be the same as the instructor's understanding. Answer (C) is incorrect. While an instructor should explain technical terms (s)he uses, the student still needs to understand what they mean and how and when they apply to a given situation.

52. What is the term for when a symbol is different from the intended meaning?

A. Interference.

B. Confusion.

C. Abstraction.

Answer (B) is correct. *(FAA-H-8083-9A Chap 3)*

DISCUSSION: Confusion between the symbol and the symbolized object results when a word is confused with what it is meant to represent.

Answer (A) is incorrect. Interference, or the prevention of a process or activity from being carried out properly, is composed of factors outside the control of the instructor. Answer (C) is incorrect. Abstractions serve as shorthand symbols that sum up large areas of experience.

53. Because words and symbols do not always represent the same thing to each person, speakers and instructors should

A. use technical terms to accurately explain the subject being covered.

B. employ words and symbols that are concrete to narrow the image being produced in the listener's mind.

C. choose words and symbols that represent what is intended.

Answer (C) is correct. *(FAA-H-8083-9A Chap 3)*

DISCUSSION: To communicate effectively, speakers and instructors should choose words and symbols that represent what is intended. Thus, confusion will be avoided.

Answer (A) is incorrect. Technical terms do not necessarily accurately explain the subject being covered. This requires the listener to have background knowledge of what is being presented. Answer (B) is incorrect. Concrete words and symbols, while narrowing the images produced in the mind of a listener, can still confuse a student if they do not represent what is intended.

54. Interference, or the prevention of a process or activity from being carried out properly, is composed of what three factors outside the control of the instructor?

A. Physiological, Psychological, Environmental.

B. Psychological, Physiological, Biological.

C. Physical, Environmental, Psychological.

Answer (A) is correct. *(FAA-H-8083-9A Chap 3)*
DISCUSSION: The three factors that compose interference are physiological, environmental, and psychological.
Answer (B) is incorrect. Any biological problem that may inhibit symbol reception is known as physiological interference. The three factors that compose interference are physiological, environmental, and psychological. Answer (C) is incorrect. Any physical problem, such as hearing loss, injury, or illness, is a type of a physiological interference. The three factors that compose interference are physiological, environmental, and psychological.

55. Physiological interference is defined as

A. the product of how the instructor and student feel at the time communication process is occurring.

B. interference caused by external physical conditions.

C. interference resulting from any biological problem.

Answer (C) is correct. *(FAA-H-8083-9A Chap 3)*
DISCUSSION: Physiological interference results from a biological problem that may inhibit reception.
Answer (A) is incorrect. Physiological interference results from a biological problem that may inhibit reception. Psychological interference is a product of how the instructor and student feel at the time communication process is occurring. Answer (B) is incorrect. Physiological interference results from a biological problem that may inhibit reception. Interference caused by external physical conditions is an environmental factor in interference.

56. Aircraft noise, vibration, or lighting conditions are a type of what factor that causes interference?

A. Environmental.

B. Physiological.

C. Psychological.

Answer (A) is correct. *(FAA-H-8083-9A Chap 3)*
DISCUSSION: Environmental factors could include aircraft noise or vibration or lighting conditions.
Answer (B) is incorrect. Physiological factors could include hearing loss, injury, or physical illness. Answer (C) is incorrect. If either the instructor or student is not committed to the communication process, communication is impaired.

57. Which factor is displayed in the example of a student who is not actively engaged in the learning process and seems distracted?

A. Physiological.

B. Psychological.

C. Environmental.

Answer (B) is correct. *(FAA-H-8083-9A Chap 3)*
DISCUSSION: If the student is not committed to the communication process, as seen by seeming distracted or not engaged, communication is impaired and describes the psychological factor of interference.
Answer (A) is incorrect. An example of a physiological interference could include hearing loss, injury, or physical illness. Answer (C) is incorrect. An example of an environmental interference could include aircraft noise or vibration or lighting conditions.

3.6 Instructor Responsibilities

58. Evaluation of demonstrated ability during flight instruction must be based upon

A. the progress of the student.

B. the instructor's opinion concerning the maneuver(s).

C. established standards of performance.

Answer (C) is correct. *(FAA-H-8083-9A Chap 7)*
DISCUSSION: Evaluation of demonstrated student ability during flight instruction must be based upon established standards of performance, suitably modified to apply to the student's experience and stage of development as a pilot.
Answer (A) is incorrect. Evaluation must be based on established standards of performance, not the progress of the student. Answer (B) is incorrect. Evaluation must be based on established standards of performance, not on the instructor's opinion.

59. Evaluation of demonstrated ability during flight instruction must be based upon

A. the instructor's background and experience relating to student pilots at this stage of training.

B. the progress of the student, considering the time and experience attained since beginning training.

C. established standards of performance, suitably modified to apply to the student's experience.

Answer (C) is correct. *(FAA-H-8083-9A Chap 7)*

DISCUSSION: Evaluation of demonstrated student ability during flight instruction must be based upon established standards of performance, suitably modified to apply to the student's experience and stage of development as a pilot.

Answer (A) is incorrect. Evaluation should be based on established standards of performance and modified based on the student's experience, not the instructor's experience. Answer (B) is incorrect. Evaluation should be based on established standards of performance, not the student's progress since beginning training, modified based on the student's experience.

60. It is important that an instructor enhance a student's acceptance of further instruction by

A. keeping the student informed of the progress made.

B. constantly reminding the student of the learning objectives that lie ahead.

C. setting standards beyond the student's abilities.

Answer (A) is correct. *(FAA-H-8083-9A Chap 8)*

DISCUSSION: In assessing piloting ability, it is important for the flight instructor to keep the student informed of progress. This may be done as each procedure or maneuver is completed or summarized during post-flight critiques. Post-flight critiques should be in a written format such as notes to aid the flight instructor in covering all areas that were noticed during the flight or lesson.

Answer (B) is incorrect. Keeping a student informed of progress made to date is a more effective motivator than drawing attention to the tasks that the student has not yet addressed. Answer (C) is incorrect. Performance standards should be realistic and achievable.

61. In evaluating student demonstrations of piloting ability, it is important for the flight instructor to

A. remain silent and observe.

B. keep the student informed of progress.

C. explain errors in performance immediately.

Answer (B) is correct. *(FAA-H-8083-9A Chap 7)*

DISCUSSION: In evaluating student demonstrations of piloting ability, it is important for the flight instructor to keep the student informed of his or her progress. This may be done as each procedure/maneuver is completed or summarized during post-flight critiques.

Answer (A) is incorrect. In evaluating student demonstrations of piloting ability, it is important for the flight instructor to keep the student informed of his or her progress, not remain silent and observe. Answer (C) is incorrect. Students should be allowed to make mistakes and correct them on their own; errors should not be pointed out immediately because students learn by correcting their mistakes. The error can be explained at the completion of the procedure/maneuver or during a post-flight critique.

62. The use of distractions by a flight instructor

A. will teach the student to divide his or her attention between the distracting task and maintaining control of the aircraft.

B. will be of little value to more experienced students.

C. will allow students to develop concentration skills so they can ignore distracting passengers.

Answer (A) is correct. *(FAA-H-8083-9A Chap 8)*

DISCUSSION: Instructor responsibilities include teaching the student to divide his or her attention between the distracting task and maintaining control of the aircraft.

Answer (B) is incorrect. Pilots at all skill levels should be aware of the increased risk of entering into an inadvertent stall or spin while performing tasks that are secondary to controlling the aircraft. Answer (C) is incorrect. The proper use of distractions will not develop concentration skills that allow students to ignore distracting passengers.

63. Examples of all common endorsements can be found in the current issue of

A. AC 61-67, Appendix A.

B. AC 91-67, Appendix A.

C. AC 61-65, Appendix A.

Answer (C) is correct. *(FAA-H-8083-9A Chap 7)*

DISCUSSION: Examples of all common endorsements can be found in the current issue of AC 61-65, Appendix A.

Answer (A) is incorrect. Examples of all common endorsements can be found in the current issue of AC 61-65, not AC 61-67, Appendix A. Answer (B) is incorrect. Examples of all common endorsements can be found in the current issue of AC 61-65, not AC 91-67, Appendix A.

64. Before endorsing a student for solo flight, the instructor should require the student to demonstrate consistent ability to perform

A. all maneuvers specified in the Student Pilot Guide.

B. all of the fundamental maneuvers.

C. slow flight, stalls, emergency landings, takeoffs and landings, and go-arounds.

Answer (B) is correct. *(FAA-H-8083-9A Chap 7)*

DISCUSSION: Before endorsing a student for solo flight, the instructor should require the student to demonstrate the consistent ability to perform all of the fundamental maneuvers.

Answer (A) is incorrect. Before endorsing a student for solo flight, the instructor should require the student to demonstrate the consistent ability to perform all of the fundamental maneuvers, not all maneuvers specified in the Student Pilot Guide (which contains no maneuvers). Answer (C) is incorrect. Before endorsing a student for solo flight, the instructor should require the student to demonstrate the consistent ability to perform all of the fundamental maneuvers, not just slow flight, stalls, emergency landings, takeoffs, landings, and go-arounds.

65. The student should be capable of handling problems that might occur, such as traffic pattern congestion, change in active runway, or unexpected crosswinds prior to

A. the first solo cross-country flight.

B. initial solo.

C. being recommended for a Recreational or Private Pilot Certificate.

Answer (B) is correct. *(FAA-H-8083-9A Chap 7)*

DISCUSSION: Flight instructors have a responsibility to provide guidance and restraint regarding the solo operations of their students. Before receiving an instructor endorsement for solo flight, a student should be required to demonstrate the consistent ability to perform all of the fundamental maneuvers and should be capable of handling ordinary problems that might occur, such as traffic pattern congestion, a change in the active runway, or unexpected crosswinds.

Answer (A) is incorrect. The student should be capable of handling problems that might occur prior to initial solo, not the first solo cross-country flight. Answer (C) is incorrect. The student should be capable of handling problems that might occur prior to initial solo, not being recommended for a recreational or private pilot certificate.

66. Goals students consider difficult, but possible, tend to

A. provide a challenge and promote learning.

B. cause frustration and lead to failure.

C. be appropriate only for students lacking motivation.

Answer (A) is correct. *(FAA-H-8083-9A Chap 8)*

DISCUSSION: Assignment of goals the student considers difficult, but possible, usually provides a challenge and promotes learning. Motivation also declines when a student believes the instructor is making unreasonable demands for performance and progress.

Answer (B) is incorrect. The assignment of impossible or unreasonable goals discourages the student, diminishes effort, and retards the learning process. Answer (C) is incorrect. All students will benefit from the assignment of reasonable goals that offer a challenge to complete.

67. What are the five main responsibilities of aviation instructors?

A. Helping students learn, providing adequate instruction, emphasizing the positive, providing pilot endorsements, and ensuring aviation safety.

B. Helping students learn, providing adequate instruction, demanding adequate standards of performance, emphasizing the positive, and ensuring aviation safety.

C. Helping students learn, providing adequate instruction, emphasizing the positive, practical test recommendations, and ensuring aviation safety.

Answer (B) is correct. *(FAA-H-8083-9A Chap 7)*

DISCUSSION: The five main responsibilities of aviation instructors include helping students learn, providing adequate instruction, demanding adequate standards of performance, emphasizing the positive, and ensuring aviation safety.

Answer (A) is incorrect. Providing pilot endorsements, while a responsibility of an aviation instructor, is not one of the five main responsibilities. Answer (C) is incorrect. Practical test recommendations, while a responsibility of an aviation instructor, is not one of the five main responsibilities.

68. The use of standards, and measurement against those standards, is key to

A. ensuring aviation safety.

B. pilot supervision.

C. helping students learn.

Answer (C) is correct. *(FAA-H-8083-9A Chap 7)*

DISCUSSION: The use of standards, and measurement against standards, is key to helping students learn.

Answer (A) is incorrect. The use of standards, and measurement against standards, is key to helping students learn, not to ensuring aviation safety. Answer (B) is incorrect. The use of standards, and measurement against standards, is key to helping students learn, not pilot supervision.

69. What is one of the best actions an instructor can take to emphasize aviation safety?

A. By setting the example.

B. By informing the student of his or her progress as each procedure is completed.

C. By analyzing the student's personality, thinking, and ability to tailor his or her teaching technique to the student.

Answer (A) is correct. *(FAA-H-8083-9A Chap 7)*

DISCUSSION: Emphasizing safety by example is one of the best actions an instructor can take to ensure aviation safety.

Answer (B) is incorrect. Informing the student of his or her progress as each procedure is completed is an example of evaluating the student's piloting ability. Emphasizing safety by example is one of the best actions an instructor can take to ensure aviation safety. Answer (C) is incorrect. Analyzing a student's personality, thinking, and ability and then tailoring a teaching technique to fit the student is an example of providing adequate instruction.

70. Which would more likely result in students becoming frustrated?

A. Giving the students meaningless praise.

B. Telling students their work is unsatisfactory with no explanation.

C. An instructor freely admitting mistakes causing lack of trust.

Answer (B) is correct. *(FAA-H-8083-9A Chap 7)*

DISCUSSION: It does not help to tell students they have made errors and not provide explanations. If a student has made an earnest effort but is told that the work is unsatisfactory, with no other explanation, frustration occurs. Errors cannot be corrected if they are not identified, and if they are not identified, they will probably be perpetuated through faulty practice. On the other hand, if the student is briefed on the errors and is told how to correct them, progress can be made.

Answer (A) is incorrect. While you are not providing effective instruction by offering a student meaningless praise, you are also not creating frustration on the part of the student. This instructional error offers many other negative consequences, though, and should be avoided. Answer (C) is incorrect. While failing to admit your own errors might frustrate a student pilot, freely acknowledging your mistakes to the student is more likely to increase rather than decrease trust on the part of the student. You are also acting as a good example to the student pilot by acknowledging and talking through your errors.

71. What is one method of keeping students aware of their progress?

A. Students should keep attempting a maneuver even if they are making the same mistake.

B. Repeating a demonstration, showing the students the standard their performance must ultimately meet.

C. Students are usually aware of their progress without instructor intervention.

Answer (B) is correct. *(FAA-H-8083-9A Chap 2)*

DISCUSSION: One way to make students aware of their progress is to repeat a demonstration or example and to show them the standards their performance must ultimately meet.

Answer (A) is incorrect. They should be told as soon after the performance as possible and should not be allowed to practice mistakes. It is more difficult to unlearn a mistake, and then learn the skill correctly, than to learn correctly in the first place. Answer (C) is incorrect. Mistakes are not always apparent. A student may know that something is wrong but not know how to correct it. In any case, the instructor provides a helpful and often critical function in making certain that the students are aware of their progress.

3.7 Instructor Professionalism

72. Which statement is true regarding true professionalism as an instructor?

A. Anything less than sincere performance destroys the effectiveness of the professional instructor.

B. To achieve professionalism, actions and decisions must be limited to standard patterns and practices.

C. A single definition of professionalism would encompass all of the qualifications and considerations which must be present.

Answer (A) is correct. *(FAA-H-8083-9A Chap 7)*

DISCUSSION: Professionalism demands a code of ethics. Professionals must be true to themselves and to those they serve. Anything less than a sincere performance will be detected by students and immediately destroy instructor effectiveness.

Answer (B) is incorrect. Professionalism requires good judgment. Professionals cannot limit their actions and decisions to standard patterns and practice. Answer (C) is incorrect. Professionalism is so multi-dimensional that no single definition can encompass all of the qualifications and considerations.

73. Aviation instructors should be constantly alert for ways to improve the services they provide to their students, their effectiveness, and their

A. appearance.

B. qualifications.

C. demeanor.

Answer (B) is correct. *(FAA-H-8083-9A Chap 7)*
DISCUSSION: Professional aviation instructors must never become complacent or satisfied with their own qualifications and abilities. Aviation instructors should be constantly alert for ways to improve the services they provide to their students, their effectiveness, and their qualifications.
Answer (A) is incorrect. While an instructor's personal appearance is important to maintaining a professional image, aviation instructors should be constantly alert for ways to improve the services they provide to their students, their effectiveness, and their qualifications. Answer (C) is incorrect. While an instructor's demeanor is important to maintaining a professional image, aviation instructors should be constantly alert for ways to improve the services they provide to their students, their effectiveness, and their qualifications.

74. Student confidence tends to be destroyed if instructors

A. bluff whenever in doubt about some point.

B. continually identify student errors and failures.

C. direct and control the student's actions and behavior.

Answer (A) is correct. *(FAA-H-8083-9A Chap 7)*
DISCUSSION: No one, including students, expects an instructor to be perfect. An instructor can gain the respect of students by honestly acknowledging mistakes. If the instructor tries to cover up or bluff, students will be quick to sense it and lose their confidence in the instructor.
Answer (B) is incorrect. Identifying the student's errors and failures helps the student to progress and gain confidence. Answer (C) is incorrect. Directing the student's actions and behavior is a basic responsibility of the flight instructor.

75. Students quickly become apathetic when they

A. realize material is being withheld by the instructor.

B. understand the objectives toward which they are working.

C. recognize that the instructor is not adequately prepared.

Answer (C) is correct. *(FAA-H-8083-9A Chap 8)*
DISCUSSION: Students become apathetic when they recognize that the instructor has made inadequate preparations for the instruction being given or when the instruction appears to be deficient, contradictory, or insincere.
Answer (A) is incorrect. Students will lose respect for the instructor (not become apathetic) when they realize material is being withheld by the instructor. Answer (B) is incorrect. It is optimal that both the student and instructor understand the objectives so that they may work cooperatively toward them.

76. Which is true regarding professionalism as an instructor?

A. Professionalism demands a code of ethics.

B. To achieve professionalism, actions and decisions must be limited to standard patterns and practices.

C. Professionalism does not require extended training and preparation.

Answer (A) is correct. *(FAA-H-8083-9A Chap 7)*
DISCUSSION: Professionalism demands a code of ethics. Professionals must be true to themselves and to those they serve. Anything less than a sincere performance will be detected by students and immediately destroy instructor effectiveness.
Answer (B) is incorrect. Professionalism requires good judgment. Professionals cannot limit their actions and decisions to standard patterns and practices. Answer (C) is incorrect. Professionalism is achieved only after extended training and preparation.

77. Which statement is true regarding the achievement of an adequate standard of performance?

A. A flight instructor should devote major effort and attention to the continuous evaluation of student performance.

B. Flight instructors can affect a genuine improvement in the student/instructor relationship by not strictly enforcing standards.

C. Flight instructors fail to provide competent instruction when they permit students to partially learn an important item of knowledge or skill.

Answer (C) is correct. *(FAA-H-8083-9A Chap 7)*
DISCUSSION: Flight instructors fail to provide competent instruction when they permit their students to partially learn an important item of knowledge or skill. More importantly, such deficiencies may in themselves allow hazardous inadequacies in the student's later piloting performance.
Answer (A) is incorrect. A flight instructor should devote major effort and attention to all areas of the teaching process, not only to the evaluation of student performance. Answer (B) is incorrect. It is a fallacy to believe that a flight instructor can affect a genuine improvement in the student/instructor relationship by not strictly enforcing standards. Reasonable standards strictly enforced are not resented by an earnest student.

78. True performance as a professional is based on study and

A. perseverance.

B. research.

C. attitude.

Answer (B) is correct. *(FAA-H-8083-9A Chap 7)*

DISCUSSION: True performance as a professional is based on study and research.

Answer (A) is incorrect. True performance as a professional is based on study and research, not perseverance. Answer (C) is incorrect. True performance as a professional is based on study and research, not attitude.

79. The professional relationship between the instructor and the student should be based on what?

A. A predetermined code of ethics.

B. A mutual acknowledgment that both the student and the instructor are working toward the same objective.

C. The knowledge that the instructor will maintain the highest level of knowledge, training, and currency during training.

Answer (B) is correct. *(FAA-H-8083-9A Chap 7)*

DISCUSSION: The professional relationship between the instructor and the student should be based on a mutual acknowledgment that both the student and the instructor are important to each other and that both are working toward the same objective.

Answer (A) is incorrect. While professionalism demands a code of ethics, this is not what a professional relationship is based on. Answer (C) is incorrect. A relationship is two-sided and does not rest solely on the instructor to be knowledgeable and prepared. The professional relationship between the instructor and the student should be based on a mutual acknowledgment that both the student and the instructor are working toward the same objective.

STUDY UNIT FOUR
TEACHING METHODS

(9 pages of outline)

4.1 LECTURE METHOD

1. The lecture is used primarily for
   a. Introducing students to new subject material,
   b. Summarizing ideas,
   c. Showing relationships between theory and practice, and
   d. Reemphasizing main points.
2. There are four types of lectures:
   a. The illustrated talk, in which the speaker relies heavily on visual aids to convey his or her ideas to the listeners;
   b. The briefing, in which the speaker presents a concise array of facts to the listeners, who do not expect elaboration or supporting material;
   c. The formal speech, in which the speaker's purpose is to inform, persuade, or entertain; and
   d. The teaching lecture, for which the instructor must plan and deliver an oral presentation in a manner that helps the students reach the desired learning outcomes.
3. One advantage of a teaching lecture is that the instructor can present many ideas in a relatively short time. Facts and ideas that have been logically organized can be concisely presented in rapid sequence.
   a. Thus, a teaching lecture is the most economical of all teaching methods in terms of the time required to present a given amount of material.
4. One disadvantage of a teaching lecture is that the instructor does not receive a direct reaction (either words or actions) from the students.
   a. Thus, the instructor must develop a keen perception for subtle responses from the class and must be able to interpret the meaning of these indirect reactions and adjust the lesson accordingly.
      1) These reactions could be in the form of facial expressions, manner of taking notes, and apparent interest or lack of interest in the lesson.
   b. The instructor must recognize that the lecture method is least useful for evaluating student performance.

5. The following four steps should be followed in preparing a lecture:
    a. Establish the objective and desired outcomes,
    b. Research the subject,
    c. Organize the material, and
    d. Plan productive classroom activities.
6. The teaching lecture is best delivered extemporaneously – but from a written outline.
    a. Because the exact words used to express an idea are chosen at the moment of delivery, the lecture can be personalized or suited to the moment more easily than one that is read or spoken from memory.
7. In the teaching lecture, use simple rather than complex words whenever possible.
    a. Picturesque slang and colloquialisms, if they suit the subject, can add variety and vividness to a teaching lecture.
    b. Errors in grammar and use of vulgarisms detract from an instructor's dignity and reflect upon the intelligence of the students.
8. The lecture can be formal or informal.
    a. A formal lecture provides no active student participation.
    b. The distinguishing characteristic of an informal lecture is the active student participation.
        1) The instructor can inspire active student participation during informal lectures through the use of questions.

4.2 COOPERATIVE OR GROUP LEARNING METHOD

1. Cooperative group learning is an instructional strategy used to organize students into small groups so that they can work together to maximize their own and each other's learning.
    a. The most significant characteristic of group learning is that it continually requires active participation of the student.
    b. The main reason that students are put in cooperative learning groups is so they can individually achieve greater success than if they were to study alone.
    c. Students in cooperative learning groups tend to interact and achieve in ways and at levels that are rarely found with other instructional strategies.
2. Instructor planning is key to achieving meaningful learning.
    a. Instructors must determine and outline clear lesson objectives and completion standards. Evidence of mastery of targeted content and skills must be stated to inform students of the intended results.
3. Instructors should organize small heterogeneous groups of students who have different academic abilities, ethnic backgrounds, race, and gender.
    a. The main advantage of heterogeneous groups is that students tend to interact and achieve in ways and at levels that are rarely found with other instructional strategies.
    b. Heterogeneous groups lead students to learn to work together, to seek more support for opinions, to tolerate each other's viewpoints, and to consider viewpoints dissimilar to their own.

4.3 GUIDED DISCUSSION METHOD

1. Fundamentally, the guided discussion method of teaching is the reverse of the lecture method. The instructor uses questions to guide and stimulate discussion among students. The instructor does not present new ideas.
2. In the guided discussion, learning is achieved through the skillful use of questions.
   a. Questions facilitate discussion, which in turn develops an understanding of the subject.
3. Questions used in a guided discussion can be broken into several types, each with its usefulness in the guided discussion:
   a. **Overhead** -- directed to the entire group to stimulate thought and response from each group member.
   b. **Rhetorical** -- also stimulates thought, but the instructor will answer it himself or herself. This is normally used in a lecture, not a guided discussion.
   c. **Direct** -- question addressed to an individual for a response.
   d. **Reverse** -- The instructor answers a student's question by redirecting the question for that student to provide the answer.
   e. **Relay** -- The reverse question is addressed to the entire group, not the individual.
4. In preparing questions, the instructor should remember that the purpose is to bring about discussion, not merely to get answers.
   a. Leadoff questions should be open-ended; i.e., they should start with "how" or "why."
   b. Avoid questions that begin with "what," "when," or "does" because they only require short, categorical answers such as "yes," "no," "green," "one," etc.
5. Each question, in order to be effective, should
   a. Have a specific purpose,
   b. Be clear in meaning,
   c. Contain a single idea,
   d. Stimulate thought,
   e. Require definite answers, and
   f. Relate to previously taught information.
6. When it appears the students have adequately discussed the ideas that support a particular part of the lesson, the instructor should summarize what they have accomplished.
   a. This interim summary is one of the most effective tools available to the instructor.
      1) This summary can be made immediately after the discussion of each learning outcome.
      2) It consolidates what students learned, emphasizes how much they know already, and points out any aspects they missed.
7. Unless the students have some knowledge to exchange with each other, they cannot reach the desired learning outcomes.
   a. Students without some background in a subject should not be asked to discuss that subject.

4.4 DEMONSTRATION/PERFORMANCE METHOD

1. The demonstration/performance method is based on the principle that we learn by doing.
   a. It is the most commonly used teaching method of flight instructors.
   b. This is the ideal method for teaching a skill that requires practice, such as using a flight computer or performing crosswind landings.

2. The demonstration/performance method of instruction has five essential steps:
   a. **Explanation** -- the instructor must clearly explain the objectives of the particular lesson to the student.
      1) Additionally, the precise steps to be completed and the desired end result should be explained.
      2) Students should be given the opportunity to ask questions to understand the requirements fully.
      3) EXAMPLE: An instructor describes the steps (power settings, flap configurations, etc.) needed to successfully perform a short-field landing. Using the Practical Test Standards (PTS)/Airman Certification Standards (ACS) as a guide, the instructor explains what the completion requirements are.
   b. **Demonstration** -- the instructor must show the student how to perform a skill.
      1) Demonstrations not closely representing the explanation should be immediately acknowledged and explained so students do not replicate improper techniques.
      2) EXAMPLE: An instructor demonstrates and completes a short-field landing within the given tolerances.
   c. **Student performance** -- the student must act and do.
      1) To learn skills, students must practice.
      2) Through doing, students learn to follow correct procedures and to reach established goals.
      3) EXAMPLE: A student practices short-field landings under the supervision of an instructor.
   d. **Instructor supervision** -- the instructor coaches, as necessary, the student's practice.
      1) Both student performance and instructor supervision are performed concurrently.
      2) EXAMPLE: During a short-field landing by the student, the instructor follows along on the controls during the demonstration of the maneuver and coaches as needed.
   e. **Evaluation** -- the instructor judges the student performance.
      1) From the measurement of student achievement, the instructor determines the effectiveness of the instruction.
      2) EXAMPLE: During a post-flight debriefing, the instructor explains the student's performance.
3. The **telling and doing technique** (or "drill and practice method") of flight instruction is basically the demonstration/performance method of instruction.
   a. It promotes learning through repetition because those things most often repeated are best remembered.
   b. Every time practice occurs, learning continues.
   c. This technique consists of performing several steps in proper order.
      1) Instructor tells -- instructor does/shows
      2) Student tells -- instructor does/shows
      3) Student tells -- student does/shows
      4) Student does/shows -- instructor evaluates
   d. Drill and practice is based on the learning principle of exercise. Connections are strengthened with practice. It promotes learning through repetition because those things most often repeated are best remembered.
      1) The human mind rarely retains, evaluates, and applies new concepts or practices after a single exposure. Students do not learn to perform crosswind landings during one instructional flight. They learn by applying what they have been told and shown.
      2) Every time practice occurs, learning continues.

4.5 PROBLEM-BASED LEARNING

1. Problem-Based Learning (PBL) describes a type of learning environment in which lessons are structured to confront students with problems encountered in real life that force them to reach real-world solutions.
   a. A characteristic of PBL is that there is no single solution to the given problem.
      1) These types of "authentic" problems allow the learner to "make meaning" of the information based on past experience and personal interpretation.
   b. Benefits of PBL include helping the learner gain a deeper understanding of the information. Students will also improve their ability to recall information in this type of learning.
   c. Effective PBL problems
      1) Relate to the real world, stimulating student desire to solve them
      2) Require students to make decisions
      3) Are open ended and not limited to one correct answer
      4) Are connected both to previously learned and new knowledge
      5) Reflect the lesson objective(s)
      6) Challenge the student to think critically
   d. The three types of PBL instruction are **scenario-based training**, the **collaborative problem-solving method**, and the **case study method**.
2. **Scenario-Based Training Method (SBT)**
   a. SBT is a realistic situation that allows the student to rehearse mentally for a situation and requires practical application of various pieces of knowledge.
   b. SBT scenarios challenge students to manage available resources, exercise sound judgment, and make timely decisions with the goal of reducing accidents. The overall learning objective is for the student to be more prepared to make good decisions based on a variety of real-world situations.
   c. SBT is a powerful tool because the future is unpredictable and there is no way to train a pilot for every combination of events that may happen in the future.
   d. A good scenario
      1) Is not a test,
      2) Will not have only one correct answer,
      3) Does not offer an obvious answer,
      4) Should not promote errors,
      5) Should promote situational awareness and opportunities for decision making, and
      6) Usually tells a story that begins with a reason to fly, because a pilot's decisions will differ depending on the motivation to fly.
         a) EXAMPLE: "A newly rated private pilot is heading out on a cross country to see his son graduate from college. He has already gotten a late start because of poor weather at his home field. Halfway through his flight he encounters low visibility and increased turbulence. ATC and AWOS both confirm the weather is IMC at his destination airport and several others nearby. What will he do now?"
3. **Collaborative Problem-Solving Method**
   a. The collaborative problem-solving method combines collaboration with problem solving when the instructor provides a problem to a group of two or more people working together who then solve the problem.
   b. This type of instruction is similar to SBT in that it includes open ended "what if" questions.

4. **Case Study Method**
   a. This method uses a written or oral account of a real-world situation that contains an educational message for the student.
   b. The instructor presents the case to the students who then analyze it, reach conclusions, and offer possible solutions. Case studies require students to use critical thinking skills.
   c. A good resource for source material for the creation of case studies can be found at the National Transportation Safety Board's (NTSB) website.
      1) The flight instructor will have the student analyze the information and suggest possible reasons for the accident. This analysis will both reinforce positive decision-making skills and provide the student with the consequences of improper decision making.
5. Operational pitfalls are classic behavioral traps that can ensnare the unwary pilot. Pilots, particularly those with considerable experience, try to complete a flight as planned, please passengers, and meet schedules. This basic drive to demonstrate achievements can have an adverse effect on safety.
   a. These tendencies ultimately may lead to practices that are dangerous and sometimes illegal. Students develop awareness and learn to avoid many of these operational pitfalls through effective ADM training. The scenarios and examples provided by instructors during ADM instruction should involve these pitfalls.
   b. Lack of effective ADM training may lead to overconfidence, disregard for applicable regulations, or disregard of flight planning.
      1) An overconfident pilot may not properly plan for minimum fuel reserves during preflight planning or may neglect the preflight planning altogether.

4.6 ELECTRONIC LEARNING (E-LEARNING)

1. Electronic learning (e-learning) is defined as any type of education that involves an electronic component (e.g., Internet, stand-alone software, simulators, etc.).
   a. Advantages of e-learning include less time spent on instruction and higher levels of mastery and retention.
      1) E-learning often seems more enjoyable from the student standpoint because it allows students to feel as if they are in control of what they are learning and at a rate that is comfortable for them.
   b. **Distance learning**, the use of electronic media to deliver instruction when the instructor and student are separated, is another advantage of e-learning.
   c. Improper or excessive use of e-learning should be avoided. It will always be the responsibility of the instructor to monitor and oversee student progress and to intervene when necessary.
   d. Limitations of e-learning include
      1) Lack of peer interaction and personal feedback,
      2) Lack of instructor control and oversight, and
      3) Costs associated with equipment/programs.

2. **Computer-Assisted Learning (CAL)** is a specific form of e-learning that integrates a personal computer with multimedia software to create a training device.
   a. The major advantage of CAL is that it is interactive in that the computer will respond in different ways depending on student input.
      1) Some of the more advanced CAL applications allow students to progress through a series of interactive segments in which the presentation varies as a result of their responses.
         a) CAL responds quickly to student input.
         b) When CAL is combined with multimedia, students can control the pace of instruction.
   b. Other advantages of CAL include the fact that students can progress at a rate that is comfortable for them and are often able to access material at locations and times convenient to them.
   c. Both initial and recurrent training can be accomplished with CAL.
      1) Aviation companies that incorporate CAL reduce the amount of manpower, and associated costs, needed to train employees.
   d. CAL can be used to test a student's achievement, compare results with past performance, and indicate a student's weak or strong areas.
      1) EXAMPLE: In preparing for an FAA knowledge test, students may use test prep software to practice tests, evaluate scores, and review missed questions.
   e. CAL should be thought of and used as a reference aid, not as the sole means of accomplishing a training program.
   f. Instructors should remain actively involved with the students by using close supervision, questions, exams, or guided discussions to constantly assess student progress.
3. Simulation, role playing, and video gaming are other forms of e-learning that, while not thought of as primary means of instruction, are still valuable tools for aviation training.
   a. Many flight schools incorporate flight simulation into a student's training regimen to have them practice scenarios that would otherwise be unwise or unsafe to perform in an actual aircraft.
   b. Depending on the type of device, use of flight simulators can be credited for actual flight time.

4.7 INTEGRATED METHOD OF FLIGHT INSTRUCTION

1. Integrated flight instruction is flight instruction during which students are taught to perform flight maneuvers, both by outside visual references and by inside reference to flight instruments for the same operations. As an instructor, your primary goal is safety. You must develop the habit of constantly monitoring the student's performance and the aircraft's performance while maintaining an appropriate scan for traffic.
   a. For this type of instruction to be fully effective, the use of instrument references should begin the first time each new maneuver is introduced.
   b. It is also important for the student to learn the feel of the aircraft while conducting maneuvers.
      1) EXAMPLE: Determining, by feeling, that the aircraft is out of trim or in an unusual attitude.
   c. Students who have been taught by means of integrated flight instruction will develop the habit of continuously monitoring both their own performance and that of the aircraft.

2. The habitual attention to instrument indications leads to improved pilot competency, operating efficiency of the aircraft, and an overall increase in safety.
   a. EXAMPLE: Landings will be improved due to more precise airspeed control, and average cruising flight performance increases by holding precise headings and altitudes.
   b. The ability to fly in instrument meteorological conditions (IMC) is not the objective of this type of primary training yet will provide a good foundation for later training for an instrument rating.
3. During the conduct of integrated flight instruction, you are responsible for collision avoidance while your student is flying by simulated instruments, i.e., under the hood.
   a. You must guard against diverting your attention to the student's performance for extended periods.
4. At the same time, you must be sure that your student develops, from the first lesson, the habit of looking for other traffic when (s)he is not operating under simulated instrument conditions.
   a. Any observed tendency of a student to enter a maneuver without clearing the area must be corrected immediately.

4.8 THE POSITIVE APPROACH IN FLIGHT INSTRUCTION

1. In flight instruction, an effective positive approach will point out the pleasurable features of flying before the unpleasant possibilities are discussed.
2. EXAMPLE of a positive first flight lesson:
   a. A preflight inspection familiarizing the student with the airplane and its components
   b. A perfectly normal flight to a nearby airport and back
      1) The instructor calls the student's attention to how easy the trip was in comparison with other ways to travel and the fact that no critical incidents were encountered or expected.
3. EXAMPLE of a negative first flight lesson:
   a. An exhaustive indoctrination on preflight procedures with emphasis on the potential for disastrous mechanical failures in flight.
   b. Instructions on the dangers of taxiing an airplane too fast.
   c. A series of stalls with emphasis on the difficulties in recovering from them. (The side effect of this performance is likely to be airsickness.)
   d. A series of simulated forced landings, stating that every pilot should always be prepared to cope with an engine failure.

4.9 TESTING THE LIMITS OF STUDENT KNOWLEDGE

1. Presenting your students with problems that require them to make a decision to test the limits of their understanding is an effective way to help them acquire knowledge. Some examples may include the following:
   a. Ask students to recite or practice newly acquired knowledge.
   b. Ask questions that probe student understanding and prompt them to think about what they have learned in different ways.
   c. Present opportunities for students to apply what they know to solving problems or making decisions.
   d. Demonstrate the benefits of understanding and being able to apply knowledge.
   e. Introduce new topics that support the objectives of the lesson whenever possible.

2. Fatigue is one of the most treacherous hazards to flight safety as it may not be apparent to a pilot until serious errors are made.
   a. The amount of training any student can absorb without incurring debilitating fatigue varies.
   b. Complex operations tend to induce fatigue more rapidly than simpler procedures do, regardless of the physical effort involved.
   c. Fatigue is the primary consideration in determining the length and frequency of flight instruction periods, and flight instruction should be continued only as long as the student is alert, receptive to instruction, and performing at a level consistent with experience.

QUESTIONS AND ANSWER EXPLANATIONS: All of the Fundamentals of Instructing knowledge test questions chosen by the FAA for release as well as additional questions selected by Gleim relating to the material in the previous outlines are provided on the following pages. These questions have been organized into the same subunits as the outlines. To the immediate right of each question are the correct answer and answer explanations. You should cover these answers and answer explanations while responding to the questions. Refer to the general discussion in the Introduction on how to take the FAA knowledge test.

Remember that the questions from the FAA knowledge test bank have been reordered by topic and organized into a meaningful sequence. Also, the first line of the answer explanation gives the citation of the authoritative source for the answer.

QUESTIONS

4.1 Lecture Method

1. In the teaching process, which method of presentation is suitable for presenting new material, for summarizing ideas, and for showing relationships between theory and practice?

A. Lecture method.

B. Integrated instruction method.

C. Demonstration/performance method.

Answer (A) is correct. *(FAA-H-8083-9A Chap 4)*
DISCUSSION: The lecture is used primarily to introduce students to new material. It is also valuable for summarizing ideas, showing relationships between theory and practice, and reemphasizing main points. The lecture is the most efficient teaching method in terms of time and student numbers, if not in other ways.
Answer (B) is incorrect. The integrated method of flight instruction is designed to teach students to perform maneuvers both by outside visual references and by reference to flight instruments. Answer (C) is incorrect. The demonstration/performance method is better suited to teaching a skill (i.e., flight instruction).

2. What is one advantage of a lecture?

A. A lecture is effective in showing relationships between theory and practice.

B. Excellent when additional research is required.

C. Allows for maximum attainment of certain types of learning outcomes.

Answer (A) is correct. *(FAA-H-8083-9A Chap 4)*
DISCUSSION: In a lecture, the instructor can present many ideas in a relatively short time. Facts and ideas that have been logically organized can be concisely presented in rapid sequence. Lecturing is unquestionably the most economical of all teaching methods in terms of time required to present a given amount of material.
Answer (B) is incorrect. One advantage of the lecture is that it can be used to present information without requiring students to do additional research. Answer (C) is incorrect. A disadvantage, not an advantage, of a lecture is that the lecture does not enable the instructor to estimate the student's progress; thus, learning may not be maximized.

3. When an instructor is teaching in a lecture environment (s)he should

A. maintain a consistent tone of voice and pace of speaking.

B. try to use simple rather than complex words.

C. move from the unknown to the known.

Answer (B) is correct. *(FAA-H-8083-9A Chap 4)*
DISCUSSION: In the teaching lecture, simple rather than complex words should be used whenever possible. The instructor should not, however, use substandard English. Errors in grammar and vulgarisms detract from an instructor's dignity and insult the intelligence of the students.
Answer (A) is incorrect. Instructors should attempt to add life to the lecture by varying the tone of voice and pace of speaking. Answer (C) is incorrect. Instructors should always move from the known to the unknown.

4. During a teaching lecture, what would detract from an instructor's dignity and reflect upon the student's intelligence?

A. Use of figurative language.

B. Errors in grammar and use of vulgarisms.

C. Using picturesque slang and colloquialisms.

Answer (B) is correct. *(FAA-H-8083-9A Chap 4)*

DISCUSSION: During a teaching lecture, errors in grammar and the use of vulgarisms detract from an instructor's dignity and reflect upon the student's intelligence.

Answer (A) is incorrect. Figurative language, when used properly, can add interest and color to a lecture. Answer (C) is incorrect. Picturesque slang and colloquialisms, if they suit the subject, can add variety and vividness to a lecture.

5. Which teaching method is most economical in terms of the time required to present a given amount of material?

A. Briefing.

B. Teaching lecture.

C. Demonstration/performance.

Answer (B) is correct. *(FAA-H-8083-9A Chap 4)*

DISCUSSION: The teaching lecture is unquestionably the most economical of all teaching methods in terms of the time required to present a given amount of material. The instructor can concisely present many ideas that have been logically organized in rapid sequence.

Answer (A) is incorrect. Although a briefing is a type of lecture, it is used to present a concise array of facts to the listeners who do not expect elaboration or supporting material. Answer (C) is incorrect. The demonstration/performance method is the least, not the most, economical in terms of time required to present a given amount of material.

6. Which is a true statement regarding the teaching lecture?

A. Delivering the lecture in an extemporaneous manner is not recommended.

B. Instructor receives direct feedback from students which is easy to interpret.

C. Instructor must develop a keen perception for subtle responses and be able to interpret the meaning of these reactions.

Answer (C) is correct. *(FAA-H-8083-9A Chap 4)*

DISCUSSION: In the teaching lecture, the instructor must develop a keen perception for subtle responses from the class (e.g., facial expressions, manner of taking notes, and apparent interest or lack of interest in the lesson), and must be able to interpret the meaning of these reactions and adjust the lesson accordingly.

Answer (A) is incorrect. The lecture is best delivered extemporaneously but from a written outline. The lecture can thus be personalized to suit different audience moods. Answer (B) is incorrect. In the teaching lecture, the instructor's feedback is not as direct as other teaching methods and therefore is harder, not easier, to interpret.

7. The first step in preparing a lecture is to

A. research the subject.

B. develop the main ideas or key points.

C. establish the objective and desired outcome.

Answer (C) is correct. *(FAA-H-8083-9A Chap 4)*

DISCUSSION: The following four steps, in order, should be used in preparing a lecture:

1. Establish the objectives and desired outcomes.
2. Research the subject.
3. Organize the material.
4. Plan productive classroom activities.

Answer (A) is incorrect. Researching the subject is the second, not the first, step in preparing a lecture. Answer (B) is incorrect. Developing the main ideas or key points is the third, not the first, step in preparing a lecture.

8. The distinguishing characteristic of an informal lecture is the

A. use of visual aids.

B. student's participation.

C. requirement for informal notes.

Answer (B) is correct. *(FAA-H-8083-9A Chap 4)*

DISCUSSION: The distinguishing characteristic of an informal lecture is the active student participation. A formal lecture does not include student participation.

Answer (A) is incorrect. Visual aids can be used in either the formal or informal lecture. Answer (C) is incorrect. The requirement for informal notes is not the distinguishing characteristic of an informal lecture. Notes may or may not be used in the formal or informal lecture.

9. An instructor can inspire active student participation during informal lectures through the use of

A. questions.

B. visual aids.

C. encouragement.

Answer (A) is correct. *(FAA-H-8083-9A Chap 4)*

DISCUSSION: An instructor can inspire student participation during informal lectures through the use of questions. In this way, the students are encouraged to make contributions that supplement the lecture.

Answer (B) is incorrect. Visual aids emphasize and enhance the lecture but do not help get the students actively involved. Answer (C) is incorrect. Encouragement aids learning in all situations, not just participation during lectures.

4.2 Cooperative or Group Learning Method

10. An instructional strategy which organizes students into small groups so that they can work together to maximize their own and each other's learning is called

A. workshop learning.

B. heterogeneous group learning.

C. cooperative or group learning.

Answer (C) is correct. *(FAA-H-8083-9A Chap 4)*

DISCUSSION: Cooperative group learning is an instructional strategy which organizes students into small groups so that they can work together to maximize their own and each other's learning.

Answer (A) is incorrect. Workshop learning may take place individually; it does not necessarily involve groups. Answer (B) is incorrect. Cooperative group learning is an instructional strategy which organizes students into small groups so that they can work together to maximize their own and each other's learning. Heterogeneous groups are recommended for effective cooperative group learning.

11. The most significant characteristic of group learning is that students tend to

A. actively participate in the learning process.

B. continually requires active participation of both the student and the instructor.

C. usually requires passive participation of the student.

Answer (A) is correct. *(FAA-H-8083-9A Chap 4)*

DISCUSSION: Many positive characteristics have been attributed to group learning, the most significant of which is that it continually requires active participation in the learning process by the student.

Answer (B) is incorrect. The most significant characteristic of group learning is that it continually requires active participation of the student, not the instructor. The instructor must allow groups to work by themselves if the students are to maximize each other's learning. Answer (C) is incorrect. Group learning requires active, not passive, participation of the student.

12. The main reason that students are put in cooperative learning groups is so they

A. learn and help each other.

B. can individually achieve greater success than if they were to study alone.

C. learn that teamwork is essential if all members are to learn equally well.

Answer (B) is correct. *(FAA-H-8083-9A Chap 4)*

DISCUSSION: The main reason that students are put in cooperative learning groups is so they can individually achieve greater success than if they were to study alone.

Answer (A) is incorrect. While students do learn and help each other, the main reason that students are put in cooperative learning groups is so they can individually achieve greater success than if they were to study alone. Answer (C) is incorrect. While teamwork is essential to group learning, it is unlikely that all members will learn equally well. Students are put in cooperative learning groups so they can individually achieve greater success than if they were to study alone.

13. The main advantage(s) with heterogeneous groups are that students tend to

A. think for themselves since they are in a group of dissimilar students.

B. interact and achieve in ways and at levels that are rarely found with other instructional strategies.

C. interact and achieve since they are in a group of similar students.

Answer (B) is correct. *(FAA-H-8083-9A Chap 4)*

DISCUSSION: Instructors should organize small heterogeneous groups of students who have different academic abilities, ethnic backgrounds, race, and gender. The main advantage of heterogeneous groups is that students tend to interact and achieve in ways and at levels that are rarely found with other instructional strategies.

Answer (A) is incorrect. Heterogeneous groups lead students to learn to work together, to seek more support for opinions, and to tolerate each other's viewpoints, not to think for themselves. Answer (C) is incorrect. Heterogeneous groups contain dissimilar, not similar, students.

14. To achieve meaningful learning on the part of all in a group, instructors must

A. interact with individuals in the group so as to ensure lesson objectives are being met.

B. determine and outline clearly what the lesson objectives and completion standards are.

C. consider the background abilities of students.

Answer (B) is correct. *(FAA-H-8083-9A Chap 4)*

DISCUSSION: To achieve meaningful learning, instructors must determine and outline clear lesson objectives and completion standards.

Answer (A) is incorrect. Interaction with individuals in a group does not guarantee lesson objectives are being met. By providing clear lesson objectives and explaining the completion standards, meaningful learning can be achieved. Answer (C) is incorrect. The background of the student is not a factor in group learning as all individuals will be sharing ideas and potentially new thoughts. To achieve meaningful learning, instructors must determine and outline clear lesson objectives and completion standards.

4.3 Guided Discussion Method

15. In a guided discussion, learning is achieved through the

A. skillful use of questions.

B. use of questions, each of which contains several ideas.

C. use of reverse questions directed to the class as a whole.

Answer (A) is correct. *(FAA-H-8083-9A Chap 4)*

DISCUSSION: The guided discussion method relies on the students to provide ideas, experiences, opinions, and information. The instructor guides the discussion by use of questions aimed at drawing out what the students know. Thus, learning is achieved through the skillful use of questions.

Answer (B) is incorrect. In a guided discussion, each question used should contain only one, not several, ideas. Answer (C) is incorrect. A relay, not reverse, question is redirected to the class as a whole.

16. A question directed to an entire group to stimulate thought and response from each group member is identified as

A. Relay.

B. Overhead.

C. Rhetorical.

Answer (B) is correct. *(FAA-H-8083-9A Chap 4)*

DISCUSSION: In the guided discussion, learning is produced through skillful use of questions. To begin a guided discussion, the instructor should use an overhead question. This type of question is directed to the entire group to stimulate thought and response from each student.

Answer (A) is incorrect. A relay question responds to a student's question by redirecting it back to the rest of the group. Answer (C) is incorrect. A rhetorical question is similar in nature to an overhead question, but the instructor answers the question. This is more commonly used in lecturing than in guided discussion.

17. In a guided discussion, leadoff questions should usually begin with

A. why.

B. what.

C. when.

Answer (A) is correct. *(FAA-H-8083-9A Chap 4)*

DISCUSSION: In preparing questions, the instructor should remember that the purpose is to bring about discussion, not merely to get only short categorical answers (e.g., yes, no, one, etc.). Thus, leadoff questions should usually begin with "how" or "why."

Answer (B) is incorrect. A question beginning with "what" usually requires only a short categorical answer and will not encourage a discussion. Answer (C) is incorrect. A question beginning with "when" usually requires a short answer and will not encourage a discussion.

18. To begin a guided discussion, instructors should ask a leadoff question that begins with

A. who or when.

B. what.

C. why or how.

Answer (C) is correct. *(FAA-H-8083-9A Chap 4)*

DISCUSSION: Leadoff questions should usually begin with "how" or "why." For example, it is better to ask "Why does an aircraft normally require a longer takeoff run at Denver than at New Orleans?" than "Would you expect an aircraft to require a longer takeoff run at Denver or at New Orleans?" Students can answer the second question by merely saying "Denver," but the first question is likely to start a discussion of air density, engine efficiency, and the effect of temperature on performance.

Answer (A) is incorrect. Leadoff questions should contain "why" or "how," not "who" or "when." The former type of question creates a chance for deeper thought on the part of the student, which can stimulate a more productive discussion. Answer (B) is incorrect. Leadoff questions should contain "why" or "how," not "what." The former type of question creates a chance for deeper thought on the part of the student, which can stimulate a more productive discussion.

19. Which question would be best as a leadoff question for a guided discussion on the subject of torque?

A. Does torque affect an airplane?

B. How does torque affect an airplane?

C. What effect does torque have on an airplane in a turn?

Answer (B) is correct. *(FAA-H-8083-9A Chap 4)*

DISCUSSION: In preparing questions to lead off a guided discussion, the instructor should remember that the purpose is to bring about discussion, not merely answers. Avoid questions that require only short, categorical (i.e., yes or no) answers. Leadoff questions should usually begin with "how" or "why."

Answer (A) is incorrect. A question beginning with "does" only requires a yes or no answer and will not encourage a discussion. Answer (C) is incorrect. A question beginning with "what" only requires a short, categorical answer and will not encourage a discussion.

20. When it appears students have adequately discussed the ideas presented during a guided discussion, one of the most valuable tools an instructor can use is

A. a session of verbal testing.

B. a written test on the subject discussed.

C. an interim summary of what the students accomplished.

Answer (C) is correct. *(FAA-H-8083-9A Chap 4)*

DISCUSSION: When it appears the students have discussed the ideas that support a particular part of the lesson, the instructor should summarize what the students have accomplished. This interim summary is one of the most effective tools available to the instructor in a guided discussion. To bring ideas together and help in transition, an interim summary should be made after the discussion of each desired learning outcome.

Answer (A) is incorrect. A session of verbal testing goes against the intention of the guided discussion, where the instructor aims to "draw out" what the students know in a structured but personable manner. Answer (B) is incorrect. A written test on the subject without an instructor summary would be testing student opinions and experiences rather than facts.

21. Which statement about the guided discussion method of teaching is true?

A. The lesson objective becomes apparent at the application level of learning.

B. Students without a background in the subject can also be included in the discussion.

C. Unless the students have some knowledge to exchange with each other, they cannot reach the desired learning outcomes.

Answer (C) is correct. *(FAA-H-8083-9A Chap 4)*

DISCUSSION: Throughout the time the instructor prepares the students for their discussion (e.g., early lectures, homework assignments), the students should be made aware of the lesson objectives. This gives them the background for a fruitful guided discussion. Students without some background in a subject should not be asked to discuss that subject.

Answer (A) is incorrect. The lesson objective should be known while the students are preparing for the guided discussion, or at least during the introduction, not afterward at the application level of learning. Answer (B) is incorrect. Students with no background in the subject will not be able to contribute to an effective discussion.

4.4 Demonstration/Performance Method

22. The drill and practice method of instruction is based on which of the following learning principles?

A. Primary.

B. Effect.

C. Exercise.

Answer (C) is correct. *(FAA-H-8083-9A Chap 5)*

DISCUSSION: The drill and practice method is based on the learning principle of exercise, which holds that connections are strengthened with continued practice. It promotes learning through repetition because those things most often repeated are best remembered.

Answer (A) is incorrect. Primacy, the state of being first, is an important learning principle, but it is not the basis of the drill and practice method. Primacy often creates a strong, almost unshakable impression and underlies the reason an instructor must teach correctly the first time and the student must learn correctly the first time. For example, a student learns a faulty technique. Now the instructor must correct the bad habit and reteach the correct technique. Relearning is more difficult than initial learning. Answer (B) is incorrect. Effect is an important learning principle, but it is not the basis of the drill and practice method. All learning involves the formation of connections, and connections are strengthened or weakened according to the law of effect. Responses to a situation that are followed by satisfaction are strengthened, while responses followed by discomfort are weakened, either strengthening or weakening the connection of learning, respectively. Thus, learning is strengthened when accompanied by a pleasant or satisfying feeling and weakened when associated with an unpleasant feeling.

23. Which method of presentation is desirable for teaching a skill such as ground school lesson on the flight computer?

A. Lecture/application.

B. Presentation/practice.

C. Demonstration/performance.

Answer (C) is correct. *(FAA-H-8083-9A Chap 4)*

DISCUSSION: The demonstration/performance method of teaching is based on the principle that you learn by doing. Students learn physical or mental skills best by actually performing them under supervision. Learning to use a flight computer is an ideal application of this teaching method.

Answer (A) is incorrect. The lecture method is not suitable to teach flight computer use because the lecture does not provide for student participation and, as a consequence, lets the instructor do all the work. Answer (B) is incorrect. Presentation/practice is not a method of presentation.

24. What are the essential steps in the demonstration/ performance method of teaching?

A. Demonstration, practice, and evaluation.

B. Demonstration, student performance, and evaluation.

C. Explanation, demonstration, student performance, instructor supervision, and evaluation.

Answer (C) is correct. *(FAA-H-8083-9A Chap 4)*

DISCUSSION: The demonstration/performance method of teaching is based on the principle that we learn by doing. Thus, it is used by flight instructors in teaching procedures and maneuvers. The five essential steps are

1. Explanation
2. Demonstration
3. Student performance
4. Instructor supervision
5. Evaluation

Answer (A) is incorrect. The five, not three, essential steps in the demonstration/performance method of teaching are explanation, demonstration, student performance (not practice), instructor supervision, and evaluation. Answer (B) is incorrect. The five, not three, essential steps in the demonstration/ performance method of teaching are explanation, demonstration, student performance, instructor supervision, and evaluation.

25. What is the last step in the demonstration/ performance method?

A. Summary.

B. Evaluation.

C. Student performance.

Answer (B) is correct. *(FAA-H-8083-9A Chap 4)*

DISCUSSION: The demonstration/performance method of teaching is based on the principle that we learn by doing. Thus, it is used by flight instructors in teaching procedures and maneuvers. The five essential steps are

1. Explanation
2. Demonstration
3. Student performance
4. Instructor supervision
5. Evaluation

Answer (A) is incorrect. Summary is not a step in the demonstration/performance method. Answer (C) is incorrect. Student performance is the third, not last, step in the demonstration/performance method.

26. The basic demonstration/performance method of instruction consists of several steps in proper order. They are

A. instructor tells--student does; student tells-- student does; student does--instructor evaluates.

B. instructor tells--instructor does; student tells-- instructor does; student does--instructor evaluates.

C. instructor tells--instructor does; student tells-- instructor does; student tells--student does; student does--instructor evaluates.

Answer (C) is correct. *(FAA-H-8083-9A Chap 8)*

DISCUSSION: The telling and doing technique of flight instruction (basically the demonstration/performance method) is very effective and valuable in teaching procedures and maneuvers. First, the instructor explains, then demonstrates. Then the student performs, first by explaining as the instructor does, then by explaining and doing it him/herself while the instructor supervises. Finally, the instructor evaluates how the student performs.

Answer (A) is incorrect. It omits the first step, which is instructor tells--instructor does. The second step is student tells-- instructor does, not vice versa. Answer (B) is incorrect. It omits the third step of student tells--student does.

27. Students should be given the opportunity to ask questions during which step of the demonstration/ performance method?

A. Instructor supervision.

B. Evaluation.

C. Explanation.

Answer (C) is correct. *(FAA-H-8083-9A Chap 4)*

DISCUSSION: Students should be given the opportunity to ask questions so as to understand the requirements fully during the explanation stage.

Answer (A) is incorrect. Instructor supervision occurs when the instructor watches student performance and coaches as necessary. Answer (B) is incorrect. Evaluation occurs at the end of a task, and any questions relating to the desired outcome of the task should have already been asked.

28. A post-flight debriefing is an example of which step in the demonstration/performance method?

A. Instructor supervision.

B. Evaluation.

C. Explanation.

Answer (B) is correct. *(FAA-H-8083-9A Chap 4)*

DISCUSSION: During a post-flight debriefing, the instructor explains the student's performance. This is known as evaluation.

Answer (A) is incorrect. Instructor supervision occurs when the instructor watches student performance and coaches as necessary. Answer (C) is incorrect. Explanation is the first step in the demonstration/performance method and occurs before a task is performed. A post-flight debriefing would not occur during this step.

29. The telling and doing technique promotes learning because

A. students learn more by passively watching a task rather than engaging in it themselves.

B. things that are most often repeated are best remembered.

C. it consists of one simple step to remember; that of the instructor telling and doing.

Answer (B) is correct. *(FAA-H-8083-9A Chap 4)*

DISCUSSION: The telling and doing technique promotes learning through repetition because those things most often repeated are best remembered.

Answer (A) is incorrect. Students do not learn better by passively watching. An engaged student with proper supervision and who gets evaluated learns better; this happens in the telling and doing technique. Answer (C) is incorrect. The telling and doing technique consists of four steps, not one. They are as follows: instructor tells--instructor does/shows, student tells--instructor does/shows, student tells--student does/shows, and student does/shows--instructor evaluates. The telling and doing technique promotes learning through repetition because those things most often repeated are best remembered.

30. In the demonstration/performance method of instruction, which two separate actions are performed concurrently?

A. Instructor explanation and demonstration.

B. Student performance and instructor supervision.

C. Instructor explanation and student demonstration.

Answer (B) is correct. *(FAA-H-8083-9A Chap 4)*

DISCUSSION: In the demonstration/performance method of instruction, student performance and instructor supervision are performed concurrently. As the student practices to learn, the instructor supervises and coaches as necessary.

Answer (A) is incorrect. During the explanation phase, the instructor explains to the student the actions they are to perform. This is accomplished during the preflight discussion. The demonstration is done in the airplane as the instructor shows the student how to perform a maneuver. Answer (C) is incorrect. Instructor supervision, not explanation, and student performance, not demonstration, are performed concurrently.

4.5 Problem-Based Learning

31. The overall learning objective of scenario-based training (SBT) is

A. that students will improve their ability to recall previously learned information.

B. for the student to be more prepared to make good decisions based on a variety of real world situations.

C. to promote situational awareness and opportunities for decision making.

Answer (B) is correct. *(FAA-H-8083-9A Chap 4)*

DISCUSSION: The overall learning objective of scenario-based training is for the student to be more prepared to make good decisions based on a variety of real-world situations.

Answer (A) is incorrect. A benefit of problem-based learning is that students will improve their ability to recall information. Answer (C) is incorrect. A good scenario should promote situational awareness and opportunities for decision making.

32. The three types of problem-based learning instruction are:

A. Scenario-based training, the collaborative problem-solving method, and the case study method.

B. Scenario-based training, the critical thinking method, and the case study method.

C. Scenario-based training, the cooperative problem-solving method, and the case study method.

Answer (A) is correct. *(FAA-H-8083-9A Chap 4)*

DISCUSSION: The three types of PBL instruction are scenario-based training, the collaborative problem-solving method, and the case study method.

Answer (B) is incorrect. The critical thinking method is not a type of problem-based learning. Answer (C) is incorrect. The collaborative problem-solving method, not the cooperative problem-solving method, is one of the three types of problem-based learning.

33. What is a characteristic of an effective scenario?

A. It should not promote errors.

B. It should be in the form of a test.

C. It should include an account of a real world situation that contains an educational message.

Answer (A) is correct. *(FAA-H-8083-9A Chap 4)*

DISCUSSION: A effective scenario should not promote errors.

Answer (B) is incorrect. A good scenario should not be in the form of a test. Answer (C) is incorrect. An account of a real-world situation that contains an educational message is a case study method.

34. "A type of learning environment in which lessons are structured to confront students with problems encountered in real life that force them to reach real world solutions" is the definition of what?

A. Problem-Based Learning.

B. Case Study Method.

C. Collaborative Problem-Solving Method.

Answer (A) is correct. *(FAA-H-8083-9A Chap 4)*

DISCUSSION: Problem-Based Learning (PBL) describes a type of learning environment in which lessons are structured to confront students with problems encountered in real life that force them to reach real-world solutions.

Answer (B) is incorrect. A written or oral account of a real-world situation that contains an educational message is the definition of the case study method. Answer (C) is incorrect. The collaborative problem-solving method combines collaboration with problem solving when the instructor provides a problem to a group of two or more people working together who then solve the problem.

35. Which of the following is true concerning effective problem-based learning?

A. Effective PBL problems are open ended and not limited to one correct answer.

B. Effective PBL problems are only connected to previously learned information.

C. Effective PBL problems begin with a reason to fly because a pilot's decisions will differ depending on the motivation.

Answer (A) is correct. *(FAA-H-8083-9A Chap 4)*

DISCUSSION: Effective PBL problems are open ended and not limited to one correct answer.

Answer (B) is incorrect. Effective PBL problems are connected both to previously learned and new knowledge. Answer (C) is incorrect. A good scenario usually tells a story that begins with a reason to fly because a pilot's decisions will differ depending on the motivation to fly.

36. A written or oral account of a real world situation that contains an educational message for the student describes what?

A. The Collaborative Problem-Solving Method.

B. The Scenario-Based Training Method.

C. The Case Study Method.

Answer (C) is correct. *(FAA-H-8083-9A Chap 4)*

DISCUSSION: The case study method is a written or oral account of a real-world situation that contains an educational message for the student.

Answer (A) is incorrect. The collaborative problem-solving method combines collaboration with problem solving when the instructor provides a problem to a group of two or more people working together who then solve the problem. Answer (B) is incorrect. The scenario-based training method is a realistic situation that allows the student to rehearse mentally for a situation and requires practical application of various pieces of knowledge.

37. The likely cause of a pilot ignoring the requirements for minimum fuel reserve is most likely overconfidence, disregard for applicable regulations, or

A. lack of flight planning.

B. acute fatigue.

C. learning plateau.

Answer (A) is correct. *(FAA-H-8083-9A Chap 9)*

DISCUSSION: Operating without adequate fuel reserves or ignoring minimum fuel reserve requirements is generally the result of overconfidence, lack of flight planning, or disregarding applicable regulations.

Answer (B) is incorrect. Acute fatigue, a normal occurrence of everyday living, is the tiredness felt after long periods of physical and mental strain, including strenuous muscular effort, immobility, heavy mental workload, strong emotional pressure, monotony, and lack of sleep. Answer (C) is incorrect. A learning plateau is a phenomenon where progress appears to cease or slow down for a significant period of time before once again increasing.

4.6 Electronic Learning (E-Learning)

38. Which statement is true regarding e-learning?

A. The instructor need not be actively involved with the student when using a form of e-learning.

B. E-learning can be used as the sole means of instruction for a student.

C. An advantage of e-learning includes higher levels of mastery and retention.

Answer (C) is correct. *(FAA-H-8083-9A Chap 4)*

DISCUSSION: Advantages of e-learning include less time spent on instruction and higher levels of mastery and retention.

Answer (A) is incorrect. Instructors should still be actively involved with students using e-learning so as to monitor and oversee student progress. Answer (B) is incorrect. E-learning, while having many advantages, should not be solely relied upon to ensure proper knowledge transfer has taken place.

39. What is one reason why flight schools use flight simulation in training students?

A. All flight simulation time can be credited for actual flight time.

B. Students can practice scenarios that would be unwise or unsafe to perform in real-life.

C. Instructor oversight is not required when students perform maneuvers on a flight simulator.

Answer (B) is correct. *(FAA-H-8083-9A Chap 4)*

DISCUSSION: Many flight schools incorporate flight simulation into a student's training regimen to have them practice scenarios that would otherwise be unwise or unsafe to perform in an actual aircraft.

Answer (A) is incorrect. Not all time spent on a simulator may be credited toward actual flight time. Credit toward logging actual flight time also depends on the type of device being used for simulation. Answer (C) is incorrect. Instructors should still be on hand to oversee all types of e-learning, including that of flight simulation.

40. The capabilities of the most recently developed computer-based training (CBT) systems allow the presentation to be customized based on the user's

A. responses.

B. previous experience.

C. wants and desires.

Answer (A) is correct. *(FAA-H-8083-9A Chap 4)*

DISCUSSION: Some of the more recent CBT applications allow students to progress through a series of interactive segments where the presentation varies as a result of their responses.

Answer (B) is incorrect. The presentation can be varied based on the user's responses, not his or her previous experience. Answer (C) is incorrect. The presentation can be varied by the user's responses, not his or her wants and desires.

41. Which method allows a student to control the pace of instruction?

A. Simulation.

B. Role playing games.

C. Computer-assisted learning (CAL).

Answer (C) is correct. *(FAA-H-8083-9A Chap 4)*

DISCUSSION: Real interactivity with CAL means the student is fully engaged with the instruction by doing something meaningful, which makes the subject of study come alive. For example, the student controls the pace of instruction, reviews previous material, jumps forward, and receives instant feedback.

Answer (A) is incorrect. Simulation gives the learner a stake in the outcome, placing him or her in the shoes of a character in a real-world scenario. This valuable teaching method does not offer a student direct control over the pace of instruction. Answer (B) is incorrect. Role playing games give the learner a stake in the outcome, placing him or her in the shoes of a character in a real-world scenario. This valuable teaching method does not offer a student direct control over the pace of instruction.

42. Among the many advantages of computer-based training (CBT) over other forms of instruction is that the computer can respond in different ways depending on the student's

A. age.

B. mathematical ability.

C. input.

Answer (C) is correct. *(FAA-H-8083-9A Chap 4)*

DISCUSSION: The major advantage of CBT is that it is interactive–the computer responds in different ways, depending on student input. When using CBT, the instructor should remain actively involved with the students by using close supervision, questions, examinations, quizzes, or guided discussions on the subject matter to constantly assess student progress.

Answer (A) is incorrect. The student's age is not a factor used by the computer to determine a response. Answer (B) is incorrect. The student's mathematical ability is not a factor used by the computer to determine a response.

43. Which statement is true regarding e-learning?

A. A major limitation of e-learning is that it can be conducted from alternate locations.

B. Improper or excessive use of e-learning should be avoided.

C. E-learning requires a student to learn at the pace provided by the monitoring instructor.

Answer (B) is correct. *(FAA-H-8083-9A Chap 4)*

DISCUSSION: Improper or excessive use of e-learning should be avoided. It will always be the responsibility of the instructor to monitor and oversee student progress and to intervene when necessary.

Answer (A) is incorrect. A major advantage, not limitation, of e-learning is that users can be in alternate locations from an instructor. This is termed distance learning. Answer (C) is incorrect. E-learning allows students to feel as if they are in control of what they are learning and at a rate that is comfortable for them, not at a pace required by an instructor.

44. Which statement is true regarding Computer-Assisted Learning, or CAL?

A. CAL will not be able to indicate a student's weak or strong areas.

B. CAL is used by flight schools so students can practice scenarios that are unwise to perform in an actual aircraft.

C. The student controls the pace and content of instruction.

Answer (C) is correct. *(FAA-H-8083-9A Chap 4)*

DISCUSSION: With CAL, the student controls the pace and content of the instruction.

Answer (A) is incorrect. Many CAL programs can and will indicate a student's weak or strong areas. An example of this is software used in preparing for an FAA knowledge test. Answer (B) is incorrect. Flight simulation, not CAL, is used to practice scenarios that are unwise or unsafe to perform in an actual aircraft.

45. The major advantage of Computer-Assisted Learning (CAL) is that it is interactive; the computer will respond in different ways depending on student

A. background.

B. input.

C. training.

Answer (B) is correct. *(FAA-H-8083-9A Chap 4)*

DISCUSSION: The major advantage of CAL is that it is interactive in that the computer will respond in different ways depending on student input.

Answer (A) is incorrect. The computer responds based on the student's input, not background. The choice of CAL training may depend on the student's academic or experimental background. Answer (C) is incorrect. The computer responds based on the student's input, not training.

4.7 Integrated Method of Flight Instruction

46. Which of the following is the primary objective of integrated flight instruction?

A. To develop the student's habit of constantly monitoring both his or her performance and the aircraft's performance.

B. To develop a proper scan while relating the instrument indications to the horizon.

C. To develop multitasking skills.

Answer (A) is correct. *(FAA-H-8083-9A Chap 8)*

DISCUSSION: It is important for the student to establish the habit of observing and relying on flight instruments from the beginning of flight training. It is equally important for the student to learn the feel of the airplane while conducting maneuvers, such as being able to feel when the airplane is out of trim or in a nose-high or nose-low attitude. Students who have been required to perform all normal flight maneuvers by reference to instruments, as well as by outside references, develop from the start the habit of continuously monitoring their own and the aircraft's performance.

Answer (B) is incorrect. The primary objective of integrated flight instruction is to develop the habit of constantly monitoring the pilot's own performance and the aircraft's performance. Answer (C) is incorrect. The primary objective of integrated flight instruction is to develop the habit of constantly monitoring the pilot's own performance and the aircraft's performance.

47. During integrated flight instruction, the instructor must be sure the student

A. develops the habit of looking for other traffic.

B. is able to control the aircraft for extended periods under IMC.

C. can depend on the flight instruments when maneuvering by outside references.

Answer (A) is correct. *(FAA-H-8083-9A Chap 8)*

DISCUSSION: If students are allowed to believe that the instructor assumes all responsibility for avoiding other traffic, they cannot develop the habit of keeping a constant watch, which is essential to safety. Any observed tendency of a student to enter flight maneuvers without first making a careful check for other possible air traffic must be corrected immediately.

Answer (B) is incorrect. The ability to control the aircraft for extended periods under IMC is not the objective of integrated flight instruction. Answer (C) is incorrect. The instructor must be sure not to let the student focus his attention on the instruments at the expense of looking for other traffic.

48. What is integrated flight instruction?

A. Flight instruction during which the student learns by sole reference to the flight instruments.

B. Flight instruction that combines the use of flight simulation with actual flight.

C. Flight instruction during which students are taught to perform flight maneuvers by outside visual references and reference to flight instruments.

Answer (C) is correct. *(FAA-H-8083-9A Chap 8)*

DISCUSSION: Integrated flight instruction is flight instruction during which students are taught to perform flight maneuvers, both by outside visual references and by inside reference to flight instruments for the same operations.

Answer (A) is incorrect. Integrated flight instruction is not accomplished by sole reference to the flight instruments. It also includes outside visual references for the same operations or maneuvers. Answer (B) is incorrect. Simulation, not integrated flight instruction, uses flight simulators in conjunction with actual flight to train students.

49. For integrated flight instruction to be fully effective, what must take place?

A. A student must rely on the instructor for collision avoidance.

B. The use of instrument references should begin the first time each new maneuver is introduced.

C. Students must already have learned the feel of the aircraft while conducting maneuvers.

Answer (B) is correct. *(FAA-H-8083-9A Chap 8)*
DISCUSSION: For integrated flight instruction to be fully effective, the use of instrument references should begin the first time each new maneuver is introduced.
Answer (A) is incorrect. A student should develop the habit of scanning for other traffic from the first flight lesson. The student will rely on the instructor to ensure adequate collision avoidance while flying by simulated instruments, but this is not a factor in effectively conducting integrated flight instruction. Answer (C) is incorrect. Student feel for the aircraft during a maneuver is learned during integrated flight training and is not necessary to effective integrated flight training.

50. Foremost among the objectives of integrated flight instruction is

A. encouraging habit patterns for observing and referencing the flight instruments.

B. developing the student's ability to operate in IMC.

C. ensuring the student is completely dependent on the instruments during VFR flight.

Answer (A) is correct. *(FAA-H-8083-9A Chap 8)*
DISCUSSION: The early establishment of proper habits of instrument cross-check, instrument interpretation, and aircraft control are highly useful to the student. The habitual attention to instrument indications leads to improved landings because of more precise airspeed control. Effective use of instruments also results in superior cross-country navigation, better coordination of the aircraft, and generally a better overall pilot competency level.
Answer (B) is incorrect. The habits formed during integrated flight instruction provide a firm foundation for later training for an instrument rating but are not intended to provide the skills required to operate in IMC. Answer (C) is incorrect. Integrated flight instruction ensures the student is able to operate the aircraft using visual references as well as the flight instruments.

51. Which of the following statements about integrated flight instruction is true?

A. Devote certain training lessons entirely to instrument or visual flight.

B. Instruction in the control of an aircraft by outside visual references is integrated with instruction in the use of flight instrument indications for the same operations.

C. Introduce maneuvers using visual references, then repeat the maneuvers using only the instruments.

Answer (B) is correct. *(FAA-H-8083-9A Chap 8)*
DISCUSSION: Integrated flight instruction is flight instruction during which students are taught to perform flight maneuvers both by outside visual references and by reference to flight instruments. For this type of instruction to be fully effective, the use of instrument references should begin the first time each new maneuver is introduced. No distinction in the pilot's operation of the flight controls is permitted, regardless of whether outside references or instrument indications are used for the performance of the maneuver. When this training technique is used, instruction in the control of an aircraft by outside visual references is integrated with instruction in the use of flight instrument indications for the same operations.
Answer (A) is incorrect. In integrated flight instruction, students must learn to use both the visual references and flight instruments simultaneously. Answer (C) is incorrect. In integrated flight instruction, students must learn to use both the visual references and flight instruments simultaneously.

52. What is a benefit of learning to habitually give attention to instrument indications during primary training?

A. Cruising performance will increase by holding precise headings and altitudes.

B. Students will be completely prepared for their instrument checkride.

C. Students will be more likely to watch for other traffic.

Answer (A) is correct. *(FAA-H-8083-9A Chap 8)*
DISCUSSION: A benefit of habitually giving attention to instrument indications is better cruising performance because a student will hold more precise headings and altitudes.
Answer (B) is incorrect. Additional training on the specifics of flying solely by reference to flight instruments will be needed. Giving habitual attention to instrument indications during primary flight training will, however, provide a basis for future training for an instrument rating. Answer (C) is incorrect. Instructors must be careful that students develop the habit of looking for other traffic when operating by reference to instruments, even during VFR conditions. It can actually be a disadvantage if a student focuses solely on an aircraft's instruments during primary flight training.

4.8 The Positive Approach in Flight Instruction

53. Which is an example of a positive approach in the first flight lesson of a student with no previous aviation experience?

A. Conducting a thorough preflight.

B. A normal flight to a nearby airport and return.

C. Instruction in the care which must be taken when taxiing an airplane.

Answer (B) is correct. *(FAA-H-8083-9A Chap 7)*

DISCUSSION: A normal flight to a nearby airport and back shows the student some of the pleasant aspects of aviation. Such an introductory lesson leaves a positive impression in the new student's mind. Positive teaching results in positive learning.

Answer (A) is incorrect. In the first flight lesson of a student with no aviation experience, conducting a thorough, exhaustive preflight is an example of a negative, not a positive, approach. The student may question whether learning to fly is a good idea or not. Answer (C) is incorrect. In the first flight lesson of a student with no aviation experience, instruction in the care that must be taken when taxiing an airplane is an example of a negative, not a positive, approach. The student may question whether learning to fly is a good idea or not.

54. Which statement is true regarding positive or negative approaches in aviation instructional techniques?

A. A student with normal abilities should not be affected by an instructor who emphasizes emergency procedures early in training.

B. A positive approach, to be effective, will point out the pleasurable features of aviation before the unpleasant possibilities are discussed.

C. The introduction of emergency procedures before the student is acquainted with normal operations is likely to be neither discouraging nor affect learning.

Answer (B) is correct. *(FAA-H-8083-9A Chap 7)*

DISCUSSION: Flight instructor success depends, in large measure, on the ability to frame instructions so that students develop a positive image of flying. A positive approach, to be effective, will point out the pleasurable features of aviation before the unpleasant possibilities are discussed. A negative approach generally results in negative learning because the student's perceptual process would be adversely affected by fear.

Answer (A) is incorrect. An instructor who emphasizes emergency procedures early in training will most likely have a negative effect on the learning process regardless of a student's abilities. The student new to aviation is still quite impressionable. Answer (C) is incorrect. The introduction of emergency procedures before the student is acquainted with normal operations most likely will be discouraging or threatening and will adversely affect learning.

4.9 Testing the Limits of Student Knowledge

55. Which of the following is the primary consideration when determining the length and frequency of flight instruction periods?

A. Inattention.

B. Fatigue.

C. Distractibility.

Answer (B) is correct. *(FAA-H-8083-9A Chap 8)*

DISCUSSION: Fatigue is the primary consideration in determining the length and frequency of flight instruction periods. Flight instruction should be continued only as long as the student is alert, receptive to instruction, and performing at a level consistent with experience.

Answer (A) is incorrect. Inattention is one of the symptoms of fatigue; it is not the same as fatigue. Answer (C) is incorrect. Distractibility is one of the symptoms of fatigue; it is not the same as fatigue.

56. Asking students about problems or decisions that test the limits of their knowledge is

A. ineffective, only promoting rote level learning.

B. beneficial to gauge understanding and determines that the student is able to apply the knowledge.

C. an effective method to help students acquire knowledge.

Answer (C) is correct. *(FAA-H-8083-9A Chap 2)*

DISCUSSION: To help students acquire knowledge, the instructor should ask students questions about problems or decisions that test the limits of their knowledge.

Answer (A) is incorrect. For students to fully understand a task or concept, instructors must push the limits of the students' knowledge. This technique encourages learning beyond merely the rote level of learning. Answer (B) is incorrect. Asking questions about problems or decisions to test the limits of a student's knowledge is beneficial to gauge understanding but is not a determination that the student has the ability to apply the knowledge.

STUDY UNIT FIVE
PLANNING INSTRUCTIONAL ACTIVITY

(7 pages of outline)

5.1 COURSE DEVELOPMENT

1. A course of training is a complete series of studies leading to attainment of a goal, such as a certificate of completion, graduation, etc.
2. A determination of objectives and standards is necessary before any important instruction can be presented. Any instructional activity must be competently planned and organized if it is to achieve the desired learning outcomes.
   a. The broad overall objective of any pilot training is to qualify the student to be a competent, efficient, safe pilot.
   b. There are two types of objectives in aviation: performance-based objectives and decision-based objectives.
3. **Performance-based objectives** are used to set measurable, reasonable standards that describe the required student performance.
   a. They provide a way of stating what performance level is desired of a student before progressing to the next stage of instruction.
   b. Written objectives are clear, measurable, and repeatable.
   c. These objectives consist of three elements: description of the skill or behavior, conditions, and criteria.
      1) **Description of the skill or behavior:** desired outcome of training stated in concrete terms that can be measured.
         a) EXAMPLE: "The student should be able to repeat the steps to a proper engine start."
      2) **Conditions:** used to explain the rules under which the skill or behavior is to be demonstrated.
         a) EXAMPLE: "Using an approved airplane checklist and referencing the Pilot's Operating Handbook, perform a normal engine start."
      3) **Criteria:** the standards used to measure the accomplishment of the objective. The performance-based objectives must fit the desired outcome for a particular lesson, and the criteria should be stated so that there is no question whether the objective has been met.
         a) EXAMPLE: "Using an approved airplane checklist and referencing the Pilot's Operating Handbook, perform a normal engine start. Engine power should be reduced to below 1000 RPM after the engine is engaged, and fuel pump adjustments should be made as required in the POH."
   d. Practical Test Standards (PTS)/Airman Certification Standards (ACS) provide specific performance-based objectives based on the standards that must be met for the issuance of a particular aviation certificate or rating.

4. **Decision-based objectives** allow for a more dynamic training environment and are designed to develop pilot judgment and ADM skills.
   a. Combined with traditional task and maneuver training, decision-based objectives facilitate a higher level of learning and application and thus reduce improper pilot decision making and increase overall flight safety.
5. Instructors must identify the blocks of learning that make up the necessary parts of the total objective.
   a. You must ensure that each block of learning identified is truly an integral part of the overall objective.
      1) Extraneous blocks of instruction are expensive frills, especially in flight instruction, and detract from the completion of the final objective.
   b. The blocks of learning must be developed and arranged in their proper sequence.
      1) In this way, a student can master the segments of the overall pilot performance requirements individually and can progressively combine these with other related segments until their sum meets the final objective.
   c. Students will master segments of blocks individually and can progressively combine these with other related segments until the overall training objectives are reached.
      1) EXAMPLE: Flight training may be divided into the following major blocks: achievement of the knowledge and skills necessary for solo flight, achievement of the knowledge and skills necessary for solo cross-country flight, and achievement of the knowledge and skills appropriate for achieving a private pilot certificate.
   d. Using this approach provides the student with a boost of self-confidence as each block is successfully completed.
6. A training syllabus is an abstract or digest of the course of training. It consists of the blocks of learning to be completed in the most efficient order.
   a. All syllabi should stress well-defined objectives and standards for each lesson.
   b. The order of training can and should be altered when necessary to suit the progress of the student and the demands of special circumstances, such as weather conditions.
      1) However, it is often preferable to skip to a completely different part of the syllabus when the conduct of a scheduled lesson is impossible, rather than proceeding to the next lesson, which may be predicated completely on skills to be developed during the lesson being postponed.
      2) EXAMPLE: If a student is having a difficult time with normal approach and landings, it might be wise for the instructor to skip the next proposed lesson on short field landings and instead review another area of training. This would enable the student to gain confidence and reinforce skills needed to perform normal landings.

5.2 ORGANIZATION OF TRAINING MATERIAL

1. Once a determination of objectives and standards has been made, an instructor must formulate a plan of action to lead students through the course in a logical manner toward the desired goal. One effective way to organize a lesson is by introduction, development, and conclusion.
   a. The **introduction** sets the stage for everything to come. The introduction can be divided into three subparts:
      1) **Attention** -- The instructor must gain the students' attention and focus it on the subject.
         a) EXAMPLE: Stories, video clips, questions, or jokes can be used to gain student attention.
      2) **Motivation** -- The instructor should offer specific reasons why they need to learn the material. This motivation should appeal to each student personally and accentuate the desire to learn.
         a) EXAMPLE: The instructor may talk about where the knowledge in the lesson was or will be applied in real life or remind students of an upcoming test on the material.
      3) **Overview** -- Each lesson introduction should contain an overview that tells the student(s) what is to be covered during the period.
         a) The overview is presented as a clear, concise presentation of the objective.
   b. The **development** is the main part of the lesson during which the instructor organizes the explanations and demonstrations in a manner that helps the students achieve the desired learning outcomes.
      1) The instructor must logically organize the material to show the relationships of the main points to each other. This is done by developing the main points in one of the following ways:
         a) Chronologically; from past to present or present to past
         b) From simple to complex
         c) From known to unknown (i.e., using a student's previous experiences and knowledge to acquire new concepts)
         d) From most frequently used (most familiar) to least frequently used
   c. The **conclusion** retraces the important elements of the lesson and relates them to the objective.
      1) This reinforces the students' learning and improves retention of what has been learned.
      2) New ideas should not be introduced in the conclusion because doing so at this point in the lesson will only confuse students.

5.3 LESSON PLAN

1. Each lesson of the training syllabus includes an objective, content, and completion standards.
2. A lesson plan is an organized outline that is developed for a single instructional period.
   a. A properly constructed lesson plan will provide an outline that tells the instructor what to do, in what order to do it, and what teaching procedure to use.
   b. The lesson plan must be appropriate for the particular student.
      1) Standard lesson plans may not be effective for students requiring a different approach.
      2) Therefore, the main concern in developing a lesson plan is the student.
3. A lesson plan should be prepared in writing for each instructional period to show what specific knowledge and/or skills will be taught during a lesson.
   a. A so-called mental outline is not a lesson plan.
   b. Another instructor should be able to take the lesson plan and know what to do in conducting the same period of instruction.
4. Lesson plans are designed to ensure that each student receives the best possible instruction under existing circumstances. Lesson plans help instructors keep a constant check on their own activity, as well as that of their students.
5. Steps to ensuring a quality lesson:
   a. Determine the objective of the lesson,
   b. Instructor research,
   c. Determine the method of instruction,
   d. Identify the lesson planning format,
   e. Decide how to organize the lesson and supporting material,
   f. Assemble training aids, and
   g. Write the lesson plan outline.
6. A characteristic of a well-planned lesson is that it should contain new material that is related to the lesson previously presented.
   a. In flight training, a short review of earlier lessons is usually necessary.
   b. Each lesson should also fall logically into the four steps of the teaching process: preparation, presentation, application, and review/evaluation.
   c. An adequate lesson plan, when properly developed, should
      1) Assure a wise selection of material and the elimination of unimportant details.
      2) Make certain that due consideration is given to each part of the lesson.
      3) Aid the instructor in presenting the material in a suitable sequence for efficient learning.
      4) Provide an outline of the teaching procedure to be used.
      5) Serve as a means of relating the lesson to the objectives of the course of training.
      6) Give the inexperienced instructor confidence.
      7) Promote uniformity of instruction regardless of the instructor or the date on which the lesson is given.

7. Each lesson plan should contain the following items: lesson objective, content, schedule, equipment, instructor's actions, student's actions, and completion standards. See the illustration below.

LESSON Ground reference maneuvers	**STUDENT** **DATE** / /
OBJECTIVE	To develop the student's skill in planning and following a pattern over the ground compensating for wind drift at varying angles.
CONTENT	Use of ground references to control path Observation and control of wind effect Control of airplane attitude, altitude, and heading
SCHEDULE	Preflight discussion :10 Instructor demonstrations :25 Student practice :45 Postflight critique :10
EQUIPMENT	Chalkboard for preflight discussion IFR visor for maneuvers reviewed
INSTRUCTOR'S ACTIONS	Preflight—discuss lesson objective. Diagram "S" turns, eight along a road, and rectangular course on a chalkboard. Inflight—demonstrate elements. Demonstrate following a road, "S" turns, eights along a road, and rectangular course, coach student practice. Postflight—critique student performance and make study assignment.
STUDENT'S ACTIONS	Preflight—discuss lesson objective and resolve questions. Inflight—review previous maneuvers including power-off stalls and flight at minimum controllable airspeed. Perform each new maneuver as directed. Postflight—ask pertinent questions.
COMPLETION STANDARDS	Student should demonstrate competency in maintaining orientation, airspeed within 10 knots, altitude within 100 feet, and headings within 10 degrees, and in making proper correction for wind drift.

8. Also see Figure 1A on the next page for an example of a ground lesson plan.

LESSON PLAN

Introduction (3 minutes)

A ______ Relates aircraft accident in which a multi-engine ran off the end of the runway. This could have been avoided by correctly computing the landing distance. Relate similar personal experience of the same type of mishap.

B ______ Tell students how landing distance can affect then (any aircraft, plus future application).

C ______ Explain what will be learned. Explain how the lesson will proceed. Define landing distance and explain the normal landing distance chart. Then, demonstrate how to solve for landing distance. The students will practice the procedure: at least once with supervision and at least once with as little help as possible. Next, the students will be evaluated according to the standards. Finally, the lesson will conclude with questions and answers, followed by a brief summary.

Body (29 minutes)

D ______ Define landing distance. Explain the normal landing distance chart to include the scale and interpolation. Ensure students can see demonstrations and encourage questions. Demonstrate the procedure using °C with a headwind and °F with a tailwind. Show the normal landing distance chart with given data in the following order:

1. temperature
2. pressure altitude
3. gross weight
4. headwind-tailwind component
5. read ground roll distance from graph

E ______ Review standards. Hand out chart and practice problems. Remind students to use a pencil, to make small tick marks, and to work as accurately as possible. Explain that they should follow the procedure on the chart to work the practice problems. Encourage students to ask questions. Check progress of each student continually so they develop skill proficiency within acceptable standards. Reteach any area(s) of difficulty to the class as they go along.

F ______ Review procedure again from the chart. Reemphasize standards of acceptable performance including time available. Prepare area for evaluation by removing the task step chart and practice problem sheets, and by handing out the evaluation problems. Ask students to work the three problems according to conditions and standards specified. Terminate evaluation after 6 minutes. Evaluate each student's performance and tactfully reveal results. Record results for use in reteaching any area(s) of difficulty in the summary.

Conclusion (3 minutes)

G ______ Review lessons with emphasis on any weak area(s).

H ______ Remind students that landing distance will be an important consideration in any aircraft they fly.

I ______ Advise students that this lesson will be used as a starting point for the next lesson. Assign study materials for the next lesson.

Figure 1A. Lesson Plan (not in supplement).

Figure 1A above is a sample ground lesson plan in contrast to the sample flight lesson plan illustrated in the previous figure. You can also view the FAA's various sample lesson plans in PDF format at www.faa.gov/regulations_policies/handbooks_manuals/aviation/aviation_instructors_handbook/. Use the lesson plan on the first page of that PDF to write in the section titles in Figure 1A above, so you will be more familiar with lesson plans for ground training.

NOTE: Figure 1A has been omitted from the testing supplement since the one released by the FAA in June 2016. We left it in our materials because we believe it will help you to better understand ground lesson plans.

9. The objectives of each lesson, content to support these objectives, and completion standards should be clearly stated.
   a. The objective is the reason for the lesson -- what the student is expected to know or be able to do at the end of the lesson.
   b. Keeping the student informed of lesson objectives and completion standards minimizes the student's insecurity.
10. When planning time for student performance, a primary consideration is the length of the practice session.
    a. A beginning student reaches a point where additional practice is not only unproductive but may be harmful. As a student gains experience, longer periods of practice become profitable.
       1) **Overlearning** is the continued study of a skill after initial proficiency has been achieved. Practice proceeds beyond the point at which the act can be performed with the required degree of excellence.
       2) One common effect of overlearning is the development of automated routines rather than development of concept application skills.
    b. As a student gains experience, longer periods of practice are profitable.
11. A blank lesson plan is provided on page 323 so you may make copies for your use.

5.4 INSTRUCTIONAL AIDS AND TRAINING TECHNOLOGY

1. Instructional aids are useful tools that emphasize, support, supplement, or reinforce the key points or concepts in a lesson and assist an instructor in the teaching-learning process.
   a. Instructional aids include models, chalkboards, charts, and projected material (e.g., videotapes, movies, slides, etc.).
2. Reasons for using instructional aids include the following:
   a. Helping students remember important information,
   b. Gaining and holding student attention,
   c. Clarifying the relationship between material objects and concepts, and
   d. Giving support when topics involve the use of more senses (i.e., sight, hearing, or a combination of others).
3. The following four-step procedure should be used to determine if and when instructional aids are necessary:
   a. Clearly establish the lesson objective, being certain what must be communicated.
   b. Gather the necessary data by researching for support material.
   c. Organize the material into an outline or lesson plan. The outline should include all key points to be presented.
   d. Finally, determine what ideas should be supported with instructional aids.
      1) They should be compatible with the learning outcomes to be achieved.
      2) They should be designed to cover the key points in a lesson.
4. Instructional aids used in the teaching/learning process should not be used as a crutch by the instructor.

QUESTIONS AND ANSWER EXPLANATIONS: All of the Fundamentals of Instructing knowledge test questions chosen by the FAA for release as well as additional questions selected by Gleim relating to the material in the previous outlines are provided on the following pages. These questions have been organized into the same subunits as the outlines. To the immediate right of each question are the correct answer and answer explanations. You should cover these answers and answer explanations while responding to the questions. Refer to the general discussion in the Introduction on how to take the FAA knowledge test.

Remember that the questions from the FAA knowledge test bank have been reordered by topic and organized into a meaningful sequence. Also, the first line of the answer explanation gives the citation of the authoritative source for the answer.

QUESTIONS

5.1 Course Development

1. In planning any instructional activity, the first consideration should be to

A. determine the overall objectives and standards.

B. establish common ground between the instructor and student.

C. identify the blocks of learning which make up the overall objective.

Answer (A) is correct. *(FAA-H-8083-9A Chap 6)*
DISCUSSION: The first step in planning any instructional activity is to determine the overall objectives and standards. If the instructor does not have a logical view of what is to be achieved, then the students will not.
Answer (B) is incorrect. Establishing a common ground between the instructor and student is the purpose of a lesson introduction, not the first step in planning instructional activity. Answer (C) is incorrect. The second, not the first, consideration in planning for any instructional activity is to identify the blocks of learning that make up the overall objective.

2. Which statement is true concerning extraneous blocks of instruction during a course of training?

A. They are usually necessary parts of the total objective.

B. They detract from the completion of the final objective.

C. They assist in the attainment of the lesson's objective.

Answer (B) is correct. *(FAA-H-8083-9A Chap 6)*
DISCUSSION: While identifying the blocks of learning to be used in the course, the instructor must examine each carefully to see that it is truly an integral part of the structure. Extraneous blocks of instruction can detract from, rather than assist, in the completion of the final objective.
Answer (A) is incorrect. Extraneous blocks of instruction are unnecessary parts of the total objective. Answer (C) is incorrect. Extraneous blocks of instruction detract, not assist, in the attainment of the lesson's objective.

3. When it is impossible to conduct a scheduled lesson, it is preferable for the instructor to

A. review and possibly revise the training syllabus.

B. proceed to the next scheduled lesson, or if this is not practical, cancel the lesson.

C. conduct a lesson that is not predicated completely on skills to be developed during the lesson which was postponed.

Answer (C) is correct. *(FAA-H-8083-9A Chap 6)*
DISCUSSION: It is preferable for the instructor to skip to a completely different part of the syllabus when it is impossible to conduct a scheduled lesson, rather than proceeding to the next lesson, which may be predicated completely on skills to be developed during the lesson that was postponed.
Answer (A) is incorrect. An instructor should review and possibly revise the training syllabus when there is an applicable change to the Federal Aviation Regulations or PTSs/ACSs, not because a lesson had to be postponed. Answer (B) is incorrect. The next lesson may need skills that were to be learned in the postponed lesson.

4. Performance-based objectives consist of which three elements?

A. Flight training scenarios, judgment assessment, and maneuver assessment.

B. Cognitive skills, affective skills, and psychomotor skills.

C. Description of the skill or behavior, conditions, and criteria.

Answer (C) is correct. *(FAA-H-8083-9A Chap 4)*
DISCUSSION: Performance-based objectives are used to set measurable, reasonable standards that describe the desired performance of the student. Performance-based objectives consist of three elements: description of the skill or behavior, conditions, and criteria.
Answer (A) is incorrect. This answer choice describes elements of decision-based, not performance-based, objectives. Answer (B) is incorrect. This answer choice describes the three domains of learning, not the elements of performance-based objectives.

5. Development and assembly of blocks of learning in their proper relationship will provide a means for

A. both the instructor and student to easily correct faulty habit patterns.

B. challenging the student by progressively increasing the units of learning.

C. allowing the student to master the segments of the overall pilot performance requirements individually and combining these with other related segments.

Answer (C) is correct. *(FAA-H-8083-9A Chap 6)*

DISCUSSION: Training for a skill as complicated and involved as piloting an aircraft requires the development and assembly, in their appropriate sequence, of many segments or blocks of learning. In this way, a student can master the segments of the overall pilot performance requirements individually and can progressively combine these with other related segments until (s)he learns to fly, which is the final objective.

Answer (A) is incorrect. Organizing the appropriate blocks of learning in their proper relationship should prevent the formation of bad habits. This is the basic reason for the building block technique of instruction. Answer (B) is incorrect. The challenge presented to the student is one way to test for a useful size of a minimum block of learning, but progressively increasing the blocks of learning may deter the student's progress.

6. As an instructor you should write performance-based objectives that

A. fit the desired outcome of a particular lesson.

B. do not require the consideration of conditions.

C. must be open to interpretation by knowledgeable readers.

Answer (A) is correct. *(FAA-H-8083-9A Chap 4)*

DISCUSSION: An instructor should write performance-based objectives to fit the desired outcome of the lesson.

Answer (B) is incorrect. Conditions are necessary to specifically explain the rules under which the skill or behavior is demonstrated. If a desired capability is to navigate from point A to point B, the objective as stated is not specific enough for all students to do it in the same way. Information such as equipment, tools, reference material, and limiting parameters should be included. Answer (C) is incorrect. Performance-based objectives must be clear, measurable, and repeatable. In other words, they must mean the same thing to any knowledgeable reader.

7. A series of studies leading to an attainment of a goal is

A. a determination of objective.

B. a course of training.

C. a decision based objective.

Answer (B) is correct. *(FAA-H-8083-9A Chap 4)*

DISCUSSION: A course of training is a complete series of studies leading to attainment of a goal, such as a certificate of completion, graduation, etc.

Answer (A) is incorrect. A determination of objectives and standards is necessary before any important instruction can be presented. Answer (C) is incorrect. Decision-based objectives are a type of objective designed to develop pilot judgment and ADM skills.

8. What is the overall objective of any pilot training?

A. To make sure all objectives are clear, measurable, and repeatable.

B. To facilitate a higher level of learning and application.

C. To qualify the student to be a competent, efficient, safe pilot.

Answer (C) is correct. *(FAA-H-8083-9A Chap 4)*

DISCUSSION: The broad overall objective of any pilot training is to qualify the student to be a competent, efficient, safe pilot.

Answer (A) is incorrect. Making sure written objectives are clear, measurable, and repeatable is an element of a performance-based objective. Answer (B) is incorrect. Decision-based objectives facilitate a higher level of learning and application and thus reduce improper pilot decision making and increase overall flight safety.

9. Which is not a type of objective used in aviation training?

A. Performance-based objectives.

B. Decision-based objectives.

C. Description-based objectives.

Answer (C) is correct. *(FAA-H-8083-9A Chap 4)*

DISCUSSION: A description-based objective is not a type of objective in aviation training.

Answer (A) is incorrect. There are two types of objectives in aviation: performance-based objectives and decision-based objectives. Performance-based objectives are used to set measurable, reasonable standards that describe the required student performance. Answer (B) is incorrect. There are two types of objectives in aviation: performance-based objectives and decision-based objectives. Decision-based objectives allow for a more dynamic training environment and are designed to develop pilot judgment and ADM skills.

10. Which element of a performance-based objective explains the standards used to measure the accomplishment of the objective?

A. Description of the skill or behavior.

B. Conditions.

C. Criteria.

Answer (C) is correct. *(FAA-H-8083-9A Chap 4)*

DISCUSSION: Criteria are the standards used to measure the accomplishment of the objective.

Answer (A) is incorrect. The description of the skill or behavior is the desired outcome of training stated in concrete terms that can be measured. Answer (B) is incorrect. Conditions are used to explain the rules under which the skill or behavior is to be demonstrated.

11. What is true of all syllabi?

A. The order of training should not be altered as this will detract from the completion of the final objective.

B. All syllabi should stress well-defined objectives and standards for each lesson.

C. Common ground between the student and instructor will be established by using a syllabus.

Answer (B) is correct. *(FAA-H-8083-9A Chap 4)*

DISCUSSION: All syllabi should stress well-defined objectives and standards for each lesson.

Answer (A) is incorrect. The order of training can and should be altered when necessary to suit the progress of the student and the demands of special circumstances, such as weather conditions. Answer (C) is incorrect. Establishing a common ground between the instructor and student is the purpose of a lesson introduction and is not dependent on a syllabus.

12. After the instructor establishes the overall training objectives, his or her next step is

A. the identification of the blocks of learning which constitute the necessary parts of the total objective.

B. create a lesson plan for the unit of instruction.

C. create a syllabus for the training objective.

Answer (A) is correct. *(FAA-H-8083-9A Chap 6)*

DISCUSSION: After the overall training objectives have been established, the next step is the identification of the blocks of learning which constitute the necessary parts of the total objective.

Answer (B) is incorrect. A lesson plan cannot be developed until the appropriate blocks of learning have been identified. Answer (C) is incorrect. A syllabus cannot be developed until the appropriate blocks of learning have been identified.

5.2 Organization of Training Material

13. The method of arranging lesson material from the simple to complex, past to present, and known to unknown, is one that

A. creates student thought pattern departures.

B. shows the relationships of the main points of the lesson.

C. requires students to actively participate in the lesson.

Answer (B) is correct. *(FAA-H-8083-9A Chap 4)*

DISCUSSION: An instructor must logically organize the lesson material to show the relationships of the main points. This can be done by arranging the material from the simple to the complex, past to present, known to unknown, and from the most frequently used to the least frequently used.

Answer (A) is incorrect. By arranging lesson material from the simple to complex, past to present, and known to unknown, the instructor will make meaningful transitions from one point to another and thus keep the students oriented, not creating thought pattern departures. Answer (C) is incorrect. The objective of each lesson, not the method of arranging material, should require students to actively participate (either directly or indirectly) in the lesson in order to achieve the desired learning outcomes.

14. In organizing lesson material, which step sets the stage for everything to come?

A. Overview.

B. Conclusion.

C. Introduction.

Answer (C) is correct. *(FAA-H-8083-9A Chap 4)*

DISCUSSION: The introduction to a lesson should set the stage for everything to come. The introduction is made up of three elements: attention, motivation, and overview.

Answer (A) is incorrect. The overview is included in the introduction and tells the group what is to be covered during the period of instruction, not how it relates to the entire course. Answer (B) is incorrect. The conclusion retraces the important elements of the lesson and relates them to the lesson objective. It does not set the stage for everything to come because it is at the end of a lesson.

15. The proper sequence for the subparts of an introduction is

A. attention, motivation, and overview.

B. attention, development, and overview.

C. overview, motivation, and conclusion.

Answer (A) is correct. *(FAA-H-8083-9A Chap 4)*

DISCUSSION: The proper sequence for the subparts of an introduction is attention, motivation, and overview. First, the instructor must gain the student's attention and focus it on the subject at hand. Second, the introduction should offer the students specific reasons for needing to be familiar with, to know, to understand, to apply, or to be able to perform whatever they are about to learn. This motivation should appeal to each student personally and accentuate the desire to learn. Third, every lesson introduction should contain an overview that tells the group what is to be covered during the period.

Answer (B) is incorrect. Development is the main part of the lesson, not a subpart of the introduction. Answer (C) is incorrect. Conclusion is the review portion of the lesson, not a subpart of the introduction.

16. Instructors should utilize the proper sequence for the subparts of an introduction. These are

A. attention, motivation, and overview.

B. application, correlation, and understanding.

C. anecdote or story, motivation, and overview.

Answer (A) is correct. *(FAA-H-8083-9A Chap 4)*

DISCUSSION: The basic introduction to a period of instruction consists of three elements: attention, motivation, and overview. By organizing the content in this manner, the instructor helps the student obtain a firm grasp of the subject matter while minimizing the possibility of a rambling discussion.

Answer (B) is incorrect. Application, correlation, and understanding are levels of learning, not the elements of an introduction to instruction. Answer (C) is incorrect. The introduction should be free of stories, jokes, or incidents that do not help the students focus their attention on the lesson objective.

17. In developing a lesson, the instructor should organize explanations and demonstrations to help the student

A. achieve the desired learning outcome.

B. acquire a thorough understanding of the material presented.

C. acquire new concepts, generally progressing from the known to the unknown.

Answer (A) is correct. *(FAA-H-8083-9A Chap 4)*

DISCUSSION: In developing a lesson, the instructor should organize the subject matter (explanations and demonstrations) in a manner that helps the student achieve the desired learning outcome.

Answer (B) is incorrect. The student's ability to acquire a thorough understanding of the material is dependent on more than an instructor's organized presentation, e.g., motivation, needs, etc. Answer (C) is incorrect. Progressing from the known to the unknown is a way of logically organizing the lesson material to show the relationships of the main points, not the intent of developing a lesson, which is to help the student achieve the desired learning outcome.

18. When teaching from the known to the unknown, an instructor is using the student's

A. current knowledge of the subject.

B. previous experiences and knowledge.

C. previously held opinions, both valid and invalid.

Answer (B) is correct. *(FAA-H-8083-9A Chap 4)*

DISCUSSION: Teaching from the known to the unknown allows the instructor to use the student's previous experience and knowledge as the point of departure from which to lead into new ideas and concepts.

Answer (A) is incorrect. When teaching from the known to the unknown, an instructor is using a student's knowledge of related subjects, not the subject at hand. Answer (C) is incorrect. Organizing lessons using the known to the unknown pattern requires students' previous knowledge, not their previously held opinions.

19. The known to unknown pattern helps the instructor lead the student into new ideas and concepts by

A. anxieties and insecurities.

B. using something the student already knows.

C. previously held opinions, both valid and invalid.

Answer (B) is correct. *(FAA-H-8083-9A Chap 4)*

DISCUSSION: By using something the student already knows as the point of departure, the instructor can lead into new ideas and concepts. For example, in developing a lesson on heading indicators, the instructor could begin with a discussion of the vacuum-driven heading indicator before proceeding to a description of the radio magnetic indicator (RMI).

Answer (A) is incorrect. The known to unknown pattern helps the instructor lead the student into new ideas and concepts by using something the student already knows, not through anxieties and insecurities. Answer (C) is incorrect. By using something the student already knows as the point of departure, the instructor can lead into new ideas and concepts, not through previously held opinions.

20. Examples of methods to gain student attention include

A. Jokes, video clips, questions.

B. Lectures, guided discussions, demonstrations.

C. Review problems, case studies, explanations.

Answer (A) is correct. *(FAA-H-8083-9A Chap 4)*

DISCUSSION: Stories, video clips, questions, or jokes can all be used to gain student attention.

Answer (B) is incorrect. Lectures do not prompt student attention. Stories, video clips, questions, or jokes are all methods to gain student attention. Answer (C) is incorrect. While case studies are a type of story, they are a type of problem-based learning and are used in the development stage of a lesson, not in the introduction.

21. Reinforcement of student learning occurs primarily during which state of lesson organization?

A. Introduction.

B. Development.

C. Conclusion.

Answer (C) is correct. *(FAA-H-8083-9A Chap 4)*

DISCUSSION: Conclusions retrace important elements of the lesson and relate them to the objective. This reinforces the student's learning and improves retention.

Answer (A) is incorrect. The introduction sets the stage for everything to come. Answer (B) is incorrect. The development is the main part of the lesson during which the instructor organizes the explanations and demonstrations in a manner that helps the students achieve the desired learning outcomes.

5.3 Lesson Plan

22. Which statement is true regarding lesson plans?

A. Lesson plans should not be directed toward the course objective; only to the lesson objective.

B. A well-thought-out mental outline of a lesson may be used any time as long as the instructor is well prepared.

C. Lesson plans help instructors keep a constant check on their own activity as well as that of their students.

Answer (C) is correct. *(FAA-H-8083-9A Chap 6)*

DISCUSSION: Lesson plans help instructors keep a constant check on their own activity, as well as that of their students. The development of lesson plans by instructors signifies, in effect, that they have taught the lesson to themselves prior to attempting to teach the lesson to students.

Answer (A) is incorrect. A lesson plan should serve as a means of relating the lesson to the objectives of the course, as well as the lesson. Answer (B) is incorrect. A mental outline of a lesson is not a lesson plan. A lesson plan should be in written form regardless of an instructor's preparation.

23. When the instructor keeps the student informed of lesson objectives and completion standards, it minimizes the student's feelings of

A. insecurity.

B. resignation.

C. aggressiveness.

Answer (A) is correct. *(FAA-H-8083-9A Chap 7)*

DISCUSSION: Students feel insecure when they do not know the lesson objectives and the completion standards to which they will be held. Instructors can minimize such feelings of insecurity by telling students what is expected of them and what to anticipate.

Answer (B) is incorrect. Resignation occurs when a student completes the early phase of training without understanding the fundamentals, not the objectives or completion standards, and becomes lost in the advanced phase. Answer (C) is incorrect. Aggression occurs when a student becomes angry at something or someone. Aggression (or any other defense mechanism) may be used to defend a feeling of insecurity when a student is not kept informed.

24. Which statement is true about lesson plans?

A. Lesson plans should follow a prescribed format.

B. Standard prepared lesson plans are effective for teaching all students.

C. The use of standard lesson plans may not be effective for students requiring a different approach.

Answer (C) is correct. *(FAA-H-8083-9A Chap 6)*

DISCUSSION: A lesson plan for an instructional period should be appropriate to the background, experience, and ability of the particular student(s). If the procedures outlined in the lesson plan are not leading to the desired results, the instructor should change the approach. Thus, the use of standard lesson plans may not be effective for students requiring a different approach.

Answer (A) is incorrect. Although lesson plans should all contain certain items, the format to be followed should be tailored to the particular student(s). Answer (B) is incorrect. Lesson plans are only an outline of the lesson. An instructor may have to adapt the procedures in a standard prepared lesson plan so it will be effective with different students.

25. A well developed lesson plan should

A. promote uniformity of instruction regardless of the instructor teaching it.

B. be a sketch of a program or teaching lecture.

C. be a document that will not require changes or alterations.

Answer (A) is correct. *(FAA-H-8083-9A Chap 6)*

DISCUSSION: A well-developed lesson plan should

- Ensure the proper material is included and eliminate unimportant details.
- Make certain that due consideration is given to each part of the lesson.
- Aid the instructor in presenting the material in a suitable sequence for efficient learning.
- Provide an outline of the teaching procedure to be used.
- Serve as a means of relating the lesson to the objectives of the course of training.
- Give the inexperienced instructor confidence.
- Promote uniformity of instruction regardless of the instructor or the date on which the lesson is given.

Answer (B) is incorrect. A well-developed lesson plan should be a well-written outline, not a vague sketch. Answer (C) is incorrect. A well-developed lesson plan should be a working document that can and should be revised as changes occur or are needed.

26. The main concern in developing a lesson plan is the

A. format.

B. content.

C. student.

Answer (C) is correct. *(FAA-H-8083-9A Chap 6)*

DISCUSSION: The lesson plan must be appropriate for the particular student. Because standard lesson plans may not be effective for students who require a different approach, the main concern in developing a lesson plan is the student.

Answer (A) is incorrect. The format of the lesson plan will be developed based on the needs of the student and the subject being taught. One lesson plan format does not work well for all students; therefore, the format of a lesson plan is an ending point, not a starting point, in lesson plan development. Answer (B) is incorrect. While the content of a lesson plan is a concern in its development (e.g., how much time should be devoted to which subjects), the main concern in developing a lesson plan is the student.

27. With regard to the characteristics of a well-planned lesson, each lesson should contain

A. new material that is related to the lesson previously presented.

B. one basic element of the principle, procedure, or skill appropriate to that lesson.

C. every bit of information needed to reach the objective of the training syllabus.

Answer (A) is correct. *(FAA-H-8083-9A Chap 6)*

DISCUSSION: One characteristic of a well-planned lesson is content, which means each lesson should contain new material. However, the new facts, principles, or skills should be related to the lesson previously presented. A short review of earlier lessons is usually necessary, especially in flight training.

Answer (B) is incorrect. All of the elements, not only one, necessary to learn a simple procedure, principle, or skill should be presented. Answer (C) is incorrect. Each lesson should include all of the information needed to reach the objective of a particular lesson but not everything needed for the entire syllabus.

28. A primary consideration in planning for student performance is the

A. student's motivational level.

B. student's intellectual level.

C. length of the practice session.

Answer (C) is correct. *(FAA-H-8083-9A Chap 2)*

DISCUSSION: In planning for student performance, a primary consideration is the length of time devoted to practice. A beginning student reaches a point where additional practice is not only unproductive but may even be harmful. When that point is reached, errors increase and motivation declines. As a student gains experience, longer periods of practice are profitable.

Answer (A) is incorrect. A student's motivational level is important to an instructor since it directly relates to the student's progress and ability to learn, not as a primary consideration in planning for student performance. Answer (B) is incorrect. A primary consideration in student performance is the length of time devoted to practice, not the student's intellectual level.

29. (Refer to Figure 1 on page 115.) Section A is titled:

A. Overview.

B. Objective.

C. Introduction.

Answer (B) is correct. *(FAA-H-8083-9A Chap 6)*

DISCUSSION: Section A of Fig. 1 is titled "Objective." The objective of the lesson is the reason for the lesson and should clearly state what the instructor expects the student to know or do at the completion of the lesson.

Answer (A) is incorrect. An overview is a subpart of an introduction to a lesson, not a titled section of a lesson plan. Answer (C) is incorrect. An introduction is part of an effective way to organize a lesson, not a titled section of a lesson plan.

30. (Refer to Figure 1 on page 115.) Section B is titled:

A. Content.

B. Elements.

C. Course of Training.

Answer (A) is correct. *(FAA-H-8083-9A Chap 6)*

DISCUSSION: Section B of Fig. 1 is titled "Content." This is a statement of the knowledge and skill necessary for the fulfillment of the lesson objective. This may include both elements previously learned and those to be introduced during this lesson.

Answer (B) is incorrect. "Elements" is not a titled section of a lesson plan. Answer (C) is incorrect. The course of training is the overall objective of the instruction and is comprised of many different lesson plans, not a titled section of a lesson plan.

31. (Refer to Figure 1 on page 115.) Section C is titled:

A. Schedule.

B. Overview.

C. Training Schedule.

Answer (A) is correct. *(FAA-H-8083-9A Chap 6)*

DISCUSSION: Section C of Fig. 1 is titled "Schedule." The instructor should estimate the amount of time to be devoted to the presentation of the elements of that lesson.

Answer (B) is incorrect. An overview is a subpart of an introduction to a lesson, not a titled section of a lesson plan. Answer (C) is incorrect. The correct title is "Schedule," not "Training Schedule."

32. (Refer to Figure 1 on page 115.) Section D is titled:

A. Instructor's Actions.

B. Equipment.

C. Content.

Answer (B) is correct. *(FAA-H-8083-9A Chap 6)*

DISCUSSION: Section D of Fig. 1 is titled "Equipment." This includes all instructional materials and training aids required to teach the lesson.

Answer (A) is incorrect. "Instructor's Actions" is the title of the section of a lesson plan that contains a statement of the instructor's proposed procedures for presenting the elements of knowledge and performance involved in the lesson (Section E). Answer (C) is incorrect. "Content" is a statement of the knowledge and skill necessary for fulfillment of the lesson objective, not a list of instructional materials to be used in the lesson.

33. (Refer to Figure 1 on page 115.) Section E is titled:

A. Content.

B. Discussion.

C. Instructor's Actions.

Answer (C) is correct. *(FAA-H-8083-9A Chap 6)*

DISCUSSION: Section E of Fig. 1 is titled "Instructor's Actions." This is a statement of the instructor's proposed procedures for presenting the elements of knowledge and performance involved in the lesson.

Answer (A) is incorrect. "Content" is a statement of the knowledge and skill necessary for fulfillment of the lesson objective, not a list of the instructor's actions. Answer (B) is incorrect. While this section states that a discussion will take place, it is specifically those actions taken by the instructor and not the student.

34. (Refer to Figure 1 on page 115.) Section F is titled:

A. Application.

B. Understanding.

C. Student's Actions.

Answer (C) is correct. *(FAA-H-8083-9A Chap 6)*

DISCUSSION: Section F of Fig. 1 is titled "Student's Actions." This is a statement of desired student responses to instruction.

Answer (A) is incorrect. While this involves application of what the instructor has presented to the student, this section is the instructor's desired student's action during the lesson. Answer (B) is incorrect. Understanding is a level of learning, not a titled section of a lesson plan.

35. (Refer to Figure 1 below.) Section G is titled:

A. Summary.

B. Evaluation.

C. Completion Standards.

Answer (C) is correct. *(FAA-H-8083-9A Chap 6)*

DISCUSSION: Section G of Fig. 1 is titled "Completion Standards." This is the evaluation basis for determining how well the student has met the objective of the lesson in terms of knowledge and skill.

Answer (A) is incorrect. A summary of a lesson would take place during the postflight discussion. Answer (B) is incorrect. Evaluation is part of the teaching process and would be used by the instructor to compare the student's performance to the completion standards.

LESSON Ground reference maneuvers **STUDENT** ________ **DATE** / /

A ________	To develop the student's skill in planning and following a pattern over the ground compensating for wind drift at varying angles.
B ________	Use of ground references to control path Observation and control of wind effect Control of airplane attitude, altitude, and heading
C ________	Preflight discussion :10 Instructor demonstrations :25 Student practice :45 Postflight critique :10
D ________	Chalkboard for preflight discussion IFR visor for maneuvers reviewed
E ________	Preflight—discuss lesson objective. Diagram "S" turns, eight along a road, and rectangular course on a chalkboard. Inflight—demonstrate elements. Demonstrate following a road, "S" turns, eights along a road, and rectangular course, coach student practice. Postflight—critique student performance and make study assignment.
F ________	Preflight—discuss lesson objective and resolve questions. Inflight—review previous maneuvers including power-off stalls and flight at minimum controllable airspeed. Perform each new maneuver as directed. Postflight—ask pertinent questions.
G ________	Student should demonstrate competency in maintaining orientation, airspeed within 10 knots, altitude within 100 feet, and headings within 10 degrees, and in making proper correction for wind drift.

Figure 1. Lesson Plan.

36. A lesson plan, if constructed properly, will provide an outline for

A. proceeding from the unknown to the known.

B. the teaching procedure to be used in a single instructional period.

C. establishing blocks of learning that become progressively larger in scope.

Answer (B) is correct. *(FAA-H-8083-9A Chap 6)*

DISCUSSION: A properly constructed lesson plan is an organized outline or blueprint for a single instructional period. It is a necessary guide for the instructor in that it tells what to do, in what order to do it, and what procedure to use in teaching the material of the lesson.

Answer (A) is incorrect. The lesson plan will usually proceed from the known to the unknown, not unknown to known. Answer (C) is incorrect. A syllabus, not a lesson plan, will provide an outline for establishing blocks of learning that become progressively larger in scope.

37. Each lesson of a training syllabus includes

A. attention, motivation, and overview.

B. introduction, development, and conclusion.

C. objective, content, and completion standards.

Answer (C) is correct. *(FAA-H-8083-9A Chap 6)*

DISCUSSION: Each lesson of a written training syllabus includes an objective, content, and completion standards.

Answer (A) is incorrect. Attention, motivation, and overview are the parts of an introduction to a lesson. Answer (B) is incorrect. The structure of every lesson as it is being presented to a student, not as found in a written syllabus, should be based on an introduction, a development, and a conclusion.

38. A primary consideration in planning for student performance is the

A. length of time devoted to practice.

B. length of time devoted to evaluation.

C. segmentation of the practice session.

Answer (A) is correct. *(FAA-H-8083-9A Chap 2)*

DISCUSSION: In planning for student performance, a primary consideration is the length of time devoted to practice. A beginning student reaches a point where additional practice is not only unproductive, but may even be harmful. When this point is reached, errors increase, and motivation declines. As a student gains experience, longer periods of practice are profitable.

Answer (B) is incorrect. In the initial stages of learning, practical suggestions are more valuable to the student than a grade. Early evaluation is usually teacher-oriented. It provides a check on teaching effectiveness; thus, it is not a primary consideration in student performance planning. Answer (C) is incorrect. While the consideration of how to properly divide or segment a practice session is important, it is futile without first determining the appropriate length of the practice session itself.

39. Which of the following statements is true in regards to the properties of overlearning?

A. Overlearning allows the student to bypass the learning plateau phenomenon.

B. Overlearning is the continued study of a skill after initial proficiency has been achieved.

C. Targets the student's deep memory.

Answer (B) is correct. *(FAA-H-8083-9A Chap 2)*

DISCUSSION: Overlearning is the continued study of a skill after initial proficiency has been achieved. Practice proceeds beyond the point at which the act can be performed with the required degree of excellence. The phenomenon of overlearning sometimes occurs when knowledge used frequently begins to take on the properties of a skill.

Answer (A) is incorrect. The learning plateau phenomenon can be present whether overlearning takes place or not. Answer (C) is incorrect. Overlearning does not pertain to the concept of deep memory.

40. Which is true regarding the overlearning of knowledge?

A. Overlearning can result in automatic responses that are undesirable.

B. Overlearning is helpful in increasing student proficiency of a topic.

C. Overlearning develops higher-order thinking skills.

Answer (A) is correct. *(FAA-H-8083-9A Chap 2)*

DISCUSSION: Overlearning is the continued study of a skill after initial proficiency has been achieved. Practice proceeds beyond the point at which the act can be performed with the required degree of excellence. One common effect of overlearning is the development of automated routines rather than development of concept application skills.

Answer (B) is incorrect. Overlearning generally degrades student proficiency by creating automatic responses on the part of the student, which limit the student's understanding of a given topic. Answer (C) is incorrect. On the contrary, overlearning creates a barrier to the development of higher-order thinking skills by creating automated responses from the student rather than actual concept mastery.

41. When teaching new material, the teaching process can be divided into which steps?

A. Preparation, presentation, application, and review and evaluation.

B. Preparation, demonstration, practice, and review.

C. Explanation, demonstration, practice, and evaluation.

Answer (A) is correct. *(FAA-H-8083-9A Chap 4)*

DISCUSSION: The four basic steps in the teaching process are preparation, presentation, application, and review and evaluation.

Answer (B) is incorrect. Demonstration and practice are examples of teaching methods, not basic steps in the teaching process. Answer (C) is incorrect. Explanation, demonstration, and practice are examples of teaching methods, not basic steps in the teaching process.

42. Every lesson, when adequately developed, falls logically into the four steps of the teaching process -

A. preparation, introduction, presentation, and review and evaluation.

B. preparation, introduction, presentation, and review and application.

C. preparation, presentation, application, and review and evaluation.

Answer (C) is correct. *(FAA-H-8083-9A Chap 6)*

DISCUSSION: Every lesson, when developed adequately, falls logically into the four steps of the teaching process: preparation, presentation, application, and review/evaluation.

Answer (A) is incorrect. The second basic step in the teaching process is presentation, not introduction, and the third basic step is application, not presentation. Answer (B) is incorrect. The second basic step in the teaching process is presentation, not introduction, the third basic step is application, not presentation, and the fourth basic step is review and evaluation, not review and application.

43. Which is not a step to ensuring a quality lesson?

A. Instructor research.

B. Assembling training aids.

C. Determining the length of the practice session.

Answer (C) is correct. *(FAA-H-8083-9A Chap 6)*

DISCUSSION: While a primary consideration in planning for student performance, determining the length of the practice session is not a step to ensuring a quality lesson.

Answer (A) is incorrect. Instructor research is a step to ensuring a quality lesson is provided to the student. Answer (B) is incorrect. Assembling training aids is a step to ensuring a quality lesson is provided to the student.

44. What are lesson plans designed to ensure?

A. That each student receive the best possible instruction under existing circumstances.

B. To reinforce student learning and retention of the stated objective.

C. To provide a boost of self-confidence to each student.

Answer (A) is correct. *(FAA-H-8083-9A Chap 6)*

DISCUSSION: Lesson plans are designed to ensure that each student receives the best possible instruction under existing circumstances.

Answer (B) is incorrect. Conclusions reinforce student learning and improve retention of what has been learned previously. Answer (C) is incorrect. Upon successful completion of a given block of learning, a student's self-confidence should be boosted. Lesson plans are not designed to accomplish this.

45. How long should a flight lesson be?

A. Shorter lessons for new students.

B. Longer lessons for new students.

C. Shorter lessons as students gain experience.

Answer (A) is correct. *(FAA-H-8083-9A Chap 2)*

DISCUSSION: In planning for student skill acquisition, a primary consideration is the length of time devoted to practice. A beginning student reaches a point where additional practice is not only unproductive but may even be harmful. As a student gains experience, longer periods of practice become profitable.

Answer (B) is incorrect. Lessons for new students should be shorter, not longer, in length. Answer (C) is incorrect. As students gain experience, the lesson length can be increased.

5.4 Instructional Aids and Training Technology

46. Which is a true statement concerning the use of instructional aids?

A. Instructional aids ensure getting and holding the student's attention.

B. Instructional aids should be designed to cover the key points in a lesson.

C. Instructional aids should not be used simply to cover a subject in less time.

Answer (B) is correct. *(FAA-H-8083-9A Chap 4)*

DISCUSSION: Instructional aids are a good way to improve communication between the instructor and the students. Instructional aids should be designed to cover the key points in a lesson.

Answer (A) is incorrect. Appropriate instructional aids will help get the student's attention, but they cannot ensure that it will hold the student's attention. Answer (C) is incorrect. Instructional aids can help get a point across quickly and clearly, thus reducing the time spent on some subjects.

47. The use of instructional aids should be based on their ability to support a specific point in the lesson. What is the first step in determining if and where instructional aids are necessary?

A. Organize subject material into an outline or a lesson plan.

B. Determine what ideas should be supported with instructional aids.

C. Clearly establish the lesson objective, being certain what must be communicated.

Answer (C) is correct. *(FAA-H-8083-9A Chap 4)*

DISCUSSION: The first step in developing a lesson plan using instructional aids is, as in any lesson plan, to establish the lesson objective. Visual or other aids must help achieve the overall lesson objective. They should be strategically placed to recapture interest, shift to a new topic, or provide emphasis.

Answer (A) is incorrect. Organizing the outline or lesson plan is the third, not first, step in the process. Answer (B) is incorrect. The final, not first, step in determining if and where instructional aids are necessary is to determine what ideas in the lesson should be supported with instructional aids.

48. Instructional aids used in the teaching/learning process should be

A. self-supporting and require no explanation.

B. compatible with the learning outcomes to be achieved.

C. selected prior to developing and organizing the lesson plan.

Answer (B) is correct. *(FAA-H-8083-9A Chap 4)*

DISCUSSION: After establishing lesson objectives, researching the subject, and organizing the material into a lesson plan, the instructor should determine what needs to be supported by visual or other instructional aids. The aids should be compatible with the learning outcomes to be achieved.

Answer (A) is incorrect. Instructional aids are not self-supporting and will require explanation. Answer (C) is incorrect. Instructional aids should be compatible with the desired learning outcomes, which can best be done after, not prior to, developing and organizing the lesson plan.

49. Instructional aids used in the teaching/learning process should not be used

A. as a crutch by the instructor.

B. for teaching more in less time.

C. to visualize relationships between abstracts.

Answer (A) is correct. *(FAA-H-8083-9A Chap 4)*

DISCUSSION: Aids used in conjunction with oral presentation should emphasize, not distract from, the oral message. Also, the instructor should realize that such aids do not take the place of a sound lesson plan or instructor's input.

Answer (B) is incorrect. Aids do help teach more in less time because they clarify and emphasize the lecture. The class can move to new material sooner. Answer (C) is incorrect. Instructional aids should be used to help students to visualize relationships between abstracts.

50. What is one reason an instructor would use an instructional aid?

A. To describe a desired outcome of training.

B. To gain and hold student attention.

C. To describe the standards used to measure the objective.

Answer (B) is correct. *(FAA-H-8083-9A Chap 4)*

DISCUSSION: A reason to use instructional aids in the teaching/learning process is that they will gain and hold the attention of students.

Answer (A) is incorrect. An element of a performance-based objective, the description of the skill or behavior describes a desired outcome of training in concrete terms that can be measured. Answer (C) is incorrect. Criteria describe the standards used to measure the accomplishment of the objective.

51. Instructional aids may be used

A. to clarify the relationships between material objects and concepts.

B. to cover broad subject areas.

C. to add to the time it takes instructors to teach students.

Answer (A) is correct. *(FAA-H-8083-9A Chap 4)*

DISCUSSION: One use for instructional aids is to clarify the relationships between material objects and concepts. When relationships are presented visually, they often are much easier to understand.

Answer (B) is incorrect. Ideally, instructional aids should be designed to cover the key points and concepts rather than broad subject areas or abstractions. Answer (C) is incorrect. Instructors are frequently asked to teach more and more in a smaller time frame. Instructional aids can help them do this. For example, instead of using many words to describe a sound, object, or function, the instructor plays a recording of the sound, shows a picture of the object, or presents a diagram of the function. Consequently, the student learns faster and more accurately, and the instructor saves time in the process.

STUDY UNIT SIX
CRITIQUE AND EVALUATION

(10 pages of outline)

6.1 THE INSTRUCTOR'S ASSESSMENT

1. No instructor skill is more important than the ability to analyze, appraise, and judge student performance. Assessment is an essential and continuous component of the teaching and learning process.
   a. **Assessment** is the process of gathering measurable information to meet evaluation needs. It involves judgment by the instructor and collaboration with the student during the evaluation stage.
   b. A student looks to the instructor for guidance, suggestions for improvement, and encouragement.
   c. To enhance a student's acceptance of further instruction, the instructor should keep the student informed of the progress made.
      1) This will help minimize student frustrations, which will keep the student motivated to learn.
   d. Assessment helps the instructor see where more emphasis is needed and determine the readiness of the student to move forward.
2. In order to provide direction and increase student performance, assessments must be factual and must be aligned with the completion standards of the lesson.
3. An assessment should be **objective**.
   a. The effective assessment is focused on student performance and should not reflect the personal opinions, likes, dislikes, and biases of the instructor.
   b. The assessment must be honest and based on the performance as it was, not as it could have been.
4. An assessment should be **flexible**.
   a. The instructor must fit the tone, technique, and content of the critique to the occasion and the student.
   b. The instructor must evaluate the entire performance in the context it was accomplished and allow for variables, whether they occur on the part of the student or from factors outside the student's control.
5. An assessment should be **acceptable**.
   a. Before students willingly accept their instructor's assessment, they must first willingly accept the instructor.
   b. The students must have confidence in the instructor's qualifications, teaching ability, sincerity, competence, and authority.
      1) An instructor's manner, attitude, and familiarity with the subject at hand does much to serve this purpose.
   c. Instructors cannot rely solely on their position to make an assessment acceptable to their students.

6. An assessment should be **comprehensive**.
   a. A comprehensive assessment is not necessarily long, nor must it treat every aspect of the performance in detail.
   b. The instructor must decide whether the greater benefit will come from a discussion of a few major points or a number of minor points.
   c. An effective assessment covers strengths as well as weaknesses.
7. An assessment should be **constructive**.
   a. An assessment is meaningless unless a student profits from it.
   b. Praise for praise's sake is of no value if a student is not taught how to capitalize on things that are done well and to improve in areas of lesser accomplishment.
   c. An instructor must give positive guidance when identifying a mistake or weakness.
      1) Negative comments that discourage should be omitted altogether.
8. An assessment must be **organized**.
   a. Almost any pattern is acceptable as long as it is logical and makes sense to the student.
   b. An organizational pattern might be the sequence of the performance itself.
      1) EXAMPLE: A flight instructor may explain the sequence of events that lead to an undesirable performance on a given flight maneuver.
9. An assessment should be **thoughtful**.
   a. An effective assessment reflects an instructor's thoughtfulness toward the student's need for self-esteem, recognition, and approval from others.
      1) The assessment must not minimize the inherent dignity and importance of the individual.
   b. Ridicule, anger, or fun at the expense of the student has no place in the assessment.
      1) EXAMPLE: An instructor should try to deliver the assessment in private rather than in a group setting.
10. An assessment should be **specific**.
   a. The instructor's comments and recommendations should be specific, not so general that the student can find nothing to hold onto.
      1) Students cannot act on recommendations and strive to improve unless they know specifically what the recommendations are.
   b. Instructors should express ideas with firmness and authority in terms that cannot be misunderstood.
      1) Students should have no doubt what they did well, what they did poorly, and specifically how they can improve.

6.2 TYPES OF ASSESSMENT

1. There are two categories of assessment: traditional assessment and authentic assessment.
   a. Assessments can be either formal or informal.
      1) Formal assessments usually involve documentation, such as quizzes or written exams.
      2) Informal assessments can include verbal critique and generally occur as needed.

2. **Traditional assessment** often involves written testing and is more likely to be used to evaluate a student's progress at the rote level of learning.
   a. In a traditional assessment, one single answer will be correct (i.e., multiple choice, true/false, etc.).
      1) EXAMPLE: The FAA knowledge test for a given certificate or rating is a traditional assessment.
   b. Traditional assessments are formal in nature.
3. **Authentic assessment** requires the student to demonstrate not only the rote and understanding levels, but also the application and correlation levels of learning. Authentic assessment generally requires the student to perform real-world tasks.
   a. In an authentic assessment, specific standards are used to define acceptable performance on a task.
      1) EXAMPLE: The practical, or flight, portion of the FAA test is an authentic assessment.
   b. Students must generate responses from skills and concepts previously learned.
   c. Authentic assessment focuses on the learning process, enhances the development of real-world skills, encourages higher order thinking skills (HOTS), and teaches students to assess their own work and performance.
   d. Authentic assessment may not be as useful as traditional assessment in the early phases of training because the student may not have enough information or knowledge about the concepts to participate fully.
4. Collaborative assessment, an aspect of authentic assessment, is a form of student-centered grading that uses open-ended questions to guide the student through a self-assessment. The purpose of self-assessment is to stimulate growth in the student's thought process and, in turn, behaviors. The four steps in this process include the following:
   a. **Replay** – Asking the student to verbally replay the flight or procedure.
   b. **Reconstruct** – The student identifies key things that (s)he should or could have done differently during the flight or maneuver.
   c. **Reflect** – Questions that require reflection on the event, often leading to insight.
      1) EXAMPLE: "Did you perform in accordance with the PTS?"
   d. **Redirect** – Helps the student relate the lessons learned to other experiences and consider how they might help in future sessions.
      1) EXAMPLE: "Which aspects of this flight might apply to future situations, and how?"
5. Collaborative assessment uses two broad grading rubrics: one that assesses proficiency in skill-focused maneuvers or procedures, and one that focuses on the decision-making aspect of flight training (referred to as Single-Pilot Resource Management, or SRM).
   a. Advantages of these forms of assessment include the following:
      1) It actively involves the student,
      2) It establishes the habit of reflection and self-assessment, and
      3) These grades are not self-esteem related because they describe a level of performance. A student cannot flunk a lesson.

6. The grading dimensions of maneuvers or procedures include the following:
   a. **Describe** – Student is able to describe the elements of the scenario but needs assistance to execute the maneuver properly.
   b. **Explain** – Student is able to describe the elements of the scenario and understands the concepts and principles that comprise the activity but needs assistance to execute the maneuver properly.
   c. **Practice** – Student is able to plan and execute the scenario with some coaching.
   d. **Perform** – Student is able to perform the activity without instructor assistance and identifies and makes corrections in a timely manner. Indicates satisfactory demonstration.
   e. **Not observed** – Any event not accomplished or required.
7. The grading dimensions of SRM include the following:
   a. **Explain** – Student can verbally identify, describe, and understand risks but needs to be prompted to make decisions.
   b. **Practice** – Student properly identifies, understands, and applies SRM principles and corrects minor deviations identified by the instructor.
   c. **Manage-Decide** – Student correctly gathers information, identifies proper courses of action, evaluates risks for each course of action, and makes the appropriate decision without instructor input.
8. To choose an effective assessment method, flight instructors can use a four-step process.
   a. Determine Level-of-Learning Objectives
      1) The individual objectives are stated as general level-of-learning objectives.
      2) Because it defines the scope of the learning task, this is a good starting point for developing a test.
   b. List Indicators/Samples of Desired Behaviors
      1) List the indicators of behavior that give the best indication of the achievement of the objective.
      2) By carefully choosing these indicators of behavior, an instructor can obtain adequate evidence of learning.
   c. Establish Criterion Objectives
      1) Define criterion (performance-based) objectives that state the conditions under which the behavior is to be performed and the criteria that must be met.
      2) Criterion objectives provide the framework for developing test items that will measure the level of learning objectives.
         a) EXAMPLE: "The student will demonstrate understanding of navigational charts and their symbols by completing a quiz with a minimum passing score of 70%."
   d. Develop Criterion-Referenced Assessment Items
      1) Criterion-referenced testing measures a student's performance against a carefully written, measurable standard or criterion.
         a) Practical tests for pilot certification are an example of criterion-referenced testing because they are based on the predetermined Practical Test Standards (PTS)/Airman Certification Standards (ACS) as set forth by the FAA.
         b) The objective of the PTS/ACS is to ensure the certification of pilots at a high level of performance and proficiency, consistent with safety.

c) The PTS/ACS should not be used merely to "teach the test;" rather, the document should be used as both a training tool and an assessment tool during flight training to ensure students are adequately prepared for the practical test.

d) The PTS/ACS is not a teaching tool. It is a testing tool. The overall focus of flight training should be on education, learning, and understanding why the standards are there and how they were set.

i) Instructors should not introduce the PTS/ACS until the last 3 hours of training prior to the practical test.

2) Criterion-referenced tests feature performance-based objectives that can be reliably, rather than subjectively, measured. Performance testing is desirable for evaluating training that involves an operation, a procedure, or a process.

a) EXAMPLE: A pretest constructed to measure knowledge and skills necessary to begin a course is a criterion-referenced test, as is a pre-solo aeronautical knowledge test.

3) The results of the test (questions missed) identify areas that were not adequately covered.

9. Airman Certification Standards (ACS) for Private Pilot – Airplane (PAR), Commercial Pilot – Airplane (CAX), and Instrument Rating – Airplane (IRA) recently became effective. Therefore, the Practical Test Standards (PTS) documents for PAR, CAX, and IRA have been canceled.

a. Since September 2011, the FAA has worked closely with a diverse group of aviation community stakeholders to help the agency improve the testing and training standards, guidance, and test development and management components of the airman certification process. The industry participants in this effort developed the ACS framework to improve airman training and testing by providing an integrated, holistic system that clearly aligns airman testing with certification standards and guidance.

b. Built on the existing PTS, which explicitly define the performance metrics and tolerances for each flight proficiency element listed in the Federal Aviation Regulations, the ACS enhances the PTS by defining the specific task elements for aeronautical knowledge, risk management, and skills needed to support each Area of Operation and Task.

1) Simply, the ACS describes what an applicant must know, consider, and do to pass the knowledge and practical tests for a given airman certificate or rating. It is thus the single-source set of standards for both the knowledge test and practical test for a certificate or rating.

2) By presenting the elements of knowledge, risk management, and skill in the integrated ACS format, the ACS approach better serves the applicant, the instructor, and the evaluator. In addition, the ACS approach enables the FAA to create and maintain a clear link among the regulations, knowledge and skill performance standards, guidance, and test materials.

NOTE: Most of the study questions for this subunit are based on known questions relevant to the PTS only and specific guidance from the FAA's *Aviation Instructor's Handbook.* If more questions specific to the ACS become available, an update will be published.

6.3 CRITIQUES AND ORAL ASSESSMENTS

1. A critique is an instructor-to-student assessment.
   a. A critique is not necessarily negative in content. It considers the good along with the bad, the individual parts, the parts in relation to each other, and overall performance.
   b. It may be written, oral, or both.
   c. A critique should always be conducted immediately after the student's performance while the details are easy to recall.
   d. The instructor may critique any activity that a student performs or practices to improve skill, proficiency, and learning.
   e. A critique can and usually should be as varied in content as the performance being evaluated.
2. Types of Critiques
   a. **Instructor/Student Critique**
      1) Group discussion in which members of the class are invited to offer criticism of a performance
      2) Should be carefully controlled and organized by the instructor
   b. **Student-Led Critique**
      1) Student-led assessment that, while generating student interest, may not be effective because of student inexperience
   c. **Small Group Critique**
      1) Small groups are assigned to analyze a specific area of performance.
      2) Once combined, a comprehensive assessment results.
   d. **Individual Student Critique by Another Student**
      1) This type of critique often allows the group to accept more ownership of the ideas expressed.
      2) Careful oversight should be maintained by the instructor to control the process.
   e. **Self-Critique**
   f. **Written Critique**
      1) Instructors can devote more time and thought to it than an oral assessment.
      2) Students can refer to them as needed.
      3) Student has a permanent record of suggestions, recommendations, and opinions.
3. The most common means of assessment is direct or indirect oral questioning of students by the instructor. Questions may be loosely classified as fact questions and HOTS questions.
   a. The answer to a fact question is based on memory or recall (i.e., who, what, where, when, why).
   b. HOTS questions require the student to combine a knowledge of facts with an ability to analyze situations, solve problems, and arrive at conclusions.
4. Proper quizzing by the instructor can have a number of desirable results. It can
   a. Reveal the effectiveness of the instructor's training methods,
   b. Check student retention and comprehension of what has been learned,
   c. Review material already presented to the student,
   d. Help retain student interest and stimulate thinking,
   e. Emphasize the important points of training,
   f. Identify points that need more emphasis, and
   g. Promote active student participation.

5. Characteristics of effective questions:
   a. Objective, or fact, questions have only one correct answer, while the answer to open-ended HOTS (higher order thinking skills) questions can be expressed in a variety of possible situations. Each question should call for a specific answer that can be readily evaluated by the instructor.
   b. Effective questions must
      1) Apply to the subject being taught
      2) Be brief and concise, but also clear and definite
      3) Be adapted to the ability, experience, and stage of training of the student
      4) Center on only one idea (who, what, when, where, how, or why; not a combination)
      5) Present a challenge to the student
         a) A question must be of suitable difficulty for the students at that particular stage of training.
6. The following types of questions should be avoided:
   a. Yes/no questions. For example: "Do you understand?"
   b. Puzzling questions – ones that do not provide a clear, definite objective. For example: "Which of the airplane systems is the most responsive to pilot inputs?"
   c. Oversize questions – ones that are too broad in scope and could have multiple correct/incorrect responses. Again, no definite objective is stated. For example: "What is required before going flying?"
   d. Toss-up questions – more than one correct response is possible. For example: "In an emergency, should you squawk 7700 or pick a landing spot?"
   e. Bewilderment questions – questions that mentally confuse. For example: "In reading the altimeter, if you take temperature into account, as when flying from a cold air mass through a warm front, what precaution should you take when in mountainous areas?"
   f. Trick questions – questions that cause the student to feel (s)he is engaged in a battle of wits with the instructor, thus changing student focus from the message to the messenger. For example: Using double negatives. "What is not a characteristic of not relying solely on flight instruments during flight in IMC?"
   g. Irrelevant questions – diversions that introduce unrelated facts and thoughts and slow student progress. For example: "How would the wing produce lift in outer space?"
7. When answering student questions, the instructor needs to clearly understand the question before attempting an answer.
   a. The instructor should display interest in the student's questions and give as direct and accurate an answer as possible.
   b. If a student's question is too advanced for the particular lesson and confusion may result from a complete answer, the instructor may
      1) Carefully explain that the question was good and pertinent;
      2) Explain that to answer would unnecessarily complicate the learning task at hand; and
      3) Advise the student to reintroduce the question later at the appropriate point in training or meet outside class for a more complete discussion.
8. Occasionally, a student will ask a question the instructor cannot answer. The best course is to freely admit not knowing the answer.
   a. The instructor should then promise to find out or offer to help the student look it up in appropriate references.

6.4 TYPES OF WRITTEN TEST QUESTIONS

1. Written test questions fall into two general categories:
   a. Supply-type and
   b. Selection-type.
2. Supply-type questions require the student to furnish a response in the form of a word, sentence, or paragraph.
   a. Supply-type test items
      1) Require students to organize their thoughts and ideas
      2) Demand the ability to express ideas
         a) This makes them valuable in measuring the learner's generalized understanding of a subject.
      3) Are subjective
         a) Thus, their main disadvantage is that they cannot be graded uniformly.
         b) The same test graded by different instructors probably would be assigned different scores.
      4) Take longer for students to answer and for instructors to grade, which is a disadvantage
3. Selection-type questions include items for which two or more alternative responses are provided and there is only one single correct response.
   a. Selection-type test items
      1) Are highly objective.
         a) Thus, they are graded uniformly regardless of the student or grader.
      2) Allow direct comparison of students' accomplishments. For example, it is possible to compare student performance
         a) Within the same class,
         b) Between classes, and
         c) Under different instructors.
   b. True/false, multiple-choice, and matching type questions are prime examples of selection-type questions.
4. The **true/false** test item is well adapted to the testing of knowledge of facts and detail, especially when there are only two possible answers.
   a. The chief disadvantage of the true/false test item is it creates the greatest probability of guessing because the student always has a 50% chance of guessing correctly.
   b. Guidelines for effective use of true/false questions
      1) Include only one idea in each statement
      2) Make the statement either entirely true or entirely false
      3) Avoid the unnecessary use of negatives
      4) Avoid absolutes such as "all," "every," "only," "never," etc.
5. **Multiple-choice** test items may be used to determine student achievement, ranging from acquisition of facts to understanding, reasoning, and ability to apply what has been learned.
   a. Multiple-choice test items consist of two parts: the stem and a list of possible responses.
      1) The **stem** includes the question, statement, or problem.
      2) Incorrect responses are called distractors.
   b. When multiple-choice items are intended to measure achievement at a higher level of learning, some or all of the alternatives should be acceptable, but one should be clearly better than the others.

c. Multiple-choice test items should have all alternatives of approximately equal length.
   1) A common error made by instructors is to make the correct alternative longer than the incorrect ones.
d. Three major challenges are common in the construction of multiple-choice test items.
   1) Developing a question or item stem that must be expressed clearly and without ambiguity
   2) Developing a statement or correct answer choice that cannot be refuted
   3) Writing distractors that are attractive to learners who do not possess the knowledge or understanding necessary to recognize the correct response
e. The following are popular distractors:
   1) An incorrect response related to the situation that sounds convincing
   2) A common misconception
   3) A true statement that does not satisfy the requirements of the problem
   4) A statement that is too broad or too narrow for the requirements of the problem

6. **Matching** test items are particularly good for measuring the student's ability to recognize relationships and to make associations between terms, parts, words, phrases, or symbols listed in one column with related items in another column.
   a. Matching reduces the probability of guessing correct responses compared to a series of multiple-choice items covering the same material.

6.5 CHARACTERISTICS OF A GOOD TEST

1. **Reliability**
   a. The degree to which test results are consistent with repeated measurements.
   b. The reliability of a written test is determined by whether it gives consistent measurement to a particular individual or group.
   c. EXAMPLE: A written test that has reliability yields consistent results.
2. **Validity**
   a. The extent to which a test measures what it is supposed to measure.
   b. This is the most important consideration in test evaluation.
   c. EXAMPLE: A written test has validity when it measures what it is supposed to measure and nothing else.
3. **Usability**
   a. The functionality of a test.
   b. EXAMPLE: A written test is usable when it is easy to give, easy to read, the wording is clear and concise, figures are appropriate to the test items and clearly drawn, and it is easily graded.
4. **Objectivity**
   a. Describes singleness of scoring a test.
   b. Selection-type test items (true/false, multiple-choice) are much easier to grade with objectivity.
   c. EXAMPLE: In essay questions, it is nearly impossible to prevent an instructor's own biases from affecting the grade subject.
5. **Comprehensiveness**
   a. The degree to which a test measures the overall objectives.
   b. A written test must sample an appropriate cross-section of the objectives of instruction.
   c. EXAMPLE: A written test is said to be comprehensive when it liberally samples whatever is being measured.

6. **Discrimination**
   a. The degree to which a test distinguishes the differences between students.
   b. Three features of a test constructed to identify the difference in achievement of students are
      1) A wide range of scores,
      2) All levels of difficulty, and
      3) Items that distinguish between students with differing levels of achievement of the course objectives.
   c. EXAMPLE: A written test having the characteristic of discrimination will measure small differences in achievement between students.

6.6 REVIEW AND EVALUATION

1. Review and evaluation of the student's learning should be an integral part of each lesson.
   a. Evaluation of student performance and accomplishment should be based on the objectives and goals established in the lesson plan.
2. Performance testing is desirable for evaluating training that involves an operation, procedure, or process.
   a. This method of evaluation is particularly suited to the measurement of a student's ability in performing a task, either mental or physical.
3. Students may perform a procedure or maneuver correctly but not fully understand the principles and objectives involved. If the instructor suspects this, students should be required to vary the performance of the maneuver or procedure slightly.
   a. Students who do not understand the principles involved will probably not be able to successfully complete the revised maneuver or procedure.

GLEIM SUCCESS TIPS

QUESTIONS AND ANSWER EXPLANATIONS: All of the Fundamentals of Instructing knowledge test questions chosen by the FAA for release as well as additional questions selected by Gleim relating to the material in the previous outlines are provided on the following pages. These questions have been organized into the same subunits as the outlines. To the immediate right of each question are the correct answer and answer explanations. You should cover these answers and answer explanations while responding to the questions. Refer to the general discussion in the Introduction on how to take the FAA knowledge test.

Remember that the questions from the FAA knowledge test bank have been reordered by topic and organized into a meaningful sequence. Also, the first line of the answer explanation gives the citation of the authoritative source for the answer.

QUESTIONS

6.1 The Instructor's Assessment

1. To be effective, an assessment should

A. not contain negative remarks.

B. treat every aspect of the performance in detail.

C. be flexible enough to satisfy the requirements of the moment.

Answer (C) is correct. *(FAA-H-8083-9A Chap 5)*

DISCUSSION: An effective assessment is one that is flexible enough to satisfy the requirements of the moment. The instructor must fit the tone, technique, and content of the assessment to the occasion and the student. Thus, the instructor is faced with the problem of what to say, what to omit, and what to minimize. The challenge of the assessment is that the instructor must determine what to say at the proper moment.

Answer (A) is incorrect. An assessment may contain negative remarks as long as they point toward improvement or a higher level of performance. Answer (B) is incorrect. A comprehensive assessment is not necessarily a long one, nor must it treat every aspect of the performance in detail. The instructor must decide whether the greater benefit will come from discussing a few major points or a number of minor points.

2. An instructor's assessment of a student's performance should

A. treat every aspect of the performance in detail.

B. be conducted in private so that the student is not embarrassed.

C. provide direction and guidance to improve performance.

Answer (C) is correct. *(FAA-H-8083-9A Chap 5)*

DISCUSSION: An assessment should improve a student's performance and provide something constructive with which (s)he can work and advance. It should provide direction and guidance to improve performance.

. Answer (A) is incorrect. A comprehensive assessment is not necessarily a long one, nor must it treat every aspect of the performance in detail. The instructor must decide whether the greater benefit will come from discussing a few major points or a number of minor points. Answer (B) is incorrect. An assessment may be conducted in private or before the entire class. An assessment presented before the entire class can be beneficial to every student in the classroom as well as to the student who performed the exercise.

3. Which is true about an instructor's assessment of a student's performance?

A. Praise for praise's sake is of value.

B. It should be constructive and objective.

C. It should treat every aspect of the performance in detail.

Answer (B) is correct. *(FAA-H-8083-9A Chap 5)*

DISCUSSION: An assessment must be constructive by explaining to the student how to capitalize on things that are done well and to use them to compensate for lesser accomplishments. An assessment must also be objective by basing it on the performance as it was, not as it could have been.

Answer (A) is incorrect. Praise for praise's sake is of no value if a student is not taught how to capitalize on things that are done well and to use them to compensate for lesser accomplishments. Answer (C) is incorrect. A comprehensive assessment is not necessarily a long one, nor must it treat every aspect of the performance in detail. The instructor must decide whether the greater benefit will come from discussing a few major points or a number of minor points.

4. Which statement is true about instructors' assessment?

A. Instructors should rely on their personality to make an assessment more acceptable.

B. A comprehensive assessment should emphasize positive aspects of student performance.

C. Before students willingly accept their instructor's assessment, they must first accept the instructor.

Answer (C) is correct. *(FAA-H-8083-9A Chap 5)*

DISCUSSION: Students must have confidence in the instructor's qualifications, teaching ability, sincerity, competence, and authority before they will willingly accept their instructor's assessment. An assessment holds little weight if the student has no respect for the instructor.

Answer (A) is incorrect. The effective assessment is focused on student performance and should not reflect the personal opinions, likes, dislikes, and biases (i.e., personality) of the instructor. Answer (B) is incorrect. A comprehensive assessment means that good and bad points are covered adequately but not necessarily in exhaustive detail.

5. Which statement is true regarding an assessment that is constructive?

A. An instructor's manner and attitude make an assessment constructive.

B. Constructive assessments can inspire a student to improve in areas of lesser accomplishment.

C. A constructive assessment should express ideas with authority in terms that cannot be misunderstood.

Answer (B) is correct. *(FAA-H-8083-9A Chap 5)*

DISCUSSION: Constructive assessments, including praise, can inspire a student to improve in areas of lesser accomplishment.

Answer (A) is incorrect. An instructor's manner and attitude make an assessment acceptable to the student. Answer (C) is incorrect. For an assessment to be specific, ideas should be expressed with firmness and in terms the student cannot misunderstand.

6. What must an instructor do to ensure an assessment is thoughtful?

A. The instructor must not minimize the importance and dignity of the individual.

B. The instructor must give positive guidance when identifying a student's mistakes.

C. The instructor must limit negative comments that discourage.

Answer (A) is correct. *(FAA-H-8083-9A Chap 5)*

DISCUSSION: The assessment given by the instructor must not minimize the inherent dignity and importance of the individual.

Answer (B) is incorrect. Instructor guidance should be constructive, which will not necessarily contain only positive comments. Answer (C) is incorrect. Negative comments that discourage should be omitted altogether, not simply limited.

7. Which of the following statements is true?

A. Instructor critiques should focus on only positive areas of the student's performance.

B. Instructor critiques should only focus on areas where the student needs to improve.

C. For an instructor's critique to be effective, the student must first accept the instructor.

Answer (C) is correct. *(FAA-H-8083-9A Chap 5)*
DISCUSSION: The student must accept the instructor in order to accept his or her assessment willingly. Students must have confidence in the instructor's qualifications, teaching ability, sincerity, competence, and authority.
Answer (A) is incorrect. A proper critique should focus on both positive and negative aspects of the student's performance. Answer (B) is incorrect. A proper critique should focus on both positive and negative aspects of the student's performance.

8. The process of gathering measurable information to meet evaluation needs of a student is known as what?

A. Critique.

B. Assessment.

C. Appraisal.

Answer (B) is correct. *(FAA-H-8083-9A Chap 5)*
DISCUSSION: Assessment is the process of gathering measurable information to meet evaluation needs.
Answer (A) is incorrect. The critique is an instructor-to-student assessment used in conjunction with either a traditional or an authentic assessment. Answer (C) is incorrect. While an assessment includes a combination of the ability to analyze, appraise, and judge student performance, appraisal is not as all-encompassing a term as an assessment.

6.2 Types of Assessment

9. FAA Practical Test Standards are

A. criterion-referenced.

B. diagnostic-assessed.

C. formative-assessed.

Answer (A) is correct. *(FAA-H-8083-9A Chap 5)*
DISCUSSION: Practical tests for maintenance technicians and pilots are criterion-referenced tests because the objective is for all successful applicants to meet the high standards of knowledge, skill, and safety required by one core standards document (the PTS) rather than other applicants seeking certification.
Answer (B) is incorrect. Diagnostic assessments are used to assess student knowledge or skills prior to a course of instruction. Answer (C) is incorrect. Formative assessments, which are not graded, are used as a wrap-up of the lesson and to set the stage for the next lesson. This type of assessment, which is limited to what transpired during that lesson, informs and guides the instructor on which areas to reinforce.

10. Practical tests for pilot certification are

A. evaluation-referenced.

B. selection type tests.

C. criterion-referenced.

Answer (C) is correct. *(FAA-H-8083-9A Chap 5)*
DISCUSSION: Criterion-referenced tests measure an applicant's performance against carefully written, measurable standards or criteria. Practical tests for pilot certification are criterion-referenced. The PTS are the criteria.
Answer (A) is incorrect. Practical tests are a form of evaluation, not evaluation-referenced. Evaluation-referenced is not a type of testing. Answer (B) is incorrect. Selection type tests require the student to select an answer from two or more alternatives.

11. The Practical Test Standards should be used in

A. flight training and testing.

B. flight training only.

C. testing only.

Answer (A) is correct. *(FAA-H-8083-9A Chap 5)*
DISCUSSION: Because the Practical Test Standards (PTS) documents are the primary evaluation tool of the FAA for the issuance of a pilot certificate, they obviously are testing documents. Because this information is publicly accessible, these documents absolutely should be used to train pilot applicants to ensure they meet the PTS requirements. This training should not be merely to "teach the test," but the PTS is a very valuable resource in evaluating a pilot applicant's eligibility to take the practical test.
Answer (B) is incorrect. The PTS documents are the primary evaluation tool of the FAA for the issuance of a pilot certificate; therefore, they are to be used as testing documents in addition to their use as flight training skill standards. Answer (C) is incorrect. While the PTS documents are the primary evaluation tool of the FAA for the issuance of a pilot certificate, they are also a very valuable resource in evaluating a pilot applicant's eligibility to take the practical test.

12. To evaluate a student's ability to use critical thinking skills in performing real-world tasks, which assessment method is most appropriate?

A. Authentic.

B. Supply-type.

C. Collaborative.

Answer (A) is correct. *(FAA-H-8083-9A Chap 5)*

DISCUSSION: Authentic assessment is a type of assessment in which the student is asked to perform real-world tasks and demonstrate a meaningful application of skills and competencies. Authentic assessment lies at the heart of training today's aviation students to use critical thinking skills.

Answer (B) is incorrect. A supply-type test can be very helpful, for example, on a pre-solo knowledge test in determining whether the pilot in training has adequate knowledge of procedures, but it would not offer insight into a student's critical thinking skills in performing real-world tasks. Answer (C) is incorrect. Collaborative assessment is a component of authentic assessment, but it is not the same thing.

13. The objective of the Airman Certification Standards (ACS) is to ensure the certification of pilots at a high level of performance and proficiency, consistent with

A. the time available.

B. safety.

C. their abilities.

Answer (B) is correct. *(FAA-H-8083-9A Chap 5)*

DISCUSSION: The objective of the ACS is to ensure the certification of pilots at a high level of performance and proficiency, consistent with safety.

Answer (A) is incorrect. The objective of the ACS is to ensure the certification of pilots at a high level of performance and proficiency, consistent with safety, not the time available. Answer (C) is incorrect. The objective of the ACS is to ensure the certification of pilots at a high level of performance and proficiency, consistent with safety, not their abilities.

14. Instructors must be aware of the fact that

A. FAA Practical Test Standards (PTS) books are testing documents only.

B. FAA Practical Test Standards (PTS) books should be introduced early in training and used as a measuring stick for student performance and progress.

C. FAA Practical Test Standards (PTS) books should be introduced 6 hours prior to the practical test.

Answer (A) is correct. *(FAA-H-8083-9A Chap 7)*

DISCUSSION: The PTS is a testing tool, not a teaching tool. The overall focus of flight training should be on education, learning, and understanding why the standards are there and how they were set. The minimum standards to pass the checkride should not be introduced until the 3 hours of preparation for the checkride. To accommodate this, the FAA requires 3 hours of training in the 60 days preceding the Practical Test.

Answer (B) is incorrect. The PTS should only be introduced in the last 3 hours of flight training prior to the checkride. Answer (C) is incorrect. The PTS should be introduced 3 hours, not 6 hours, prior to the checkride.

15. The FAA Practical Test Standards

A. should be used as a primary training tool.

B. contain tasks in addition to those presented in 14 CFR Part 61.

C. contain testing standards only.

Answer (B) is correct. *(FAA-H-8083-9A Chap 5)*

DISCUSSION: The PTS Areas of Operation for each pilot certificate and rating are listed in 14 CFR Part 61. The PTS documents list specific tasks that must be performed for each Area of Operation during an FAA Practical Test for a given certificate or rating.

Answer (A) is incorrect. Instructors should avoid merely teaching from the PTS as this encourages student pilots to aim for the minimum passing standard. While the PTS should obviously be a measuring standard, it should not be the primary teaching tool for a course of training. Instead, CFIs should use a training syllabus appropriate to the training that addresses the PTS tasks in a logical, productive way. Answer (C) is incorrect. In addition to testing standards, the PTS documents also contain important information on the conduct of the test, special emphasis items, pilot/instructor/examiner considerations, and test checklists.

16. When should an instructor introduce a student to the Practical Test Standards (PTS)?

A. Not before 6 hours prior to the practical test.

B. Not before 9 hours prior to the practical test.

C. Not before 3 hours prior to the practical test.

Answer (C) is correct. *(FAA-H-8083-9A Chap 8)*

DISCUSSION: The PTS are not a teaching tool. They are a testing tool. The overall focus of flight training should be on education, learning, and understanding why the standards are there and how they were set. The minimum standards to pass the practical test should not be introduced until the 3 hours of preparation for the practical test. To accommodate this, the FAA requires 3 hours of training in the 60 days preceding the practical test.

Answer (A) is incorrect. The PTS should be introduced 3 hours, not 6 hours, prior to the practical test. Answer (B) is incorrect. The PTS should be introduced 3 hours, not 9 hours, prior to the practical test.

17. A pretest constructed to measure knowledge and skills necessary to begin a course is referred to as a

A. virtual-reality test.

B. evaluation-referenced.

C. criterion-referenced test.

Answer (C) is correct. *(FAA-H-8083-9A Chap 5)*

DISCUSSION: A pretest is a criterion-referenced test constructed to measure the knowledge and skills that are necessary to begin a course. Criterion-referenced tests measure a student's performance against carefully written, measurable standards or criteria.

Answer (A) is incorrect. Virtual reality is a potential future method of computer-based training (CBT) that can simulate environments very realistically. It is not a type of test. Answer (B) is incorrect. Practical tests are a form of evaluation, not evaluation-referenced. Evaluation-referenced is not a type of testing.

18. Criterion-based assessment items would most likely be part of

A. performance-based tests.

B. multiple choice tests.

C. oral quizzing.

Answer (A) is correct. *(FAA-H-8083-9A Chap 5)*

DISCUSSION: Criterion-based tests are performance-based tests. In addition to the behavior expected, criterion objectives state the conditions under which the behavior is to be performed and the criteria that must be met. If the instructor developed performance-based objectives during the creation of lesson plans, criterion objectives have already been formulated. The criterion objective provides the framework for developing the test items used to measure the level of learning objectives.

Answer (B) is incorrect. Criterion-based assessments are performance-based tests that may be administered through multiple formats. Answer (C) is incorrect. Criterion-based assessments are performance-based tests that may be administered through multiple formats.

19. Performance-based objectives are a distinguishable characteristic of

A. formative assessments.

B. subjective grading.

C. criterion-referenced testing.

Answer (C) is correct. *(FAA-H-8083-9A Chap 5)*

DISCUSSION: Performance-based objectives serve as a reference for the development of test items in criterion-referenced testing. Criterion-referenced tests evaluate based on carefully written, measurable standards or criteria.

Answer (A) is incorrect. Formative assessments, which are not graded, are used as a wrap-up of the lesson and to set the stage for the next lesson. This type of assessment, which is limited to what transpired during that lesson, informs and guides the instructor on which areas to reinforce. Answer (B) is incorrect. Performance-based objectives provide carefully written, measurable standards or criteria for testing. They do not allow for subjective grading.

20. What is true of traditional assessments?

A. They require the student to demonstrate meaningful application of skills.

B. They evaluate a student's progress at a rote level of learning.

C. There are multiple correct responses in traditional assessments.

Answer (B) is correct. *(FAA-H-8083-9A Chap 5)*

DISCUSSION: Traditional assessments often involve written tests and are more likely to be used to evaluate a student's progress at the rote level of learning.

Answer (A) is incorrect. Authentic assessment, not traditional assessment, requires the student to demonstrate meaningful application of skills and competencies. Answer (C) is incorrect. In a traditional assessment, only one single answer will be correct.

21. Which of the following assessment types focuses on real-world tasks?

A. Traditional.

B. Formal.

C. Authentic.

Answer (C) is correct. *(FAA-H-8083-9A Chap 5)*

DISCUSSION: Authentic assessment requires the student to demonstrate not just the rote and understanding levels, but also the application and correlation levels of learning. Authentic assessment generally requires the student to perform real-world tasks.

Answer (A) is incorrect. During traditional assessment, the student usually has a set amount of time to recognize or reproduce memorized terms, formulas, or data. There is a single answer that is correct. Consequently, the traditional assessment is more likely to be used to judge or evaluate the student's progress at the rote and understanding levels of learning. Answer (B) is incorrect. Whether traditional or authentic, an assessment can be either formal or informal. Formal assessments usually involve documentation, such as a quiz or written examination. They are used periodically throughout a course, as well as at the end of a course, to measure and document whether or not the course objectives have been met.

22. Which type of assessment is more beneficial during the early stages of training?

A. Collaborative assessments.

B. Traditional assessments.

C. Authentic assessments.

Answer (B) is correct. *(FAA-H-8083-9A Chap 5)*

DISCUSSION: Traditional assessments are generally more useful in the early phases of training, as the student may not have enough information or knowledge about the concepts to participate fully.

Answer (A) is incorrect. A collaborative assessment, an aspect assessment, is a form of student-centered grading that uses open-ended questions to guide the student through a self-assessment. Answer (C) is incorrect. Authentic assessments may not be as useful as traditional assessment in the early phases of training, as the student may not have enough information or knowledge about the concepts to participate fully.

23. What are the four steps in the collaborative assessment process?

A. Replay, reconstruct, redesign, redirect.

B. Replay, reconstruct, reflect, redirect.

C. Replay, repeat, reflect, redirect.

Answer (B) is correct. *(FAA-H-8083-9A Chap 5)*

DISCUSSION: The four steps in the collaborative assessment process are replay, reconstruct, reflect, redirect.

Answer (A) is incorrect. Redesign is not a step in the collaborative assessment process. The four steps in the collaborative assessment process are replay, reconstruct, reflect, redirect. Answer (C) is incorrect. Repeat is not a step in the collaborative assessment process and is the same as replay. The four steps in the collaborative assessment process are replay, reconstruct, reflect, redirect.

24. What step in the collaborative assessment process helps the student relate the lessons learned to other experiences?

A. Redirect.

B. Replay.

C. Reconstruct.

Answer (A) is correct. *(FAA-H-8083-9A Chap 5)*

DISCUSSION: The last step, that of redirecting, helps the student relate the lessons learned to other experiences and consider how they might help in future sessions.

Answer (B) is incorrect. Replay occurs when a student is asked to verbally replay or repeat the flight or procedure. Answer (C) is incorrect. Reconstruction occurs when the student identifies key things that (s)he should or could have done differently during the flight or maneuver.

25. What grading dimension or level has a student reached when they correctly gather information, identify proper courses of action, evaluate risk, and make an appropriate decision without instructor input?

A. Explain.

B. Practice.

C. Manage-Decide.

Answer (C) is correct. *(FAA-H-8083-9A Chap 5)*

DISCUSSION: A student who correctly gathers information, identifies proper courses of action, evaluates risks for each course of action, and makes the appropriate decision without instructor input is at the “Manage-Decide” grading dimension of Single-Pilot Management.

Answer (A) is incorrect. The grading dimension “Explain” describes when a student can verbally identify, describe, and understand risks but needs to be prompted to make decisions. Answer (B) is incorrect. The grading dimension “Practice” describes a student who properly identifies, understands, and applies SRM principles and corrects minor deviations identified by the instructor.

6.3 Critiques and Oral Assessments

26. Which is a valid reason for the use of proper oral quizzing during a lesson?

A. Promotes active student participation.

B. Identifies points that need less emphasis.

C. Helps the instructor determine the general intelligence level of the students.

Answer (A) is correct. *(FAA-H-8083-9A Chap 5)*

DISCUSSION: A valid reason for the use of proper oral quizzing during a lesson is to promote active student participation, which is important to effective teaching.

Answer (B) is incorrect. A valid reason for the use of proper oral quizzing during a lesson is that it identifies points that need more, not less, emphasis. Answer (C) is incorrect. A valid reason for the use of proper oral quizzing during a lesson is to check the students’ comprehension of what has been learned, not their general intelligence level.

27. Proper oral quizzing by the instructor during a lesson can have which result?

A. Alerts the instructor to the level of student motivation.

B. Identifies points which need more emphasis.

C. Can serve as a lead-in to introduce new material.

Answer (B) is correct. *(FAA-H-8083-9A Chap 5)*

DISCUSSION: One desirable result of oral quizzing is that it helps the instructor identify points that need more emphasis. By noting students’ answers, the instructor can quickly spot weak points in understanding and give these extra attention.

Answer (A) is incorrect. Student performance on oral quizzes can indicate weak points in understanding but will not help the instructor gauge student motivation. Answer (C) is incorrect. The introduction of new material is accomplished during the presentation, not evaluation, step of the teaching process.

28. One desirable result of proper oral quizzing by the instructor is to

A. reveal the effectiveness of the instructor's training procedures.

B. fulfill the requirements set forth in the overall objectives of the course.

C. reveal the essential information from which the student can determine progress.

Answer (A) is correct. *(FAA-H-8083-9A Chap 5)*

DISCUSSION: One desirable result of proper oral quizzing by the instructor is that it reveals the effectiveness of the instructor's training procedures.

Answer (B) is incorrect. Quizzing can only measure achievement, not fulfill the requirements, of the overall objectives of the course. Answer (C) is incorrect. An instructor should use the critique, not a quiz, to reveal the essential information from which the student can determine progress.

29. During oral quizzing, which type of questions should an instructor expect a student to answer based on memory or recall?

A. Trick questions.

B. Fact questions.

C. HOTS (higher order thinking skills) questions.

Answer (B) is correct. *(FAA-H-8083-9A Chap 5)*

DISCUSSION: The most common means of assessment is direct or indirect oral questioning of students by the instructor. Questions may be loosely classified as fact questions and HOTS questions. The answer to a fact question is based on memory or recall. This type of question usually concerns who, what, when, and where. HOTS questions involve why or how, and they require the student to combine knowledge of facts with an ability to analyze situations, solve problems, and arrive at conclusions.

Answer (A) is incorrect. Trick questions should be avoided because they are a detriment to the learning process, but they can exist as either fact questions or HOTS questions. Answer (C) is incorrect. A HOTS question involves why or how, and it requires the student to combine knowledge of facts with an ability to analyze situations, solve problems, and arrive at conclusions.

30. To be effective in oral quizzing during the conduct of a lesson, a question should

A. be of suitable difficulty for that stage of training.

B. include a combination of where, how, and why.

C. divert the student's thoughts to subjects covered in other lessons.

Answer (A) is correct. *(FAA-H-8083-9A Chap 5)*

DISCUSSION: During oral quizzing, an effective question must present a challenge to the student. A question must be of suitable difficulty for the student at that particular stage of training. These types of questions stimulate learning.

Answer (B) is incorrect. An effective question should be limited to who, what, when, where, how, or why, not a combination. Answer (C) is incorrect. An effective question must apply to the subject of instruction, not divert the student's thoughts to subjects covered in other lessons.

31. During oral quizzing in a given lesson, effective questions should

A. be brief and concise.

B. provide answers that can be expressed in a variety of ways.

C. divert the student's thoughts to subjects covered in previous lessons.

Answer (A) is correct. *(FAA-H-8083-9A Chap 5)*

DISCUSSION: During oral quizzing, an effective question should be brief and concise but should also be clear and definite. Enough words must be used to establish the conditions or situations exactly so that instructor and students will have the same mental picture.

Answer (B) is incorrect. All effective questions will have only one correct answer. Answer (C) is incorrect. An effective question must apply to the subject of instruction, not divert the student's thoughts to subjects covered in previous lessons.

32. In all quizzing as a portion of the instruction process, the questions should

A. include catch questions to develop the student's perceptive power.

B. call for specific answers and be readily evaluated by the instructor.

C. include questions with more than one central idea to evaluate how completely a student understands the subject.

Answer (B) is correct. *(FAA-H-8083-9A Chap 5)*

DISCUSSION: In any kind of testing, questions should have one specific answer so that the instructor can readily evaluate the student's response. General questions tend to confuse rather than help, and unanswered questions serve no useful purpose at all.

Answer (A) is incorrect. Catch questions should be avoided at all times. The students will feel they are engaged in a battle of wits with the instructor, and the whole significance of the subject of instruction will be lost. Answer (C) is incorrect. Effective questions used in quizzing should center on only one central idea.

33. To answer a student's question, it is most important that the instructor

A. clearly understand the question.

B. have complete knowledge of the subject.

C. introduce more complicated information to partially answer the question, if necessary.

Answer (A) is correct. *(FAA-H-8083-9A Chap 5)*

DISCUSSION: The answering of students' questions can be an effective teaching method. To answer a student's question, it is most important that the instructor clearly understands the question.

Answer (B) is incorrect. While an instructor may have knowledge of a subject, occasionally a student will ask a question the instructor cannot answer. The instructor should admit not knowing the answer and should promise to get the answer or help the student to find it. Answer (C) is incorrect. Introducing more complicated information to partially answer the question is normally unwise. Doing so would confuse the student and complicate the learning task at hand.

34. With regards to oral quizzing, which type of question requires the student to combine knowledge with the ability to analyze, solve problems, and arrive at conclusions?

A. Fact questions.

B. HOTS questions.

C. Provocative questions.

Answer (B) is correct. *(FAA-H-8083-9A Chap 5)*

DISCUSSION: HOTS, or higher order thinking skills, questions usually involve why or how and require the student to combine knowledge of facts with the ability to analyze situations, solve problems, and arrive at conclusions.

Answer (A) is incorrect. Fact questions involve answers that are based on memory or recall. This type of question usually concerns who, what, when, and where. Answer (C) is incorrect. Provocative, or controversial, questions are a type that should be avoided in oral quizzing.

35. For oral quizzing to be effective during a lesson, a question should

A. be limited to who, what, when, where, why, or how, not a combination.

B. include a combination of where, how, and why.

C. be easy for the student at that particular stage of training.

Answer (A) is correct. *(FAA-H-8083-9A Chap 5)*

DISCUSSION: To be effective in oral quizzing, each question should center on only one idea, which is limited to who, what, where, when, how, or why, not a combination.

Answer (B) is incorrect. A single question should be limited to who, what, when, where, how, or why, not a combination. Answer (C) is incorrect. Questions of suitable difficulty serve to stimulate learning. To be effective, questions must be adapted to the ability, experience, and stage of training of the students and be of suitable difficulty.

36. When an instructor critiques a student, it should always be

A. done in private.

B. subjective rather than objective.

C. conducted immediately after the student's performance.

Answer (C) is correct. *(FAA-H-8083-9A Chap 5)*

DISCUSSION: The critique should always be conducted immediately after the student's performance while the performance is still fresh in the student's mind. Specific comments on "your third turn," for instance, would have little value a week after the maneuver was performed.

Answer (A) is incorrect. A critique may be conducted in private or before the entire class. A critique presented before the entire class can be beneficial to every student in the classroom as well as to the student who performed the exercise. Answer (B) is incorrect. The critique should be objective rather than subjective.

37. Using double negatives is an example of which type of question that should be avoided?

A. Irrelevant questions.

B. Oversize questions.

C. Trick questions.

Answer (C) is correct. *(FAA-H-8083-9A Chap 5)*

DISCUSSION: Trick questions, such as double negatives, cause a student to feel (s)he is engaged in a battle of wits with the instructor, thus changing student focus from the message to the messenger.

Answer (A) is incorrect. Irrelevant questions are diversions that introduce unrelated facts and thoughts and slow student progress. Answer (B) is incorrect. Oversize questions are too broad in scope and could have multiple correct/incorrect responses. An example might be: "What is required before going flying?"

38. Which of the following is not a type of critique?

A. Written critique.

B. Instructor-absence critique.

C. Individual student critique by another student.

Answer (B) is correct. *(FAA-H-8083-9A Chap 5)*

DISCUSSION: Instructor-absence is not a type of critique. During all types of critiques, the instructor should be present to carefully control the process.

Answer (A) is incorrect. The written critique is a type of critique. Answer (C) is incorrect. Individual student critique by another student is a type of critique.

39. What is a benefit of a written critique?

A. The student will have a permanent record of suggestions.

B. Students get to work together, thus sharing ideas.

C. The written critique is always positive.

Answer (A) is correct. *(FAA-H-8083-9A Chap 5)*
DISCUSSION: Students will have a permanent record of suggestions, recommendations, and opinions to reference at a later date if needed.
Answer (B) is incorrect. The sharing of ideas is a characteristic of the small group critique, not the written critique. Answer (C) is incorrect. All critiques, no matter what the format, can include both positive and negative comments.

40. What is true of irrelevant questions?

A. They are too broad in scope and could have multiple correct responses.

B. They change the student's focus from the message to the messenger.

C. They introduce unrelated facts and slow student progress.

Answer (C) is correct. *(FAA-H-8083-9A Chap 5)*
DISCUSSION: Irrelevant questions are diversions that introduce unrelated facts and thoughts and slow student progress.
Answer (A) is incorrect. Oversize questions, not irrelevant questions, are too broad in scope and could have multiple correct/incorrect responses. Answer (B) is incorrect. Trick questions are questions that cause the student to feel (s)he is engaged in a battle of wits with the instructor, thus changing student focus from the message to the messenger.

41. An instructor's critique of a student's performance should be

A. as varied in content as the performance being evaluated.

B. an opportunity for an instructor to be critical of a student's performance.

C. always conducted in private.

Answer (A) is correct. *(FAA-H-8083-9A Chap 5)*
DISCUSSION: An effective critique considers good as well as bad performance, the individual parts, relationships of the individual parts, and the overall performance. A critique can and usually should be as varied in content as the performance being evaluated.
Answer (B) is incorrect. The word "critique" sometimes has a negative connotation, and the instructor needs to avoid using this method as an opportunity to be overly critical of student performance. Answer (C) is incorrect. A critique may be conducted privately or before the entire class. A critique presented before the entire class can be beneficial to every student in the classroom, as well as to the student who performed the exercise or assignment. In this case, however, the instructor should avoid embarrassing the student in front of the class.

42. The purpose of a critique is to

A. identify only the student's faults and weaknesses.

B. give a delayed evaluation of the student's performance.

C. provide direction and guidance to raise the level of the student's performance.

Answer (C) is correct. *(FAA-H-8083-9A Chap 5)*
DISCUSSION: A critique provides the student with constructive feedback (s)he can build upon. It should provide direction and guidance to raise the student's level of performance.
Answer (A) is incorrect. An effective critique considers good as well as bad performance. It is not necessarily negative in content. Answer (B) is incorrect. A critique is not the same thing as an evaluation, as it does not determine a student's progress in a course. Even as part of an evaluation, a critique (guidance) should not be delayed.

6.4 Types of Written Test Questions

43. What is a characteristic of supply-type test items?

A. They are easily adapted to testing knowledge of facts and details.

B. Test results would be graded the same regardless of the student or the grader.

C. The same test graded by different instructors would probably be given different scores.

Answer (C) is correct. *(FAA-H-8083-9A Chap 5)*
DISCUSSION: A characteristic of supply-type test items is that they cannot be graded with uniformity. The same test graded by different instructors would probably be assigned different scores. The same test graded by the same instructor on consecutive days might be assigned two different scores. There is no assurance that the grade assigned is the grade deserved.
Answer (A) is incorrect. True/false, not supply-type, test items are easily adapted to testing knowledge of facts and details. Answer (B) is incorrect. Selection-type, not supply-type, test items would be graded the same regardless of the student or the grader.

44. Which is the main disadvantage of supply-type test items?

A. They cannot be graded with uniformity.

B. They are readily answered by guessing.

C. They are easily adapted to statistical analysis.

Answer (A) is correct. *(FAA-H-8083-9A Chap 5)*

DISCUSSION: The main disadvantage of supply-type test items is that they cannot be graded with uniformity. The same test graded by different instructors would probably be assigned different scores. The same test graded by the same instructor on consecutive days might be assigned two different scores. There is no assurance that the grade assigned is the grade deserved.

Answer (B) is incorrect. The main disadvantage of true/false, not supply-type, test items is they are readily answered by guessing. Answer (C) is incorrect. An advantage, not disadvantage, of selection-type, not supply-type, test items is that they are easily adapted to statistical analysis.

45. The primary advantage of supply-type testing is that

A. it can be graded quickly.

B. the learner is required to organize knowledge.

C. it can be graded with an answer key.

Answer (B) is correct. *(FAA-H-8083-9A Appendix B)*

DISCUSSION: Supply-type test items require the learner to furnish a response in the form of a word, sentence, or paragraph. The supply-type item requires the learner to organize knowledge. It demands an ability to express ideas and is thus valuable in measuring the learner's generalized understanding of a subject. For example, the supply-type item on a pre-solo knowledge test can be very helpful in determining whether the pilot in training has adequate knowledge of procedures.

Answer (A) is incorrect. Supply-type tests require more time for the learner to complete and more time for the instructor to grade. Answer (C) is incorrect. Supply-type tests cannot be effectively graded with an answer key. The same test graded by different instructors could be assigned different scores. Even the same test graded by the same instructor on consecutive days might be assigned altogether different scores.

46. One of the main advantages of selection-type test items over supply-type test items is that the selection-type

A. decreases discrimination between responses.

B. would be graded objectively regardless of the student or the grader.

C. precludes comparison of students under one instructor with those under another instructor.

Answer (B) is correct. *(FAA-H-8083-9A Chap 5)*

DISCUSSION: One of the main advantages of selection-type test items over supply-type test items is that the selection-type are graded objectively regardless of the student or grader.

Answer (A) is incorrect. An advantage of the selection-type test item over the supply-type test item is that more areas of knowledge can be tested in a given time, thus increasing, not decreasing, comprehensiveness, validity, and discrimination. Answer (C) is incorrect. An advantage of the selection-type test item over supply-type test item is the ability to compare, not to preclude comparison of, student performance under one instructor with those of another instructor.

47. Which statement is true about multiple-choice test items that are intended to measure achievement at a higher level of learning?

A. It is unethical to mislead students into selecting an incorrect alternative.

B. Some or all of the alternatives should be acceptable, but only one should be clearly better than the others.

C. The use of common errors as distracting alternatives to divert the student from the correct response is ineffective and invalid.

Answer (B) is correct. *(FAA-H-8083-9A Chap 5)*

DISCUSSION: When multiple-choice test items are intended to measure achievement at a higher level of learning, some or all of the alternatives should be acceptable, but only one should be clearly better than the others. The instructions given should direct the student to select the best alternative.

Answer (A) is incorrect. When using multiple-choice test items, the students are not supposed to guess the correct answer; they should select it only if they know it is correct. Thus, it is ethical, not unethical, to mislead students into selecting an incorrect alternative. Answer (C) is incorrect. When using multiple-choice test items, the use of common errors as distracting alternatives to divert the student from the correct response is effective, not ineffective, and valid, not invalid.

48. Which statement is true relative to effective multiple-choice test items?

A. Negative words or phrases need not be emphasized.

B. Items should call for abstract background knowledge.

C. Keep all alternatives of approximately equal length.

Answer (C) is correct. *(FAA-H-8083-9A Chap 5)*

DISCUSSION: In preparing and reviewing the alternatives to a multiple-choice item, it is advisable to keep all alternatives approximately the same length. Research of instructor-made tests reveals that, in general, correct alternatives are longer than incorrect ones.

Answer (A) is incorrect. When negative words or phrases are used, they should be emphasized in order to be effective. Answer (B) is incorrect. Items should call for essential knowledge rather than for abstract background knowledge or unimportant facts.

49. Which type of test item creates the greatest probability of guessing?

A. True/false.

B. Supply-type.

C. Multiple-choice.

Answer (A) is correct. *(FAA-H-8083-9A Chap 5)*

DISCUSSION: The true/false test item creates the greatest probability of guessing because the student always has a 50% chance of guessing correctly.

Answer (B) is incorrect. The true/false, not the supply-type, test item creates the greatest probability of guessing. Answer (C) is incorrect. The true/false, not the multiple-choice, test item creates the greatest probability of guessing.

50. Which is one of the major difficulties encountered in the construction of multiple-choice test items?

A. Adapting the items to statistical item analysis.

B. Keeping all responses approximately equal in length.

C. Inventing distractors which will be attractive to students lacking knowledge or understanding.

Answer (C) is correct. *(FAA-H-8083-9A Chap 5)*

DISCUSSION: Three major difficulties are encountered in the construction of multiple-choice test items:

1. Development of a question or an item stem that can be expressed clearly without ambiguity.
2. Statement of an answer that cannot be refuted.
3. The invention of lures or distractors attractive to those students who do not possess the knowledge or understanding necessary to recognize the correct answer.

Answer (A) is incorrect. It is a major advantage, not difficulty, for a multiple-choice test item to be well adapted to statistical item analysis. Answer (B) is incorrect. A principle, not difficulty, of constructing a multiple-choice test item is to keep all responses approximately equal in length.

51. In a written test, which type of selection-type test items reduces the probability of guessing correct responses?

A. Essay.

B. Matching.

C. Multiple-choice.

Answer (B) is correct. *(FAA-H-8083-9A Chap 5)*

DISCUSSION: In a written test, matching test items reduces the probability of guessing correct responses compared to a series of multiple-choice items covering the same material, especially if alternatives are used more than once.

Answer (A) is incorrect. An essay question is a supply-type, not selection-type, test item. Answer (C) is incorrect. Matching, not multiple-choice, test items reduce the probability of guessing correct responses.

52. Which part of a multiple-choice test includes the question, statement, or problem?

A. The response.

B. The root.

C. The stem.

Answer (C) is correct. *(FAA-H-8083-9A Chap 5)*

DISCUSSION: The stem includes the question, statement, or problem.

Answer (A) is incorrect. The responses in a multiple-choice test are the combination of both the distractors and the one correct answer. Answer (B) is incorrect. The stem, not the root, of a question includes the question, statement, or problem.

6.5 Characteristics of a Good Test

53. A written test that has reliability

A. yields consistent results.

B. measures small differences in the achievement of students.

C. actually measures what it is supposed to measure and nothing else.

Answer (A) is correct. *(FAA-H-8083-9A Chap 5)*

DISCUSSION: A written test that has reliability is one that yields consistent results.

Answer (B) is incorrect. A written test that shows discrimination, not reliability, measures small differences in the achievement of students. Answer (C) is incorrect. A written test that has validity, not reliability, actually measures what it is supposed to measure and nothing else.

54. A written test has validity when it

A. yields consistent results.

B. samples liberally whatever is being measured.

C. measures what it is supposed to measure.

Answer (C) is correct. *(FAA-H-8083-9A Chap 5)*

DISCUSSION: A written test has validity when it measures what it is supposed to measure.

Answer (A) is incorrect. A written test has reliability, not validity, when it yields consistent results. Answer (B) is incorrect. A written test has comprehensiveness, not validity, when it samples liberally whatever is being measured.

55. Comprehensiveness is the degree to which a test

A. measures the overall objectives.

B. consists of an appropriate mix of easy, medium, and difficult questions.

C. includes multiple-choice, essay, and true/false questions.

Answer (A) is correct. *(FAA-H-8083-9A Chap 5)*

DISCUSSION: Comprehensiveness is the degree to which a test measures the overall objectives. A written test must sample an appropriate cross-section of the objectives of instruction. The instructor has to make certain the evaluation includes a representative and comprehensive sampling of the objectives of the course.

Answer (B) is incorrect. Determining an "appropriate" mix of the difficulty level of questions is not necessary for a test to be comprehensive. Answer (C) is incorrect. The degree to which a test measures the overall objectives is not determined by the question type, but instead by the question content.

56. A written test is said to be comprehensive when it

A. includes all levels of difficulty.

B. samples liberally whatever is being measured.

C. measures knowledge of the same topic in many different ways.

Answer (B) is correct. *(FAA-H-8083-9A Chap 5)*

DISCUSSION: A written test is said to be comprehensive when it samples liberally whatever is being measured.

Answer (A) is incorrect. A written test shows discrimination, not comprehensiveness, when it includes all levels of difficulty. Answer (C) is incorrect. A written test shows discrimination, not comprehensiveness, when it measures knowledge of the same topic in many different ways.

57. The characteristic of a written test, which measures small differences in achievement between students, is its

A. validity.

B. reliability.

C. discrimination.

Answer (C) is correct. *(FAA-H-8083-9A Chap 5)*

DISCUSSION: The characteristic of a written test that measures small differences in achievement between students is its discrimination.

Answer (A) is incorrect. A written test has validity when it measures what it is supposed to and nothing else, not when it measures small differences in achievement between students. Answer (B) is incorrect. A written test that has reliability is one that yields consistent results, not which measures small differences in achievement between students.

58. A written test having the characteristic of discrimination will

A. be easy to give and be easily graded.

B. distinguish between students both low and high in achievement.

C. include a representative and comprehensive sampling of the course objectives.

Answer (B) is correct. *(FAA-H-8083-9A Chap 5)*

DISCUSSION: When a written test has the characteristic of discrimination, each item will distinguish between students who are low and students who are high in achievement of the course objectives.

Answer (A) is incorrect. A written test having the characteristic of usability, not discrimination, will be easy to give and be easily graded. Answer (C) is incorrect. A written test having the characteristic of comprehensiveness, not discrimination, will include a representative and comprehensive sampling of the course objectives.

59. A written test that is objective

A. distinguishes the differences between students.

B. measures what is supposed to be measured.

C. describes the singleness of scoring a test.

Answer (C) is correct. *(FAA-H-8083-9A Chap 5)*

DISCUSSION: Objectivity describes singleness of scoring a test.

Answer (A) is incorrect. Discrimination, not objectivity, distinguishes the differences between students. Answer (B) is incorrect. Validity, not objectivity, measures what is supposed to be measured.

60. The most important consideration in test evaluation is what?

A. Usability.

B. Validity.

C. Comprehensiveness.

Answer (B) is correct. *(FAA-H-8083-9A Chap 5)*

DISCUSSION: Validity is the most important consideration in test evaluation.

Answer (A) is incorrect. Validity, not usability, is the most important consideration in test evaluation. Answer (C) is incorrect. Validity, not comprehensiveness, is the most important consideration in test evaluation.

6.6 Review and Evaluation

61. Evaluation of student performance and accomplishment during a lesson should be based on

A. objectives and goals established in the lesson plan.

B. performance of each student compared to an objective standard.

C. each student's ability to make an objective evaluation of their own progress.

Answer (A) is correct. *(FAA-H-8083-9A Chap 4)*

DISCUSSION: The evaluation of student performance and accomplishment during a lesson should be based on the objectives and goals that were established in the instructor's lesson plan.

Answer (B) is incorrect. A critique, not an evaluation, is based on comparing a student's performance to an objective standard. Answer (C) is incorrect. A student's own evaluation can only be subjective, not objective. Only the instructor can provide a realistic evaluation of performance and progress.

62. Which statement is true regarding student evaluation?

A. The student's own evaluations can only be objective.

B. Evaluation of the student's learning should be an integral part of each lesson.

C. If deficiencies or faults not associated with the present lesson are revealed, they should be corrected immediately.

Answer (B) is correct. *(FAA-H-8083-9A Chap 4)*

DISCUSSION: Review and evaluation should be an integral part of each classroom or flight lesson. At the end of each class period, the instructor should review what has been covered during the lesson and require the students to demonstrate the extent to which the lesson objectives have been met. Evaluation can be formal (performance, written tests) or informal (oral quiz or guided discussion).

Answer (A) is incorrect. The student's own evaluations can only be subjective, not objective. Answer (C) is incorrect. If deficiencies or faults not associated with the present lesson are revealed, they should be noted and pointed out. Corrective measures that are practicable at the time should be taken immediately, but more thorough remedial actions must be included in future lesson plans.

63. Which type test is desirable for evaluating training that involves an operation, procedure, or process?

A. Oral.

B. Performance.

C. Proficiency.

Answer (B) is correct. *(FAA-H-8083-9A Chap 5)*

DISCUSSION: Performance testing is desirable for evaluating training that involves an operation, procedure, or process. This method of evaluation is particularly suited to the measurement of a student's ability in performing a task, either mental or physical.

Answer (A) is incorrect. Performance, not oral, testing is desirable for evaluating training that involves an operation, procedure, or process. Answer (C) is incorrect. There is no proficiency-type test in evaluation, only oral, written, or performance.

64. When a student performs a maneuver correctly but the instructor suspects the student does not fully understand the principles and objectives involved, the instructor should

A. defer on the matter to avoid lowering student confidence.

B. point out the suspected flaw to the student.

C. vary the performance of the maneuver slightly.

Answer (C) is correct. *(FAA-H-8083-9A Chap 8)*

DISCUSSION: Students may perform a procedure or maneuver correctly but not fully understand the principles and objectives involved. If the instructor suspects this, students should be required to vary the performance of the maneuver or procedure slightly. Students who do not understand the principles involved will probably not be able to successfully complete the revised maneuver or procedure.

Answer (A) is incorrect. While it is important to prevent student discouragement, it is more important to ensure that the student possesses the required level of skill in each phase of training. Rather than ignoring the situation, an instructor can require that the student repeat the maneuver in a slightly different way, thus evaluating the depth of the student's mastery of the maneuver. Answer (B) is incorrect. Rather than projecting negativity onto the student in a situation where the instructor could well be mistaken, it is best to have the student perform the maneuver in a slightly different way, thus evaluating the depth of the student's mastery of the maneuver.

APPENDIX A
FUNDAMENTALS OF INSTRUCTING PRACTICE TEST

The following 50 questions have been randomly selected from the fundamentals of instructing questions in our flight and ground instructor test bank. Topical coverage in this practice test is similar to that of the FAA pilot knowledge test. Use the correct answer listing on page 146 to grade your practice test.

1. To communicate effectively, instructors must

A — recognize the level of comprehension.
B — provide an atmosphere which encourages questioning.
C — reveal a positive attitude while delivering their message.

2. A communicator's words cannot communicate the desired meaning to another person unless the

A — words have meaningful referents.
B — words give the meaning that is in the mind of the receiver.
C — listener or reader has had some experience with the objects or concepts to which these words refer.

3. During integrated flight instruction, the instructor must be sure the student

A — develops the habit of looking for other traffic.
B — is able to control the aircraft for extended periods under IMC.
C — can depend on the flight instruments when maneuvering by outside references.

4. Which statement is true regarding lesson plans?

A — Lesson plans should not be directed toward the course objective; only to the lesson objective.
B — A well-thought-out mental outline of a lesson may be used any time as long as the instructor is well prepared.
C — Lesson plans help instructors keep a constant check on their own activity as well as that of their students.

5. (Refer to Figure 1 on page 115.) Section A is titled:

A — Overview.
B — Objective.
C — Introduction.

6. (Refer to Figure 1 on page 115.) Section C is titled:

A — Schedule.
B — Overview.
C — Training Schedule.

7. Which statement is true regarding true professionalism as an instructor?

A — Anything less than sincere performance destroys the effectiveness of the professional instructor.
B — To achieve professionalism, actions and decisions must be limited to standard patterns and practices.
C — A single definition of professionalism would encompass all of the qualifications and considerations which must be present.

8. Student confidence tends to be destroyed if instructors

A — bluff whenever in doubt about some point.
B — continually identify student errors and failures.
C — direct and control the student's actions and behavior.

9. Students quickly become apathetic when they

A — realize material is being withheld by the instructor.
B — understand the objectives toward which they are working.
C — recognize that the instructor is not adequately prepared.

10. In the learning process, fear or the element of threat will

A — narrow the student's perceptual field.
B — decrease the rate of associative reactions.
C — cause a student to focus on several areas of perception.

11. When under stress, normal individuals usually react

A — by showing excellent morale followed by deep depression.
B — by responding rapidly and exactly, often automatically, within the limits of their experience and training.
C — inappropriately such as extreme overcooperation, painstaking self-control, and inappropriate laughing or singing.

12. When students display the defense mechanism called repression, they

A — refuse to accept reality.
B — place uncomfortable thoughts into inaccessible areas of the unconscious mind.
C — attempt to justify actions by asking numerous questions.

13. When a student presents a belief opposite to what (s)he truly believes, it usually is an indication of the defense mechanism known as

A — fantasy.
B — reaction formation.
C — displacement.

14. Which of the student's human needs offer the greatest challenge to an instructor?

A — Physiological.
B — Psychological.
C — Self-Actualization.

15. What should an instructor do with a student who assumes that correction of errors is not important?

A — Divide complex flight maneuvers into elements.
B — Try to reduce the student's overconfidence to reduce the chance of an accident.
C — Raise the standard of performance for each lesson, demanding greater effort.

16. By using abstractions in the communication process, the communicator will

A — bring forth specific items of experience in the minds of the receivers.
B — be using words which refer to objects or ideas that human beings can experience directly.
C — not evoke in the listener's or reader's mind the specific items of experience the communicator intends.

17. To ensure proper habits and correct techniques during training, an instructor should

A — use the building block technique of instruction.
B — repeat subject matter the student has already learned.
C — introduce challenging material to continually motivate the student.

18. During the flight portion of a practical test, the examiner simulates complete loss of engine power by closing the throttle and announcing "simulated engine failure." What level of learning is being tested?

A — Application.
B — Correlation.
C — Understanding.

19. According to one theory, some forgetting is due to the unconscious practice of submerging an unpleasant experience into the subconscious. This is called

A — suppression.
B — immersion.
C — repression.

20. Responses that produce a pleasurable return are called

A — reward.
B — praise.
C — positive feedback.

21. A change in behavior as a result of experience can be defined as

A — learning.
B — knowledge.
C — understanding.

22. Individuals make more progress learning if they have a clear objective. This is one feature of the principle of

A — primacy.
B — readiness.
C — willingness.

23. Things most often repeated are best remembered because of which principle of learning?

A — Principle of effect.
B — Principle of recency.
C — Principle of exercise.

24. Which principle of learning often creates a strong impression?

A — Principle of primacy.
B — Principle of intensity.
C — Principle of readiness.

25. The factor which contributes most to a student's failure to remain receptive to new experiences and which creates a tendency to reject additional training is

A — basic needs.
B — element of threat.
C — negative self-concept.

26. Instruction, as opposed to the trial and error method of learning, is desirable because competent instruction speeds the learning process by

A — motivating the student to a better performance.
B — emphasizing only the important points of training.
C — teaching the relationship of perceptions as they occur.

27. The best way to prepare a student to perform a task is to

A — explain the purpose of the task.
B — provide a clear, step-by-step example.
C — give the student an outline of the task.

28. To be effective, an assessment should

A — not contain negative remarks.
B — treat every aspect of the performance in detail.
C — be flexible enough to satisfy the requirements of the moment.

29. Which statement is true regarding an assessment that is constructive?

A — An instructor's manner and attitude make an assessment constructive.
B — Constructive assessments can inspire a student to improve in areas of lesser accomplishment.
C — A constructive assessment should express ideas with authority in terms that cannot be misunderstood.

30. One desirable result of proper oral quizzing by the instructor is to

A — reveal the effectiveness of the instructor's training procedures.
B — fulfill the requirements set forth in the overall objectives of the course.
C — reveal the essential information from which the student can determine progress.

31. To be effective in oral quizzing during the conduct of a lesson, a question should

A — be of suitable difficulty for that stage of training.
B — include a combination of where, how, and why.
C — divert the student's thoughts to subjects covered in other lessons.

32. One of the main advantages of selection-type test items over supply-type test items is that the selection-type

A — decreases discrimination between responses.
B — would be graded objectively regardless of the student or the grader.
C — precludes comparison of students under one instructor with those under another instructor.

33. In a written test, which type of selection-type test items reduces the probability of guessing correct responses?

A — Essay.
B — Matching.
C — Multiple-choice.

34. A written test that has reliability

A — yields consistent results.
B — measures small differences in the achievement of students.
C — actually measures what it is supposed to measure and nothing else.

35. A written test is said to be comprehensive when it

A — includes all levels of difficulty.
B — samples liberally whatever is being measured.
C — measures knowledge of the same topic in many different ways.

36. Which statement is true regarding student evaluation?

A — The student's own evaluations can only be objective.
B — Evaluation of the student's learning should be an integral part of each lesson.
C — If deficiencies or faults not associated with the present lesson are revealed, they should be corrected immediately.

37. What is the last step in the demonstration/performance method?

A — Summary.
B — Evaluation.
C — Student performance.

38. The basic demonstration/performance method of instruction consists of several steps in proper order. They are

A — instructor tells--student does; student tells--student does; student does--instructor evaluates.
B — instructor tells--instructor does; student tells--instructor does; student does--instructor evaluates.
C — instructor tells--instructor does; student tells--instructor does; student tells--student does; student does--instructor evaluates.

39. What is one advantage of a lecture?

A — A lecture is effective in showing relationships between theory and practice.
B — Excellent when additional research is required.
C — Allows for maximum attainment of certain types of learning outcomes.

40. Which teaching method is most economical in terms of the time required to present a given amount of material?

A — Briefing.
B — Teaching lecture.
C — Demonstration/performance.

41. The first step in preparing a lecture is to

A — research the subject.
B — develop the main ideas or key points.
C — establish the objective and desired outcome.

42. In a guided discussion, learning is achieved through the

A — skillful use of questions.
B — use of questions, each of which contains several ideas.
C — use of reverse questions directed to the class as a whole.

43. When it appears students have adequately discussed the ideas presented during a guided discussion, one of the most valuable tools an instructor can use is

A — a session of verbal testing.
B — a written test on the subject discussed.
C — an interim summary of what the students accomplished.

44. Which is generally the more effective way for an instructor to properly motivate students?

A — Maintain pleasant personal relationships with students.
B — Provide positive motivations by the promise or achievement of rewards.
C — Reinforce their self-confidence by requiring no tasks beyond their ability to perform.

45. Which statement is true concerning motivations?

A — Motivations must be tangible to be effective.
B — Motivations may be very subtle and difficult to identify.
C — Negative motivations often are as effective as positive motivations.

46. The overall learning objective of scenario-based training (SBT) is

A — that students will improve their ability to recall previously learned information.
B — for the student to be more prepared to make good decisions based on a variety of real world situations.
C — to promote situational awareness and opportunities for decision making.

47. What is a characteristic of an effective scenario?

A — It should not promote errors.
B — It should be in the form of a test.
C — It should include an account of a real world situation that contains an educational message.

48. Development and assembly of blocks of learning in their proper relationship will provide a means for

A — both the instructor and student to easily correct faulty habit patterns.
B — challenging the student by progressively increasing the units of learning.
C — allowing the student to master the segments of the overall pilot performance requirements individually and combining these with other related segments.

49. The method of arranging lesson material from the simple to complex, past to present, and known to unknown, is one that

A — creates student thought pattern departures.
B — shows the relationships of the main points of the lesson.
C — requires students to actively participate in the lesson.

50. Instructional aids used in the teaching/learning process should not be used

A — as a crutch by the instructor.
B — for teaching more in less time.
C — to visualize relationships between abstracts.

Page Intentionally Left Blank

PRACTICE TEST LIST OF ANSWERS

The listing below gives the correct answers for your fundamentals of instructing practice knowledge test and the page number in this book on which you will find each question with the complete Gleim answer explanation.

Q. #	Answer	Page	Q. #	Answer	Page	Q. #	Answer	Page	Q. #	Answer	Page
1.	C	72	14.	C	64	27.	B	37	40.	B	90
2.	C	73	15.	C	51	28.	C	128	41.	C	90
3.	A	98	16.	C	74	29.	B	129	42.	A	92
4.	C	112	17.	A	31	30.	A	134	43.	C	93
5.	B	114	18.	B	33	31.	A	134	44.	B	64
6.	A	114	19.	C	30	32.	B	137	45.	B	66
7.	A	78	20.	B	30	33.	B	138	46.	B	95
8.	A	79	21.	A	24	34.	A	138	47.	A	95
9.	C	79	22.	B	24	35.	B	139	48.	C	109
10.	A	26	23.	C	24	36.	B	140	49.	B	110
11.	B	47	24.	A	25	37.	B	94	50.	A	118
12.	B	46	25.	C	44	38.	C	94			
13.	B	46	26.	C	27	39.	A	89			

APPENDIX B
REPRINTS FROM THE FAA'S
AVIATION INSTRUCTOR'S HANDBOOK

The FAA's *Aviation Instructor's Handbook* (FAA-H-8083-9A) consists of nine chapters, which are briefly outlined in Study Units 1 through 6 of this book. The chapters are reprinted for your reference as you prepare for your FAA knowledge test and your FAA practical test. These chapters may also be useful to you whether you are already an active flight instructor or are becoming a flight instructor.

Chapter 1: Human Behavior
Chapter 2: The Learning Process
Chapter 3: Effective Communication
Chapter 4: The Teaching Process
Chapter 5: Assessment
Chapter 6: Planning Instructional Activity
Chapter 7: Instructor Responsibilities and Professionalism
Chapter 8: Techniques of Flight Instruction
Chapter 9: Risk Management

They are reprinted beginning on the next page and continue through page 308. Please note that we do not reproduce the six appendixes found in the FAA text because they are beyond the scope of preparing for the knowledge test. However, they are important and reference practical content that you will need to be familiar with as you begin working as a CFI. You should certainly reference the appendixes and learn from them.

FAA Errata as of March 7, 2014

1. In Figure 9-3 on page 9-5 (Gleim page 295), the bottom line of the checklist should be changed to: "Emotion -- am I emotionally upset?"
2. Item 6. at the top of the left column on page 9-6 (Gleim page 296) should be changed to: "The emotions of anger, depression, and anxiety from such events as a serious argument; death in the family; separation or divorce; loss of employment; and/or financial problems not only decrease alertness, but also may lead to taking risks that border on self-destruction. Any pilot who experiences an emotionally upsetting event should refrain from flying until the pilot has satisfactorily recovered."

Chapter 1

Human Behavior

Derek's student Jason is very smart and able to retain a lot of information, but has a tendency to rush through the less exciting material and shows interest and attentiveness only when doing tasks that he finds to be interesting. This concerns Derek because he is worried that Jason will overlook many important details and rush through procedures. For a homework assignment Jason was told to take a very thorough look at Preflight Procedures, and that for his next flight lesson, they would discuss each step in detail. As Derek predicted, Jason found this assignment to be boring and was not prepared. Derek knows that Jason is a "thrill seeker" as he talks about his business, which is a wilderness adventure company. Derek must find a way to keep Jason focused and help him find excitement in all areas of learning so that he will understand the complex art of flying and aircraft safety.

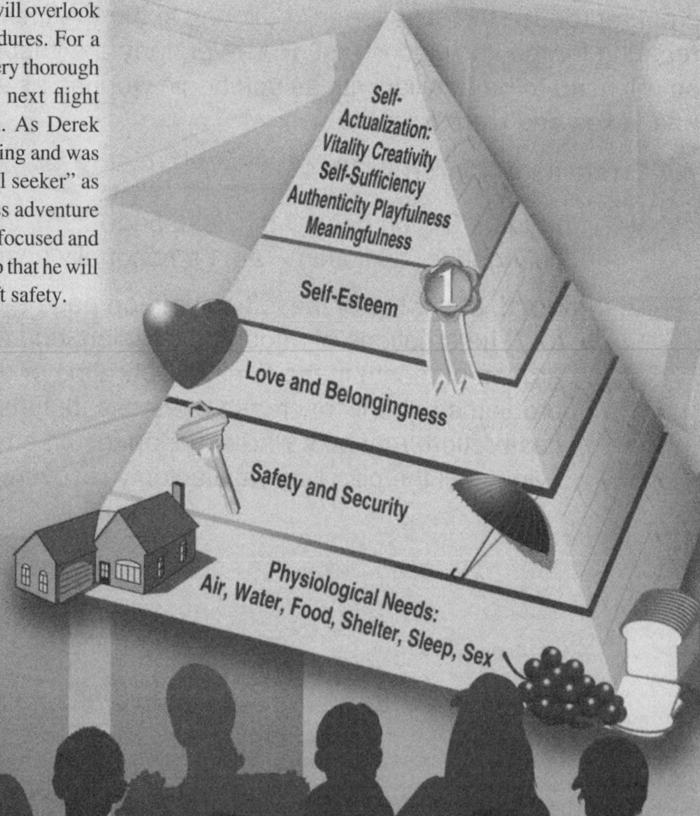

Introduction

This chapter discusses human behavior and how it affects the learning process. Learning is the acquisition of knowledge or understanding of a subject or skill through education, experience, practice, or study. A change of behavior results from learning. To successfully bring about learning, the instructor must know why people act the way they do, how people learn, and then use this understanding to teach. The study of applied educational psychology underlies the information and theories that are discussed. To be an effective instructor, knowledge of human behavior, basic human needs, the defense mechanisms humans use that prevent learning, as well as how adults learn is essential for organizing student activities and promoting a productive learning experience for students.

Definitions of Human Behavior

The study of human behavior is an attempt to explain how and why humans function the way they do. A complex topic, human behavior is a product both of innate human nature and of individual experience and environment. Definitions of human behavior abound, depending on the field of study. In the scientific world, human behavior is seen as the product of factors that cause people to act in predictable ways.

For example, speaking in public is very high on the list of fears modern humans have. While no two people react the same to any given fear, fear itself does trigger certain innate biological responses in humans such as an increase in breathing rate. How a person handles that fear is a product of individual experiences. The person who has never spoken in public may be unable to fulfill the obligation. Another person, knowing his or her job requires public speaking, may chose to take a class on public speaking to learn how to cope with the fear.

Human behavior is also defined as the result of attempts to satisfy certain needs. These needs may be simple to understand and easy to identify, such as the need for food and water. They also may be complex, such as the need for respect and acceptance. A working knowledge of human behavior can help an instructor better understand a student. It is also helpful to remember that to a large extent thoughts, feelings, and behavior are shared by all men or women, despite seemingly large cultural differences. For example, fear causes humans to either fight or flee. In the public speaking example above, one person may "flee" by not fulfilling the obligation. The other person may "fight" by learning techniques to deal with fear.

Another definition of human behavior focuses on the typical life course of humans. This approach emphasizes human development or the successive phases of growth in which human behavior is characterized by a distinct set of physical, physiological, and behavioral features. The thoughts, feelings, and behavior of an infant differ radically from those of a teen. Research shows that as an individual matures, his or her mode of action moves from dependency to self-direction. Therefore, the age of the student impacts how the instructor designs the curriculum. Since the average age of a student can vary, the instructor needs to offer a curriculum that addresses the varying student tendency to self-direct. *[Figure 1-1]*

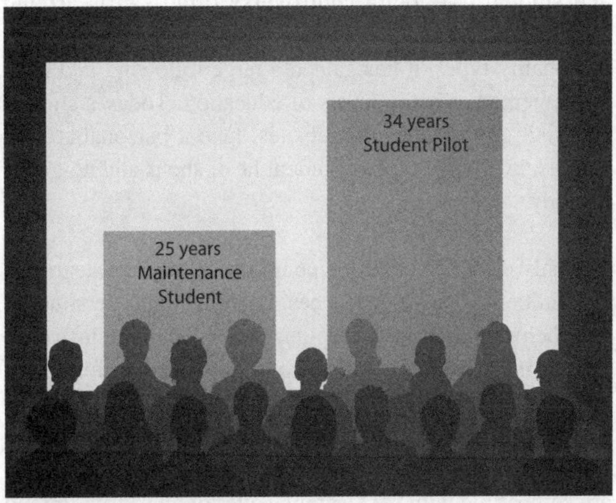

Figure 1-1. *The average age of a student pilot is 34, while the average age of a maintenance student is 25.*

By observing human behavior, an instructor can gain the knowledge needed to better understand him or herself as an instructor as well as the learning needs of students. Understanding human behavior leads to successful instruction.

Personality Types

In a continuing quest to figure out why humans do what they do, the mother-daughter team of Katharine Cook Briggs and Isabel Briggs Myers pioneered the Myers-Briggs Type Indicator (MBTI) test in 1962. The MBTI was based on Jungian theory, previous research into personality traits, and lengthy personal observations of human behavior by Myers and Briggs. They believed that much seemingly random variation in human behavior is actually quite orderly and consistent, being due to basic differences in the ways individuals prefer to use their perception and judgment. They distilled human behavior into sixteen distinct personality types. Inspired by their research, clinical psychologist and author, Dr. David Keirsey condensed their sixteen types into four groups he calls Guardian, Artisan, Rational, and Idealist. Others have either contributed or continued to expand personality research and its influence on human behavior. Personality type testing now runs the gamut from helping people make career choices to helping people choose marriage partners.

Instructor and Student Relationship

How does personality type testing affect instructors and students? Research has led many educational psychologists to feel that based on personality type, everyone also has an individual style of learning. In this theory, working with that style, rather than against it, benefits both instructor and student. Although controversy often swirls around the educational benefits of teaching students according to personality types, it has gained a large following and been implemented at many levels of education. Today's student can visit any number of websites, take a personality test, and discover what type of student he or she is and how best to study.

Not only does personality type influence how one learns, it also influences how one teaches. Learning one's personality type helps an instructor recognize how he or she instructs. Why is it important to recognize personal instruction style? The match or mismatch between the way an instructor teaches and the way a student learns contributes to student satisfaction or dissatisfaction. Students whose learning styles are compatible with the teaching styles of an instructor tend to retain information longer, apply it more effectively, learn more, and have a more positive attitude toward the course in general. Although an instructor cannot change his or her preferred style of teaching to match a learning style, steps can be taken to actively bridge the differences.

Consider Derek's dilemma with Jason. Derek knows he is the type of instructor who provides a clear, precise syllabus and has a tendency to explain with step-by-step procedures. His teaching style relies on traditional techniques and he often finds himself teaching as he was taught. Observation leads Derek to believe Jason is the type of person who needs the action, excitement, and variation reflected in his career choice. In an effort to focus Jason on the need to learn all aspects of flight, Derek sets up a scenario for the day that features how to scout locations for future adventure tours.

By adjusting the flight scenario, Derek pushes himself out of his lock-step approach to teaching. He has also added an element of variation to the lesson that not only interests Jason, but is one of the reasons he wants to learn to fly.

Human Needs and Motivation

Human needs are things all humans require for normal growth and development. These needs have been studied by psychologists and categorized in a number of ways. Henry A. Murray, one of the founders of personality psychology who was active in developing a theory of motivation, identified a list of core psychological needs in 1938. He described these needs as being either primary (based on biological needs, such as the need for food) or secondary (generally psychological, such as the need for independence). Murray believed the interplay of these needs produce distinct personality types and are internal influences on behavior.

Murray's research underpins the work of psychologist Abraham Maslow who also studied human needs, motivation, and personality. While working with monkeys during his early years of research, he noticed that some needs take precedence over others. For example, thirst is relieved before hunger because the need for water is a stronger need than the need for food. In 1954, Maslow published what has become known as Maslow's Hierarchy of Needs which remains valid today for understanding human motivation. *[Figure 1-2]* According to Maslow, human needs go beyond the obvious physical needs of food and shelter to include psychological needs, safety and security, love and belongingness, self esteem, and self actualization to achieve one's goals.

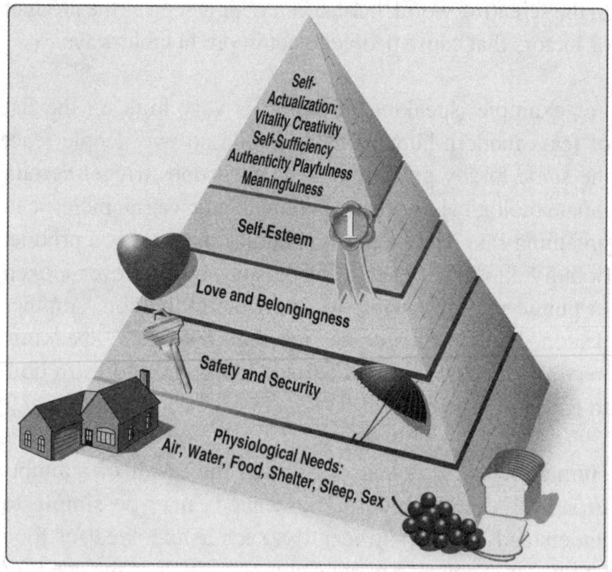

Figure 1-2. *Maslow's Hierarchy of Needs.*

Human needs are satisfied in order of importance. Once a need is satisfied, humans work to satisfy the next level of need. Need satisfaction is an ongoing behavior that determines everyday actions.

Human Needs That Must Be Met To Encourage Learning

Physiological

These are biological needs. They consist of the need for air, food, water, and maintenance of the human body. If a student is unwell, then little else matters. Unless the biological needs are met, a person cannot concentrate fully on learning, self-expression, or any other tasks. Instructors should monitor their students to make sure that their basic physical needs have been met. A hungry or tired student may not be able to perform as expected.

Security

Once the physiological needs are met, the need for security becomes active. All humans have a need to feel safe. Security needs are about keeping oneself from harm. If a student does not feel safe, he or she cannot concentrate on learning. The aviation instructor who stresses flight safety during training mitigates feelings of insecurity.

Belonging

When individuals are physically comfortable and do not feel threatened, they seek to satisfy their social needs of belonging. Maslow states that people seek to overcome feelings of loneliness and alienation. This involves both giving and receiving love, affection, and the sense of belonging. For example, aviation students are usually out of their normal surroundings during training, and their need for association and belonging is more pronounced. Instructors should make every effort to help new students feel at ease and to reinforce their decision to pursue a career or hobby in aviation.

Esteem

When the first three classes of needs are satisfied, the need for esteem can become dominant. Humans have a need for a stable, firmly based, high level of self-respect and respect from others. Esteem is about feeling good about one's self. Humans get esteem in two ways: internally or externally. Internally, a person judges himself or herself worthy by personally defined standards. High self-esteem results in self-confidence, independence, achievement, competence, and knowledge.

Most people, however, seek external esteem through social approval and esteem from other people, judging themselves by what others think of them. External self-esteem relates to one's reputation, such as status, recognition, appreciation, and respect of associates.

When esteem needs are satisfied, a person feels self-confident and valuable as a person in the world. When these needs are frustrated, the person feels inferior, weak, helpless, and worthless. Esteem needs not only have a strong influence on the instructor-student relationship, but also may be the main reason for a student's interest in aviation training.

Cognitive and Aesthetic

In later years, Maslow added cognitive (need to know and understand) and aesthetic (the emotional need of the artist) needs to the pyramid. He realized humans have a deep need to understand what is going on around them. If a person understands what is going on, he or she can either control the situation or make informed choices about what steps might be taken next. The brain even reinforces this need by giving humans a rush of dopamine whenever something is learned, which accounts for that satisfying "eureka!" moment. For example, a flight student usually experiences a major "eureka!" moment upon completing the first solo flight.

Aesthetic needs connect directly with human emotions, which makes it a subtle factor in the domain of persuasion. When someone likes another person, a house, a painting, or a song, the reasons are not examined—he or she simply likes it. This need can factor into the student-instructor relationship. If an instructor does not "like" a student, this subtle feeling may affect the instructor's ability to teach that student.

Self-Actualization

When all of the foregoing needs are satisfied, then and only then are the needs for self-actualization activated. Maslow describes self-actualization as a person's need to be and do that which the person was "born to do." To paraphrase an old Army recruiting slogan, self-actualization is to "be all you can be."

Self-actualized people are characterized by:

- Being problem-focused.
- Incorporating an ongoing freshness of appreciation of life.
- A concern about personal growth.
- The ability to have peak experiences.

Helping a student achieve his or her individual potential in aviation training offers the greatest challenge as well as reward to the instructor.

Instructors should help students satisfy their human needs in a manner that creates a healthy learning environment. In this type of environment, students experience fewer frustrations and, therefore, can devote more attention to their studies. Fulfillment of needs can be a powerful motivation in complex learning situations.

Human Nature and Motivation

Human nature refers to the general psychological characteristics, feelings, and behavioral traits shared by all humans. Motivation (discussed more fully in Chapter 2, The Learning Process) is the reason one acts or behaves in a certain way and lies at the heart of goals. A goal is the object of a person's effort.

Consider Jason, who came to aviation because he wanted to participate more actively in another realm of his business. Derek needs to capitalize on this motivation to keep Jason interested in the step-by-step procedures that must be learned in order to fly safely. There is a gap between Jason and his goal of earning a pilot certificate. It is Derek's job to close the gap. The successful instructor channels student motivation and guides the student toward the goal of learning aviation skills through education, experience, practice, and study.

Building on Maslow's hierarchy of needs, social psychologist Douglas McGregor set out two opposing assumptions about human nature and motivation in 1960. *[Figure 1-3]* Although McGregor's famous X-Y Theory was designed for use in human resource management, it offers information about how people view human behavior at work and organizational life which makes it useful for aviation instructors.

Theory X assumes that management's role is to coerce and control employees because people need control and direction. Managers who think in Theory X terms believe people have an inherent dislike for work, avoid it whenever possible, and must be coerced, controlled, directed, or threatened with punishment in order to get them to achieve the objectives.

McGregor believed these assumptions were false, that the role of managers (or instructors) is to develop the potential in employees (students) and help them to release that potential

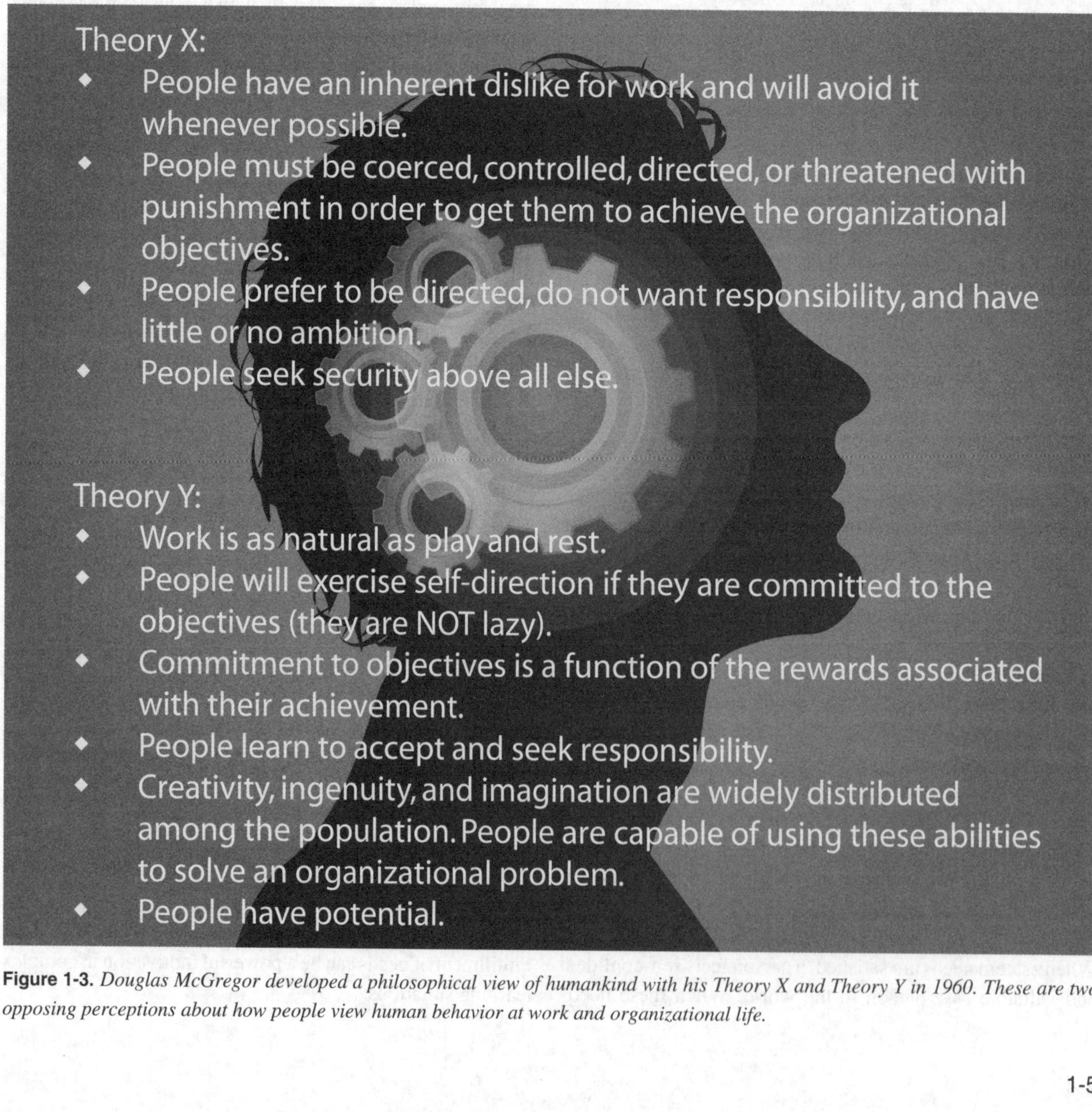

Figure 1-3. *Douglas McGregor developed a philosophical view of humankind with his Theory X and Theory Y in 1960. These are two opposing perceptions about how people view human behavior at work and organizational life.*

toward common goals. This view of humans he termed "Theory Y" and holds that:

- Work is as natural as play and rest. The average person does not inherently dislike work. Depending on conditions, work may be a source of satisfaction and, if so, it is performed voluntarily. On the other hand, when work is a form of punishment, it is avoided, if possible.
- People exercise self-direction if they are committed to the goals (they are not lazy).
- Commitment to goals relates directly to the rewards associated with their achievement.
- People learn to accept and seek responsibility. Shirking responsibility and lack of ambition are not inherent in human nature, but are usually the consequences of experience.
- Creativity, ingenuity, and imagination are widely distributed among the population. People are capable of using these abilities to solve problems.
- People have potential.

Since it is human nature to be motivated, the responsibility for discovering how to realize the potential of the student lies with the instructor. How to mold a solid, healthy, productive relationship with a student depends on the instructor's knowledge of human behavior and needs. Being able to recognize factors that inhibit the learning process also helps the instructor in this process.

Human Factors That Inhibit Learning

Defense Mechanisms

Defense mechanisms can be biological or psychological. The biological defense mechanism is a physiological response that protects or preserves organisms. For example, when humans experience a danger or a threat, the "fight or flight" response kicks in. Adrenaline and other chemicals are activated and physical symptoms such as rapid heart rate and increased blood pressure occur.

An example of this might occur when an anxious student pilot is learning to place the aircraft (helicopter) in an autorotative descent, which is used in the event of engine failure or tail rotor failure. Emergency procedure training is necessary to practice as the outcome of a true emergency is directly related to the pilot's ability to react instantly and correctly, and in taking the proper corrective action since there may be limited time to analyze the problem. The anxiety that the student pilot may feel while practicing such maneuvers may resolve itself into a "fight or flight" response.

The instructor needs to recognize the student's apprehension about performing the autorotation and help the student gain the necessary skill level to feel comfortable with the maneuver. In this case, the instructor could take the procedure apart and demonstrate each stage of an autorotation. Allowing the student to then practice the stages at various heights should instill the confidence needed to perform the autorotation.

Sigmund Freud introduced the psychological concept of the ego defense mechanism in 1894. The ego defense mechanism is an unconscious mental process to protect oneself from anxiety, unpleasant emotions, or to provide a refuge from a situation with which the individual cannot currently cope. For example, someone who blots out the memory of being physically assaulted is using a defense mechanism. People use these defenses to prevent unacceptable ideas or impulses from entering the conscience. Defense mechanisms soften feelings of failure, alleviate feelings of guilt, help an individual cope with reality, and protect one's self-image. *[Figure 1-4]*

Figure 1-4. *Several common defense mechanisms may apply to aviation students.*

When anxiety occurs, the mind tries to solve the problem or find an escape, but if these tactics do not work, defense mechanisms are triggered. Defense mechanisms share two common properties:

- They often appear unconsciously.
- They tend to distort, transform, or otherwise falsify reality.

Because reality is distorted, perception changes, which allows for a lessening of anxiety, with a corresponding reduction in tension. Repression and denial are two primary defense mechanisms.

Repression

Repression is the defense mechanism whereby a person places uncomfortable thoughts into inaccessible areas of the unconscious mind. Things a person is unable to cope with now are pushed away, to be dealt with at another time, or hopefully never because they faded away on their own accord. The level of repression can vary from temporarily forgetting an uncomfortable thought to amnesia, where the events that triggered the anxiety are deeply buried. Repressed memories do not disappear and may reappear in dreams or slips of the tongue ("Freudian slips"). For example, a student pilot may have a repressed fear of flying that inhibits his or her ability to learn how to fly.

Denial

Denial is a refusal to accept external reality because it is too threatening. It is the refusal to acknowledge what has happened, is happening, or will happen. It is a form of repression through which stressful thoughts are banned from memory. Related to denial is minimization. When a person minimizes something, he or she accepts what happened, but in a diluted form.

For example, the instructor finds a screwdriver on the wing of an aircraft the maintenance student was repairing and explains the hazards of foreign object damage (FOD). The student, unwilling to accept the reality that his or her inattention could have caused an aircraft accident, denies having been in a hurry the previous day. Or, the student minimizes the incident, accepting he or she left the tool but pointing out that nothing bad happened as a result of the action.

Other defense mechanisms include but are not limited to the following:

Compensation

Compensation is a process of psychologically counterbalancing perceived weaknesses by emphasizing strength in other areas. Through compensation, students often attempt to disguise the presence of a weak or undesirable quality by emphasizing a more positive one. The "I'm not a fighter, I'm a lover" philosophy can be an example of compensation. Compensation involves substituting success in a realm of life other than the realm in which the person suffers a weakness.

Projection

Through projection, an individual places his or her own unacceptable impulses onto someone else. A person relegates the blame for personal shortcomings, mistakes, and transgressions to others or attributes personal motives, desires, characteristics, and impulses to others. The student pilot who fails a flight exam and says, "I failed because I had a poor examiner" believes the failure was not due to a lack of personal skill or knowledge. This student projects blame onto an "unfair" examiner.

Rationalization

Rationalization is a subconscious technique for justifying actions that otherwise would be unacceptable. When true rationalization takes place, individuals sincerely believe in the plausible and acceptable excuses which seem real and justifiable. For example, a student mechanic performs poorly on a test. He or she may justify the poor grade by claiming there was not enough time to learn the required information. The student does not admit to failing to join the class study group or taking the computer quiz offered by the instructor.

Reaction Formation

In reaction formation a person fakes a belief opposite to the true belief because the true belief causes anxiety. The person feels an urge to do or say something and then actually does or says something that is the opposite of what he or she really wants. For example, a student may develop a who-cares-how-other-people-feel attitude to cover up feelings of loneliness and a hunger for acceptance.

Fantasy

Fantasy occurs when a student engages in daydreams about how things should be rather than doing anything about how things are. The student uses his or her imagination to escape from reality into a fictitious world—a world of success or pleasure. This provides a simple and satisfying escape from problems, but if a student gets sufficient satisfaction from daydreaming, he or she may stop trying to achieve goals altogether. Perhaps the transitioning pilot is having trouble mastering a more complex aircraft, which jeopardizes his or her dream of becoming an airline pilot. It becomes easier to daydream about the career than to achieve the certification. Lost in the fantasy, the student spends more time dreaming about being a successful airline pilot than working toward the goal. When carried to extremes, the worlds of fantasy and reality can become so confused that the dreamer cannot distinguish one from the other.

Displacement

This defense mechanism results in an unconscious shift of emotion, affect, or desire from the original object to a more acceptable, less threatening substitute. Displacement avoids the risk associated with feeling unpleasant emotions and puts them somewhere other than where they belong. For example, the avionics student is angry with the instructor over a grade received, but fears displaying the anger could cause the instructor to lower the grade. The student might choose to express the anger but redirects it toward another, safer person such as a spouse. Maybe the student yells at the spouse, but the student knows the spouse either forgives the anger or ignores it. The student is allowed to express anger without risking failure in a class.

Psychology textbooks or online references offer more in-depth information about defense mechanisms. While most defense mechanisms fall within the realm of normal behavior and serve a useful purpose, in some cases they may be associated with mental health problems. Defense mechanisms involve some degree of self-deception and distortion of reality. Thus, they alleviate the symptoms, not the causes, and do not solve problems. Moreover, because defense mechanisms operate on an unconscious level, they are not subject to normal conscious checks and balances. Once an individual realizes there is a conscious reliance on one of these devices, behavior ceases to be an unconscious adjustment mechanism and becomes, instead, an ineffective way of satisfying a need.

It may be difficult for an instructor to identify excessive reliance on defense mechanisms by a student, but a personal crisis or other stressful event is usually the cause. For example, a death in the family, a divorce, or even a failing grade on an important test may trigger harmful defensive reactions. Physical symptoms such as a change in personality, angry outbursts, depression, or a general lack of interest may point to a problem. Drug or alcohol abuse also may become apparent. Less obvious indications may include social withdrawal, preoccupation with certain ideas, or an inability to concentrate.

An instructor needs to be familiar with typical defense mechanisms and have some knowledge of related behavioral problems. A perceptive instructor can help by using common sense and discussing the problem with the student. The main objective should be to restore motivation and self-confidence. It should be noted that the human psyche is fragile and could be damaged by inept measures. Therefore, in severe cases involving the possibility of deep psychological problems, timely and skillful help is needed. In this event, the instructor should recommend that the student use the services of a professional counselor.

Student Emotional Reactions

While it is not necessary for a flight instructor to be a certified psychologist, it is helpful to learn how to analyze student behavior before and during each flight lesson. This ability helps a flight instructor develop and use appropriate techniques for instruction.

Anxiety

Anxiety is probably the most significant psychological factor affecting flight instruction. This is true because flying is a potentially threatening experience for those who are not accustomed to flying and the fear of falling is universal in human beings. Anxiety also is a factor in maintenance training because lives may depend on consistently doing the job right the first time. The following paragraphs are primarily concerned with flight instruction and student reactions.

Anxiety is a feeling of worry, nervousness, or unease, often about something that is going to happen, typically something with an uncertain outcome. It results from the fear of anything, real or imagined, which threatens the person who experiences it, and may have a potent effect on actions and the ability to learn from perceptions.

The responses to anxiety range from a hesitancy to act to the impulse to do something even if it's wrong. Some people affected by anxiety react appropriately, adequately, and more rapidly than they would in the absence of threat. Many, on the other hand, may freeze and be incapable of doing anything to correct the situation that has caused their anxiety. Others may do things without rational thought or reason.

Both normal and abnormal reactions to anxiety are of concern to the flight instructor. The normal reactions are significant because they indicate a need for special instruction to relieve the anxiety. The abnormal reactions are even more important because they may signify a deep-seated problem.

Anxiety can be countered by reinforcing the students' enjoyment of flying and by teaching them to cope with their fears. An effective technique is to treat fears as a normal reaction, rather than ignoring them. Keep in mind that anxiety for student pilots is usually associated with certain types of flight operations and maneuvers. Instructors should introduce these maneuvers with care, so that students know what to expect and what their reactions should be. When introducing stalls, for example, instructors should first review the aerodynamic principles and explain how stalls affect flight characteristics. Then, carefully describe the physical sensations to be expected, as well as the recovery procedures.

Student anxiety can be minimized throughout training by emphasizing the benefits and pleasurable experiences that can be derived from flying, rather than by continuously citing the unhappy consequences of faulty performances. Safe flying practices should be presented as conducive to satisfying, efficient, uninterrupted operations, rather than as necessary only to prevent catastrophe.

Normal Reactions to Stress

As mentioned earlier in the chapter, when a threat is recognized or imagined, the brain alerts the body. The adrenal gland activates hormones, which prepare the body to meet the threat or to retreat from it—the fight or flight syndrome.

Normal individuals begin to respond rapidly and exactly, within the limits of their experience and training. Many responses are automatic, highlighting the need for proper training in emergency operations prior to an actual emergency. The affected individual thinks rationally, acts rapidly, and is extremely sensitive to all aspects of the surroundings.

Abnormal Reactions to Stress

Reactions to stress may produce abnormal responses in some people. With them, response to anxiety or stress may be completely absent or at least inadequate. Their responses may be random or illogical, or they may do more than is called for by the situation.

During flight instruction, instructors are normally the only ones who can observe students when they are under pressure. Instructors, therefore, are in a position to differentiate between safe and unsafe piloting actions. Instructors also may be able to detect potential psychological problems. The following student reactions are indicative of abnormal reactions to stress. None of them provides an absolute indication, but the presence of any of them under conditions of stress is reason for careful instructor evaluation.

- Inappropriate reactions, such as extreme over-cooperation, painstaking self-control, inappropriate laughter or singing, and very rapid changes in emotions.
- Marked changes in mood on different lessons, such as excellent morale followed by deep depression.
- Severe anger directed toward the flight instructor, service personnel, and others.

In difficult situations, flight instructors must carefully examine student responses and their own responses to the students. These responses may be the normal products of a complex learning situation, but they also can be indicative of psychological abnormalities that inhibit learning or are potentially very hazardous to future piloting operations. *[Figure 1-5]*

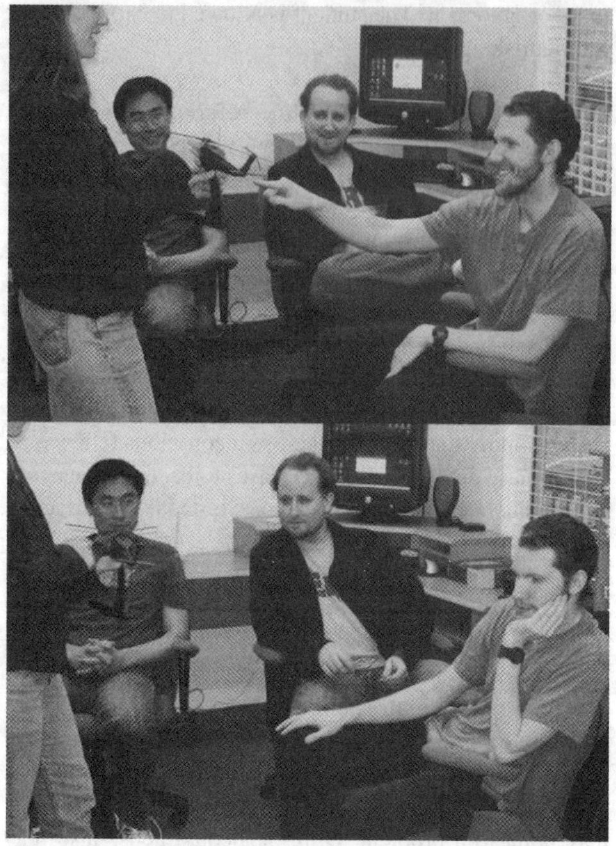

Figure 1-5. *A student with marked changes in mood during different lessons, such as excellent morale followed by deep depression, is indicative of an abnormal reaction to stress.*

Flight Instructor Actions Regarding Seriously Abnormal Students

A flight instructor who believes a student may be suffering from a serious psychological abnormality has a responsibility to refrain from instructing that student. In addition, a flight instructor has the personal responsibility of assuring that such a person does not continue flight training or become certificated as a pilot. To accomplish this, the following steps are available:

- If an instructor believes that a student may have a disqualifying psychological defect, arrangements should be made for another instructor, who is not acquainted with the student, to conduct an evaluation flight. After the flight, the two instructors should confer to determine whether they agree that further investigation or action is justified.
- The flight instructor's primary legal responsibility concerns the decision whether to endorse the student to be competent for solo flight operations, or to make a recommendation for the practical test leading to certification as a pilot. If, after consultation with an unbiased instructor, the instructor believes that the student may have a serious psychological deficiency, such endorsements and recommendations must be withheld.

Teaching the Adult Student

While aviation instructors teach students of all ages, the average aviation student age is 30 years old. This means the aviation instructor needs to be versed in the needs of adult students. The field of adult education is relatively young, having been established in the late twentieth century by Dr. Malcolm Knowles. His research revealed certain traits that need to be recognized when teaching adult students as well as ways instructors can use these traits to teach older students.

Adults as learners possess the following characteristics:

- Adults who are motivated to seek out a learning experience do so primarily because they have a use for the knowledge or skill being sought. Learning is a means to an end, not an end in itself.
- Adults seek out learning experiences in order to cope with specific life-changing events—marriage, divorce, a new job. They are ready to learn when they assume new roles.
- Adults are autonomous and self-directed; they need to be independent and exercise control.
- Adults have accumulated a foundation of life experiences and knowledge and draw upon this reservoir of experience for learning.
- Adults are goal oriented.
- Adults are relevancy oriented. Their time perspective changes from one of postponed knowledge application to immediate application.
- Adults are practical, focusing on the aspects of a lesson most useful to them in their work.
- As do all learners, adults need to be shown respect.
- The need to increase or maintain a sense of self-esteem is a strong secondary motivator for adult learners.
- Adults want to solve problems and apply new knowledge immediately.

Instructors should:

- Provide a training syllabus (see Chapter 8, Planning Instructional Activity) that is organized with clearly defined course objectives to show the student how the training helps him or her attain specific goals.
- Help students integrate new ideas with what they already know to ensure they keep and use the new information.
- Assume responsibility only for his or her own expectations, not for those of students. It is important to clarify and articulate all student expectations early on.
- Recognize the student's need to control pace and start/stop time.
- Take advantage of the adult preference to self-direct and self-design learning projects by giving the student frequent scenario based training (SBT) opportunities.
- Remember that self-direction does not mean isolation. Studies of self-directed learning indicate self-directed projects involve other people as resources, guides, etc.
- Use books, programmed instruction, and computers which are popular with adult learners.
- Refrain from "spoon-feeding" the student.
- Set a cooperative learning climate.
- Create opportunities for mutual planning.

An aviation student may be the retired business executive who always wanted to learn how to fly, an Army helicopter pilot who wants to learn how to fly an airplane, or a former automobile mechanic who decides to pursue avionics. These students may be financially stressed, or they may be financially secure. They may be healthy, but they may be experiencing such age-related problems as diminished hearing or eyesight. Whatever the personal circumstances of the student, he or she wants the learning experience to be problem-oriented, personalized, and the instructor to be accepting of the student's need for self-direction and personal responsibility.

Chapter Summary

This chapter discussed how human behavior affects learning, human needs that must be met before students can learn, defense mechanisms students use to prevent learning, how adults learn, and the flight instructor's role in determining a student's future in the aviation community. For more information on these topics, it is recommended the instructor read a general educational psychology text or visit one of the many online sites devoted to education.

Chapter 2

The Learning Process

Introduction

The First Flight

When Beverly (student) enthusiastically presents herself for her first day of flight instruction, Bill, her Certificated Flight Instructor (CFI), decides to spend some time in the classroom. Beverly knows a lot of facts about flying and shares her knowledge with Bill, but when he asks questions to test her understanding of the facts, she cannot answer them. During their first flight, Bill discovers Beverly has mastered a few basic skills, but her performance is awkward, as if she were working from a list of memorized steps.

In the early stages of flight training, Beverly focuses all her attention on performing each skill. If Bill asks her a question or to perform two tasks at once, she loses her place and must restart. As she flies, she makes errors. When she catches herself making an error, she becomes visibly frustrated. Then sometimes she does not notice an error and keeps moving ahead as if nothing were amiss. Since she is a beginner, Bill is patient.

The Check Ride

Months later, Bill is helping Beverly prepare for her practical test. Remembering her first days of instruction, Bill feels as if he were working with a different person. The breadth and depth of her classroom knowledge has grown. Beverly does not simply reiterate facts—she applies her knowledge to solve the problems Bill gives her. In addition to the required knowledge listed in the Practical Test Standards (PTS), she also knows about her local environment, such as the nuances of local weather patterns.

In the aircraft, once awkward and tentative actions are now performed with a steady hand and confidence. Skills she struggled to learn in the past have become second nature. When asked to do several things simultaneously, she performs well. When Bill interrupts her, she mentally bookmarks where she is, contends with the interruption, and then returns to the task at hand. She still makes errors, but they are small ones that she notices and corrects right away. She still gets frustrated when she makes an error, but she takes a deep breath, and continues on her way. She makes flying look easy, and Bill is confident that tomorrow's meeting with the examiner will go well.

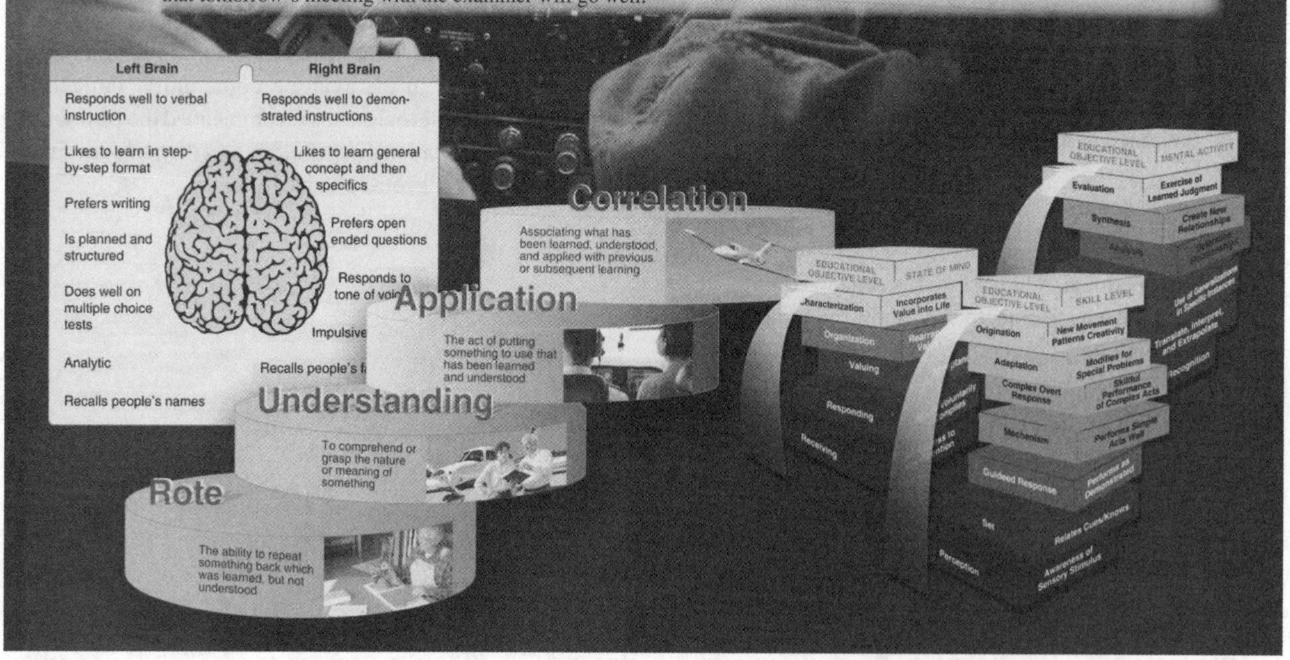

Discussion of First Flight and Check Ride

Between Beverly's first day of training and the day before her practical test, she has undergone some remarkable changes:

1. She has developed a collection of memorized facts into an in-depth understanding of how to fly and learned to apply this knowledge to problem-solving and decision-making.
2. Skills once performed awkwardly and deliberately are now performed smoothly and efficiently.
3. She comfortably performs several tasks at once, deals with distractions and interruptions, and maintains her focus in demanding situations. Knowledge and skills are now orchestrated.
4. She still makes errors, but they are less frequent, smaller in magnitude, and she quickly identifies and corrects them.
5. Her motivation and enthusiasm remain as high as they were on the first day of training.
6. She displays proficiency in all areas now: those at which she naturally excels as well as those she struggled to master in the past.
7. She deals with psychological obstacles, such as frustration, that initially got in the way of her learning.
8. She recognizes the importance of regular study and practice.

This scenario illustrates the goal of an aviation instructor: to teach each student in such a way that he or she will become a competent pilot or aviation maintenance technician (AMT). In order to take a pilot or AMT from memorized facts to higher levels of knowledge and skill that include the ability to exercise judgment and solve problems, an instructor needs to know how people learn. Designed as a basic guide in applied educational psychology, this chapter addresses how people learn.

What Is Learning?

Learning can be defined in many ways:

- A change in the behavior of the learner as a result of experience. The behavior can be physical and overt, or it can be intellectual or attitudinal.
- The process by which experience brings about a relatively permanent change in behavior.
- The change in behavior that results from experience and practice.
- Gaining knowledge or skills, or developing a behavior, through study, instruction, or experience.
- The process of acquiring knowledge or skill through study, experience, or teaching. It depends on experience and leads to long-term changes in behavior potential. Behavior potential describes the possible behavior of an individual (not actual behavior) in a given situation in order to achieve a goal.
- A relatively permanent change in cognition, resulting from experience and directly influencing behavior.

The effective instructor understands the subject being taught, the student, the learning process, and the interrelationships that exist. An effective instructor also realizes learning is a complex procedure and assists each student in reaching the learning outcomes while helping the student build self-esteem and confidence. *[Figure 2-1]*

Figure 2-1. *An effective instructor understands the characteristics of learning and assists students accordingly.*

The Framework for Learning

Research into how people learn gained momentum with the Swiss scientist and psychologist Jean Piaget, who studied the intellectual development of children in the early twentieth century. *[Figure 2-2]* His studies influenced others to research not only how people learn, but also the best ways to teach them, leading eventually to the establishment of the field of educational psychology.

Learning Theory

Learning theory is a body of principles advocated by psychologists and educators to explain how people acquire skills, knowledge, and attitudes. Various branches of learning theory are used in formal training programs to improve and accelerate the learning process. Key concepts such as desired learning outcomes, objectives of the training, and depth of training also apply. When properly integrated, learning principles can be useful to aviation instructors and developers of instructional programs for both pilots and AMTs.

Figure 2-2. *Jean Piaget, Swiss scientist and psychologist.*

Many psychologists and educators have attempted to explain how people learn. While variations abound, modern learning theories grew out of two concepts of how people learn: behaviorism and cognitive theory.

Behaviorism

Behaviorism is a school of psychology that explains animal and human behavior entirely in terms of observable and measurable responses to stimuli. Behaviorism was introduced in the early twentieth century and its followers believed all human behavior is conditioned more or less by events in the environment. Thus, human behavior can be predicted based on past rewards and punishments. Classic behaviorist theory in education stressed a system of rewards and punishment or the "carrot and stick" approach to learning. In modern education circles, behaviorism stresses the importance of having a particular form of behavior positively reinforced by someone (other than the learner) who shapes or controls what is learned rather than no reinforcement or punishment. In aviation training, the instructor provides the reinforcement.

Although the popular therapeutic system of behavior modification has emerged from this theory, behaviorism is now used more to break unwanted behaviors, such as smoking, than in teaching. The popularity of behaviorism has waned due to research that indicates learning is a much more complex process than a response to stimuli. Humans, far from being passive products of experience, are always actively interacting with the environment.

Cognitive Theory

Cognitive theory focuses on what is going on inside the mind. It is more concerned with cognition (the process of thinking and learning)—knowing, perceiving, problem-solving, decision-making, awareness, and related intellectual activities—than with stimulus and response. Learning is not just a change in behavior; it is a change in the way a learner thinks, understands, or feels. Theories based on cognition are concerned with the mental events of the learner. Much of the recent psychological thinking and experimentation in education includes some facets of the cognitive theory.

Early theories of cognitive learning were established by psychologists and educators such as John Dewey, Jean Piaget, Benjamin Bloom, and Jerome Bruner. *[Figure 2-3]* Over the past century, there have been many interpretations of the increasingly large amount of research data dealing with cognitive theories. This has led to many different models for learning as well as catch phrases.

Figure 2-3. *Psychologists and educators who established the early theories of cognitive learning.*

For example, educator, psychologist, and philosopher, John Dewey introduced the concept "reflective thought" in a 1910 book designed for teachers. Dewey believed learning improves to the degree that it arises out of the process of reflection. Over the years, terminology describing reflection has spawned a host of synonyms, such as "critical thinking," "problem-solving," and "higher level thought."

For Dewey, the concept of reflective thought carried deep meaning. He saw reflection as a process that moves a learner from one experience into the next with deeper understanding of its relationships with and connections to other experiences and ideas. Thus, reflection leads the learner from the unclear to the clear.

Jean Piaget, who spent 50 years studying how children develop intellectually, became a major figure in the school of cognitive thought. His research led him to conclude there is always tension between assimilation (old ideas meeting new situations) and accommodation (changing the old ideas to meet the new situations). The resolution of this tension results in intellectual growth. Thus, humans develop cognitive skills through active interaction with the world (a basic premise of scenario-based training (SBT), discussed later in this chapter).

An American psychologist who studied with Piaget, Jerome Bruner became interested in how intellectual development related to the process of learning, His research led him to advocate learning from the known to the unknown, or from the concrete to the abstract, because humans best learn when relating new knowledge to existing knowledge. He introduced and developed the concept of the spiral curriculum, which revisits basic ideas repeatedly and builds on them in increasingly sophisticated ways as the student matures and develops.

Consider the opening scenario with Bill and Beverly. Bill might effectively use this theory with Beverly because she arrived at her first class with a store of aviation facts. Building upon this knowledge, Bill can teach her how to keep the aircraft in straight and level flight while he reinforces what she knows about basic aerodynamics via demonstration and discussion. Since aerodynamics is a constant thread in the flight lessons, Bill is also able to employ the spiral curriculum concept in future lesson by repeatedly revisiting the basic concepts and building upon them as Beverly's skill and knowledge increase.

In the mid-1900s, a group of educators led by Benjamin Bloom tried to classify the levels of thinking behaviors thought to be important in the processes of learning. *[Figure 2-4]* They wanted to classify education goals and objectives based on the assumption that abilities can be measured along a continuum from simple to complex. The result, which remains a popular framework for cognitive theory, was Bloom's Taxonomy of the Cognitive Domain. The taxonomy (a classification system according to presumed relationships) comprises six levels of intellectual behavior and progresses from the simplest to the most complex: knowledge, comprehension, application, analysis, synthesis, and evaluation. For more detailed information about the taxonomy, see Domains of Learning.

Continued research into cognitive theory has led to theories such as information processing and constructivism.

Information Processing Theory

Information processing theory uses a computer system as a model for human learning. The human brain processes incoming information, stores and retrieves it, and generates responses to the information. This involves a number of cognitive processes: gathering and representing information (encoding), retaining of information, and retrieving the information when needed.

This learning system has limitations and must be operated properly. A computer gets input from a keyboard, mouse, etc., whereas the human brain gets input from the senses of sight, hearing, touch, taste, and smell. The amount of sensory input the brain receives per second ranges from thousands to millions of bits of information according to various theories. Regardless of the number, that is a lot of information for the brain to track and process.

One way the brain deals with all this information is to let many of the habitual and routine things go unnoticed. For example, a pilot who uses the rudder when entering a turn is usually unaware of pressing the pedal, even though it involves moving a leg, exerting pressure on the pedal, etc. The human unconscious takes charge, leaving conscious thought processes free to deal with issues that are not habitual.

Since information processing theorists approach learning primarily through a study of memory, this learning concept is revisited during the discussion of memory.

Constructivism

A derivative of cognitive theory, constructivism is a philosophy of learning that can be traced to the eighteenth century. This theory holds that learners do not acquire knowledge and skills passively but actively build or construct them based on their experiences. As implied by its name, constructivism emphasizes the constructing or building that goes on in a learner's mind when he or she learns. Therefore, it creates a learner-centered learning environment in which learners assume responsibility for their own learning.

According to constructivism, humans construct a unique mental image by combining preexisting information with the information received from sense organs. Learning is the result of the learner matching new information against this preexisting information and integrating it into meaningful connections. In constructivist thinking, learners are given more latitude to become effective problem solvers, identifying and evaluating problems, as well as deciphering ways in which to transfer their learning to these problems, all of which foster critical thinking skills. While the student is at the center of the learning process, an experienced teacher is necessary to guide them through the information jungle. Constructivism techniques are good for some types of learning, some situations, and some learners, but not all. This school of thought also encourages teaching students how to use what are known as the higher order thinking skills (HOTS) from Bloom's Taxonomy and training based on problems or scenarios.

Figure 2-4. *Bloom's Taxonomy of the Cognitive Domain.*

Higher Order Thinking Skills (HOTS)

The constructivist theory of learning explains and supports the learning of HOTS, which is commonly called aeronautical decision-making (ADM) in aviation. HOTS lie in the last three categories on Bloom's Taxonomy of Learning: analysis, synthesis, and evaluation skills. Teaching the higher level thinking skills which are essential to judgment, decision-making, and critical thinking is important to aviation because a common thread in aviation accidents is the absence of higher order thinking skills (see Appendix F).

HOTS are taught like other cognitive skills, from simple to complex and from concrete to abstract. To teach HOTS effectively involves strategies and methods that include (1) using problem-based learning (PBL) instruction, (2) authentic problems, (3) real world problems, (4) student-centered learning, (5) active learning, (6) cooperative learning, and (7) customized instruction to meet the individual learner's needs. These strategies engage the learner in some form of mental activity, have the learner examine that mental activity and select the best solution, and challenge the learner to explore other ways to accomplish the task or the problem.

It must be remembered that critical thinking skills should be taught in the context of subject matter. Learners progress from simple to complex; therefore, they need some information before they can think about a subject beyond rote learning. For example, knowing that compliance with the weight-and-balance limits of any aircraft is critical to flight safety will not help an aviation student interpret weight-and-balance charts unless he or she knows something about how center of gravity interacts with weight and balance.

If the student does not yet have much subject matter knowledge, draw on the student's experiences to gain entry into complex concepts. For example, most students probably played on a seesaw during their childhood. Thus, they have a basic experience of how weight and balance work around a center of gravity.

Additionally, HOTS must be emphasized throughout a program of study for best results. For aviation, this means HOTS should be taught in the initial pilot training program and in every subsequent pilot training program. Instructors need to teach the cognitive skills used in problem-solving until these techniques become automated and transferable to new situations or problems. Cognitive research has shown the learning of HOTS is not a change in observable behavior but the construction of meaning from experience.

Scenario-Based Training (SBT)

At the heart of HOTS lies scenario-based training (SBT) which is an example of the PBL instructional method and facilitates the enhancement of learning and the development and transference of thinking skills. SBT provides more realistic decision-making opportunities because it presents tasks in an operational environment; it correlates new information with previous knowledge, and introduces new information in a realistic context.

SBT is a training system that uses a structured script of "real world" scenarios to address flight-training objectives in an operational environment. Such training can include initial training, transition training, upgrade training, recurrent training, and special training.

The instructor should adapt the scenarios to the aircraft, its specific flight characteristics and the likely flight environment, and should always require the student to make real-time decisions in a realistic setting. The scenarios should always be planned and led by the student (with the exception of the first flight or two or until the student has developed the required skills).

SBT not only meets the challenge of teaching aeronautical knowledge to the application level of learning, but also enables the instructor to teach the underlying HOTS needed to improve ADM. The best use of scenarios draws the learner into formulating possible solutions, evaluating the possible solutions, deciding on a solution, judging the appropriateness of that decision and finally, reflecting on the mental process used in solving the problem. It causes the learner to consider whether the decision led to the best possible outcome and challenges the learner to consider other solutions.

SBT scenarios help learners better understand the decisions they have to make and also helps focus the learner on the decisions and consequences involved. It is being used to train people in everything from emergency response to hotel management. The strength of SBT lies in helping the learner gain a deeper understanding of the information and in the learner improving his or her ability to recall the information. This goal is reached when the material is presented as an authentic problem in a situated environment that allows the learner to "make meaning" of the information based on his or her past experience and personal interpretation.

SBT has become one of the primary methods to teach today's aviation learners how to make good aeronautical decisions which in turn enhances the safety of all aviation related activities. For information on how to incorporate SBT into a training syllabus, refer to chapter 9.

Perceptions

Initially, all learning comes from perceptions, which are directed to the brain by one or more of the five senses: sight, hearing, touch, smell, and taste. Psychologists have also found that learning occurs most rapidly when information is received through more than one sense. *[Figure 2-5]*

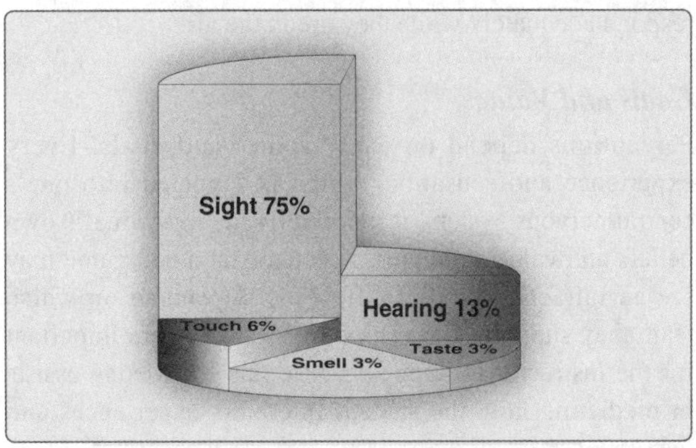

Figure 2-5. *Most learning occurs through sight, but the combination of sight and hearing accounts for about 88 percent of all perception.*

Perception involves more than the reception of stimuli from the five senses; it also involves a person giving meaning to sensations. People base their actions on the way they believe things to be. The experienced AMT, for example, perceives an engine malfunction quite differently than does an inexperienced student. This occurs because the beginning aviation student is overwhelmed by stimuli and often focuses on meaningless things, thus missing key information. It is important for the instructor to direct trainee's perceptions initially so that the student detects and perceives relevant information.

Real meaning comes only from within a person, even though the perceptions, which evoke these meanings, result from external stimuli. The meanings, which are derived from perceptions, are influenced not only by the individual's experience, but also by many other factors. Knowledge of the factors that affect the perceptual process is very important to the aviation instructor because perceptions are the basis of all learning.

Factors That Affect Perception

Both internal and external factors affect an individual's ability to perceive:

- Physical organism
- Goals and values
- Self-concept
- Time and opportunity
- Element of threat

Physical Organism

The physical organism provides individuals with the perceptual apparatus for sensing the world around them. Pilots, for example, must be able to see, hear, feel, and respond adequately while they are in the air.

Goals and Values

Perceptions depend on one's values and goals. Every experience and sensation, which is funneled into one's central nervous system, is colored by the individual's own beliefs and value structures. Spectators at a ball game may see an infraction or foul differently depending on which team they support. The values of the student are important for the instructor to know, because this knowledge assists in predicting how the student interprets experiences and instructions.

Goals are also a product of one's value structure. Things that are more highly valued and cherished are pursued; those accorded less value and importance are not sought after.

Self-Concept

Self-concept is a powerful determinant in learning. A student's self-image, described in such terms as "confident" or "insecure," has a great influence on the total perceptual process. If a student's experiences tend to support a favorable self-image, the student tends to remain receptive to subsequent experiences. If a student has negative experiences, which tend to contradict self-concept, there is a tendency to reject additional training.

A negative self-concept inhibits the perceptual processes by introducing psychological barriers, which tend to keep the student from perceiving. They may also inhibit the ability to properly implement what is perceived. That is, self-concept affects the ability to actually perform or do things unfavorably. Students who view themselves positively, on the other hand, are less defensive and more receptive to new experiences, instructions, and demonstrations.

Time and Opportunity

It takes time and opportunity to perceive. Learning some things depends on other perceptions, which have preceded these learnings, and on the availability of time to sense and relate these new things to the earlier perceptions. Thus, proper sequence and time are necessary.

A student could probably stall an aircraft on the first attempt, regardless of previous experience. Stalls cannot really be learned, however, unless some experience in normal flight has been acquired. Even with such experience, time and practice are needed to relate the new sensations and experiences associated with stalls in order to develop a perception of the stall. In general, lengthening an experience and increasing its frequency are the most obvious ways to speed up learning, although this is not always effective. Many factors, in addition to the length and frequency of training periods, affect the rate of learning. The effectiveness of the use of a properly planned training syllabus is proportional to the consideration it gives to the time and opportunity factor in perception.

Element of Threat

The element of threat does not promote effective learning. In fact, fear adversely affects perception by narrowing the perceptual field. Confronted with threat, students tend to limit their attention to the threatening object or condition. The field of vision is reduced, for example, when an individual is frightened and all the perceptual faculties are focused on the thing that has generated fear.

Flight instruction provides many clear examples of this. During the initial practice of steep turns, Beverly may focus her attention on the altimeter and completely disregard outside visual references. Anything Bill does that is interpreted as threatening makes Beverly less able to accept the experience Bill is trying to provide. It adversely affects all her physical, emotional, and mental faculties.

Learning is a psychological process, not necessarily a logical one. Trying to frighten a student through threats of unsatisfactory reports or reprisals may seem logical, but is not effective psychologically. The effective instructor organizes teaching to fit the psychological needs of the student. If a situation seems overwhelming, the student feels unable to handle all of the factors involved; a threat exists. As long as the student feels capable of coping with a situation, each new experience is viewed as a challenge.

A good instructor recognizes that behavior is directly influenced by the way a student perceives, and perception is affected by all of these factors. Therefore, it is important for the instructor to facilitate the learning process by avoiding any actions which may inhibit or prevent the attainment of teaching goals. Teaching is consistently effective only when those factors that influence perception are recognized and taken into account.

Insight

Insight involves the grouping of perceptions into meaningful wholes. Creating insight is one of the instructor's major responsibilities. To ensure that this occurs, it is essential to keep each student constantly receptive to new experiences and to help the student understand how each piece relates to all other pieces of the total pattern of the task to be learned.

For example, during straight-and-level flight in an aircraft with a fixed-pitch propeller, the revolutions per minute (rpm) increase when the throttle is opened and decrease when it is closed. On the other hand, rpm changes can also result from changes in aircraft pitch attitude without changes in power setting. Obviously, engine speed, power setting, airspeed, and aircraft attitude are all related.

True learning requires an understanding of how each factor may affect all of the others and, at the same time, knowledge of how a change in any one of them may affect all of the others. This mental relating and grouping of associated perceptions is called insight.

Insight almost always occurs eventually, whether or not instruction is provided. For this reason, it is possible for a person to become an electrician by trial and error, just as one may become a lawyer by reading law. Instruction, however, speeds this learning process by teaching the relationship of perceptions as they occur, thus promoting the development of the student's insight.

As perceptions increase in number, the student develops insight by assembling them into larger blocks of learning. As a result, learning becomes more meaningful and more permanent. Forgetting is less of a problem when there are more anchor points for tying insights together. It is a major responsibility of the instructor to organize demonstrations and explanations, and to direct practice so that the student has better opportunities to understand the interrelationship of the many kinds of experiences that have been perceived. Pointing out the relationships as they occur, providing a secure and nonthreatening environment in which to learn, and helping the student acquire and maintain a favorable self-concept are key steps in fostering the development of insight.

Acquiring Knowledge

Part of an aviation instructor's job is helping students acquire knowledge. In this context, knowledge refers to information that humans are consciously aware of and can articulate. For example, knowledge of the fuel capacity of a particular aircraft, understanding how an internal combustion engine works, and the ability to determine the weight and balance of an aircraft are examples of knowledge.

Figure 2-6 shows the three phases of knowledge, a progression of how students acquire knowledge. Some practical considerations about learning new knowledge and instructor actions that help students acquire knowledge are summarized.

Memorization

A student's first attempt to acquire knowledge about a new topic amounts to memorizing facts about steps in a procedure. For example, when Beverly is learning to use an altimeter, she may have memorized that the knob on the instrument is used to dial the current barometric pressure and that this number must be obtained from the recorded broadcast and set prior to flight.

Memorizing facts and steps has an advantage: it allows students to get started quickly. For example, as soon as Beverly memorizes the purpose of the knob on the altimeter and the procedure for obtaining the current barometric pressure, she is able to properly configure the instrument for flight.

The limitations of memorization become apparent when a student is asked to solve a problem or provide an explanation of something that is not covered by the newly acquired knowledge. For example, when asked whether she would rather have the altimeter mistakenly set too high or too low

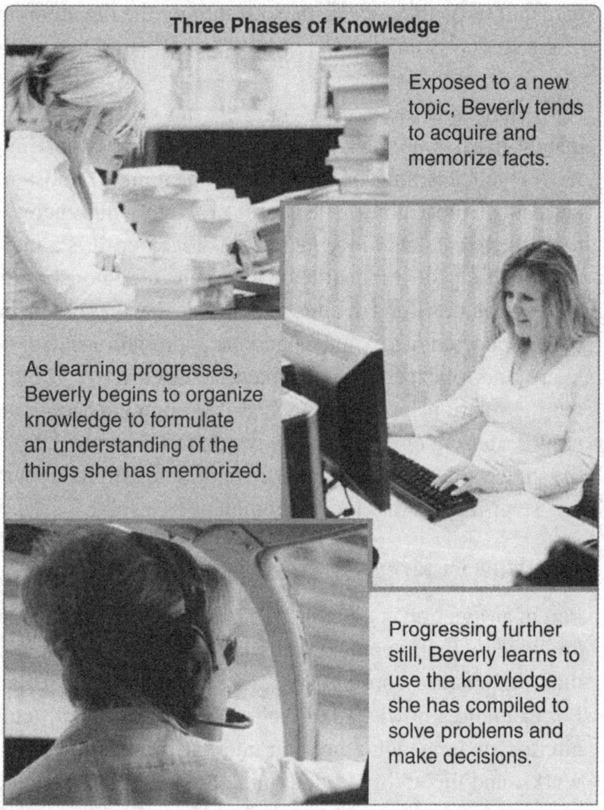

Figure 2-6. *A student acquires knowledge through memorization, understanding, and application.*

when flying in mountainous terrain, Beverly may not have an answer.

Understanding

A more experienced pilot can answer the altimeter question because she or he understands the ramifications of the question. Understanding, or the ability to notice similarities and make associations between the facts and procedural steps learned, is an important next stage in the knowledge acquisition process. At this stage, the learner begins to organize knowledge in useful ways and a collection of memorized facts gives way to understanding.

Understanding develops when students begin to organize known facts and steps into coherent groups that come together to form an understanding of how a thing or a process works. For example, after learning to adjust the mixture control in cruise flight, Beverly learns that combustion requires a certain mixture of fuel and air, and that air becomes less dense as altitude increases.

Combining these two ideas, she now understands the purpose of the mixture control is to keep these two quantities in balance as the aircraft changes altitude. "Mental model" or self-explanation is often used to refer to an organized collection of ideas that forms a learner's understanding of a thing or process.

The advantages of possessing this type of understanding include the following:

1. The learner is no longer limited to answering questions that match the memorized facts. For example, armed with the understanding of the mixture control, Beverly may now be able to produce answers to more challenging questions, such as what would happen if the mixture were set too rich or too lean.
2. Learners who understand a process have an easier time mastering variations of the processes, such as unfamiliar aircraft, new avionics systems, and unfamiliar airport procedures.
3. Understanding shared between people allows them to communicate more efficiently. For example, an experienced pilot might mention to an experienced mechanic that a magneto ran a bit rough during an engine run-up. This brief communication triggers access to a wealth of knowledge in the mind of the mechanic who instantly knows what must be done.
4. Learners who understand the purpose behind procedure steps are better able to remember the procedure steps later, or reconstruct them when they are forgotten.

Mental models evolve as learners take in new information. For example, Bill could ask Beverly why flying with an inappropriate mixture setting is bad. A learner whose understanding includes knowledge about spark plugs and carbon deposits might answer correctly. If this same learner's understanding later extends to include knowledge about thermal efficiency and the stoichiometric equation for the combustion of gasoline, the explanations are likely to become much more sophisticated. No individual's understanding of anything is ever "complete."

Concept Learning

Concept learning is based on the assumption that humans tend to group objects, events, ideas, people, etc., that share one or more major attributes that set them apart. It also involves discrimination between types of things or ideas inside or outside of a concept set. By grouping information into concepts, humans reduce the complexities of life and create manageable categories. Although many theories about concept learning exist, categorization has always been a central aspect.

Concept learning enhances student understanding when students formulate generalized concepts from particular facts or steps. Generalized concepts are more powerful than facts because instead of literally describing one thing, they describe many things at once.

For example, a new flight student who sees several examples of weight-shift control (WSC) aircraft may formulate a category for WSC aircraft based on the wing, which is large and fabric covered. The power of the category becomes obvious when the student sees a sport plane. Because of the similar wing, he or she immediately categorizes it as an ultra light and ascribes many of the properties of ultra light aircraft to the sport plane. In this way, the student has used a generalized concept to begin understanding something new.

Most learners exhibit a natural tendency to categorize and become adept at recognizing members of most any category they create. If something is encountered that does not fit into a category, these learners formulate a new category or revise the definitions of existing categories. In the above example, the student eventually must revise the category of ultra light to light-sport aircraft which encompasses both types of aircraft. Therefore, an important part of the learning process is continual revision of the categories used when learners encounter new things or exceptions to things previously catalogued.

Another type of generalization is a schema (the cognitive framework that helps people organize and interpret information). Schemas can be revised by any new information and are useful because they allow people to take shortcuts in interpreting a vast amount of information.

Humans form schemas when they notice reoccurring patterns in things frequently observed or done. Schemas help learners interpret things they observe by priming them to expect certain elements that match the schema. For example, schemas demonstrate why an experienced pilot is able to listen to and read back a lengthy departure clearance issued by air traffic control (ATC). Beginning flight students often remember the controller's use of the words "the" and "and" and fail to note more important words that describe assigned altitudes or radio frequencies. The experienced pilot is successful because he or she possesses a schema for this type of event and knows in advance that the clearance contains five key pieces of information. While listening to the clearance, the pilot anticipates and is primed to capture those five things.

Similarly, students create schemas for preflight inspection procedures and procedures required to operate advanced flight deck systems such as autopilots or multifunction displays. As with categories, humans continuously learn new schemas and revise old ones to accommodate new things as they continue to learn. While schemas help humans deal with information, they can also make it difficult to retain new information that does not conform to established schemas.

Thorndike and the Laws of Learning

One of the pioneers of educational psychology, E.L. Thorndike formulated three laws of learning in the early 20th century. *[Figure 2-7]* These laws are universally accepted and apply to all kinds of learning: the law of readiness, the law of exercise, and the law of effect. Since Thorndike set down his laws, three more have been added: the law of primacy, the law of intensity, and the law of recency.

Figure 2-7. *E. L. Thorndike (1874–1949).*

Readiness

The basic needs of the learner must be satisfied before he or she is ready or capable of learning (see Chapter 1, Human Behavior). The instructor can do little to motivate the learner if these needs have not been met. This means the learner must want to learn the task being presented and must possess the requisite knowledge and skill. In SBT, the instructor attempts to make the task as meaningful as possible and to keep it within the learner's capabilities.

Students best acquire new knowledge when they see a clear reason for doing so, often show a strong interest in learning what they believe they need to know next, and tend to set aside things for which they see no immediate need. For example, beginning flight students commonly ignore the flight instructor's suggestion to use the trim control. These students believe the control yoke is an adequate way to manipulate the aircraft's control surfaces. Later in training, when they must divert their attention away from the controls to other tasks, they realize the importance of trim.

Instructors can take two steps to keep their students in a state of readiness to learn. First, instructors should communicate a clear set of learning objectives to the student and relate each new topic to those objectives. Second, instructors should introduce topics in a logical order and leave students with a need to learn the next topic. The development and use of a well-designed curriculum accomplish this goal.

Readiness to learn also involves what is called the "teachable moment" or a moment of educational opportunity when a person is particularly responsive to being taught something. One of the most important skills to develop as an instructor is the ability to recognize and capitalize on "teachable moments" in aviation training. An instructor can find or create teachable moments in flight training activity: pattern work, air work in the local practice area, cross-country, flight review, or instrument proficiency check.

Teachable moments present opportunities to convey information in a way that is relevant, effective, and memorable to the student. They occur when a learner can clearly see how specific information or skills can be used in the real world.

For example, while on final approach several deer cross the runway. Bill capitalizes on this teachable moment to stress the importance of always being ready to perform a go-around.

Effect

All learning involves the formation of connections and connections are strengthened or weakened according to the law of effect. Responses to a situation that are followed by satisfaction are strengthened; responses followed by discomfort are weakened, either strengthening or weakening the connection of learning. Thus, learning is strengthened when accompanied by a pleasant or satisfying feeling, and weakened when associated with an unpleasant feeling. Experiences that produce feelings of defeat, frustration, anger, confusion, or futility are unpleasant for the student. For example, if Bill teaches landings to Beverly during the first flight, she is likely to feel inferior and be frustrated, which weakens the learning connection.

The learner needs to have success in order to have more success in the future. It is important for the instructor to create situations designed to promote success. Positive training experiences are more apt to lead to success and motivate the learner, while negative training experiences might stimulate forgetfulness or avoidance. When presented correctly, SBT provides immediate positive experiences in terms of real world applications.

To keep learning pleasant and to maintain student motivation, an instructor should make positive comments about the student's progress before discussing areas that need improving. Flight instructors have an opportunity to do this during the flight debriefing. For example, Bill praises Beverly on her aircraft control during all phases of flight, but offers constructive comments on how to better maintain the runway centerline during landings.

Exercise

Connections are strengthened with practice and weakened when practice is discontinued, which reflects the adage "use it or lose it." The learner needs to practice what has been learned in order to understand and remember the learning. Practice strengthens the learning connection; disuse weakens it. Exercise is most meaningful and effective when a skill is learned within the context of a real world application.

Primacy

Primacy, the state of being first, often creates a strong, almost unshakable impression and underlies the reason an instructor must teach correctly the first time and the student must learn correctly the first time. For example, a maintenance student learns a faulty riveting technique. Now the instructor must correct the bad habit and reteach the correct technique. Relearning is more difficult than initial learning.

Also, if the task is learned in isolation, it is not initially applied to the overall performance, or if it must be relearned, the process can be confusing and time consuming. The first experience should be positive, functional, and lay the foundation for all that is to follow.

Intensity

Immediate, exciting, or dramatic learning connected to a real situation teaches a learner more than a routine or boring experience. Real world applications (scenarios) that integrate procedures and tasks the learner is capable of learning make a vivid impression and he or she is least likely to forget the experience. For example, using realistic scenarios has been shown to be effective in the development of proficiency in flight maneuvers, tasks, and single-pilot resource management (SRM) skills.

Recency

The principle of recency states that things most recently learned are best remembered. Conversely, the further a learner is removed in time from a new fact or understanding, the more difficult it is to remember. For example, it is easy for a learner to recall a torque value used a few minutes earlier, but it is more difficult or even impossible to remember an unfamiliar one used a week earlier.

Instructors recognize the principle of recency when they carefully plan a summary for a ground school lesson, a shop period, or a postflight critique. The instructor repeats, restates, or reemphasizes important points at the end of a lesson to help the learner remember them. The principle of recency often determines the sequence of lectures within a course of instruction.

In SBT, the closer the training or learning time is to the time of the actual scenario, the more apt the learner is to perform successfully. This law is most effectively addressed by making the training experience as much like the scenario as possible.

Domains of Learning

As mentioned during the discussion of Cognitive Theory, Dr. Bloom played a central role in transforming the field of educational psychology. Interested in what and how people learn, he proposed a framework to help understand the major areas of learning and thinking. He first classified them into three large groups *[Figure 2-8]* called the domains of learning:

- Cognitive (thinking)
- Affective (feeling)
- Psychomotor (doing)

Cognitive Domain

The group effort to classify the levels of thinking behaviors thought to be important in the processes of learning mentioned earlier in the chapter led to Bloom's Taxonomy of the Cognitive Domain. One of the best known educational domains, it includes remembering specific facts (content knowledge) and concepts that help develop intellectual abilities and skills. There are six major categories, starting from the simplest behavior (recalling facts) to the most complex (evaluation). *[Figure 2-9]*

The four practical learning levels are rote, understanding, application, and correlation. *[Figure 2-10]* The lowest level is the ability to repeat something which one has been taught, without understanding or being able to apply what has been learned. This is referred to as rote learning. The fact level is a single concept. The key verbs which describe or measure this activity are words such as define, identify, and label. The comprehension or understanding level puts two or more concepts together and uses verbs such as describe, estimate, or explain. The application level puts two or more concepts together to form something new. Typical verbs at this level include "determine," "develop," and "solve."

For example, Bill may explain the procedure for entering a level, left turn to Beverly. The procedure includes several steps: (1) visually clear the area, (2) add a slight amount of power to maintain airspeed, (3) apply aileron control pressure to the left, (4) add sufficient rudder pressure in the direction of the turn to avoid slipping and skidding, and (5) increase back pressure to maintain altitude. When Beverly verbally repeats this instruction, she has learned the procedure by rote. This will not be very useful to her if there is never an opportunity to make a turn in flight, or if she has no knowledge of the function of aircraft controls.

With proper instruction on the effect and use of the flight controls, and experience in controlling the aircraft during straight-and-level flight, Beverly can consolidate old and new perceptions into an insight on how to make a turn. At this point, she has developed an understanding of the procedure for turning the aircraft in flight. This understanding is basic to effective learning, but may not necessarily enable her to make a correct turn on the first attempt.

When Beverly understands the procedure for entering a turn, has had turns demonstrated, and has practiced turn entries until consistency has been achieved, she has developed the skill to apply what has been learned. This is a major level of learning, and one at which the instructor is too often willing to stop. Discontinuing instruction on turn entries at this point and directing subsequent instruction exclusively to other elements of piloting performance is characteristic of piecemeal instruction, which is usually inefficient.

The correlation level of learning, which should be the objective of aviation instruction, is that level at which the student becomes able to associate an element which has been learned with other segments or blocks of learning. The other segments may be items or skills previously learned, or new learning tasks to be undertaken in the future. When Beverly has achieved this level of learning in turn entries, for example,

Cognitive	Affective	Psychomotor
Knowledge	Attitude	Skills
Recall information	Awareness	Observation
Understanding	Respond	Imitation
Application	Valuing	Practice
Analyze	Organization	Habit
Synthesize	Integration	
Evaluate		

Figure 2-8. *An overview of the three learning domains.*

	Competence	Skills Demonstrated	Example
I	Knowledge: remembering information	Define, identify, label, state, list, match, select	1. State the standard temperature at sea level. 2. Define a logbook entry.
II	Comprehension: explaining the meaning of information	Describe, generalize, paraphrase, summarize, estimate, discuss	1. In one sentence explain why aviation uses a standard temperature. 2. Describe why a log entry is required by the FAA.
III	Application: using abstractions in concrete situation	Determine, chart, implement, prepare, solve, use, develop, explain, apply, relate, instruct, show, teaches	1. Using a standard lapse rate, determine what the temperature would be at a pressure altitude of 4000'. 2. Determine when a logbook entry is required.
IV	Analysis: breaking down a whole into component parts	Points out, differentiate distinguish, examine discriminate, compare, outline, prioritize, recognize, subdivide	1. Compare what the different temperatures would be at certain pressure altitudes based on the standard lapse rate. 2. Determine information required for logbook entry.
V	Synthesis: putting parts together to form a new and integrated whole	Create, design, plan, organize, generate, write, adapt, compare, formulate, devise, model, revise, incorporate	1. Generate a chart depicting temperatures for altitudes up to 12,000'. 2. Write a logbook entry for an oil change.
VI	Evaluation: making judgments about the merits of ideas, materials, or phenomena	Appraise, critique, judge, weigh, evaluate, select, compare and contrast, defend, interpret, support	1. Evaluate the importance of this information for a pilot. 2. Evaluate the necessity of keeping logbook entries.

Figure 2-9. *The six major levels of Bloom's Taxonomy of the Cognitive Domain with types of behavior and examples of objectives.*

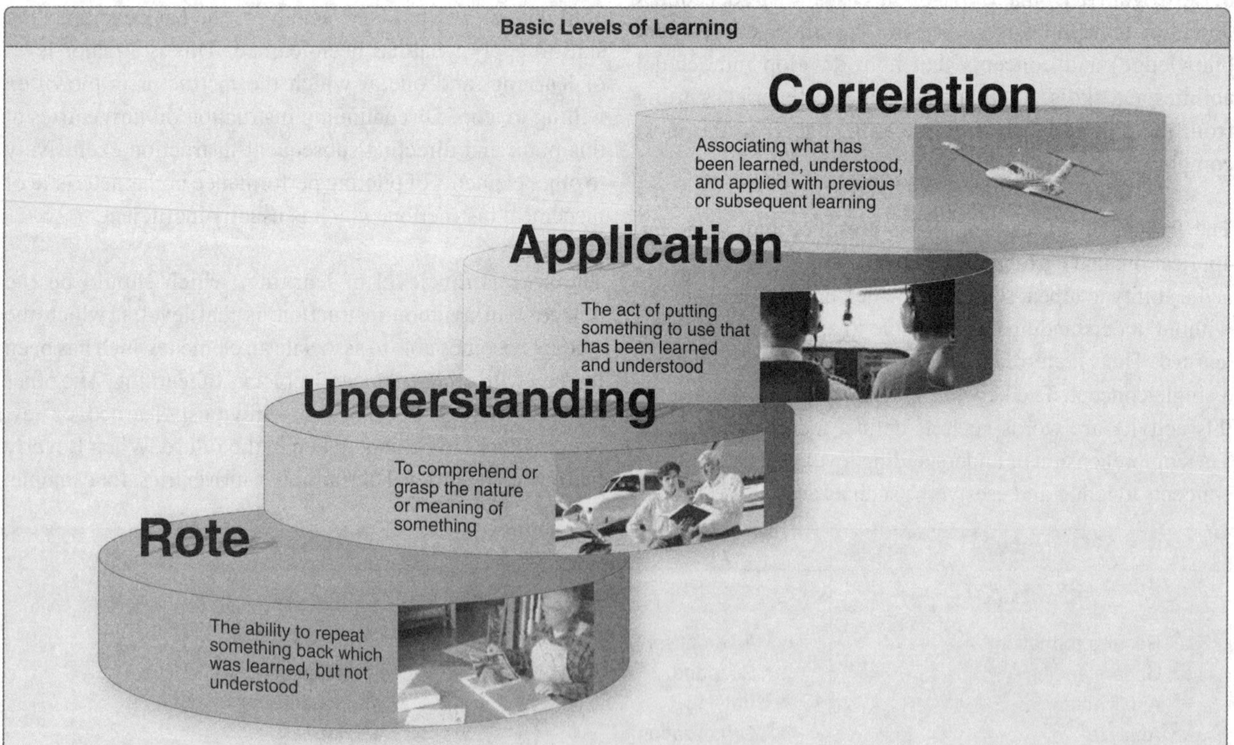

Figure 2-10. *Learning is progressive and occurs at several basic levels.*

she has developed the ability to correlate the elements of turn entries with the performance in traffic patterns.

The three higher thinking skills instructional levels include analysis, synthesis and evaluation (or HOTS level previously mentioned in the learning theory section). The analysis level involves breaking the information into its component parts, examining, and trying to understand the information in order to develop conclusions, make inferences, and/or find evidence to support generalizations. This level uses such verbs as points out, differentiate distinguish, examine, discriminate, compare, outline, prioritize, recognize, or subdivide.

Synthesis involves putting parts together to form a new and integrated whole. Typical verbs for this level include create, design, plan, organize, generate, write, adapt, compare, formulate, devise, model, revise, or incorporate. The final level in the taxonomy is evaluation and involves making judgments about the merits of ideas, materials, or phenomena. The following example demonstrates the difference between learning on the first three levels versus learning critical thinking skills.

Bill provides a detailed explanation on how to control for wind drift. The explanation includes a thorough coverage of heading, speed, angle of bank, altitude, terrain, and wind direction plus velocity. The explanation is followed by a demonstration and repeated practice of a specific flight maneuver, such as turns around a point or S-turns across the road until the maneuver can be consistently accomplished in a safe and effective manner within a specified limit of heading, altitude, and airspeed. At the end of this lesson, Beverly is only capable of performing the maneuver.

Then Bill asks Beverly to plan for the arrival at a specific nontowered airport. The planning should take into consideration the possible wind conditions, arrival paths, airport information and communication procedures, available runways, recommended traffic patterns, courses of action, and preparation for unexpected situations. Upon arrival at the airport, Beverly makes decisions (with guidance and feedback as necessary) to safely enter and fly the traffic pattern. This is followed by a discussion of what was done, why it was done, the consequences, and other possible courses of action and how it applies to other airports. At the end of this lesson the student is capable of explaining the safe arrival at any nontowered airport in any wind condition.

For aviation instructors, educational objectives for the first three levels (knowledge, comprehension, and application) are generally gained as the result of attending a ground school, reading about aircraft systems, listening to a preflight briefing, or taking part in computer-based training. The highest educational objective levels in this domain (analysis, synthesis, and evaluation) can be acquired through SBT training. For example, the student pilot learns to correctly evaluate a flight maneuver or the maintenance student repairs an aircraft engine. Sample questions for each level of the cognitive domain are provided in the graph. Thus, SBT correctly utilized reinforces the three higher level thinking skills.

Affective Domain

The affective domain addresses a learner's emotions toward the learning experience. It includes feelings, values, enthusiasms, motivations, and attitudes. *[Figure 2-11]* For the aviation instructor, this may mean how the student approaches learning. Is he or she motivated to learn? Does he or she exhibit confidence in learning? Does the student have a positive attitude toward safety?

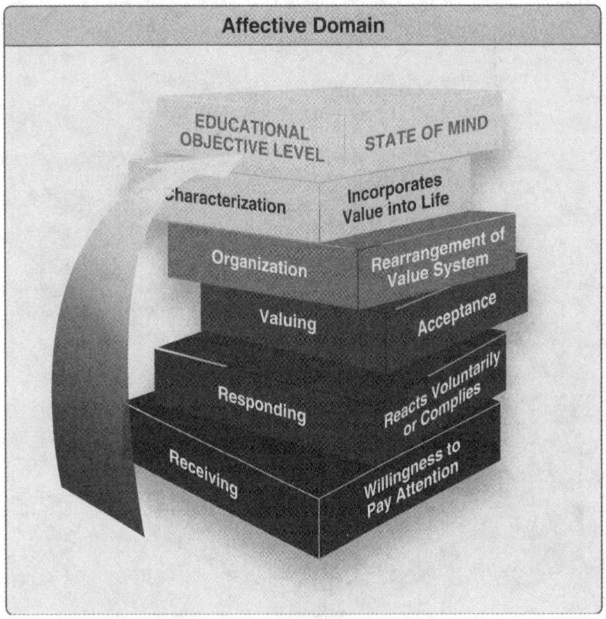

Figure 2-11. *The affective domain (attitudes, beliefs, and values) contains five educational objective levels.*

The affective domain provides a framework for teaching in five levels: awareness, response, value, organizing, and integration. In this taxonomy, the learner begins on the awareness level and is open to learning, willing to listen to the instructor. As the learner traverses the taxonomy, he or she responds by participating actively in the training, decides the value of the training, organizes the training into his or her personal belief system, and finally internalizes it.

The affective domain is more difficult to measure, but motivation and enthusiasm are important components of any learning. Therefore, the aviation instructor should be acquainted with this facet of learning. Motivation is discussed in depth later in the chapter.

Psychomotor Domain

The psychomotor domain is skill based and includes physical movement, coordination, and use of the motor-skill areas. *[Figure 2-12]* Development of these skills requires repetitive practice and is measured in terms of speed, precision, distance, and techniques. While various examples of the psychomotor domain exist, the practical instructional levels for aviation training purposes include observation, imitation, practice, and habit. This domain is an important component of instruction when aviation instructors prepare students for the practical test.

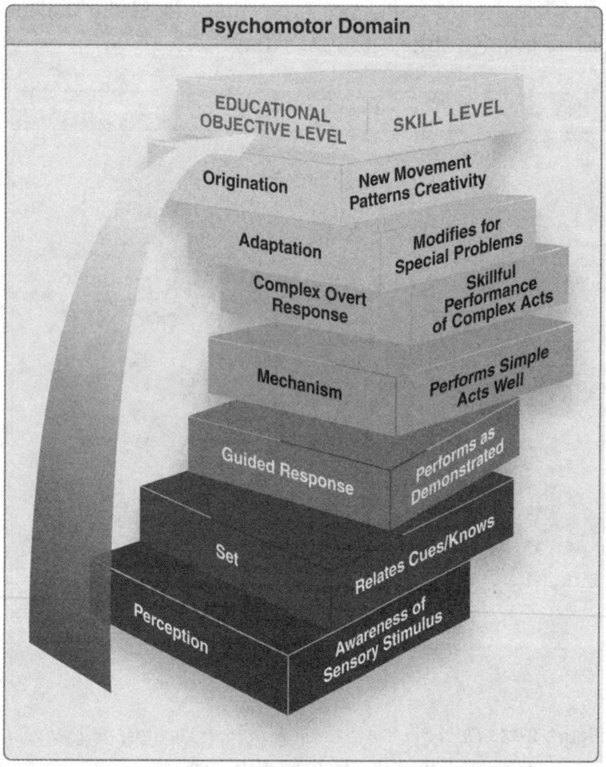

Figure 2-12. *The psychomotor domain (physical skills) consists of seven educational objective levels.*

At the first level, the learner observes a more experienced person perform the skill. The instructor has the learner observe sequences and relationships that lead to the finished product. Observation may be supplemented by reading, watching a DVD, or computer-based training. The second level is imitation in which the learner attempts to copy the skill under the watchful eye of the instructor.

The practice level is a proficiency building experience in which the learner tries a specific activity over and over. It may be conducted by the learner without direct oversight of the instructor, such as touch-and-go landings for the flight student who has flown a successful solo flight. The habit level is reached when the student can perform the skill in twice the time that it takes the instructor or an expert to perform. The evaluation of ability is a performance or skill test. If a person continues to perfect a skill, it eventually becomes a skill performed at the expert level.

Skills involving the psychomotor domain include learning to fly a precision instrument approach procedure, programming a global positioning system (GPS) receiver, or using sophisticated maintenance equipment. As physical tasks and equipment become more complex, the requirement for integration of cognitive and physical skills increases.

Summary of Instructor Actions

To help students acquire knowledge, the instructor should:

- Ask students to recite or practice newly acquired knowledge.
- Ask questions that probe student understanding and prompt them to think about what they have learned in different ways.
- Present opportunities for students to apply what they know to solving problems or making decisions.
- Present students with problems and decisions that test the limits of their knowledge.
- Demonstrate the benefits of understanding and being able to apply knowledge.
- Introduce new topics as they support the objectives of the lesson, whenever possible.

These additional levels of learning are the basis of the knowledge, attitude, and skill learning objectives commonly used in advanced qualification programs for airline training. They also can be tied to the PTS to show the level of knowledge or skill required for a particular task. A list of action verbs for the three domains shows appropriate behavioral objectives at each level. *[Figure 2-13]* Instructors who are familiar with curriculum development recognize that the action verbs are examples of performance-based objectives.

Characteristics of Learning

The ability to learn is one of the most outstanding human characteristics. Learning occurs continuously throughout a person's lifetime. To understand how people learn, it is necessary to understand what happens to the individual during the process. In spite of numerous theories and contrasting views, psychologists generally agree there are many characteristics of learning.

Domain	Objective Level	Action Verbs for Each Level
COGNITIVE DOMAIN	Evaluation	assess, evaluate, interpret, judge, rate, score, or write
	Synthesis	compile, compose, design, reconstruct, or formulate
	Analysis	compare, discriminate, distinguish, or separate
	Application	compute, demonstrate, employ, operate, or solve
	Comprehension	convert, explain, locate, report, restate, or select
	Knowledge	describe, identify, name, point to, recognize, or recall
AFFECTIVE DOMAIN	Characterization	assess, delegate, practice, influence, revise, and maintain
	Organization	accept responsibility, adhere, defend, and formulate
	Valuing	appreciate, follow, join, justify, show concern, or share
	Responding	conform, greet, help, perform, recite, or write
	Receiving	ask, choose, give, locate, select, rely, or use
PSYCHOMOTOR DOMAIN	Origination	combine, compose, construct, design, or originate
	Adaptation	adapt, alter, change, rearrange, reorganize, or revise
	Complex Overt Response	same as guided response except more highly coordinated
	Mechanism	same as guided response except with greater proficiency
	Guided Response	assemble, build, calibrate, fix, grind, or mend
	Set	begin, move, react, respond, start, or select
	Perception	choose, detect, identify, isolate, or compare

Figure 2-13. *A listing such as the one shown here is useful for development of almost any training program.*

Knowledge of the general characteristics of learning help an aviation instructor use them in a learning situation. If learning is a change in behavior as a result of experience, then instruction must include a careful and systematic creation of those experiences that promote learning. This process can be quite complex because, among other things, an individual's background strongly influences the way that person learns. To be effective, the learning situation also should be purposeful, based on experience, multifaceted, and involve an active process.

Learning Is Purposeful

Each student sees a learning situation from a different viewpoint. Each student is a unique individual whose past experiences affect readiness to learn and understanding of the requirements involved. For example, an instructor may give two aviation maintenance students the assignment of learning certain inspection procedures. One student may learn quickly and be able to competently present the assigned material. The combination of an aviation background and future goals may enable that student to realize the need and value of learning the procedures. A second student's goal may only be to comply with the instructor's assignment, and may result in only minimum preparation. The responses differ because each student acts in accordance with what he or she sees in the situation.

Most people have fairly definite ideas about what they want to do and achieve. Their goals sometimes are short term, involving a matter of days or weeks. On the other hand, their goals may be carefully planned for a career or a lifetime. Each student has specific intentions and goals. Some may be shared by other students. Students learn from any activity that tends to further their goals. Their individual needs and attitudes may determine what they learn as much as what the instructor is trying to get them to learn. In the process of learning, the student's goals are of paramount significance. To be effective, aviation instructors need to find ways to relate new learning to the student's goals.

Learning Is a Result of Experience

Since learning is an individual process, the instructor cannot do it for the student. The student can learn only from personal experiences; therefore, learning and knowledge cannot exist apart from a person. A person's knowledge is a result of experience, and no two people have had identical experiences. Even when observing the same event, two people react differently; they learn different things from it, according to the manner in which the situation affects their individual needs. Previous experience conditions a person to respond to some things and to ignore others.

All learning is by experience, but learning takes place in different forms and in varying degrees of richness and depth. For instance, some experiences involve the whole person while others may be based only on hearing and memory. Aviation instructors are faced with the problem of providing learning experiences that are meaningful, varied, and appropriate. As an example, students can learn to say a list of words through repeated drill, or they can learn to recite certain principles of flight by rote. However, they can make them meaningful only if they understand them well enough to apply them correctly to real situations. If an experience challenges the students, requires involvement with feelings, thoughts, memory of past experiences, and physical activity, it is more effective than a learning experience in which all the students have to do is commit something to memory.

It seems clear enough that the learning of a physical skill requires actual experience in performing that skill. Student pilots learn to fly aircraft only if their experiences include flying them; student AMTs learn to overhaul power plants only by actually performing that task. Mental habits are also learned through practice. If students are to use sound judgment and develop decision-making skills, they need learning experiences that involve knowledge of general principles and require the use of judgment in solving realistic problems.

Learning Is Multifaceted

If instructors see their objective as being only to train their students' memory and muscles, they are underestimating the potential of the teaching situation. Students learn much more than expected if they fully exercise their minds and feelings. The fact that these items were not included in the instructor's plan does not prevent them from influencing the learning situation.

Psychologists sometimes classify learning by types, such as verbal, conceptual, perceptual, motor, problem-solving, and emotional. Other classifications refer to intellectual skills, cognitive strategies, and attitudinal changes, along with descriptive terms like surface or deep learning. However useful these divisions may be, they are somewhat artificial. For example, a class learning to apply the scientific method of problem-solving may learn the method by trying to solve real problems. But in doing so, the class also engages in verbal learning and sensory perception at the same time. Each student approaches the task with preconceived ideas and feelings, and for many students, these ideas change as a result of experience. Therefore, the learning process may include verbal elements, conceptual elements, perceptual elements, emotional elements, and problem-solving elements all taking place at once. This aspect of learning will become more evident later in this handbook when lesson planning is discussed.

Learning is multifaceted in still another way. While learning the subject at hand, students may be learning other things as well. They may be developing attitudes about aviation—good or bad—depending on what they experience. Under a skillful instructor, they may learn self-reliance. The list is seemingly endless. This type of learning is sometimes referred to as incidental, but it may have a great impact on the total development of the student.

Learning Is an Active Process

Students do not soak up knowledge like a sponge absorbs water. The instructor cannot assume that students remember something just because they were in the classroom, shop, or aircraft when the instructor presented the material. Neither can the instructor assume the students can apply what they know because they can quote the correct answer verbatim. For students to learn, they need to react and respond, perhaps outwardly, perhaps only inwardly, emotionally, or intellectually.

Learning Styles

Learning styles are simply different approaches or ways of learning based on the fact that people absorb and process information in different ways. Learning style is an individual's preference for understanding experiences and changing them into knowledge. It denotes the typical strategy a learner adopts in a learning situation. For example, information may be learned in a variety of ways: by seeing or hearing, by reflecting or acting, analyzing or visualizing, or it may be learned piecemeal or steadily. Just as people learn differently, they also have different teaching methods. Some instructors rely on lectures, others demonstrate, and others may prefer computer simulation training. Everyone has a mixture of strengths and preferences, not a single style or preference to the complete exclusion of any other. Please bear this in mind when using these ideas.

As mentioned in chapter 1 and the discussion of personality types and learning, underpinning the idea of learning style is the theory that everyone has an individual style of learning. According to this approach to learning, if the student and instructor work with that style, rather than against it, both benefit. Currently, 71 different theories of learning styles have been identified. These theories run from simple to complex, usually reflecting scientific research about how the brain processes information. While the scientific community may be surprised at how the research has been used, many educators and school systems have become advocates of applying learning style to teaching methods.

Another model for learning, the Approaches to Learning model, bases its theory on the student's learning intentions. For example, is the student interested in short-term memorization of the material or long-term knowledge? Does the student want a passing grade on a pop quiz or the ability to use the material learned to repair an engine? One feature of the Approaches to Learning is that the learner's approach to learning depends on his or her reasons for learning. This theory reflects the chapter 1 discussion of adult learners who come to aviation training with definite reasons for learning.

While controversy exists over the scientific value of learning styles as well as approaches to learning, many educational psychologists advocate their use in the learning process. Knowledge of learning styles and approaches can help an instructor make adjustments in how material is presented if his or her learning/teaching style differs from the way a student learns. Since a student's information processing technique, personality, social interaction tendencies, and the instructional methods used are all significant factors, training programs should be sensitive to different learning styles.

Right Brain/Left Brain

According to research on the human brain, people have a preferred side of the brain to use for understanding and storing information. While both sides of the brain are involved in nearly every human activity, it has been shown that those with right-brain dominance are characterized as being spatially oriented, creative, intuitive, and emotional. Those with left-brain dominance are more verbal, analytical, and objective. Generally, the brain functions as a whole. For example, the right hemisphere may recognize a face, while the left associates a name to go with the face.

While most people seem to have a dominant side, it is a preference, not an absolute. On the other hand, when learning is new, difficult, or stressful, the brain seems to go on autopilot to the preferred side. Recognizing a student's dominant brain hemisphere gives the instructor a guide for ways to teach and reinforce learning. There are also some people who use both sides of the brain equally well for understanding and storing information. *[Figure 2-14]*

Left Brain	Right Brain
Responds well to verbal instruction	Responds well to demonstrated instructions
Likes to learn in step-by-step format	Likes to learn general concept and then specifics
Prefers writing	Prefers open-ended questions
Is planned and structured	Responds to tone of voice
Does well on multiple choice tests	Impulsive
Analytic	Recalls people's faces
Recalls people's names	Holistic or global

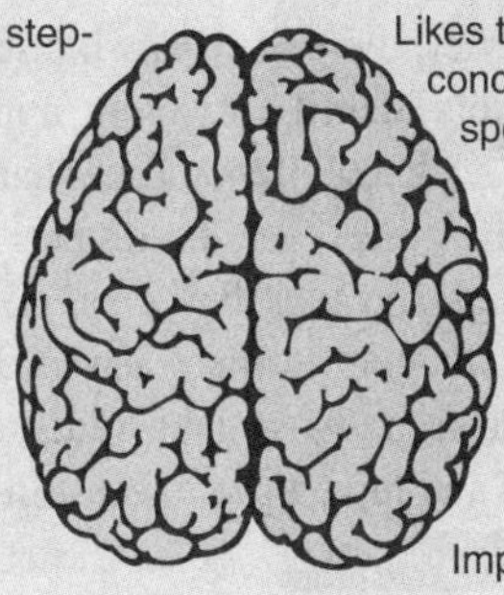

Figure 2-14. *The importance of recognizing a dominant brain hemisphere gives the instructor a guide for ways to teach and reinforce learning.*

Holistic/Serialist Theory

As seen in *Figure 2-14,* right and left brain learners have preferences for how they process information. Based on information processing theory, left brain learners or serialist learners have an analytic approach to learning. Because they gain understanding in linear steps, with each step logically following the previous one, these learners need well-defined, sequential steps where the overall picture is developed slowly, thoroughly, and logically. This is a bottom-up strategy.

Right brain or holistic learners favor the holist strategy and prefer a big picture or global perspective. This is a top-down strategy and learners tend to learn in large jumps, absorbing material almost randomly without seeing connections, until suddenly "it" clicks and they get it. Global learners solve complex problems rapidly once they have grasped the big picture, but they often have difficulty explaining how they did it. This type of learner seeks overall comprehension; analogies help this learner.

Index of Learning Styles (ILS)

In 1988, Richard Felder and Linda Silverman designed a learning style model with parallel learning styles that classified students as having learning preferences in sensing or intuitive, visual or verbal, active or reflective, sequential or global (discussed under holistic/serialist learning style. Dr. Felder maintains a website at www4.ncsu.edu/unity/lockers/users/f/felder/public/RMF.html that offers learners the opportunity to assess learning preferences at no cost for noncommercial purposes. *[Figure 2-15]*

Learning Style	Traits
Active	Tends to retain and understand information by doing something with it
Reflective	Prefers to think about information quietly
Sensing	Likes learning facts
Intuitive	Prefers discovering possibilities and relationships
Visual	Remembers best what is seen
Verbal	Learns more from words–written and spoken explanations
Sequential	Learns best with step-by-step explanations
Global	Tends to learn in large jumps

Figure 2-15. *Some of the different traits utilized by each learning style.*

Visual, Auditory, Kinesthetic Learners (VAK)

One of the most popular learning styles is based on the three main sensory receptors: vision, hearing, and touch. These are called visual, auditory, and kinesthetic learning styles (VAK). *[Figure 2-16]* Research in this area dates back to the early 20th century and the concepts were developed over many years by psychologists and teaching specialists. Others have augmented the VAK model with the addition of R for "reading" (VARK), or the addition of T for "tactile" (VAKT), or even a combination of the terms for VARKT.

Learning Style	Traits	Teaching Tips
Visual	Seeing, reading	Use graphs, charts,videos.
Auditory	Hearing, speaking	Have learner verbalize questions.
Kinesthetic	Touching, doing	Use demonstrations of skills.

Figure 2-16. *Visual, auditory, and kinesthetic learning styles (VAK).*

Learners generally use all three styles to receive information, but one of these three ways of receiving information is dominant. Once again, the dominant style of receiving information is the best way for a person to learn new information, but this style may not be the same for every task. The learner may use one style of learning or a combination of styles depending on the learning task.

Visual learners rely on seeing to learn. They learn best if a major component of the lesson is something they can see, and work best with printed and graphic materials, and visual displays including diagrams, illustrated text books, overhead transparencies, videos, flip charts, and hand-outs. They store information in their brains as pictures or images. They like to take extensive notes. Statistically, most people are visual learners.

Auditory learners transfer knowledge through listening and speaking. These learners need an oral component to the lesson such as verbal instructions. These learners have excellent listening skills and remember what was discussed over what was seen. They are better at verbally explaining than at writing. Since auditory learners prefer to listen to material, they are not good note takers.

Kinesthetic learners process and store information through physical experience such as touching, manipulating, using, or doing. They like to move around while trying to solve a problem and learn best when the material being taught involves hands-on practical experiences. Their concentration tends to wander when there is no external stimulation. They also learn from demonstration by watching carefully, then imagining or mirroring the demonstrator's movements.

Learners may prefer one of these three learning styles over another, but most learners employ all three depending on the material being learned. For example, when Beverly makes her first landing with Bill guiding her attempt, she employs visual, auditory, and kinesthetic learning. As the aircraft enters downwind, Beverly uses visual cues to recognize the airport and landing strip as she lines the aircraft up to land. As Bill talks her through the procedures, Beverly is using her auditory learning skills to learn how to land the aircraft. Finally, she needs to use kinesthetic skills to perform the actual landing.

Remember, good learners are capable of processing information in a variety of ways. The key to meeting individual student needs is to ensure a variety of learning styles are addressed in every lesson.

Superlinks

In a theory proposed by Ricki Linksman, the learning style ideas discussed in the preceding paragraphs have been melded into a concept based on the VAKT learning styles plus brain hemisphere preference. This "superlink," as she calls it, is the easiest way for a learner to process information in order to understand, remember, and retain it. Matching visual, auditory, kinesthetic, and tactile with right- and left-brain research, Linksman created eight superlinks: visual left-brain, visual right-brain, auditory left-brain, auditory right-brain, tactile left-brain, tactile right-brain, kinesthetic left-brain, and kinesthetic right-brain. These superlinks accelerate learning by targeting the best way a person learns.

Summary

As mentioned earlier, there are many models of how people learn. Some models identify styles or approaches that are easily recognized such as collaborative, sharing students who enjoy working with others, versus competitive students who are grade conscious and feel they must do better than their peers. Participant students normally have a desire to learn and enjoy attending class, and avoidant students do not take part in class activities and have little interest in learning.

The learning environment also influences learning style. In real life, most students find it necessary to adapt to a traditional style-learning environment provided by a school, university, or other educational/training establishment. Sometimes, the student's way of learning may or may not be compatible with his or her environment.

Instructors who recognize either the learning style or learning approach of students and problems associated with them are more effective teachers than those who do not. Also, these instructors are prepared to develop appropriate lesson plans and provide guidance, counseling, or other advisory services, as required.

Acquiring Skill Knowledge

An aviation instructor also helps a student acquire skill knowledge, which is knowledge reflected in motor or manual skills and in cognitive or mental skills, that manifests itself in the doing of something. Thus, skill knowledge differs from declarative knowledge because the student is not usually aware of it consciously or able to articulate the skill. Evidence of skill knowledge is gained through observations of performance. This knowledge of how to do things is based on extensive practice, which leads to the storage of skill knowledge. An everyday example of skill knowledge is the ability to ride a bicycle.

Skill knowledge is acquired slowly through related experience. For example, a maintenance student who is learning to weld typically burns or cracks the metal being welded while an expert welder's work is free of such imperfections. What does the experienced welder "know" that the beginner does not? The expert welder has had many hours of practice and a knowing-is-in-the-doing ability the inexperienced welder lacks. It isn't always possible to reduce to mere words that which one knows or knows how to do.

Stages of Skill Acquisition

Students make their way from beginner to expert via three stages of skill knowledge acquisition, helping students transition from beginner to expert. The development of any skill acquisition (or the learning process) has three characteristic stages: cognitive, associative, and automaticity. An instructor must learn to recognize each stage in student performance in order to assess student progress.

Cognitive Stage

Cognitive learning has a basis in factual knowledge. Since the student has no prior knowledge of flying, the instructor first introduces him or her to a basic skill. The student then memorizes the steps required to perform the skill. As the student carries out these memorized steps, he or she is often unaware of progress, or may fixate on one aspect of performance. Performing the skill at this stage typically requires all the student's attention; distractions introduced by an instructor often cause performance to deteriorate or stop.

The best way to prepare the student to perform a task is to provide a clear, step-by-step example. Having a model to follow permits students to get a clear picture of each step in the sequence so they understand what is required and how to do it. In flight or maintenance training, the instructor provides the demonstration, emphasizing the steps and techniques. During classroom instruction, an outside expert may be used, either in person or in a video presentation. In any case, students need to have a clear impression of what they are to do.

For example, Beverly enters a steep turn after increasing power by a prescribed amount and adjusting the pitch trim. She fixates on the attitude indicator as she attempts to achieve the desired bank angle. The bank angle exceeds tolerances as she struggles to correct it, making many abrupt control inputs.

Associative Stage

Even demonstrating how to do something does not result in the student learning the skill. Practice is necessary in order for the student to learn how to coordinate muscles with visual and tactile senses. Learning to perform various aircraft maintenance skills or flight maneuvers requires practice. Another benefit of practice is that as the student gains proficiency in a skill, verbal instructions become more meaningful. A long, detailed explanation is confusing before the student begins performing, whereas specific comments are more meaningful and useful after the skill has been partially mastered.

As the storage of a skill via practice continues, the student learns to associate individual steps in performance with likely outcomes. The student no longer performs a series of memorized steps, but is able to assess his or her progress along the way and make adjustments in performance. Performing the skill still requires deliberate attention, but the student is better able to deal with distractions.

For example, Beverly enters the steep turn and again struggles to achieve the desired bank angle. Still working on the bank angle, she remembers the persistent altitude control problem and glances at the altimeter. Noticing that the aircraft has descended almost 100 feet, she increases back pressure on the control and adjusts the trim slightly. She goes back to a continuing struggle with the bank angle, keeping it under control with some effort, and completes the turn 80 feet higher than started.

Automatic Response Stage

Automaticity is one of the by-products of practice. As procedures become automatic, less attention is required to carry them out, so it is possible to do other things simultaneously, or at least do other things more comfortably. By this stage, student performance of the skill is rapid and smooth. The student devotes much less deliberate attention to performance, and may be able to carry on a conversation or perform other tasks while performing the skill. The student makes far fewer adjustments during his or her performance and these adjustments tend to be small. The student may no longer be able to remember the individual steps in the procedure, or explain how to perform the skill.

For example, the student smoothly increases power, back pressure on the yoke, and trim as a turn is entered. During the turn, the instructor questions the student on an unrelated topic. The student answers the questions, while making two small adjustments in pitch and trim, and then rolls out of the turn with the altimeter centered on the target altitude. Noting the dramatically improved performance, the instructor asks "What are you doing differently?" The student seems unsure and says, "I have developed a feel for it."

Knowledge of Results

In learning some simple skills, students can discover their own errors quite easily. In other cases, such as learning complex aircraft maintenance skills, flight maneuvers, or flight crew duties, mistakes are not always apparent. A student may know that something is wrong, but not know how to correct it. In any case, the instructor provides a helpful and often critical function in making certain that the students are aware of their progress. It is perhaps as important for students to know when they are right as when they are wrong. They should be told as soon after the performance as possible, and should not be allowed to practice mistakes. It is more difficult to unlearn a mistake, and then learn the skill correctly, than to learn correctly in the first place. One way to make students aware of their progress is to repeat a demonstration or example and to show them the standards their performance must ultimately meet.

How To Develop Skills

Theories about how a skill evolves from the awkward and deliberate performance associated with the cognitive stage to the smooth and steady-handed performance of the automatic response stage have one thing in common: progress appears to depend on repeated practice. Making progress toward automating a skill seems to be largely a matter of performing the skill over and over again. In skill learning, the first trials are slow and coordination is lacking. Mistakes are frequent, but each trial provides clues for improvement in subsequent trials. The student modifies different aspects of the skill such as how to hold the yoke or weld correctly.

How long does it take to become proficient at a skill? Studies of skill learning have demonstrated that progress tends to follow what is known as a power law of practice. This law simply states that the speed of performance of a task improves as a power of the number of times that the task is performed. The logarithm of the reaction time for a particular task decreases linearly with the logarithm of the number of practice trials taken. Qualitatively, the law simply says that practice improves performance.

The graph in *Figure 2-17* shows how the power law of practice relates the time required to perform a skill to the number of times the skill has been practiced. While it is impossible to predict how many practice trials a student will recquire to develop a skill to maturity, the general shape of the power law of practice offers some clues. Learning progress proceeds at a fast pace in the beginning (when there is ample room for improvement) and tends to slow down as performance becomes more skilled. In later stages of learning, improvement is more gradual. Once the curve levels off, it may stay level for a significant period of time. Further improvement may even seem unlikely. This is called a learning plateau.

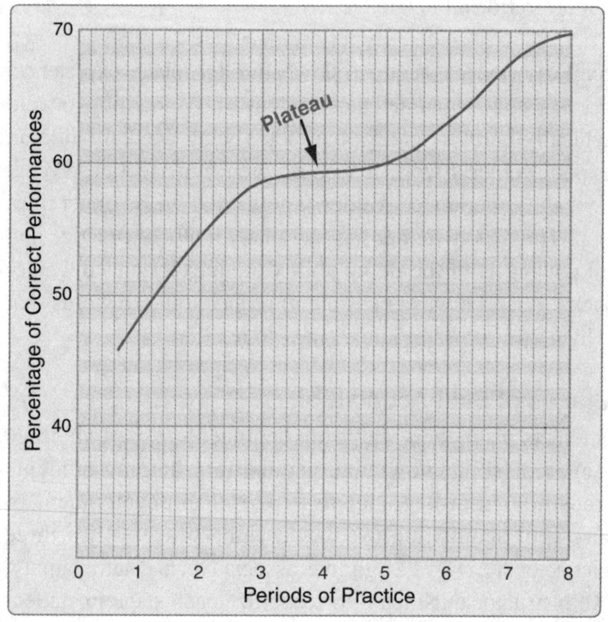

Figure 2-17. *Students will probably experience a learning plateau at some point in their training.*

Learning Plateaus

Learning plateaus are a normal part of the learning process and tend to be temporary, but instructors and students should be prepared for them. A learning plateau may signify any number of conditions. For example, the student may have reached capability limits, may be consolidating levels of skill, interest may have waned, or the student may need a more efficient method for increasing progress. Instructors themselves can bring on a learning plateau by overpractice. After repeating any task three or four times, give it a break to avoid causing a learning plateau. Keep in mind that the apparent lack of increasing proficiency does not necessarily mean that learning has ceased. The point is that, in learning motor skills, a leveling off process, or plateau, is normal and should be expected after an initial period of rapid improvement. The instructor should prepare the student for this situation to avert discouragement. If the student is aware of this learning plateau, frustration may be minimized.

Instructors can help students who fall into a learning plateau by moving the student to a different place in the curriculum and giving the current task a break. Instructors should also be aware that they can bring on a learning plateau by over-practice. Learning plateau problems can sometimes be alleviated also by the instructor better explaining the lesson, the reason for the lesson, and how it applies to the student.

Types of Practice

Once a student learns the skill, it is important to continue some practice to improve retention, but the power law of practice raises the question of whether or not there is a point at which continued practice no longer leads to improvement. Since athletic coaches, among others, are very interested in maximizing performance, much research has been done on the subject. Within the last few years, research has shown that how practice is structured makes an important impact on how well people retain what they have learned.

There are three types of practice, each of which yields particular results in acquiring skills: deliberate, blocked, and random.

Deliberate Practice

In order for a student to gain skill knowledge and learn how to perform the skill on the automatic level, a student must engage in deliberate practice. This practice is aimed at a particular goal. During deliberate practice, the student practices specific areas for improvement and receives specific feedback after practice. The feedback points out discrepancies between the actual performance and the performance goal sought. During deliberate practice, a student focuses on eliminating these discrepancies. *[Figure 2-18]*

Figure 2-18. *A student exhibits deliberate practice by plotting courses for his next training flight.*

Studies of skill learning suggest a student achieves better results if distractions are avoided during deliberate practice. When feedback is needed to correct student performance, it should be brief and explicit. Examples of individual skills for pilots are landings, stalls, steep turns, and procedure flows. Examples for maintenance technicians are correct installation of piston rings on a reciprocating engine, setting timing on an aircraft engine, and installing a tach generator.

Unlike the acquisition of knowledge, skill learning does not benefit from the instructor introducing the student to new ideas or prompting the student to think about old ones in different ways. On the other hand, instructors should not confuse distractions during skill learning with the legitimate use of distractions to help a student learn how to manage his or her attention while coordinating several tasks that have been mastered to some degree.

Blocked Practice

Blocked practice is practicing the same drill until the movement becomes automatic. Doing the same task over and over leads to better short-term performance, but poorer long-term learning. It tends to fool not only the student but the instructor into thinking the skills have been well learned. While blocked practice enhances current performance, it does not improve either concept learning or retrieval from long-term memory. *[Figure 2-19]*

Random Practice

Random practice mixes up the skills to be acquired throughout the practice session. This type of practice leads to better retention because by performing a series of separate skills in a random order, the student starts to recognize the similarities and differences of each skill which makes it more meaningful. The learner also is able to store the skill more effectively in the long-term memory. Students are then required to retrieve

Figure 2-19. *Pilot practices cross-wind landings repeatedly to improve performance.*

steps and parameters from long-term memory which helps students recognize patterns between tasks.

Blocked practice performance scores well during the actual practice when compared to random practice performance. But on a test given the next day, random practice does better than blocked practice. For long-term retention of aviation knowledge, the instructor who uses well-written SBT which encourages random practice and leads to better retention of information.

How much practice is needed to attain proficiency? In planning for student skill acquisition, a primary consideration is the length of time devoted to practice. A beginning student reaches a point where additional practice is not only unproductive, but may even be harmful. When this point is reached, errors increase, and motivation declines. As a student gains experience, longer periods of practice are profitable.

Another consideration is the problem of whether to divide the practice period. Perhaps even the related instruction should be broken down into segments, or it may be advantageous to plan one continuous, integrated sequence. The answer depends on the nature of the skill. Some skills are composed of closely related steps, each dependent on the preceding one. Learning to pack a parachute is a good example. Other skills are composed of related subgroups of skills. Learning to overhaul an aircraft engine is a good example.

One way to structure practice to get the most from learning is to expose the student to the same knowledge and skill in different contexts. For example, after practicing the short field landing in the aircraft, return to the classroom and rehearse the procedure using the toy airplane. Then, watch a video that shows a variety of back-to-back landings and have the student describe what went right and what went wrong. Each of these learning methods gives the student the chance practice the maneuver while adding new perceptions and insights to his or her skill base.

Evaluation Versus Critique

In the initial stages of skill acquisition, practical suggestions are more valuable to the student than a grade. Early evaluation is usually teacher oriented. It provides a check on teaching effectiveness, can be used to predict eventual student learning proficiency, and can help the teacher locate special problem areas. The observations on which the evaluations are based also can identify the student's strengths and weaknesses, a prerequisite for making constructive criticism. For additional information, refer to Chapter 5, Assessment.

As a student practices a skill, it is important he or she perform the skill correctly and that the skill being practiced is one that needs to be developed to maturity. An instructor ensures a skill is practiced correctly by monitoring the practice and providing feedback about the skill development. The student profits by having someone watch the performance and provide constructive criticism to help eliminate errors. Providing compliments on aspects of the skill that were performed correctly help keep the evaluation positive. Allowing the student to critique his or her performance enhances student-centered training.

Instructors should note students can develop deviations from the intended method of performance at any stage of skill acquisition.

Overlearning of Knowledge

Overlearning is the continued study of a skill after initial proficiency has been achieved. Practice proceeds beyond the point at which the act can be performed with the required degree of excellence. The phenomenon of overlearning sometimes occurs when knowledge used frequently begins to take on the properties of a skill. For example, a student's everyday knowledge about weight-and-balance concepts tends to center on the routine use of familiar charts found in the aircraft. Eventually, the student's performance is characterized less by an understanding of weight-and-balance concepts, and more by an automatic process in which rows and columns of familiar charts give desired numbers.

In some cases, the overlearning of knowledge has the advantage of making application of knowledge more streamlined and efficient. In other cases, the development of automated routines can lead to problems. For example, a verbal checklist procedure becomes so automatic that a streamlined recitation of checklist items becomes decoupled from the thoughts and actions the checklist items are intended to trigger. In this case, the pilot or mechanic may not stop to consider each item.

The development of automated skills can impede further learning or lead to forgetting general knowledge. In one study, student pilots and flight instructors were asked to solve weight-and-balance problems using charts taken from two different aircraft: (1) a small single-engine airplane they flew on a daily basis and (2) a different small single-engine airplane in which they had no experience. Test scores were surprisingly low when the charts for the unfamiliar airplane were used, and this was as true for instructors as it was for students. The results suggest pilots had focused on developing streamlined, automatic procedures tuned to the details of the familiar aircraft charts while their ability to use their understanding of overall weight-and-balance concepts seemed to have diminished.

Instructors must remain aware of skills students develop as a result of overlearning and help make sure that their actions continue to be accompanied by a use of their underlying knowledge. As a student progresses, the key difference between knowledge and skill becomes apparent. Memorized facts about a topic that once supported the beginner's awkward performance of the skill tend to develop into deeper understanding. Skill acquisition involves learning many individual steps that eventually meld into a seemingly continuous automated process, at which point the student has entered the procedural knowledge realm, and may no longer be consciously aware of the individual steps.

Application of Skill

The final and critical question is "Can the student use what has been learned?" It is not uncommon to find that students devote weeks and months in school learning new abilities, and then fail to apply these abilities on the job. To solve this problem, two conditions must be present. First, the student must learn the skill so well that it becomes easy, even habitual. Second, the student must recognize the types of situations where it is appropriate to use the skill. This second condition involves the question of transfer of learning, which is discussed later in this chapter.

Summary of Instructor Actions

To help students acquire skills, the instructor should:

- Explain that the key to acquiring and improving any skill is continued practice.
- Monitor student practice of skills and provide immediate feedback.
- Avoid conversation and other distractions when students are practicing individual skills.
- Explain that learning plateaus are common and that continued practice leads to continued improvement.

Putting It All Together

Many skills are learned before a student can fly an airplane or a maintenance student can rebuild an aircraft engine. Just as practicing scales is a fundamental part of learning to play the piano, the student does not "make music" until the ability to combine the notes in a variety of ways is acquired. For the student pilot or technician, practicing specific skills is essential, but flying a cross-country trip or repairing a collapsed landing gear requires "putting it all together" in the right way to achieve success.

The following section looks at the challenge of learning to perform several tasks at once, dealing with distractions and interruptions, overcoming problems with fixation and inattention. It also describes the benefits of using realistic training scenarios to develop these abilities.

Multitasking

Multitasking is the simultaneous execution of two or more tasks. A hallmark of the proficient pilot or mechanic is the ability to multitask. In aviation, multitasking involves two different abilities: attention switching and simultaneous performance. It is useful to distinguish between the two types of multitasking because developing both types of abilities is an important part of aviation training.

Attention Switching

Continuously switching attention back and forth between two or more tasks is attention switching. For example, when Beverly uses a checklist to perform a preflight inspection, she must continuously switch her attention between the checklist and the equipment she is inspecting. She looks at the checklist to retrieve the next step in the procedure, and then looks at the equipment to perform the step.

For many kinds of tasks, attention switching is the only way to accomplish multitasking. For example, it is generally impossible to look at two different things at the same time. The area of focused vision (called the fovea) is only a few degrees in span and can only be directed to one location at a time. Similarly, people cannot listen to two conversations at the same time. While both conversations fall upon the ears at once, people must devote their attention to the comprehension of one, to the exclusion of the other.

Psychologists sometimes refer to these limiting features of human information-processing capabilities as bottlenecks. For example, people have bottlenecks within the individual perceptual channels of hearing and seeing. Another important bottleneck becomes apparent when people attempt to process the information perceived or retrieved from memories.

Indeed, it seems impossible to think about two different things at the same time.

Simultaneous Performance

Performing several tasks at once, or simultaneous performance, is the second type of multitasking. *[Figure 2-20]* This type of multitasking becomes possible when no bottlenecks are present and when one or more of the tasks being performed are skills developed to the point of being automatic. For example, the experienced instrument pilot is able to perform basic attitude instrument flying while communicating with ATC. For these pilots, scanning instruments and responding to minor attitude deviations with small control inputs has become automatic. The attentional resources of the pilot are free to devote to thinking and talking about other topics.

It is important to note that the ability to simultaneously perform tasks is a fragile phenomenon. For example, suppose Beverly is performing the basic attitude control task and communicating with ATC when she suddenly encounters turbulence. The attitude control task quickly increases in difficulty and begins to require more and more deliberate attention. Her ability to perform both tasks simultaneously quickly degrades.

Learning To Multitask

Since doing several things at once is a natural part of aviation, instructors need to help students develop both types of multitasking abilities: attention switching and simultaneous performance. Before students are asked to perform several tasks at once, instructors should ensure that the student has devoted enough time to study and practice such that the individual tasks can be performed reasonably well in isolation.

Inexperience with an individual task can often hinder attempts to learn combinations of it and other tasks. For example, a student distracted by trying to interpret unfamiliar symbols on a sectional chart inadvertently deviates from assigned attitude or heading. An instructor recognizes the need to spend more time with these skills in isolation. In this case, there is nothing about the experience of controlling the aircraft that helps students better understand chart symbols.

Distractions and Interruptions

A distraction is an unexpected event that causes the student's attention to be momentarily diverted. Students must learn to decide whether or not a distraction warrants further attention or action on their part. Once this has been decided, the students must either turn their attention back to what they were doing, or act on the distraction.

An interruption is an unexpected event for which the student voluntarily suspends performance of one task in order to complete a different one. Interruptions are a significant source of errors and students must be made aware of the

Figure 2-20. *A pilot is required to perform several tasks at once during approach and landings.*

potential for errors caused by interruptions and develop procedures for dealing with them. A classic example is an interruption that occurs while a student is following the steps in a written procedure or checklist. The student puts down the checklist, deals with the interruption, and then returns to the procedure—but erroneously picks up at a later point in the procedure, omitting one or more steps.

Fixation and Inattention

Since human attention is limited in focus and highly prone to distraction, people are vulnerable to two other types of problems: fixation and inattention.

Fixation occurs when a student becomes absorbed in performing one task to the exclusion of other tasks. Instructors see many examples of this in student performance. Beginning instrument pilots characteristically fixate on particular instruments, attempting to control one aspect of their performance while other aspects deteriorate. Fixation on a task is often a sign that the task has not received enough practice in isolation. That is, the student has not yet mastered the task well enough to perform it in addition to other tasks. Fixation can happen even when individual skills have been reasonably mastered, when students have not yet learned the importance of managing their own limited attentional resources.

Inattention occurs when a student fails to pay attention to a task that is important. Inattention is sometimes a natural by-product of fixation. Students fixate on one task and become too busy to attend to other tasks. Inattention also happens when students are not busy: attention may drift when they become bored or think that a task does not deserve their attention. In some cases, this type of inattention is difficult to eliminate through training and practice. For example, it is well known that humans perform poorly when placed in the role of passive monitor. Many studies have shown how performance rapidly deteriorates when humans are asked to passively monitor gauges or the progress of an automated system such as a GPS navigation computer or autopilot. Furthermore, it seems that the more reliable the system becomes, the poorer the human performance becomes at the monitoring task. The first line of defense against this type of inattention is to alert the student to the problem, and to help students develop habits that keep their attention focused.

How To Identify Fixation or Inattention Problems

One way for instructors to identify problems with fixation and inattention is to try and follow where students look. To accomplish this, instructors can glance at a student's eyes to try to determine where the student is looking. Students who appear to look at one instrument for an extended period of time might have a problem with fixation. Students whose gaze is never directed toward engine instruments might have a problem with inattention.

The technique of following student eye movements is useful, but has limitations since looking in the same direction as the student is not the same as "seeing" what the student sees.

Scenario-Based Training

Research and practical experience have demonstrated the usefulness of practicing in realistic scenarios—ones that resemble the environment in which knowledge and skills are later used. Instructors must devise scenarios that allow students to practice what they have learned. This is challenging because different students need to practice different things at different times, and because different working environments present different practice opportunities.

What makes a good scenario? A good scenario:

- Has a clear set of objective.
- Is tailored to the needs of the student.
- Capitalizes on the nuances of the local environment.

For example, Bill is introducing Beverly to a low-fuel emergency. His objective at this early stage is to simply enable Beverly to recall the sorts of actions that are appropriate for a low-fuel emergency. He decides to use the classroom environment as a first practice scenario. He asks Beverly about what sorts of actions she might take if such an event would occur. She has some good ideas but he asks her to think more about before her next lesson. On her next lesson he gives her the same exercise. This time her answers are consistent and insightful. Bill decides that this scenario has served its purpose and moves on.

During their next flight, Bill's objective is having Beverly recall and carry out the steps that she was able to cite in the classroom. As they arrive at their home airport, he presents Beverly with a low-fuel scenario. He notes that she remembers much of what she was able to recall in the classroom, but amidst the excitement, has forgotten a few things. He uses the same scenario at a different airport on their next flight, and she performs admirably.

Later in her training, Bill's next objective is to enable her to recall and perform the emergency steps in concert with other piloting duties. They depart on a cross-country flight from a populated area to a remote area. While en route, Bill presents Beverly with a low-fuel emergency scenario knowing that there is only one airport nearby and that it is not easy to spot. She successfully uses her available navigational resources to locate and arrive at the airport. Upon returning home, Bill attempts to generalize her new abilities and put yet a different spin on the same problem. He presents the low-fuel scenario, taking advantage of the fact that there are eight nearby airports. All of the airports are in plain view, and she must choose one.

Each of these scenarios taught Beverly something she needed to learn next, and made good use of the surroundings and available circumstances. As these examples illustrate, there is no list of "canned" scenarios that can be used for all students. Instructors must learn to devise their own scenarios by considering what each student needs to practice, and exploiting features of the local environment that allow them to do it.

The Learning Route to Expertise

What does it take to successfully orchestrate all of the knowledge and skills the student has learned into what instructors, evaluators, and other pilots and mechanics would regard as true expertise? All evidence seems to point once again to the idea of practice. Just as the perfection of an individual skill seems to rely on repeated practice, so does the combination of knowledge and skills that make up our abilities to do the real-world job of pilot or mechanic.

How much practice does it take to become a true expert? In a study of expert performers in fields ranging from science to music to chess, one psychologist found that no performer had reached true expertise without having invested at least ten years of practice in his or her field. Experts have been found to use two tools to help them gain expertise in their field: cognitive strategies and problem-solving tactics.

Cognitive Strategies

The idea of cognitive strategies emerged over 50 years ago in the context of human information processing theory. Cognitive strategies refer to the knowledge of procedures or knowledge about how to do something in contrast with the knowledge of facts. They use the mind to solve a problem or complete a task and provide a structure for learning that actively promotes the comprehension and retention of knowledge. A cognitive strategy helps the learner develop internal procedures that enable him or her to perform higher level operations.

As students acquire experience, they develop their own strategies for dealing with problems that arise frequently. For example, a student develops the following strategy for avoiding inadvertent flight into instrument meteorological conditions (IMC) at night. He or she checks the weather prior to departure, obtains updates on the weather every hour, and plans to divert to an alternate destination at the first suspicion of unexpected weather ahead.

One approach to helping students develop cognitive strategies is to study and identify the strategies that experts use and then teach these strategies to the students. Expert strategies were identified by researchers who presented experts with problems to solve and asked them to think aloud as they attempted to solve the problems. These cognitive strategies can be taught to students, usually with successful results.

Problem-Solving Tactics

Problem-solving tactics are specific actions intended to get a particular result, and this type of knowledge represents the most targeted knowledge in the expert's arsenal. For example, a student notices how easy it is to make a mistake with a takeoff distance chart after using it several times. She notices her finger drifts upward or downward when sliding it across a row of numbers on the chart, sometimes landing on the wrong number. The student formulates several tactics to ensure she obtains the correct figures: (1) work slowly and deliberately, (2) use a ruler, and (3) double-check the work.

But even the experts had to practice. In a study of violinists at a music academy in Berlin, researchers compared the "best" students to those who were regarded as merely "very good." Using estimates of how many total hours each student had spent practicing during his or her lifetime, the researchers found that the best violinists had spent an average of 7,000 hours practicing, while the very good violinists had logged about 5,000 hours. The scientific study of expertise reiterates the adage: "Practice makes perfect."

Awareness of Existence of Unknowns

An important aspect of an expert's knowledge is an awareness of what he or she does not know. This is not always the case with a student. It's important that an instructor be aware of situations in which students have acquired "book" knowledge, but not yet acquired the more in-depth understanding that comes from association and experience. For example, after acquiring substantial knowledge of a single-engine training aircraft, students should understand that a four-seat aircraft by the same manufacturer should be approached with caution and not overconfidence.

Summary of Instructor Actions

To help students exercise their knowledge and skills in a concerted fashion, the instructor should:

- Explain the two types of multitasking and give examples of each type.
- Ensure that individual skills are reasonably well-practiced before asking students to perform several tasks at once.

- Teach students how to deal with distractions and interruptions and provide them with opportunities to practice.
- Point out fixation and inattention when it occurs.
- Devise scenarios that allow students to use their knowledge and skill to solve realistic problems and make decisions.
- Explain to the student that continued practice with the goal of improving leads to continued improvement.

Errors

Errors are a natural part of human performance. Beginners, as well as the most highly skilled experts, are vulnerable to error, and this is perhaps the most important thing to understand about error. To believe people can eliminate errors from their performance is to commit the biggest error of all. Instructors and students alike should be prepared for occasional errors by learning about common kinds of errors, how errors can be minimized, how to learn from errors, and how to recover from errors when they are made.

Kinds of Error

There are two kinds of error: slip and mistake.

Slip

A slip occurs when a person plans to do one thing, but then inadvertently does something else. Slips are errors of action. Slips can take on a variety of different forms. One of the most common forms of slips is to simply neglect to do something. Other forms of slips occur when people confuse two things that are similar. Accidentally using a manual that is similar to the one really needed is an example of this type of slip.

Other forms of slips happen when someone is asked to perform a routine procedure in a slightly different way. For example, Beverly has been assigned runway 30 for many days in a row. This morning she approaches to land and ATC assigns runway 12 instead. As she approaches the traffic pattern, she turns to enter the pattern for runway 30 out of habit.

Time pressure is another common source of slips. Studies of people performing a variety of tasks demonstrated a phenomenon called the speed-accuracy tradeoff. The more hurried one's work becomes the more slips one is likely to make.

Mistake

A mistake occurs when a person plans to do the wrong thing and is successful. Mistakes are errors of thought. Mistakes are sometimes the result of gaps or misconceptions in the student's understanding. One type of mistake happens when a student formulates an understanding of a phenomenon and then later encounters a situation that shows how this understanding was incorrect or incomplete. For example, overly simplistic understanding of weather frequently leads inexperienced students into situations that are unexpected.

Experts are not immune to making mistakes, which sometimes arise from the way an expert draws upon knowledge of familiar problems and responds to them using familiar solutions. *[Figure 2-21]* Mistakes can occur when the expert categorizes a particular case incorrectly. For example, an experienced pilot may become accustomed to ignoring nuisance alerts issued by his traffic alerting system when approaching his home airport, as many aircraft on the ground turn on their transponders prior to takeoff. One night, he ignores an alert that was generated not by an aircraft on the ground, but rather by another aircraft that has turned in front of him on final approach.

Figure 2-21. *Other mistakes arise under pressure. For example, a technician or pilot might perform a cursory inspection of an aircraft to save time, only to have a problem manifest itself later.*

Reducing Error

Although it is impossible to eliminate errors entirely, there are ways to reduce them, as described in the following paragraphs.

Learning and Practicing

The first line of defense against errors is learning and practice. Higher levels of knowledge and skill are associated with a lower frequency and magnitude of error.

Taking Time

Errors can often be reduced by working deliberately at a comfortable pace. Hurrying does not achieve the same results as faster performance that is gained by increasing one's skill through continued practice.

Checking for Errors

Another way to help avoid errors is to look actively for evidence of them. Many tasks in aviation offer a means of checking work. Students should be encouraged to look for new ways of checking their work.

Using Reminders

Errors are reduced when visible reminders are present and actively used. Checklists and other published procedures are examples of reminders. Many aircraft instruments such as altimeters offer bugs that can be used to remind the pilot about assigned altitudes, airspeeds, headings, and courses. Mechanics and pilots alike can use notepads to jot down reminders or information that must otherwise be committed to memory.

Developing Routines

The use of standardized procedures for routine tasks is widely known to help reduce error. Even when a checklist procedure is unavailable or impractical, students can help reduce the occurrence of error by adopting standardized procedures.

Raising Awareness

Another line of defense against errors is to raise one's awareness when operating in conditions under which errors are known to happen (e.g., changes in routine, time pressure), or in conditions under which defenses against errors have been compromised (e.g., fatigue, lack of recent practice).

Error Recovery

Given that the occasional error is inevitable, it is a worthwhile exercise to practice recovering from commonly made errors, or those that pose serious consequences. All flight students are required to learn and practice a lost procedure to ensure that they can recover from the situation in which they have lost their way. It is useful to devote the same sort of preparation to other common student errors.

Learning From Error

Error can be a valuable learning resource. Students naturally make errors, which instructors can utilize to help students learn while being careful not to let the student practice doing the wrong thing. When a student makes an error, it is useful to ask the student to consider why the error happened, and what could be done differently to prevent the error from happening again in the future. In some cases, errors are slips that simply reveal the need for more practice. In other cases, errors point to aspects of student methods or habits that might be improved. For example, beginning instrument flight students commonly make errors when managing two communications radios, each with an active and standby frequency. When the same students learn to use each radio for a specific purpose (e.g., ATIS, ground, tower frequencies), error rates often drop quickly.

Instructors and students should be aware of a natural human tendency to resist learning from errors. That is, there is a tendency to "explain away" errors, dismissing them as one-time events that will likely never happen again. The same phenomenon occurs when observing errors made by others. Reading an accident or incident report, it is easy to spot where a pilot or mechanic made an error and regard the error as something that could never happen to the reader. It is important to note that this type of bias is not necessarily the result of ego or overconfidence; rather, it is something to which we are all susceptible. Psychologist Baruch Fischoff studied hindsight explanations given by people who were presented with descriptions of situations and their ultimate outcomes. When asked to provide explanations for events that had already occurred and for which the outcome was known, people explained that the outcomes were "obvious" and "predictable." When the same events without the outcomes were presented to a second group, peoples' prediction of the outcome was no better than chance guessing. The study nicely illustrates the popular adage that "hindsight is 20/20."

Summary of Instructor Actions

To help students learn from errors they make and be prepared for them in the future, an instructor should:

- Explain that pilots and mechanics at all levels of skill and experience make occasional errors.
- Explain that the magnitude and frequency of errors tend to decrease as skill and experience increases.
- Explain the difference between slips and mistakes and provide examples of each.
- Explain ways in which the student can help minimize errors.
- Allow the student to practice recovering from common errors.
- Point out errors when they occur and ask the student to explain why they occurred.

Motivation

As defined in chapter 1, motivation is the reason one acts or behaves in a certain way and lies at the heart of goals. A goal is the object of a person's effort. Motivation prompts students to engage in hard work and affects student success. Being smart or coordinated seldom guarantees success, but motivation routinely propels students to the top. An important part of an aviation instructor's job is to discover what motivates each student and to use this information to encourage him or her to work hard.

Motivation is probably the dominant force that governs the student's progress and ability to learn and can be used to advantage by the instructor. Motivation comes in many guises. It may be negative or positive. Negative motivation may engender fear, for example. While negative motivation may be useful in certain situations, characteristically it is not as effective in promoting efficient learning as positive motivation. *[Figure 2-22]* Positive motivation is provided by the promise or achievement of rewards. These rewards may be personal or social, they may involve financial gain, satisfaction of the self-concept, personal gain, or public recognition.

Figure 2-22. *Insecure and unpleasant training situations inhibit learning.*

Motivation may be tangible or intangible. Students seeking intangible rewards are motivated by the desires for personal comfort and security, group approval, and the achievement of a favorable self-image. The desire for personal comfort and security is a form of motivation which instructors often forget. All students want secure, pleasant conditions and a safe environment. If they recognize that what they are learning may promote these objectives, their attention is easier to attract and hold. Insecure and unpleasant training situations inhibit learning. Students also want a tangible return for their efforts. For motivation to be effective on this level, students must believe that their efforts are suitably rewarded. These rewards must be constantly apparent to the student during instruction, whether they are to be financial, self-esteem, or public recognition.

The tangible rewards of aviation are not always obvious during training. Traditional syllabi often contain lessons with objectives that are not immediately obvious to the student. These lessons may pay dividends during later instruction, a fact the student may not appreciate and resulting in less learning than if the student could relate all objectives to an operational need (law of readiness). The instructor should ensure that the student is aware of those applications which are not immediately apparent. To reduce this issue, the instructor should develop appropriate scenarios that contain the elements to be practiced.

Everyone wants to avoid pain and injury. Students normally are eager to learn operations or procedures that help prevent injury or loss of life. This is especially true when the student knows that the ability to make timely decisions, or to act correctly in an emergency, is based on sound principles.

The attractive features of the activity to be learned also can be a strong motivational factor. Students are anxious to learn skills that may be used to their advantage. If they understand that each task is useful in preparing for future activities, they are more willing to pursue it.

Another strong motivating force is group approval. Every person wants the approval of peers and superiors. Interest can be stimulated and maintained by building on this natural desire. Most students enjoy the feeling of belonging to a group and are interested in accomplishment, which gives them prestige among their fellow students.

Every person seeks to establish a favorable self-image. In certain instances, this self-image may be submerged in feelings of insecurity or despondency. Fortunately, most people engaged in a task believe that success is possible under the right combination of circumstances and good fortune. This belief can be a powerful motivating force for students. An instructor can effectively foster this motivation by the introduction of perceptions that are solidly based on previously learned factual information easily recognized by the student. Each additional block of learning should help formulate insight, contributing to the ultimate training goals, and promoting student confidence in the overall training program. At the same time, it helps the student develop a favorable self-image. As this confirmation progresses and confidence increases, advancement is more rapid and motivation is strengthened.

Positive motivation is essential to true learning. Negative motivation in the form of reproofs or threats should be avoided with all but the most overconfident and impulsive students. Slumps in learning are often due to declining motivation. Motivation does not remain at a uniformly high level. It may be affected by outside influences, such as physical or mental disturbances or inadequate instruction. The instructor should strive to maintain motivation at the highest possible level. In addition, the instructor should be alert to detect and counter any lapses in motivation.

Where Does the Motivation To Learn Come From?

Motivation to learn can come from many sources. Some students have a fundamental interest in aviation and experience sheer fascination with aircraft or with the experience of flight. Other students may decide that aviation provides an opportunity to develop a wide variety of technical, physical, communication, and problem-solving abilities. Some see aviation as a way to boost their self-image or ego. Other students are motivated by tradition and wish to follow in the footsteps of a relative or close friend. Some students are motivated to pursue aviation training because it offers a promising career. To others, aviation offers prestige or acceptance within social groups. Some may think that aviation offers fun and excitement or simply a more convenient form of transportation. All of these sources of motivation have one thing in common: they all offer some type of reward in exchange for performing the hard work.

Teaching the adult learner was discussed in chapter 1, but aviation instructors should keep in mind that adult learners who are motivated to seek out a learning experience do so primarily because they have a use for the knowledge or skill being sought. Learning is a means to an end, not an end in itself. Based on this, it is important instructors determine why a student enrolled in the course. Based on preference and/or class size, an instructor can conduct a brief personal interview with the student or have the student complete a student information form. *[Figure 2-23]* Asking questions such as "Why are you taking this course?" or "How do you plan to use the information you learn in this course?" may be all that is necessary.

Figure 2-23. *An instructor's first task with a student is to learn about personal goals to help him or her stay motivated to learn.*

Student Questionnaire

A short questionnaire can be helpful in gathering additional student background information. For example, it is helpful to know a student's familiarity with the subject matter. Questions such as "Have you ever taken a course in aircraft maintenance?" or "Have you ever flown a small airplane?" or "Have you had any on-the-job training in avionics?" should garner the type of information needed.

A short questionnaire also offers an instructor the chance to discover how the student learns best (small groups, independent study, etc.). Another possible way to gather information about a student is to have him or her write a brief autobiography which includes any experience with the subjects being taught. However an instructor gathers information about students, the information helps the instructor allow for not only personal learning goals for the course, but also the goals and motivations of the students, their background in aviation training, as well as their learning preferences. An instructor armed with this information can make the learning experience beneficial to all involved.

Maintaining Motivation

Motivation is generally not something that can be transferred from one person to another. Instructors must become skillful at recognizing problems with motivation and at encouraging students to continue to do their best.

Rewarding Success

Positive feedback encourages students. Practice positive feedback frequently by:

- Praising incremental successes during training.
- Relating daily accomplishments to lesson objectives.
- Commenting favorably on student progress and level ability.

For example, as the student progresses through training, remark on the milestones. When a student first performs a task alone, congratulate him or her on having learned it.

When that same skill reaches an intermediate level, point out that the student's performance is almost consistent with the requirements of the PTS. When performance is equal to the PTS requirements, comment favorably on the skill acquisition. When student performance exceeds PTS requirements, point out what a benefit this will be when the student must perform under pressure during a practical test or on the job.

Presenting New Challenges

With each declaration of success, be sure to present students with the next challenge. For example, when a student begins to perform a skill consistently to PTS requirements, challenge him or her to continue to improve it so the skill can be performed under pressure or when distracted. Instructors can also present new challenges by presenting the student with new problems or situations.

Drops in Motivation

Instructors must be prepared to deal with a number of circumstances in which motivation levels drop. It is natural for motivation to wane somewhat after the initial excitement of the student's first days of training, or between major training events such as solo, evaluations, or practical tests. Drops in motivation appear in several different ways. Students may come to lessons unprepared or give the general sense that aviation training is no longer a priority. During these times, it is often helpful to remind students of their own stated goals for seeking aviation training.

Learning plateaus are a common source of frustration, discouragement, and decreased student motivation. A first line of defense against this situation is to explain that learning seldom proceeds at a constant pace—no student climbs the ladder of success by exactly one rung per day. Students should be encouraged to continue to work hard and be reassured that results will follow.

Summary of Instructor Actions

To ensure that students continue to work hard, the instructor should:

- Ask new students about their aviation training goals.
- Reward incremental successes in learning.
- Present new challenges.
- Occasionally remind students about their own stated goals for aviation training.
- Assure students that learning plateaus are normal and that improvement will resume with continued effort.

Memory

Memory is the vital link between the student learning/retaining information and the cognitive process of applying what is learned. It is the ability of people and other organisms to encode (initial perception and registration of information), store (retention of encoded information over time), and retrieve (processes involved in using stored information) information. *[Figure 2-24]* When a person successfully recalls a past experience (or skill), information about the experience has been encoded, stored, and retrieved.

Although there is no universal agreement of how memory works, a widely accepted model has three components: sensory memory, short-term memory, and long-term memory.

Sensory Memory

Sensory memory is the part of the memory system that receives initial stimuli from the environment and processes them according to the individual's preconceived concept of what is important. Other factors can influence the reception of information by sensory memory. For example, if the input is dramatic and impacts more than one of the five senses, that information is more likely to make an impression. The sensory memory processes stimuli from the environment within seconds, discards what is considered extraneous, and processes what is determined by the individual to be relevant. This is a selective process where the sensory register is set to recognize certain stimuli and immediately transmit them to the short-term memory (STM) for action. The process is called precoding. An example of sensory precoding is recognition of a fire alarm. No matter what is happening at the time, when the sensory register detects a fire alarm, the working memory is immediately made aware of the alarm and preset responses begin to take place. Sensory memory is capable of retaining information for only a very short period of time and within seconds the relevant information is passed to the STM.

Short-Term Memory (STM)

Short-term memory is the part of the memory system where information is stored for roughly 30 seconds, after which it may rapidly fade or be consolidated into long-term memory, depending on the individual's priorities. Several common steps help retention in STM. These include rehearsal or repetition of the information and sorting or categorization into systematic chunks. The sorting process is usually called coding or chunking. A key limitation of STM is that it takes 5–10 seconds to properly code information and if the coding process is interrupted, that information is easily lost since it is stored for only 30 seconds. The goal of the STM is to put the information to immediate use.

The STM is not only time limited, it also has limited capacity, usually about seven bits or chunks of information. A seven-digit telephone number is an example. As indicated, the time limitation may be overcome by rehearsal. This means learning the information by a rote memorization process. Of course, rote memorization is subject to imperfections in both the duration of recall and in its accuracy. The coding process is more useful in a learning situation. In addition, the coding process may involve recoding to adjust the information to individual experiences. This is when actual learning begins to take place. Therefore, recoding may be described as a process of relating incoming information to concepts or knowledge already in memory.

Brain research has led to the conclusion that STM resembles the control tower of a major airport and is responsible for scheduling and coordinating all incoming and outgoing flights. STM has three basic operations: iconic memory, acoustic memory, and working memory. Iconic memory is

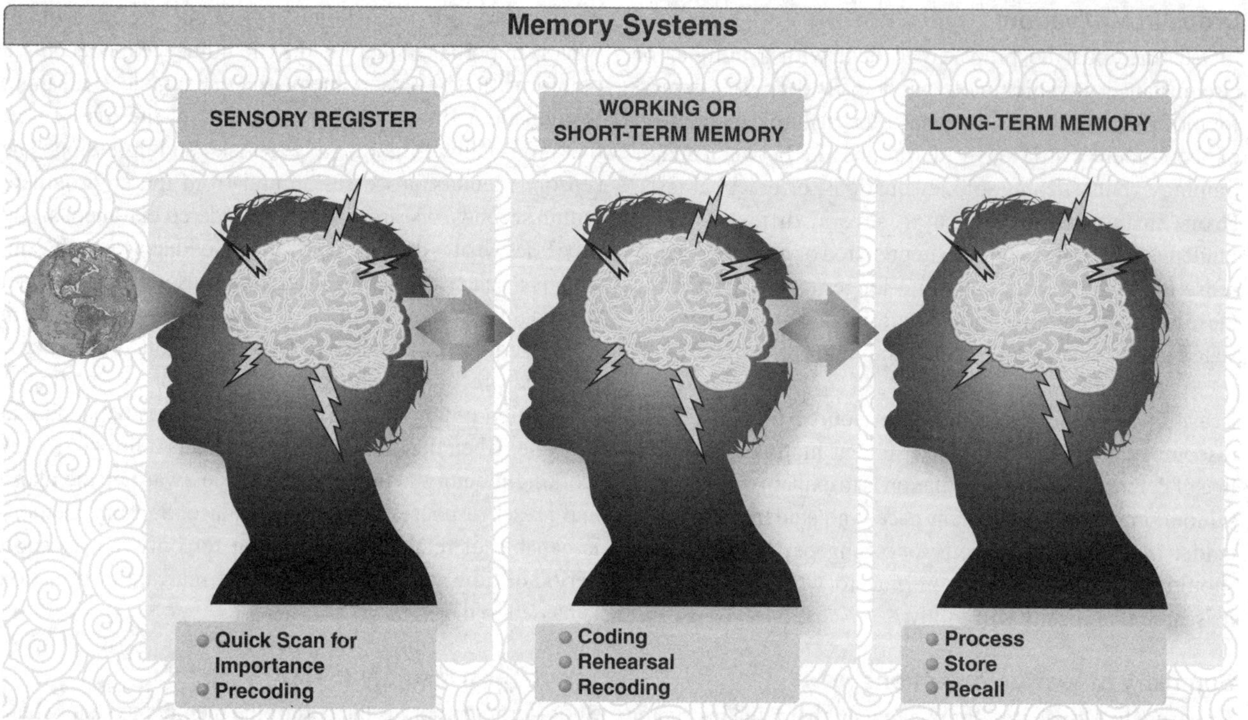

Figure 2-24. *Information processing within the sensory register, working on short-term memory, and long-term memory includes complex coding, sorting, storing, and recall functions.*

the brief sensory memory of visual images. Acoustic memory is the encoded memory of a brief sound memory or the ability to hold sounds in STM. Of the two, acoustic memory can be held longer than iconic memory. Working memory is an active process to keep information until it is put to use (think of a phone number repeated until used). It is useful in remembering a spoken sentence or a string of digits.

Also called "scratch-pad" memory, working memory is of short duration and has limited capacity. It simultaneously stores and manipulates information. The goal of the working memory is not really to move the information from STM to long-term memory (LTM), but merely put the information to immediate use.

STM retention makes information available long enough for it to be rehearsed. For example, if the learner repeats the number to himself, it can be transferred to some sort of longer term storage. To retain information for extended periods of time, it must be transferred from STM to LTM. This process involves encoding or consolidation of information into LTM where it can then be retrieved.

Long-Term Memory (LTM)

Long-term memory (LTM) is relatively permanent storage of unlimited information and it is possible for memories in LTM to remain there for a lifetime. What is stored in LTM affects a person's perceptions of the world and affects what information in the environment is noticed. Information that passes from STM to LTM typically has some significance attached to it. For example, imagine how difficult it would be for a pilot to forget the first day he or she soloed. This is a significant day in any pilot's training, so when the information was processed, significance was attached to it, the information was deemed important, and it was transferred into LTM.

There must be other reasons information is transferred to LTM because the average human brain stores numerous insignificant facts. One explanation is repetition; people tend to remember things the more they are rehearsed. Information also ends up in LTM because it is somehow attached to something significant. A man may remember the color of the dress his girlfriend was wearing on the day he proposed marriage to her. The color of the dress plays no important role, but is attached to the memory of proposing marriage.

For the stored information to be useful, some special effort must have been expended during the encoding or consolidation of information in STM. The encoding should provide meaning and connections between old and new information. If initial encoding is not properly accomplished, recall is distorted and it may be impossible. The more effective the encoding process, the easier the recall. However, it should be noted that the LTM is a reconstruction, not a pure recall of information or events. It is also subject to limitations, such as time, biases, and, in many cases, personal inaccuracies. This is why two people who view the same event often have totally different recollections. Memory also applies to psychomotor skills. For example, with practice, a tennis player may be able to serve a tennis ball at a high rate of speed and with accuracy. This may be accomplished with very little thought. For a pilot, the ability to instinctively perform certain maneuvers or tasks that require manual dexterity and precision, provides obvious benefits. For example, it allows the pilot more time to concentrate on other essential duties such as navigation, communications with ATC facilities, and visual scanning for other aircraft.

Information in LTM is stored in interrelated networks of schemas which are the cognitive frameworks that help people organize and interpret information. Schemas guide recognition and understanding of new information by providing expectations about what should occur. Since LTM is organized into schemas, instructors must consciously look for ways to make training relevant and meaningful enough for the learner to transfer new information to LTM. This can be accomplished by activating existing schemas before presenting new information. For example, a brief review of the previous lesson via discussion, video, questions, etc.

Remembering What Has Been Learned

The moment people learn something new and add it to their repertoire of knowledge and skill, they are confronted with a second task: the task of remembering it. Remembering is a challenge because of a natural feature of human memory-forgetting. Forgetting is such an apparent part of human memory that it is often the first thing that people think of when they bring up the topic of memory.

The following section discusses how remembering and forgetting happens in predictable ways that help keep human memories tuned to the demands of everyday life. Memories help people keep fresh precisely those things needed next, and let slip those things that have outlived their usefulness. Understanding the factors that determine what is remembered and what is forgotten helps instructor and student get the most from memory.

How Usage Affects Memory

The ability to retrieve knowledge or skills from memory is primarily related to two things: (1) how often that knowledge has been used in the past; and (2) how recently the knowledge has been used. These two factors are called frequency and recency of use. Frequency and recency can be present individually or in combination.

Frequency and recency—knowledge that enjoys both frequency and recency is likely to be retrieved easily and quickly. This is knowledge much used in the past that continues to be used in the present. This is the ideal situation for knowledge and skills that need to be used.

Frequency only—knowledge that has been used much in the past but that has not been used recently is vulnerable to being forgotten. This type of knowledge is likely to be retrieved slowly or not at all. To retrieve this knowledge and skill, some recent rehearsal or practice must be added in order to refresh the memory.

Recency only—knowledge that has been recently used but has not been used in the past is knowledge that has been recently acquired. This type of knowledge is particularly vulnerable to being forgotten since there is little to distinguish it from "throw away" knowledge, such as an hourly weather broadcast. To remember this knowledge requires a program of regular rehearsal to build up its frequency.

Forgetting

Forgetting, which refers to loss of a memory, typically involves a failure in memory retrieval. The failure may be due to the decay or overwriting of information which has been temporarily stored in STM, but generally forgetting refers to loss of information from LTM. The information is not lost, per se, it is somewhere in the person's LTM, but he or she is not able to retrieve and remember it.

Why do people forget? Why don't we remember everything? Do we need to remember everything? Most of the information people are exposed to each day has a short period of usefulness with little need to retain it. For example, why would anyone need to remember the details of an hourly weather broadcast ten years ago?

Thus, forgetting knowledge is not always a bad thing. For example, forgetting old information keeps new information up to date. Many theories on why people forget have been offered to explain the phenomenon, among them retrieval failure, fading, interference, and repression or suppression.

Retrieval Failure

Retrieval failure is simply the inability to retrieve information, that tip-of-the-tongue phenomenon when a person knows the meaning of a word, or the answer to a question, but cannot retrieve it. It is also caused by the fact that sometimes people simply do not encode information well, and the information never makes it to LTM or is lost before it can attach itself to the LTM. This is sometimes referred to as failure to store.

Fading

The theory of fading or decay suggests that a person forgets information that is not used for an extended period of time, that it fades away or decays. It had been suggested that humans are physiologically preprogrammed to eventually erase data that no longer appears pertinent.

On the other hand, experimental studies show that a hypnotized person can describe specific details of an event, which normally is beyond recall. Apparently the memory is there, locked in the recesses of the mind. The difficulty is summoning the memory to consciousness or retrieving the link that leads to it.

Interference

Interference theory suggests that people forget something because a certain experience has overshadowed it, or that the learning of similar things has intervened. This theory might explain how the range of experiences after graduation from school causes a person to forget or to lose knowledge. In other words, new events displace many things that had been learned. From experiments, at least two conclusions about interference may be drawn. First, similar material seems to interfere with memory more than dissimilar material; and second, material not well learned suffers most from interference.

Repression or Suppression

Freudian psychology advances the view that some forgetting is caused by repression or suppression. In repression or suppression, a memory is pushed out of reach because the individual does not want to remember the feelings associated with it. Repression is an unconscious form of forgetting while suppression is a conscious form.

Forgetting information does not mean it is gone forever. Sometimes it is still there, just inaccessible.

Retention of Learning

Each of the theories of forgetting implies that when a person forgets something, it is not actually lost. Rather, it is simply unavailable for recall. The instructor's problem is how to make certain that the student's learning is readily available for recall. The following suggestions can help.

Teach thoroughly and with meaning. Material thoroughly learned is highly resistant to forgetting. This is suggested by experimental studies and it also was pointed out in the sections on skill learning. Meaningful learning builds patterns of relationships in the learner's consciousness, which is one reason to conduct scenario-based training (SBT). In contrast, rote learning is superficial and is not easily retained. Meaningful learning goes deep because it involves principles and concepts anchored in the student's own experiences. The following discussion emphasizes five principles, which are generally accepted as having a direct application to remembering.

Praise Stimulates Remembering

Responses that give a pleasurable return tend to be repeated. Absence of praise or recognition tends to discourage, and any form of negativism in the acceptance of a response tends to make its recall less likely.

Recall Is Promoted by Association

As discussed earlier, each bit of information or action, which is associated with something to be learned, tends to facilitate its later recall by the student. Unique or disassociated facts tend to be forgotten unless they are of special interest or application.

Favorable Attitudes Aid Retention

People learn and remember only what they wish to know. Without motivation there is little chance for recall. The most effective motivation is based on positive or rewarding objectives.

Learning With All Senses Is Most Effective

Although people generally receive what is learned through the eyes and ears, other senses also contribute to most perceptions. When several senses respond together, a fuller understanding and greater chance of recall is achieved.

Meaningful Repetition Aids Recall

Each repetition gives the student an opportunity to gain a clearer and more accurate perception of the subject to be learned, but mere repetition does not guarantee retention. Practice provides an opportunity for learning, but does not cause it. Further, some research indicates that three or four repetitions provide the maximum effect, after which the rate of learning and probability of retention fall off rapidly.

Along with these five principles, there is a considerable amount of additional literature on retention of learning during a typical academic lesson. After the first 10–15 minutes, the rate of retention drops significantly until about the last 5–10 minutes when students wake up again. Students passively listening to a lecture have roughly a five percent retention rate over a 24-hour period, but students actively engaged in the learning process have a much higher retention. This clearly reiterates the point that active learning is superior to just listening.

Mnemonics

A mnemonic uses a pattern of letters, ideas, visual images, or associations to assist in remembering information. It is a memory enhancing strategy that involves teaching learners to link new information to information they already know. Its chief value lies in helping learners recall information that needs to be recalled in a particular order by encoding difficult-to-remember information in a way that makes it easier to remember. Research shows that providing students with memorization techniques improves their ability to recall information. Mnemonics include but are not limited to acronyms, acrostics, rhymes, or chaining.

Acronyms form a word from the first letters of other words. For example, "AIM" is the acronym for Aeronautical Information Manual.

An acrostic is a poem, word puzzle, or other composition in which the first letter of each line or word is a cue to the idea the learner wishes to remember. For example, Every Good Boy Does Fine is used to remember the order of the G-clef notes in music. An example of a useful aviation acrostic is the memory aid for one of the magnetic compass errors. The letters "ANDS" indicate:

Accelerate
North
Decelerate
South

Rhymes and melody are another way to remember information. Rhymes such as "In 1492, Columbus sailed the ocean blue." Most children learn the alphabet using a familiar melody "Twinkle, Twinkle, Little Star." A well-known mnemonic rhyme for remembering the days of the month is the familiar, "30 days hath September, April, June, and November..."

Chaining is used for ordered or unordered lists and consists of creating a story in which each word or idea that needs to be remembered cues the next idea.

Variations of the encoding process are practically endless. Developing a logical strategy for encoding information is a significant step in the learning process.

Transfer of Learning

Transfer of learning is broadly defined as the ability to apply knowledge or procedures learned in one context to new contexts. Learning occurs more quickly and the learner develops a deeper understanding of the task if he or she brings some knowledge or skills from previous learning. A positive transfer of learning occurs when the learner practices under a variety of conditions, underscoring again the value of SBT.

A distinction is commonly made between near and far transfer. Near transfer consists of transfer from initial learning that is situated in a given setting to ones that are closely related. Far transfer refers both to the ability to use what was learned in one setting to a different one as well as the ability to solve novel problems that share a common structure with the knowledge initially acquired. There is a third way to talk about transfer called generativity. In this context it means learners have the ability on their own to come up with novel solutions.

During a learning experience, things learned previously usually aid the student, but sometimes previous learning interferes with the current learning task. Consider the learning of two skills. If the learning of skill A helps to learn skill B, positive transfer occurs. If learning skill A hinders the learning of skill B, negative transfer occurs. For example, the practice of slow flight (skill A) helps Beverly learn short-field landings (skill B). However, practice in making a landing approach in an airplane (skill A) may hinder learning to make an approach in a helicopter (skill B). It should be noted that the learning of skill B might affect the retention or proficiency of skill A, either positively or negatively. While these processes may help substantiate the interference theory of forgetting, they are still concerned with the transfer of learning.

It is clear that some degree of transfer is involved in all learning. This is true because, except for certain inherent responses, all new learning is based upon previously learned experience. People interpret new things in terms of what they already know.

Many aspects of teaching profit by this type of transfer, perhaps explaining why students of apparently equal ability have differing success in certain areas. Negative transfer may hinder the learning of some; positive transfer may help others. This points to a need to know a student's past experience and what has already been learned. In lesson and syllabus development, instructors can plan for transfer by organizing course materials and individual lesson materials in a meaningful sequence. Each phase should help the student learn what is to follow.

The cause of transfer and exactly how it occurs is difficult to determine, but no one disputes the fact that transfer occurs. For the instructor, the significance of transference lies in the fact that the students can be helped to achieve it. The following suggestions are representative of what educational psychologists believe should be done:

- Plan for transfer as a primary objective. As in all areas of teaching, the chance for success is increased if the instructor deliberately plans to achieve it.
- Ensure that the students understand that what is learned can be applied to other situations. Prepare them to seek other applications.

- Maintain high-order learning standards. Overlearning may be appropriate. The more thoroughly the students understand the material, the more likely they are to see its relationship to new situations. Avoid unnecessary rote learning, since it does not foster transfer.
- Provide meaningful learning experiences that build student confidence in their ability to transfer learning. This suggests activities that challenge them to exercise their imagination and ingenuity in applying their knowledge and skills.
- Use instructional material that helps form valid concepts and generalizations. Use materials that make relationships clear.

Habit Formation

The formation of correct habit patterns from the beginning of any learning process is essential to further learning and for correct performance after the completion of training. Remember, primacy is one of the fundamental principles of learning. Therefore, it is the instructor's responsibility to insist on correct techniques and procedures from the outset of training to provide proper habit patterns. It is much easier to foster proper habits from the beginning of training than to correct faulty ones later.

Due to the high level of knowledge and skill required in aviation for both pilots and maintenance technicians, training has traditionally followed a building block concept. This means new learning and habit patterns are based on a solid foundation of experience and/or old learning. Everything from intricate cognitive processes to simple motor skills depends on what the student already knows and how that knowledge can be applied in the present. As knowledge and skill increase, there is an expanding base upon which to build for the future.

How Understanding Affects Memory

The ability to remember is greatly affected by the level of understanding of what has been learned. Many studies have demonstrated a depth-of-processing effect on memory: the more deeply humans think about what they have learned, the more likely they are able to retrieve that knowledge later. Depth-of-processing is the natural result of the kinds of learning activities described earlier: beginning with memorized information and then elaborating upon it, making associations, constructing explanations, all in pursuit of furthering understanding.

The effects of depth of processing on memory are quite powerful and result from even the simplest attempts to elaborate on what has been learned. One study asked participants to memorize sentences such as "The pilot arrived late." Half of the participants simply memorized the sentences as they were. The other participants were asked to develop an elaboration for the sentence such as "because of the bad weather."

When put to a test, participants who created elaborations were significantly better able to recall the sentences. When memories for sentences had decayed, it seems that remembered words from the elaborations helped people recall them.

Remembering During Training

Remembering what is learned on a day-to-day basis is the first challenge students must meet. As students are presented with new knowledge each day, they must work to maintain that new knowledge plus all the knowledge they learned on previous days. Indeed, remembering during training is a challenge that increases in magnitude each day.

The first threat to newly acquired knowledge is a lack of frequent usage in the past. To address this threat, the student must engage in regular practice of what they have learned. Students often put off daily studying in favor of "cramming" the night before an evaluation. These students should be made aware that shorter and regularly spaced study sessions produce memory results that far exceed those obtained from cramming.

A second threat to newly acquired knowledge is a lack of understanding that might serve to assist the student in recalling it. It has been demonstrated that study practices that combine repetition of knowledge along with efforts to increase one's understanding of the knowledge lead to best results. The idea of reading with "study questions" in mind is one that has received much attention by memory researchers.

Experiments have found that not only does answering study questions lead to better memory, but so does the very act of creating study questions. In one experiment in which students read a text and were then tested on their comprehension, students who wrote their own study questions and then discarded them unanswered exhibited better recall than students who simply read the text.

Remembering After Training

Students must leave the training environment with a sound understanding that a certificate is in no sense a guarantee that they will remember anything that they have learned. It seems that no one is exempt from the process of forgetting. Continued practice of their knowledge and skill is the only means of retaining what they learned, and practice is important after they become certificated pilots and mechanics as it is during their training.

One study of pilots' retention of aeronautical knowledge showed that students' retention of some topics was superior to that of their own instructors. It seems that the students' active use and recent rehearsal of these knowledge topics in preparation for knowledge and practical tests outweighed the effects of the more frequent (but less recent) usage on the part of the instructors. This finding nicely demonstrates that an instructor's knowledge is just as vulnerable to forgetting when it has not been recently practiced.

In the same study, the ability of certificated pilots to remember details about regulations was related to the number of months since each pilot's last flight review. This suggests that pilots may take steps to sharpen their knowledge before a flight review and allow it to decay between reviews. Even skills that become automatic during training may not remain automatic after a period of disuse.

Sources of Knowledge

Aviation students obtain knowledge from a variety of sources while training to be pilots or mechanics. The aviation instructor is the student's primary source of knowledge, but an instructor also recommends other sources of knowledge. These include books, photographs, videos, diagrams and charts, and other instructional materials. These sources are important for the student because they allow information to be archived and easily transferred from one person to another. They also allow the reader to self-pace the acquisition of information and permit the reader to pause, think, formulate, and reformulate his or her understanding.

The instructor also encourages the student to gain experience in the real world of aviation. These experiences enhance the student's incidental learning: observation of other pilots or mechanics, thinking about what has been learned, formulation of schemas, and ability to make correlations about what has been learned. Interactive computer-based instruction programs, another excellent source of knowledge, often go hand-in-hand with the flight training syllabus, assuring academics are delivered just-in-time to complement lessons.

Summary of Instructor Actions

To help students remember what they have learned, the instructor should:

- Discuss the difference between short-term memory and long-term memory.
- Explain the effect of frequent and recent usage of knowledge on remembering and forgetting.
- Explain the effect of depth of understanding on remembering and forgetting.
- Encourage student use of mnemonic devices while studying.
- Explain the benefits of studying at regularly spaced intervals, and the disadvantages of "cramming."

Chapter Summary

Learning theory has caused instruction to move from basic skills and pure facts to linking new information with prior knowledge, from relying on a single authority to recognizing multiple sources of knowledge, and from novice-like to expert-like problem-solving. While educational theories facilitate learning, no one learning theory is good for all learning situations and all learners. Instruction in aviation should utilize a combination of learning theories.

Chapter 3

Effective Communication

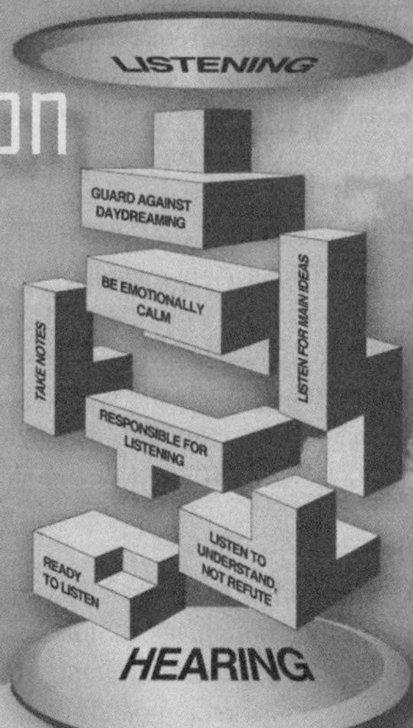

Introduction

Carol, a Certified Flight Instructor (CFI), has planned the first tailwheel flight with Jacob, her student pilot. She begins the preflight briefing with an explanation of the tendency of tailwheel aircraft to yaw in normal takeoff. This yawing tendency gives the illusion that the tailwheel aircraft is unstable during the takeoff. Since this yawing tendency occurs on every takeoff, it is predictable and the pilot is able to compensate for it. Carol then discusses the precession, which causes the noticeable yaw when the tail is raised from a three point attitude to a level flight attitude. This change of attitude tilts the horizontal axis of the propeller, and the resulting precession produces a forward force on the right side (90° ahead in the direction of rotation), yawing the aircraft's nose to the left. To demonstrate the yawing tendency, she places a model aircraft prop under a desk lamp. *[Figure 3-1]* By moving the prop, the shadow it casts illustrates the pitch change of the propeller when the aircraft is on its tailwheel and when the aircraft is raised to a level flight attitude.

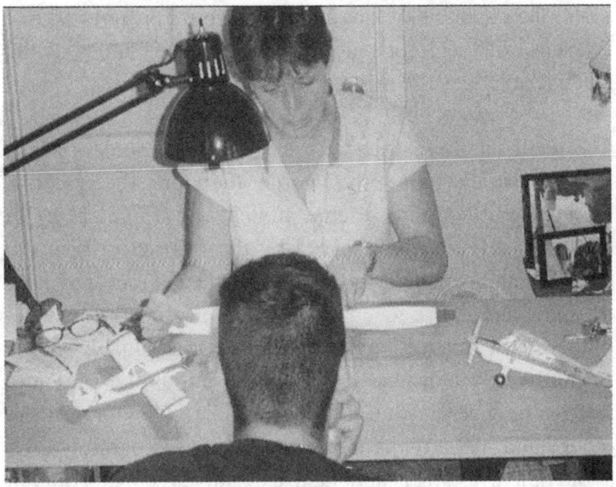

Figure 3-1. *An aviation instructor communicates with her student using model airplanes to ensure the student's understanding of the principles discussed.*

Effective communication is an essential element of instruction. An aviation instructor may possess a high level of technical knowledge, but he or she needs to cultivate the ability to communicate effectively in order to share this knowledge with students. While communication is a complex process, aviation instructors need to develop a comfortable style of communication that meets the goal of passing on desired information to students. The elements of effective communication, the barriers to communication, and the development of communication skills are discussed in this chapter. It is also important to recognize that communication is a two-way process.

Basic Elements of Communication

Communication takes place when one person transmits ideas or feelings to another person or group of people. The effectiveness of the communication is measured by the similarity between the idea transmitted and the idea received. The process of communication is composed of three elements:

- Source (sender, speaker, writer, encoder, transmitter, or instructor)
- Symbols used in composing and transmitting the message (words or signs (model prop/desk lamp in *Figure 3-1*))
- Receiver (listener, reader, decoder, or student)

The three elements are dynamically interrelated since each element is dependent on the others for effective communication to take place. The relationship between the source and the receiver is also dynamic and depends on the two-way flow of symbols between the source and the receiver. The source depends on feedback from the receiver to properly tailor the communication to the situation. The source also provides feedback to the receiver to reinforce the desired receiver responses.

Source

As indicated, the source in communication is the sender, speaker, writer, encoder, transmitter, or instructor. The effectiveness of persons acting in the role of communicators is related to at least three basic factors.

First, their ability to select and use language is essential for transmitting symbols that are meaningful to listeners and readers. It is the responsibility of the speaker or writer, as the source of communication, to realize that the effectiveness of the communication is dependent on the receiver's understanding of the symbols or words being used. For example, if an aviation maintenance instructor were to use aviation acronyms like ADs, TCDS or STCs or a flight instructor were to use aviation acronyms like ILS, TCAS, or TAWS with a new maintenance student or student pilot respectively, effective communication would be difficult if not impossible. Use of aviation acronyms or technical language is necessary, but the student must be taught the language first. Conversely, a speaker or writer may rely on highly technical or professional background with its associated vocabulary while addressing a receiver with a similar background.

Second, communicators consciously or unconsciously reveal attitudes toward themselves as a communicator, toward the ideas being communicated, and toward the receivers. These attitudes must be positive while delivering the message if they are to communicate effectively. Communicators must be confident; they should illustrate that the message is important and that the receiver has a need to know the ideas presented.

Third, communicators are more likely to be successful when they speak or write from accurate, up-to-date, and stimulating material. Communicators must constantly strive to have the most current and interesting information possible. In this way, the receiver's interest can be held. Out-of-date information causes the instructor to lose credibility in the eyes of the receiver. Use of monotonous or uninteresting information runs the risk of losing the receiver's attention.

Symbols

At its basic level, communication is achieved through symbols, which are simple oral and visual codes. The words in the vocabulary constitute a basic code. Common gestures and facial expressions form another, but words and gestures alone do not communicate ideas. Ideas are communicated only when symbols are combined in meaningful wholes, as in ideas, sentences, paragraphs, speeches, or chapters that mean something to the receiver. When symbols are combined into these units, each portion becomes important to effective communication.

On a higher level, communication through symbols is achieved by their interpretation through different perceptions, sometimes referred to as channels. While many theories have been proposed, one popular theory indicates that the symbols are perceived through one of three sensory channels: either visual, auditory, or kinethestic. As discussed in Chapter 2, visual learners rely on seeing, auditory prefers listening and speaking, while kinesthetic learners process and store information through physical experience such as touching, manipulating, using, or doing.

The instructor will be more successful in gaining and retaining the student's attention by using a variety of channels. As an example, instead of telling a student to adjust the trim, the instructor can move the trim wheel while the student tries to maintain a given aircraft attitude. The student experiences by feel that the trim wheel affects the amount of control stick pressure needed to maintain the attitude. At the same time, the instructor can explain to the student that what is felt is forward or back pressure on the control stick. After that, the student begins to understand the correct meaning of control pressure and trim, and when told to adjust the trim to relieve control pressure, the student responds in the manner desired by the instructor. Most frequently, communicators select the channels of hearing and seeing. For motor skills, the sense of touch, or kinesthetic learning, is added as the student practices the skill.

The feedback an instructor is getting from a student needs to be constantly monitored in order to modify the symbols, as required, to optimize communication. *[Figure 3-2]* In addition to feedback received by the instructor from the students, students need feedback from the instructor on how they are doing. The feedback not only informs the students of their performance, but can also serve as a valuable source of motivation. An instructor's praise builds the student's self-confidence and reinforces favorable behavior. On the other hand, negative feedback must be used carefully. To avoid embarrassing a student, use negative feedback only in private. This information should be delivered as a description of actual performance and given in a nonjudgmental manner. For example, it would be appropriate to tell a maintenance student that a safety wire installation is not satisfactory. To refer to the work as careless would not be good and could do harm to the student's feeling of self-worth.

The parts of the total idea should be analyzed to determine which are most suited to starting or ending the communication, and which are best for the purpose of explaining, clarifying, or emphasizing. All of these functions are required for effective transmission of ideas. The process finally culminates in the determination of the medium best suited for their transmission.

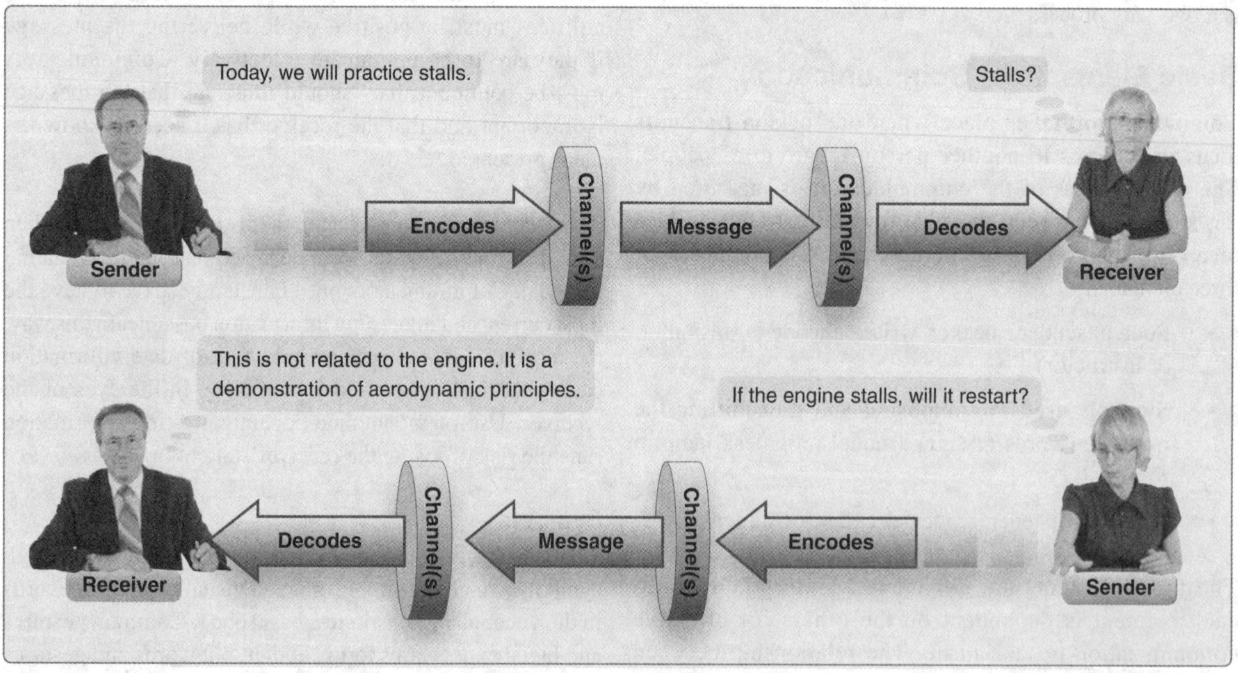

Figure 3-2. *The instructor realizes from the response of the student that "stall" has been interpreted by the student to have something to do with the engine quitting. Recognizing that the student has misunderstood, the instructor is able to clarify the information and help the student to obtain the desired outcome.*

Receiver

The receiver is the listener, reader, decoder, or student—the individual or individuals to whom the message is directed. Effective communicators should always keep in mind that communication succeeds only in relation to the reaction of their receivers. When the receiver reacts with understanding and changes his or her behavior according to the intent of the source, effective communication has taken place.

In order to understand the process of communication, three characteristics of receivers must be understood: abilities, attitudes, and experiences.

First, an instructor needs to determine the abilities of the student in order to properly communicate. One factor that can have an effect on student ability is his or her background. For example, consider how familiar the student may be with aviation. Their familiarity may range from having grown up around aviation to absolutely no familiarity at all. Some students may have highly developed motor skills, and others have not had opportunities to develop these skills. These factors must be taken into consideration when presenting information to a student.

Instructors in aviation enjoy a unique advantage over other teachers, in that the aviation student, as an adult learner, usually exhibits a much more developed sense of motivation and self-concept. The aviation student generally wants to be in the learning environment, as opposed to a typical school student, and is willing to expend his or her own time and money to learn. Additionally, they usually come into the learning environment with a significant amount of prior knowledge, many life experiences, and have already developed a number of decision-making skills.

The instructor also must understand that the viewpoint and background of people may vary significantly because of cultural differences. However, this consciousness of the differences between people should not be overdone. The instructor should be aware of possible differences, but not overreact or assume certain values because of these differences. For example, just because a student is a college graduate does not guarantee rapid advancement in aviation training. Student education certainly affects the instructor's style of presentation, but that style should be based on the evaluation of the student's knowledge of the aviation subject being taught.

Second, the attitudes students exhibit may indicate resistance, willingness, or passive neutrality. To gain and hold student attention, attitudes should be molded into forms that promote reception of information. A varied communicative approach works best in reaching most students since they have different attitudes.

Third, student experience, background, and educational level determine the approach an instructor takes. What the student knows, along with student abilities and attitudes, guides the instructor in communicating. It is essential to understand the dynamics of communication, but the instructor also needs to be aware of several barriers to communication that can inhibit learning.

Barriers to Effective Communication

The nature of language and the way it is used often lead to misunderstandings. These misunderstandings can be identified by four barriers to effective communication: lack of common experience, confusion between the symbol and the symbolized object, overuse of abstractions, and interference. *[Figure 3-3]*

Lack of Common Experience

Lack of common experience between the communicator (instructor) and the receiver (student) is probably the greatest single barrier to effective communication. Communication can be effective only to the extent that the experiences (physical, mental, and emotional) of the people concerned are similar.

Many people seem to believe that words transport meanings from speaker to listener in the same way that a truck carries bricks from one location to another. Words, however, rarely carry precisely the same meaning from the mind of the instructor to the mind of the student. In fact, words, in themselves, do not transfer meanings at all. Whether spoken or written, words are merely stimuli used to arouse a response in the student.

The student's past experience with the words and things to which they refer determines how the student responds to what the instructor says. A communicator's words cannot communicate the desired meaning to another person unless the listener or reader has had some experience with the objects or concepts to which these words refer. Since it is the students' experience that forms vocabulary, it is also essential that instructors speak the same language as the students. If the instructor's terminology is necessary to convey the idea, some time needs to be spent making certain the students understand that terminology.

For example, a maintenance instructor tells a student to time the magnetos. A student new to the maintenance field might think a stopwatch or clock would be necessary to do the requested task. Instruction would be necessary for the student to understand that the procedure has nothing to do with the usual concept of time.

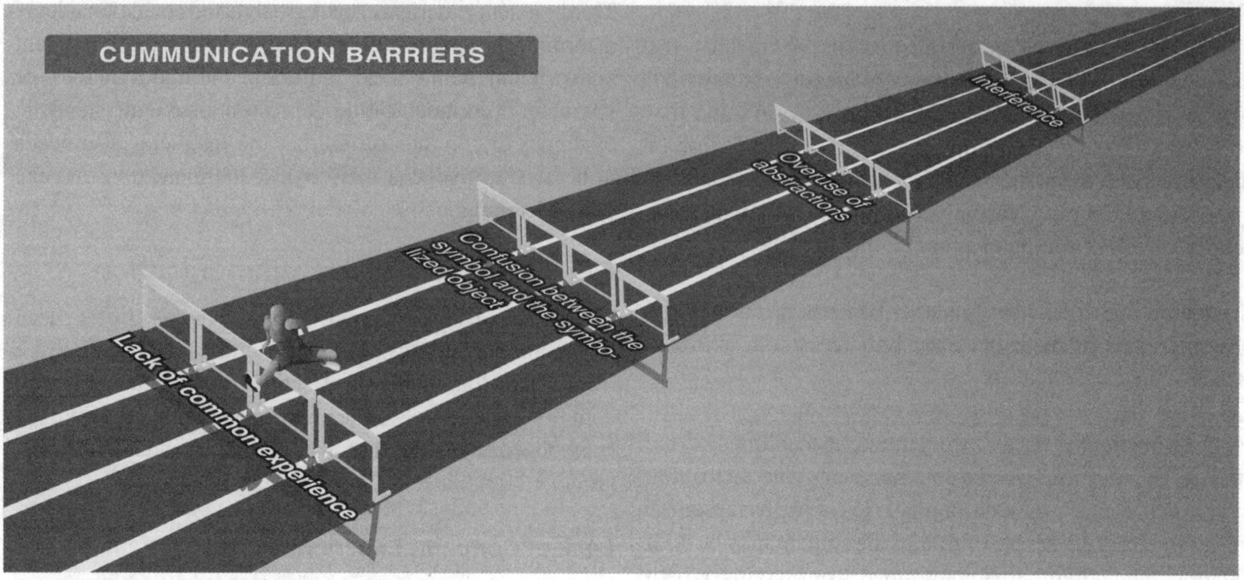

Figure 3-3. *Misunderstandings stem primarily from four barriers to effective communication.*

The English language abounds in words that mean different things to different people. To a farmer, the word "tractor" means the machine that pulls the implements to cultivate the soil; to a trucker, it is the vehicle used to pull a semi trailer; in aviation, a tractor propeller is the opposite of a pusher propeller. Each technical field has its own vocabulary. Technical words might mean something entirely different to a person outside that field, or perhaps mean nothing at all. In order for communication to be effective, the students' understanding of the meaning of the words needs to be the same as the instructor's understanding.

Confusion Between the Symbol and the Symbolized Object

Confusion between the symbol and the symbolized object results when a word is confused with what it is meant to represent. Although it is obvious that words and the connotations they carry can be different, people sometimes fail to make the distinction. An aviation maintenance technician (AMT) might be introduced as a mechanic. To many people, the term mechanic conjures up images of a person laboring over an automobile. Being referred to as an aircraft mechanic might be an improvement in some people's minds, but neither really portrays the training and skill of the AMT. Words and symbols do not always represent the same thing to every person. To communicate effectively, speakers and writers should be aware of these differences. Words and symbols can then be chosen to represent what the speaker or writer intends.

Overuse of Abstractions

Abstractions are words that are general rather than specific. Concrete words or terms refer to objects people can relate directly to their own experiences. These words or terms specify an idea that can be perceived or a thing that can be visualized. Abstract words, on the other hand, stand for ideas that cannot be directly experienced, things that do not call forth mental images in the minds of the students. The word aircraft is an abstract word. It does not call to mind a specific aircraft in the imaginations of various students. One student may visualize an airplane, another student might visualize a helicopter, and still another student might visualize an airship. *[Figure 3-4]* Although the word airplane is more specific, various students might envision anything from a Boeing 777 to a Piper Cub.

Aircraft engines represent another example of abstractions. When an instructor refers to aircraft engines in general, some students might think of jet engines, while others would think of reciprocating engines. Even reciprocating engine is too abstract since it could be a radial engine, an inline engine, a V-type engine, or an opposed type engine. Use of the technical language of engines, as in Lycoming IO-360, would narrow the engine type, but would only be understood by students who have learned the terminology particular to aircraft engines.

Abstractions should be avoided in most cases, but there are times when abstractions are necessary and useful. Aerodynamics is applicable to all aircraft and is an example of an abstraction that can lead to understanding aircraft flight characteristics. The danger of abstractions is that they do not evoke the same specific items of experience in the minds of the students that the instructor intends. When such terms are used, they should be linked with specific experiences through examples and illustrations.

Figure 3-4. *Overuse of abstract terms can interfere with effective communication.*

For instance, when an approach to landing is going badly, telling a student to take appropriate measures might not result in the desired action. It would be better to tell the student to conduct a go-around since this is an action that has the same meaning to both student and instructor. When maintenance students are being taught to torque the bolts on an engine, it would be better to tell them to torque the bolts in accordance with the maintenance manual for that engine rather than simply to torque the bolts to the proper values. Whenever possible, the level of abstraction should be reduced by using concrete, specific terms. This better defines and gains control of images produced in the minds of the students.

Interference

Some barriers to effective communication can be controlled by the instructor. Interference, or the prevention of a process or activity from being carried out properly, is composed of factors outside the control of the instructor These factors include physiological, environmental, and psychological interference. To communicate effectively, the instructor should consider the effects of these factors.

Physiological interference is any biological problem that may inhibit symbol reception, such as hearing loss, injury, or physical illness. These and other physiological factors can inhibit communication because the student is not comfortable. The instructor must adapt the presentation to allow the student to feel better about the situation and be more receptive to new ideas. Adaptation could be as simple as putting off a lesson until the student is over an illness. Another accommodation could be the use of a seat cushion to allow a student to sit properly in the airplane.

With the advent of advanced avionics, multitasking has become a form of physiological interference. The term multitask comes from a computer's ability to simultaneously execute more than one program or task at a time. Although it now refers to humans performing multiple tasks simultaneously, humans are not computers. Research shows that although human comprehension can handle two simple, low-level cognitive tasks at once, a higher level cognitive task takes brain function and concentration to perform optimally. Adding even a simple activity diminishes the comprehension and recall of both. Research shows that multitasking is just a series of constant micro-interruptions and "stop-go" decisions, all of which tend to reduce mental and motor performance.

Environmental interference is caused by external physical conditions. One example of this is the noise level found in many light aircraft. Noise not only impairs the communication process, but also can result in long-term damage to hearing. One solution to this problem is the use of headphones and an intercom system. If an intercom system is not available, a good solution is the use of earplugs. It has been shown that in addition to protecting hearing, use of earplugs actually clarifies speaker output. Vibration is another possible example of environmental interference, applicable to rotary wing aircraft.

Psychological interference is a product of how the instructor and student feel at the time the communication process is occurring. If either instructor or student is not committed to the communication process, communication is impaired. Fear of the situation or mistrust between the instructor and student could severely inhibit the flow of information.

Developing Communication Skills

Communication skills must be developed; they do not occur automatically. The ability to effectively communicate stems from experience. The experience of instructional communication begins with role playing during the training to be an instructor, continues during the actual instruction, and is enhanced by additional training.

Role Playing

Role playing is a method of learning in which students perform a particular role. In role playing, the learner is provided with a general description of a situation and then applies a new skill or knowledge to perform the role. Experience in instructional communication comes from actually doing it and is learned in the beginning by role playing during the instructor's initial training. For example, a flight instructor applicant can fly with a CFI who assumes the role of a student pilot. In the role of student pilot, the CFI can duplicate known student responses and then critique the applicant's role as instructor. A mentor or supervisor can play the student AMT for a maintenance instructor applicant.

It is essential for the flight instructor to develop good ground instruction skills, as well as flight instruction skills to prepare students for what is to transpire in the air. Likewise, the maintenance instructor must develop skills in the classroom to prepare the maintenance student for practical, hands-on tasks. In both cases, effective communication is necessary to reinforce the skills that have been attempted and to assess or critique the results. This development continues as an instructor progresses in experience. What worked early on might be refined or replaced by some other technique as the instructor gains more experience.

A new instructor is more likely to find a comfortable style of communication in an environment that is not threatening. For a prospective maintenance instructor, this might take the form of conducting a class on welding while under the supervision of a maintenance supervisor; the flight instructor applicant usually flies with a CFI who role plays the student.

Current Federal Aviation Administration (FAA) training emphasis has moved from a maneuvers-based training standard to what is called scenario-based training (SBT). SBT is a highly effective approach that allows students to learn, then apply their knowledge as they participate in realistic scenarios. This method of instruction and learning allows students to move from theory to practical application of skills during their training. Instructor applicants, flight or maintenance, need to learn to think in terms of SBT while they are students. Not only does it prepare them to react appropriately in the situations they encounter in the workplace, it also helps them as instructors when they are responsible for creating scenarios for their students.

For example, James (the flight instructor applicant) designs a scenario in which Ray (the CFI playing the role of student) is learning to perform stalls to Practical Test Standards (PTS). James briefs Ray on the maneuver before the flight, demonstrates the stall, and then talks Ray through the maneuver. Ray pretends to be an anxious student pilot, replicating several reactions he himself has experienced with flight students. After the flight, James critiques their instruction period. As increased emphasis is placed on SBT, there will be a corresponding increase in the importance of role playing.

Instructional Communication

Instruction has taken place when the instructor has explained a particular procedure and subsequently determined that the desired student response has occurred. The instructor can improve communication by adhering to several techniques of good communication.

One of the basic principles used in public speaking courses is to encourage students to talk about something they understand. It would not be good if an instructor without a maintenance background tried to teach a course for aviation maintenance. Instructors perform better when speaking of something they know very well and for which they have a high level of confidence.

The instructor should not be afraid to use examples of past experiences to illustrate particular points. When teaching the procedures to be used for transitioning from instrument meteorological conditions (IMC) to visual cues during an approach, it would be helpful to be able to tell the student about encountering these same conditions. An instructor's personal experiences make instruction more valuable than reading the same information in a textbook. The instructor should be cautioned, however, to exercise restraint with this technique of illustration, as these types of discussions frequently degrade into a "war story" or "there I was" discussion.

Communication has not occurred unless desired results of the communication have taken place. The instructor needs some way of determining results, and the method used should be related to the expected outcome. In the case of flight training, the instructor can judge the actual performance of a maneuver. For a maintenance student, the instructor can judge the level of accomplishment of a maintenance procedure. In both cases, the instructor must determine whether the student has actually received and retained the knowledge or if acceptable performance was a one-time event.

The aviation student should know how and why something should be done. For example, a maintenance student may know how to tighten a particular fastener to a specified torque, but it is more important for the student to know that the security and integrity of any fastener depends on proper torque. In this way, the student would be more likely to torque all fasteners properly in the future. For a flight student, simply knowing the different airspeeds for takeoffs and landings is not enough. It is essential to know the reasons for different airspeeds in specific situations to fully understand the importance of proper airspeed control. Normally, the instructor must determine the level of understanding by use of some type of evaluation. See Chapter 5, Assessment, for more information.

Listening

Instructors must know something about their students in order to communicate effectively. As discussed earlier, an instructor needs to determine the abilities of the students and understand the students to properly communicate. One way of becoming better acquainted with students is to be a good listener. Instructors can use a number of techniques to become better at listening. It is important to realize that in order to master the art of listening, an attitude of wanting to listen must be developed. *[Figure 3-4]*

Just as it is important for instructors to want to listen in order to be effective listeners, it is necessary for students to want to listen. Wanting to listen is just one of several techniques that allow a student to listen effectively. Instructors can improve the percentage of information transfer by teaching students how to listen. *[Figure 3-5]*

Figure 3-4. *Instructors can use a number of tools to become better at listening.*

Listening is more than hearing. Most instructors are familiar with the concept that listening is "hearing with comprehension." When the student hears something being communicated, he or she may or may not comprehend what is being transmitted. On the other hand, when the student truly hears the communication, he or she then interprets the communication based on their knowledge to that point, processes the information to a level of understanding, and attempts to make a correlation of that communicated information to the task at hand. The increased level of motivation of typical flight and aviation maintenance students makes this process much easier.

Students also need to be reminded that emotions play a large part in determining how much information is retained. One emotional area to concentrate on is listening to understand rather than refute. For example, an instrument student pilot anticipating drastic changes in requested routing becomes anxious. With this frame of mind, it is very difficult for the student to listen to the routing instructions and then retain very much. In addition, instructors must ensure that students are aware of their emotions concerning certain subjects. If certain areas arouse emotion in a student, the student should be aware of this and take extra measures to listen carefully. For example, if a student who is terrified of the prospect of spins is listening to a lesson on spins, the emotions felt by the student might overwhelm the attempt to listen. If the student, aware of this possibility, made a conscious effort to put that fear aside, listening would probably be more successful.

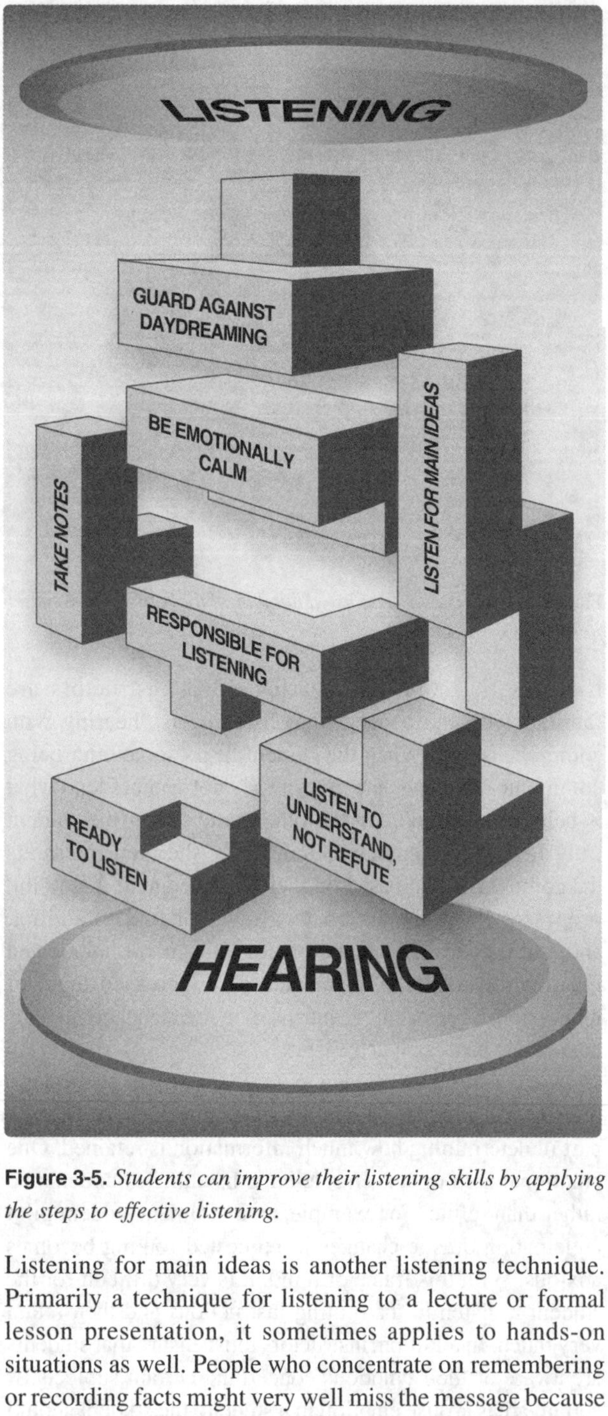

Figure 3-5. *Students can improve their listening skills by applying the steps to effective listening.*

Listening for main ideas is another listening technique. Primarily a technique for listening to a lecture or formal lesson presentation, it sometimes applies to hands-on situations as well. People who concentrate on remembering or recording facts might very well miss the message because they have not picked up on the big picture. A listener must always ask, what is the purpose of what I am listening to? By doing this, the listener can relate the words to the overall concept.

The instructor must ensure that the student is aware of the danger of daydreaming. Most people can listen much faster than even the fastest talker can speak. This leaves room for the mind to get off onto some other subject. The listener who is aware of this problem can concentrate on repeating, paraphrasing, or summarizing the speaker's words. Doing so uses the extra time to reinforce the speaker's words, allowing the student to retain more of the information.

Nobody can remember everything. Teaching a student to take notes allows the student to use an organized system to reconstruct what was said during the lesson. Every student has a slightly different system, but no attempt to record the lecture verbatim should be made.

In most cases, a shorthand or abbreviated system of the student's choosing should be encouraged. Notetaking is merely a method of allowing the student to recreate the lecture so that it can be studied. The same notetaking skills can be used outside the classroom any time information needs to be retained. For example, copying an instrument clearance word for word is very difficult. By knowing the format of a typical clearance, student instrument pilots can develop their own system of abbreviations. This allows them to copy the clearance in a useful form for read back and for flying the clearance. By incorporating all or some of these techniques, students retain more information. Instructors can vastly improve their students' retention of information by making certain their students have the best possible listening skills.

Questioning

Good questioning can determine how well the student understands what is being taught. It also shows the student that the instructor is paying attention and that the instructor is interested in the student's response. An instructor should ask focused, open-ended questions and avoid closed-ended questions.

Focused questions allow the instructor to concentrate on desired areas. An instructor may ask for additional details, examples, and impressions from the student. This allows the instructor to ask further questions if necessary. The presentation can then be modified to fit the understanding of the student.

Open-ended questions are designed to encourage full, meaningful answers using the student's own knowledge and perceptions while closed-ended questions encourage a short or single-word answer. Open-ended questions, which typically begin with words such as "why" and "how" tend to be more objective and less leading than closed-ended questions. Often open-ended questions are not technically questions, but statements that implicitly ask for completion. An instructor's ability to ask open-ended questions is an important skill to develop.

In contrast, closed-ended questions tend to evaluate the student's understanding only at the rote level of learning. Closed-ended questions can be answered by "yes" or "no." When used in a multiple choice scenario, closed-ended questions have a finite set of answers from which the respondent chooses. One of the choices may be "other." It is a good idea to allow respondents to write in an optional response if they choose "other" because developing the student response may lead to insights into the learning process.

One benefit of closed-ended questions is that they are relatively easy to standardize and the data gathered easily lend themselves to statistical analysis. The down side to closed-ended questions is that they are more difficult to write than open-ended questions, generally lead the student towards the desired answer, and may under certain circumstances direct the conversation toward the instructor's own agenda.

To be effective, questions, regardless of the type, must be adapted to the ability, experience, and stage of training of the student. Effective questions and, therefore, effective communications center on only one idea. A single question should be limited to who, what, when, where, why, or how and not a combination of these. Effective questioning must present a challenge to the student. Questions of suitable difficulty serve to stimulate learning.

Two ways of confirming that the student and instructor understand things in the same way are the use of paraphrasing and perception checking. The instructor can use paraphrasing to show what the student's statement meant to the instructor. In this way, the student can then make any corrections or expansions on the statement in order to clarify. Perception checking gets to the feelings of the student, again by stating what perceptions the instructor has of the student's behavior that the student can then clarify as necessary.

Since it is important that the instructor understand as much as possible about the students, instructors can be much more effective by using improved listening skills and effective questions to help in putting themselves in the place of the students. Questions should be phrased to focus the student on the decision-making process and the exercise of good judgment.

Knowledge of the subject material and skill at instructional communication are necessary to be an instructor. Increasing the depth of knowledge in either area makes the instructor more effective.

Instructional Enhancement

An instructor never stops learning. While professional development is discussed in greater detail in Chapter 8, the more an instructor knows about a subject, the better the instructor is at conveying that information. For example, a maintenance instructor teaching basic electricity might be able to teach at a minimally satisfactory level if the instructor had only the same training level as that being taught. If asked a question that exceeded the instructor's knowledge, the instructor could research the answer and get back to the student. If would be much better if the instructor, through experience or additional training, was prepared to answer the question initially. Additional knowledge and training would also bolster the instructor's confidence and give the instructional presentation more depth. It is important for an instructor to tailor whatever information that is being presented with the learning level of the students.

Chapter Summary

An awareness of the basic elements of the communicative process (source, symbols, and receiver) indicates the beginning of the understanding required for the successful communicator. Recognizing the various barriers to communication further enhances the flow of ideas between an instructor and the student. The instructor must develop communications skills in order to convey desired information to the students and must recognize that communication is a two-way process. In the end, the true test of whether successful communication has taken place is to determine if the desired results have been achieved.

Chapter 4

The Teaching Process

Introduction

Bob, an aviation maintenance instructor, arrives thirty minutes before a scheduled class to prepare for the lesson he plans to present that day. A quick visual scan tells him the classroom is well lit, the desks are in order, and the room presents a neat overall appearance. He places his lecture notes on the podium, checking to make sure they are all there and in the correct order. Then, he turns on the computer and projector to ensure the audio visual components are working correctly. A quick run of his visual presentation reassures him this portion of his lecture is ready. Next, he counts the handouts he plans to distribute to the class. By now, students are beginning to filter into the classroom. With his preparations made, Bob is free to greet the students, chat with them socially, or answer any questions they might have about the previous class.

Today's class is Bob's introductory lecture on aircraft weight and balance. Using a software program, he has created a slide show featuring examples of safety problems caused by out-of-balance aircraft. He uses these images to introduce the class to the importance of aircraft weight and balance in safe flying. Then, Bob teaches the class how to compute weight and balance for a generic aircraft. To reinforce the lecture, Bob divides the class into small groups and distributes the handouts which contain sample weight and balance problems. Working as a group, the students solve the first weight and balance problem. During this time, Bob and the students freely discuss how to figure weight and balance for that particular aircraft. Once the problem is solved, Bob reiterates the steps used to calculate weight and balance. Now Bob assigns another problem to the students to be solved independently in the class. After each student complete this assignment, Bob is confident they will be able to successfully complete the remaining three weight and balance problems as homework for the next class.

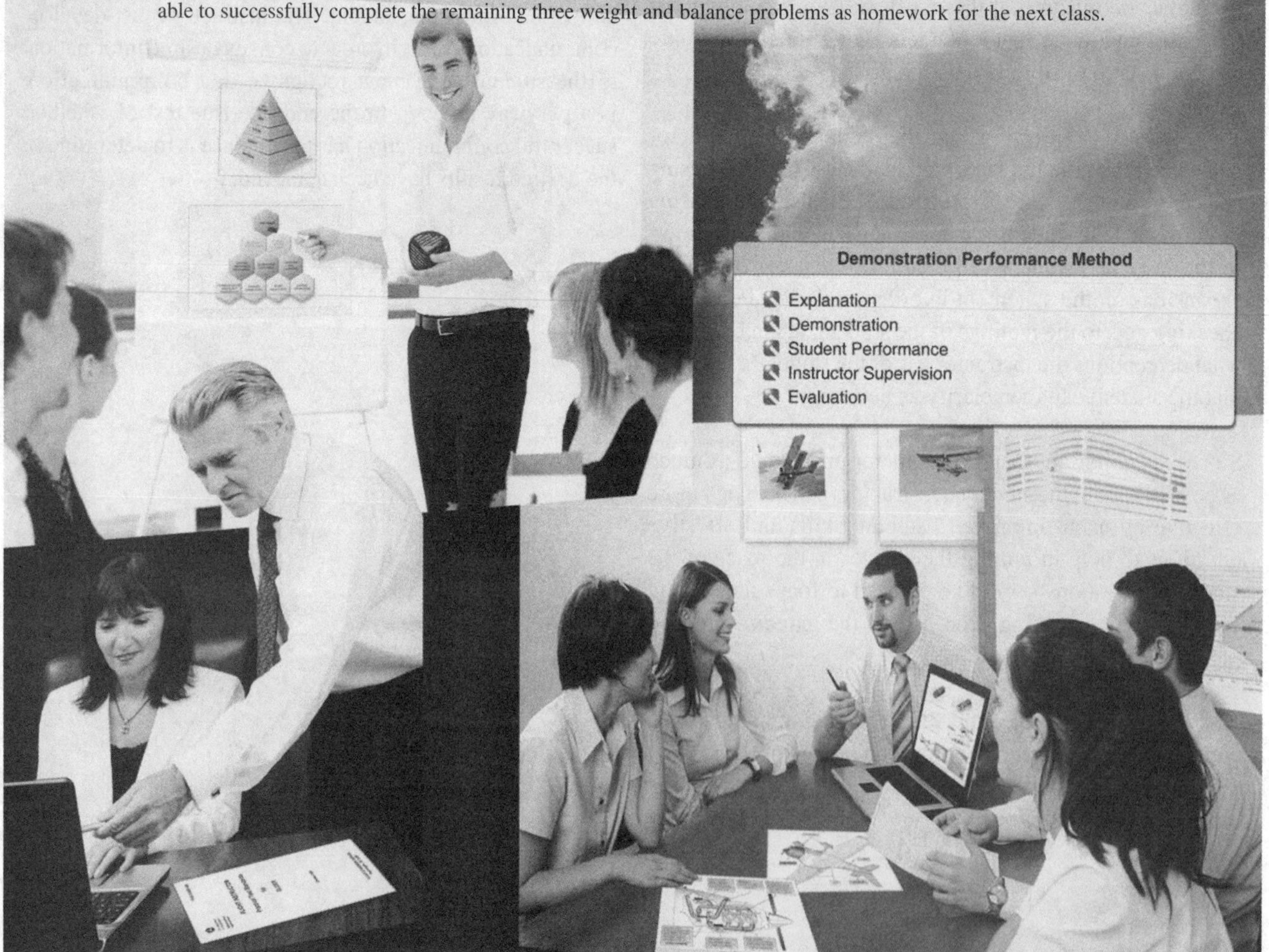

By using a combination of teaching methods (lecture, group learning, and discussion) and instructional aids (audio/visual and handouts), Bob achieves his instructional objective, which is for the students to learn how to compute weight and balance. In order to present the lesson on weight and balance, Bob has taken the theoretical information presented in previous chapters—concepts and principles pertinent to human behavior, how people learn, and effective communication—into the classroom. He has turned this knowledge into practical knowledge utilized in the teaching process. Drawing on previously discussed theoretical knowledge, this chapter discusses specific recommendations on how to use this information to teach aviation students.

What Is Teaching?

Teaching is to instruct or train someone, or the profession of someone who teaches. Someone who teaches is, of course, a teacher or, for the purposes of this handbook, an instructor. Measured in number of people in the profession, teaching is one of the world's largest professions. To be a teacher implies one has completed some type of formal training, has specialized knowledge, has been certified or validated in some way, and adheres to a set of standards of performance. Defining a "good instructor" has proven more elusive, but in *The Essence of Good Teaching* (1985), psychologist Stanford C. Ericksen wrote "good teachers select and organize worthwhile course material, lead students to encode and integrate this material in memorable form, ensure competence in the procedures and methods of a discipline, sustain intellectual curiosity, and promote how to learn independently."

Essential Teaching Skills

Much research has been devoted to trying to discover what makes a "good" or effective instructor. This research has revealed that effective instructors come in many forms, but they generally possess four essential teaching skills: people skills, subject matter expertise, management skills, and assessment skills. *[Figure 4-1]*

Figure 4-1. *A good aviation instructor organizes worthwhile course material and ensures competence in the procedures and methods used to promote learning.*

People Skills

People skills are the ability to interact, talk, understand, empathize, and connect with people. Effective instructors relate well to people. Communication, discussed in Chapter 3, Effective Communication, underlies people skills. It is important for instructors to remember:

- Technical knowledge is useless if the instructor fails to communicate it effectively.
- The two-way process of effective communication means actively listening to the student, as well as teaching him or her.

In the previous scenario, Bob uses the guided group discussion period to listen to his students discuss the weight and balance problem. By listening to their discussion and questions, he can pinpoint problem areas and explain them more fully during the review of the solved problem.

People skills also include the ability to interact respectfully with students, pick up when students are not following along, motivate students to learn, and adapt to the needs of the student when necessary. Another important people skill used by effective instructors is to challenge students intellectually while supporting their efforts to learn. Effective instructors also display enthusiasm for their subject matter and express themselves clearly. The willingness to look for ways to match student learning styles to personal instructional style is another element of effective instruction.

Subject Matter Expertise

A subject matter expert (SME) is a person who possesses a high level of expertise, knowledge, or skill in a particular area. For example, the instructor in the opening scenario is an aviation maintenance SME.

Effective instructors are not only knowledgeable about aviation, they are also knowledgeable about teaching. As mentioned earlier, possession of a high level of technical knowledge does not equate to the ability to teach it. An effective instructor possesses a strong motivation to teach, as well as a positive attitude toward learning. Research into how people learn has been ongoing for almost one hundred years. This handbook is a compilation of that research and is designed to help aviation instructors become experts in the field of education.

Effective instructors have a sincere interest in learning and professional growth. There are a number of professional development opportunities for aviation instructors, such as Federal Aviation Administration (FAA) seminars, industry conventions, professional organizations, and online classes. Networking with and observing other instructors to learn new strategies is also helpful. By being a lifelong learner, the aviation professional remains current in both aviation and education. This topic is explored more thoroughly in Chapter 9, Professional Development.

Management Skills

Management skills generally include the ability to plan, organize, lead, and supervise. For the effective instructor, these skills are reflected in the ability to plan, organize, and carry out a lesson. A well-planned lesson means the instructor is also practicing time management skills and ensures the time allocated for the lesson is well used. As discussed in Chapter 1, Human Behavior, the average age of aviation students is 34 years old. Unlike younger students, no law requires they attend school, they are paying for the training, and they expect the instructor to make wise use of their time.

To manage time well, it is important that an instructor look at the time available and plan how to use the time to achieve the lesson goals. An effective instructor understands what can be realistically achieved within the allotted time, makes the best use of the time available, allows enough time for what must be done, preserves contingency time to handle the unexpected, and minimizes stress by not planning too much for the allotted time.

Management skills also come into play for the aviation instructor who is teaching a class of students. For this instructor, effective management of the classroom promotes learning. Consider the opening scenario in which Bob arrived early for the class and ensured the classroom was well lit, the desks in order, and that the room presented a neat overall appearance. He also made sure the computer and projector were in working order. These steps contribute to a positive learning environment.

Another management skill that enhances the effectiveness of aviation instructors is supervision of the students. For the flight instructor, this may entail overseeing the preflight procedures. For the maintenance instructor, this may mean monitoring the replacement of a carburetor. While it is important to provide hands-on tasks in the lesson plan to engage students in active learning, it is also important to ensure the tasks are completed safely and correctly.

Assessment Skills

In Chapter 2, The Learning Process, learning was defined as "a change in the behavior of the learner as a result of experience. The behavior can be physical and overt, or it can be intellectual or attitudinal." This change is measurable and therefore can be assessed.

Assessment of learning is a complex process and it is important to be clear about the purposes of the assessment. There are several points at which assessments can be made: before training, during training, and after training. Learning assessment is another important skill of an effective instructor. *[Figure 4-2]* This topic is discussed in detail in Chapter 5, Assessment.

Figure 4-2. *An effective instructor uses a variety of tools to evaluate how students learn, as well as what they know.*

Instructor's Code of Conduct

While many of the characteristics of effective instructors discussed in the previous paragraphs hold true for any instructor, the aviation instructor has the added responsibility of molding an aviation citizen—a pilot or maintenance technician the instructor feels confident will be an asset to the rest of the aviation community. The following code describes the concept of an aviation citizen.

An aviation instructor needs to remember he or she is teaching a pilot or technician who should:

- Make safety the number one priority,
- Develop and exercise good judgment in making decisions,

- Recognize and manage risk effectively,
- Be accountable for his or her actions,
- Act with responsibility and courtesy,
- Adhere to prudent operating practices and personal operating parameters, and
- Adhere to applicable laws and regulations.

In addition, the Certificated Flight Instructor (CFI) needs to remember he or she is teaching a pilot who should:

- Seek proficiency in control of the aircraft,
- Use flight deck technology in a safe and appropriate way,
- Be confident in a wide variety of flight situations, and
- Be respectful of the privilege of flight.

The teaching process organizes the material an instructor wishes to teach in such a way that the learner understands what is being taught. The teaching process consists of four steps: preparation, presentation, application, and assessment. Regardless of the teaching or training delivery method used, the teaching process remains the same. To be effective, an instructor utilizes people skills, subject matter expertise, management skills, and assessment skills.

This chapter explores the teaching process in general terms of how to prepare, present, apply, and assess lesson material. Teaching methods or training delivery methods are discussed, as well as the use of instructional aids.

Course of Training

In education, a course of training is a complete series of studies leading to attainment of a specific goal. The goal might be a certificate of completion, graduation, or an academic degree. For example, a student pilot may enroll in a private pilot certificate course, and upon completion of all course requirements, be awarded a graduation certificate. A course of training also may be limited to something like the additional training required for operating high-performance airplanes.

Other terms closely associated with a course of training include curriculum, syllabus, and training course outline. In many cases, these terms are used interchangeably, but there are important differences.

A curriculum is a set of courses in an area of specialization offered by an educational institution. A curriculum for a pilot school usually includes courses for the various pilot certificates and ratings, while the curriculum for an aviation maintenance technician (AMT) addresses the subject areas described in Title 14 of the Code of Federal Regulations (14 CFR) part 147. A syllabus is a summary or outline of a course of study that generally contains a description of each lesson, including objectives and completion standards. In aviation, the term "training syllabus" is commonly used and in this context it is a step-by-step, building block progression of learning with provisions for regular review and assessments at prescribed stages of learning. *[Figure 4-3]* And, finally, a training course outline within a curriculum is the content of a particular course. It normally includes statements of objectives, descriptions of teaching aids, definitions of assessment criteria, and indications of desired outcome.

Preparation of a Lesson

A determination of objectives and standards is necessary before any important instruction can be presented. Although some schools and independent instructors may develop their own syllabus, in practice, many instructors use a commercially developed syllabus that already has been selected by a school for use in their aviation training program. For the aviation instructor, the objectives listed in the syllabus are a beginning point for instruction.

Training Objectives and Standards

Aviation training involves two types of objectives: performance based and decision based. Performance-based objectives are essential in defining exactly what needs to be done and how it is done during each lesson. As the student progresses through higher levels of performance and understanding, the instructor should shift the training focus to decision-based training objectives. Decision-based training objectives allow for a more dynamic training environment and are ideally suited to scenario type training. The instructor uses decision-based training objectives to teach aviation students critical thinking skills, such as risk management and aeronautical decision-making (ADM).

The desired level of learning should also be incorporated into the objectives, and these level of learning objectives may apply to one or more of the three domains of learning—cognitive (knowledge), affective (attitudes, beliefs, and values), and psychomotor (physical skills). Normally, aviation training aspires to a level of learning at the application level or higher.

Standards are closely tied to objectives since they include a description of the desired knowledge, behavior, or skill stated in specific terms, along with conditions and criteria. When a student is able to perform according to well-defined standards, evidence of learning is apparent. Comprehensive examples of the desired learning outcomes, or behaviors, should be included in the standards. As indicated in chapter 2, standards for the level of learning in the cognitive and

Lesson 1	**Flight Planning**
Objective:	To develop student skill in flight planning/obtaining a weather briefing
Elements:	• Observe wind and weather conditions from the weather channel, radio, and/or visually • Call flight service station for weather briefing • Select launch site
Equipment:	• Weather information form • Sectional chart and road map • Plotter • Compass • Pilot balloon (Pibal)
Instructor Action:	• Discuss lesson • Obtain weather information • Observe surface winds with pibal • Determine launch site • Locate launch site on chart • Draw dead reckoning line in direction of flight and mark off distance or time on the line • Suggest landmarks to verify position in flight • Ascertain airspace considerations • Critique plan
Student Action:	• Obtain weather briefing from AFSS (1-800-WX-BRIEF) • Recommend launch site based on accurate weather information recorded on form • Draw flight plan approved by instructor
Completion Standards:	• Demonstrates ability to obtain complete weather briefing from the Automated Flight Service Station and correlate this information with observed weather conditions • Locates launch site on chart • Draws proposed course with time ticks on dead reckoning line • Understands need for flexibility to adjust flight plan • Selects landmarks in flight to verify position

Figure 4-3. *The syllabus defines the unit of training, states by objective what the student is expected to accomplish during the unit of training, shows an organized plan for instruction, and dictates the assessment process for either the unit or stages of learning.*

psychomotor domains are easily established. However, writing standards to evaluate a student's level of learning or overt behavior in the affective domain (attitudes, beliefs, and values) is more difficult.

The overall objective of an aviation training course is usually well established, and the general standards are included in various rules and related publications. For example, eligibility, knowledge, proficiency, and experience requirements for pilots and AMT students are stipulated in the regulations, and the standards are published in the applicable PTS or oral and practical tests (O&Ps). It should be noted that PTS and O&P standards are limited to the most critical job tasks. Certification tests do not represent an entire training syllabus.

A broad, overall objective of any pilot training course is to qualify the student to be a competent, efficient, safe pilot for the operation of specific aircraft types under stated conditions. The established criteria or standards to determine whether the training has been adequate are the passing of knowledge and practical tests required by 14 CFR for the issuance of pilot certificates. Similar objectives and standards are established for AMT students. Professional instructors should not limit their objectives to meeting only the published requirements for pilot or AMT certification.

Instructional objectives should also extend beyond those listed in official publications. Successful instructors teach their students not only how, but also why and when. By incorporating ADM and risk management into each lesson, the aviation instructor helps the student learn, develop, and reinforce the decision-making process which ultimately leads to sound judgment and good decision-making skills.

Performance-Based Objectives

Performance-based objectives are used to set measurable, reasonable standards that describe the desired performance of the student. This usually involves the term behavioral objective, although it may be referred to as a performance, instructional, or educational objective. All refer to the same thing, the behavior of the student.

These objectives provide a way of stating what performance level is desired of a student before the student is allowed to progress to the next stage of instruction. Again, the objectives must be clear, measurable, and repeatable. In other words, they must mean the same thing to any knowledgeable reader. The objectives must be written. If they are not written, they become subject to the fallibility of recall, interpretation, or loss of specificity with time.

Performance-based objectives consist of three elements: description of the skill or behavior, conditions, and criteria. Each part is required and must be stated in a way that leaves every reader with the same picture of the objective, how it is performed, and to what level of performance. *[Figure 4-4]*

Figure 4-4. *Performance-based objectives are made up of a description of the skill or behavior, conditions, and criteria.*

Description of the Skill or Behavior

The description of the skill or behavior explains the desired outcome of the instruction. It is actually a learned capability, which may be defined as knowledge, a skill, or an attitude. The description should be in concrete terms that can be measured. Terms such as "knowledge of ..." and "awareness of ..." cannot be measured very well, and words like this should be avoided. Phrases like "able to select from a list of ..." or "able to repeat the steps to ..." are better because they describe something that can be measured. Furthermore, the skill or behavior described should be logical and within the overall instructional plan.

Conditions

Conditions are necessary to specifically explain the rules under which the skill or behavior is demonstrated. If a desired capability is to navigate from point A to point B, the objective as stated is not specific enough for all students to do it in the same way. Information such as equipment, tools, reference material, and limiting parameters should be included. For example, inserting conditions narrows the objective as follows: "Using sectional charts, a flight computer, and Cessna 172, navigate from point A to point B while maintaining standard hemispheric altitudes." Sometimes, in the process of writing the objective, a difficulty is encountered. This might be someone saying, "But, what if ...?" This is a good indication that the original version was confusing to that person. If it is confusing to one person, it will be confusing to others and should be corrected.

Criteria

Criteria are the standards that measure the accomplishment of the objective. The criteria should be stated so that there is no question whether the objective has been met. In the previous example, the criteria may include that navigation from point A to point B be accomplished within 5 minutes of the preplanned flight time and that en route altitude be maintained within 200 feet. The revised performance-based objective may now read, "Using a sectional chart and a flight computer, plan a flight and fly from point A to point B in a Cessna 172. Arrival at point B should be within 5 minutes of planned arrival time and cruise altitude should be maintained within 200 feet during the en route phase of the flight." The alert reader has already noted that the conditions and criteria changed slightly during the development of these objectives, and that is exactly the way it will occur. Conditions and criteria should be refined as necessary. As noted earlier, a PTS already has many of the elements needed to formulate performance-based objectives. In most cases, the objective is listed along with sufficient conditions to describe the scope of the objective. The PTS also has specific criteria or standards upon which to grade performance; however, the criteria may not always be specific enough for a particular lesson. An instructor should write performance-based objectives to fit the desired outcome of the lesson. The objective formulated in the last few paragraphs, for instance, is a well-defined lesson objective from the task, Pilotage and Dead Reckoning, in the Private Pilot PTS.

The Importance of the PTS in Aviation Training Curricula

PTS hold an important position in aviation training curricula because they supply the instructor with specific performance objectives based on the standards that must be met for the issuance of a particular aviation certificate or rating. *[Figure 4-5]* The FAA frequently reviews the test items in an attempt to maintain their validity in the current

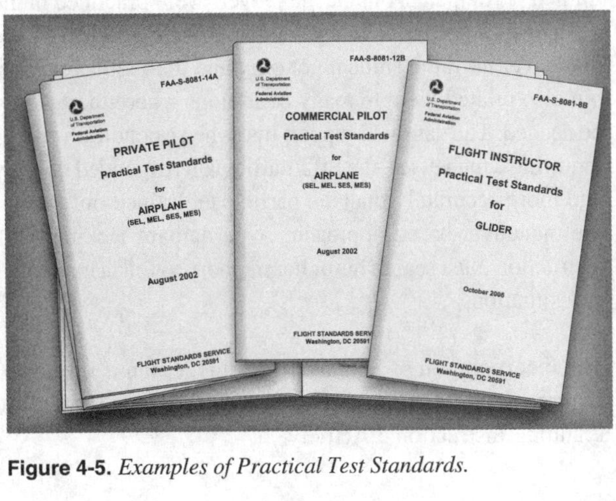

Figure 4-5. *Examples of Practical Test Standards.*

aviation environment. It is a widely accepted belief in the aviation community that test items included as part of a test or evaluation should be both content valid and criterion valid. Content validity means that a particular maneuver or procedure closely mimics what is required. Criterion validity means that the completion standards for the test are reflective of acceptable standards.

For example, in flight training, content validity is reflected by a particular maneuver closely mimicking a maneuver required in actual flight, such as the student pilot being able to recover from a power-off stall. Criterion validity means that the completion standards for the test are reflective of acceptable standards in actual flight. Thus, the student pilot exhibits knowledge of all the elements involved in a power-off stall as listed in the PTS.

As discussed in chapter 2, humans develop cognitive skills through active interaction with the world. This concept has led to the adoption of scenario-based training (SBT) in many fields, including aviation. An effective aviation instructor uses the maneuver-based approach of the PTS but presents the objectives in a scenario situation.

It has been found that flight students using SBT methods demonstrate stick-and-rudder skills equal to or better than students trained under the maneuver-based approach only. Of even more significance is that the same data also suggest that SBT students demonstrate better decision-making skills than maneuver based students—most likely because their training occurred while performing realistic flight maneuvers and not artificial maneuvers designed only for the test.

Research also indicates SBT may lead to improved piloting and navigation skills over traditional maneuver-based training techniques. SBT trained participants demonstrated the same skills and knowledge as the maneuver-based trained participants, but the maneuvers were practiced in the context of a scenario. Many scenarios were coupled to the maneuver until the student not only had the requisite skills, but also related them to many conditions where they would be needed. The data also support that when a condition occurs requiring a maneuver, the SBT participant responded quickly and more accurately than the participant trained only under the maneuver-based approach. A participant lacking SBT instruction must search his or her memory to link a maneuver to a situation.

The incorporation of SBT as part of the lesson is discussed in more detail later in this chapter, as well as in Chapter 6, Planning Instructional Activity.

Decision-Based Objectives

Decision-based objectives are designed specifically to develop pilot judgment and ADM skills. Improper pilot decisions cause a significant percentage of all accidents, and the majority of fatal accidents in light single- and twin-engine aircraft. Often combined with traditional task and maneuver training within a given scenario, decision-based objectives facilitate a higher level of learning and application. By using dynamic and meaningful scenarios, the instructor teaches the student how to gather information and make informed, safe, and timely decisions.

Decision-based training is not a new concept. Experienced CFIs have been using scenarios that require dynamic problem solving to teach cross-country operations, emergency procedures, and other flight skills for years.

Decision-based learning objectives and the use of flight training scenarios do not preclude traditional maneuver-based training. Rather, flight maneuvers are integrated into the flight training scenarios and conducted as they would occur in the real world. Those maneuvers requiring repetition may still be taught during concentrated settings. However, once they are learned, they are integrated into more realistic and dynamic flight situations.

Decision-based objectives are also important for the aviation instructor planning AMT training. An AMT uses ADM and risk management skills not only on the job site but also in the repair and maintenance of aircraft.

Other Uses of Training Objectives

Performance-based and decision-based objectives are also helpful for an instructor designing a lesson plan. Having decided on the objectives, an instructor can use this information to complete many of the steps on the lesson plan. For example, once the instructor decides how the student will accomplish the objective, most of the work that determines the elements of the lesson and the schedule of events has been done. The equipment necessary and the instructor and student actions anticipated during the lesson have also been specified. By listing the criteria for the training objectives, the instructor has already established the completion standards normally included as part of the lesson plan.

Use of training objectives also provides the student with a better understanding of the big picture, as well as knowledge of what is expected. This overview can alleviate a significant source of uncertainty and frustration on the part of the student.

As indicated in chapter 1, training objectives apply to all three domains of learning—cognitive (knowledge), affective (attitudes, beliefs, values), and psychomotor (physical skills). In addition, since each domain includes several educational or skill levels, training objectives may easily be adapted to a specific performance level of knowledge or skill. Clearly defined training objectives that the student understands are essential to the teaching process regardless of the teaching technique used.

Presentation of a Lesson

Research into how people learn has led many experts to recommend ways to present lessons that keep the attention of a class. The steps in *Figure 4-6* form a guideline for lesson presentation. Many of them can be combined during the actual presentation. For example, consider a video presentation given during the weight and balance lecture. The video adds a multimedia element to the lecture, is a good attention getter, and can be used to visually demonstrate the learning objective.

Organization of Material

Even the most knowledgeable instructor must properly organize the material. Once a determination of objectives and standards has been made, an instructor formulates a plan of action to lead students through the course in a logical manner toward the desired goal. Usually the goal for students is a certificate or rating. It could be a private pilot certificate, an instrument rating, or an AMT certificate or rating. In all cases, a systematic plan of action requires the use of an appropriate training syllabus. Generally, the syllabus contains a description of each lesson, including objectives and completion standards. Refer to Chapter 6, Planning Instructional Activity, for detailed information on requirements for an aviation training syllabus and the building-block concept for curriculum development.

The main concern of the instructor is usually the more manageable task of organizing a block of training with integrated lesson plans. The traditional organization of a lesson plan is introduction, development, and conclusion.

Introduction

The introduction sets the stage for everything to come. Efforts in this area pay great dividends in terms of quality of instruction. In brief, the introduction is made up of three elements: attention, motivation, and an overview of what is to be covered.

Attention

The purpose of the attention element is to focus each student's attention on the lesson. The instructor begins by telling a story, showing a video clip, asking a question, or telling a joke. Any of these may be appropriate at one time or another. Regardless of which is used, it should relate to the subject and establish a background for developing the learning outcomes. Telling a story or a joke that is not related in some way to the subject distracts from the lesson. The main concern is to gain the attention of everyone and concentrate on the subject. *[Figure 4-7]*

Before the Lesson

- Decide on the topic.
- Determine the amount of time for the lesson.
- Write an outline.
- Develop a flow or order to the concepts being introduced.
- Avoid overloading the students with too much detail.
- Rehearse the lesson.
- Think about delivery—is a microphone needed?
- Arrive early, create a welcoming atmosphere for students.
- Be available to students before class.
- Set a positive tone for learning.

During the Lesson

- Grab the students' attention (have a beginning).
- Maintain sustained eye contact.
- Make learning goals explicit for each assignment.
- Plan an activity for students.
- Progress through the lesson smoothly, begin with an introduction, support the lesson in the middle, and flow into the conclusion.
- Use time efficiently and effectively.
- Use multimedia such as slide presentations, video clips, etc.
- Break the lesson up with small tasks for the students to help them concentrate.
- Move around during the lesson. Students today are conditioned by television and movies to movement.
- Give students time to answer questions before rephrasing them.

After the Lesson

- Plan an ending to the lesson.
- Summarize the day's main points.
- Have a final task for students to do at the end in case the lesson ends too soon.
- Leave time for questions at the end.
- Treat student questions with courtesy no matter how basic the question seems.
- Have students do something with the lecture material (accountability) outside of the class.
- Provide other resources for students.
- Encourage students to keep up and do well.
- Be available to students after class.
- Critique the lesson: jot down notes about what went well and what could have gone better.

Figure 4-6. *Guidelines for presenting lessons.*

Figure 4-7. *The attention element causes students to focus on the upcoming lesson.*

Motivation

The purpose of the motivation element is to offer the students specific reasons why the lesson content is important to know, understand, apply, or perform concepts of Thorndike's law of readiness. For example, the instructor may talk about an occurrence where the knowledge in the lesson was applied. Or the instructor may remind the students of an upcoming test on the material. This motivation should appeal to each student personally and engender a desire to learn the material.

Overview

Every lesson introduction should contain an overview that tells the group what is to be covered during the period. A clear, concise presentation of the objective and the key ideas gives the students a road map of the route to be followed. A good visual aid can help the instructor show the students the path that they are to travel. The introduction should be free of stories, jokes, or incidents that do not help the students focus their attention on the lesson objective. Also, the instructor should avoid a long apologetic introduction, because it only serves to dampen the students' interest in the lesson.

Development

Development is the main part of the lesson. Here, the instructor develops the subject matter in a manner that helps the students achieve the desired learning outcomes. The instructor must logically organize the material to show the relationships of the main points. The instructor usually shows these primary relationships by developing the main points in one of the following ways: from past to present, simple to complex, known to unknown, and most frequently used to least used.

Past to Present

In this pattern of development, the subject matter is arranged chronologically, from the present to the past or from the past to the present. Time relationships are most suitable when history is an important consideration, as in tracing the development of radio navigation systems.

Simple to Complex

The simple-to-complex pattern helps the instructor lead the student from simple facts or ideas to an understanding of the phenomena or concepts involved. In studying jet propulsion, for example, the student might begin by considering the action involved in releasing air from a toy balloon and finish by taking part in a discussion of a complex gas turbine engine.

Do not be afraid to omit "less important" information at first in order to simplify the learning process. If Class D, E, and G airspace are the only airspace types being utilized by a student, save the discussion of A, B, and C airspace until they have operating familiarity with the other types. Less information at first is easier to absorb.

Known to Unknown

By using something the student already knows as the point of departure, the instructor can lead into new ideas and concepts. For example, in developing a lesson on heading indicators, the instructor could begin with a discussion of the vacuum-driven heading indicator before proceeding to a description of the radio magnetic indicator (RMI).

Most Frequently Used to Least Used

In some subjects, certain information or concepts are common to all who use the material. This fourth organizational pattern starts with common usage before progressing to the rarer ones. Even though most aircraft are equipped with some sort of navigational system, instructors should teach students the basics of navigation. For example, basic map reading is a perishable skill that should be practiced often. Another example is dead reckoning, which forces pilots to be aware of there surroundings at all times. Basic VOR/NDB radio navigation procedures are also perishable and could save lives if proficiency is maintained. Before using a global positioning system (GPS) as the sole means of navigation, students should be taught the basics.

Under each main point in a lesson, the subordinate points should lead naturally from one to another. With this arrangement, each point leads logically to and serves as a reminder of the next. Meaningful transition from one main point to another keeps the students oriented, aware of where they have been, and where they are going. This permits effective sorting or categorizing chunks of information in the working or short-term memory. Organizing a lesson so the students grasp the logical relationships of ideas is not an easy task, but it is necessary if the students are to learn and remember what they have learned. Poorly organized information is of little or no value to the student because it cannot be readily understood or remembered.

Conclusion

An effective conclusion retraces the important elements of the lesson and relates them to the objective. This review and wrap-up of ideas reinforces student learning and improves the retention of what has been learned. New ideas should not be introduced in the conclusion because at this point they are likely to confuse the students.

By organizing the lesson material into a logical format, the instructor maximizes the opportunity for students to retain the desired information. Since each teaching situation is unique, the setting and purpose of the lesson determines which teaching method is used.

Training Delivery Methods

Today's instructor can choose from a wealth of ways to present instructional material: lecture, discussion, guided discussion, problem based, group learning, demonstration-performance, or e-learning. It is important to remember that a training delivery method is rarely used by itself. In a typical lesson, an effective instructor normally uses a combination of methods. For example, Bob lectures in the opening scenario, but after giving the students knowledge of how to compute weight and balance, he uses group learning to reinforce the lecture. To be an effective instructor, it is important to determine which teaching methods best convey the information being taught.

Lecture Method

In the lecture method, the instructor delivers his knowledge via lectures to students who are more or less silent participants. Lectures are best used when an instructor wishes to convey a general understanding of a subject that students lack. While this is the most widely used form of presentation and instructors should know how to develop and present a lecture, they also should understand the advantages and limitations of this method.

Lectures are used for introduction of new subjects, summarizing ideas, showing relationships between theory and practice, and reemphasizing main points. The lecture method is adaptable to many different settings, including small or large groups. Lectures also may be used to introduce a unit of instruction or a complete training program. Finally, lectures may be combined with other teaching methods to give added meaning and direction.

The lecture method of teaching needs to be very flexible since it may be used in different ways. For example, there are several types of lectures, such as the illustrated talk where the speaker relies heavily on visual aids to convey ideas to the listeners. With a briefing, the speaker presents a concise array of facts to the listeners who normally do not expect elaboration of supporting material. During a formal lecture, the speaker's purpose is to inform, to persuade, or to entertain with little or no verbal participation by the students. When using a teaching lecture, the instructor plans and delivers an oral presentation in a manner that allows some participation by the students and helps direct them toward the desired learning outcomes.

In general lectures, begin with an introduction of the topic to be discussed. It is also a good idea at this time to let students know whether or not questions during the lecture are welcomed. The body of the lecture follows with a summary of the lecture's main points at the end.

Teaching Lecture

The teaching lecture is favored by aviation instructors because it allows some active participation by the students. The instructor must determine the method to be used in developing the subject matter. The instructor also should carefully consider the class size and the depth of the presentation. As mentioned in chapter 3, covering a subject in too much detail is as bad or worse than sketchy coverage. Regardless of the method of development or depth of coverage, the success of the teaching lecture depends upon the instructor's ability to communicate effectively with the class.

In other methods of teaching such as demonstration-performance or guided discussion, the instructor receives direct reaction from the students, either verbally or by some form of body language. However in the teaching lecture, the feedback is not nearly as obvious and is much harder to interpret. In the teaching lecture, the instructor must develop a keen perception for subtle responses from the class—facial expressions, manner of taking notes, and apparent interest or disinterest in the lesson. The effective instructor is able to interpret the meaning of these reactions and adjust the lesson accordingly.

Preparing the Teaching Lecture

Careful preparation is one key to successful performance as a classroom lecturer. This preparation should start well in advance of the presentation. The following four steps should be followed in the planning phase of preparation:

- Establishing the objective and desired outcomes
- Researching the subject
- Organizing the material
- Planning productive classroom activities

In all stages of preparing for the teaching lecture, the instructor should support any point to be covered with meaningful examples, comparisons, statistics, or testimony. The instructor should consider that the student may neither believe nor understand any point without the use of testimony from SMEs or without meaningful examples, statistics, or comparisons. While developing the lesson, the instructor also should strongly consider the use of examples and personal experiences related to the subject of the lesson.

After completing the preliminary planning and writing of the lesson plan, the instructor should rehearse the lecture to build self-confidence. Rehearsals, or dry runs, help smooth out the mechanics of using notes, visual aids, and other instructional devices. If possible, the instructor should have another knowledgeable person, preferably another instructor, observe the practice sessions and act as a critic. This critique helps the instructor judge the adequacy of supporting materials and visual aids, as well as the presentation. *[Figure 4-8]*

Figure 4-8. *Instructors should try a dry run with another instructor to get a feel for the lecture presentation.*

Suitable Language

In the teaching lecture, simple rather than complex words should be used whenever possible. Good newspapers offer examples of the effective use of simple words. Picturesque slang and free-and-easy colloquialisms, if they suit the subject, can add variety and vividness to a teaching lecture. The instructor should not, however, use substandard English. Errors in grammar and vulgarisms detract from an instructor's dignity and insult the intelligence of the students.

If the subject matter includes technical terms, the instructor should clearly define each one so that no student is in doubt about its meaning. Whenever possible, the instructor should use specific rather than general words. For example, the specific words, "a leak in the fuel line" tell more than the general term "mechanical defect."

Another way the instructor can add life to the lecture is to vary his or her tone of voice and pace of speaking. In addition, using sentences of different length helps, since consistent use of short sentences results in a choppy style. On the other hand, poorly constructed long sentences are difficult to follow and can easily become tangled. To ensure clarity and variety, the instructor should normally use sentences of short and medium length.

Types of Delivery

Depending on the requirements of any particular circumstances, a lecture is usually delivered in one of four ways:

- Reading from a typed or written manuscript
- Reciting memorized material without the aid of a manuscript
- Speaking extemporaneously from an outline
- Speaking impromptu without preparation

The teaching lecture is probably best delivered in an extemporaneous manner. The instructor speaks from a mental or written outline, but does not read or memorize the material to be presented. Because the exact words to express an idea are spontaneous, the lecture is more personalized than one that is read or spoken from memory.

Since the instructor talks directly to the students, their reactions can be readily observed, and adjustments can be made based on their responses. The instructor has better control of the situation, can change the approach to meet any contingency, and can tailor each idea to suit the responses of the students. For example, if the instructor realizes from puzzled expressions that a number of students fail to grasp an idea, that point can be further elaborated until the reactions of the students indicate they understand. The extemporaneous presentation reflects the instructor's personal enthusiasm and is more flexible than other methods. For these reasons, it is likely to hold the interest of the students.

Use of Notes

An instructor who is thoroughly prepared or who has made the presentation before can usually speak effectively without notes. If the lecture has been carefully prepared, and the instructor is completely familiar with the outline, there should be no real difficulty.

Notes used wisely can ensure accuracy, jog the memory, and dispel the fear of forgetting. They are essential for reporting complicated information. For an instructor who tends to ramble, notes are a must because they help keep the lecture on track. The instructor who requires notes should use them sparingly and unobtrusively, but at the same time should make no effort to hide them from the students. Notes may be written legibly or typed, and they should be placed where they can be consulted easily, or held, if the instructor walks about the room. *[Figure 4-9]*

Figure 4-9. *Notes allow the accurate dissemination of complicated information.*

Formal Versus Informal Lectures

The lecture may be conducted in either a formal or an informal manner. The informal lecture includes active student participation. The primary consideration in the lecture method, as in all other teaching methods, is the achievement of desired learning outcomes. Learning is best achieved if students participate actively in a friendly, relaxed atmosphere. Therefore, the use of the informal lecture is encouraged. At the same time, it must be realized that a formal lecture is still to be preferred on some subjects and occasions, such as lectures introducing new subject matter.

The instructor can achieve active student participation in the informal lecture through the use of questions. In this way, the students are encouraged to make contributions that supplement the lecture. The instructor can use questions to determine the experience and background of the students in order to tailor the lecture to their needs, and/or to add variety, stimulate interest, and check student understanding. However, it is the instructor's responsibility to plan, organize, develop, and present the major portion of a lesson.

Advantages and Disadvantages of the Lecture

There are a number of advantages to lectures. For example, a lecture is a convenient way to instruct large groups. If necessary, a public address system can be used to amplify the speaker's voice. Lectures can be used to present information that would be difficult for the students to get in other ways, particularly if the students do not have the time required for research, or if they do not have access to reference material. Lectures also can usefully and successfully supplement other teaching devices and methods. A brief introductory lecture can give direction and purpose to a demonstration or prepare students for a discussion by telling them something about the subject matter to be covered.

In a lecture, the instructor can present many ideas in a relatively short time. Facts and ideas that have been logically organized can be concisely presented in rapid sequence. Lecturing is unquestionably the most economical of all teaching methods in terms of the time required to present a given amount of material.

The lecture is particularly suitable for introducing a new subject and for explaining the necessary background information. By using a lecture in this way, the instructor can offer students with varied backgrounds a common understanding of essential principles and facts. Although the lecture method is useful in providing information, it is not an effective method of learning large amounts of information in a short time. Nor do lectures easily allow an instructor to estimate student understanding of the material covered. Within a single period, the instructor may unwittingly present more information than students can absorb, and the lecture method provides no accurate means of checking student progress.

Many instructors find it difficult to hold the attention of all students in a lecture throughout the class period. To achieve desired learning outcomes through the lecture method, an instructor needs considerable skill in speaking.

As indicated in chapter 2, a student's rate of retention drops off significantly after the first 10-15 minutes of a lecture and improves at the end. The pure lecture format also inhibits student participation. Research has shown that learning is an active process—the more involved students are in the process, the better they learn. On the other hand, a student needs knowledge in order to build understanding of a subject.

One last disadvantage of the lecture is that it does not foster attainment of certain types of learning outcome, such as motor skills, need to be perfected via hands-on practice. Thus, an instructor who introduces some form of active student participation in the middle of a lecture greatly increases student retention. One way to increase retention during a lecture is to use the discussion method of training delivery.

Discussion Method

The discussion method modifies the pure lecture form by using lecture and then discussion to actively integrate the student into the learning process. In the discussion method, the instructor provides a short lecture, no more than 20 minutes in length, which gives basic knowledge to the students. This short lecture is followed by instructor-student and student-student discussion.

This method relies on discussion and the exchange of ideas. Everyone has the opportunity to comment, listen, think, and participate. By being actively engaged in discussing the lecture, students improve their recall and ability to use the information in the future.

It is important for the instructor to play the part of guide, keeping the discussion focused on the subject matter. That may mean the instructor needs to initiate leading questions, referee if the discussions cause conflict, ensure that all students participate, and at the end summarize what has been learned.

Tying the discussion method into the lecture method not only provides active student participation, it also allows students to develop higher order thinking skills (HOTS). The give and take of the discussion method also helps students learn to evaluate ideas, concepts, and principles. When using this method, instructors should keep their own discussion to a minimum since the goal is student participation.

Instructors can also use another form of discussion, the guided discussion method, to ensure the student has correctly received and interpreted subject information.

Guided Discussion Method

The guided discussion method relies on student possession of a level of knowledge about the topic to be discussed, either through reading prior to class or a short lecture to set up the topic to be discussed. This training method employs instructor-guided discussion with the instructor maintaining control of the discussion. It can be used during classroom periods and preflight and postflight briefings. The discussions reflect whatever level of knowledge and experience the students have gained.

The goal of guided discussions is to draw out what the students know. The instructor should remember that the more intense the discussion and the greater the participation, the more effective the learning. All members of the group should follow the discussion. The instructor should treat everyone impartially, encourage questions, exercise patience and tact, and comment on all responses. Sarcasm and/or ridicule should never be used, since they inhibit the spontaneity of the participants. In a guided discussion, the instructor guides the discussion with the goal of reinforcing a learning objective related to the lesson. The instructor acts as a facilitator to encourage discussion between students.

Use of Questions in a Guided Discussion

In the guided discussion, learning is achieved through the skillful use of questions. Questions can be categorized by function and by characteristics. Understanding these distinctions helps the instructor become a more skilled user of questions.

The instructor often uses a question to open up an area for discussion. This is the lead-off question and its purpose is to get the discussion started. After the discussion develops, the instructor may ask a follow-up question to guide the discussion. The reasons for using a follow-up question may vary. The instructor may want a student to explain something more thoroughly, or may need to bring the discussion back to a point from which it has strayed.

In terms of characteristics, questions can be identified as overhead, rhetorical, direct, reverse, and relay. The overhead question is directed to the entire group to stimulate thought and response from each group member. The instructor may use an overhead question to pose the lead-off question. The rhetorical question is similar in nature, because it also spurs group thought. However, the instructor provides the answer to the rhetorical question. Consequently, it is more commonly used in lecturing than in guided discussion.

The instructor who wants to phrase a question for follow-up purposes may choose the overhead type. If, however, a response is desired from a specific individual, a direct question may be asked of that student. A reverse question is a question asked by a learner and the instructor returns the question to the same learner for response. A relay question is asked by a learner and the instructor requests another student to respond.

Questions are so much a part of teaching that they are often taken for granted. Effective use of questions may result in more student learning than any other single technique used by instructors. Instructors should avoid questions that can be answered by short factual statements or yes or no responses and ask open-ended questions that are thought provoking and require more mental activity. Since most aviation training is at the understanding level of learning or higher, questions should require students to grasp concepts, explain similarities and differences, and to infer cause-and-effect relationships. *[Figure 4-10]*

Characteristics of an Effective Question

- Has a specific purpose
- Is clear in meaning
- Contains a single idea
- Stimulates thought
- Requires definite answers
- Relates to previously covered information

Figure 4-10. *If the objectives of a lesson are clearly established in advance, instructors will find it much easier to ask appropriate questions that keep the discussion moving in the planned direction.*

Planning a Guided Discussion

Planning a guided discussion is similar to planning a lecture. Instructors will find the following suggestions helpful in planning a discussion lesson. (Note that these same suggestions include many that are appropriate for planning cooperative learning, to be discussed later in the chapter.)

- Select a topic the students can profitably discuss. Unless the students have some knowledge to exchange with each other, they cannot reach the desired learning outcomes by the discussion method. If necessary, make assignments that give the students an adequate background for discussing the lesson topic.
- Establish a specific lesson objective with desired learning outcomes. Through discussion, the students develop an understanding of the subject by sharing knowledge, experiences, and backgrounds. Consequently, the objective normally is stated at the understanding level of learning. The desired learning outcomes should stem from the objective.
- Conduct adequate research to become familiar with the topic. While researching, the instructor should always be alert for ideas on the best way to tailor a lesson for a particular group of students. Similarly, the instructor can prepare the prediscussion assignment more effectively while conducting research for the classroom period. During this research process, the instructor should also earmark reading material that appears to be especially appropriate as background material for students. Such material should be well organized and based on fundamentals.
- Organize the main and subordinate points of the lesson in a logical sequence. The guided discussion has three main parts: introduction, discussion, and conclusion. The introduction consists of three elements: attention, motivation, and overview. In the discussion, the instructor should be certain that the main points discussed build logically with the objective. The conclusion consists of the summary of the main points. By organizing in this manner, the instructor phrases the questions to help the students obtain a firm grasp of the subject matter and to minimize the possibility of a rambling discussion.
- Plan at least one lead-off question for each desired learning outcome. In preparing questions, the instructor should remember that the purpose is to stimulate discussion, not merely to get answers. Lead-off questions should usually begin with how or why. For example, it is better to ask "Why does an aircraft normally require a longer takeoff run at Denver than at New Orleans?" instead of "Would you expect an aircraft to require a longer takeoff run at Denver or at New Orleans?" Students can answer the second question by merely saying "Denver," but the first question is likely to start a discussion of air density, engine efficiency, and the effect of temperature on performance.

Student Preparation for a Guided Discussion

It is the instructor's responsibility to help students prepare themselves for the discussion. Each student should be encouraged to accept responsibility for contributing to the discussion and benefiting from it. Throughout the time the instructor prepares the students for their discussion, they should be made aware of the lesson objective(s). In certain instances, the instructor has no opportunity to assign preliminary work and must face the students for the first time. In such cases, it is practical and advisable to give the students a brief general survey of the topic during the introduction. Normally, students should not be asked to discuss a subject without some background in that subject.

Guiding a Discussion—Instructor Technique

The techniques used to guide a discussion require practice and experience. The instructor needs to keep up with the discussion and know when to intervene with questions or redirect the group's focus. The following information provides a framework for successfully conducting the guided discussion.

Introduction

A guided discussion lesson is introduced in the same manner as the lecture. The introduction should include an attention element, a motivation element, and an overview of key points. To encourage enthusiasm and stimulate discussion, the instructor should create a relaxed, informal atmosphere. Each student should be given the opportunity to discuss the various aspects of the subject, and feel free to do so. Moreover, the student should feel a personal responsibility to contribute. The instructor should try to make the students feel that their ideas and active participation are wanted and needed.

Discussion

The instructor opens the discussion by asking one of the prepared lead-off questions. Discussion questions should be easy for students to understand, put forth decisively by the instructor, and followed by silence. An instructor should also be patient and give students a chance to react. While the instructor should have the answer in mind before asking the question, the students need to think about the question before answering. Keep in mind that it takes time to recall data, determine how to answer, or to think of an example.

The more difficult the question, the more time the students need to answer. If the instructor sees puzzled expressions, denoting that the students do not understand the question, it should be rephrased in a slightly different form. The nature of the questions should be determined by the lesson objective and desired learning outcomes.

Once the discussion is underway, the instructor should listen attentively to the ideas, experiences, and examples contributed by the students during the discussion. Remember that during the preparation, the instructor listed some of the anticipated responses that would, if discussed by the students, indicate that they had a firm grasp of the subject. As the discussion proceeds, the instructor may find it necessary to guide the direction to stimulate the students to explore the subject in greater depth or to encourage them to discuss the topic in more detail. By using "how" and "why" follow-up questions, the instructor should be able to guide the discussion toward the objective of helping students understand the subject.

When it appears the students have discussed the ideas that support this particular part of the lesson, the instructor should summarize what the students have accomplished using an interim summary. This type of summary is one of the most effective tools available to the instructor. It can be made immediately after the discussion of each learning outcome to bring ideas together and help in transition, showing how the ideas developed by the group relate to and support the idea discussed. The interim summary may be omitted after discussing the last learning outcome when it is more expedient for the instructor to present the first part of the conclusion. An interim summary reinforces learning in relation to a specific learning outcome. In addition to its uses as a summary and transitional device, the interim summary may also be used to keep the group on the subject or to divert the discussion to another member.

Conclusion

A guided discussion is closed by summarizing the material covered. In the conclusion the instructor should tie together the various points or topics discussed, and show the relationships between the facts brought forth and the practical application of these facts. For example, in concluding a discussion on density altitude, an instructor might give a fairly complete description of an accident which occurred due to a pilot attempting to take off in an overloaded airplane from a short runway at a high-altitude airport on a hot day.

The summary should be succinct, but not incomplete. If the discussion has revealed that certain areas are not understood by one or more members of the group, the instructor should clarify or cover this material again.

Advantages

As with any training method that involves discussion, students are encouraged to listen to and learn from their instructor and/or each other. Also as mentioned earlier, discussion involves critical thinking skill. Open-ended questions of the type used in guided discussion lend themselves readily to concepts of risk management and ADM. The constant use of "What If?" discussions provide the student with increased exposure to proper decision-making.

From the description of guided discussion, it is obvious this method works best in a group situation, but it can be modified for an interactive one-on-one learning situation. *[Figure 4-11]* Planning the guided discussion as well as learning how to ask the type of questions used in guided discussions are assets for any aviation instructor.

Problem-Based Learning

In 1966, the McMaster University School of Medicine in Canada pioneered a new approach to teaching and curriculum design called problem-based learning (PBL). In the intervening years, PBL has helped shift the focus of learning from an instructor-centered approach to a student-centered approach. (See Appendix F.) There are many

Figure 4-11. *As the student grows in flight knowledge, he or she should be able to lead the postflight review while the instructor guides the discussion with targeted questions.*

definitions for PBL, but for the purposes of this handbook, it is defined as the type of learning environment in which lessons are structured in such a way as to confront students with problems encountered in real life that force them to reach real world solutions.

PBL starts with a carefully constructed problem to which there is no single solution. The benefit of PBL lies in helping the learner gain a deeper understanding of the information and in the learner improving his or her ability to recall the information. This results when the material is presented as an authentic problem in a situated environment that allows the learner to "make meaning" of the information based on his or her past experience and personal interpretation. This type of problem encourages the development of HOTS, which include cognitive processes such as problem solving and decision-making, as well as the cognitive skills of analysis, synthesis and evaluation.

Developing good problems that motivate, focus, and initiate student learning are an important component of PBL. Effective problems:

- Relate to the real world so students want to solve them.
- Require students to make decisions.
- Are open ended and not limited to one correct answer.
- Are connected to previously learned knowledge as well as new knowledge.
- Reflect lesson objective(s).
- Challenge students to think critically.

Teaching Higher Order Thinking Skills (HOTS)

Risk management, ADM, automation management, situational awareness, and Controlled Flight into Terrain (CFIT) awareness are the skills encompassed by HOTS. To teach the cognitive skills needed in making decisions and judgments effectively, an instructor should incorporate analysis, synthesis, and evaluation into lessons using PBL. HOTS should be taught throughout the curriculum from simple to complex and from concrete to abstract.

Basic approach to teaching HOTS:

1. Set up the problem.
2. Determine learning outcomes for the problem.
3. Solve the problem or task.
4. Reflect on problem-solving process.
5. Consider additional solutions through guided discovery.
6. Reevaluate solution with additional options.
7. Reflect on this solution and why it is the best solution.
8. Consider what "best" means (is it situational).

Types of Problem-Based Instruction

While there are many variations as to how a problem-based lesson might work, it usually involves an incentive or need to solve the problem, a decision on how to find a solution, a possible solution, an explanation for the reasons used to reach that solution, and then reflection on the solution. Three types of problem-based instruction are discussed: scenario based, collaborative problem-solving, and case study.

Scenario-Based Training Method (SBT)

SBT uses a highly structured script of real-world experiences to address aviation training objectives in an operational environment. It is a realistic situation that allows the student to rehearse mentally for a situation and requires practical application of various bits of knowledge. Such training can include initial training, transition training, upgrade training, recurrent training, and special training. Because improper pilot decisions cause a significant percentage of all accidents and the majority of fatal accidents in light single- and twin-engine aircraft, SBT challenges the student or transitioning pilot with a variety of flight scenarios with the goal of reducing accidents. These scenarios require the pilot to manage the resources available in the flight deck, exercise sound judgment, and make timely decisions. Since it has been documented that students learn more effectively when actively involved in the learning process, SBT is also used to train AMTs.

The aviation instructor is the key to successful SBT and the overall learning objective in this method of training delivery is for the student to be more ready to exercise sound judgment and make good decisions. The scenario may not have one right or one wrong answer, which reflects situations faced in the real world. It is important for the instructor to understand in advance which outcomes are positive and/or negative and give the student freedom to make both good and poor decisions without jeopardizing safety. This allows the student to make decisions that fit his or her experience level and result in positive outcomes.

Once the class has mastered the ability to compute weight and balance, Bob decides to give them the following scenario with the objective of teaching them how to reconfigure weight and balance in the real world. A customer wants a tail strobe light installed on his Piper Cherokee 180. How will this installation affect the weight and balance of the aircraft?

Since the student must remove the position light, install a power supply, and also install the tail strobe light, he or she needs to make several decisions that effect the final weight and balance of the aircraft. The real world problem forces the student to analyze, evaluate, and make decisions about the procedures required.

For the flight instructor, a good scenario tells a story that begins with a reason to fly because a pilot's decisions differ depending on the motivation to fly. For example, Mark's closest friends bought him a ticket for a playoff game at their alma mater and they paid him to rent an airplane. He is flying the four of them to the "big" football game. Another friend is planning to meet them at the airport and drive everyone to the game and back.

Mark has strong motivation to fly his friends to the game so he keys up College Airport AWOS which reports clear and unrestricted visibility. His flight is a go, yet, 15 miles from College Airport he descends to 1,000 feet to stay below the lowering clouds and encounters rain and lowering visibility to 3 miles. The terrain is flat farmland with no published obstacles. What will he do now?

Remember, a good inflight scenario is more than an hour of flight time; it is also a learning experience. SBT is a powerful tool because the future is unpredictable and there is no way to train a pilot for every combination of events that may happen in the future.

A good scenario:

- Is not a test;
- Will not have one, right answer;
- Does not offer an obvious answer;
- Should not promote errors; and
- Should promote situational awareness and opportunities for decision-making.

Collaborative Problem-Solving Method

Collaboration (two or more people working together) to solve problems has been used throughout time. In education, the collaborative problem-solving method combines collaboration with problem solving when the instructor provides a problem to a group who then solves it. The instructor provides assistance when needed, but he or she needs to remember that learning to solve the problem or task without assistance is part of the learning process. This method uses collaboration and can be modified for an interactive one-on-one learning situation such as an independent aviation instructor might encounter. The instructor provides the problem to the student, offering only limited assistance as the student solves it, but participating in finding solutions. Once again, open-ended "what if" problems encourage the students an opportunity to develop HOTS.

Case Study Method

A case study is a written or oral account of a real world situation that contains a message that educates the student. An increasingly popular form of teaching, the case study contains a story relative to the student that forces him or her to deal with situations encountered in real life.

The instructor presents the case to the students who then analyze it, come to conclusions, and offer possible solutions. Effective case studies require the student to use critical thinking skills.

An excellent source of real-world case studies for flight instructors can be found at the National Transportation Safety Board (NTSB) where descriptions of more than 140,000 aviation accidents are located. By removing the NTSB's determination of probable cause, a flight instructor can use the description as a case study. The following paragraph is an example of one such accident.

"The private pilot was on a visual flight rules (VFR) cross-country flight when he began encountering instrument conditions. The pilot continued into the instrument conditions for about 30 minutes before asking Atlanta Approach Control for directions to the nearest airport for landing. The controller directed the pilot to two different nearby airports, but both were below minimums. The pilot informed the controller that he was low on fuel and needed to land as soon as possible. The controller directed the pilot to the Columbus Metropolitan Airport, Columbus, Georgia. The pilot told the controllers that he would attempt an instrument approach. The pilot attempted four unsuccessful approaches with the controllers talking him through each approach. On the fifth approach, at five miles from the runway, the pilot stated that both engines quit due to fuel exhaustion. The pilot called "mayday" and during the forced landing the airplane collided with trees and the ground separating the right wing, half of the left wing, and coming to rest inverted. The pilot did not report any mechanical deficiencies with the airplane during the attempted approaches. Injuries: one serious, one minor, one uninjured."

The flight instructor has the student analyze the information and suggest possible reasons for the accident. The instructor then shares the NTSB's determination of probable cause: "The pilot's inadequate decision to continue VFR flight into IMC conditions, which resulted in a loss of engine power due to fuel exhaustion" which can lead to further discussions of how to avoid this type of accident. Accident data is available at NTSB's Aviation Accident Database & Synopses at www.ntsb.gov/ntsb/query.asp/.

Electronic Learning (E-Learning)

Electronic learning or e-learning has become an umbrella term for any type of education that involves an electronic component such as the Internet, a network, a stand-alone computer, CD/DVDs, video conferencing, websites, or e-mail in its delivery. *[Figure 4-12]* E-learning comes in many formats. It can be a stand-alone software program that takes a learner from lecture to exam or it can be an interactive web-based course of instruction that involves a mixture of mandatory class attendance with e-mail discussions and assignments. E-learning can be as basic as an online college course taken via e-mail or as sophisticated as refining flight techniques in a helicopter simulator.

Figure 4-12. *E-learning encompasses a variety of electronic educational media.*

Time flexible, cost competitive, learner centered, easily updated, accessible anytime, and anywhere, e-learning has many advantages that make it a popular addition to the field of education. Predictions are that more and more learning will take place via e-learning.

E-learning is now used for training at many different levels. For example, technology flight training devices and flight simulators are used by everyone from flight schools to major airlines, as well as the military. Fixed-base operators (FBOs) who offer instrument training may use personal computer-based aviation training devices (PCATDs) or flight training devices (FTDs) for a portion of the instrument time a pilot needs for the instrument rating. Major airlines have high-level flight simulators that are so realistic that transitioning crews meet all qualifications in the flight simulator. Likewise, military pilots use flight training devices or flight simulators to prepare for flying aircraft, such as the A-10, for which there are no two-seat training versions. With e-learning, sophisticated databases can organize vast amounts of information that can be quickly sorted, searched, found, and cross-indexed.

Due to the active nature of e-learning, the overall learning process is enhanced in several ways. Well-designed programs allow students to feel as if they are in control of what they are learning and how fast they learn it. They can explore areas that interest them and discover more about a subject on their own. In addition, e-learning often seems more enjoyable than learning from a regular classroom lecture. The main advantages are less time spent on instruction compared to traditional classroom training, and higher levels of mastery and retention.

Distance learning, or the use of electronic media to deliver instruction when the instructor and student are separated, is another advantage to e-learning. Participants in a class may be located on different continents, yet share the same teaching experience. Distance learning also may be defined as a system and process that connects students with resources for learning. As sources for access to information expand, the possibilities for distance learning increases.

While e-learning has many training advantages, it also has limitations which can include the lack of peer interaction and personal feedback, depending on what method of e-learning is used. For the instructor, maintaining control of the learning situation may be difficult. It also may be difficult to find good programs for certain subject areas, and the expense associated with the equipment, software, and facilities must be considered. In addition, instructors and students may lack sufficient experience with personal computers to take full advantage of the software programs that are available.

Improper or excessive use of e-learning should be avoided. For example, a flight instructor should not rely exclusively on a software program on traffic patterns and landings to do the ground instruction for a student pilot, then expect the student to demonstrate patterns and landings in the aircraft.

Likewise, it would be unfair to expect a maintenance student to safely and properly perform a compression check on an aircraft engine if the student received only e-learning.

Along with the many types of e-learning, there are a variety of terms used to describe the educational use of the computer. While there are subtle nuances to the different terms which include computer-assisted learning (CAL), computer-assisted instruction (CAI), computer-based training (CBT), and computer-based instruction (CBI), this handbook will use the term "computer-assisted learning" in the following discussion.

Computer-Assisted Learning (CAL) Method

Computer-assisted learning (CAL) couples the personal computer (PC) with multimedia software to create a training device. For example, major aircraft manufacturers have developed CAL programs to teach aircraft systems and maintenance procedures to their employees, reducing the amount of manpower necessary to train aircrews and maintenance technicians on the new equipment. End users of the aircraft, such as the major airlines, can purchase the training materials with the aircraft in order to accomplish both initial and recurrent training of their personnel. Major advantages of CAL are that students can progress at a rate which is comfortable for them and are often able to access the CAL at their own convenience.

Another benefit of CAL is the test prep study guides, useful for preparation for the FAA knowledge tests. These programs typically allow the students to select a test, complete the questions, and find out how they did on the test. The student may then conduct a review of questions missed.

Some of the more advanced CAL applications allow students to progress through a series of interactive segments where the presentation varies as a result of their responses. If students wish to learn about a particular area, they do so by clicking the mouse on a particular portion of the screen. They can focus on the area they either need to study or want to study. For example, a maintenance student who wants to find information on the refueling of a specific aircraft could use a CAL program to access the refueling section, and study the entire procedure. If the student wishes to repeat a section or a portion of the section, it can be done at any time merely by clicking on the appropriate icon.

In teaching aviation students, CAL programs can be used by the instructor as another type of reference for students to study. Just as a student can reread a section in a text, a student can review portions of a CAL program until it is understood. The instructor must continue to monitor and evaluate the progress of the student as usual. This is necessary to be certain a student is on track with the training syllabus. At times, instructors may feel that they are doing more one-on-one instruction than in a normal classroom setting, but repetitive forms of teaching may be accomplished by computer. This actually gives the instructor more time for one-on-one teaching. Remember, the computer has no way of knowing when a student is having difficulty, and it will always be the responsibility of the instructor to provide monitoring and oversight of student progress and to intervene when necessary. *[Figure 4-13]*

Figure 4-13. *The instructor must continually monitor student performance when using CAL, as with all instructional aids.*

Real interactivity with CAL means the student is fully engaged with the instruction by doing something meaningful which makes the subject of study come alive. For example, the student controls the pace of instruction, reviews previous material, jumps forward, and receives instant feedback. With advanced tracking features, CAL also can be used to test the student's achievement, compare the results with past performance, and indicate the student's weak or strong areas.

For most aviation training, the computer should be thought of as a valuable instructional aid and entrusting an entire aviation training program to a computer is not practical. Even airline simulator programs require tailoring and hands-on interaction with a human instructor. On the other hand, CAL is a useful tool for aviation instructors. For example, in teaching aircraft maintenance, CAL programs produced by various aircraft manufacturers can be used to expose students to equipment not normally found at a maintenance school. Another use of computers would allow students to review procedures at their own pace while the instructor is involved in hands-on training with other students. The major advantage of CAL is that it is interactive—the computer responds in different ways, depending on student input. When using CAL, the instructor should remain actively involved with the students by using close supervision, questions, examinations, quizzes, or guided discussions on the subject matter to constantly assess student progress.

Simulation, Role-Playing, and Video Gaming

Simulation (the appearance of real life), role-playing (playing a specific role in the context of a real world situation), and video gaming have taken e-learning in new directions. *[Figure 4-14]* The popularity of simulation games that provide players with complex situations and opportunities to learn have drawn educators into the gaming field as they seek interactive educational games that help students retain subject matter learning.

Figure 4-14. *Flight simulator.*

The advantages of simulation/role-playing games come as the student learns new information, develops skills, connects and manipulates information. A game gives the learner a stake in the outcome by putting the learner into the shoes of a character (role playing) who needs to overcome a real world scenario. Learning evolves as a result of the student's interactions with the game, and these games usually promote the development of critical thinking skills.

Not every aviation learning objective can be delivered via this teaching method, but it should prove to be a useful tool in the instructor's tool box as the number and content of educational games increase.

Cooperative or Group Learning Method

Cooperative or group learning organizes students into small groups who can work together to maximize their own and each other's learning. Research indicates that students completing cooperative learning group tasks tend to have higher test scores, higher self-esteem, improved social skills, and greater comprehension of the subjects they are studying. Perhaps the most significant characteristic of group learning is that it continually requires active participation of the student in the learning process.

Conditions and Controls

In spite of its advantages, success with cooperative or group learning depends on conditions and controls. First of all, instructors need to begin planning early to determine what the student group is expected to learn and to be able to do on their own. The group task may emphasize academic achievement, cognitive abilities, or physical skills, but the instructor must use clear and specific learning objectives to describe the knowledge and/or abilities the students are to acquire and then demonstrate on their own.

The following conditions and controls are useful for cooperative learning, but do not need to be used every time an instructor assigns a group learning project:

1. Small, heterogeneous groups
2. Clear, complete instructions of what students are to do, in what order, with what materials, and when appropriate—what students are to do as evidence of their mastery of targeted content and skills
3. Student perception of targeted objectives as their own, personal objectives
4. The opportunity for student success
5. Student access to and comprehension of required information
6. Sufficient time for learning
7. Individual accountability
8. Recognition and rewards for group success
9. Time after completion of group tasks for students to systematically reflect upon how they worked together as a team

In practice, cooperative or group learning in aviation training is normally modified to adapt to school policy or for other valid reasons. For example, collaborative, student-led, instructor-led, or working group strategies are alternatives to a pure form of group learning. In these examples, the student leader or the instructor serves as a coach or facilitator who interacts with the group, as necessary, to keep it on track or to encourage everyone in the group to participate.

Demonstration-Performance Method

Best used for the mastery of mental or physical skills that require practice, the demonstration-performance method is based on the principle that people learn by doing. In this method, students observe the skill and then try to reproduce it. It is well suited for the aircraft maintenance instructor who uses it in the shop to teach welding, and the flight instructor who uses it in teaching piloting skills.

Every instructor should recognize the importance of student performance in the learning process. Early in a lesson that is to include demonstration and performance, the instructor should identify the most important learning outcomes. Next, explain and demonstrate the steps involved in performing the skill being taught. Then, allow students time to practice each step, so they can increase their ability to perform the skill.

The demonstration-performance method is divided into five phases: explanation, demonstration, student performance, instructor supervision, and evaluation. *[Figure 4-15]*

Demonstration Performance Method

- Explanation
- Demonstration
- Student Performance
- Instructor Supervision
- Evaluation

Figure 4-15. *The demonstration-performance method of teaching has five essential phases.*

Explanation Phase

Explanations must be clear, pertinent to the objectives of the particular lesson to be presented, and based on the known experience and knowledge of the students. In teaching a skill, the instructor must convey to the students the precise actions they are to perform. In addition to the necessary steps, the instructor should describe the end result of these efforts. Before leaving this phase, the instructor should encourage students to ask questions about any step of the procedure that they do not understand.

Demonstration Phase

The instructor must show students the actions necessary to perform a skill. As little extraneous activity as possible should be included in the demonstration if students are to clearly understand the instructor is accurately performing the actions previously explained. If, due to some unanticipated circumstances, the demonstration does not closely conform to the explanation, this deviation should be immediately acknowledged and explained.

Student Performance and Instructor Supervision Phases

Because these two phases, which involve separate actions, are performed concurrently, they are discussed here under a single heading. The first of these phases is the student's performance of the physical or mental skills that have been explained and demonstrated. The second activity is the instructor's supervision.

Student performance requires students to act and do. To learn skills, students must practice. The instructor must, therefore, allot enough time for meaningful student activity. Through doing, students learn to follow correct procedures and to reach established standards. It is important that students be given an opportunity to perform the skill as soon as possible after a demonstration. In flight training, the instructor may allow the student to follow along on the controls during the demonstration of a maneuver. Immediately thereafter, the instructor should have the student attempt to perform the maneuver, coaching as necessary. In the opening scenario, students performed a task (weight and balance computation) as a group, and prior to terminating the performance phase, they were allowed to independently complete the task at least once with supervision and coaching as necessary.

Evaluation Phase

In this phase, the instructor judges student performance. The student displays whatever competence has been attained, and the instructor discovers just how well the skill has been learned. To test each student's ability to perform, the instructor requires students to work independently throughout this phase and makes some comment about how each performed the skill relative to the way it was taught. From this measurement of student achievement, the instructor determines the effectiveness of the instruction.

Drill and Practice Method

A time-honored training delivery method, drill and practice is based on the learning principle of exercise discussed in chapter 2, which holds that connections are strengthened with practice. It promotes learning through repetition because those things most often repeated are best remembered. The human mind rarely retains, evaluates, and applies new concepts or practices after a single exposure. Students do not learn to weld during one shop period or to perform crosswind landings during one instructional flight. They learn by applying what they have been told and shown. Every time practice occurs, learning continues. Effective use of drill and practice revolves around knowing what skill is being developed. The instructor must provide opportunities for students to practice and, at the same time, make sure that this process is directed toward a learning objective.

Conclusion

A successful instructor needs to be familiar with as many teaching methods as possible. Although lecture and demonstration-performance may be the methods used most often, being aware of other methods and teaching tools such as guided discussion, cooperative learning, and computer-assisted learning better prepares an instructor for a wide variety of teaching situations.

Obviously, the aviation instructor is the key to effective teaching. An experienced instructor's knowledge and skill regarding methods of instruction may be compared to a maintenance technician's toolbox. The instructor's tools are teaching methods. Just as the technician uses some tools more than others, the instructor uses some methods more often than others. As is the case with the technician, there are times when a less used tool is the exact tool needed for a particular situation. The instructor's success is determined to a large degree by the ability to organize material and to select and utilize a teaching method appropriate to a particular lesson.

Application of the Lesson

Application is student use of the instructor's presented material. If it is a classroom presentation, the student may be asked to explain the new material. If it is a new flight maneuver, the student may be asked to perform the maneuver that has just been demonstrated. In most instructional situations, the instructor's explanation and demonstration activities are alternated with student performance efforts. Usually the instructor has to interrupt the student's efforts for corrections and further demonstrations. This is necessary because it is very important that each student perform the maneuver or operation the right way the first few times to establish a good habit. Faulty habits are difficult to correct and must be addressed as soon as possible. Flight instructors in particular must be aware of this problem since students often do a lot of their practice without an instructor. Only after reasonable competence has been demonstrated should the student be allowed to practice certain maneuvers on solo flights. Periodic review and assessment by the instructor is necessary to ensure that the student has not acquired any bad habits.

As the student becomes proficient with the fundamentals of flight and aircraft maneuvers or maintenance procedures, the instructor should increasingly emphasize ADM as a means of applying what has been previously learned. For example, the flight student may be asked to plan for the arrival at a specific nontowered airport. The planning should take into consideration the wind conditions, arrival paths, communication procedures, available runways, recommended traffic patterns, and courses of action in the event the unexpected occurs. Upon arrival at the airport the student makes decisions (with guidance and feedback as necessary) to safely enter and fly the traffic pattern.

Assessment of the Lesson

Before the end of the instructional period, the instructor should review what has been covered during the lesson and require the students to demonstrate how well the lesson objectives have been met. Review and assessment are integral parts of each classroom, and/or flight lesson. The instructor's assessment may be informal and recorded only for the instructor's own use in planning the next lesson for the students, or it may be formal. More often, the assessment is formal and results recorded to certify the student's progress in the course. Assessment is explored in more detail in chapter 5.

Instructional Aids and Training Technologies

Instructional aids are devices that assist an instructor in the teaching-learning process. Instructional aids are not self-supporting; they support, supplement, or reinforce what is being taught. In contrast, training media are generally described as any physical means that communicates an instructional message to students. For example, the instructor's voice, printed text, video cassettes, interactive computer programs, part-task trainers, flight training devices, or flight simulators, and numerous other types of training devices are considered training media.

In school settings, instructors may become involved in the selection and preparation of instructional aids, but they often are already in place. For the independent instructor setting, the instructor may need to select and prepare instructional aids. Whatever the setting, instructors need to learn how to effectively use them.

Instructional Aid Theory

For many years, educators have theorized about how the human brain and the memory function during the communicative process. There is general agreement about certain factors that seem pertinent to understanding the use of instructional aids.

- During the communicative process, the sensory register of the memory acts as a filter. As stimuli are received, the individual's sensory register works to sort out the important bits of information from the routine or less significant bits. Within seconds, what is perceived as the most important information is passed to the working or short-term memory where it is processed for possible storage in the long-term memory. This complex process is enhanced by the use of appropriate instructional aids that highlight and emphasize the main points or concepts.

- The working or short-term memory functions are limited by both time and capacity. Therefore, it is essential that the information be arranged in useful bits or chunks for effective coding, rehearsal, or recording. The effectiveness of the instructional aid is critical for this process. Carefully selected charts, graphs, pictures, or other well-organized visual aids are examples of items that help the student understand, as well as retain, essential information.
- Ideally, instructional aids should be designed to cover the key points and concepts. In addition, the coverage should be straightforward and factual so it is easy for students to remember and recall. Generally, instructional aids that are relatively simple are best suited for this purpose.

Reasons for Use of Instructional Aids

In addition to helping students remember important information, instructional aids have other advantages. When properly used, they help gain and hold the attention of students. Audio or visual aids can be very useful in supporting a topic, and the combination of both audio and visual stimuli is particularly effective since the two most important senses are involved. Instructors should keep in mind that they are often salesmen of ideas, and many of the best sales techniques that attract the attention of potential clients are well worth considering. One caution—the instructional aid should keep student attention on the subject; it should not be a distracting gimmick.

Clearly, a major goal of all instruction is for the student to be able to retain as much knowledge of the subject as possible, especially the key points. Numerous studies have attempted to determine how well instructional aids serve this purpose. Indications from the studies vary greatly—from modest results, which show a 10 to 15 percent increase in retention, to more optimistic results in which retention is increased by as much as 80 percent. *[Figure 4-16]*

Good instructional aids also can help solve certain language barrier problems. Consider the continued expansion of technical terminology in everyday usage. This, coupled with culturally diverse backgrounds of today's students, makes it necessary for instructors to be precise in their choice of terminology. Words or terms used in an instructional aid should be carefully selected to convey the same meaning for the student as they do for the instructor. They should provide an accurate visual image and make learning easier for the student.

Another use for instructional aids is to clarify the relationships between material objects and concepts. When relationships are presented visually, they often are much easier to understand. For example, the subsystems within a physical unit are relatively easy to relate to each other through the use of schematics or diagrams. Symbols, graphs, and diagrams can also show relationships of location, size, time, frequency,

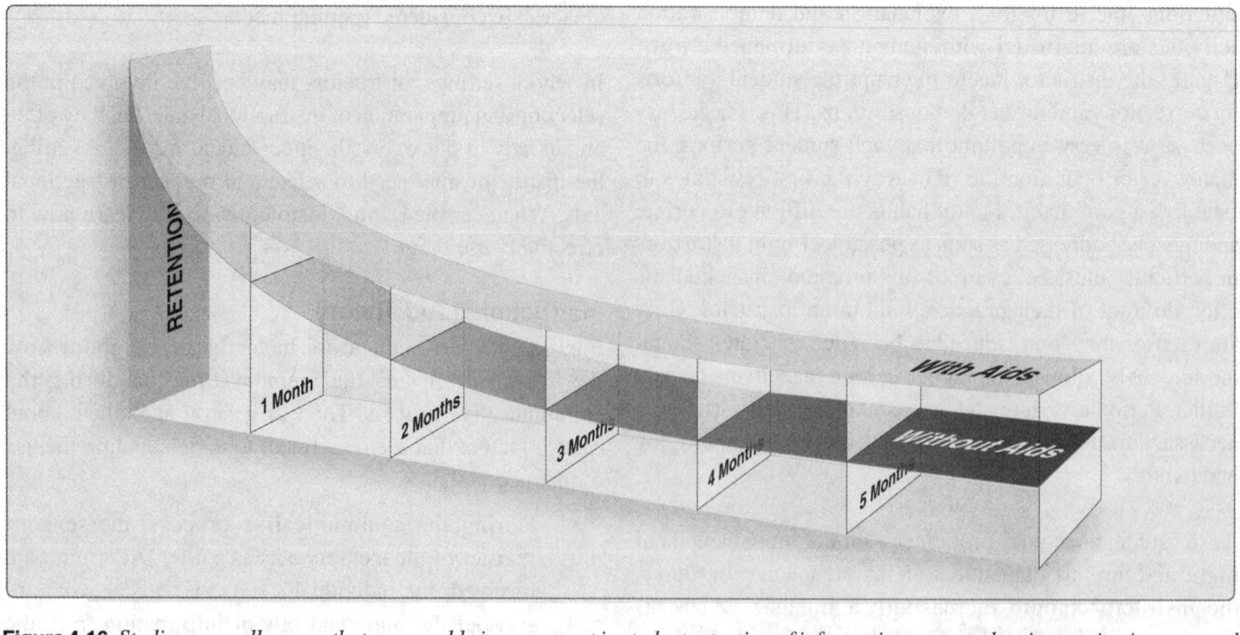

Figure 4-16. *Studies generally agree that measurable improvement in student retention of information occurs when instruction is supported by appropriate instructional aids.*

and value. By symbolizing the factors involved, it is even possible to visualize abstract relationships.

Instructors are frequently asked to teach more and more in a smaller time frame. Instructional aids can help them do this. For example, instead of using many words to describe a sound, object, or function, the instructor plays a recording of the sound, shows a picture of the object, or presents a diagram of the function. Consequently, the student learns faster and more accurately, and the instructor saves time in the process.

Guidelines for Use of Instructional Aids

The use of any instructional aid must be planned, based on its ability to support a specific point in a lesson. A simple process can be used to determine if and where instructional aids are necessary.

- Clearly establish the lesson objective. Be certain of what is to be communicated.
- Gather the necessary data by researching for support material.
- Organize the material into an outline or a lesson plan. The plan should include all key points that need to be covered. This may include important safety considerations.
- Select the ideas to be supported with instructional aids. The aids should be concentrated on the key points. Aids are often appropriate when long segments of technical description are necessary, when a point is complex and difficult to put into words, when instructors find themselves forming visual images, or when students are puzzled by an explanation or description.

Aids should be simple and compatible with the learning outcomes to be achieved. Obviously, an explanation of elaborate equipment may require detailed schematics or mock-ups, but less complex equipment may lend itself to only basic shapes or figures. Since aids are normally used in conjunction with a verbal presentation, words on the aid should be kept to a minimum. In many cases, visual symbols and slogans can replace in-depth explanations. The instructor should avoid the temptation to use the aids as a crutch. The tendency toward unnecessarily distracting artwork also should be avoided.

Instructional aids should appeal to the student and be based on sound principles of instructional design. When practical, they should encourage student participation. They also should be meaningful to the student, lead to the desired behavioral or learning objectives, and provide appropriate reinforcement. Aids that involve learning a physical skill should guide students toward mastery of the skill or task specified in the lesson objective.

Instructional aids have no value in the learning process if they cannot be heard or seen. Recordings of sounds and speeches should be tested for correct volume and quality in the actual environment in which they will be used. Visual aids must be visible to the entire class. All lettering and illustrations must be large enough to be seen easily by the students farthest from the aids. Colors, when used, should provide clear contrast and easily be visible.

The usefulness of aids can be improved by proper sequencing to build on previous learning. Frequently, good organization and natural patterns of logic dictate the sequence. However, use of standardized materials, including a syllabus, is recommended. Sequencing also can be enhanced simply by using overlays on transparencies, stripping techniques on charts and chalk or marker boards, and by imaginative use of magnetic boards. Sequencing can be emphasized and made clearer by the use of contrasting colors.

The effectiveness of aids and the ease of their preparation can be increased by initially planning them in rough draft form. Revisions and alterations are easier to make at that time than after their completion. The rough draft should be carefully checked for technical accuracy, proper terminology, grammar, spelling, basic balance, clarity, and simplicity. Instructional aids should also be reviewed to determine whether their use is feasible in the training environment and whether they are appropriate for the students. *[Figure 4-17]*

Instructional Aids ...

- Support the lesson objective.
- Are student centered.
- Build on previous learning.
- Contain useful and meaningful content that is consistent with sound principles of learning.
- Appeal to students.
- Maintain student attention and interest.
- Encourage student participation, when appropriate.
- Lead students in the direction of the behavior or learning outcomes specified in the learning objective.
- Provide proper stimuli and reinforcement.
- Contain quality photo, graphs, and text, as required.
- Are checked prior to use for completeness and technical accuracy.
- Contain appropriate terminology for the student.
- Are properly sequenced.
- Are easy to understand.
- Include appropriate safety precautions.

Figure 4-17. *Guidelines for effective instructional aids.*

In practice, the choice of instructional aids depends on several factors. Availability, feasibility, or cost may impose realistic limitations. The number of students in a class and the existing facilities are other considerations. In some school situations, the designers of the curriculum determine the use of instructional aids. In this case, the instructor may have little control over their use. On the other hand, an independent instructor may have considerable latitude, but limited resources. Often, instructors must improvise and adapt to the existing circumstances in order to incorporate quality instructional aids.

Types of Instructional Aids

Some of the most common and economical aids are chalk or marker boards, and supplemental print materials, including charts, diagrams, and graphs. Other aids, which are usually more expensive, are projected materials, video, computer-based programs, and models, mock-ups, or cut-aways.

Chalk or Marker Board

The chalk or marker board is a widely used tool for instructors. Its versatility and effectiveness provide several advantages for most types of instruction. First, the material presented can be erased, allowing the surface to be used again and again; and second, the boards serve as an excellent medium for joint student-instructor activity in the classroom. The following practices are fundamental in the use of the chalk or marker board:

- Keep the chalk or marker board clean.
- Erase all irrelevant material.
- Keep chalk, markers, erasers, cleaning cloths, rulers, and related items readily available to avoid interruption of the presentation.
- Organize and practice the chalk or marker board presentation in advance.
- Write or draw large enough for everyone in the group to see.
- Leave a margin around the material and sufficient space between lines of copy so the board is not overcrowded.
- Present material simply and briefly.
- Make only one point at a time. A complete outline tends to distract students and makes a logical presentation difficult. If writing has been previously prepared, it should be covered and then revealed one step at a time.
- If necessary, use a ruler, compass, or other devices in making drawings.
- Use colored chalk or marker for emphasis.
- Underline statements for emphasis.
- Use the upper part of the board. In many classrooms, students may not be able to see the lower half.
- Stand to one side of the board to avoid hiding the essential information.
- Use a pointer when appropriate.
- Adjust lighting as necessary to remove glare.

Supplemental Print Material

Print media, including photographs, reproductions of pictures, drawings, murals, cartoons, and other print materials are valuable supplemental aids. Charts, diagrams, and graphs are also in this category. Many of these items are suitable for long-term use on bulletin boards and in briefing areas. Pictures, drawings, and photographs are especially effective because they provide common visual imagery for both instructors and students. In addition, they also provide realistic details necessary for visual recognition of important subject material. In many cases, this type of supplemental training media may be reproduced in a format for projection on a screen or other clear surface.

Charts, diagrams, and graphs include any printed material which gives information in tabular form. There are several types of charts that can be used in presenting data such as pie charts, flow charts, and organizational charts, among others. The type of chart selected for use depends largely on the type of information the instructor wants to convey. An important factor is chart format. Since charts may consist of a series of single sheets or be tied together in a flip-chart format with several pages, the location and handling of them should be planned in advance.

A graph is a symbolic drawing which shows relationships or makes comparisons. The most common types are the line graph and the bar graph. The selection of a graph for use in any given situation depends upon the type of information the instructor wants to convey.

Charts, diagrams, and graphs can be used effectively to show relationships, chronological changes, distributions, components, and flow. They are easy to construct and can be produced in the same manner as pictures. In addition, they can be drawn on a chalk or marker board and can be duplicated. Care must be taken to display only a small amount of material and to make the material as simple but meaningful as possible.

Numerous other useful print items may be considered as supplemental training aids. Some of these include study guides, exercise books, course outlines, and syllabi. Well-designed course outlines are especially useful to students because they list the key points and help students organize note taking during a lecture.

Enhanced Training Materials

Aviation instructors must cover a broad range of aeronautical knowledge and skill training for pilots and AMTs. The actual training requirements are based in the Code of Federal Regulations (CFR) and other publications used by designated pilot and maintenance examiners when they conduct practical tests. While aviation instructors are expected to be familiar with all regulatory training requirements, use of instructor-oriented training materials which are enhanced for regulatory compliance can be very beneficial for ensuring required training is being accomplished, endorsed, and properly documented. Whether working as an individual instructor or employed by a flight or maintenance school, the instructor must ensure that each student accomplishes a number of important benchmarks. Enhanced training materials that include these benchmarks can help aviation instructors complete, endorse, and document required training.

For example, the training syllabi represent enhanced training material and contain provisions for instructor endorsements and recordkeeping. Such syllabi not only present the course of training in a logical step-by-step, building block sequence, they contain provisions to remind both students and instructors of critical regulatory training benchmarks which are approaching. Blocks for instructor endorsements also may be included at appropriate points. Provisions for logging training time can be incorporated so the syllabus could also serve as the training record for the student, instructor, or school. When required endorsements and recordkeeping provisions are designed into training syllabi, it is much easier, from the instructor's standpoint, to conduct required training, track student progress, and certify records. The training record can be reviewed and the student's training status easily assessed in case the student transfers to another school or instructor.

Another example of enhanced, instructor-oriented material for pilot training is a maneuvers guide or handbook which includes the PTS as an integral part of the description of maneuvers and procedures. Students learn from the beginning how to perform the maneuver or procedure and also become familiar with the performance criteria. Instructors need not refer to another document to evaluate student performance. The examiner for the Airframe and Powerplant (A&P) is required to ask four questions in each of the subject areas, which are required by the regulations to be taught. The examiner also is required to assign a practical project from each subject area. Individual maintenance instructors, as well as publishers, have compiled lists of typical questions and projects. Use of these questions and projects as part of the syllabus helps an instructor ensure that all subject areas for a particular class have been covered.

There are many ways to incorporate design features in training materials in order to facilitate regulatory compliance, required endorsements, and recordkeeping. Computer-based training also can be designed so the progress of the student can be tracked and documented. As training becomes more detailed and complex, instructor-oriented materials can be a valuable instructional aid for aviation instructors. More information on enhanced training materials is presented in chapter 6.

Projected Material

Traditional aids in this group include slides, filmstrips, and transparencies for overhead projection. In recent years, video (VHS, compact disks (CDs), digital video disks (DVDs), or computer files), and computer slide shows incorporating text, graphics, video, and animations, have pushed aside traditional training aids. Whatever type of projected training aid used, it is essential for the content to be current and support the lesson.

Use of projected materials requires planning and practice. The instructor should set up and adjust the equipment and lighting beforehand and then preview the presentation. During a classroom session, the instructor should provide students with an overview of the presentation before showing it. After the presentation, the instructor should allow time for questions and a summary of key points.

Computer-generated slide shows have changed the way information is presented to today's student. While a computer, screen, and projector may be needed for the classroom, a laptop computer may be all that is needed for the one-on-one presentation. These slide shows can be only bulleted information or incorporate animation and video clips. The instructor can tailor the presentation for the class and also include graphics at appropriate points. A wireless mouse can be used to activate the slide changes from anywhere in the room.

Another convenient and cost effective instructional aid is the overhead transparency and projector. Instructors can create their own overhead acetate or plastic transparencies, or they may purchase commercially produced ones. Material composed on a computer word processing and graphics program can also be printed onto transparencies.

The equipment can be placed at the front of the room, allowing the instructor to maintain eye contact with students. *[Figure 4-18]* The brilliant light source concentrated at a short distance makes it possible to use the projector in lighted areas. The instructor also can write on a blank transparency

Figure 4-18. *Interior of a lecture room designed for trainings with enhanced training materials utilizing projection equipment.*

as the lesson progresses, much like a chalk or marker board. Additional transparencies can be overlaid onto the original to show development or buildup of an event or display. Overlays can also be cut into various shapes and moved about in relation to the base transparency. This is a useful technique for displaying dial indications or fitting several parts of a component together so relative motion can be simulated.

With any projection equipment, instructors should ensure the projector does not obstruct the students' line of sight. The projection angle should be adjusted to eliminate image distortion. Finally, although the overhead projector is simple to operate and requires little maintenance, it has disadvantages. Most projectors are bulky to handle and store, and the projector cooling fan may be noisy.

Although vastly different from other projection equipment, the opaque projector reflects light from the surface of the picture or three-dimensional object onto a regular projection screen. The height of usable objects is limited to the space between the top of the lowered projection plate and the body of the projector, usually about two or three inches. The area of the picture or object is limited to approximately 10 inches by 10 inches.

Items which may be projected are practically limitless. A postage stamp, typed material, textbook illustrations, or a defective spark plug are representative of the items that may be projected. This equipment is especially adapted to enlarging diagrams and small charts for display purposes. Since the material projected requires no special preparation, the cost is very low. Many of the limitations of the overhead projector are also true of the opaque projector.

Video

CDs and DVDs are today's popular video instructional aids. Some educators believe that television and the film industry have produced a visual culture that has actually changed the way people learn.

Passive video, or video that the student watches like a movie, provide motion, color, sound, and in many cases, special effects with advanced graphic and animation techniques. High-quality, commercially produced CDs and DVDs are available for almost every aviation training subject. Consequently, CDs and DVDs have replaced many of the projection-type instructional aids.

For instructors, the convenience of CDs and DVDs is certainly an advantage. The capability to stop, freeze, and replay information is helpful for both instructors and students. CDs and DVDs and the associated equipment, although more expensive than some of the more basic instructional aid equipment, are fairly economical. Unlike other forms of projected material, CDs and DVDs can also be played on a laptop computer.

On the other hand, CDs and DVDs offer their own disadvantages. Students are often accustomed to dramatic, action-packed movies or games designed as entertainment. They also tend to watch movies or TV in a passive way without attempting to absorb what they are seeing and hearing. Instructional CDs and DVDs, in comparison, are perceived as much less exciting and less stimulating visually. This, coupled with an inattentive viewing style, can diminish the instructional value of the CD or DVD.

As is true for any instructional aid, instructors need to follow some basic guidelines when using CDs and DVDs. For example, the presentation is not designed to replace the instructor. Prior planning and rehearsal will help determine the important points and concepts that should be stressed, either during the presentation or as part of a summary. Instructors should also try to prepare students for viewing CD/DVD programs by telling them what to watch carefully, what is important or, possibly, what is incorrect. In addition, instructors should be available to summarize the presentation and answer any questions students may have regarding content.

Interactive CDs and DVDs

"Interactive" refers broadly to computer software that responds quickly to certain choices and commands by the user. A typical system consists of a CD or DVD and a computer. A major advantage of CDs and DVDs is the capability to store enormous amounts of information. As an example, a single CD or DVD may contain all pertinent aviation regulations, plus the complete AIM. With search-and-find features incorporated, a CD or DVD is a powerful information source. The software may include additional features such as image banks with full color photos and graphics, as well as questions or directions which are programmed to create interactivity for students as they progress through the course.

The questions or directions are programmed using a branching technique, which provides several possible courses of action for the user to choose in order to move from one sequence to another. For example, a program may indicate, "That was incorrect. Go back to … and try again."

Interactive CDs and DVDs solve one of the main problems of passive video in that it increases involvement of the student in the learning process. Well-designed interactive video, when properly used, is highly effective as an instructional aid. Each student essentially receives a customized learning experience.

Computer-Assisted Learning (CAL)

As mentioned earlier, CAL has become a popular training delivery method. In its basic form, CAL is a combination of more than one instructional media, such as audio, text, graphics, and video (or film) usually shown on a PC.

With CAL, the roles of both student and instructor change. Students become more involved in their own learning, and instructors may no longer occupy a center-stage position in a typical classroom setting. Instead, instructors become supportive facilitators. As such, they serve as guides or resource experts and circulate among students who are working individually or in small groups. This results in considerable one-on-one instructor-student interaction. Thus, the instructor provides assistance, reinforcement, and answers for those who need it most.

In this situation, the CAL should still be considered as an add-on instructional aid to improve traditional classroom instruction. The instructor, although no longer the center of attention, must continue to maintain complete control over the learning environment to ensure learning objectives are being achieved. *[Figure 4-19]*

A more advanced application of computer-based training may involve less instructor control. For example, a laboratory-type environment may be configured with separate study areas for each student. With this setup, the physical facility is usually referred to as a learning center or training center.

Figure 4-19. *In a computer-assisted learning environment, the instructor must still ensure that learning objectives are being achieved.*

Students in these centers are often monitored by a teacher's aide or other trained personnel who can provide guidance, answer questions, and act as a conduit to the instructor who is responsible for the training. In this case, the responsible instructor needs to establish procedures to make sure the required training is accomplished, since he or she must certify student competency at the end of the course.

Models, Mock-ups, and Cut-Aways

Models, mock-ups, and cut-aways are additional instructional aids. A model is a copy of a real object. It can be an enlargement, a reduction, or the same size as the original. The scale model represents an exact reproduction of the original, while simplified models do not represent reality in all details. Some models are solid and show only the outline of the object they portray, while others can be manipulated or operated.

Although a model may not be a realistic copy of an actual piece of equipment, it can be used effectively in explaining operating principles of various types of equipment. Models are especially adaptable to small group discussions in which students are encouraged to ask questions. A model is even more effective if it works like the original, and if it can be taken apart and reassembled. With the display of an operating model, the students can observe how each part works in relation to the other parts. When the instructor points to each part of the model while explaining these relationships, the students can better understand the mechanical principles involved. As instructional aids, models are usually more practical than originals because they are lightweight and easy to manipulate.

A mock-up is a three-dimensional or specialized type of working model made from real or synthetic materials. It is used for study, training, or testing in place of the real object, which is too costly or too dangerous, or which is impossible to obtain. The mock-up may emphasize or highlight elements or components for learning and eliminate nonessential elements.

Cut-aways, another type of model, are built in sections and can be taken apart to reveal the internal structure. Whenever possible, the various parts should be labeled or colored to clarify relationships.

Production and equipment costs are limiting factors to consider in developing and using models, mock-ups, and cut-aways. Depending on the nature of the representation, cost can vary. For instance, scale replicas are often very expensive. In general, if a two-dimensional representation will satisfy the instructor's requirement, it should be used.

Test Preparation Material

Test preparation material applies to an array of paper, video, and computer software products that are designed by commercial publishers to help student applicants prepare for FAA tests. While test preparation materials may be effective in preparing students for FAA tests, the danger is that students may learn to pass a given test, but fail to learn other critical information essential to safe piloting and maintenance practices. In addition, FAA inspectors and designated examiners have found that student applicants often exhibit a lack of knowledge during oral questioning, even though many have easily passed the FAA knowledge test. A major shortcoming of test preparation materials is that the emphasis is on rote learning, which is the lowest of all levels of learning.

Test preparation materials, as well as instructors, that dwell on teaching the test are shortchanging student applicants. All instructors who use test preparation publications should stress that these materials are not designed as stand-alone learning tools. They should be considered as a supplement to instructor-led training.

Future Developments

Electronic communications, including use of computer databases, voice mail, e-mail, Internet, World Wide Web, and satellite-based, wireless communications, are routine and this explosion of information access affects aviation training. It will be even more significant in the future.

Computer technology continues to advance in quantum leaps, challenging traditional ways of teaching. For example, voice-recognition technology, which lets computers accept spoken rather than keyed input, is highly effective for technical training.

Miniature electro-optical devices allow computer-aided information to be projected electronically on sunglass-style eye wear which is connected to a lightweight, belt mounted computer. Computer-aided information is particularly useful for aviation maintenance activities. For example, it would be possible for a technician's eyes to easily move back and forth from computer-generated technical data to the actual hardware while diagnosing and correcting a maintenance problem.

Trends in training indicate a shift from the typical classroom to more extensive use of a lab-type environment with computer work or study stations. Using simulation devices, computer networks, and multimedia programs, students become more actively involved and responsible for their own training. Aviation-related learning centers are usually associated with colleges, universities, and research centers. The airlines, as well as aeronautical programs at some colleges and universities, have used similar facilities for many years.

Another type of computer-based technology, virtual reality (VR), creates a sensory experience that allows a participant to believe and barely distinguish a virtual experience from a real one. VR uses graphics with animation systems, sounds, and images to reproduce electronic versions of real-life experience. Despite enormous potential, VR, in its current stage of development, has drawbacks. It is extremely expensive, and versions with a head-mounted display sometimes produce unfavorable side effects.

For those engaged in aviation training, the challenge is staying abreast of technological changes that apply to training and adopting those that are the most useful and cost effective. Since much of the new technology is based on computer technology, instructors with well-developed computer skills are in demand.

Although the explosion of training technology offers new opportunities, instructors must remember their main teaching goals and be selectively receptive to new possibilities. Electronic information on computer networks and bulletin boards is from commercial providers, as well as community, state, and national government agencies. There is no guarantee that all of this information is current, or even accurate.

Chapter Summary

As indicated by this discussion, the teaching process organizes the material an instructor wishes to teach in such a way that the learner understands what is being taught. An effective instructor uses a combination of teaching methods as well as instructional aids to achieve this goal.

By being well prepared, an effective instructor presents and applies lesson material, and also periodically assesses how well the learner is learning. An effective instructor never stops learning. He or she maintains currency in the subject matter being taught, as well as how to teach it by reading professional journals and other aviation publications, many of which can be viewed or purchased via the Internet, another source of valuable aviation information for professional instructors.

Chapter 5

Assessment

Introduction

The afternoon before a flight lesson, Linda, a Certificated Flight Instructor, sends an e-mail to her student, Brian, and asks him to plan tomorrow's flight. She attaches a copy of the syllabus and task list to the e-mail and emphasizes the need to work on both flight deck automation (Multi-Function Display (MFD), Global Positioning System (GPS), and Primary Flight Display (PFD)), and pattern and landing skills. Brian puts together a short, two-leg cross-country flight plan that allows for plenty of pattern entry and landing work, while using the en route legs to explore the flight deck electronic displays.

Brian also adds a stall series because he did not really understand the aerodynamics of power-off stalls during the last lesson. The next day, Brian briefs Linda on his plan and presents his completed paperwork for the flight. Linda notes the addition of stalls and approves the plan. Next, she and her student engage in a discussion of the areas of the flight that he still does not understand, and she quizzes him on proper procedures as well as possible situations and decisions they may encounter.

Once in the air, Brian plans and executes the flight. Linda interjects comments and questions as the need arises. Linda alternates between demonstration, questioning, and suggesting an alternate course of action, always allowing Brian time to participate in the discussion.

After landing, Brian and Linda sit down to assess the flight. Linda begins by asking Brian to discuss the flight from his perspective. As he talks, she listens for areas where her assessment of Brian's performance differs from his own perceptions. After Brian completes his self-assessment, Linda offers her view, and she and Brian discuss the areas of disagreement. By asking Brian to lead the initial post-flight assessment and discussing areas where her perceptions of his performance differ, Linda is both instilling the self-assessment habits Brian will need throughout his flying career and helping him learn to make accurate perceptions.

Assessment is an essential and continuous (ongoing) component of the teaching and learning processes. No skill is more important to an instructor than the ability to continuously analyze, appraise, and judge a student's performance. The student looks to the instructor for guidance, suggestions for improvement, and encouragement. The instructor must gather the information needed to evaluate student progress throughout the course. This information helps to shape the learning process by guiding an instructor regarding what needs to be reinforced during instruction, as well as helping the instructor determine the readiness of the aviation student to move forward.

This chapter examines the instructor's role in assessing levels of learning, describes methods of assessment, and discusses how to construct and conduct effective assessments. The techniques and methods described in this chapter apply as much to the aviation instructor in the classroom as to the aircraft maintenance instructor in the shop, or to the flight instructor in the aircraft or in the briefing area. Since each student is different and each learning situation is unique, the outcome may not be what the instructor expected. Whatever the outcome, the instructor must be able to assess student performance and convey this information to the student. To do so, the instructor utilizes several different types of assessment.

Assessment Terminology

Most instructors and students are familiar with the term "grading." A more useful term is "assessment," which is the process of gathering measurable information to meet evaluation needs. The Latin root "assess" means "to judge, to sit beside." This term thus conveys the idea that assessment involves both judgment by the instructor and collaboration with the student during the evaluation stage.

This chapter presents and discusses two broad categories of assessment. The first is traditional assessment, which often involves the kind of written testing (e.g., multiple choice, matching) and grading that is most familiar to instructors and students. To achieve a passing score on a traditional assessment, the student usually has a set amount of time to recognize or reproduce memorized terms, formulas, or data. There is a single answer that is correct. Consequently, the traditional assessment is more likely to be used to judge, or evaluate, the student's progress at the rote and understanding levels of learning.

The second category of assessment is authentic assessment. Authentic assessment requires the student to demonstrate not just rote and understanding, but also the application and correlation levels of learning. Authentic assessment generally requires the student to perform real-world tasks, and demonstrate a meaningful application of skills and competencies. In other words, the authentic assessment requires the student to exhibit in-depth knowledge by generating a solution instead of merely choosing a response.

In authentic assessment, there are specific performance criteria, or standards, that students know in advance of the actual assessment. The terms "criteria/criterion" and "standard" are often used interchangeably. They refer to the characteristics that define acceptable performance on a task. Another term used in association with authentic assessment is "rubric." A rubric is a guide used to score performance assessments in a reliable, fair, and valid manner. It is generally composed of dimensions for judging student performance, a scale for rating performances on each dimension, and standards of excellence for specified performance levels.

Whether traditional or authentic, an assessment can be either formal or informal. Formal assessments usually involve documentation, such as a quiz or written examination. They are used periodically throughout a course, as well as at the end of a course, to measure and document whether or not the course objectives have been met. Informal assessments, which can include verbal critique, generally occur as needed and are not part of the final grade.

Other terms associated with assessment include diagnostic, formative, and summative.

- Diagnostic assessments are used to assess student knowledge or skills prior to a course of instruction.
- Formative assessments, which are not graded, are used as a wrap-up of the lesson and to set the stage for the next lesson. This type of assessment, which is limited to what transpired during that lesson, informs and guides the instructor on which areas to reinforce.
- Summative assessments are used periodically throughout the training to measure how well learning has progressed to that point. For example, a chapter quiz or an end-of-course test can measure the student's overall mastery of the training. These assessments are an integral part of the lesson, as well as the course of training.

Purpose of Assessment

Assessment is an essential and continuous (ongoing) component of the teaching and learning processes. An effective assessment provides critical information to both the instructor and the student. Both instructor and student need to know how well the student is progressing. A good assessment provides practical and specific feedback to students, including direction and guidance on how to raise their level of performance. Most importantly, a well-designed and effective assessment process contributes to the development of aeronautical decision-making and judgment skills by helping develop the student's ability to evaluate his or her own knowledge and performance accurately.

A well-designed and effective assessment is also a very valuable tool for the instructor. By highlighting the areas in which a student's performance is incorrect or inadequate, it helps the instructor see where more emphasis is needed. If, for example, several students falter when they reach the same step in a weight-and-balance problem, the instructor might recognize the need for a more detailed explanation, another demonstration of the step, or special emphasis in the assessment of subsequent performance.

General Characteristics of Effective Assessment

In order to provide direction and raise the student's level of performance, assessment must be factual, and it must be aligned with the completion standards of the lesson. An effective assessment displays the characteristics shown in *Figure 5-1.*

Figure 5-1. *Effective assessments share a number of characteristics.*

Objective

The effective assessment is objective, and focused on student performance. It should not reflect the personal opinions, likes, dislikes, or biases of the instructor. Instructors must not permit judgment of student performance to be influenced by their personal views of the student, favorable or unfavorable. Sympathy or over-identification with a student, to such a degree that it influences objectivity, is known as "halo error." A conflict of personalities can also distort an opinion. If an assessment is to be objective, it must be honest; it must be based on the performance as it was, not as it could have been.

Flexible

The instructor must evaluate the entire performance of a student in the context in which it is accomplished. Sometimes a good student turns in a poor performance, and a poor student turns in a good one. A friendly student may suddenly become hostile, or a hostile student may suddenly become friendly and cooperative. The instructor must fit the tone, technique, and content of the assessment to the occasion, as well as to the student. An assessment should be designed and executed so that the instructor can allow for variables. The ongoing challenge for the instructor is deciding what to say, what to omit, what to stress, and what to minimize at the proper moment.

Acceptable

The student must accept the instructor in order to accept his or her assessment willingly. Students must have confidence in the instructor's qualifications, teaching ability, sincerity, competence, and authority. Usually, instructors have the opportunity to establish themselves with students before the formal assessment arises. If not, however, the instructor's manner, attitude, and familiarity with the subject at hand must serve this purpose. Assessments must be presented fairly, with authority, conviction, sincerity, and from a position of recognizable competence. Instructors must never rely on their position to make an assessment more acceptable to students.

Comprehensive

A comprehensive assessment is not necessarily a long one, nor must it treat every aspect of the performance in detail. The instructor must decide whether the greater benefit comes from a discussion of a few major points or a number of minor points. The instructor might assess what most needs improvement, or only what the student can reasonably be expected to improve. An effective assessment covers strengths as well as weaknesses. The instructor's task is to determine how to balance the two.

Constructive

An assessment is pointless unless the student benefits from it. Praise for its own sake is of no value, but praise can be very effective in reinforcing and capitalizing on things that are done well, in order to inspire the student to improve in areas of lesser accomplishment. When identifying a mistake or weakness, the instructor must give positive guidance for correction. Negative comments that do not point toward improvement or a higher level of performance should be omitted from an assessment altogether.

Organized

An assessment must be organized. Almost any pattern is acceptable, as long as it is logical and makes sense to the student. An effective organizational pattern might be the sequence of the performance itself. Sometimes an assessment can profitably begin at the point at which a demonstration failed, and work backward through the steps that led to the failure. A success can be analyzed in similar fashion. Alternatively, a glaring deficiency can serve as the core of an assessment. Breaking the whole into parts, or building the parts into a whole, is another possible organizational approach.

Thoughtful

An effective assessment reflects the instructor's thoughtfulness toward the student's need for self-esteem, recognition, and approval. The instructor must not minimize the inherent dignity and importance of the individual. Ridicule, anger, or fun at the expense of the student never has a place in assessment. While being straightforward and honest, the instructor should always respect the student's personal feelings. For example, the instructor should try to deliver criticism in private.

Specific

The instructor's comments and recommendations should be specific. Students cannot act on recommendations unless they know specifically what the recommendations are. A statement such as, "Your second weld wasn't as good as your first," has little constructive value. Instead, the instructor should say why it was not as good, and offer suggestions on how to improve the weld. If the instructor has a clear, well-founded, and supportable idea in mind, it should be expressed with firmness and authority, and in terms that cannot be misunderstood. At the conclusion of an assessment, students should have no doubt about what they did well and what they did poorly and, most importantly, specifically how they can improve.

Traditional Assessment

As defined earlier, traditional assessment generally refers to written testing, such as multiple choice, matching, true/false, fill in the blank, etc. Written assessments must typically be completed within a specific amount of time. There is a single, correct response for each item. The assessment, or test, assumes that all students should learn the same thing, and relies on rote memorization of facts. Responses are often machine scored, and offer little opportunity for a demonstration of the thought processes characteristic of critical thinking skills.

One shortcoming is that traditional assessment approaches are generally instructor centered, and that they measure performance against an empirical standard. In traditional assessment, fairly simple grading matrices such as shown in *Figure 5-2* are used. The problem with this type of assessment has always been that a satisfactory grade for the first lesson may be an unsatisfactory on lesson number three.

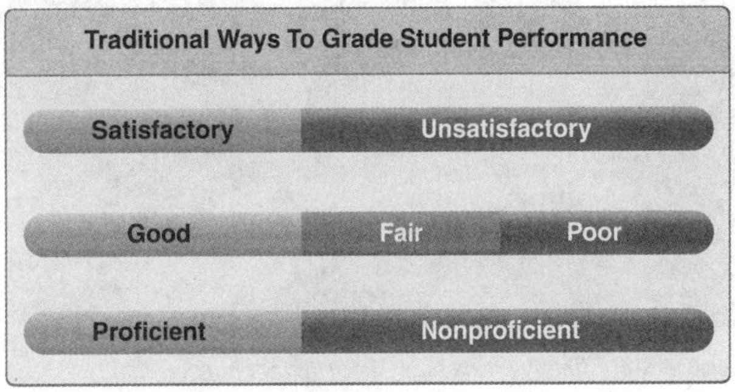

Figure 5-2. *Traditional grading.*

Still, tests of this nature do have a place in the assessment hierarchy. Multiple choice, supply type, and other such tests are useful in assessing the student's grasp of information, concepts, terms, processes, and rules—factual knowledge that forms the foundation needed for the student to advance to higher levels of learning.

Characteristics of a Good Written Assessment (Test)

Whether or not an instructor designs his or her own tests or uses commercially available test banks, it is important to know the components of an effective test. *(Note: This section is intended to introduce basic concepts of written test design. Please see Appendix A for testing and test writing publications.)*

A test is a set of questions, problems, or exercises intended to determine whether the student possesses a particular knowledge or skill. A test can consist of just one test item, but it usually consists of a number of test items. A test item measures a single objective, and calls for a single response. The test could be as simple as the correct answer to an essay question or as complex as completing a knowledge or practical test. Regardless of the underlying purpose, effective tests share certain characteristics. *[Figure 5-3]*

Reliability is the degree to which test results are consistent with repeated measurements. If identical measurements are obtained every time a certain instrument is applied to a certain dimension, the instrument is considered reliable. The reliability of a written test is judged by whether it gives consistent measurement to a particular individual or group. Keep in mind, though, that knowledge, skills, and understanding can improve with subsequent attempts at taking the same test, because the first test serves as a learning device.

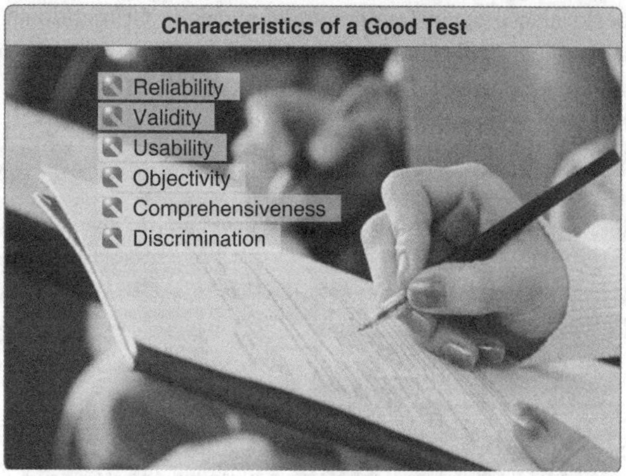

Figure 5-3. *Effective tests have six primary characteristics.*

Validity is the extent to which a test measures what it is supposed to measure, and it is the most important consideration in test evaluation. The instructor must carefully consider whether the test actually measures what it is supposed to measure. To estimate validity, several instructors read the test critically and consider its content relative to the stated objectives of the instruction. Items that do not pertain directly to the objectives of the course should be modified or eliminated.

Usability refers to the functionality of tests. A usable written test is easy to give if it is printed in a type size large enough for students to read easily. The wording of both the directions for taking the test and of the test items needs to be clear and concise. Graphics, charts, and illustrations appropriate to the test items must be clearly drawn, and the test should be easily graded.

Objectivity describes singleness of scoring of a test. Essay questions provide an example of this principle. It is nearly impossible to prevent an instructor's own knowledge and experience in the subject area, writing style, or grammar from affecting the grade awarded. Selection-type test items, such as true/false or multiple choice, are much easier to grade objectively.

Comprehensiveness is the degree to which a test measures the overall objectives. Suppose, for example, an AMT wants to measure the compression of an aircraft engine. Measuring compression on a single cylinder would not provide an indication of the entire engine. Similarly, a written test must sample an appropriate cross-section of the objectives of instruction. The instructor has to make certain the evaluation includes a representative and comprehensive sampling of the objectives of the course.

Discrimination is the degree to which a test distinguishes the difference between students. In classroom evaluation, a test must measure small differences in achievement in relation to the objectives of the course. A test constructed to identify the difference in the achievement of students has three features:

- A wide range of scores
- All levels of difficulty
- Items that distinguish between students with differing levels of achievement of the course objectives

Please see the reference section for information on the advantages and disadvantages of multiple-choice, supply-type, and other written assessment instruments, as well as guidance on creating effective test items.

Authentic Assessment

Authentic assessment is a type of assessment in which the student is asked to perform real-world tasks, and demonstrate a meaningful application of skills and competencies. Authentic assessment lies at the heart of training today's aviation student to use critical thinking skills. Rather than selecting from predetermined responses, students must generate responses from skills and concepts they have learned. By using open-ended questions and established performance criteria, authentic assessment focuses on the learning process, enhances the development of real-world skills, encourages higher order thinking skills (HOTS), and teaches students to assess their own work and performance.

Collaborative Assessment

There are several aspects of effective authentic assessment. The first is the use of open-ended questions in what might be called a "collaborative critique," which is a form of student-centered grading. As described in the scenario that introduced this chapter, the instructor begins by using a four-step series of open-ended questions to guide the student through a complete self-assessment.

Replay—ask the student to verbally replay the flight or procedure. Listen for areas in which the instructor's perceptions differ from the student's perceptions, and discuss why they do not match. This approach gives the student a chance to validate his or her own perceptions, and it gives the instructor critical insight into his or her judgment abilities.

Reconstruct—the reconstruction stage encourages the student to learn by identifying the key things that he or she would have, could have, or should have done differently during the flight or procedure.

Reflect—insights come from investing perceptions and experiences with meaning, requiring reflection on the events. For example:

- What was the most important thing you learned today?
- What part of the session was easiest for you? What part was hardest?
- Did anything make you uncomfortable? If so, when did it occur?
- How would you assess your performance and your decisions?
- Did you perform in accordance with the PTS?

Redirect—the final step is to help the student relate lessons learned in this session to other experiences, and consider how they might help in future sessions. Questions:

- How does this experience relate to previous lessons?
- What might be done to mitigate a similar risk in a future situation?
- Which aspects of this experience might apply to future situations, and how?
- What personal minimums should be established, and what additional proficiency flying and/or training might be useful?

The purpose of the self-assessment is to stimulate growth in the student's thought processes and, in turn, behaviors. The self-assessment is followed by an in-depth discussion between the instructor and the student, which compares the instructor's assessment to the student's self-assessment. Through this discussion, the instructor and the student jointly determine the student's progress on a rubric. As explained earlier, a rubric is a guide for scoring performance assessments in a reliable, fair, and valid manner. It is generally composed of dimensions for judging student performance, a scale for rating performances on each dimension, and standards of excellence for specified performance levels.

The collaborative assessment process in student-centered grading uses two broad rubrics: one that assesses the student's level of proficiency on skill-focused maneuvers or procedures, and one that assesses the student's level of proficiency on single-pilot resource management (SRM), which is the cognitive or decision-making aspect of flight training.

The performance assessment dimensions for each type of rubric are as follows:

Maneuver or Procedure "Grades"

- Describe—at the completion of the scenario, the student is able to describe the physical characteristics and cognitive elements of the scenario activities, but needs assistance to execute the maneuver or procedure successfully.
- Explain—at the completion of the scenario, the student is able to describe the scenario activity and understand the underlying concepts, principles, and procedures that comprise the activity, but needs assistance to execute the maneuver or procedure successfully.
- Practice—at the completion of the scenario, the student is able to plan and execute the scenario. Coaching, instruction, and/or assistance will correct deviations and errors identified by the instructor.
- Perform—at the completion of the scenario, the student is able to perform the activity without instructor assistance. The student will identify and correct errors and deviations in an expeditious manner. At no time will the successful completion of the activity be in doubt. ("Perform" is used to signify that the student is satisfactorily demonstrating proficiency in traditional piloting and systems operation skills).
- Not observed—any event not accomplished or required.

For example, a student can describe a landing and can tell the flight instructor about the physical characteristics and appearance of the landing. On a good day, with the wind straight down the runway, the student may be able to practice landings with some success while still functioning at the rote level of learning. However, on a gusty crosswind day the student needs a deeper level of understanding to adapt to the different conditions. If a student can explain all the basic physics associated with lift/drag and crosswind correction, he or she is more likely to practice successfully and eventually perform a landing under a wide variety of conditions.

Single-Pilot Resource Management (SRM) "Grades"

- Explain—the student can verbally identify, describe, and understand the risks inherent in the flight scenario, but needs to be prompted to identify risks and make decisions.

- Practice—the student is able to identify, understand, and apply SRM principles to the actual flight situation. Coaching, instruction, and/or assistance quickly corrects minor deviations and errors identified by the instructor. The student is an active decision maker.
- Manage-Decide—the student can correctly gather the most important data available both inside and outside the flight deck, identify possible courses of action, evaluate the risk inherent in each course of action, and make the appropriate decision. Instructor intervention is not required for the safe completion of the flight.

In SRM, the student may be able to describe basic SRM principles during the first flight. Later, he or she is able to explain how SRM applies to different scenarios that are presented on the ground and in the air. When the student actually begins to make quality decisions based on good SRM techniques, he or she earns a grade of manage-decide. The advantage of this type of grading is that both flight instructor and student know exactly where the student learning has progressed.

Let's look at how the rubric in *Figure 5-4* might be used in the flight training scenario at the beginning of this chapter. During the postflight debriefing, CFI Linda asks her student, Brian, to assess his performance for the day, using the Replay – Reconstruct – Reflect – Redirect guided discussions questions described in the Collaborative Assessment subsection. Based on this assessment, she and Brian discuss where Brian's performance falls in the rubrics for maneuvers/procedures and SRM. This part of the assessment may be verbally discussed or, alternatively, Brian and Linda separately create an assessment sheet for each element of the flight.

When Brian studies the sheet, he finds "Describe, Explain, Practice, and Perform." He decides he was at the perform level since he had not made any mistakes. The flight scenario had been a two-leg Instrument Flight Rules (IFR) scenario to a busy class B airport about 60 miles to the east. Brian felt he had done well in keeping up with programming the GPS and MFD until he reached the approach phase. He had attempted to program the Instrument Landing System (ILS) for runway 7L and had actually flown part of the approach until air traffic control (ATC) asked him to execute a missed approach.

When he compares the sheet he has completed to Linda's version, Brian discovers that most of their assessments appear to match. An exception is the item labeled "programming the approach." Here, where he had rated the item as "Perform," Linda had rated it as "Explain." During the ensuing discussion, Brian realizes that he had selected the correct approach, but he had not activated it. Before Linda could intervene, traffic dictated a go-around. Her "explain" designation tells Brian that he did not really understand how the GPS worked, and he agrees.

This approach to assessment has several key advantages. One is that it actively involves the student in the assessment process, and establishes the habit of healthy reflection and self-assessment that is critical to being a safe pilot. Another is that these grades are not self-esteem related, since they do not describe a recognized level of prestige (such as A+ or "Outstanding"), but rather a level of performance. The student cannot flunk a lesson. Instead, he or she can only fail to demonstrate a given level of flight and SRM skills.

Both instructors and students may initially be reluctant to use this method of assessment. Instructors may think it requires more time, when in fact it is merely a more structured, effective, and collaborative version of a traditional postflight critique. Also, instructors who learned in the more traditional assessment structure must be careful not to equate or force the dimensions of the rubric into the traditional grading mold of A through F. One way to avoid this temptation is to remember that evaluation should be progressive: the student should achieve a new level of learning during each lesson. For example, in flight one, the automation management area might be a "describe" item. By flight three, it is a "practice" item, and by flight five, it is a "manage-decide" item.

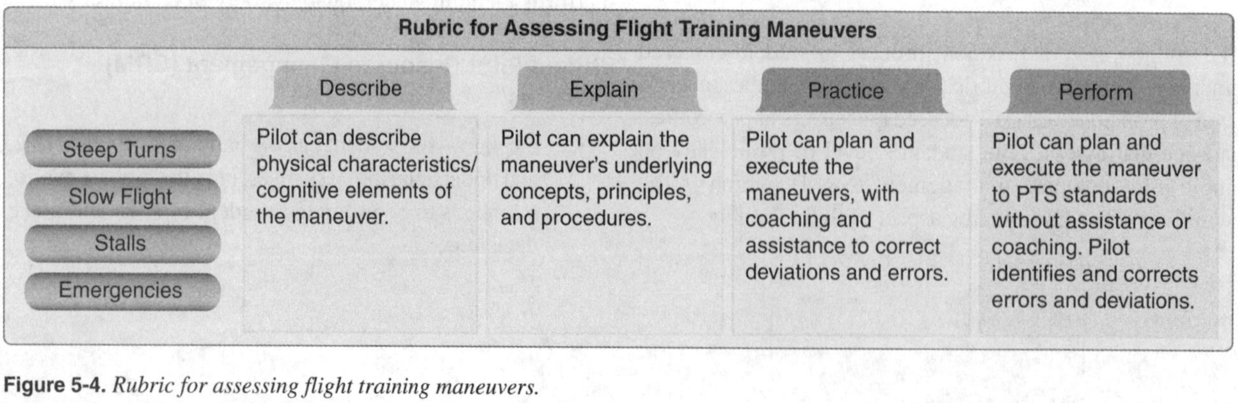

Figure 5-4. *Rubric for assessing flight training maneuvers.*

The student may be reluctant to self-assess if he or she has not had the chance to participate in such a process before. Therefore, the instructor may need to teach the student how to become an active participant in the collaborative assessment.

Choosing an Effective Assessment Method

When deciding how to assess student progress, aviation instructors can follow a four-step process.

- First, determine level-of-learning objectives.
- Second, list indicators of desired behaviors.
- Third, establish criterion objectives.
- Fourth, develop criterion-referenced test items.

This process is useful for tests that apply to the cognitive and affective domains of learning, and also can be used for skill testing in the psychomotor domain. The development process for criterion-referenced tests follows a general-to-specific pattern. *[Figure 5-4]*

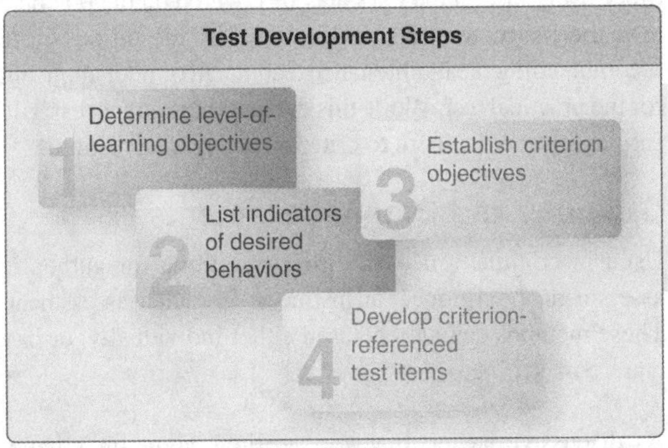

Figure 5-4. *The development process for criterion-referenced tests follows a general-to-specific pattern.*

Instructors should be aware that authentic assessment may not be as useful as traditional assessment in the early phases of training, because the student does not have enough information about the concepts or knowledge to participate fully. As discussed in Chapter 2, The Learning Process, when exposed to a new topic, students first tend to acquire and memorize facts. As learning progresses, they begin to organize their knowledge to formulate an understanding of the things they have memorized. When students possess the knowledge needed to analyze, synthesize, and evaluate (i.e., application and correlation levels of learning), they can participate more fully in the assessment process.

Determine Level-of-Learning Objectives

The first step in developing an appropriate assessment is to state the individual objectives as general, level-of-learning objectives. The objectives should measure one of the learning levels of the cognitive, affective, or psychomotor domains described in chapter 2. The levels of cognitive learning include knowledge, comprehension, application, analysis, synthesis, and evaluation.

For the understanding level, an objective could be stated as, "Describe how to perform a compression test on an aircraft reciprocating engine." This objective requires a student to explain how to do a compression test, but not necessarily perform a compression test (application level). Further, the student would not be expected to compare the results of compression tests on different engines (application level), design a compression test for a different type of engine (correlation level), or interpret the results of the compression test (correlation level). A general level-of-learning objective is a good starting point for developing a test because it defines the scope of the learning task.

List Indicators/Samples of Desired Behaviors

The second step is to list the indicators or samples of behavior that give the best indication of the achievement of the objective. Some level of learning objectives often cannot be directly measured. As a result, behaviors that can be measured are selected in order to give the best evidence of learning. For example, if the instructor is expecting the student to display the understanding level of learning on compression testing, some of the specific test question answers should describe appropriate tools and equipment, the proper equipment setup, appropriate safety procedures, and the steps used to obtain compression readings. The overall test must be comprehensive enough to give a true representation of the learning to be measured. It is not usually feasible to measure every aspect of a level of learning objective, but by carefully choosing samples of behavior, the instructor can obtain adequate evidence of learning.

Establish Criterion Objectives

The next step in the test development process is to define criterion (performance-based) objectives. In addition to the behavior expected, criterion objectives state the conditions under which the behavior is to be performed, and the criteria that must be met. If the instructor developed performance-based objectives during the creation of lesson plans, criterion objectives have already been formulated. The criterion objective provides the framework for developing the test items used to measure the level of learning objectives. In the compression test example, a criterion objective to measure the understanding level of learning might be stated as, "The student will demonstrate understanding of compression test procedures for reciprocating aircraft engines by completing a quiz with a minimum passing score of 70 percent."

Develop Criterion-Referenced Assessment Items

The last step is to develop criterion-referenced assessment items. The development of written test questions is covered in the reference section. While developing written test questions, the instructor should attempt to measure the behaviors described in the criterion objective(s). The questions in the exam for the compression test example should cover all of the areas necessary to give evidence of understanding the procedure. The results of the test (questions missed) identify areas that were not adequately covered.

Performance-based objectives serve as a reference for the development of test items. If the test is the pre-solo knowledge test, the objectives are for the student to understand the regulations, the local area, the aircraft type, and the procedures to be used. The test should measure the student's knowledge in these specific areas. Individual instructors should develop their own tests to measure the progress of their students. If the test is to measure the readiness of a student to take a knowledge test, it should be based on the objectives of all the lessons the student has received.

Aviation training also involves performance tests for maneuvers or procedures. The flight instructor does not administer the practical test for a pilot certificate, nor does the aviation maintenance instructor administer the oral and practical exam for certification as an aviation maintenance technician (AMT). However, aviation instructors do get involved with the same skill or performance testing that is measured in these tests. Performance testing is desirable for evaluating training that involves an operation, a procedure, or a process. The job of the instructor is to prepare the student to take these tests. Therefore, each element of the practical test should be evaluated prior to sending an applicant for the practical exam.

Practical tests for maintenance technicians and pilots are criterion-referenced tests. The practical tests, defined in the Practical Test Standards (PTS), are criterion referenced because the objective is for all successful applicants to meet the high standards of knowledge, skill, and safety required by the regulations. The purpose of the PTS is to delineate the standards by which FAA inspectors, designated pilot examiners (DPEs), and designated maintenance examiners (DMEs) conduct tests for ratings and certificates. The standards are in accordance with the requirements of Title 14 of the Code of Federal Regulations (14 CFR) parts 61, 65, 91, and other FAA publications, including the Aeronautical Information Manual (AIM) and pertinent advisory circulars and handbooks.

The objective of the PTS is to ensure the certification of pilots and maintenance technicians at a high level of performance and proficiency, consistent with safety. The PTS for aeronautical certificates and ratings include areas of operation and tasks that reflect the requirements of the FAA publications mentioned above. Areas of operation define phases of the practical test arranged in a logical sequence within each standard. They usually begin with preflight preparation and end with postflight procedures. Tasks are titles of knowledge areas, flight procedures, or maneuvers appropriate to an area of operation. Included are references to the applicable regulations or publications. Private pilot applicants are evaluated in all tasks of each area of operation. Flight instructor applicants are evaluated on one or more tasks in each area of operation. In addition, certain tasks are required to be covered and are identified by notes immediately following the area of operation titles.

Since every task in the PTS may be covered on the practical test, the instructor must evaluate all of the tasks before recommending the maintenance technician or pilot applicant for the practical test. While this evaluation is not necessarily formal, it should adhere to criterion-referenced testing.

Critiques and Oral Assessments

Used in conjunction with either traditional or authentic assessment, the critique is an instructor-to-student assessment. These methods can also be used either individually, or in a classroom setting.

As discussed earlier, the word critique sometimes has a negative connotation, and the instructor needs to avoid using this method as an opportunity to be overly critical of student performance. An effective critique considers good as well as bad performance, the individual parts, relationships of the individual parts, and the overall performance. A critique can and usually should be as varied in content as the performance being evaluated.

A critique may be oral, written, or both. It should come immediately after a student's performance, while the details of the performance are easy to recall. An instructor may critique any activity a student performs or practices to improve skill, proficiency, and learning. A critique may be conducted privately or before the entire class. A critique presented before the entire class can be beneficial to every student in the classroom, as well as to the student who performed the exercise or assignment. In this case, however, the instructor should avoid embarrassing the student in front of the class.

There are several useful ways to conduct a critique.

Instructor/Student Critique

The instructor leads a group discussion in an instructor/student critique in which members of the class are invited to offer criticism of a performance. This method should be controlled carefully and directed with a clear purpose. It should be organized, and not allowed to degenerate into a random free-for-all.

Student-Led Critique

The instructor asks a student to lead the assessment in a student-led critique. The instructor can specify the pattern of organization and the techniques or can leave it to the discretion of the student leader. Because of the inexperience of the participants in the lesson area, student-led assessments may not be efficient, but they can generate student interest and learning and, on the whole, be effective.

Small Group Critique

For the small group critique, the class is divided into small groups, each assigned a specific area to analyze. Each group must present its findings to the class. It is desirable for the instructor to furnish the criteria and guidelines. The combined reports from the groups can result in a comprehensive assessment.

Individual Student Critique by Another Student

The instructor may require another student to present the entire assessment. A variation is for the instructor to ask a number of students questions about the manner and quality of performance. Discussion of the performance and of the assessment can often allow the group to accept more ownership of the ideas expressed. As with all assessments incorporating student participation, it is important that the instructor maintain firm control over the process.

Self-Critique

A student critiques personal performance in a self-critique. Like all other methods, a self-critique must be controlled and supervised by the instructor.

Written Critique

A written critique has three advantages. First, the instructor can devote more time and thought to it than to an oral assessment in the classroom. Second, students can keep written assessments and refer to them whenever they wish. Third, when the instructor requires all students to write an assessment of a performance, the student-performer has the permanent record of the suggestions, recommendations, and opinions of all the other students. The disadvantage of a written assessment is that other members of the class do not benefit.

Whatever the type of critique, the instructor must resolve controversial issues and correct erroneous impressions. The instructor must make allowances for the students' relative inexperience. Normally, the instructor should reserve time at the end of the student assessment to cover those areas that might have been omitted, not emphasized sufficiently, or considered worth repeating.

Oral Assessment

The most common means of assessment is direct or indirect oral questioning of students by the instructor. Questions may be loosely classified as fact questions and HOTS questions. The answer to a fact question is based on memory or recall. This type of question usually concerns who, what, when, and where. HOTS questions involve why or how, and require the student to combine knowledge of facts with an ability to analyze situations, solve problems, and arrive at conclusions.

Proper quizzing by the instructor can have a number of desirable results:

- Reveals the effectiveness of the instructor's training methods
- Checks student retention of what has been learned
- Reviews material already presented to the student
- Can be used to retain student interest and stimulate thinking
- Emphasizes the important points of training
- Identifies points that need more emphasis
- Checks student comprehension of what has been learned
- Promotes active student participation, which is important to effective learning

Characteristics of Effective Questions

The instructor should devise and write pertinent questions in advance. One method is to place them in the lesson plan. Prepared questions merely serve as a framework, and as the lesson progresses, should be supplemented by such impromptu questions as the instructor considers appropriate. Objective questions have only one correct answer, while the answer to an open-ended HOTS question can be expressed in a variety of possible solutions.

To be effective, questions must:

- Apply to the subject of instruction.
- Be brief and concise, but also clear and definite.
- Be adapted to the ability, experience, and stage of training of the students.
- Center on only one idea (limited to who, what, when, where, how, or why, not a combination).
- Present a challenge to the students.

Types of Questions To Avoid

Effective quizzing does not ever include yes/no questions such as "Do you understand?" or "Do you have any questions?" Instructors should also avoid the following types of questions:

- Puzzle—"What is the first action you should take if a conventional gear airplane with a weak right brake is swerving left in a right crosswind during a full flap, power-on wheel landing?"
- Oversize—"What do you do before beginning an engine overhaul?"
- Toss-up—"In an emergency, should you squawk 7700 or pick a landing spot?"
- Bewilderment—"In reading the altimeter—you know you set a sensitive altimeter for the nearest station pressure—if you take temperature into account, as when flying from a cold air mass through a warm front, what precaution should you take when in a mountainous area?"
- Trick questions—these questions cause the students to develop the feeling that they are engaged in a battle of wits with the instructor, and the whole significance of the subject of the instruction involved is lost. An example of a trick question would be one in which the response options are 1, 2, 3, and 4, but they are placed in the following form.

  A. 4

  B. 3

  C. 2

  D. 1
- Irrelevant questions—diversions that introduce only unrelated facts and thoughts and slow the student's progress. Questions unrelated to the test topics are not helpful in evaluating the student's knowledge of the subject at hand. An example of an irrelevant question would be to ask a question about tire inflation during a test on the timing of magnetos.

Answering Student Questions

Tips for responding effectively to student questions, especially in a classroom setting:

- Be sure that you clearly understand the question before attempting to answer.
- Display interest in the student's question and frame an answer that is as direct and accurate as possible.
- After responding, determine whether or not the student is satisfied with the answer.

Sometimes it is unwise to introduce considerations more complicated or advanced than necessary to completely answer a student's question at the current point in training. In this case, the instructor should carefully explain to the student that the question was good and pertinent, but that a detailed answer would, at this time, unnecessarily complicate the learning tasks. The instructor should invite the student to reintroduce the question later at the appropriate point in training.

Occasionally, a student asks a question that the instructor cannot answer. In such cases, the instructor should freely admit not knowing the answer, but should promise to get the answer or, if practicable, offer to help the student look it up in available references.

Chapter Summary

This chapter has offered the aviation instructor techniques and methods for assessing how, what, and how well a student is learning. Well-designed assessments define what is worth knowing, thereby improving student learning. Since today's students want to know the criteria by which they are assessed, as well as practical and specific feedback, it is important for aviation instructors to be familiar with the different types of assessments available for monitoring student progress throughout a course of training, and how to select the most appropriate assessment method.

Chapter 6

Planning Instructional Activity

Introduction

Susan (student) and Bill (Certificated Flight Instructor (CFI)) are flying a lesson scenario which consists of a short cross-country leg to a local airport for some practice landings followed by a return to the home airport located in Class C airspace. While practicing landings at the nontowered airport, the student notes that the ceiling is lowering and the crosswind is beginning to increase. In his own mind, Bill is convinced that they can practice landings for another 30 minutes to an hour and still return to home base. However, instead of telling Susan this, while taxiing back after a full stop landing, he first asks her several questions.

- Has the flight situation changed since they left the home field?
- What does she think of the weather situation?
- How can we gain more information?
  - Check with Automated Flight Service Station (AFSS) on the radio?
  - Stop at the Fixed Based Operator (FBO) and call back to the FBO to check on weather and the schedule?
- Are there other issues?
  - Fuel?
  - Schedule?
- Aircraft equipment (instrument flight rules (IFR)/visual flight rules (VFR)) and pilot capability?

Susan decides that she would be more comfortable returning to the home airport and practicing landings there to stay out of the weather. Although not his plan, it is a good plan based on accurate situational awareness and good risk management skills, so Bill agrees. Susan is now beginning to gain confidence by practicing her judgment and decision-making skills. In the postflight critique, Susan leads a discussion of this and other decisions she has made in order to learn more about the process.

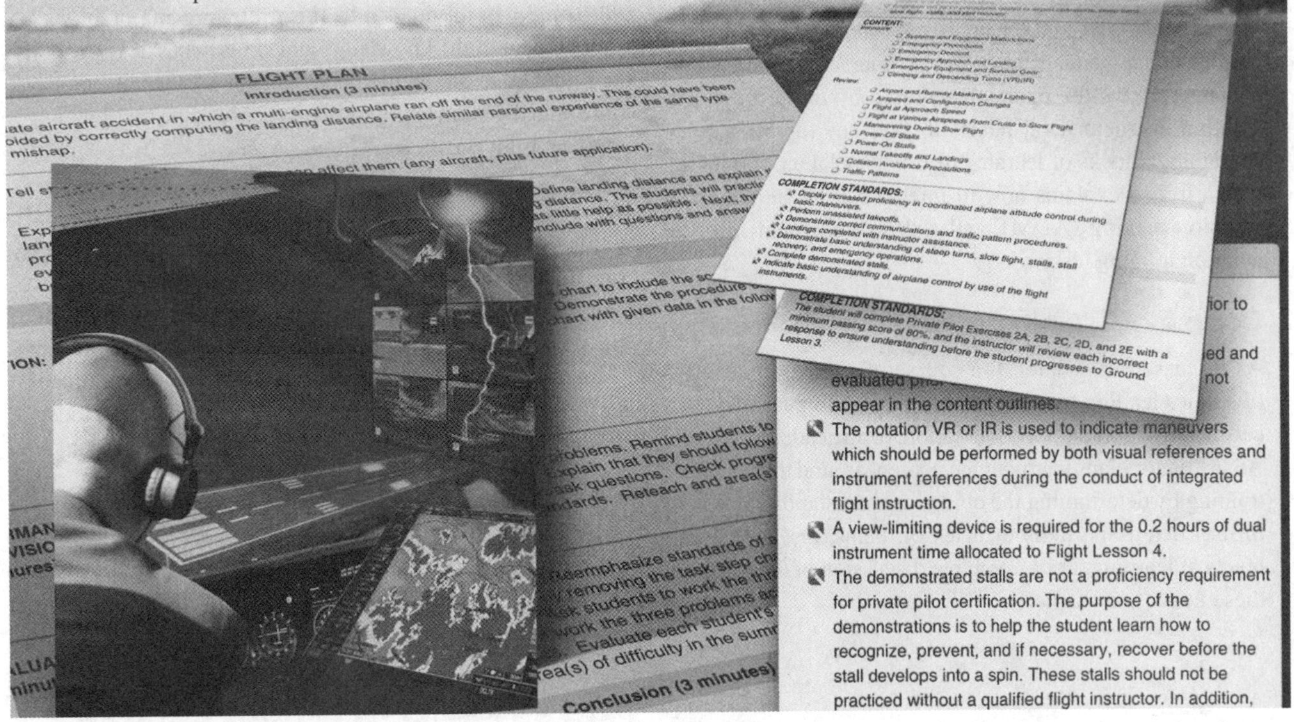

In the past, the aviation instructor was a capable pilot or aviation technician with a rather general understanding of basic teaching methods and techniques. More recently, the Federal Aviation Administration (FAA) has paid more attention to the instructor's role as teacher and mentor, and has provided a much better grounding in instructional techniques. The instructor is now required to master the teaching methods, write lesson objectives, outline and write lesson plans, and motivate students by example. The instructor is responsible for what is taught in the aircraft and classroom. The amount of learning that takes place is a direct result of how well the lesson is prepared and the teaching skill of the instructor.

Historically, aviation instruction focused on the performance of specific procedures and/or maneuvers, and learning was measured with objective standards. Changing technology and innovations in learning provide today's aviation instructors with the opportunity to use new methods and teach to new standards. One of these methods, introduced in Chapter 4, The Teaching Process, is scenario-based training (SBT). While SBT is an integral component of today's aviation training, the instructor is crucial to its implementation. By emphasizing SBT, the instructor functions in the learning environment as an advisor and guide for the learner.

Whatever the method of teaching, the key to developing well-planned and organized aviation instruction includes using lesson plans and a training syllabus that meet all regulatory certification requirements. Much of the basic planning necessary for the flight instructor and maintenance instructor is provided by the knowledge and proficiency requirements published in Title 14 of the Code of Federal Regulations (14 CFR) parts 61 and 65, approved school syllabi, and the various texts, manuals, and training courses available. This chapter reviews the planning required by the professional aviation instructor as it relates to four key topics—course of training, blocks of learning, training syllabus, and lesson plans. It also explains how to integrate SBT, aeronautical decision-making (ADM), and risk management into the aviation training lesson.

Course of Training

As discussed in chapter 4, a course of training is a series of studies leading to attainment of a specific goal such as a certificate of completion, graduation, or an academic degree. An instructor plans instructional content around the course of training by determining the objectives and standards, which in turn determine individual lesson plans, test items, and levels of learning. For a complete discussion of determining these items, see chapter 4.

Blocks of Learning

After the overall training objectives have been established, the next step is the identification of the blocks of learning which constitute the necessary parts of the total objective. Just as in building a pyramid, some blocks are submerged in the structure and never appear on the surface, but each is an integral and necessary part of the structure. Thus, the various blocks are not isolated subjects, but essential parts of the whole. During the process of identifying the blocks of learning to be assembled for the proposed training activity, the instructor must also examine each block to ensure it is an integral part of the structure. Extraneous blocks of instruction are expensive frills, especially in flight instruction, and detract from, rather than assist in, the completion of the final objective.

While determining the overall training objectives is a necessary first step in the planning process, early identification of the foundation blocks of learning is also essential. Training for any such complicated and involved task as piloting or maintaining an aircraft requires the development and assembly of many segments or blocks of learning in their proper relationships. In this way, a student can master the segments or blocks individually and can progressively combine these with other related segments until their sum meets the overall training objectives.

The blocks of learning identified during the planning and management of a training activity should be fairly consistent in scope. They should represent units of learning which can be measured and evaluated—not a sequence of periods of instruction. For example, the flight training of a private pilot might be divided into the following major blocks: achievement of the knowledge and skills necessary for solo, the knowledge and skills necessary for solo cross-country flight, and the knowledge and skills appropriate for obtaining a private pilot certificate. *[Figure 6-1]*

Use of the building block approach provides the student with a boost in self-confidence. This normally occurs each time a block is completed. Otherwise, an overall goal, such as earning a mechanic's certificate, may seem unobtainable. If the larger blocks are broken down into smaller blocks of instruction, each on its own is more manageable. Humans learn from the simple to the complex. For example, an student airplane pilot should understand and master the technique of a normal landing prior to being introduced to short and soft field landings. A helicopter pilot must be proficient in running landings before the instructor introduces a no hydraulics approach and landing.

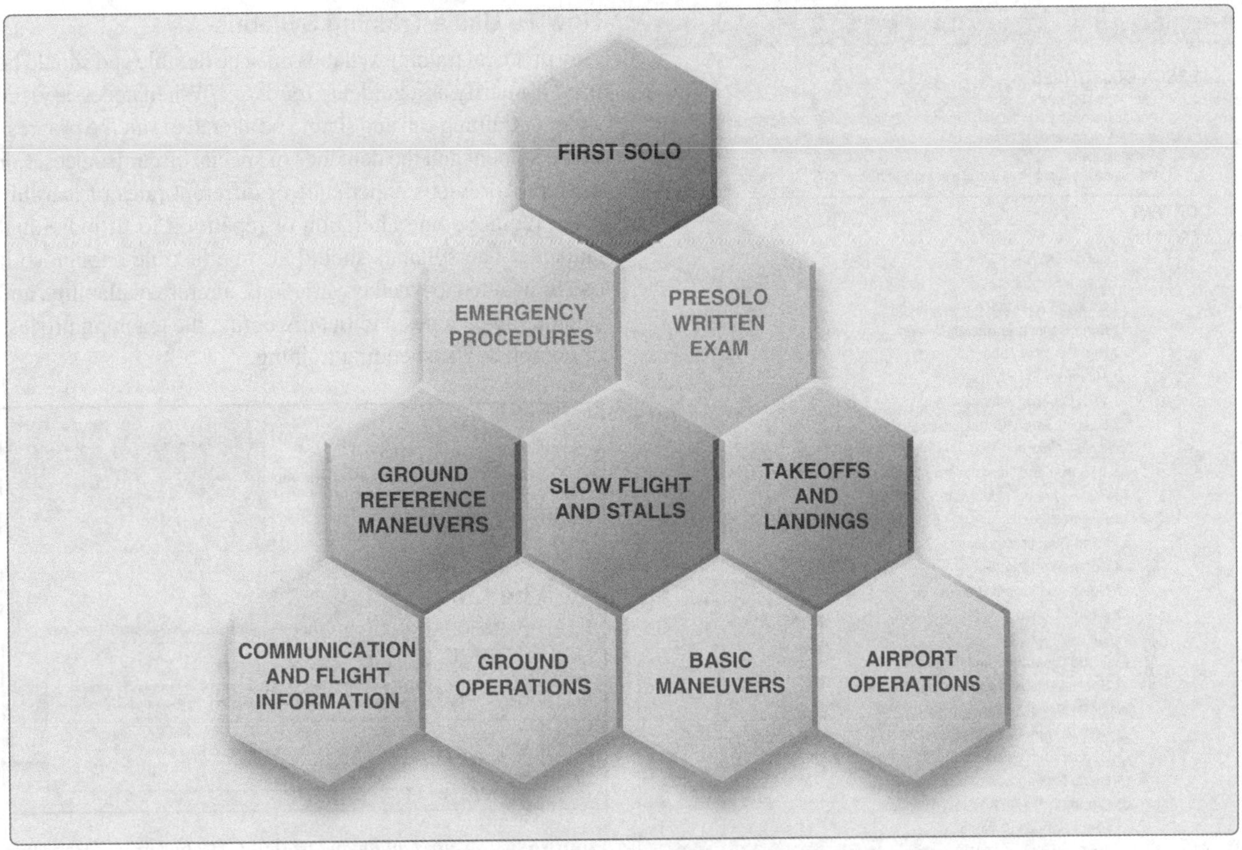

Figure 6-1. *The presolo stage or phase of private pilot training is comprised of several basic building blocks. These blocks of learning, which should include coordinated ground and flight training, lead up to the first solo.*

By becoming familiar with the student's aviation background, an instructor can plan the sequence of instruction blocks. Does the applicant have previous aeronautical experience or posses a pilot certificate in another category? This information will help the instructor design appropriate training blocks. For example, if the student is a helicopter pilot who is transitioning to an airplane, he or she will understand speed control, but not necessarily know how to achieve it in an airplane. The instructor can plan blocks of instruction that build on what the student already knows.

Training Syllabus

Aviation instructors use a training syllabus because as technology advances, training requirements become more demanding. At the same time, new, and often more complicated, rules continue to be proposed and implemented. In addition, the rules for instruction in other than an approved aviation school are still quite specific about the type and duration of training. These factors, along with the continuing growth of aviation, add to the complexity of aviation training and certification. Instructors need a practical guide to help them make sure the training is accomplished in a logical sequence and that all of the requirements are completed and properly documented. A well organized, comprehensive syllabus can fulfill these needs.

Syllabus Format and Content

The format and organization of the syllabus may vary, but it always should be in the form of an abstract or digest of the course of training. It should contain blocks of learning to be completed in the most efficient order. Since a syllabus is intended to be a summary of a course of training, it should be fairly brief, yet comprehensive enough to cover essential information. This information is usually presented in an outline format with lesson-by-lesson coverage. Some syllabi include tables to show recommended training time for each lesson, as well as the overall minimum time requirements. *[Figure 6-2]*

While many instructors may develop their own training syllabi, there are many well-designed commercial products that may be used. These are found in various training manuals, approved school syllabi, and other publications available from industry.

Syllabi developed for approved flight schools contain specific information that is outlined in 14 CFR parts 141 and 142. In contrast, syllabi designed for training in other than approved schools may not provide certain details such as enrollment

STAGE 1 | GROUND LESSON 2

LESSON OBJECTIVES

- Learn important safety of flight considerations.
- Become thoroughly familiar with airports, including marking and lighting aids.
- Learn the significance of airspace divisions and how to use the radio for communications.
- Understand the capabilities and use of radar and other ATC services.

CONTENT

Introduce:

Section A—Safety of Flight

- ❑ Visual Scanning
- ❑ Collision Avoidance Precautions
- ❑ Blind Spots and Aircraft Design
- ❑ Right-of-Way Rules
- ❑ Minimum Safe Altitudes
- ❑ VFR Cruising Altitudes
- ❑ Special Safety Considerations

Section B—Airports

- ❑ Towered and Nontowered Airports
- ❑ Runway and Taxiway Markings
- ❑ Airport Signs
- ❑ Wind Direction Indicators
- ❑ Segmented Circle
- ❑ Noise Abatement Procedures
- ❑ Airport Lighting

Section C—Airspace

- ❑ Cloud Clearance and Visibility
- ❑ Special Use and Other Airspace Areas

Section D—Radio Communications

- ❑ VHF Communications Equipment
- ❑ Coordinated Universal Time
- ❑ Radio Procedures
- ❑ Common Traffic Advisory Frequency
- ❑ Flight Service Stations

Section E—Radar and ATC Services

- ❑ Radar
- ❑ Transponder
- ❑ FAA Radar Systems

COMPLETION STANDARDS

The student will complete Private Pilot Exercises 2A, 2B, 2C, 2D, and 2E with a minimum passing score of 80%. The instructor will review each incorrect response to ensure understanding before the student progresses to Ground Lesson 3.

Figure 6-2. *This excerpt of a ground lesson shows a unit of ground instruction. In this example, neither the time nor the number of ground training periods to be devoted to the lesson is specified. The lesson should include three parts—objective, content, and completion standards.*

prerequisites, planned completion times, and descriptions of checks and tests to measure student accomplishments for each stage of training.

Since effective training relies on organized blocks of learning, all syllabi should stress well-defined objectives and standards for each lesson. Appropriate objectives and standards should be established for the overall course, the separate ground and flight segments, and for each stage of training. Other details may be added to a syllabus in order to explain how to use it and describe the pertinent training and reference materials. Examples of the training and reference materials include textbooks, video, compact disks, exams, briefings, and instructional guides.

How To Use a Training Syllabus

Any practical training syllabus must be flexible and should be used primarily as a guide. *[Figure 6-3]* When necessary, the order of training can and should be altered to suit the progress of the student and the demands of special circumstances. For example, previous experience or different rates of learning often require some alteration or repetition to fit individual students. The syllabus should also be flexible enough so it can be adapted to weather variations, aircraft availability, and scheduling changes without disrupting the teaching process or completely suspending training.

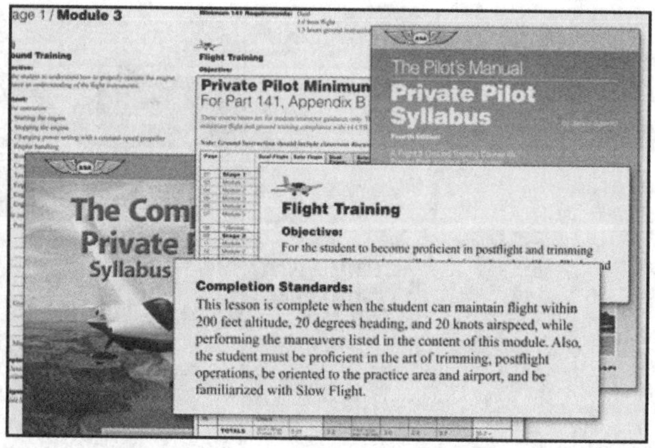

Figure 6-3. *The curriculum and training syllabus provide teaching guidelines.*

In departing from the order prescribed by the syllabus, however, it is the responsibility of the instructor to consider how the relationships of the blocks of learning are affected. For example, if the student is having a difficult time with normal approaches and landings, the instructor might decide to delay adding short field landings, which were originally to be the next step in his block of instruction. To prevent the student from becoming frustrated with his or her poor landing technique, the instructor may choose to review the block on slow flight, which offers the student a chance to do well and regain confidence. This exercise also builds the skills necessary for the student to master approaches and normal landings.

Each approved training course provided by a certificated aviation school should be conducted in accordance with a training syllabus specifically approved by the FAA. At certificated schools, the syllabus is a key part of the training course outline. The instructional facilities, airport, aircraft, and instructor personnel must be able to support the course of training specified in the syllabus. Compliance with the appropriate, approved syllabus is a condition for graduation from such courses. Therefore, effective use of a syllabus requires that it be referred to throughout the entire course of training. Both the instructor and the student should have a copy of the approved syllabus. However, as previously mentioned, adherence to a syllabus should not be so stringent that it becomes inflexible or unchangeable. It must be flexible enough to adapt to the special needs of individual students.

Ground training lessons and classroom lectures concentrate on the cognitive domain of learning. A typical lesson might include defining, labeling, or listing what the student has learned so far. Many of the knowledge areas are directly or indirectly concerned with safety, ADM, and judgment. Since these subjects are associated with the affective domain of learning (emotion), instructors who find a way to stress safety, ADM, and judgment, along with the traditional aviation subjects, can favorably influence a student's attitude, beliefs, and values.

Flight training lessons or aviation technical lab sessions also include knowledge areas, but they generally emphasize the psychomotor domain of learning because the student is "doing" something. The lesson plan shown in *Figure 6-4* shows the main elements of a ground lesson for a flight student. The affective domain of learning is also important in this type of training; a student's attitude toward safety, ADM, and judgment, should be a major concern of the instructor.

The flight training syllabus should include special emphasis items that have been determined to be cause factors in aircraft accidents or incidents. For example, the instructor should emphasize collision and wake turbulence avoidance procedures throughout a student's flight training. The aviation technician syllabus should also emphasize what constitutes unsafe practices, such the ease of introducing foreign object damage (FOD) to an aircraft when the location of tools is not monitored.

STAGE 1 | FLIGHT LESSON 4

Dual—Local (1.0)

Note: A view-limiting device is required for 0.2 hours of dual instrument time allocated to Flight Lesson 4.

LESSON OBJECTIVES
- Practice the maneuvers listed for review to gain additional proficiency and demonstrate the ability to recognize and recover from stalls.
- The student will also receive instruction and practice in the maneuvers and procedures listed for introduction, including emergency operations and additional practice of airplane control by instrument reference (IR).
- Instructor may demonstrate secondary, accelerated maneuver, crossed-control, and elevator trim stalls.
- Emphasis will be on procedures related to airport operations, steep turns, slow flight, stalls, and stall recovery.

CONTENT

Introduce:
- ❑ Systems and Equipment Malfunctions
- ❑ Emergency Procedures
- ❑ Emergency Descent
- ❑ Emergency Approach and Landing
- ❑ Emergency Equipment and Survival Gear
- ❑ Climbing and Descending Turns (VR)(IR)

Review:
- ❑ Airport and Runway Markings and Lighting
- ❑ Airspeed and Configuration Changes
- ❑ Flight at Approach Speed
- ❑ Flight at Various Airspeeds From Cruise to Slow Flight
- ❑ Maneuvering During Slow Flight
- ❑ Power-Off Stalls
- ❑ Power-On Stalls
- ❑ Normal Takeoffs and Landings
- ❑ Collision Avoidance Precautions
- ❑ Traffic Patterns

COMPLETION STANDARDS
- Displays increased proficiency in coordinated airplane attitude control during basic maneuvers.
- Performs unassisted takeoffs.
- Demonstrates correct communications and traffic pattern procedures.
- Completes landings with instructor assistance.
- Demonstrates basic understanding of steep turns, slow flight, stalls, stall recovery, and emergency operations.
- Completes demonstrated stalls.
- Indicates basic understanding of airplane control by use of the flight instruments.

Figure 6-4. *A flight training lesson, like a ground training lesson, should include an objective, content, and completion standards. More than one objective could, and often does, apply to a single flight lesson.*

A syllabus may include several other items that add to or clarify the objective, content, or standards. A lesson may specify the recommended class time, reference or study materials, recommended sequence of training, and study assignment for the next lesson. Both ground and flight lessons may have explanatory information notes added to specific lessons. *[Figure 6-5]*

While a syllabus is designed to provide a road map showing how to accomplish the overall objective of a course of training, it may be useful for other purposes. As already mentioned, it can be used as a checklist to ensure that required training has successfully been completed. Thus, a syllabus can be an effective tool for recordkeeping. Enhanced syllabi, which also are designed for recordkeeping, can be very beneficial to the independent instructor.

This recordkeeping function is usually facilitated by boxes or blank spaces adjacent to the knowledge areas, procedures, or maneuvers in a lesson. Most syllabi introduce each procedure or maneuver in one lesson and review them in subsequent lessons. Some syllabi also include provisions for grading student performance and recording both ground and flight training time. Accurate recordkeeping is necessary to keep both the student and the instructor informed on the status of training. These records also serve as a basis for endorsements and recommendations for knowledge and practical tests. Some training syllabi or records may include

Typical syllabus notes

- Students should read Chapter 1 of the textbook prior to Ground Lesson 1.
- All preflight duties and procedures will be performed and evaluated prior to each flight. Therefore, they will not appear in the content outlines.
- The notation "VR" or "IR" is used to indicate maneuvers which should be performed by both visual references and instrument references during the conduct of integrated flight instruction.
- A view-limiting device is required for the 0.2 hours of dual instrument time allocated to Flight Lesson 4.
- The demonstrated stalls are not a proficiency requirement for private pilot certification. The purpose of the demonstrations is to help the student learn how to recognize, prevent, and if necessary, recover before the stall develops into a spin. These stalls should not be practiced without a qualified flight instructor. In addition, some stalls may be prohibited in some airplanes.

Figure 6-5. *Information in the form of notes may be added to individual ground or flight lessons in a syllabus when they are necessary.*

coded numbers or letters for other instructors to record their evaluation of a student's progress and knowledge or skill level. *[Figure 6-6]*

Another benefit of using a syllabus is that it helps in the development of lesson plans. A well constructed syllabus already contains much of the essential information that is required in a lesson plan, including objectives, content, and completion standards.

Lesson Plans

A lesson plan is an organized outline for a single instructional period. It is a necessary guide for the instructor because it tells what to do, in what order to do it, and what procedure to use in teaching the material of a lesson. Lesson plans should be prepared for each training period and be developed to show specific knowledge and/or skills to be taught.

A mental outline of a lesson is not a lesson plan. A lesson plan should be put into writing. Another instructor should be able to take the lesson plan and know what to do in conducting the same period of instruction. Written out, the lesson plan can be analyzed for adequacy and completeness.

Lesson plans make excellent recordkeeping forms that can become a permanent part of a pilot's training record. They can be formatted for the instructor to carry in the aircraft and include a checklist for indicating what portions of the lesson were completed, date of completion, the flight instructor's signature, and time flown. The lesson plan can also have a notation section for flight instructor comments.

A training folder for each student helps an instructor keep all pertinent data in one place. The folder should include items such as lesson plans, training requirements, flight or ground instruction received, 14 CFR part 61 requirements met, solo endorsements, and any other training information. These records should be kept in a safe area for at least 3 years. Good recordkeeping also provides each instructor with the number of students he or she has trained, which is helpful information for an instructor who needs to renew his or her certificate. For sample lesson plans, please refer to Appendix A.

Purpose of the Lesson Plan

Lesson plans are designed to assure that each student receives the best possible instruction under the existing conditions. Lesson plans help instructors keep a constant check on their own activity, as well as that of their students. The development of lesson plans by instructors signifies, in effect, that they have taught the lessons to themselves prior to attempting to teach the lessons to students. An adequate lesson plan, when properly used, should:

- Assure a wise selection of material and the elimination of unimportant details.
- Make certain that due consideration is given to each part of the lesson.
- Aid the instructor in presenting the material in a suitable sequence for efficient learning.
- Provide an outline of the teaching procedure to be used.
- Serve as a means of relating the lesson to the objectives of the course of training.
- Give the inexperienced instructor confidence.
- Promote uniformity of instruction regardless of the instructor or the date on which the lesson is given.

Characteristics of a Well-Planned Lesson

The quality of planning affects the quality of results. Successful professionals understand that the price of excellence is hard work and thorough preparation. The effective instructor realizes that the time and energy spent in planning and preparing each lesson is well worth the effort in the long run.

A complete cycle of planning usually includes several steps. After the objective is determined, the instructor must research the subject as it is defined by the objective. Once the research is complete, the instructor determines the method of

FLIGHT INSTRUCTION LOG (GLIDER)

Student: **Instructor:**

Flight Number	1	2	3	4	5	6	7	8	9	10	11	12	13	14	15	16
Lesson Number																
Glider Assembly																
Preflight Inspection																
Ground Handling																
Takeoff (Normal)																
Crosswind Takeoff																
Tow (High-Tow & Low-Tow)																
Boxing the Wake																
Slack Line Recovery																
Straight Glides																
Turns (Shallow & Medium)																
Steep Turns (50 to 60 Degrees of Bank)																
Slow Flight & Minimum Controllable Airspeed																
Straight-Ahead Stalls																
Turning Stalls																
Accelerated Stalls																
Spin Recovery																
Traffic Pattern																
Use of Spoilers																
Forward Slips (With & Without Spoilers)																
Landings (Normal)																
Crosswind Landings (Simulated)																
Off-Airport Landings (Simulated)																
Airspeed Control																
Vigilance & Collision Avoidance																
Judgment																
Use of Checklists																
Flight Time (This flight)																
Total Flight Time																

Figure 6-6. *Glider training log.*

instruction and identifies a useful lesson planning format. The decision of how to organize the lesson and the selection of suitable support material come next. The final steps include assembling training aids and writing the lesson plan outline. One technique for writing the lesson plan outline is to prepare the beginning and ending first. Then, complete the outline and revise as required. A lesson plan should be a working document that can and should be revised as changes occur or are needed.

The following are some of the important characteristics that should be reflected in all well-planned lessons.

Unity—each lesson should be a unified segment of instruction. A lesson is concerned with certain limited objectives, which are stated in terms of desired student learning outcomes. All teaching procedures and materials should be selected to attain these objectives.

Content—each lesson should contain new material. However, the new facts, principles, procedures, or skills should be related to the lesson previously presented. A short review of earlier lessons is usually necessary, particularly in flight training.

Scope—each lesson should be reasonable in scope. A person can master only a few principles or skills at a time, the number depending on complexity. Presenting too much material in a lesson results in confusion; presenting too little material results in inefficiency.

Practicality—each lesson should be planned in terms of the conditions under which the training is to be conducted. Lesson plans conducted in an airplane or ground trainer will differ from those conducted in a classroom. Also, the kinds and quantities of instructional aids available have a great influence on lesson planning and instructional procedures.

Flexibility—although the lesson plan provides an outline and sequence for the training to be conducted, a degree of flexibility should be incorporated. For example, the outline of content may include blank spaces for add-on material, if required.

Relation to course of training—each lesson should be planned and taught so that its relation to the course objectives is clear to each student. For example, a lesson on short field takeoffs and landings should be related to both the certification and safety objectives of the course of training.

Instructional steps—every lesson, when adequately developed, falls logically into the four steps of the teaching process: preparation, presentation, application, and review and evaluation.

How To Use a Lesson Plan Properly

Be familiar with the lesson plan. The instructor should study each step of the plan and should be thoroughly familiar with as much information related to the subject as possible.

Use the lesson plan as a guide. The lesson plan is an outline for conducting an instructional period. It assures that pertinent materials are at hand and that the presentation is accomplished with order and unity. Having a plan prevents the instructor from getting off track, omitting essential points, and introducing irrelevant material. Students have a right to expect an instructor to give the same attention to teaching that they give to learning. The most certain means of achieving teaching success is to have a carefully reviewed lesson plan.

Adapt the lesson plan to the class or student. In teaching a class, the instructor may find that the procedures outlined in the lesson plan are not leading to the desired results. In this situation, the instructor should change the approach. There is no certain way of predicting the reactions of different groups of students. An approach that has been successful with one group may not be equally successful with another.

A lesson plan for an instructional flight period should be appropriate to the background, flight experience, and ability of the particular student. A lesson plan may have to be modified considerably during flight, due to deficiencies in the student's knowledge or poor mastery of elements essential to the effective completion of the lesson. In some cases, the entire lesson plan may have to be abandoned in favor of review.

Revise the lesson plan periodically. After a lesson plan has been prepared for a training period, a continuous revision may be necessary. This is true for a number of reasons such as availability or non-availability of instructional aids, changes in regulations, or new manuals and textbooks.

Lesson Plan Formats

The format and style of a lesson plan depends on several factors. Certainly the subject matter helps determine how a lesson is presented and what teaching method is used. Individual lesson plans may be quite simple for one-on-one training, or they may be elaborate and complicated for large, structured classroom lessons. Preferably, each lesson should have somewhat limited objectives that are achievable within a reasonable period of time. This principle should apply to both ground and flight training. However, as previously noted, aviation training is not simple. It involves all three domains of learning, and the objectives usually include the higher levels of learning, at least at the application level.

In spite of need for varied subject coverage, diverse teaching methods, and relatively high level learning objectives, most aviation lesson plans have the common characteristics already discussed. All should include objectives, content to support the objectives, and completion standards. Various authorities often divide the main headings into several subheadings; terminology, even for the main headings, varies extensively. For example, completion standards may be called assessment, review and feedback, performance evaluation, or some other related term.

Commercially developed lesson plans are acceptable for most training situations, including use by flight instructor applicants during their practical tests. However, all instructors should recognize that even well-designed preprinted lesson plans may need to be modified. Therefore, instructors are encouraged to use creativity when adapting preprinted lesson plans or when developing their own lesson plans for specific students or training circumstances.

In the traditional lesson plan illustrated by *Figure 6-7,* the objective is "The student will learn to control for wind drift." The content has the instructor pilot giving a thorough

Traditional Lesson Plan

LESSON OBJECTIVE
The student will learn to control for wind drift.

COMPLETION STANDARDS
The student will demonstrate the ability to consistently control for wind drift in a safe and effective manner within a specified limit of heading, altitude, and airspeed.

CONTENT
Preflight Discussion:

- Lesson objective and completion standards
- Normal checklist procedures
- Weather analysis

Review:

- Heading
- Speed
- Angle of bank
- Altitude
- Terrain
- Wind direction plus velocity

Introduction:

- Aerodynamics Demonstration
  i. Turns around a point
  ii. S-turns across a road

Postflight Discussion:

- Critique student performance, preview next lesson, and give study assignment

EXAMPLE

Figure 6-7. *Example of a traditional training lesson plan.*

coverage of heading, speed, angle of bank, altitude, terrain, and wind direction plus velocity. This explanation is followed by a demonstration and repeated practice of a specific flight maneuver, such as turns around a point or S-turns across the road until the maneuver can be consistently accomplished in a safe and effective manner within a specified limit of heading, altitude, and airspeed. At the end of this lesson, the student is only capable of practicing the maneuver with assistance from the instructor.

The traditional type of training lesson plan with its focus on the task and maneuver or procedure continues to meet many aviation learning requirements, but as discussed earlier in the chapter, it is being augmented by more realistic and fluid forms of problem-based learning such as SBT. For the CFI, this type of training does not preclude traditional maneuver-based training. Rather, flight maneuvers are integrated into the flight scenarios and conducted as they would occur in the real world. Those maneuvers requiring repetition are still taught during concentrated settings; once learned, they are then integrated into realistic flight situations.

For the aviation technician instructor, SBT enhances traditional classroom instruction. By integrating SBT into the lesson, students are required to deal with problems they will encounter in the real world.

Scenario-Based Training (SBT)

Improper pilot decisions cause a significant percentage of all accidents and the majority of fatal accidents in light single- and twin-engine aircraft. The goal of SBT is to challenge the student or transitioning pilot with a variety of flight scenarios to improve decision-making skills. These scenarios require the pilot to manage the resources available in the flight deck, exercise sound judgment, and make timely decisions.

As defined in chapter 4, SBT is a training method that uses a highly structured script of real world experiences to address aviation training objectives in an operational environment. Such training can include initial training, transition training, upgrade training, recurrent training, and special training. Since humans develop cognitive skills through active interaction with the world, an effective aviation instructor uses the maneuver- or procedure-based approach of the PTS but presents the objectives in a scenario situation.

Although some CFIs have used the SBT approach as a teaching method for many years, the recent emphasis on SBT in aviation training reflects education research that shows students learn more effectively when actively involved in the learning process. The introduction of advanced avionics is also a factor. Advanced avionics have changed the role of general aviation (GA) from an industry dominated by pleasure flying to a viable alternative to the scheduled airlines. With glass displays, GPS, and autopilot, advanced avionics may allow easier and safer operation, but are more complex.

Advanced avionics have contributed to a shift in the focus of aviation training to include aeronautical decision-making (ADM) and risk management. For the pilot, this is called Single-Pilot Resource Management (SRM). Since SRM training requires the student or transitioning pilot to practice the decision-making process in real-world situations, it combines traditional task and maneuver-based training with SBT to enhance ADM, risk management, and SRM skills without compromising basic stick and rudder skills. Instead of training pilots to pass practical tests, this program focuses on expertly managed real-world challenges.

Duties, Responsibilities, and Authority of the Aviation Instructor

The duties, responsibilities, and authority of the aviation instructor include the following:

1. Orient new learners to the SBT approach.
2. Help the learner become a confident planner and a critical evaluator of his or her own performance.
3. Help the learner understand the knowledge requirements present in real world applications.
4. Diagnose learning difficulties and help the individual overcome them.

5. Evaluate student progress and maintain appropriate records.
6. Provide continuous review of student learning.

The aviation instructor is the key to the success of SBT. Remember, the overall learning objective is for the student to be ready to exercise sound judgment and make good decisions. For example, the flight instructor must be ready to turn the responsibility for planning and execution of the flight over to the student as soon as possible. The flight instructor continues to demonstrate and instruct skill maneuvers in the traditional manner; but, when the student begins to make decisions, the flight instructor should revert to the role of mentor and/or learning facilitator.

A situation a student faces may not have one right or one wrong answer. Instead, a student encounters situations in training that may have several "good" outcomes and few "poor" ones. Rather than requiring the student to make a decision that matches the instructor's personal preference, he or she should understand in advance which outcomes are positive and/or negative and give the student the freedom to make both good and poor decisions. This does not mean that the student should be allowed to make an unsafe decision or commit an unsafe act. However, it does allow the student to make decisions that fit his or her experience level and result in positive outcomes.

SBT Lesson Plan

The SBT lesson plan differs from the traditional lesson plan. *[Figure 6-8]* In this example, the instructor pilot tells the student to plan for arrival at a specific nontowered airport. The planning should take into consideration the possible wind conditions, arrival paths, airport information and communication procedures, available runways, recommended traffic patterns, courses of action, and preparation for unexpected situations. Upon arrival at the airport, the student makes decisions (with guidance and feedback, as necessary) to safely enter and fly the traffic pattern. This is followed by a discussion of what was done, why it was done, the consequences, other possible courses of action, and how it applies to other airports. In contrast to the student who trained under the traditional lesson plan, the student who trains under the SBT format is not only capable of a specific flight maneuver, he or she is now capable of detailing the safe arrival at any nontowered airport in any wind condition.

Scenario-Based Training Lesson Plan

TYPE OF TRAINING
Initial

MANEUVER OR TRAINING OBJECTIVE
Plan for arrival at a specific nontowered airport.

SCENARIO
Prepare to fly to the Enterprise Municipal Airport (EDN) in order to visit the Army Aviation Museum at Fort Rucker.

COMPLETION STANDARDS
The student is capable of explaining the safe arrival at any nontowered airport in any wind condition.

POSSIBLE HAZARDS OR CONSIDERATIONS
- Ground-based obstructions/hazards
- Winds conditions
- Visibility/ceiling
- Engine-out procedures
- Airport traffic

MITIGATION STRATEGIES AND RESOURCES **(Every hazard or consideration should be addressed through the use of some mitigating strategy or resource. Those provided below serve only as an example to illustrate the system safety methodology.)**

Ground-based obstructions/hazards:
The instructor and student will review all available resources, including sectional/terminal area charts, A/FD, and Notices To Airmen (NOTAMs). Using aircraft performance data found in the POH/FM, the potential impact of any obstructions or hazards during departure, en route, and arrival will be assessed and a strategy developed to address any concerns.

Wind conditions:
The instructor and student will use the aircraft POH/FM and assess the runway environment prior to making a determination. This would also be an excellent catalyst for a discussion of personal minimums and any additional training requirements.

Visibility/ceiling:
The instructor and student will discuss the impact of visibility/ceiling as it relates to departure, en route, and landing at an nontowered airport in various wind conditions. For example, if circumstances demand the conduct of a circling approach under marginal VFR conditions, does the student have the confidence and proficiency to fly a tight pattern while managing airspeed, aircraft coordination, etc? Under such circumstances, would it be more desirable to conduct a straight-in approach with a slight tailwind (if that is even an option)? How much wind would be too much? What other variables/options should be considered (perhaps a diversion to a more suitable airport)?

Engine-out procedures:
Should an engine fail or partial loss of power occur, the student and instructor should discuss and simulate in a manner consistent with safety, engine-out procedures as part of a comprehensive training program.

Airport traffic:
Traffic at both towered and nontowered airports often necessitates wide variations in landing patterns. While issues stemming from airport traffic may largely be addressed through sound flying technique, the instructor can take an otherwise routine lesson and introduce other risk elements, thus promoting the student's development of critical decision-making skills.

FLY THE SCENARIO

POSTFLIGHT REVIEW
This review should include a dialogue between the instructor pilot and the student or transitioning pilot encompassing the flight scenario. Generally, the instructor pilot should lead the discussion with questions that generate reflective thinking on how the overall flight went. The instructor pilot should use this to assist in evaluating the student or transitioning pilot's assessment skills, judgment, and decision-making skills. Typically, the discussion should begin with student self-critique; the instructor pilot enables the student to solve the problems and draw conclusions. Based on this analysis, the student and instructor pilot should discuss methods for improvement, even on those items that were considered successful.

Figure 6-8. *SBT lesson plan.*

Prescenario Planning

For SBT instruction to be effective, it is vital that the aviation instructor and student establish the following information:

Flight scenario:

- Scenario destination(s)
- Desired student learning outcomes
- Desired level of student performance
- Possible inflight scenario changes

Nonflight scenario:

- Narrative of the task goal
- Desired student learning outcomes
- Desired level of student performance
- Possible scenario changes

The aviation industry is moving from traditional knowledge-related learning outcomes to an emphasis on increased internalized learning in which learners assess situations and react appropriately. Knowledge components are becoming an important side effect of a dynamic learning experience.

Reality is the ultimate learning situation and SBT attempts to get as close as possible to this ideal. It addresses learning that occurs in a context or situation. It is based on the concept of situated cognition, which is the idea that knowledge cannot be known and fully understood independent of its context. In other words, humans learn better, the more realistic the situation is and the more they are counted on to perform.

For example, realistic cross-country flight scenarios planned and executed by the pilot in training with assistance from the flight instructor begin the early development of flight deck management skills, situational awareness, and ADM. Continued engagement by the student in the planning, executing, and assessment of each scenario reinforces it throughout the training. It is important to remember the student is responsible for planning the flight scenario from a menu of short cross-country flights developed by the training provider. While the flight instructor will certainly assist the student in aircraft performance data, weight and balance, and general aircraft layout prior to the first lesson, the sooner the student assumes these responsibilities, the better the learning environment. The scenario descriptions offered in the FAA generic syllabi are a starting point for the training provider. Scenarios can be tailored for the local weather and terrain conditions and are most effective when they replicate the environment most likely encountered by the students.

SBT is a compilation of basic learning theory, adult learning concepts, and the best of the traditional aviation training procedures. Above all, it is about learning complex tasks in a realistic environment at a pace and in a structure the individual student can comprehend and process. *[Figure 6-9]* Good teaching techniques are still important, but only if they aid in student learning. More detailed information about SBT can be found at www.faa.gov/education_research/training/fits/.

The Main Points To Remember About Scenario-Based Training

- SBT is situated in a real context and is based on the idea that knowledge cannot be gained and fully integrated independent of its context.
- SBT accords with a performance improvement and behavior change philosophy of the learning function.
- SBT is different from traditional instructional design; one must be aware of the differences to successfully employ SBT.
- Most learning solutions should employ both traditional training and SBT.
- Traditional learning elements should enhance the SBT elements.
- It is essential to place boundaries around scenarios to make the transitions between scenarios and traditional learning as efficient as possible.
- Open-ended qualitative learner feedback is key to successful scenario revision, but revisions should not further complicate the scenario unless highly justified.

Figure 6-9. *Points to remember about scenario-based training.*

Single-Pilot Resource Management

SRM is the art and science of managing all the resources (both on-board the aircraft and from outside sources) available to a single pilot (prior and during flight) to ensure that the successful outcome of the flight is never in doubt.

The emergence of very light jet (VLJ) aircraft will revolutionize the way America travels. *[Figure 6-10]* Central to their economic success is the concept of single-pilot operations. Since the aircraft is heavily automated, the pilot's workload may actually be less than the current workload in a high performance single-engine aircraft of today. This allows more time for the pilot to gather and analyze information about weather, winds, landing conditions, fuel state, pilot physical condition, and passenger desires.

Figure 6-10. *Very light jet aircraft in flight.*

However, unless the pilot is trained to manage all of these factors and to let the aircraft automation assist, the workload may be very high. SRM training helps the pilot maintain situational awareness by managing the automation and associated aircraft control and navigation tasks. This enables the pilot to accurately assess, manage risk, and make accurate and timely decisions. SBT enhances SRM because SBT helps pilots learn how to gather information, analyze it, and make decisions.

Chapter Summary

As indicated by this chapter, it is possible to develop well-planned and organized instruction by using a training syllabus and lesson plans that meet all regulatory certification requirements. By identifying and incorporating "blocks of learning" into the teaching of objectives, the instructor can plan lessons that build on prior knowledge. Maneuver and/or procedure training coupled with SBT will help the aviation instructor train professional aviators and technicians who are able to gather and analyze information to aid in making good aeronautical decisions and decrease risk factors, leading to a successful flight or maintenance outcome.

As this training program evolves and new resources are introduced, aviation instructors will have immediate, web-based access to documents such as the generic transition syllabus through http://www.faa.gov/.

Another helpful website for SBT is:
www.faa.gov/education_research/training/fits/training/flight_instructor/media/Volume1.pdf

Chapter 7

Instructor Responsibilities and Professionalism

Introduction

Since students look to aviation instructors as authorities in their respective areas, it is important that instructors not only know how to teach, but that they project a knowledgeable and professional image. This chapter addresses the responsibilities of aviation instructors in the training process and role as safety advocates, discusses how aviation instructors can enhance their professional image, and offers suggestions and sources of information to assist in professional development.

Responsibilities of All Aviation Instructors

- Helping Students Learn
- Providing Adequate Instruction
- Demanding Adequate Standards of Performance
- Emphasizing the Positive
- Ensuring Safety of Flight

Additional Responsibilities of Flight Instr

- Evaluation of Student Piloting Ability
- Pilot Supervision
- Practical Test Recommendations
- Flight Instructor Endorsements
- Additional Training and Endorsements
- Pilot Proficiency
- See and Avoid Responsibility
- Student's Pre-solo Flight Thought Process

Special Emphasis Areas

- Positive aircraft control
- Procedures for positive exchange of flight
- Stall and spin awareness (if appropriate)
- Collision avoidance
- Wake turbulence and low level wind shear avoidance
- Runway incursion avoidance
- Controlled flight into terrain (CFIT)
- ADM/risk management
- Checklist usage
- Spatial disorientation
- Temporary flight restrictions (TFR)
- Special use airspace (SUA)
- Aviation security
- Wire strike avoidance
- Other areas deemed appropriate to any phase of the practical test or proficiency check

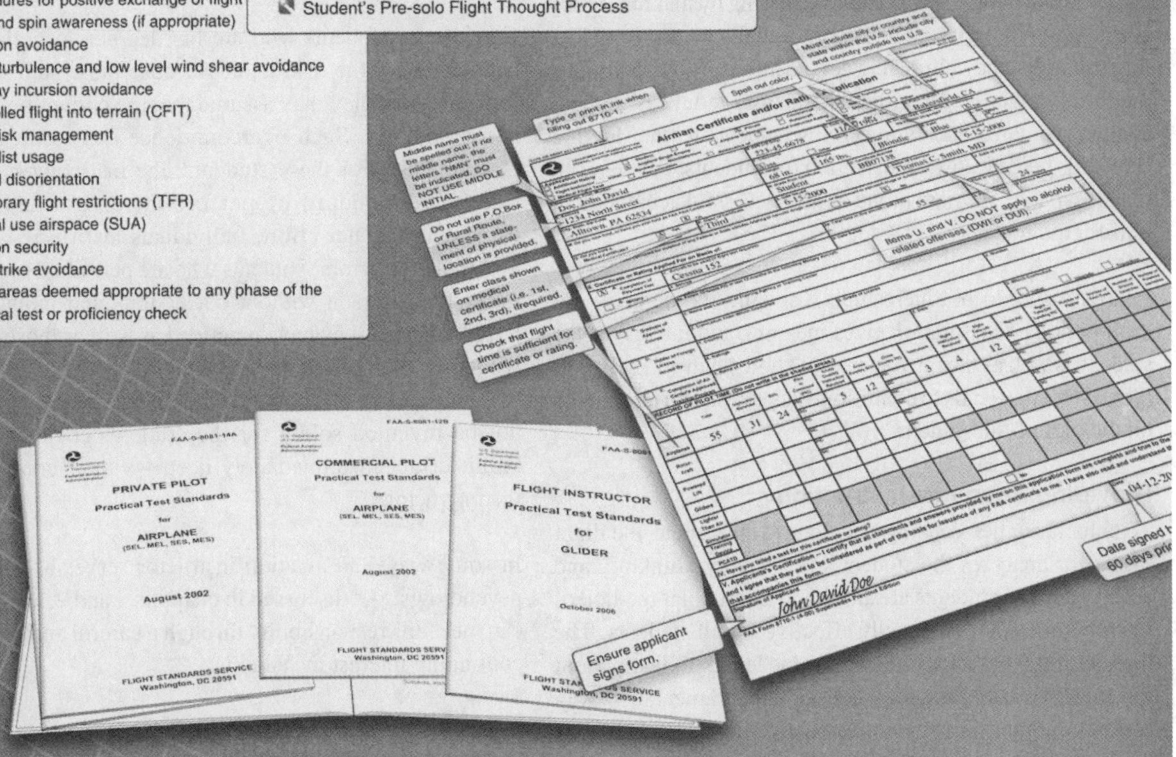

Aviation Instructor Responsibilities

The job of an aviation instructor is to teach. Previous chapters have discussed how people learn, the teaching process, and teaching methods. As indicated, the learning process can be made easier by helping students learn, providing adequate instruction to meet established standards, measuring student performance against those standards, and emphasizing the positive. *[Figure 7-1]*

Responsibilities of All Aviation Instructors

- Helping students learn
- Providing adequate instruction
- Demanding adequate standards of performance
- Emphasizing the positive
- Ensuring aviation safety

Figure 7-1. *There are five main responsibilities of aviation instructors.*

Helping Students Learn

Learning should be an enjoyable experience. By making each lesson a pleasurable experience for the student, the instructor can maintain a high level of student motivation. This does not mean the instructor makes things easy for the student or sacrifices standards of performance to please the student. The student experiences satisfaction from doing a good job or from successfully meeting the challenge of a difficult task.

The idea that people must be led to learning by making it easy is a fallacy. Though students might initially be drawn to less difficult tasks, they ultimately devote more effort to activities that bring rewards. The use of standards, and measurement against standards, is key to helping students learn. Meeting standards holds its own satisfaction for students. People want to feel capable; they are proud of the successful achievement of difficult goals.

Learning should be interesting. Knowing the objective of each period of instruction gives meaning and interest to the student as well as the instructor. Not knowing the objective of the lesson often leads to confusion, disinterest, and uneasiness on the part of the student.

Providing Adequate Instruction

To tailor his or her teaching technique to the student, the flight instructor analyzes the student's personality, thinking, and ability. No two students are alike, and a particular method of instruction cannot be equally effective for all students. The instructor talks with a student at some length to learn about the student's background, interests, temperament, and way of thinking, and is prepared to change his or her methods of instruction as the student advances through successive stages of training.

An instructor who incorrectly analyzes a student may find the instruction does not produce the desired results. For example, the instructor at first thinks the student is not a quick learner because that student is quiet and reserved. Such a student may fail to act at the proper time due to lack of self-confidence, even though the situation is correctly understood. In this case, instruction is directed toward developing student self-confidence, rather than drill on flight fundamentals. In another case, too much criticism may discourage a timid person, whereas brisk instruction may force a more diligent application to the learning task. A student requiring more time to learn also requires instructional methods that combine tact, keen perception, and delicate handling. If such a student receives too much help and encouragement, a feeling of incompetence may develop.

A student whose slow progress is due to discouragement and a lack of confidence should be assigned subgoals that can be attained more easily than the usual learning goals. For this purpose, complex lessons can be separated into elements, and each element practiced until an acceptable performance is achieved before the whole maneuver or operation is attempted. For example, instruction in S-turns may begin with consideration for headings only. Elements of altitude control, drift correction, and coordination can be introduced one at a time. As the student gains confidence and ability, goals are increased in difficulty until progress is normal.

Conversely, students who are fast learners can also create challenges for the instructor. Because these students make few mistakes, they may assume that the correction of errors is unimportant. Such overconfidence can result in faulty performance. For these students, the instructor constantly raises the standard of performance for each lesson, demanding greater effort. Individuals learn when they are aware of their errors. Students who are permitted to complete every flight lesson without corrections and guidance will not retain what they have practiced as well as those students who have their attention constantly directed to an analysis of their performance. On the other hand, deficiencies should not be invented solely for the students' benefit because unfair criticism immediately destroys their confidence in the instructor.

In some ways, an aviation instructor serves as a practical psychologist. As discussed in chapters 1 and 2, an instructor can meet this responsibility through a careful analysis of and continuing interest in students.

Most new instructors tend to adopt the teaching methods used by their own instructors. The fact that one has learned under a certain system of instruction does not mean that the instructor, though well respected by the former student, used the best method. The new instructor needs to continue to grow in his or her role of instructor, seeking other resources and information to enhance his or her own teaching skills.

Standards of Performance

An aviation instructor is responsible for training an applicant to acceptable standards in all subject matter areas, procedures, and maneuvers included in the tasks within each area of operation in the appropriate Practical Test Standard (PTS). It must be emphasized that the PTS book is a testing document, not a teaching document. *[Figure 7-2]*

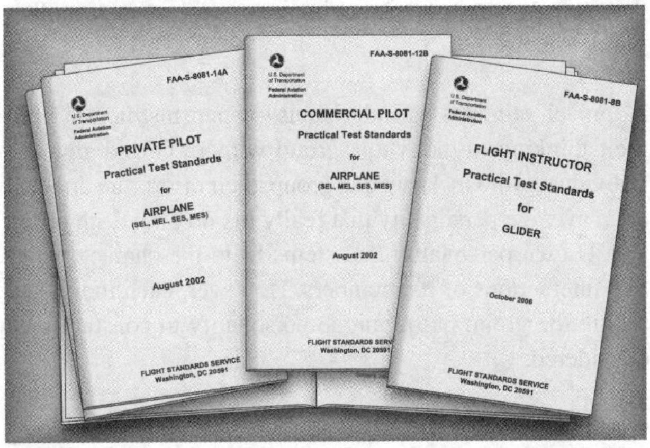

Figure 7-2. *Acceptable standards in all subject matter areas, procedures, and maneuvers are included in the appropriate Practical Test Standards.*

When teaching a particular procedure, an instructor might be tempted to point out the consequences of doing it differently, perhaps telling the student that failure to perform the procedure as taught will court disaster. The instructor may believe this "consequence approach" is necessary to ensure the student commits the procedure to memory, but the stated reasons for performing the procedure a certain way must contribute to the learning situation to be effective.

Emphasizing the Positive

Aviation instructors have a tremendous influence on a student's perception of aviation. The way instructors conduct themselves, the attitudes they display, and the manner in which they develop instruction all contribute to the formation of either positive or negative impressions by students. The success of an aviation instructor depends greatly on his or her ability to present instruction in a manner that gives students a positive image of aviation. *[Figure 7-3]*

Figure 7-3. *Students learn more when instruction is presented in a positive and professional manner.*

Chapter 1, Human Behavior, emphasized that a negative self-concept inhibits the perceptual process, that fear adversely affects student perceptions, that the feeling of being threatened limits the ability to perceive, and that negative motivation is not as effective as positive motivation. Merely knowing about these factors is not enough. Instructors must be able to detect these factors in their students and strive to prevent negative feelings from undermining the instructional process.

Consider how the following scenarios conducted during the first lesson might influence and impress a new student pilot who has limited or no aviation experience:

- An indoctrination in preflight procedures with emphasis on the critical precautions which must be taken before every flight because "… emergencies in flight can be caused by an improper preflight and are often disastrous."
- Instruction and hands-on training in the care that must be taken in taxiing an airplane because "… if you go too fast, you may lose directional control of the aircraft."
- Introduction and demonstration of stalls, because "… this is how so many people lose their lives in airplanes."
- Illustrating and demonstrating forced landings during the first lesson, because "… one should always be prepared to cope with a rope break in a glider."

These new experiences might make the new student wonder if learning to fly is a good idea.

In contrast, consider a first flight lesson in which the preflight inspection is presented to familiarize the student with the aircraft and its components, and the flight is a perfectly normal one to a nearby airport, with return. Following the flight, the instructor can call the student's attention to the ease with which the trip was made in comparison with other modes of transportation, and the fact that no critical incidents were encountered or expected.

This does not mean stalls and emergency procedures should be omitted from training. It only illustrates the positive approach in which the student is not overwhelmed with information that he or she may not be prepared to digest. Again, this reinforces the need for the instructor to employ a syllabus that makes sense and consider student ability to comprehend new information. The introduction of emergency procedures after the student has developed an acquaintance with normal operations is not as likely to be discouraging and frightening, or to inhibit learning by the imposition of fear.

There is nothing in aviation that demands that students must suffer as part of their instruction. Every effort should be made to ensure instruction is given under positive conditions that reinforce training conducted to standard and modification of the method of instruction when students have difficulty grasping a task. In essence, a student's failure to perform is viewed as an instructor's inability to transfer the information. Otherwise, the instructor fails to consider himself or herself as part of a broken learning chain. Emphasize the positive because positive instruction results in positive learning.

Minimizing Student Frustrations

Minimizing student frustrations in the classroom, shop, or during flight training is an instructor's responsibility. By following basic rules, instructors can reduce student frustrations and create a learning environment that encourages rather than discourages learning.

For example, lesson plans used as part of an organized curriculum help the student pilot measure training progress. Since most pilots don't want to be students, the ability to measure their progress or "see an end in sight" reduces frustration and increases pilot motivation. *[Figure 7-4]*

Minimizing Student Frustration

- Motivate students
- Keep students informed
- Approach students as individuals
- Give credit when due
- Criticize constructively
- Be consistent
- Admit errors

Figure 7-4. *These are practical ways to minimize student frustration.*

Motivate students—more can be gained from wanting to learn than from being forced to learn. Too often, students do not realize how a particular lesson or course can help them reach an important goal. When students can see the benefits and purpose of the lesson or course, their enjoyment and their efforts increase.

Keep students informed—students feel insecure when they do not know what is expected of them or what is going to happen to them. Instructors can minimize feelings of insecurity by telling students what is expected of them and what they can expect in return. Instructors keep students informed in various ways, including giving them an overview of the course, keeping them posted on their progress, and giving them adequate notice of examinations, assignments, or other requirements.

Approach students as individuals—when instructors limit their thinking to the whole group without considering the individuals who make up that group, their efforts are directed at an average personality that really fits no one. Each group has its own personality that stems from the characteristics and interactions of its members. However, each individual within the group has a unique personality to constantly be considered.

Give credit when due—when students do something extremely well, they normally expect their abilities and efforts to be noticed. Otherwise, they may become frustrated. Praise or credit from the instructor is usually ample reward and provides an incentive to do even better. Praise pays dividends in student effort and achievement when deserved, but when given too freely, it becomes valueless.

Criticize constructively—although it is important to give praise and credit when deserved, it is equally important to identify mistakes and failures. It does not help to tell students they have made errors and not provide explanations. If a student has made an earnest effort but is told that the work is unsatisfactory, with no other explanation, frustration occurs. Errors cannot be corrected if they are not identified, and if they are not identified, they will probably be perpetuated through faulty practice. On the other hand, if the student is briefed on the errors and is told how to correct them, progress can be made.

Be consistent—students want to please their instructor. This is the same desire that influences much of the behavior of subordinates toward their superiors in industry and business. Naturally, students have a keen interest in knowing what is required to please the instructor. If the same thing is acceptable one day and unacceptable the next, the student becomes confused. The instructor's philosophy and actions must be consistent.

Admit errors—no one, including students, expects an instructor to be perfect. The instructor can win the respect of students by honestly acknowledging mistakes. If the instructor tries to cover up or bluff, students are quick to sense it. Such behavior tends to destroy student confidence in the instructor. If in doubt about some point, the instructor should admit it.

Flight Instructor Responsibilities

Learning to fly should provide students with an opportunity for exploration and experimentation. It should be a habit-building period during which students devote their attention, memory, and judgment to the development of correct habit patterns. All aviation instructors shoulder an enormous responsibility because their students will ultimately be flying, servicing, or repairing aircraft, but flight instructors have the additional responsibilities of evaluating student pilots and making a decision of when they are ready to solo. The flight instructor's job is to "mold" the student pilot into a safe pilot who takes a professional approach to flying. Other flight instructor responsibilities can be found in Title 14 of the Code of Federal Regulations (14 CFR) part 61 and FAA advisory circulars (ACs). *[Figure 7-5]*

Additional Responsibilities of Flight Instructors

- Evaluation of student piloting ability
- Pilot supervision
- Practical test recommendations
- Flight instructor endorsements
- Additional training and endorsements
- Pilot proficiency
- See and avoid responsibility
- Student's pre-solo flight thought process

Figure 7-5. *The flight instructor has many additional responsibilities.*

Flight instructors must provide the most comprehensive ground and flight instruction possible. They should be current and proficient in the aircraft they use for flight instruction, encouraging each pilot to learn as much as he or she can and to continually "raise the bar." Flight instructors have the responsibility of producing the safest pilots possible with the overall focus on education and learning. It is also important to convey an understanding of why pilots are trained to standards and how they are set.

Instructors should not introduce the minimum acceptable standards for passing the check ride when introducing lesson tasks. The minimum standards to pass the check ride should be introduced during the "3 hours of preparation" for the check ride. Keep the PTS in the proper perspective, with emphasis on the Practical Test Standard (PTS) increasing later in the training.

Physiological Obstacles for Flight Students

Although most student pilots have been exposed to air travel, they may not have flown in light, training aircraft. Consequently, students may react to unfamiliar noises or vibrations, or experience unfamiliar sensations due to G-force, or an uncomfortable feeling in the stomach. To teach effectively, instructors cannot ignore the existence of these negative factors, nor should they ridicule students who are adversely affected. These negative sensations can usually be overcome by understanding the nature of their causes. Remember, a sick student does not learn well.

Ensuring Student Skill Set

Flight instructors must ensure student pilots develop the required skills and knowledge prior to solo flight. The student pilot must show consistency in the required solo tasks: takeoffs and landings, ability to prioritize in maintaining control of the aircraft, proper navigation skills, proficiency in flight, proper radio procedures and communication skills, and traffic pattern operation. Student pilots should receive instruction to ask for assistance or help from the ATC system when needed.

Mastery of the skill set includes consistent use and continued growth as well as increased accuracy of performance. The instructor determines when a student is ready for his or her first solo flight. Generally this determination is made when the instructor observes the student from preflight to engine start to engine shutdown and the student performs consistently, without need of instructor assistance.

Flight instructors need to provide adequate flight and ground instruction for "special emphasis" items listed in each PTS for airplane, helicopter, and light sport aircraft. The student needs to be knowledgeable in these special emphasis areas because examiners and authorized instructors place special emphasis upon areas considered critical to flight safety. Special emphasis items include, but are not limited to:

1. Positive aircraft control
2. Procedures for positive exchange of flight controls
3. Stall and spin awareness (if appropriate)
4. Collision avoidance
5. Wake turbulence and low-level wind turbulence and wind shear avoidance
6. Runway incursion avoidance

7. Controlled flight into terrain (CFIT)
8. Aeronautical decision-making (ADM)/risk management
9. Checklist usage
10. Spatial disorientation
11. Temporary flight restrictions (TFR)
12. Special use airspace (SUA)
13. Aviation security
14. Wire strike avoidance

Flight instructors should be current on the latest procedures regarding pilot training, certification, and safety. It is the flight instructor's responsibility to maintain a current library of information. These sources are listed in the appropriate PTS, and other sources can be located on the Internet at www.faa.gov and www.faasafety.gov. The FAA website provides comprehensive information to pilots and instructors. Other aviation organizations also have excellent information. However, an instructor is bound to follow any procedures in the manner prescribed by the FAA. If an instructor needs any assistance, he or she should contact a more experienced instructor, an FAA Designated Pilot Examiner (DPE), or the local Flight Standards District Office (FSDO).

Aviator's Model Code of Conduct

The Aviator's Model Code of Conduct presents broad guidance and recommendations for General Aviation (GA) pilots to improve airmanship, flight safety, and to sustain and improve the GA community. The Code of Conduct presents a vision of excellence in GA aviation. Its principles both complement and supplement what is merely legal. The Code of Conduct is not a "standard" and is not intended to be implemented as such. The code of conduct consists of the following seven sections:

1. General Responsibilities of Aviators
2. Passengers and People on the Surface
3. Training and Proficiency
4. Security
5. Environmental Issues
6. Use of Technology
7. Advancement and Promotion of General Aviation

Each section provides flight instructors a list of principles and sample recommended practices. Successful instructor pilots continue to self-evaluate and find ways to make themselves safer and more productive instructors. The Aviator's Model Code of Conduct provides guidance and principles for the instructor to integrate into their own practices. More information about the Aviator's Model Code of Conduct can be found at www.secureav.com.

Safety Practices and Accident Prevention

Aviation instructors are on the front line of efforts to improve the safety record of the aviation industry. Safety, one of the most fundamental considerations in aviation training, is paramount. FAA regulations intended to promote safety by eliminating or mitigating conditions that can cause death, injury, or damage are comprehensive, but even the strictest compliance with regulations may not be sufficient to guarantee safety. Rules and regulations are designed to address known or suspected conditions detrimental to safety, but there is always a chance that some new combination of circumstances not contemplated by the regulations will arise. It is important for aviation instructors to be proactive to ensure the safety of flight or maintenance training activities.

The safety practices aviation instructors emphasize have a long-lasting effect on students. Generally, students consider their instructor to be a role model whose habits they attempt to imitate, whether consciously or unconsciously. The instructor's advocacy and description of safety practices mean little to a student if the instructor does not demonstrate them consistently. For example, if a maintenance student observes the instructor violating safety practices by not wearing safety glasses around hazardous equipment, the student probably will not be conscientious about using safety equipment when the instructor is not around. One of the best actions a flight or maintenance instructor can take to enhance aviation safety is to emphasize safety by example.

Another way for the instructor to advocate safety is to join the new FAA Safety Team (FAASTeam). The FAASTeam is dedicated to improving the aviation safety record by conveying safety principles and practices through training, outreach, and education. More information is available at FAASafety.gov.

Professionalism

The aviation instructor is the central figure in aviation training and is responsible for all phases of required training. The instructor, either pilot or aircraft maintenance technician, must be a professional. As professionals, aviation instructors strive to maintain the highest level of knowledge, training, and currency in the field of aviation. To achieve this goal, instructors need to commit themselves to continuous, lifelong learning and professional development through study, service, and membership in professional organizations such as the National Association of Flight Instructors (NAFI) and Professional Aviation Mechanics Association (PAMA). Professionals build a library of resources that keeps them in touch with their field through the most current procedures, publications, and educational opportunities. Being a professional also means behaving in a professional manner. *[Figure 7-6]* An aviation instructor should strive to practice the characteristics on the Instructor Do's list when teaching a student.

Instructor Do's

- Be professional at all times.
- Be sincere.
- Present a professional appearance and personal habits.
- Maintain a calm demeanor.
- Practice safety and accident prevention at all times.
- Avoid profanity.
- Define common terms.
- Continue professional development.
- Minimize student frustration.
- Motivate the student.
- Keep the student informed.
- Approach each student as an individual.
- Give credit when due.
- Criticize constructively.
- Be consistent.
- Admit errors.

Instructor Don'ts

- Ridicule the student's performance.
- Use profanity.
- Model irresponsible flight behaviors.
- Say one thing but do another.
- Forget personal hygiene.
- Disrespect the student.
- Demand unreasonable progress.
- Forget the student is new to aviation jargon.
- Set the student up for failure.
- Correct errors without an explanation of what went wrong.

Figure 7-6. *Guidelines for an aviation instructor.*

Sincerity

An aviation instructor should be straightforward and honest. Attempting to hide inadequacy behind a smokescreen of unrelated instruction makes it impossible for the instructor to command the respect and full attention of a student. Teaching an aviation student is based upon acceptance of the instructor as a competent, qualified teacher and an expert pilot or aircraft maintenance technician. Any facade of instructor pretentiousness, whether it is real or mistakenly presumed by the student, causes the student to lose confidence in the instructor, and learning is adversely affected.

Acceptance of the Student

The instructor must accept students as they are, including all their faults and problems. The student is a person who wants to learn, and the instructor is a person who is available to help in the learning process. Beginning with this understanding, the professional relationship of the instructor with the student should be based on a mutual acknowledgement that the student and the instructor are important to each other, and that both are working toward the same objective.

Under no circumstance should the instructor do anything which implies degrading the student. Acceptance (rather than ridicule) and support (rather than reproof) encourage learning. Students must be treated with respect, regardless of whether they are quick to learn or require more time to absorb certain concepts. Criticizing a student who does not learn rapidly is similar to a doctor reprimanding a patient who does not get well as rapidly as predicted.

Personal Appearance and Habits

Personal appearance has an important effect on the professional image of the instructor. Today's aviation customer expects an instructor to be neat, clean, and appropriately dressed. Since the instructor is engaged in a learning situation, the attire worn should be appropriate to professional status. *[Figure 7-7]*

Figure 7-7. *The aviation instructor should always present a professional appearance.*

Personal habits have a significant effect on the professional image. The exercise of common courtesy is perhaps the most important of these. An instructor who is rude, thoughtless, and inattentive cannot hold the respect of a student, regardless of the instructor's ability as a pilot or aviation maintenance technician. Personal cleanliness is important to aviation instruction. Frequently, an instructor and a student work in close proximity, and even little annoyances such as body odor or bad breath can cause serious distractions from learning the tasks at hand.

Demeanor

The attitude and behavior of the instructor can contribute much to a professional image. The instructor should avoid erratic movements, distracting speech habits, and capricious changes in mood. The professional image requires development of a calm, thoughtful, and disciplined demeanor.

The successful instructor avoids contradictory directions, reacting differently to similar or identical errors at different times, demanding unreasonable performance or progress, or criticizing a student unfairly, and presenting an overbearing manner or air of flippancy. Effective instruction is best conducted in a calm, pleasant, thoughtful manner that puts the student at ease. The instructor must constantly demonstrate competence in the subject matter and genuine interest in the student's well being.

Proper Language

In aviation instruction, as in other professional activities, the use of profanity and obscene language leads to distrust or, at best, to a lack of complete confidence in the instructor. Many people object to such language. The professional instructor speaks normally, without inhibitions, and speaks positively and descriptively, without profanity.

Evaluation of Student Ability

Evaluation of a student's ability is an important element of instruction. Used in this context, evaluation refers to judging a student's ability to perform a maneuver or procedure.

Demonstrated Ability

Evaluation of demonstrated ability during flight or maintenance instruction is based upon established standards of performance, suitably modified to apply to the student's experience and stage of development as a pilot or mechanic. The evaluation considers the student's mastery of the elements involved in the maneuver or procedure, rather than merely the overall performance. For example, qualification of student pilots for solo and solo cross-country privileges depends upon demonstrations of performance.

Keeping the Student Informed

In evaluating student demonstrations of ability, it is important for the aviation instructor to keep the student informed of progress. This may be done as each procedure or maneuver is completed or summarized during a postflight or class critique. These critiques should be in a written format, such as notes, to aid the instructor in covering all areas that were noticed during the flight or lesson. When explaining errors in performance, instructors point out the elements in which the deficiencies are believed to have originated and, if possible, suggest appropriate corrective measures.

Correction of Student Errors

Correction of student errors does not include the practice of taking over from students immediately when a mistake is made. Safety permitting, it is frequently better to let students progress part of the way into the mistake and find a way out. For example, in a weight-shift control aircraft the bar is moved right to turn left. A student may show an initial tendency to move the bar in the direction of the desired turn. This tendency dissipates with time, but allowing the student to see the effect of his or her control input is a valuable aid in illustrating the stability of the aircraft. It is difficult for students to learn a maneuver properly if they seldom have the opportunity to correct an error.

On the other hand, students may perform a procedure or maneuver correctly but not fully understand the principles and objectives involved. If the instructor suspects this, students should be required to vary the performance of the maneuver or procedure slightly. The maneuver or procedure may also be combined with other operations, or the same elements could be applied to the performance of other maneuvers or procedures. Students who do not understand the principles involved will probably not be able to successfully complete the revised maneuver or procedure.

Aviation Instructors and Exams

Knowledge Test

When preparing a student or applicant for the private pilot certification or higher grade rating (i.e., commercial or instrument) a test is required to ensure the student has adequate aeronautical knowledge in those subject areas listed in 14 CFR part 61. The instructor may provide the student with an endorsement to certify he or she has the required knowledge to pass the test. Some additional ratings do not require a test. For information concerning additional aircraft certifications that do not require knowledge tests, refer to AC 61-65, Certification: Pilots and Flight and Ground Instructors. Flight instructors must take a short test for each additional category.

An instructor should remember he or she is held accountable for a deficient instructional performance. This is important for any instructor who signs recommendations for applicants who were not trained by that instructor.

If the applicant fails a test, the aviation instructor must sign the test after he or she has provided additional training in the areas the applicant failed. The applicant is given a retest. Prior to certification, the aviation instructor must make a statement that he or she gave the required training in the preceding 60 days and the instructor reviewed those areas of deficiency on the applicant's knowledge test.

Practical Test

Provision is made on the airman certificate or rating application form for the written recommendation of the flight instructor who has prepared the applicant for the practical test involved. Signing this recommendation imposes a serious responsibility on the flight instructor. A flight instructor who makes a practical test recommendation for an applicant seeking a certificate or rating should require the applicant to thoroughly demonstrate the knowledge and skill level required for that certificate or rating. This demonstration should in no instance be less than the complete procedure prescribed in the applicable PTS.

When the instructor endorses the applicant for the practical test, his or her signature on the FAA form 8710-1 Airman Certificate and/or Rating Application is valid for 60 days. This is also true with the flight proficiency endorsement that is placed in the applicant's logbook or training record (AC-61-65). These two dates should be the same.

Completion of prerequisites for a practical test is another instructor task that must be documented properly. Examples of all common endorsements can be found in the current issue of AC 61-65, appendix 1. This appendix also includes references to 14 CFR part 61 for more details concerning the requirements that must be met to qualify for each respective endorsement. The examples shown contain the essential elements of each endorsement. It is not necessary for all endorsements to be worded exactly as those in the AC. For example, changes to regulatory requirements may affect the wording, or the instructor may customize the endorsement for any special circumstances of the applicant. However, at a minimum, the instructor needs to cite the appropriate 14 CFR part 61 section that has been completed.

If a flight instructor fails to ensure a student pilot or additional rating pilot meets the requirements of regulations prior to making endorsements to allow solo flight or additional rating, that instructor is exhibiting a serious deficiency in performance. The FAA holds him or her accountable. Providing a solo endorsement for a student pilot who is not proficient for solo flight operations, or providing an endorsement for an additional rating for a pilot not meeting the appropriate regulatory requirements, is also a breach of faith with the student or applicant.

Professional Development

Aviation is changing rapidly, and aviation instructors must continue to develop their knowledge and skills in order to teach successfully in this environment. The aviation instructor is well respected by other technicians and pilots because instructors must meet additional training requirements in order to be certificated. Flight instructors undergo comprehensive evaluations and a practical test to obtain a flight instructor certificate. 14 CFR part 147 requires all instructors teaching maintenance subjects to hold an FAA certificate as an aircraft maintenance technician.

Successful, professional aviation instructors do not become complacent or satisfied with their own qualifications and abilities, and are constantly alert for ways to improve their qualifications, effectiveness, and the services they provide to students. Considered by their students to be a source of up-to-date information, instructors have the opportunity and responsibility of introducing new procedures and techniques both to their students and to other aviation professionals with whom they come in contact.

Continuing Education

A professional aviation instructor continually updates his or her knowledge and skills. This goal is attained in a variety of ways, such as reading an article in a technical publication or taking a course at a technical school. There are many different sources of information the aviation instructor can use in order to remain current in aviation knowledge and teaching.

Government

One of the first educational sources for the instructor is the FAA and other governmental agencies. The FAA either sponsors or collaborates in sponsoring aviation programs, seminars, and workshops for the public. For example, the FAA conducts safety seminars around the country in conjunction with the aviation industry. These seminars, although directed at pilots, can be a useful source of knowledge for aviation instructors.

The FAA is a rich source of information that can be used to enhance an instructor's knowledge. Regulations, advisory circulars, airworthiness directives, orders, and notices are some of the documents that can be downloaded from the FAA website at www.faa.gov.

As mentioned earlier in the chapter, participation in the Pilot Proficiency Awards Program is a good way for a flight instructor to improve proficiency and to serve as an example to students. Another way is to work toward the Gold Seal Flight Instructor Certificate. Accomplishing the requirements of the certificate is evidence the instructor has performed at a very high level as a flight instructor. See AC 61-65, Certification: Pilots and Flight and Ground Instructors, for a list of requirements for earning this certificate.

Similarly, the Aviation Maintenance Awards Program affords the aviation maintenance instructor the opportunity for increased education through attendance at FAA or industry maintenance training seminars. Details for the awarding of bronze through diamond pins can be found in AC 65-25, Aviation Maintenance Technician Awards Program.

The FAA approves the sponsors who conduct Flight Instructor Refresher Clinics (FIRCs) in accordance with AC 61-83. Nationally scheduled FAA-approved industry-conducted Flight Instructor Refresher Clinics (FIRC). These courses are available for flight instructors to complete the training requirements for renewal of flight instructor certificates.

The FAA cosponsors Inspection Authorization (IA) seminars. These seminars are open to all maintenance technicians, and are a good source of additional training and education for maintenance instructors.

Educational/Training Institutions

Professional aviation instructors can further increase their knowledge and skill in aviation specialties by attending classes at local community colleges, technical schools, or universities. These schools may offer complete degree programs in aviation subjects as well as single-subject courses of benefit to instructors.

Commercial Organizations

Commercial organizations are another important source of education/training for the aviation instructor. Some may be publishers of training materials while others may provide complete ground and flight training programs for professional pilots and instructors. These companies often provide a wide variety of study programs including videos, computer-based training, and printed publications. Many offer training that can be attended either at the home base of the company or in traveling classes/seminars so instructors can more easily attend.

There are numerous organizations around the country that offer courses of training for aviation instructors. These are generally courses that are available to all pilots and technicians, but are especially useful for instructors to improve their abilities. Examples of such courses include workshops for maintenance technicians to enhance their skills in subjects such as composites, sheet metal fabrication, and fabric covering. For pilots there are courses in mountain flying, spin training, and tail wheel qualification. Flight instructors also may increase their aviation knowledge and experience by adding additional category and class ratings to their certificates.

Industry Organizations

Other significant sources of ongoing education for aviation instructors are aviation organizations. These organizations not only provide educational articles in their publications, but also present training programs or cosponsor such programs.

Many industry organizations have local affiliated chapters that make it easy to meet other pilots, technicians, and instructors. These meetings frequently include presentations by industry experts, as well as formal training sessions. Some aviation industry organizations conduct their own training sessions on areas such as flight instructor refresher clinics and Inspection Authorization (IA) seminars. Properly organized safety symposiums and training clinics are valuable sources of refresher training. They are also an excellent opportunity to exchange information with other instructors.

Sources of Material

An aviation instructor should maintain access to current flight publications or maintenance publications. For the flight instructor, this includes current copies of regulations pertinent to pilot qualification and certification, Aeronautical Information Manual (AIM), appropriate Practical Test Standards (PTS), and pilot training manuals. The aviation maintenance instructor should have copies of applicable regulations, current knowledge and PTS, and maintenance training manuals. Aviation instructors must be thoroughly familiar with current certification and rating requirements in order to provide competent instruction. AC 00.2-15, Advisory Circular Checklist, is a listing of all current advisory circulars and other FAA publications sold by the Superintendent of Documents, U.S. Government Printing Office (GPO) or available online at www.faa.gov/. Many of the advisory circulars should be considered by the aviation instructor for inclusion in a personal reference library.

In addition to government publications, a number of excellent handbooks and other reference materials are available from commercial publishers. Aviation periodicals and technical journals from the aviation industry are other sources of valuable information for instructors. Many public and institutional libraries have excellent resource material on educational psychology, teaching methods, testing, and other aviation related subjects.

The aviation instructor has two reasons to maintain a source of current information and publications. First, the instructor needs a steady supply of fresh material to make instruction interesting and up to date. Second, instructors should keep themselves well informed by maintaining familiarity with what is being written in current aviation publications. Most of these publications are in printed form, but increasingly, information is available through electronic means. *[Figure 7-8]*

Figure 7-8. *Aviation instructors can improve their knowledge by becoming familiar with information on the Internet.*

Printed Material

In aviation, documentation in the form of flight publications or maintenance data must be immediately available for referral while flying or conducting maintenance. While the portability of printed material meets this need for immediate availability, printed material has two disadvantages. First, it takes up space for storage and second, it can be time consuming to keep printed material current. Many publishers of printed material now make their information available in electronic format. For example, most FAA regulations, standards, and guides are available either in electronic form or as hard copy.

Non-FAA publications are available through the GPO and from the National Technical Information Service (NTIS). Publications not printed by the U.S. Government Printing Office are available from the many publishers and suppliers of books. Commercial publishers usually provide catalogues and toll-free numbers or websites for ordering their products.

Electronic Sources

Access to the Internet via personal computers has opened up a vast storehouse of information for the aviation instructor. In the past, aviation instructors had limited access to information, but the personal computer has greatly expanded sources of aviation information. This section lists some sources of information on the Internet. In the following discussion, several sites for accessing FAA materials are explored, and some non-FAA sites are included. Once instructors begin to navigate the Internet, they find sites which provide the information they use most frequently. Obviously, some FAA publications are more important to the aviation instructor than others. Many of the publications of interest to the aviation instructor can be accessed through the FAA website, www.faa.gov.

The FAA website is not the only source of aviation or education-related information on the Internet. The aviation instructor can access aviation-related publications at other government or non-government websites via published web addresses or by using the search function of the web browser. Keep in mind that most sites on the Internet are updated periodically, but some are not. In addition, new sites are added and old sites are discontinued on a regular basis. The aviation instructor can become more adept at obtaining information by entering and navigating around the Internet to become informed about the contents and how to best locate desired information. The more familiar aviation instructors become with the Internet, the better they are able to adapt to any changes that may occur.

Professional aviation instructors must continue to expand their knowledge and skills in order to be competent instructors. The field of aviation is advancing, and the instructor also must advance. Instructors can best do this by taking advantage of the wide variety of materials available from the FAA, other government agencies, commercial publishers and vendors, and from industry trade groups. These materials are available at training sessions and seminars, from printed books, papers, magazines, and from the Internet and other electronic sources. Instructors who commit to continuing education are able to provide the highest quality instruction to their students.

Chapter Summary

This chapter discussed the responsibilities of aviation instructors to the student, the public, and the FAA in the training process. The additional responsibilities of flight instructors who teach new student pilots as well as rated pilots seeking add-on certification, the role of aviation instructors as safety advocates, and ways in which aviation instructors can enhance their professional image and development were explored.

Chapter 8

Techniques of Flight Instruction

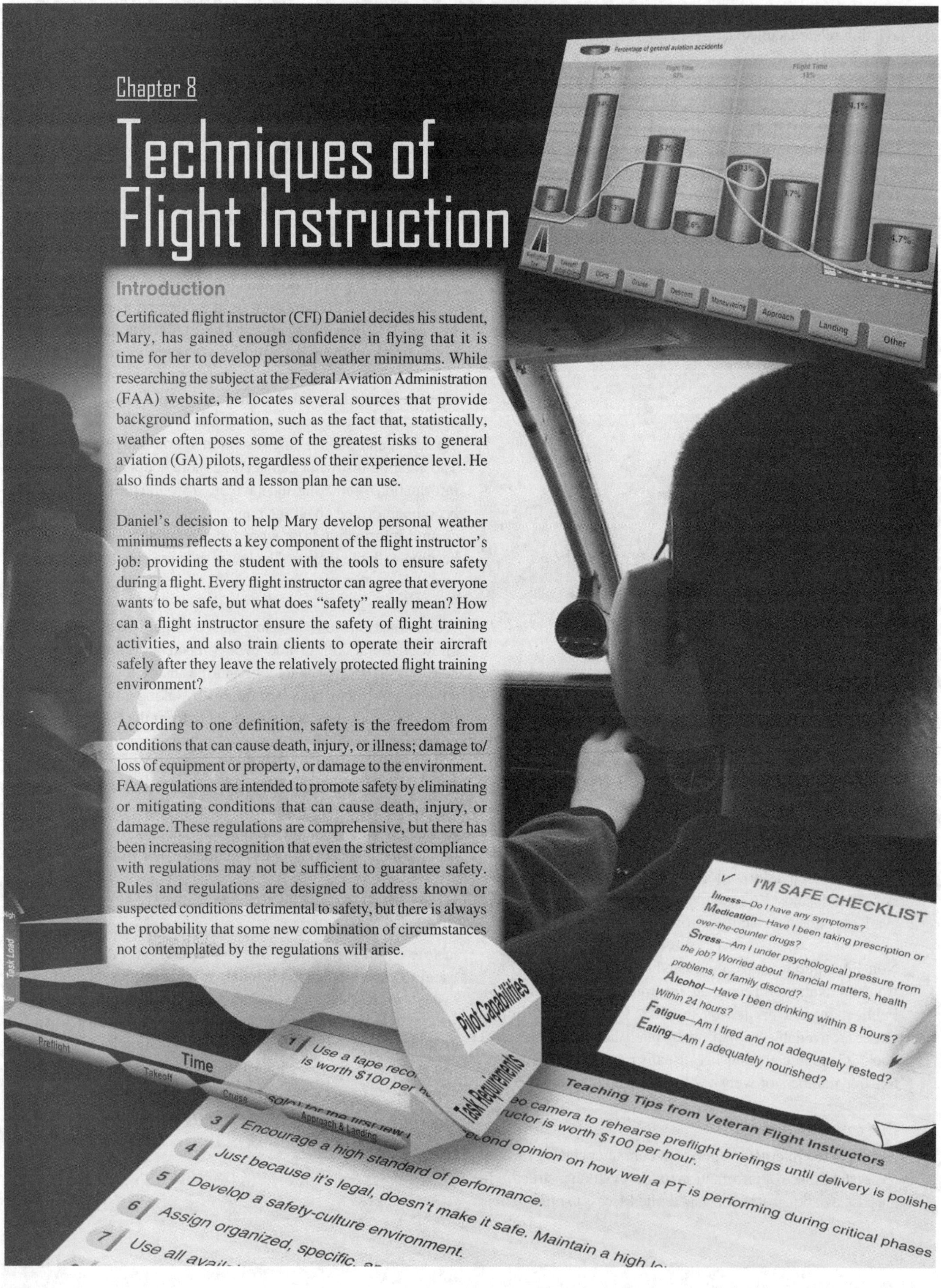

Introduction

Certificated flight instructor (CFI) Daniel decides his student, Mary, has gained enough confidence in flying that it is time for her to develop personal weather minimums. While researching the subject at the Federal Aviation Administration (FAA) website, he locates several sources that provide background information, such as the fact that, statistically, weather often poses some of the greatest risks to general aviation (GA) pilots, regardless of their experience level. He also finds charts and a lesson plan he can use.

Daniel's decision to help Mary develop personal weather minimums reflects a key component of the flight instructor's job: providing the student with the tools to ensure safety during a flight. Every flight instructor can agree that everyone wants to be safe, but what does "safety" really mean? How can a flight instructor ensure the safety of flight training activities, and also train clients to operate their aircraft safely after they leave the relatively protected flight training environment?

According to one definition, safety is the freedom from conditions that can cause death, injury, or illness; damage to/loss of equipment or property, or damage to the environment. FAA regulations are intended to promote safety by eliminating or mitigating conditions that can cause death, injury, or damage. These regulations are comprehensive, but there has been increasing recognition that even the strictest compliance with regulations may not be sufficient to guarantee safety. Rules and regulations are designed to address known or suspected conditions detrimental to safety, but there is always the probability that some new combination of circumstances not contemplated by the regulations will arise.

The recognition of aviation training and flight operations as a system led to a "system approach" to aviation safety. Since flight instructors are a critical part of the aviation safety system, this chapter introduces system safety—aeronautical decision-making (ADM), risk management, situational awareness, and single-pilot resource management (SRM)—in the modern flight training environment. It also provides methods flight instructors can teach students to use practical risk management tools and discusses how to evaluate student decision-making. The chapter begins with practical strategies flight instructors can use to enhance their instruction, the demonstration-performance training delivery method of flight instruction, integrated flight instruction, positive exchange of flight controls, use of distractions, obstacles to learning encountered during flight training, and how to evaluate students. After an intensive look at ADM, it closes with a discussion of CFI recommendations and endorsements.

Flight Instructor Qualifications

A CFI must be thoroughly familiar with the functions, characteristics, and proper use of all flight instruments, avionics, and other aircraft systems being used for training. This is especially important due to the wide variety in global positioning systems (GPS) and glass panel displays.

It is the personal responsibility of each flight instructor to maintain familiarity with current pilot training techniques and certification requirements. This may be done by frequent review of new periodicals and technical publications, personal contacts with FAA inspectors and designated pilot examiners (DPE), and by participation in pilot and flight instructor clinics. Additional information can be obtained from veteran flight instructors. *[Figure 8-1]* The application of outmoded instructional procedures or the preparation of students using obsolete certification requirements is inexcusable.

Practical Flight Instructor Strategies

During all phases of flight training, CFIs should remember they are role models for the student. The flight instructor should demonstrate good aviation sense at all times:

- Before the flight—discuss safety and the importance of a proper preflight and use of the checklist.
- During flight—prioritize the tasks of aviating, navigating, and communicating. Instill importance of "see and avoid" in the student.

Teaching Tips from Veteran Flight Instructors	
1	Use a tape recorder and/or video camera to rehearse preflight briefings until delivery is polished.
2	Find a mentor to provide a second opinion on how well a student is performing during critical phases of flight training (such as first solo) for the first few PTs.
3	Encourage a high standard of performance.
4	Just because it's legal, doesn't make it safe. Maintain a high level of supervision of PT operations.
5	Develop a safety-culture environment.
6	Assign organized, specific, appropriate homework after each flight session.
7	Use all available tools to supplement teaching and assignments: online sources, seminars, flight simulators, etc.
8	Know the background, credentials, security issues, medications, etc., of the student before climbing into the cockpit with him or her.
9	Thoroughly and carefully document all training events as though the National Transportation Safety Board (NTSB) were going to read them.
10	Postflight debriefing after an FAA checkride is an excellent opportunity for additional learning.
11	Encourage each student to establish personal minimums.
12	Include a review of NTSB accident reports during advanced instructional activity.

Figure 8-1. *Teaching tips from veteran flight instructors.*

- During landing—conduct stabilized approaches, maintain desired airspeed on final, demonstrate good judgment for go-arounds, wake turbulence, traffic, and terrain avoidance. Use ADM to correct faulty approaches and landing errors. Make power-off, stall-warning blaring, on centerline touchdowns in the first third of runway.
- Always—remember safety is paramount.

Flight instructors have the responsibility of producing the safest pilots possible. For that reason, CFIs should encourage each student to learn as much as he or she is capable of and keep raising the bar. When introducing lesson tasks, flight instructors should not introduce the minimum acceptable standards for passing the checkride. The Practical Test Standard (PTS) is not a teaching tool. It is a testing tool. The overall focus of flight training should be on education, learning, and understanding why the standards are there and how they were set. The minimum standards to pass the checkride should not be introduced until the 3 hours of preparation for the checkride.

Obstacles to Learning During Flight Instruction

Certain obstacles are common to flight instruction and may apply directly to the student's attitude, physical condition, and psychological make-up. These include but are not limited to:

- Feeling of unfair treatment
- Impatience to proceed to more interesting operations
- Worry or lack of interest
- Physical discomfort, illness, fatigue, and dehydration
- Apathy due to inadequate instruction
- Anxiety

Unfair Treatment

Students who believe their instruction is inadequate, or that their efforts are not conscientiously considered and evaluated, do not learn well. In addition, their motivation suffers no matter how intent they are on learning to fly. Motivation also declines when a student believes the instructor is making unreasonable demands for performance and progress. *[Figure 8-2]*

Assignment of goals the student considers difficult, but possible, usually provides a challenge and promotes learning. In a typical flight lesson, reasonable goals are listed in the lesson objectives and the desired levels of proficiency for the goals are included in statements that contain completion standards.

Figure 8-2. *The assignment of impossible or unreasonable goals discourages the student, diminishes effort, and retards the learning process.*

Impatience

Impatience is a greater deterrent to learning pilot skills than is generally recognized. For a student, this may take the form of a desire to make an early solo flight, or to set out on cross-country flights before the basic elements of flight have been learned.

The impatient student fails to understand the need for preliminary training and seeks only the ultimate objective without considering the means necessary to reach it. With every complex human endeavor, it is necessary to master the basics if the whole task is to be performed competently and safely. The instructor can correct student impatience by presenting the necessary preliminary training one step at a time, with clearly stated goals for each step. The procedures and elements mastered in each step should be clearly identified in explaining or demonstrating the performance of the subsequent step.

Impatience can result from instruction keyed to the pace of a slow learner when it is applied to a motivated, fast learner. It is just as important that a student be advanced to the subsequent step as soon as one goal has been attained, as it is to complete each step before the next one is undertaken. Disinterest grows rapidly when unnecessary repetition and drill are requested on operations that have already been adequately learned.

Worry or Lack of Interest

Worry or lack of interest has a detrimental effect on learning. Students who are worried or emotionally upset are not ready to learn and derive little benefit from instruction. Worry or distraction may be due to student concerns about progress in the training course, or may stem from circumstances completely unrelated to their instruction. Significant emotional upsets may be due to personal problems, psychiatric disturbances, or a dislike of the training program or the instructor.

The experiences of students outside their training activities affect behavior and performance in training; the two cannot be separated. When students begin flight training, they bring with them their interests, enthusiasms, fears, and troubles. The instructor cannot be responsible for these outside diversions, but cannot ignore them because they have a critical effect on the learning process. Instruction must be keyed to the utilization of the interests and enthusiasm students bring with them, and to diverting their attention from their worries and troubles to learning the tasks at hand. This is admittedly difficult, but must be accomplished if learning is to proceed at a normal rate.

Worries and emotional upsets that result from a flight training course can be identified and addressed. These problems are often due to inadequacies of the course or of the instructor. The most effective cure is prevention. The instructor must be alert and ensure the students understand the objectives of each step of their training, and that they know at the completion of each lesson exactly how well they have progressed and what deficiencies are apparent. Discouragement and emotional upsets are rare when students feel that nothing is being withheld from them or is being neglected in their training.

Physical Discomfort, Illness, Fatigue, and Dehydration

Physical discomfort, illness, and fatigue will materially slow the rate of learning during both classroom instruction and flight training. Students who are not completely at ease, and whose attention is diverted by discomforts such as the extremes of temperature, poor ventilation, inadequate lighting, or noise and confusion, cannot learn at a normal rate. This is true no matter how diligently they attempt to apply themselves to the learning task.

A minor illness, such as a cold, major illness, or injury, interferes with the normal rate of learning. This is especially important for flight instruction. Most illnesses adversely affect the acuteness of vision, hearing, and feeling, all of which are essential to correct performance.

Airsickness can be a great deterrent to flight instruction. A student who is airsick or bothered with incipient airsickness is incapable of learning at a normal rate. There is no sure cure for airsickness, but resistance or immunity usually can be developed in a relatively short period of time. An instructional flight should be terminated as soon as incipient sickness is experienced. As the student develops immunity, flights can be increased in length until normal flight periods are practicable.

Keeping students interested and occupied during flight is a deterrent to airsickness. They are much less apt to become airsick while operating the controls themselves. Rough air and unexpected abrupt maneuvers tend to increase the chances of airsickness. Tension and apprehension apparently contribute to airsickness and should be avoided.

Fatigue

Fatigue is one of the most treacherous hazards to flight safety as it may not be apparent to a pilot until serious errors are made. Fatigue can be either acute (short-term) or chronic (long-term). Acute fatigue, a normal occurrence of everyday living, is the tiredness felt after long periods of physical and mental strain, including strenuous muscular effort, immobility, heavy mental workload, strong emotional pressure, monotony, and lack of sleep.

Acute fatigue caused by training operations may be physical or mental, or both. It is not necessarily a function of physical robustness or mental acuity. The amount of training any student can absorb without incurring debilitating fatigue varies. Generally speaking, complex operations tend to induce fatigue more rapidly than simpler procedures do, regardless of the physical effort involved. Fatigue is the primary consideration in determining the length and frequency of flight instruction periods and flight instruction should be continued only as long as the student is alert, receptive to instruction, and is performing at a level consistent with experience.

It is important for a CFI to be able to detect fatigue, both in assessing a student's substandard performance early in a lesson, and also in recognizing the deterioration of performance. If fatigue occurs as a result of application to a learning task, the student should be given a break in instruction and practice.

A CFI who is familiar with the signs indicative to acute fatigue will be more aware if the student is experiencing them. The deficiencies listed below are apparent to others before the individual notices any physical signs of fatigue.

Acute fatigue is characterized by:

- Inattention
- Distractibility
- Errors in timing
- Neglect of secondary tasks

- Loss of accuracy and control
- Lack of awareness of error accumulation
- Irritability

Another form of fatigue is chronic fatigue which occurs when there is not enough time for a full recovery from repeated episodes of acute fatigue. Chronic fatigue's underlying cause is generally not "rest-related" and may have deeper points of origin. Therefore, rest alone may not resolve chronic fatigue.

Chronic fatigue is a combination of both physiological problems and psychological issues. Psychological problems such as financial, home life, or job-related stresses cause a lack of qualified rest that is only solved by mitigating the underlying problems before the fatigue is solved. Without resolution, human performance continues to fall off, and judgment becomes impaired so that unwarranted risks may be taken. Recovery from chronic fatigue requires a prolonged and deliberate solution. In either case, unless adequate precautions are taken, personal performance could be impaired and adversely affect pilot judgment and decision-making.

Dehydration and Heatstroke

Dehydration is the term given to a critical loss of water from the body. Dehydration reduces a pilot's level of alertness, producing a subsequent slowing of decision-making processes or even the inability to control the aircraft. The first noticeable effect of dehydration is fatigue, which in turn makes top physical and mental performance difficult, if not impossible. Flying for long periods in hot summer temperatures or at high altitudes increases susceptibility to dehydration since dry air at high altitudes tends to increase the rate of water loss from the body. If this fluid is not replaced, fatigue progresses to dizziness, weakness, nausea, tingling of hands and feet, abdominal cramps, and extreme thirst.

Heatstroke is a condition caused by any inability of the body to control its temperature. Onset of this condition may be recognized by the symptoms of dehydration, but also has been known to be recognized only by complete collapse. To prevent these symptoms, it is recommended that an ample supply of water be carried and used at frequent intervals on any long flight, whether the pilot is thirsty or not. If the airplane has a canopy or roof window, wearing light-colored, porous clothing and a hat helps provide protection from the sun. Keeping the flight deck well ventilated aids in dissipating excess heat.

Apathy Due to Inadequate Instruction

Students can become apathetic when they recognize that the instructor has made inadequate preparations for the instruction being given, or when the instruction appears to be deficient, contradictory, or insincere. To hold the student's interest and to maintain the motivation necessary for efficient learning, well-planned, appropriate, and accurate instruction must be provided. Nothing destroys a student's interest as quickly as a poorly organized period of instruction. Even an inexperienced student realizes immediately when the instructor has failed to prepare a lesson. *[Figure 8-3]*

Figure 8-3. *Poor preparation leads to spotty coverage, misplaced emphasis, unnecessary repetition, and a lack of confidence on the part of the student. The instructor should always have a plan.*

Instruction may be overly explicit and so elementary it fails to hold student interest, or it may be so general or complicated that it fails to evoke the interest necessary for effective learning. To be effective, the instructor must teach for the level of the student. The presentation must be adjusted to be meaningful to the person for whom it is intended. For example, instruction in the preflight inspection of an aircraft should be presented quite differently for a student who is a skilled aircraft maintenance technician (AMT) compared to the instruction on the same operation for a student with no previous aeronautical experience. The instruction needed in each case is the same, but a presentation meaningful to one of these students might not be appropriate for the other.

Poor instructional presentations may result not only from poor preparation, but also from distracting mannerisms, personal untidiness, or the appearance of irritation with the student. Creating the impression of talking down to the student is one of the fastest ways for an instructor to lose student confidence and attention. Once the instructor loses student confidence, it is difficult to regain, and the learning rate is unnecessarily diminished.

Anxiety

Student anxiety may place additional burdens on the instructor. This frequently limits the student's perceptive ability and retards the development of insights. The student must be comfortable, confident in the instructor and the aircraft, and at ease if effective learning is to occur. Providing this atmosphere for learning is one of the first and most important tasks of the instructor. Although doing so may be difficult at first, successive accomplishment of recognizable goals and the avoidance of alarming occurrences or situations will rapidly ease the student's mind. This is true of all flight students, but special handling by the instructor may be required for students who are obviously anxious or uncomfortable.

Demonstration-Performance Training Delivery Method

The demonstration-performance training delivery method was discussed briefly in Chapter 4, The Teaching Process, but the following in-depth discussion is geared to the flight instructor. This training method has been in use for a long time and is very effective in teaching kinesthetic skills so flight instructors find it valuable in teaching procedures and maneuvers. The demonstration-performance method is divided into four phases: explanation, demonstration, student performance with instructor supervision, and evaluation. *[Figure 8-4]*

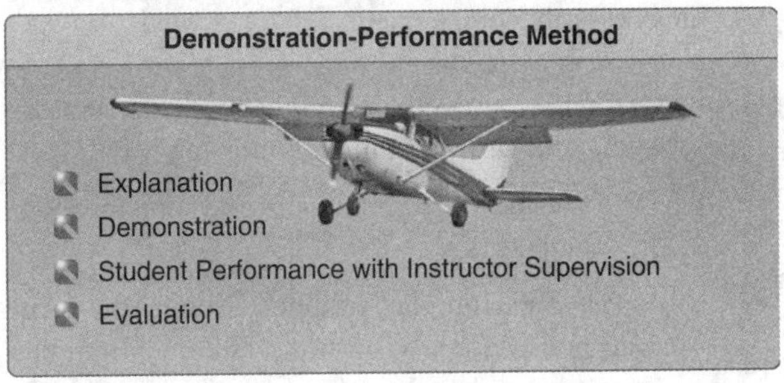

Figure 8-4. *The demonstration-performance method of teaching has five essential phases.*

Explanation Phase

The flight instructor needs to be well prepared and highly organized if complex maneuvers and procedures are to be taught effectively. The student must be intellectually and psychologically ready for the learning activity. The explanation phase is accomplished prior to the flight lesson with a discussion of lesson objectives and completion standards, as well as a thorough preflight briefing. Explanations must be clear, pertinent to the objectives of the particular lesson to be presented, and based on the known experience and knowledge of the students. Students need to know not only what they will learn, but also how they will learn it—that is, how the lesson will proceed and how they will be evaluated. In teaching a skill, the instructor must convey to the students the precise actions they are to perform. In addition to the necessary steps, the instructor should describe the end result of these efforts. The explanation phase also should include coverage of appropriate safety procedures. Before leaving this phase, the instructor should encourage students to ask questions about any step of the procedure that they do not understand.

Demonstration Phase

The instructor must show students the actions necessary to perform a skill. As little extraneous activity as possible should be included in the demonstration if students are to clearly understand that the instructor is accurately performing the actions previously explained. If, due to some unanticipated circumstances the demonstration does not closely conform to the explanation, this deviation should be immediately acknowledged and explained.

Student Performance and Instructor Supervision Phases

As discussed in chapter 4, these two phases involve separate actions that are performed concurrently. The first of these phases is the student's performance of the physical or mental skills that have been explained and demonstrated. The second activity is the instructor's supervision.

Student performance requires students to act and do. To learn skills, students must practice. The instructor must, therefore, allot enough time for meaningful student activity. Through doing, students learn to follow correct procedures and to reach established standards. It is important that students be given an opportunity to perform the skill as soon as possible after a demonstration.

Then, the instructor reviews what has been covered during the instructional flight and determines to what extent the student has met the objectives outlined during the preflight discussion. The instructor should be satisfied that the student is well prepared and understands the task before starting. The instructor observes as the student performs, and then makes appropriate comments.

Evaluation Phase

In this phase, the instructor traditionally evaluates student performance, records the student's performance, and verbally advises the student of the progress made toward the objectives. Regardless of how well a skill is taught, there may still be performance deficiencies. When pointing out areas that need improvement, offer concrete suggestions that help. If possible, avoid ending the evaluation on a negative note.

As discussed in Chapter 5, Assessment, collaborative assessment (or learner centered grading (LCG)) is a form of authentic assessment currently used in aviation training with problem-based learning (PBL). PBL structures the lessons to confront students with problems that are encountered in real life and forces them to reach real-world solutions. Scenario-based training (SBT), a type of PBL, uses a highly structured script of real world experiences to address aviation training objectives in an operational environment. Collaborative assessment is used to evaluate whether certain learning criteria were met during the SBT.

Collaborative assessment includes two parts—learner self-assessment and a detailed assessment by the flight instructor. The purpose of the self-assessment is to stimulate growth in the learner's thought processes and, in turn, behaviors. The self-assessment is followed by an in-depth discussion between the instructor and the student which compares the instructor's assessment to the student's self-assessment.

The Telling-and-Doing Technique

The demonstration-performance method can be applied to the telling-and-doing technique of flight instruction in three steps. However, the telling-and-doing technique includes specific variations for flight instruction. *[Figure 8-5]*

Instructor Tells—Instructor Does

First, the flight instructor gives a carefully planned demonstration of the procedure or maneuver with accompanying verbal explanation. While demonstrating inflight maneuvers, the instructor should explain the required power settings, aircraft attitudes, and describe any other pertinent factors that may apply. This is the only step in which the student plays a passive role. It is important for the demonstration to conform to the explanation as closely as possible. In addition, it should be demonstrated in the same sequence in which it was explained so as to avoid confusion and provide reinforcement. Since students generally imitate the instructor's performance, the instructor must demonstrate the skill exactly the way the students are expected to practice it, including all safety procedures that the students must follow. If, due to some unanticipated circumstances, the demonstration does not closely conform to the explanation, this deviation should be immediately acknowledged and explained.

Most physical skills lend themselves to a sequential pattern where the skill is explained in the same step-by-step order normally used to perform it. When the skill being taught is related to previously learned procedures or maneuvers, the known to unknown strategy may be used effectively. When teaching more than one skill at the same time, the simple-to-complex strategy works well. By starting with the simplest skill, a student gains confidence and is less likely to become frustrated when faced with building skills that are more complex.

Another consideration in this phase is the language used. Instructors should attempt to avoid unnecessary jargon and technical terms that their students do not know. Instructors should also take care to clearly describe the actions students are expected to perform. Communication is the key. It is neither appropriate nor effective for instructors to try to impress students with their expertise by using language that is unnecessarily complicated.

As an example, a level turn might be demonstrated and described by the instructor in the following way:

- Use outside visual references and monitor the flight instruments.
- After clearing the airspace around the aircraft, add power slightly, turn the aircraft in the desired direction, and apply a slight amount of back pressure on the yoke to maintain altitude. Maintain coordinated flight by applying rudder in the direction of the turn.

Traditional Teaching Process	Demonstration-Performance Method	Telling-and-Doing Technique
Preparation	Explanation	Preparation
Presentation	Demonstration	Instructor tells Instructor does
		Student tells Instructor does
Application	Student performance supervision	Student tells Student does
Review and Evaluation	Evaluation	Student does Instructor evaluates

Figure 8-5. *This comparison of steps in the teaching process, the demonstration-performance method, and the telling-and-doing technique highlights similarities as well as differences. The main difference in the telling-and-doing technique is the important transition, student tells—instructor does, which occurs between the second and third step.*

- Remember, the ailerons control the roll rate, as well as the angle of bank. The rate at which the aircraft rolls depends on how much aileron deflection is used. How far the aircraft rolls (steepness of the bank) depends on how long the ailerons are deflected, since the aircraft continues to roll as long as the ailerons are deflected. When the desired angle of bank is reached, neutralize the ailerons, and trim as appropriate.
- Lead the roll-out by approximately one-half the number of degrees of the angle of bank. Use coordinated aileron and rudder control pressures. Simultaneously begin releasing the back pressure so aileron, rudder, and elevator pressures are neutralized when the aircraft reaches the wings-level position.
- Leading the roll-out heading by one-half the bank angle is a good rule of thumb for initial training. However, keep in mind that the required amount of lead really depends on the type of turn, turn rate, and roll-out rate. As a pilot gains experience, he or she will develop a consistent roll-in and roll-out technique for various types of turns. Upon reaching a wings-level attitude, reduce power and trim to remove control pressures.

Student Tells—Instructor Does

Second, the student tells as the instructor does. In this step, the student actually plays the role of instructor, telling the instructor what to do and how to do it. Two benefits accrue from this step: the student, being freed from the need to concentrate on performance of the maneuver and from concern about its outcome, is able to organize his or her thoughts regarding the steps involved and the techniques to be used. In the process of explaining the maneuver as the instructor performs it, perceptions begin to develop into insights. Mental habits begin to form with repetition of the instructions previously received. Plus, the instructor is able to evaluate the student's understanding of the factors involved in performance of the maneuver.

According to the principle of primacy, it is important for the instructor to make sure the student gets it right the first time. The student should also understand the correct sequence and be aware of safety precautions for each procedure or maneuver. If a misunderstanding exists, it can be corrected before the student becomes absorbed in controlling the aircraft.

Student Tells—Student Does

Application is the third step in this method. This is where learning takes place and where performance habits are formed. If the student has been adequately prepared and the procedure or maneuver fully explained and demonstrated, meaningful learning occurs. The instructor should be alert during the student's practice to detect any errors in technique and to prevent the formation of faulty habits.

At the same time, the student should be encouraged to think about what to do during the performance of a maneuver, until it becomes habitual. In this step, the thinking is done verbally. This focuses concentration on the task to be accomplished, so that total involvement in the maneuver is fostered. All of the student's physical and mental faculties are brought into play. The instructor should be aware of the student's thought processes. It is easy to determine whether an error is induced by a misconception or by a simple lack of motor skills. Therefore, in addition to forcing total concentration on the part of the student, this method provides a means for keeping the instructor aware of what the student is thinking. The student is not only learning to do something, but he or she is also learning a self-teaching process that is highly desirable in development of a skill.

The exact procedures that the instructor should use during student practice depends on factors such as the student's proficiency level, the type of maneuver, and the stage of training. The instructor must exercise good judgment to decide how much control to use. With potentially hazardous or difficult maneuvers, the instructor should be alert and ready to take control at any time. This is especially true during a student's first attempt at a particular maneuver. On the other hand, if a student is progressing normally, the instructor should avoid unnecessary interruptions or too much assistance.

A typical test of how much control is needed often occurs during a student's first few attempts to land an aircraft. The instructor must quickly evaluate the student's need for help, and not hesitate to take control, if required. At the same time, the student should be allowed to practice the entire maneuver often enough to achieve the level of proficiency established in the lesson objectives. Since this is a learning phase rather than an evaluation phase of the training, errors or unsafe practices should be identified and corrected in a positive and timely way. In some cases, the student is not able to meet the proficiency level specified in the lesson objectives within the allotted time. When this occurs, the instructor should be prepared to schedule additional training.

Positive Exchange of Flight Controls

Positive exchange of flight controls is an integral part of flight training. It is especially critical during the demonstration-performance method of flight instruction. Due to the importance of this subject, the following discussion provides guidance on the recommended procedure to use for the positive exchange of flight controls between pilots when operating an aircraft.

Background

Incident/accident statistics indicate a need to place additional emphasis on the exchange of control of an aircraft by pilots. Numerous accidents have occurred due to a lack of communication or misunderstanding regarding who had actual control of the aircraft, particularly between students and flight instructors. Establishing the following procedure during initial training will ensure the formation of a habit pattern that should stay with students throughout their flying careers.

Procedure

During flight training, there must always be a clear understanding between students and flight instructors about who has control of the aircraft. The preflight briefing should include procedures for the exchange of flight controls. A positive three-step process in the exchange of flight controls between pilots is a proven procedure and one that is strongly recommended. When an instructor is teaching a maneuver to a student, the instructor normally demonstrates the maneuver first, then has the student follow along on the controls during a demonstration and, finally, the student performs the maneuver with the instructor following along on the controls. *[Figure 8-6]*

Positive Exchange of Flight Controls

1. When the flight instructor wishes the student to take control of the aircraft, the instructor says to the student,

   "You have the flight controls."

2. The student acknowledges immediately by saying,

   "I have the flight controls."

3. The flight instructor again says,

   "You have the flight controls."

Figure 8-6. *During this procedure, a visual check is recommended to see that the other person actually has the flight controls. When returning the controls to the instructor, the student should follow the same procedure the instructor used when giving control to the student. The student should stay on the controls and keep flying the aircraft until the instructor says, "I have the flight controls." There should never be any doubt about who is flying the aircraft.*

Flight instructors should always guard the controls and be prepared to take control of the aircraft. When necessary, the instructor should take the controls and calmly announce, "I have the flight controls." If an instructor allows a student to remain on the controls, the instructor may not have full and effective control of the aircraft. Anxious students can be incredibly strong and usually exhibit reactions inappropriate to the situation. If a recovery is necessary, there is absolutely nothing to be gained by having the student on the controls and having to fight for control of the aircraft. students should never be allowed to exceed the flight instructor's limits. Flight instructors should not exceed their own ability to perceive a problem, decide upon a course of action, and physically react within their ability to fly the aircraft.

Sterile Cockpit Rule

Commonly known as the "sterile cockpit rule," Title 14 of the Code of Federal Regulations (14 CFR) section 121.542 requires flight crewmembers to refrain from nonessential activities during critical phases of flight. As defined in the regulation, critical phases of flight are all ground operations involving taxi, takeoff, and landing, and all other flight operations below 10,000 feet except cruise flight. Nonessential activities include such activities as eating, reading a newspaper, or chatting. A series of aircraft accidents caused by flight crews who were distracted from their flight duties during critical phases of the flight caused the FAA to propose the rule. While the regulation grew out of accidents in the airline industry, it holds true for the entire aviation community. Pilots can improve flight safety significantly by reducing distractions during critical phases of flight. It is important the flight instructor not only teach the concept of a sterile cockpit, but also model such behavior during flight instruction.

Use of Distractions

National Transportation Safety Board (NTSB) statistics reveal that most stall/spin accidents occurred when the pilot's attention was diverted from the primary task of flying the aircraft. Sixty percent of stall/spin accidents occurred during takeoff and landing, and twenty percent were preceded by engine failure. Preoccupation inside or outside the flight deck while changing aircraft configuration or trim, maneuvering to avoid other traffic, or clearing hazardous obstacles during takeoff and climb could create a potential stall/spin situation. The intentional practice of stalls and spins seldom resulted in an accident. The real danger was inadvertent stalls induced by distractions during routine flight situations.

Pilots at all skill levels should be aware of the increased risk of entering into an inadvertent stall or spin while performing tasks that are secondary to controlling the aircraft. The FAA has established a policy for use of certain distractions on practical tests for pilot certification. The purpose is to determine that applicants possess the skills required to cope with distractions while maintaining the degree of aircraft control required for safe flight. The most effective training is the simulation of scenarios that can lead to inadvertent stalls by creating distractions while the student is practicing certain maneuvers.

Instructor responsibilities include teaching the student to divide his or her attention between the distracting task and maintaining control of the aircraft. The following are examples of distractions that can be used for this training:

- Drop a pencil. Ask the student to pick it up.
- Ask the student to determine a heading to an airport using a chart.
- Ask the student to reset the clock.
- Ask the student to get something from the back seat.
- Ask the student to read the outside air temperature.
- Ask the student to call the Automated Flight Service Station (AFSS) for weather information.
- Ask the student to compute true airspeed with a flight computer.
- Ask the student to identify terrain or objects on the ground.
- Ask the student to identify a field suitable for a forced landing.
- Have the student climb 200 feet and maintain altitude, then descend 200 feet and maintain altitude.
- Have the student reverse course after a series of S-turns.

It is a flight instructor's responsibility to teach the student how to take charge during a flight. A pilot in command (PIC) must know when to tell any passengers, even a DPE, when the PIC finds actions in the aircraft that distract and interfere with the safe conduct of the flight.

Integrated Flight Instruction

Integrated flight instruction is flight instruction during which students are taught to perform flight maneuvers both by outside visual references and by reference to flight instruments. For this type of instruction to be fully effective, the use of instrument references should begin the first time each new maneuver is introduced. No distinction in the pilot's operation of the flight controls is permitted, regardless of whether outside references or instrument indications are used for the performance of the maneuver. When this training technique is used, instruction in the control of an aircraft by outside visual references is integrated with instruction in the use of flight instrument indications for the same operations.

Development of Habit Patterns

It important for the student to establish the habit of observing and relying on flight instruments from the beginning of flight training. It is equally important for the student to learn the feel of the airplane while conducting maneuvers, such as being able to feel when the airplane is out of trim or in a nose-high or nose-low attitude. Students who have been required to perform all normal flight maneuvers by reference to instruments, as well as by outside references, develop from the start the habit of continuously monitoring their own and the aircraft's performance. The early establishment of proper habits of instrument cross-check, instrument interpretation, and aircraft control is highly useful to the student. The habitual attention to instrument indications leads to improved landings because of more precise airspeed control. Effective use of instruments also results in superior cross-country navigation, better coordination, and generally, a better overall pilot competency level.

General aviation accident reports provide ample support for the belief that reference to flight instruments is important to safety. The safety record of pilots who hold instrument ratings is significantly better than that of pilots with comparable flight time who have never received formal flight training for an instrument rating. Pilots in training who have been required to perform all normal flight maneuvers by reference to instruments, as well as by outside references, will develop from the start the habit of continuously monitoring their own and the aircraft's performance. The early establishment of proper habits of instrument cross-check, instrument interpretation, and aircraft control is highly useful to the student. The habits formed at this time also give him or her a firm foundation for later training for an instrument rating.

Operating Efficiency

As students become more proficient in monitoring and correcting their own flight technique by reference to flight instruments, the performance obtained from an aircraft increases noticeably. This is particularly true of modern, complex, or high-performance aircraft, which are responsive to the use of correct operating airspeeds.

The use of correct power settings and climb speeds and the accurate control of headings during climbs result in a measurable increase in climb performance. Holding precise headings and altitudes in cruising flight definitely increases average cruising performance.

The use of integrated flight instruction provides the student with the ability to control an aircraft in flight for limited periods if outside references are lost. In an emergency, this ability could save the pilot's life and those of the passengers.

During the conduct of integrated flight training, the flight instructor must emphasize to the students that the introduction to the use of flight instruments does not prepare them for operations in marginal weather or instrument meteorological conditions (IMC). The possible consequences, both to themselves and to others, of experiments with flight operations in weather conditions below visual flight rules (VFR) minimums before they are instrument rated should be constantly impressed on the students. According to NTSB accident data, inflight encounters with weather (attempting VFR flight into IMC) is one of the most lethal types of GA flying.

Procedures

Integrated flight instruction begins with the first briefing on the function of the flight controls. This briefing includes the instrument indications to be expected, as well as the outside references to be used to control the attitude of the aircraft.

Each new flight maneuver is introduced using both outside and instrument references with students developing the ability to maneuver an aircraft equally as well by instrument or outside references. They naturally accept the fact that the manipulation of the flight controls is identical, regardless of which references are used to determine the attitude of the aircraft. This practice should continue throughout the flight instruction for all maneuvers. To fully achieve the demonstrated benefits of this type of training, the use of visual and instrument references must be constantly integrated throughout the training. Failure to do so lengthens the flight instruction necessary for the student to achieve the competency required for a private pilot certificate.

See and Avoid

From the start of flight training, the instructor must ensure students develop the habit of looking for other air traffic at all times. If students believe the instructor assumes all responsibility for scanning and collision avoidance procedures, they do not develop the habit of maintaining a constant vigilance, which is essential to safety. Any observed tendency of a student to enter flight maneuvers without first making a careful check for other air traffic must be corrected immediately. Recent studies of midair collisions determined that:

- Flight instructors were onboard the aircraft in 37 percent of the accidents in the study.
- Most of the aircraft involved in collisions are engaged in recreational flying not on any type of flight plan.
- Most midair collisions occur in VFR weather conditions during weekend daylight hours.
- The vast majority of accidents occurred at or near nontowered airports and at altitudes below 1,000 feet.
- Pilots of all experience levels were involved in midair collisions, from pilots on their first solo, to 20,000 hour veterans.
- Most collisions occur in daylight with visibility greater than 3 miles.

It is imperative to introduce 14 CFR section 91.113 "Right-of-way" rules to the student. Practice the "see and avoid" concept at all times regardless of whether the training is conducted under VFR or instrument flight rules (IFR). For more information on how to reduce the odds of becoming involved in a midair collision, see www.faa.gov/about/office_org/headquarters_offices/ato/tracon/anchorage/pilots_info/mca/.

Assessment of Piloting Ability

Assessment is an essential component of the teaching process and determines how, what, and how well a student is learning. A well designed assessment provides a student with something constructive upon which he or she can work or build. An assessment should provide direction and guidance to raise the level of performance. Students must understand the purpose of the assessment; otherwise, they will be unlikely to accept the evaluation offered and little improvement will result. There are many types of assessment, but the flight instructor generally uses the review, collaborative assessment (LCG), written tests, and performance-based tests to ascertain knowledge or practical skill levels. Refer to chapter 5 for an in-depth discussion of the types of assessment available to the flight instructor.

An assessment can also be used as a tool for reteaching. Although not all assessments lend themselves to reteaching, the instructor should be alert to the possibility and take advantage of the opportunity when it arises. In assessing the ability of a student, the instructor initially determines if he or she understands the procedure or maneuver. Then, the instructor demonstrates the maneuver, allows the student to practice the maneuver under direction, and finally evaluates student accomplishment by observing the performance.

Demonstrated Ability

Assessment of demonstrated ability during flight instruction must be based upon established standards of performance, suitably modified to apply to the student's experience and stage of development as a pilot. The assessment must consider the student's mastery of the elements involved in the maneuver, rather than merely the overall performance.

In order for a student to be signed off for a solo flight, the CFI must determine that the student is qualified and proficient in the flight tasks necessary for the flight. The CFI bases this assessment on the student's ability to demonstrate consistent proficiency on a number of flight maneuvers. Also associated with pilot skill evaluations during flight training are the stage checks conducted in FAA-approved school courses and the practical tests for pilot certificates and ratings.

Postflight Evaluation

In assessing piloting ability, it is important for the flight instructor to keep the student informed of progress. This may be done as each procedure or maneuver is completed or summarized during postflight critiques. Postflight critiques should be in a written format, such as notes to aid the flight instructor in covering all areas that were noticed during the flight or lesson. Traditionally, flight instructors explained errors in performance, pointed out elements in which the deficiencies were believed to have originated and, if possible, suggested appropriate corrective measures. Traditional assessment depends on a grading scale of "excellent, good, fair, poor" or "exceeds standards, meets standards, needs more training" which often meets the instructor's needs but not the needs of the student.

With the advent of SBT, collaborative assessment is used whenever the student has completed a scenario. As discussed in chapters 4 and 5, SBT uses a highly structured script of real-world experiences to address aviation training objectives in an operational environment. During the postflight evaluation, collaborative assessment is used to evaluate whether certain learning criteria were met during the SBT.

Collaborative assessment includes learner self-assessment and a detailed assessment by the aviation instructor. The purpose of the self-assessment is to stimulate growth in the learner's thought processes and, in turn, behaviors. The self-assessment is followed by an in-depth discussion between the instructor and the student which compares the instructor's assessment to the student's self-assessment.

First Solo Flight

During the student's first solo flight, the instructor must be present to assist in answering questions or resolving any issues that arise during the flight. To ensure the solo flight is a positive, confidence-building experience for the student, the flight instructor needs to consider time of day when scheduling the flight. Time of day is a factor in traffic congestion, possible winds, sun angles, and reflection.

If possible, the flight instructor needs access to a portable radio during any supervised solo operations. A radio enables the instructor to terminate the solo operation if he or she observes a situation developing. The flight instructor must use good judgment when communicating with a solo student. Keep all radio communications to a minimum. Do not talk to the student on short final of the landing approach.

Post-Solo Debriefing

During a post-solo debriefing, the flight instructor discusses what took place during the student's solo flight. It is important for the flight instructor to answer any questions the student may have as result of a solo flight. Instructors need to be involved in all aspects of the flight to ensure the student utilizes correct flight procedures. It is very important for the flight instructor to debrief a student immediately after a solo flight. With the flight vividly etched in the student's memory, questions about the flight will come quickly.

Correction of Student Errors

Correction of student errors should not include the practice of immediately taking the controls away when a mistake is made. Safety permitting, it is frequently better to let students progress part of the way into the mistake and find a way out. For example, in a weight-shift control aircraft the control bar is moved right to turn left. A student may show an initial tendency to move the bar in the direction of the desired turn. This tendency will dissipate with time, but allowing the student to see the effect of his or her control input is a valuable aid in illustrating the stability of the aircraft. It is difficult for students to learn a maneuver properly if they seldom have the opportunity to correct an error.

On the other hand, students may perform a procedure or maneuver correctly and not fully understand the principles and objectives involved. When the instructor suspects this, students should be required to vary the performance of the maneuver slightly, combine it with other operations, or apply the same elements to the performance of other maneuvers. Students who do not understand the principles involved will probably not be able to do this successfully.

Pilot Supervision

Flight instructors have the responsibility to provide guidance and restraint with respect to the solo operations of their students. This is by far the most important flight instructor responsibility. The flight instructor is the only person in a position to make the determination a student is ready for solo operations. Before endorsing a student for solo flight, the instructor should require the student to demonstrate consistent ability to perform all of the fundamental maneuvers.

Dealing with Normal Challenges

Instructors should teach students how to solve ordinary problems encountered during flight. Traffic pattern congestion, change in active runway, or unexpected crosswinds are challenges the student masters individually before being able to perform them collectively.

Visualization

SBT lends itself well to visualization techniques. For example, have a student visualize how the flight may occur under normal circumstances, with the student describing how he or she would fly the flight. Then, the instructor adds unforeseen circumstances such as a sudden change in weather that brings excessive winds during final approach. Other examples of SBT can have the instructor adding undesired landing sites for balloon student pilots, rope breaks for glider students, and radio outages for instrument airplane students. Now, the student must visualize how he or she will handle the unexpected change.

During this visualization, the flight instructor can ask questions to check the student's thought processes. The job of the instructor is to challenge the student with realistic flying situations without overburdening him or her with unrealistic scenarios.

Practice Landings

The FAA recommends that in all student flights involving landings in an aircraft, the flight instructor should teach a full stop landing. Full stop landings help the student develop aircraft control and checklist usage. Aircraft speed and control take precedence over all other actions during landings and takeoffs.

Stress landing in the first third of the runway to ensure there is stopping distance for the aircraft. If the student is unable to land in the first third, teach him or her to make an immediate go around. If the student bounces an airplane on landing, teach the student to make an immediate go around. By following these teaching guidelines, the student is better equipped to properly execute landings when he or she solos. Furthermore, by requiring the first solo flight to consist of landings to a full stop, the flight instructor has the opportunity to stop the flight if necessary.

In gliders, a low energy landing is the most desirable, based on current winds. This helps the student develop good off-field landings techniques. This is dependent on current weather, such as excess winds including crosswinds.

Practical Test Recommendations

Provision is made on the airman certificate or rating application form for the written recommendation of the flight instructor who has prepared the applicant for the practical test involved. Signing this recommendation imposes a serious responsibility on the flight instructor. A flight instructor who makes a practical test recommendation for an applicant seeking a certificate or rating should require the applicant to demonstrate thoroughly the knowledge and skill level required for that certificate or rating. This demonstration should in no instance be less than the complete procedure prescribed in the applicable PTS.

When the instructor endorses the applicant for the practical test, his or her signature on the FAA Form 8710-1, Airman Certificate and/or Rating Application, is valid for 60 days. This is also true with the flight proficiency endorsement that is placed in the applicant's logbook or training record (Advisory Circular (AC) 61-65). These two dates should be the same.

Completion of prerequisites for a practical test is another instructor task that must be documented properly. Examples of all common endorsements can be found in the current issue of AC 61-65, Appendix 1. This appendix also includes references to 14 CFR Part 61, Certification: Pilots, Flight Instructors, and Ground Instructors, for more details concerning the requirements that must be met to qualify for each respective endorsement. The examples shown contain the essential elements of each endorsement. It is not mandatory, but recommended for all endorsements to be worded exactly as those in the AC. For example, changes to regulatory requirements may affect the wording, or the instructor may customize the endorsement for any special circumstances of the applicant. However, at a minimum, the instructor needs to cite the appropriate 14 CFR part 61 section that has been completed.

FAA inspectors and DPEs rely on flight instructor recommendations as evidence of qualification for certification, and proof that a review has been given of the subject areas found to be deficient on the appropriate knowledge test. Recommendations also provide assurance that the applicant has had a thorough briefing on the PTS and the associated knowledge areas, maneuvers, and procedures. If the flight instructor has trained and prepared the applicant competently, the applicant should have no problem passing the practical test.

A flight instructor who fails to ensure a student meets the requirements of regulations prior to endorsing solo flight or additional rating exhibits a serious deficiency in performance. The FAA holds him or her accountable. Providing a solo endorsement for a student who is not fully prepared to accept the responsibility for solo flight operations, or providing an endorsement for an additional rating to a pilot not meeting the appropriate regulatory requirements, is also a breach of faith with the applicant.

Aeronautical Decision-Making

As discussed on page 8-2, aviation training and flight operations are now seen as a system rather than individual concepts. The goal of system safety is for pilots to utilize all four concepts (ADM, risk management, situational awareness, and SRM) so that risk can be reduced to the lowest possible level.

ADM is a systematic approach to the mental process used by aircraft pilots to consistently determine the best course of action in response to a given set of circumstances. Risk management is a decision-making process designed to systematically identify hazards, assess the degree of risk, and determine the best course of action associated with each flight. Situational awareness is the accurate perception and understanding of all the factors and conditions within the four fundamental risk elements that affect safety before, during, and after the flight. SRM is the art and science of managing all resources (both onboard the aircraft and from outside sources) available to a single pilot (prior and during flight) to ensure the successful outcome of the flight.

These key principles are often collectively called ADM. The importance of teaching students effective ADM skills can not be overemphasized. While progress is continually being made in the advancement of pilot training methods, aircraft equipment and systems, and services for pilots, accidents still occur. Despite all the changes in technology to improve flight safety, one factor remains the same—the human factor. It is estimated that approximately 80 percent of all aviation accidents are human factors related.

By taking a system approach to aviation safety, flight instructors interweave aeronautical knowledge, aircraft control skills, ADM, risk management, situational awareness, and SRM into the training process.

Historically, the term "pilot error" has been used to describe the causes of these accidents. Pilot error means that an action or decision made by the pilot was the cause of, or contributing factor to, the accident. This definition also includes the pilot's failure to make a decision or take action. From a broader perspective, the phrase "human factors related" more aptly describes these accidents since it is usually not a single decision that leads to an accident, but a chain of events triggered by a number of factors.

The poor judgment chain, or the error chain, describes this concept of contributing factors in a human factors related accident. Breaking one link in the chain is all that is usually necessary to change the outcome of the sequence of events. The best way to illustrate this concept to students is to discuss specific situations that lead to aircraft accidents or incidents. The following is an example of the type of scenario that can be presented to illustrate the poor judgment chain.

A private pilot with 100 hours of flight time made a precautionary landing on a narrow dirt runway at a private airport. The pilot lost directional control during landing and swerved off the runway into the grass. A witness recalled later that the aircraft appeared to be too high and fast on final approach, and speculated the pilot was having difficulty controlling the aircraft in high winds. The weather at the time of the incident was reported as marginal VFR due to rain showers and thunderstorms. When the aircraft was fueled the following morning, 60 gallons of fuel were required to fill the 62-gallon capacity tanks.

By discussing the events that led to this incident, instructors can help students understand how a series of judgmental errors contributed to the final outcome of this flight.

- Weather decision—on the morning of the flight, the pilot was running late and, having acquired a computer printout of the forecast the night before, he did not obtain a briefing from flight service before his departure.
- Flight planning decision/performance chart—the pilot calculated total fuel requirements for the trip based on a rule-of-thumb figure he had used previously for another airplane. He did not use the fuel tables printed in the pilot's operating handbook (POH) for the aircraft he was flying on this trip. After reaching his destination, the pilot did not request refueling. Based on his original calculations, he believed sufficient fuel remained for the flight home.
- Fatigue/failure to recognize personal limitations—in the presence of deteriorating weather, the pilot departed for the flight home at 5:00 p.m. He did not consider how fatigue and lack of extensive night flying experience could affect the flight.
- Fuel exhaustion—with the aircraft fuel supply almost exhausted, the pilot no longer had the option of diverting to avoid rapidly developing thunderstorms. He was forced to land at the nearest airfield available.

On numerous occasions during the flight, the pilot could have made decisions which may have prevented this incident.

However, as the chain of events unfolded, each poor decision left him with fewer and fewer options. On the positive side, the pilot made a precautionary landing at a time and place of his choosing. VFR into IMC accidents often lead to fatalities. In this case, the pilot landed his aircraft without loss of life.

Teaching pilots to make sound decisions is the key to preventing accidents. Traditional pilot instruction has emphasized flying skills, knowledge of the aircraft, and familiarity with regulations. ADM training focuses on the decision-making process and the factors that affect a pilot's ability to make effective choices.

Timely decision-making is an important tool for any pilot. The student who hesitates when prompt action is required, or who makes the decision to not decide, has made a wrong decision. Sometimes, sound ADM calls for going against procedure. For example, in the event of an engine fire, the pilot initiates an emergency descent. Some POHs call for mixture to be enriched during an emergency descent, but what if the powerplant is engulfed in flames? Emergencies require the pilot to think—assess the situation, choose and execute the actions that assure safety, not act in a rote manner.

It is important for flight instructors to teach students that declaring an emergency when one occurs is an appropriate reaction. Once an emergency is declared, air traffic control (ATC) gives the pilot priority handling. 14 CFR Section 91.3, Responsibility and Authority of the Pilot in Command, states that "In an inflight emergency requiring immediate action, the pilot in command may deviate from any rule of this part to the extent required to meet that emergency."

Flight instructors should incorporate ADM, risk management, situational awareness, and SRM throughout the entire training course for all levels of students. AC 60-22, Aeronautical Decision Making, provides background references, definitions, and other pertinent information about ADM training in the GA environment. *[Figure 8-7]*

The Decision-Making Process

An understanding of the decision-making process provides students with a foundation for developing ADM skills. Some situations, such as engine failures, require a pilot to respond immediately using established procedures with little time for detailed analysis. Traditionally, pilots have been well trained to react to emergencies, but are not as well prepared to make decisions, which require a more reflective response. Typically during a flight, the pilot has time to examine any changes that occur, gather information, and assess risk before reaching a decision. The steps leading to this conclusion constitute the decision-making process. When the decision-making process is presented to students, it is essential to discuss how the process applies to an actual flight situation. To explain the decision-making process, the instructor can introduce the following steps with the accompanying scenario that places the students in the position of making a decision about a typical flight situation.

Defining the Problem

The first step in the decision-making process is to define the problem. This begins with recognizing that a change has occurred or that an expected change did not occur. A problem is perceived first by the senses, and then is distinguished through insight and experience. These same abilities, as well as an objective analysis of all available information, are used to determine the exact nature and severity of the problem.

One critical error that can be made during the decision-making process is incorrectly defining the problem. For example, failure of a landing-gear-extended light to illuminate could indicate that the gear is not down and locked into place or it could mean the bulb is burned out. The actions to be taken in each of these circumstances would be significantly different. Fixating on a problem that does not exist can divert the pilot's attention from important tasks. The pilot's failure to maintain an awareness of the circumstances regarding the flight now becomes the problem. This is why once an initial assumption is made regarding the problem, other sources must be used to verify that the pilot's conclusion is correct.

While on a cross-country flight, Brenda discovers her time en route between two checkpoints is significantly longer than the time she originally calculated. By noticing this discrepancy, she has recognized a change. Based on insight, cross-country flying experience, and knowledge of weather systems, she considers the possibility that she has an increased headwind. She verifies that the original calculations are correct and considers factors that may have lengthened the time between checkpoints, such as a climb or deviation off course. To determine if there is a change in the winds aloft forecast and to check recent pilot reports, she contacts Flight Watch. After weighing each information source, she concludes that the headwind has increased. To determine the severity of the problem, she calculates a new groundspeed and reassesses fuel requirements.

Choosing a Course of Action

After the problem has been identified, the pilot evaluates the need to react to it and determines the actions that may be taken to resolve the situation in the time available. The expected outcome of each possible action should be considered and the risks assessed before the pilot decides on a response to the situation.

Definitions

Aeronautical Decision-Making (ADM)
is a systematic approach to the mental process used by pilots to consistently determine the best course of action in response to a given set of circumstances.

Attitude
is a personal motivational predisposition to respond to persons, situations, or events in a given manner that can, nevertheless, be changed or modified through training as sort of a mental shortcut to decision making.

Attitude Management
is the ability to recognize hazardous attitudes in oneself and the willingness to modify them as necessary through the application of an appropriate antidote thought.

Crew Resource Management (CRM)
is the application of team management concepts in the flight deck environment. It was initially known as cockpit resource management, but as CRM programs evolved to include cabin crews, maintenance personnel, and others, the phrase crew resource management was adopted. This includes single pilots, as in most general aviation aircraft. Pilots of small aircraft, as well as crews of larger aircraft, must make effective use of all available resources: human resources, hardware, and information. A current definition includes all groups routinely working with the cockpit crew who are involved in decisions required to operate a flight safely. These groups include, but are not limited to: pilots, dispatchers, cabin crewmembers, maintenance personnel, and air traffic controllers. CRM is one way of addressing the challenge of optimizing the human/machine interface and accompanying interpersonal activities.

Headwork
is required to accomplish a conscious, rational thought process when making decisions. Good decision-making involves risk identification and assessment, information processing, and problem solving.

Judgment
is the mental process of recognizing and analyzing all pertinent information in a particular situation, a rational evaluation of alternative actions in response to it, and a timely decision on which action to take.

Personality
is the embodiment of personal traits and characteristics of an individual that are set at a very early age and extremely resistant to change.

Poor Judgment Chain
is a series of mistakes that may lead to an accident or incident. Two basic principles generally associated with the creation of a poor judgment chain are: (1) One bad decision often leads to another; and (2) as a string of bad decisions grows, it reduces the number of subsequent alternatives for continued safe flight. ADM is intended to break the poor judgment chain before it can cause an accident or incident.

Risk Elements in ADM
take into consideration the four fundamental risk elements: the pilot, the aircraft, the environment, and the type of operation that comprise any given aviation situation.

Risk Management
is the part of the decision-making process which relies on situational awareness, problem recognition, and good judgment to reduce risks associated with each flight.

Situational Awareness
is the accurate perception and understanding of all the factors and conditions within the four fundamental risk elements that affect safety before, during, and after the flight.

Skills and Procedures
are the procedural, psychomotor, and perceptual skills used to control a specific aircraft or its systems. They are the airmanship abilities that are gained through conventional training, are perfected, and become almost automatic through experience.

Stress Management
is the personal analysis of the kinds of stress experienced while flying, the application of appropriate stress assessment tools, and other coping mechanisms.

Figure 8-7. *Terms used in AC 60-22 to explain concepts used in ADM training.*

Brenda determines the fuel burn if she continues to her destination and considers other options: turning around and landing at a nearby airport, diverting off course, or landing prior to her destination at an airport en route. She now considers the expected outcome of each possible action and assesses the risks involved. After studying the chart, she concludes there is an airport which has fueling services within a reasonable distance along her route. She can refuel there and continue to her destination without a significant loss of time.

Implementing the Decision and Evaluating the Outcome

Although a decision may be reached and a course of action implemented, the decision-making process is not complete. It is important to think ahead and determine how the decision could affect other phases of the flight. As the flight progresses, the pilot must continue to evaluate the outcome of the decision to ensure that it is producing the desired result.

To implement her decision, Brenda plots the course changes and calculates a new estimated time of arrival. She also contacts the nearest AFSS to amend her flight plan and check weather conditions at the new destination. As she proceeds to the airport, she continues to monitor groundspeed, aircraft performance, and weather conditions to ensure no additional steps need to be taken to guarantee the safety of the flight.

Factors Affecting Decision-Making

It is important to stress to a student that being familiar with the decision-making process does not ensure he or she has the good judgment to be a safe pilot. The ability to make effective decisions as PIC depends on a number of factors. Some circumstances, such as the time available to make a decision, may be beyond the pilot's control. However, a pilot can learn to recognize those factors that can be managed, and learn skills to improve decision-making ability and judgment.

Recognizing Hazardous Attitudes

While the ADM process does not eliminate errors, it helps the pilot recognize errors, and in turn enables the pilot to manage the error to minimize its effects. Two steps to improve flight safety are identifying personal attitudes hazardous to safe flight and learning behavior modification techniques.

Flight instructors must be able to spot hazardous attitudes in a student because recognition of hazardous thoughts is the first step toward neutralizing them. CFIs should keep in mind that being fit to fly depends on more than just a pilot's physical condition and recency of experience. Hazardous attitudes contribute to poor pilot judgment and affect the quality of decisions.

Attitude can be defined as a personal motivational predisposition to respond to persons, situations, or events in a given manner. Studies have identified five hazardous attitudes that can affect a pilot's ability to make sound decisions and exercise authority properly. *[Figure 8-8]*

In order for a student to self-examine behaviors during flight, he or she must be taught the potential risks caused from hazardous attitudes and, more importantly, the antidote for each. *[Figure 8-9]* For example, if a student has an easy time with flight training and seems to understand things very quickly, there may be a potential for that student to have a "macho" hazardous attitude. A successful CFI points out

The Five Hazardous Attitudes

Anti-authority: "Don't tell me."
This attitude is found in people who do not like anyone telling them what to do. In a sense, they are saying, "No one can tell me what to do." They may be resentful of having someone tell them what to do, or may regard rules, regulations, and procedures as silly or unnecessary. However, it is always pilot prerogative to question authority if it seems to be in error.

Impulsivity: "Do it quickly."
This is the attitude of people who frequently feel the need to do something—anything—immediately. They do not stop to think about what they are about to do; they do not select the best alternative, and they do the first thing that comes to mind.

Invulnerability: "It won't happen to me."
Many people believe that accidents happen to others, but never to them. They know accidents can happen, and they know that anyone can be affected. They never really feel or believe that they will be personally involved. Pilots who think this way are more likely to take chances and increase risk.

Macho: "I can do it."
Pilots who are always trying to prove that they are better than anyone else are thinking, "I can do it, I'll show them." Pilots with this type of attitude will try to prove themselves by taking risks in order to impress others. While this pattern is thought to be a male characteristic, women are equally susceptible.

Resignation: "What's the use?"
Pilots who think, "What's the use?" do not see themselves as being able to make a great deal of difference in what happens to them. When things go well, the pilot is apt to think that it is good luck. When things go badly, the pilot may feel that "someone is out to get me," or attribute it to bad luck. The pilot will leave the action to others, for better or worse. Sometimes, such pilots will even go along with unreasonable requests just to be a "nice guy."

Figure 8-8. *Pilots should examine their decisions carefully to ensure that their choices have not been influenced by a hazardous attitude.*

Hazardous Attitude	Antidotes
Macho Steve often brags to his friends about his skills as a pilot and how close to the ground he flies. During a local pleasure flight in his single-engine airplane, he decides to buzz some friends barbecuing at a nearby park.	**Taking chances is foolish.**
Anti-authority Although he knows that flying so low to the ground is prohibited by the regulations, he feels that the regulations are too restrictive in some circumstances.	**Follow the rules. They are usually right.**
Invulnerability Steve is not worried about an accident since he has flown this low many times before and he has not had any problems.	**It could happen to me.**
Impulsivity As he is buzzing the park, the airplane does not climb as well as Steve had anticipated and, without thinking, he pulls back hard on the yoke. The airspeed drops and the airplane is close to stalling as the wing brushes a power line.	**Not so fast. Think first.**
Resignation Although Steve manages to recover, the wing sustains minor damage. Steve thinks to himself, "It doesn't really matter how much effort I put in—the end result is the same whether I really try or not."	**I'm not helpless. I can make a difference.**

Figure 8-9. *Students in training can be asked to identify hazardous attitudes and the corresponding antidotes when presented with flight scenarios.*

the potential for the behavior and teaches the student the antidote for that attitude. Hazardous attitudes need to be noticed immediately and corrected with the proper antidote to minimize the potential for any flight hazard.

Stress Management

Learning how to recognize and cope with stress is another effective ADM tool. Stress is the body's response to demands placed upon it. These demands can be either pleasant or unpleasant in nature. The causes of stress for a pilot can range from unexpected weather or mechanical problems while in flight to personal issues unrelated to flying. Stress is an inevitable and necessary part of life; it adds motivation and heightens an individual's response to meet any challenge.

Everyone is stressed to some degree all the time. A certain amount of stress is good since it keeps a person alert and prevents complacency. However, the effects of stress are cumulative and, if not coped with adequately, they eventually add up to an intolerable burden. Performance generally increases with the onset of stress, peaks, and then begins to fall off rapidly as stress levels exceed a person's ability to cope. The ability to make effective decisions during flight can be impaired by stress. Factors, referred to as stressors, can increase a pilot's risk of error in the flight deck. *[Figure 8-10]*

Stressors
Physical Stress Conditions associated with the environment, such as temperature and humidity extremes, noise, vibration, and lack of oxygen.
Physiological Stress Physical conditions, such as fatigue, lack of physical fitness, sleep loss, missed meals (leading to low blood sugar levels), and illness.
Psychological Stress Social or emotional factors, such as a death in the family, a divorce, a sick child, or a demotion at work. This type of stress may also be related to mental workload, such as analyzing a problem, navigating an aircraft, or making decisions.

Figure 8-10. *Three types of stressors that can affect pilot performance.*

One way of exploring the subject of stress with a student is to recognize when stress is affecting performance. If a student seems distracted, or has a particularly difficult time accomplishing the tasks of the lesson, the instructor can query the student. Was the student uncomfortable or tired during the flight? Is there some stress in another aspect of the student's life that may be causing a distraction? This may prompt the student to evaluate how these factors affect performance and judgment. The instructor should also try to determine if there are aspects of pilot training that are causing excessive amounts of stress for the student. For example, if the student consistently makes a decision not to fly, even though weather briefings indicate favorable conditions, it may be due to apprehension regarding the lesson content. Stalls, landings, or an impending solo flight may cause concern. By explaining a specific maneuver in greater detail or offering some additional encouragement, the instructor may be able to alleviate some of the student's stress.

To help students manage the accumulation of life stresses and prevent stress overload, instructors can recommend several techniques. For example, including relaxation time in a busy schedule and maintaining a program of physical fitness can help reduce stress levels. Learning to manage time more effectively can help pilots avoid heavy pressures imposed by getting behind schedule and not meeting deadlines. While these pressures may exist in the workplace, students may also experience the same type of stress regarding their flight training schedule. Instructors can advise students to self-assess to determine their capabilities and limitations and then set realistic goals. In addition, avoiding stressful situations and encounters can help pilots cope with stress.

Use of Resources

To make informed decisions during flight operations, students must be made aware of the resources found both inside and outside the flight deck. Since useful tools and sources of information may not always be readily apparent, learning to recognize these resources is an essential part of ADM training. Resources must not only be identified, but students must also develop the skills to evaluate whether they have the time to use a particular resource and the impact that its use would have upon the safety of flight. For example, the assistance of ATC may be very useful if a pilot is lost. However, in an emergency situation when action needs be taken quickly, time may not be available to contact ATC immediately. During training, CFIs can routinely point out resources to students.

Internal Resources

Internal resources are found in the flight deck during flight. Since some of the most valuable internal resources are ingenuity, knowledge, and skill, pilots can expand flight deck resources immensely by improving their capabilities. This can be accomplished by frequently reviewing flight information publications, such as 14 CFR and the Aeronautical Information Manual (AIM), as well as by pursuing additional training.

A thorough understanding of all the equipment and systems in the aircraft is necessary to fully utilize all resources. For example, advanced navigation and autopilot systems are valuable resources flight instructors must ensure students know how to use. If students do not fully understand how to use the equipment, or if they rely on it so much that they become complacent, it can become a detriment to safe flight. With the advent of advanced avionics with glass displays, GPS, and autopilot, flying might seem inherently easier and safer, but in reality it has become more complex. With the update of the Instrument Practical Test Standards (PTS) to include electronic flight instrument displays, flight management systems, GPS, and autopilot usage, knowledge of internal resources becomes an important component of flight training. As discussed in the section on flight instructor qualifications, instructors must be familiar with the components of each aircraft in which they instruct to ensure students understand the operation of the equipment.

Checklists are essential flight deck resources for verifying that the aircraft instruments and systems are checked, set, and operating properly, as well as ensuring that the proper procedures are performed if there is a system malfunction or inflight emergency. Students reluctant to use checklists can be reminded that pilots at all levels of experience refer to checklists, and that the more advanced the aircraft is, the more crucial checklists become. With the advent of electronic checklists, it has become easier to develop and maintain personal checklists from the manufacturer's checklist with additions for specific aircraft and operations.

In addition, the AFM/POH, which is required to be carried onboard the aircraft, is essential for accurate flight planning and for resolving inflight equipment malfunctions. Other valuable flight deck resources include current aeronautical charts and publications, such as the Airport/Facility Directory (A/FD).

It should be pointed out to students that passengers can also be a valuable resource. Passengers can help watch for traffic and may be able to provide information in an irregular situation, especially if they are familiar with flying. A strange smell or sound may alert a passenger to a potential problem. The PIC should brief passengers before the flight to make sure that they are comfortable voicing any concerns.

External Resources

Possibly the greatest external resources during flight are air traffic controllers and flight service specialists. ATC can help decrease pilot workload by providing traffic advisories, radar vectors, and assistance in emergency situations. AFSS can provide updates on weather, answer questions about airport conditions, and may offer direction-finding assistance. The services provided by ATC can be invaluable in enabling pilots to make informed inflight decisions. Instructors can help new students feel comfortable with ATC by encouraging them to take advantage of services, such as flight following and Flight Watch. If students are exposed to ATC as much as possible during training, they feel confident asking controllers to clarify instructions and are better equipped to use ATC as a resource for assistance in unusual circumstances or emergencies.

Throughout training, students can be asked to identify internal and external resources, which can be used in a variety of flight situations. For example, if a discrepancy is found during preflight, what resources can be used to determine its significance? In this case, the student's knowledge of the aircraft, the POH, an instructor or other experienced pilot, or an AMT can be a resource which may help define the problem.

During cross-country training, students may be asked to consider the following situation. On a cross-country flight, you become disoriented. Although you are familiar with the area, you do not recognize any landmarks, and fuel is running low. What resources do you have to assist you? students should be able to identify their own skills and knowledge, aeronautical charts, ATC, flight service, and navigation equipment as some of the resources that can be used in this situation.

Workload Management

Effective workload management ensures that essential operations are accomplished by planning, prioritizing, and sequencing tasks to avoid work overload. As experience is gained, a pilot learns to recognize future workload requirements and can prepare for high workload periods during times of low workload. Instructors can teach this skill by prompting their students to prepare for a high workload. For example, when en route, the student can be asked to explain the actions that need to be taken during the approach to the airport. The student should be able to describe the procedures for traffic pattern entry and landing preparation. Reviewing the appropriate chart and setting radio frequencies well in advance of need helps reduce workload as the flight nears the airport. In addition, the student should listen to the Automatic Terminal Information Service (ATIS), Automated Surface Observing Systems (ASOS), or Automated Weather Observing System (AWOS), if available, and then monitor the tower frequency or Common Traffic Advisory Frequency (CTAF) to get a good idea of what traffic conditions to expect. Checklists should be performed well in advance so there is time to focus on traffic and ATC instructions. These procedures are especially important prior to entering a high-density traffic area, such as Class B airspace.

To manage workload, items should be prioritized. This concept should be emphasized to students and reinforced when training procedures are performed. For example, during a go-around, adding power, gaining airspeed, and properly configuring the aircraft are priorities. Informing the tower of the balked landing should be accomplished only after these tasks are completed. students must understand that priorities change as the situation changes. If fuel quantity is lower than expected on a cross-country flight, the priority can shift from making a scheduled arrival time at the destination, to locating a nearby airport to refuel. In an emergency situation, the first priority is to fly the aircraft and maintain a safe airspeed.

Another important part of managing workload is recognizing a work overload situation. The first effect of high workload is that the pilot begins to work faster. As workload increases, attention cannot be devoted to several tasks at one time, and the pilot may begin to focus on one item. When the pilot becomes task saturated, there is no awareness of inputs from various sources; decisions may be made on incomplete information, and the possibility of error increases. *[Figure 8-11]*

During a lesson, workload can be gradually increased as the instructor monitors the student's management of tasks. The instructor should ensure that the student has the ability to recognize a work overload situation. When becoming overloaded, the student should stop, think, slow down, and

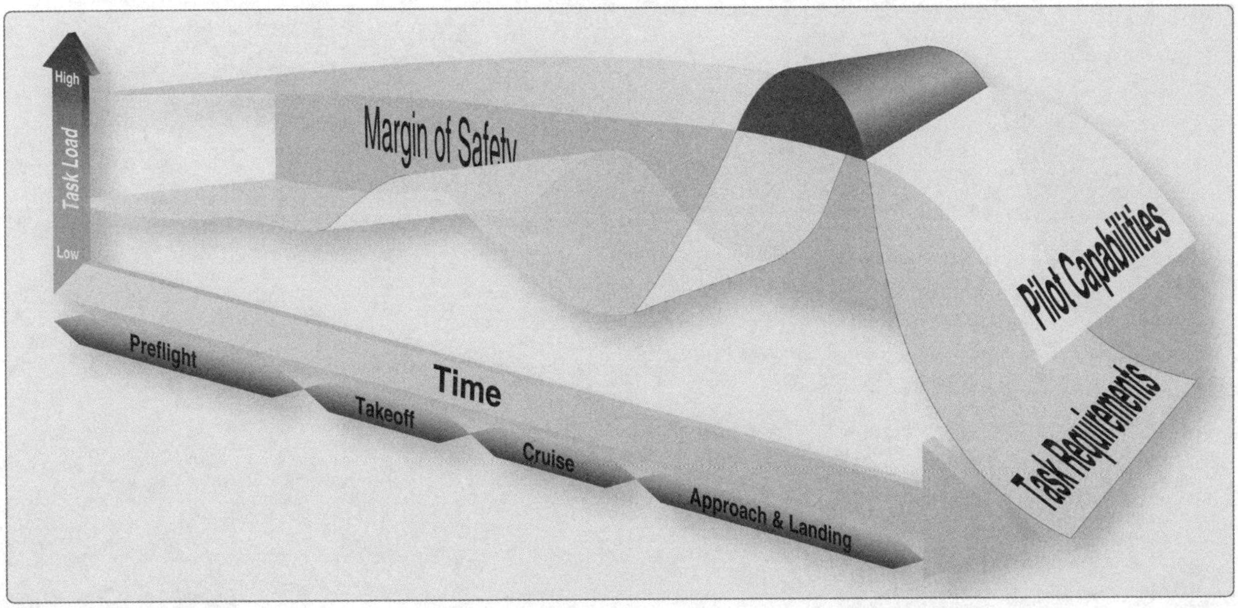

Figure 8-11. *Accidents often occur when flying task requirements exceed pilot capabilities. The difference between these two factors is called the margin of safety. Note that in this idealized example, the margin of safety is minimal during the approach and landing. At this point, an emergency or distraction could overtax pilot capabilities, causing an accident.*

prioritize. It is important that the student understand options that may be available to decrease workload. For example, locating an item on a chart or setting a radio frequency may be delegated to another pilot or passenger, an autopilot (if available) may be used, or ATC may be enlisted to provide assistance.

Chapter Summary

This chapter discussed the demonstration-performance and telling-and-doing training delivery methods of flight instruction, SBT techniques, practical strategies flight instructors can use to enhance their instruction, integrated flight instruction, positive exchange of flight controls, use of distractions, obstacles to learning encountered during flight training, and how to evaluate students. After an intensive look at ADM with suggestions for how to interweave ADM, risk management, and SRM into the teaching process, it closes with a discussion of CFI recommendations. Additional information on recommendations and endorsements can be found in Appendix E, Flight Instructor Endorsements.

Chapter 9

Risk Management

Introduction

"Pull the throttle back!" Lenore, a Certificated Flight Instructor (CFI), ordered the student, Jennifer, as the revolutions per minute (rpm) climbed past 2,000 on engine start-up. "I did, I did!"

Both Jennifer and Lenore grabbed the mixture and pulled. The engine went from a deafening roar to silence. They looked at each other. "What happened?" asked Jennifer. "I don't know. Let's check the engine," Lenore said.

Ten minutes later, they had removed the cowling from the Cessna 152. A quick engine check gave them the answer. The throttle rod-end was not connected to the carburetor arm—no bolt, no nut, just air between the rod-end and the arm. Jennifer looked at Lenore. "What if this had happened in flight?"

"What I want to know," Lenore said, "is how this happened at all. The annual inspection was signed off yesterday."

The previous day, the annual inspection had been signed off after a lengthy inspection by a local facility. Several mechanics had been involved in the inspection, including the owner/student who had installed a headliner. The mechanic with the Inspection Authorization (IA) who signed off the annual was supervising several annuals, so most of the maintenance was performed by other mechanics.

After the inspection, the engine had been run-up according to the usual post-inspection procedures. The student and instructor had flown the airplane for a half-hour familiarization flight. The next day's engine start resulted in a runaway engine with the apparent cause due to the lack of the throttle rod-end hardware being safetied.

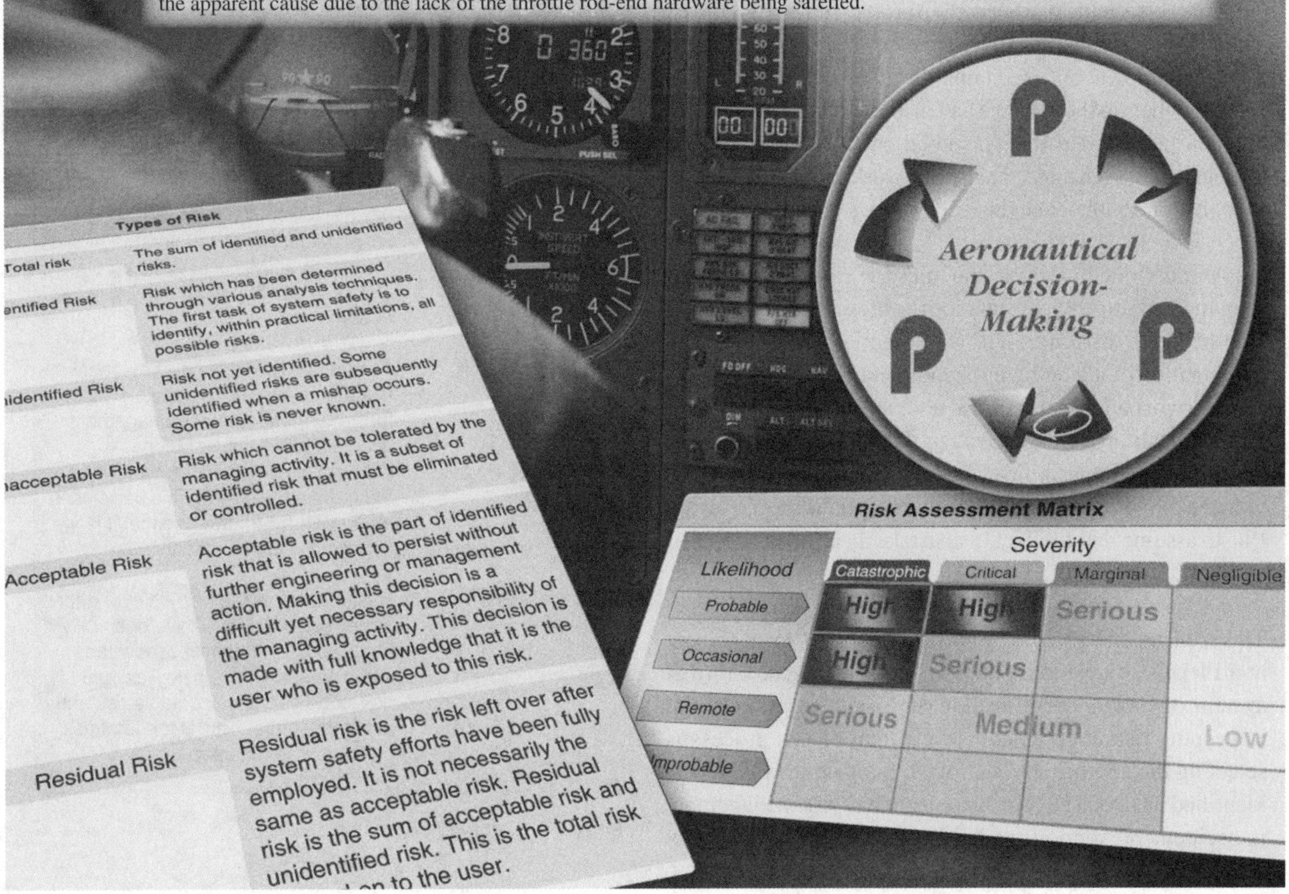

Three deficient areas in this annual inspection were identified by a round-table discussion group of aircraft and powerplant (A&P) mechanics and the student. These areas were:

- Lack of responsibility
- Checklist misuse
- Complacency

Lack of responsibility—no one took responsibility for the entire inspection. The chances of something being overlooked increase with an increase in the number of mechanics involved in an inspection. The responsible person is removed from the actual procedure. The student remembers hearing the IA ask one of the engine mechanics about the throttle. However, the question was vague, the answer was vague, and the rod-end was not safetied.

Checklist misuse—all checklists have a line item regarding inspection of the engine controls for rigging and safety. Perhaps the throttle rod-end had been disconnected for maintenance after the IA had signed off the control inspection. In that case, a discrepancy should have been entered onto the discrepancy sheet stating "reconnect and safety throttle rod-end."

Complacency—an insidious and hard-to-identify attitude. Each of the mechanics involved in the incident thought someone else had inspected the throttle rod-end. The IA signed off the annual inspection because he had either asked the mechanics about the items on the checklist or in his frequent visits to the airplane had inspected the various items himself and decided that was good enough. Complacency crippled the mechanics' quality of work by removing any thoughts of double-checking each other's work.

While a definite answer to the question of what happened remains a matter of speculation, professional mechanics should heed warning signs of potential problems. The combination of a lengthy inspection, numerous technicians, an overworked supervisor, a poor checklist, and vague communication should raise a red flag of caution. Although the ultimate responsibility for the safety of any flight rests with the pilot in command (PIC), it is not unreasonable for the PIC to assume that mechanics also take their responsibilities seriously.

This scenario underscores the need for safety risk management at all levels of aviation. Safety risk management, a formal system of hazard identification and analysis, is essential in keeping risk at acceptable levels. Part of this process is selecting the appropriate controls to mitigate the risk of the identified hazard. The primary objective of risk management is accident prevention, which is achieved by proactively identifying, assessing, and eliminating or controlling safety-related hazards to acceptable levels.

This chapter discusses safety risk management in the aviation community, looking at it as preemptive, rather than reactive. The principles of risk management and the tools for teaching risk management in the flight training environment are addressed in Chapter 8, Techniques of Flight Instruction.

Defining Risk Management

Risk is defined as the probability and possible severity of accident or loss from exposure to various hazards, including injury to people and loss of resources. *[Figure 9-1]* All Federal Aviation Administration (FAA) operations in the United States involve risk and require decisions that include risk assessment and risk management. Risk management, a formalized way of thinking about these topics, is the logical process of weighing the potential costs of risks against the possible benefits of allowing those risks to stand uncontrolled. Risk management is a decision-making process designed to

Types of Risk	
Total Risk	The sum of identified and unidentified risks.
Identified Risk	Risk which has been determined through various analysis techniques. The first task of system safety is to identify, within practical limitations, all possible risks.
Unidentified Risk	Risk not yet identified. Some unidentified risks are subsequently identified when a mishap occurs. Some risk is never known.
Unacceptable Risk	Risk which cannot be tolerated by the managing activity. It is a subset of identified risk that must be eliminated or controlled.
Acceptable Risk	Acceptable risk is the part of identified risk that is allowed to persist without further engineering or management action. Making this decision is a difficult yet necessary responsibility of the managing activity. This decision is made with full knowledge that it is the user who is exposed to this risk.
Residual Risk	Residual risk is the risk left over after system safety efforts have been fully employed. It is not necessarily the same as acceptable risk. Residual risk is the sum of acceptable risk and unidentified risk. This is the total risk passed on to the user.

Figure 9-1. *Types of risk.*

identify hazards systematically, assess the degree of risk, and determine the best course of action. Key terms are:

- Hazard—a present condition, event, object, or circumstance that could lead to or contribute to an unplanned or undesired event, such as an accident. It is a source of danger. For example, a nick in the propeller represents a hazard.
- Risk—the future impact of a hazard that is not controlled or eliminated. It is the possibility of loss or injury. The level of risk is measured by the number of people or resources affected (exposure); the extent of possible loss (severity); and likelihood of loss (probability).
- Safety—freedom from those conditions that can cause death, injury, occupational illness, or damage to or loss of equipment or property, or damage to the environment. Note that absolute safety is not possible because complete freedom from all hazardous conditions is not possible. Therefore, safety is a relative term that implies a level of risk that is both perceived and accepted.

Principles of Risk Management

Accept No Unnecessary Risk

Unnecessary risk is that which carries no commensurate return in terms of benefits or opportunities. Everything involves risk. The most logical choices for accomplishing an operation are those that meet all requirements with the minimum acceptable risk. The corollary to this axiom is "accept necessary risk" required to complete the operation or task successfully. Flying is impossible without risk, but unnecessary risk comes without a corresponding return. If flying a new airplane for the first time, a CFI might determine that the risk of making that flight in low instrument flight rules (IFR) conditions is unnecessary.

Make Risk Decisions at the Appropriate Level

Anyone can make a risk decision. However, the appropriate decision-maker is the person who can develop and implement risk controls. The decision-maker must be authorized to accept levels of risk typical of the planned operation. In a single-pilot situation, the pilot makes the decision to accept certain levels of risk. In the maintenance facility, an aviation maintenance technician (AMT) may need to elevate decisions to the next level in the chain of management upon determining that those controls available to him or her will not reduce residual risk to an acceptable level.

Accept Risk When Benefits Outweigh the Costs

All identified benefits should be compared against all identified costs. Even high-risk endeavors may be undertaken when there is clear knowledge that the sum of the benefits exceeds the sum of the costs. For example, in any flying activity, it is necessary to accept some degree of risk. A day with good weather, for example, is a much better time to fly an unfamiliar airplane for the first time than a day with low instrument flight rules (IFR) conditions.

Integrate Risk Management Into Planning at All Levels

Risks are more easily assessed and managed in the planning stages of an operation. The later changes are made in the process of planning and executing an operation, the more expensive and time consuming they become. Because risk is an unavoidable part of every flight, safety requires the use of appropriate and effective risk management not just in the preflight planning stage, but in all stages of the flight.

Risk Management Process

Risk management is a simple process which identifies operational hazards and takes reasonable measures to reduce risk to personnel, equipment, and the mission.

Step 1: Identify the Hazard

A hazard is defined as any real or potential condition that can cause degradation, injury, illness, death, or damage to or loss of equipment or property. Experience, common sense, and specific analytical tools help identify risks.

Step 2: Assess the Risk

The assessment step is the application of quantitative and qualitative measures to determine the level of risk associated with specific hazards. This process defines the probability and severity of an accident that could result from the hazards based upon the exposure of humans or assets to the hazards.

Step 3: Analyze Risk Control Measures

Investigate specific strategies and tools that reduce, mitigate, or eliminate the risk. All risks have two components:

1. Probability of occurrence
2. Severity of the hazard

Effective control measures reduce or eliminate at least one of these. The analysis must take into account the overall costs and benefits of remedial actions, providing alternative choices if possible.

Step 4: Make Control Decisions

Identify the appropriate decision-maker. That decision-maker must choose the best control or combination of controls, based on the analysis of steps 1 and 2.

Step 5: Implement Risk Controls

A plan for applying the selected controls must be formulated, the time, materials, and personnel needed to put these measures in place must be provided.

Step 6: Supervise and Review

Once controls are in place, the process must be reevaluated periodically to ensure their effectiveness. People at every level must fulfill their respective roles to assure the controls are maintained over time. The risk management process continues throughout the life cycle of the system, mission, or activity.

Implementing the Risk Management Process

To derive maximum benefit from this powerful tool, it must be used properly. The following principles are essential.

- Apply the steps in sequence—each step is a building block for the next, and must be completed before proceeding to the next. If a hazard identification step is interrupted to focus on the control of a particular hazard, more important hazards may be overlooked. Until all hazards are identified, the remainder of the process is not effective.
- Maintain a balance in the process—all steps are important. Allocate the time and resources to perform all.
- Apply the process in a cycle—the "supervise and review" step should include a brand new look at the operation being analyzed to see whether new hazards can be identified.
- Involve people in the process—ensure that risk controls are mission supportive, and the people who must do the work see them as positive actions. The people who are actually exposed to risks usually know best what works and what does not.

Level of Risk

The level of risk posed by a given hazard is measured in terms of:

- Severity (extent of possible loss)
- Probability (likelihood that a hazard will cause a loss)

Assessing Risk

Assessment of risk is an important part of good risk management. For example, the hazard of a nick in the propeller poses a risk only if the airplane is flown. If the damaged prop is exposed to the constant vibration of normal engine operation, there is a high risk is that it could fracture and cause catastrophic damage to the engine and/or airframe and the passengers.

Every flight has hazards and some level of risk associated with it. It is critical that pilots and especially students are able to differentiate in advance between a low-risk flight and a high-risk flight, and then establish a review process and develop risk mitigation strategies to address flights throughout that range.

For the single pilot, assessing risk is not as simple as it sounds. For example, the pilot acts as his or her own quality control in making decisions. If a fatigued pilot who has flown 16 hours is asked if he or she is too tired to continue flying, the answer may be no. Most pilots are goal oriented and, when asked to accept a flight, there is a tendency to deny personal limitations while adding weight to issues not germane to the mission. For example, pilots of helicopter emergency services (EMS) have been known to make flight decisions that add significant weight to the patient's welfare. These pilots add weight to intangible factors (the patient in this case) and fail to appropriately quantify actual hazards such as fatigue or weather when making flight decisions. The single pilot who has no other crew member for consultation must wrestle with the intangible factors that draw one into a hazardous position. Therefore, he or she has a greater vulnerability than a full crew.

Examining National Transportation Safety Board (NTSB) reports and other accident research can help a pilot learn to assess risk more effectively. For example, the accident rate during night VFR decreases by nearly 50 percent once a pilot obtains 100 hours, and continues to decrease until the 1,000 hour level. The data suggest that for the first 500 hours, pilots flying VFR at night might want to establish higher personal limitations than are required by the regulations and, if applicable, apply instrument flying skills in this environment.

Several risk assessment models are available to assist in the process of assessing risk. The models, all taking slightly different approaches, seek a common goal of assessing risk in an objective manner.

The most basic tool is the risk matrix. *[Figure 9-2]* It assesses two items: the likelihood of an event occurring and the consequence of that event.

Likelihood of an Event

Likelihood is nothing more than taking a situation and determining the probability of its occurrence. It is rated as probable, occasional, remote, or improbable. For example, a pilot is flying from point A to point B (50 miles) in marginal visual flight rules (MVFR) conditions. The likelihood of encountering potential instrument meteorological conditions

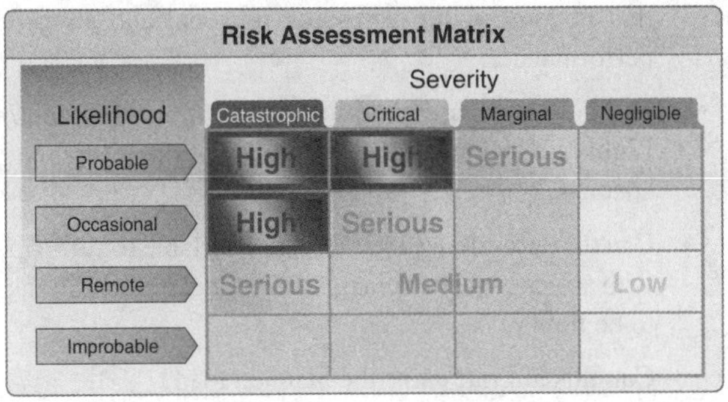

Figure 9-2. *This risk matrix can be used for almost any operation by assigning likelihood and severity. In the case presented, the pilot assigned the likelihood of occassional and the severity as catastrophic falls in the high-risk area.*

(IMC) is the first question the pilot needs to answer. The experiences of other pilots, coupled with the forecast, might cause the pilot to assign "occasional" to determine the probability of encountering IMC.

The following are guidelines for making assignments.

- Probable—an event will occur several times.
- Occasional—an event will probably occur sometime.
- Remote—an event is unlikely to occur, but is possible.
- Improbable—an event is highly unlikely to occur.

Severity of an Event

The next element is the severity or consequence of a pilot's action(s). It can relate to injury and/or damage. If the individual in the example above is not an instrument flight rules (IFR) pilot, what are the consequences of encountering inadvertent IMC? In this case, because the pilot is not IFR rated, the consequences are catastrophic. The following are guidelines for this assignment.

- Catastrophic—results in fatalities, total loss
- Critical—severe injury, major damage
- Marginal—minor injury, minor damage
- Negligible—less than minor injury, less than minor system damage

Simply connecting the two factors as shown in *Figure 9-2* indicates the risk is high and the pilot must either not fly or fly only after finding ways to mitigate, eliminate, or control the risk.

Mitigating Risk

Risk assessment is only part of the equation. After determining the level of risk, the pilot needs to mitigate the risk. For example, the pilot flying from point A to point B (50 miles) in MVFR conditions has several ways to reduce risk:

- Wait for the weather to improve to good visual flight rules (VFR) conditions.
- Take a pilot who is rated as an IFR pilot.
- Delay the flight.
- Cancel the flight.
- Drive.

IMSAFE Checklist

One of the best ways that single pilots can mitigate risk is to use the IMSAFE checklist *[Figure 9-3]* to determine physical and mental readiness for flying:

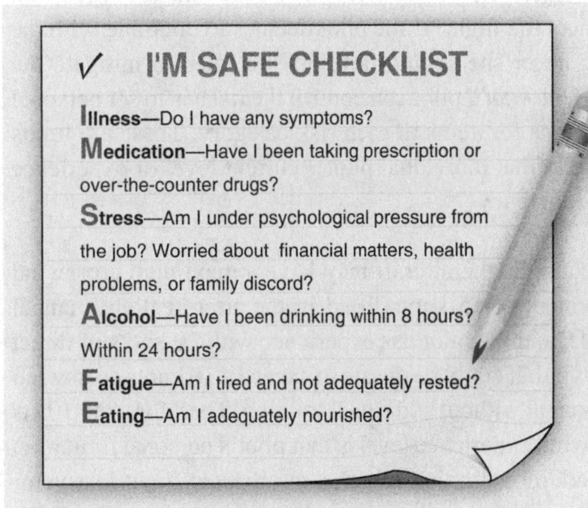

Figure 9-3. *Prior to flight, pilots should assess their fitness, just as they evaluate the aircraft's airworthiness.*

1. Illness—Am I sick? Illness is an obvious pilot risk.
2. Medication—Am I taking any medicines that might affect my judgment or make me drowsy?
3. Stress—Am I under psychological pressure from the job? Do I have money, health, or family problems? Stress causes concentration and performance problems. While the regulations list medical conditions that require grounding, stress is not among them. The pilot should consider the effects of stress on performance.
4. Alcohol—Have I been drinking within 8 hours? Within 24 hours? As little as one ounce of liquor, one bottle of beer, or four ounces of wine can impair flying skills. Alcohol also renders a pilot more susceptible to disorientation and hypoxia.
5. Fatigue—Am I tired and not adequately rested? Fatigue continues to be one of the most insidious hazards to flight safety, as it may not be apparent to a pilot until serious errors are made.

6. Eating—Have I eaten enough of the proper foods to keep adequately nourished during the entire flight?

The PAVE Checklist

Another way to mitigate risk is to perceive hazards. By incorporating the PAVE checklist into all stages of flight planning, the pilot divides the risks of flight into four categories: **P**ilot in command (PIC), **A**ircraft, en**V**ironment, and **E**xternal pressures (PAVE) which form part of a pilot's decision-making process.

With the PAVE checklist, pilots have a simple way to remember each category to examine for risk prior to each flight. Once a pilot identifies the risks of a flight, he or she needs to decide whether the risk or combination of risks can be managed safely and successfully. If not, make the decision to cancel the flight. If the pilot decides to continue with the flight, he or she should develop strategies to mitigate the risks. One way a pilot can control the risks is to set personal minimums for items in each risk category. These are limits unique to that individual pilot's current level of experience and proficiency.

For example, the aircraft may have a maximum crosswind component of 15 knots listed in the aircraft flight manual (AFM), and the pilot has experience with 10 knots of direct crosswind. It could be unsafe to exceed a 10 knots crosswind component without additional training. Therefore, the 10 kts crosswind experience level is that pilot's personal limitation until additional training with a certificated flight instructor (CFI) provides the pilot with additional experience for flying in crosswinds that exceed 10 knots.

One of the most important concepts that safe pilots understand is the difference between what is "legal" in terms of the regulations, and what is "smart" or "safe" in terms of pilot experience and proficiency.

P = Pilot in Command (PIC)

The pilot is one of the risk factors in a flight. The pilot must ask, "Am I ready for this trip?" in terms of experience, currency, physical and emotional condition. The IMSAFE checklist combined with proficiency, recency, and currency provides the answers.

A = Aircraft

What limitations will the aircraft impose upon the trip? Ask the following questions:

- Is this the right aircraft for the flight?
- Am I familiar with and current in this aircraft? Aircraft performance figures and the AFM are based on a brand new aircraft flown by a professional test pilot. Keep that in mind while assessing personal and aircraft performance.
- Is this aircraft equipped for the flight? Instruments? Lights? Navigation and communication equipment adequate?
- Can this aircraft use the runways available for the trip with an adequate margin of safety under the conditions to be flown?
- Can this aircraft carry the planned load?
- Can this aircraft operate at the altitudes needed for the trip?
- Does this aircraft have sufficient fuel capacity, with reserves, for trip legs planned?
- Does the fuel quantity delivered match the fuel quantity ordered?

V = EnVironment

Weather is an major environmental consideration. Earlier it was suggested pilots set their own personal minimums, especially when it comes to weather. As pilots evaluate the weather for a particular flight, they should consider the following:

- What are the current ceiling and visibility? In mountainous terrain, consider having higher minimums for ceiling and visibility, particularly if the terrain is unfamiliar.
- Consider the possibility that the weather may be different than forecast. Have alternative plans, and be ready and willing to divert should an unexpected change occur.
- Consider the winds at the airports being used and the strength of the crosswind component.
- If flying in mountainous terrain, consider whether there are strong winds aloft. Strong winds in mountainous terrain can cause severe turbulence and downdrafts and can be very hazardous for aircraft even when there is no other significant weather.
- Are there any thunderstorms present or forecast?
- If there are clouds, is there any icing, current or forecast? What is the temperature-dew point spread and the current temperature at altitude? Can descent be made safely all along the route?
- If icing conditions are encountered, is the pilot experienced at operating the aircraft's deicing or anti-icing equipment? Is this equipment in good condition and functional? For what icing conditions is the aircraft rated, if any?

Evaluation of terrain is another important component of analyzing the flight environment. To avoid terrain and obstacles, especially at night or in low visibility, determine safe altitudes in advance by using the altitudes shown on VFR and IFR charts during preflight planning. Use maximum elevation figures (MEFs) and other easily obtainable data to minimize chances of an inflight collision with terrain or obstacles.

Airport considerations include:

- What lights are available at the destination and alternate airports? VASI/PAPI or ILS glideslope guidance? Is the terminal airport equipped with them? Are they working? Will the pilot need to use the radio to activate the airport lights?
- Check the Notices to Airmen (NOTAMs) for closed runways or airports. Look for runway or beacon lights out, nearby towers, etc.
- Choose the flight route wisely. An engine failure gives the nearby airports (and terrain) supreme importance.
- Are there shorter or obstructed fields at the destination and/or alternate airports?

Airspace considerations include:

- If the trip is over remote areas, are appropriate clothing, water, and survival gear onboard in the event of a forced landing?
- If the trip includes flying over water or unpopulated areas with the chance of losing visual reference to the horizon, the pilot must be current, equipped, and qualified to fly IFR.
- Check the airspace and any temporary flight restriction (TFRs) along the route of flight.

Night flying requires special consideration.

- If the trip includes flying at night over water or unpopulated areas with the chance of losing visual reference to the horizon, the pilot must be prepared to fly IFR.
- Will the flight conditions allow a safe emergency landing at night?
- Preflight all aircraft lights, interior and exterior, for a night flight. Carry at least two flashlights—one for exterior preflight and a smaller one that can be dimmed and kept nearby.

E = External Pressures

External pressures are influences external to the flight that create a sense of pressure to complete a flight—often at the expense of safety. Factors that can be external pressures include the following:

- Someone waiting at the airport for the flight's arrival.
- A passenger the pilot does not want to disappoint.
- The desire to demonstrate pilot qualifications.
- The desire to impress someone. (Probably the two most dangerous words in aviation are "Watch this!")
- The desire to satisfy a specific personal goal ("get-home-itis," "get-there-itis," and "let's-go-itis").
- The pilot's general goal-completion orientation.
- Emotional pressure associated with acknowledging that skill and experience levels may be lower than a pilot would like them to be. Pride can be a powerful external factor!

Management of external pressure is the single most important key to risk management because it is the one risk factor category that can cause a pilot to ignore all the other risk factors. External pressures put time-related pressure on the pilot and figure into a majority of accidents.

The use of personal standard operating procedures (SOPs) is one way to manage external pressures. The goal is to supply a release for the external pressures of a flight. These procedures include but are not limited to:

- Allow time on a trip for an extra fuel stop or to make an unexpected landing because of weather.
- Have alternate plans for a late arrival or make backup airline reservations for must-be-there trips.
- For really important trips, plan to leave early enough so that there would still be time to drive to the destination.
- Advise those who are waiting at the destination that the arrival may be delayed. Know how to notify them when delays are encountered.
- Manage passengers' expectations. Make sure passengers know that they might not arrive on a firm schedule, and if they must arrive by a certain time, they should make alternative plans.

- Eliminate pressure to return home, even on a casual day flight, by carrying a small overnight kit containing prescriptions, contact lens solutions, toiletries, or other necessities on every flight.

The key to managing external pressure is to be ready for and accept delays. Remember that people get delayed when traveling on airlines, driving a car, or taking a bus. The pilot's goal is to manage risk, not create hazards.

During each flight, decisions must be made regarding events involving interactions between the four risk elements—PIC, aircraft, environment, and external pressures. The decision-making process involves an evaluation of each of these risk elements to achieve an accurate perception of the flight situation. *[Figure 9-4]*

Three-P Model for Pilots

Risk management is a decision-making process designed to perceive hazards systematically, assess the degree of risk associated with a hazard, and determine the best course of action (see Appendix F). For example, the Perceive, Process, Perform (3P) model for aeronautical decision-making (ADM) offers a simple, practical, and structured way for pilots to manage risk. *[Figure 9-5]*

To use the 3P model, the pilot:

- Perceives the given set of circumstances for a flight.
- Processes by evaluating the impact of those circumstances on flight safety.
- Performs by implementing the best course of action.

In the first step, the goal is to develop situational awareness by perceiving hazards, which are present events, objects, or circumstances that could contribute to an undesired future event. In this step, the pilot systematically identifies and lists hazards associated with all aspects of the flight: pilot, aircraft, environment, and external pressures. It is important to consider how individual hazards might combine. Consider, for example, the hazard that arises when a new instrument pilot with no experience in actual instrument conditions wants to make a cross-country flight to an airport with low ceilings in order to attend an important business meeting.

In the second step, the goal is to process this information to determine whether the identified hazards constitute risk, which is defined as the future impact of a hazard that is not controlled or eliminated. The degree of risk posed by a given hazard can be measured in terms of exposure (number of people or resources affected), severity (extent of possible loss), and probability (the likelihood that a hazard will cause a loss). If the hazard is low ceilings, for example, the level of risk depends on a number of other factors, such as pilot training and experience, aircraft equipment, and fuel capacity.

In the third step, the goal is to perform by taking action to eliminate hazards or mitigate risk, and then continuously evaluate the outcome of this action. With the example of low ceilings at destination, for instance, the pilot can perform good ADM by selecting a suitable alternate, knowing where to find good weather, and carrying sufficient fuel to reach it. This course of action would mitigate the risk. The pilot also has the option to eliminate it entirely by waiting for better weather.

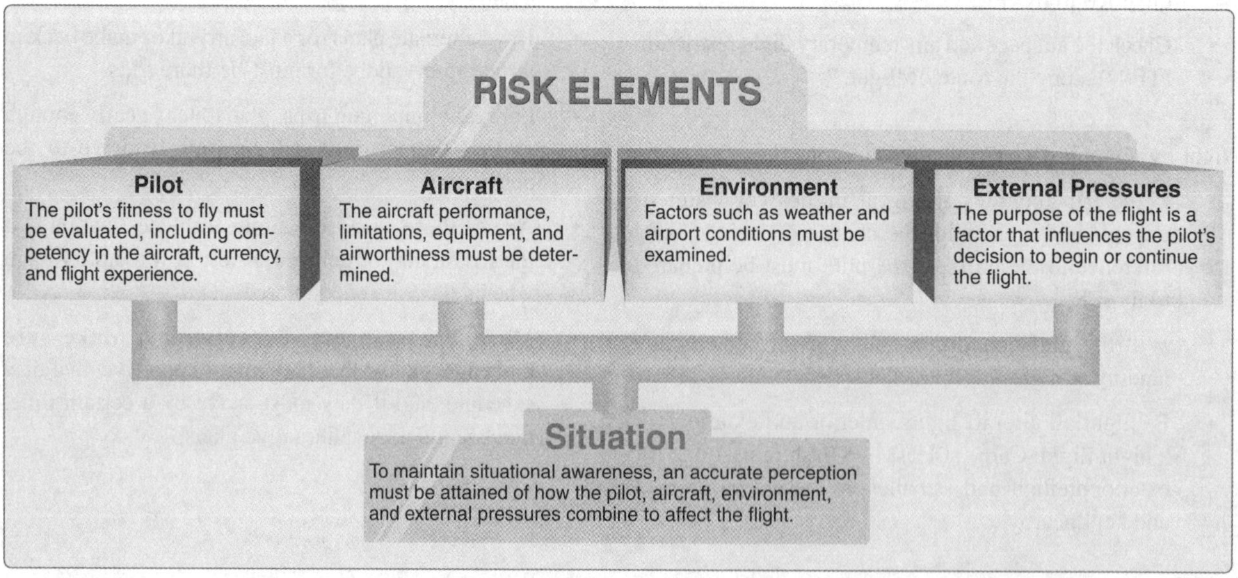

Figure 9-4. *One of the most important decisions that the pilot in command must make is the go/no-go decision. Evaluating each of these risk elements can help the pilot decide whether a flight should be conducted or continued.*

Figure 9-5. *3P Model (Perceive, Process, and Perform).*

Once the pilot has completed the 3P decision process and selected a course of action, the process begins again because the set of circumstances brought about by the course of action requires analysis. The decision-making process is a continuous loop of perceiving, processing, and performing.

It is never too early to start teaching students about risk management. Using the 3P model gives CFIs a tool to teach them a structured, efficient, and systematic way to identify hazards, assess risk, and implement effective risk controls. Practicing risk management needs to be as automatic in general aviation (GA) flying as basic aircraft control. Consider making the 3P discussion a standard feature of the preflight discussion. As is true for other flying skills, risk management habits are best developed through repetition and consistent adherence to specific procedures.

Hazard List for Aviation Technicians

AMTs should learn about risk management early in training, also. Instructors tasked with integrating risk management into instruction can turn to hazard assessments that identify the safety risks associated with the facility being used, the tools used in the procedure, and/or the job being performed.

The process for identifying hazards can be accomplished through the use of checklists, lessons learned, compliance inspections/audits, accidents/near misses, regulatory developments, and brainstorming sessions. For example, aviation accident reports from the National Transportation Safety Board (NTSB) can be used to generate discussions pertaining to faulty maintenance that led to aircraft accidents. All available sources should be used for identifying, characterizing, and controlling safety risks.

The 3P model can also be adapted for use in a nonflight environment, such as a maintenance facility. For example, the AMT perceives a hazard, processes its impact on shop or personnel safety, and then performs by implementing the best course of action to mitigate the perceived risk.

Pilot Self-Assessment

Setting personal minimums is an important step in mitigating risk, and safe pilots know how to properly self-assess. For example, in the opening scenario, the aircraft Mary plans to fly may have a maximum crosswind component of 15 knots listed in the aircraft flight manual (AFM), but she only has experience with 10 knots of direct crosswind. It could be unsafe to exceed a 10 knots crosswind component without additional training. Therefore, the 10 knot crosswind experience level is Mary's personal limitation until additional training with Daniel provides her with additional experience for flying in crosswinds that exceed 10 knots.

Pilots in training must be taught that exercising good judgment begins prior to taking the controls of an aircraft. Often, pilots thoroughly check their aircraft to determine airworthiness, yet do not evaluate their own fitness for flight. Just as a checklist is used when preflighting an aircraft, a personal checklist based on such factors as experience, currency, and comfort level can help determine if a pilot is prepared for a particular flight. The FAA's "Personal Minimums Checklist" located in Appendix D is an excellent tool for pilots to use in self-assessment. This checklist reflects the PAVE approach to risk mitigation discussed in the previous paragraphs.

Worksheets for a more in-depth risk assessment are located in the "FAA/Industry Training Standards Personal and Weather Risk Assessment Guide" located online at www.faa.gov. This guide is designed to assist pilots in developing personal standardized procedures for accomplishing PIC responsibilities and in making better preflight and inflight weather decisions. CFIs should stress that frequent review of the personal guide keeps the information fresh and increases a pilot's ability to recognize the conditions in which a new risk assessment should be made, a key element in the decision-making process.

Situational Awareness

Situational awareness is the accurate perception and understanding of all the factors and conditions within the four fundamental risk elements that affect safety before, during, and after the flight. Maintaining situational awareness requires an understanding of the relative significance of these factors and their future impact on the flight. When situationally aware, the pilot has an overview of the total operation and is not fixated on one perceived significant factor. Some of the elements inside the aircraft to be considered are the status of aircraft systems, pilot, and passengers. In addition, an awareness of the environmental conditions of the flight, such as spatial orientation of the aircraft and its relationship to terrain, traffic, weather, and airspace must be maintained.

To maintain situational awareness, all of the skills involved in ADM are used. For example, an accurate perception of the pilot's fitness can be achieved through self-assessment and recognition of hazardous attitudes. A clear assessment of the status of navigation equipment can be obtained through workload management, and establishing a productive relationship with ATC can be accomplished by effective resource use.

Obstacles to Maintaining Situational Awareness

Many obstacles exist that can interfere with a pilot's ability to maintain situational awareness. For example, fatigue, stress, or work overload can cause the pilot to fixate on a single perceived important item rather than maintaining an overall awareness of the flight situation. A contributing factor in many accidents is a distraction, which diverts the pilot's attention from monitoring the instruments or scanning outside the aircraft. Many flight deck distractions begin as a minor problem, such as a gauge that is not reading correctly, but result in accidents as the pilot diverts attention to the perceived problem and neglects to properly control the aircraft.

Fatigue, discussed as an obstacle to learning, is also an obstacle to maintaining situational awareness. It is a threat to aviation safety because it impairs alertness and performance. *[Figure 9-5]* The term is used to describe a range of experiences from sleepy, or tired, to exhausted. Two major physiological phenomena create fatigue: sleep loss and circadian rhythm disruption.

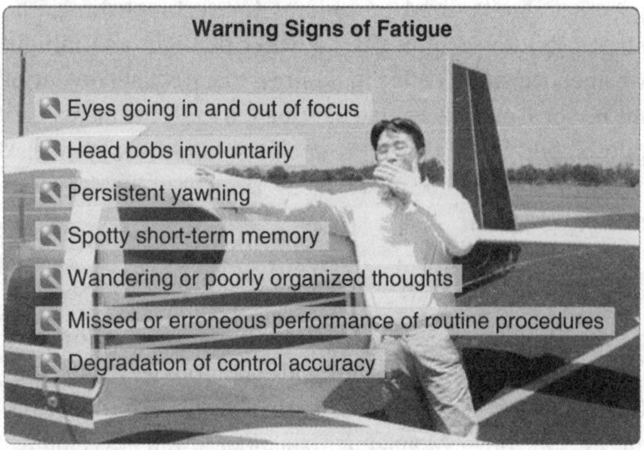

Figure 9-5. *Fatigue is a threat to aviation safety because it impairs alertness and performance.*

Fatigue is a normal response to many conditions common to flight operations because characteristics of the flight deck environment, such as low barometric pressure, humidity, noise, and vibration, make pilots susceptible to fatigue. The only effective treatment for fatigue is adequate sleep. As fatigue progresses, it is responsible for increased errors of omission, followed by errors of commission, and microsleeps, or involuntary sleep lapses lasting from a few seconds to a few minutes. For obvious reasons, errors caused by these short absences can have significant hazardous consequences in the aviation environment.

Sleep-deprived pilots may not notice sleepiness or other fatigue symptoms during preflight and departure flight operations. Once underway and established on altitude and heading, sleepiness and other fatigue symptoms tend to manifest themselves. Extreme fatigue can cause uncontrolled and involuntary shutdown of the brain. Regardless of motivation, professionalism, or training, an individual who is extremely sleepy can lapse into sleep at any time, despite the potential consequences of inattention. There are a number of countermeasures for coping with fatigue, as shown in *Figure 9-6.*

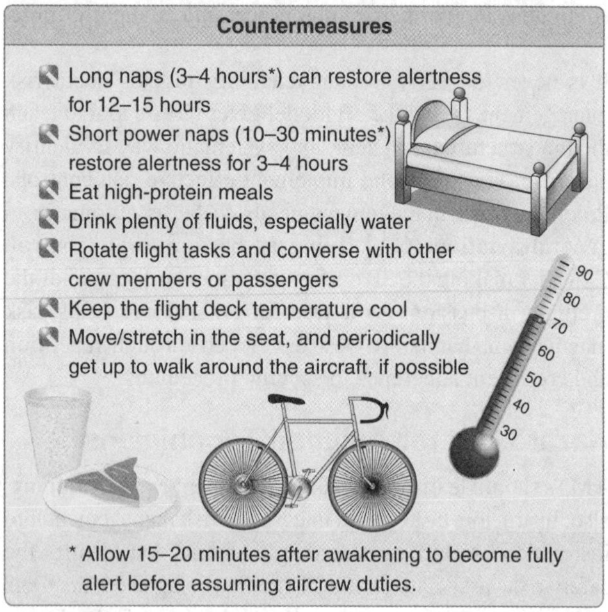

Figure 9-6. *Countermeasures for coping with fatigue.*

Complacency presents another obstacle to maintaining situational awareness. Defined as overconfidence from repeated experience on a specific activity, complacency has been implicated as a contributing factor in numerous aviation accidents and incidents. Like fatigue, complacency reduces the pilot's effectiveness in the flight deck. However, complacency is harder to recognize than fatigue, since everything is perceived to be progressing smoothly. Highly reliable automation has been shown to induce overconfidence and complacency. This can result in a pilot following the instructions of the automation even when common sense suggests otherwise. If the pilot assumes the autopilot is doing its job, he or she does not crosscheck the instruments or the aircraft's position frequently. If the autopilot fails, the pilot may not be mentally prepared to fly the aircraft manually. Instructors should be especially alert to complacency in students with significant flight experience. For example, a pilot receiving a flight review in a familiar aircraft may be prone to complacency.

Advanced avionics have created a high degree of redundancy and dependability in modern aircraft systems, which can promote complacency and inattention. During flight training, the CFI should emphasize that routine flight operations may lead to a sense of complacency, which can threaten flight safety by reducing situational awareness.

By asking about positions of other aircraft in the traffic pattern, engine instrument indications, and the aircraft's location in relation to references on a chart, the instructor can determine if the student is maintaining situational awareness. The instructor can also attempt to focus the student's attention on an imaginary problem with the communication or navigation equipment. The instructor should point out that situational awareness is not being maintained if the student diverts too much attention away from other tasks, such as controlling the aircraft or scanning for traffic. These are simple exercises that can be done throughout flight training, which help emphasize the importance of maintaining situational awareness.

Operational Pitfalls

There are numerous classic behavioral traps that can ensnare the unwary pilot. Pilots, particularly those with considerable experience, try to complete a flight as planned, please passengers, and meet schedules. This basic drive to demonstrate achievements can have an adverse effect on safety, and can impose an unrealistic assessment of piloting skills under stressful conditions. These tendencies ultimately may bring about practices that are dangerous and sometimes illegal, and may lead to a mishap. Students develop awareness and learn to avoid many of these operational pitfalls through effective ADM training. The scenarios and examples provided by instructors during ADM instruction should involve these pitfalls. *[Figure 9-7]*

Single-Pilot Resource Management (SRM)

Single pilot resource management (SRM) is defined as the art and science of managing all the resources (both onboard the aircraft and from outside sources) available to a single pilot (prior to and during flight) to ensure the successful outcome of the flight. SRM includes the concepts of ADM, Risk Management (RM), Task Management (TM), Automation Management (AM), Controlled Flight Into Terrain (CFIT) Awareness, and Situational Awareness (SA). SRM training helps the pilot maintain situational awareness by managing the automation and associated aircraft control and navigation tasks. This enables the pilot to accurately assess and manage risk and make accurate and timely decisions.

SRM is all about helping pilots learn how to gather information, analyze it, and make decisions. Although the flight is coordinated by a single person and not an onboard flightcrew, the use of available resources such as air traffic control (ATC) and automated flight service station (AFSS) replicates the principles of CRM.

Operational Pitfalls
Peer Pressure Poor decision-making may be based upon an emotional response to peers, rather than evaluating a situation objectively.
Mind Set A pilot displays mind set through an inability to recognize and cope with changes in a given situation.
Get-There-Itis This disposition impairs pilot judgment through a fixation on the original goal or destination, combined with a disregard for any alternative course of action.
Duck-Under Syndrome A pilot may be tempted to make it into an airport by descending below minimums during an approach. There may be a belief that there is a built-in margin of error in every approach procedure, or a pilot may want to admit that the landing cannot be completed and a missed approach must be initiated.
Scud Running This occurs when a pilot tries to maintain visual contact with the terrain at low altitudes while instrument conditions exist.
Continuing Visual Flight Rules (VFR) into Instrument Conditions Spatial disorientation or collision with ground/obstacles may occur when a pilot continues VFR into instrument conditions. This can be even more dangerous if the pilot is not instrument rated or current.
Getting Behind the Aircraft This pitfall can be caused by allowing events or the situation to control pilot actions. A constant state of surprise at what happens next may be exhibited when the pilot is getting behind the aircraft.
Loss of Positional or Situational Awareness In extreme cases, when a pilot gets behind the aircraft, a loss of positional or situational awareness may result. The pilot may not know the aircraft's geographical location or may be unable to recognize deteriorating circumstances.
Operating Without Adequate Fuel Reserves Ignoring minimum fuel reserve requirements is generally the result of overconfidence, lack of flight planning, or disregarding applicable regulations.
Descent Below the Minimum En Route Altitude The duck-under syndrome, as mentioned above, can also occur during the en route portion of an IFR flight.
Flying Outside the Envelope The assumed high-performance capability of a particular aircraft may cause a mistaken belief that it can meet the demands imposed by a pilot's overestimated flying skills.
Neglect of Flight Planning, Preflight Inspections, and Checklists A pilot may rely on short- and long-term memory, regular flying skills, and familiar routes instead of established procedures and published checklists. This can be particularly true of experienced pilots.

Figure 9-7. *All experienced pilots have fallen prey to, or have been tempted by, one or more of these tendencies in their flying careers.*

SRM and the 5P Check

SRM is about gathering information, analyzing it, and making decisions. Learning how to identify problems, analyze the information, and make informed and timely decisions is not as straightforward as the training involved in learning specific maneuvers. Learning how to judge a situation and "how to think" in the endless variety of situations encountered while flying out in the "real world" is more difficult. There is no one right answer in ADM; rather, each pilot is expected to analyze each situation in light of experience level, personal minimums, and current physical and mental readiness level, and make his or her own decision.

SRM sounds good on paper, but it requires a way for pilots to understand and use it in their daily flights. One practical application is called the "Five Ps" (5 Ps). *[Figure 9-8]* The 5 Ps consist of "the Plan, the Plane, the Pilot, the Passengers, and the Programming." Each of these areas consists of a set of challenges and opportunities that face a single pilot. And each can substantially increase or decrease the risk of successfully completing the flight based on the pilot's ability to make informed and timely decisions. The 5 Ps are used to evaluate the pilot's current situation at key decision points during the flight, or when an emergency arises. These decision points include preflight, pretakeoff, hourly or at the midpoint of the flight, predescent, and just prior to the final approach fix or for visual flight rules (VFR) operations, just prior to entering the traffic pattern.

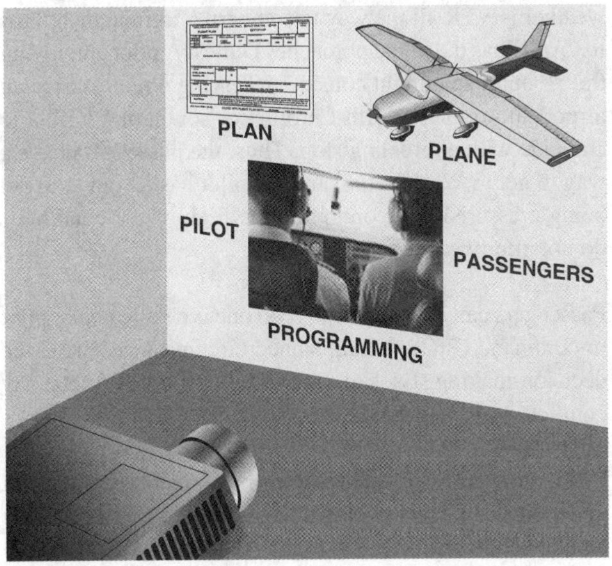

Figure 9-8. *The 5P checklist.*

The 5 Ps are based on the idea that the pilot has essentially five variables that impact his or her environment and that can cause the pilot to make a single critical decision, or several less critical decisions, that when added together can create a critical outcome. This concept stems from the belief that current decision-making models tend to be reactionary in nature. A change must occur and be detected to drive a risk management decision by the pilot. For instance, many pilots use risk management sheets that are filled out by the pilot prior to takeoff. These form a catalog of risks that may be encountered that day and turn them into numerical values. If the total exceeds a certain level, the flight is altered or cancelled. Informal research shows that while these are useful documents for teaching risk factors, they are almost never used outside of formal training programs. The 5P concept is an attempt to take the information contained in those sheets and in the other available models and use it.

The 5P concept relies on the pilot to adopt a scheduled review of the critical variables at points in the flight where decisions are most likely to be effective. For instance, the easiest point to cancel a flight due to bad weather is before the pilot and passengers walk out the door to load the aircraft. So, the first decision point is preflight in the flight planning room, where all the information is readily available to make a sound decision, and where communication and Fixed Base Operator (FBO) services are readily available to make alternate travel plans.

The second easiest point in the flight to make a critical safety decision is just prior to takeoff. Few pilots have ever had to make an emergency takeoff. While the point of the 5P check is to help the pilot fly, the correct application of the 5P before takeoff is to assist in making a reasoned go/no-go decision based on all the information available. These two points in the process of flying are critical go/no-go points on each and every flight.

The third place to review the 5 Ps is at the midpoint of the flight. Often, pilots may wait until the Automated Terminal information Service (ATIS) is in range to check weather, yet at this point in the flight many good options have already passed behind the aircraft and pilot. Additionally, fatigue and low-altitude hypoxia serve to rob the pilot of much of his or her energy by the end of a long and tiring flight day. This leads to a transition from a decision-making mode to an acceptance mode on the part of the pilot. If the flight is longer than 2 hours, the 5P check should be conducted hourly.

The last two decision points are just prior to decent into the terminal area and just prior to the final approach fix, or if VFR just prior to entering the traffic pattern, as preparations for landing commence. Most pilots execute approaches with the expectation that they will land out of the approach every time. A healthier approach requires the pilot to assume that changing conditions (the 5 Ps again) will cause the pilot to divert or execute the missed approach on every approach.

This keeps the pilot alert to all conditions that may increase risk and threaten the safe conduct of the flight. Diverting from cruise altitude saves fuel, allows unhurried use of the autopilot, and is less reactive in nature. Diverting from the final approach fix, while more difficult, still allows the pilot to plan and coordinate better, rather than executing a futile missed approach. Let's look at a detailed discussion of each of the Five Ps.

The Plan

The plan can also be called the mission or the task. It contains the basic elements of cross-country planning, weather, route, fuel, publications currency, etc. The plan should be reviewed and updated several times during the course of the flight. A delayed takeoff due to maintenance, fast moving weather, and a short notice temporary flight restriction (TFR) may all radically alter the plan. The plan is not only about the flight plan, but also all the events that surround the flight and allow the pilot to accomplish the mission. The plan is always being updated and modified and is especially responsive to changes in the other four remaining Ps. If for no other reason, the 5P check reminds the pilot that the day's flight plan is real life and subject to change at any time.

Obviously weather is a huge part of any plan. The addition of real time data link weather information give the advanced avionics pilot a real advantage in inclement weather, but only if the pilot is trained to retrieve, and evaluate the weather in real time without sacrificing situational awareness. And of course, weather information should drive a decision, even if that decision is to continue on the current plan. Pilots of aircraft without datalink weather should get updated weather in flight through an AFSS and/or Flight Watch.

The Plane

Both the plan and the plane are fairly familiar to most pilots. The plane consists of the usual array of mechanical and cosmetic issues that every aircraft pilot, owner, or operator can identify. With the advent of advanced avionics, the plane has expanded to include database currency, automation status, and emergency backup systems that were unknown a few years ago. Much has been written about single-pilot IFR flight both with and without an autopilot. While this is a personal decision, it is just that—a decision. Low IFR in a non-autopilot equipped aircraft may depend on several of the other Ps to be discussed. Pilot proficiency, currency, and fatigue are among them.

The Pilot

Flying, especially when used for business transportation, can expose the pilot to high altitude flying, long distance and endurance, and more challenging weather. An advanced avionics aircraft, simply due to its advanced capabilities can expose a pilot to even more of these stresses. The traditional "IMSAFE" checklist is a good start.

The combination of late night, pilot fatigue, and the effects of sustained flight above 5,000 feet may cause pilots to become less discerning, less critical of information, less decisive, and more compliant and accepting. Just as the most critical portion of the flight approaches (for instance, a night instrument approach in the weather after a 4-hour flight), the pilot's guard is down the most. The 5P process helps a pilot recognize the physiological situation at the end of the flight before takeoff, and continues to update personal conditions as the flight progresses. Once risks are identified, the pilot is in an infinitely better place to make alternate plans that lessen the effect of these factors and provide a safer solution.

The Passengers

One of the key differences between CRM and SRM is the way passengers interact with the pilot. The pilot of a high capability single-engine aircraft has entered into a very personal relationship with the passengers. In fact, the pilot and passengers sit within an arm's reach all of the time.

The desire of the passengers to make airline connections or important business meetings enters easily into this pilot's decision-making loop. Done in a healthy and open way, this can be a positive factor. Consider a flight to Dulles Airport and the passengers, both close friends and business partners, need to get to Washington, D.C., for an important meeting. The weather is VFR all the way to southern Virginia, then turns to low IFR as the pilot approaches Dulles. A pilot employing the 5P approach might consider reserving a rental car at an airport in northern North Carolina or southern Virginia to coincide with a refueling stop. Thus, the passengers have a way to get to Washington, and the pilot has an out to avoid being pressured into continuing the flight if the conditions do not improve.

Passengers can also be pilots. If no one is designated as pilot in command (PIC) and unplanned circumstances arise, the decision-making styles of several self-confident pilots may conflict.

Pilots also need to understand that non-pilots may not understand the level of risk involved in the flight. There is an element of risk in every flight. That is why SRM calls it risk management, not risk elimination. While a pilot may feel comfortable with the risk present in a night IFR flight, the passengers may not. A pilot employing SRM should ensure the passengers are involved in the decision-making and given tasks and duties to keep them busy and involved. If, upon a factual description of the risks present, the passengers decide to buy an airline ticket or rent a car, then a good decision has generally been made. This discussion also allows the pilot to move past what he or she thinks the passengers want to do and find out what they actually want to do. This removes self-induced pressure from the pilot.

The Programming

The advanced avionics aircraft adds an entirely new dimension to the way GA aircraft are flown. The electronic instrument displays, GPS, and autopilot reduce pilot workload and increase pilot situational awareness. While programming and operation of these devices are fairly simple and straightforward, unlike the analog instruments they replace, they tend to capture the pilot's attention and hold it for long periods of time. To avoid this phenomenon, the pilot should plan in advance when and where the programming for approaches, route changes, and airport information gathering should be accomplished as well as times it should not. Pilot familiarity with the equipment, the route, the local air traffic control environment, and personal capabilities vis-à-vis the automation should drive when, where, and how the automation is programmed and used.

The pilot should also consider what his or her capabilities are in response to last-minute changes of the approach (and the reprogramming required) and ability to make large-scale changes (a reroute for instance) while hand flying the aircraft. Since formats are not standardized, simply moving from one manufacturer's equipment to another should give the pilot pause and require more conservative planning and decisions.

The SRM process is simple. At least five times before and during the flight, the pilot should review and consider the "Plan, the Plane, the Pilot, the Passengers, and the Programming" and make the appropriate decision required by the current situation. It is often said that failure to make a decision is a decision. Under SRM and the 5 Ps, even the decision to make no changes to the current plan is made through careful consideration of all the risk factors present.

Information Management

The volume of information presented in aviation training is enormous, but part of the process of good SRM is a continuous flow of information in and actions out. How a student manages the flow of information definitely has an effect on the relative success or failure of each and every flight because proper information contributes to valid decisions. SBT plays an important part in teaching the student how to gather pertinent information from all available sources, make appropriate decisions, and assess the actions taken.

For a transitioning pilot, the primary flight display (PFD), multifunction display (MFD), and GPS/very high frequency (VHF) navigator screens seem to offer too much information presented in colorful menus and submenus. In fact, the student may be overwhelmed and unable to find a specific piece of information. The first critical information management skill for flying with advanced avionics is to understand the system at a conceptual level. Remembering how the system is organized helps the pilot manage the available information. Simulation software and books on the specific system used are of great value in furthering understanding for both the CFI and the student.

Another critical information management skill is reading. The best strategy for accessing and managing the available information from PFD to navigational charts is to stop, look, and read. The goal is for the student to learn how to monitor, manage, and prioritize the information flow to accomplish specific tasks.

Task Management (TM)

Task management (TM), a significant factor in flight safety, is the process by which pilots manage the many, concurrent tasks that must be performed to safely and efficiently fly a modern aircraft. A task is a function performed by a human, as opposed to one performed by a machine (e.g., setting the target heading in the autopilot).

The flight deck is an environment in which potentially many important tasks compete for pilot attention at any given time. TM determines which of perhaps many concurrent tasks the pilot(s) attend to at any particular point in time. More specifically, TM entails initiation of new tasks; monitoring of ongoing tasks to determine their status; prioritization of tasks based on their importance, status, urgency, and other factors; allocation of human and machine resources to high-priority tasks; interruption and subsequent resumption of lower priority tasks; and termination of tasks that are completed or no longer relevant.

Humans have a limited capacity for information. Once information flow exceeds a person's ability to mentally process the information, any additional information becomes unattended or displaces other tasks and information already being processed. Once the information flow reaches its limit, two alternatives exist: shed the unimportant tasks or perform all tasks at a less than optimal level. Like an electrical circuit being overloaded, either the consumption must be reduced or a circuit failure is experienced. Once again, SBT helps the student learn how to effectively manage tasks and properly prioritize them.

Automation Management

Automation management is the demonstrated ability to control and navigate an aircraft by means of the automated systems installed in the aircraft. One of the most important concepts of automation management is knowing when to use it and when not to use it. Ideally, the goal of the flight instructor is to train the student until he or she has learned how to perform PTS maneuvers and procedures in the aircraft, using all the available automation and/or the autopilot. However, the flight instructor must ensure the student also knows how to turn everything off and hand fly the maneuver when the safety of the flight is threatened.

Advanced avionics offers multiple levels of automation, from strictly manual flight to highly automated flight. No one level of automation is appropriate for all flight situations, but in order to avoid potentially dangerous distractions when flying with advanced avionics, the student must know how to manage the course indicator, the navigation source, and the autopilot. It is important for a student to know the peculiarities of the particular automated system being used. This ensures the student knows what to expect, how to monitor for proper operation, and promptly take appropriate action if the system does not perform as expected.

At the most basic level, managing the autopilot means knowing at all times which modes are engaged and which modes are armed to engage. The student needs to verify that armed functions (e.g., navigation tracking or altitude capture) engage at the appropriate time. Automation management is a good place to practice the callout technique, especially after arming the system to make a change in course or altitude.

Teaching Decision-Making Skills

When instructor pilots discuss system safety, they generally worry about the loss of traditional stick-and-rudder skills. The fear is that emphasis on items such as risk management, ADM, SRM, and situational awareness detracts from the training necessary in developing safe pilots.

It is important to understand that system safety flight training occurs in three phases. First, there are the traditional stick and rudder maneuvers. In order to apply the critical thinking skills that are to follow, pilots must first have a high degree of confidence in their ability to fly the aircraft. Next, the tenets of system safety are introduced into the training environment as students begin to learn how best to identify hazards, manage risk, and use all available resources to make each flight as safe as possible. This can be accomplished through scenarios that emphasize the skill sets being taught. Finally, the student is introduced to more complex scenarios demanding focus on several safety-of-flight issues. Thus, scenarios should start out rather simply, then progress in complexity and intensity as the student can handle the learning load.

A traditional stick-and-rudder maneuver such as short field landings can be used to illustrate how ADM and risk management can be incorporated into instruction. In phase I the initial focus is on developing the stick-and-rudder skills required to execute this operation safely. These include power and airspeed management, aircraft configuration, placement in the pattern, wind correction, determining the proper aim point and sight picture, etc. By emphasizing these points through repetition and practice, a student eventually acquires the skills needed to execute a short field landing.

Phase II introduces the many factors that come into play when performing a short field landing, which include runway conditions, no-flap landings, airport obstructions, and rejected landings. The introduction of such items need not increase training times. In fact, all of the hazards or considerations referenced in the short field landing lesson plan may be discussed in detail during the ground portion of the instructional program. For example, if training has been conducted at an airport that enjoys an obstruction-free 6,000-foot runway, consider the implications of operating the same aircraft out of a 1,800-foot strip with an obstruction off the departure end. Add to that additional considerations, such as operating the aircraft at close to its maximum gross weight under conditions of high density altitude, and now a single training scenario has several layers of complexity. The ensuing discussion proves a valuable training exercise, and it comes with little additional ground and no added flight training.

Finally, phase III takes the previously discussed hazards, risks, and considerations, and incorporates them into a complex scenario. This forces a student to consider not only a specific lesson item (in this case, short-field landings), but also requires that it be viewed in the greater context of the overall flight. For example, on a cross-country flight, the student is presented with a realistic distraction, perhaps the illness of a passenger. This forces a diversion to an alternate for which the student has not planned. The new destination airport has two runways, the longest of which is closed due to construction. The remaining runway is short, but while less than ideal, should prove suitable for landing. However, upon entering the pattern, the student finds the electrically driven flaps do not extend. The student must now consider whether to press on and attempt the landing, or proceed to a secondary alternate.

If he or she decides to go forward and attempt the landing, this proves an excellent time to test the requisite stick and rudder skills. If the student decides to proceed to a second alternate, this opens new training opportunities. Proceeding further tests cross-country skills, such as navigation, communication, management of a passenger in distress, as well as the other tasks associated with simply flying the aircraft. The outlined methodology simply takes a series of seemingly unrelated tasks and scripts them into a training exercise requiring both mechanical and cognitive skills to complete it successfully.

SBT helps the flight instructor effectively teach ADM and risk management. The what, why, and how of SBT has been discussed extensively throughout this handbook. In teaching ADM, it is important to remember the learning objective is for the student to exercise sound judgment and make good decisions. Thus, the flight instructor must be ready to turn the responsibility for planning and execution of the flight over to the student as soon as possible. Although the flight instructor continues to demonstrate and instruct skill maneuvers, when the student begins to make decisions, the flight instructor should revert to the role of mentor and/or learning facilitator.

The flight instructor is an integral part of the systems approach to training and is crucial to the implementation of an SBT program which underlies the teaching of ADM. Remember, for SBT instruction to be effective, it is vital the flight instructor and student establish the following information:

- Scenario destination(s)
- Desired student learning outcome(s)
- Desired level of student performance
- Possible inflight scenario changes

It is also important for the flight instructor to remember that a good scenario:

- Is not a test.
- Will not have a single correct answer.
- Does not offer an obvious answer.
- Engages all three learning domains.
- Is interactive.
- Should not promote errors.
- Should promote situational awareness and opportunities for decision-making.
- Requires time-pressured decisions.

The flight instructor should make the situation as realistic as possible. This means the student knows where he or she is going and what transpires on the flight. While the actual flight may deviate from the original plan, it allows the student to be placed in a realistic scenario. The student will plan the flight to include:

- Route
- Destination(s)
- Weather
- NOTAMS
- Possible emergency procedures

Since the scenarios may have several good outcomes and a few poor ones, the flight instructor should understand in advance which outcomes are positive and/or negative and give the student the freedom to make both good and poor decisions. This does not mean that the student should be allowed to make an unsafe decision or commit an unsafe act. However, it does allow the students to make decisions that fit their experience level and result in positive outcomes.

Teaching decision-making skills has become an integral part of flight training. The word "decision" is used several times in each PTS and applicants are judged on their ability to make a decision as well as their ability to perform a task. Thus, it is important for CFIs to remember that decision-making is a component of the PTS.

Assessing SRM Skills

A student's performance is often assessed only on a technical level. The instructor determines whether maneuvers are technically accurate and that procedures are performed in the right order. In SRM assessment, instructors must learn to assess students on a different level. How did the student arrive at a particular decision? What resources were used? Was risk assessed accurately when a go/no-go decision was made? Did the student maintain situational awareness in the traffic pattern? Was workload managed effectively during a cross-country flight? How does the student handle stress and fatigue?

Instructors should continually evaluate student decision-making ability and offer suggestions for improvement. It is not always necessary to present complex situations, which require detailed analysis. By allowing students to make decisions about typical issues that arise throughout the course of training, such as their fitness to fly, weather conditions, and equipment problems, instructors can address effective decision-making and allow students to develop judgment skills. For example, when a discrepancy is found during preflight inspection, the student should be allowed to initially determine the action to be taken. Then the effectiveness of the student's choice and other options that may be available can be discussed. Opportunities for improving decision-making abilities occur often during training. If the tower offers the student a runway that requires landing with a tailwind in order to expedite traffic, the student can be directed to assess the risks involved and asked to present alternative actions to be taken. Perhaps the most frequent choice that has to be made during flight training is the go/no-go decision based on weather. While the final choice to fly lies with the instructor, students can be required to assess the weather prior to each flight and make a go/no-go determination.

In addition, instructors should utilize SBT to create lessons that are specifically designed to test whether students are applying SRM skills. Planning a flight lesson in which the student is presented with simulated emergencies, a heavy workload, or other operational problems can be valuable in assessing the student's judgment and decision-making skills. During the flight, student performance can be evaluated for workload and/or stress management.

As discussed in chapter 5, SRM grades are based on these four components:

- Explain—the student can verbally identify, describe, and understand the risks inherent in the flight scenario. The student needs to be prompted to identify risks and make decisions.
- Practice—the student is able to identify, understand, and apply SRM principles to the actual flight situation. Coaching, instruction, and/or assistance from the CFI quickly corrects minor deviations and errors identified by the CFI. The student is an active decision maker.
- Manage/Decide—the student can correctly gather the most important data available both within and outside the flight deck, identify possible courses of action, evaluate the risk inherent in each course of action, and make the appropriate decision. Instructor intervention is not required for the safe completion of the flight.
- Not Observed—any event not accomplished or required.

Postflight, collaborative assessment or learner centered grading (LCG) (also discussed in chapter 5), is a vital component of assessing a student's SRM skills. As a reminder, collaborative assessment includes two parts: learner self-assessment and a detailed assessment by the flight instructor. The purpose of the self-assessment is to stimulate growth in the student's thought processes and, in turn, behaviors. The self-assessment is followed by an in-depth discussion between the flight instructor and the student which compares the CFI's assessment to the student's self-assessment.

An important element of SRM skills assessment is that the CFI provides a clear picture of the progress the student is making during the training. Grading should also be progressive. During each flight, the student should achieve a new level of learning. For flight one, the automation management area might be a "describe" item. By flight three, it would be a "practice" item, and by flight five, a "manage-decide" item.

Chapter Summary

This chapter introduced aviation instructors to the underlying concepts of safety risk management, which the FAA is integrating into all levels of the aviation community.

APPENDIX C
GROUND SCHOOL COURSE SUGGESTIONS

The purpose of this appendix is to suggest ideas concerning marketing, organization, and presentation of ground schools for pilot knowledge tests. We would appreciate any comments or suggestions you may have after reading this material, as will other aviation professionals when we incorporate this information into subsequent editions. Please send feedback to us at your convenience at www.GleimAviation.com/questions. Thank you.

RATIONALE FOR CONDUCTING A GROUND SCHOOL

1. **Aid to the industry.** General aviation (including flight instruction), while more financially sound than it has been in years past, is still not normally a high-profit enterprise. A ground school is the first step into aviation for many students who will one day become aircraft renters and owners--the people who sustain GA. While it will not generate large profits for a business on its own, a ground school sets the stage for a lasting relationship between a flight school/FBO and its students.
2. **Maintaining a professional level of currency and familiarity with aviation subjects.** Obtaining your flight and/or ground instructor certificate will keep you up to date on the Federal Aviation Regulations and all other academic areas of flight. Additionally, teaching will challenge you to learn and understand a wide variety of material.
3. **Finding new customers.** Many flight instructors use ground schools as a source of student pilots.
4. **Public service.** Many flight and/or ground instructors provide ground schools to Civil Air Patrol (CAP) chapters, high school classes, etc., as a public service to young people.
5. **Personal employment.** Obtaining your flight and/or ground instructor certificate can lead to opportunities for part-time work at FBOs, community colleges, and adult education programs.

POTENTIAL SPONSORS OF GROUND SCHOOLS

1. **Community colleges.** Call your local junior college and ask if a ground school is offered. Ask what division it is in and call the dean or director to indicate your interest in teaching the ground school. While talking to the dean or director, you should obtain a course outline, as well as information on the cost and class schedule. The college may already have an instructor, but you should make known your interest in teaching in case there should be an opening.
   a. Send us the dean or director's name and address and your own name and address. We will send him or her a complimentary copy of ***Private Pilot FAA Knowledge Test Prep*** or ***Sport Pilot FAA Knowledge Test Prep*** and explain that it was at your suggestion. We will reiterate your interest in presenting a ground school.
2. **Local high school adult education centers.** Call all local high schools for more information.
3. **FBOs.** Inquire at your local airport, or search on the Internet (e.g., www.airnav.com).
4. **Civil Air Patrol units.** Inquire at your local armed forces recruiting or training station for the name and telephone number of local CAP unit commanders (see the U.S. Government section of your telephone book). You can also find information about the CAP's aerospace education program at the Civil Air Patrol National Headquarters website (www.gocivilairpatrol.com).

MARKETING GROUND SCHOOLS

The objective of marketing a ground school is to contact interested students if you are beginning a new ground school and to increase enrollment if you are associated with an existing ground school. The following are only a few suggestions.

1. **Classified ads in local newspapers.** Ads usually cost only a few dollars a day for a brief description that might read

   "Private Pilot/Sport Pilot Ground School. 6 weeks in length, Tuesday and Thursday evenings, 7:00-9:00 p.m. Offered at [course location]. Tuition, books, etc., $[your price]. Call [instructor or sponsor name] at [phone number] after 7 p.m."
2. **Radio ads.** Call your local radio station and pay for an advertisement or, preferably, have it broadcast as a public service announcement. Provide the same information stated in the sample ad above.
3. **Posters.** Prepare posters and provide a telephone number, again with the above information. Post them at your local community college, university, airport, stores, etc.
4. **Internet.** Create a simple website or have one built for you to advertise your services, schedule, location, etc. Gleim can provide you with buttons leading directly to our products in our aviation store.
5. **Social media.** Advertise your services on various social media platforms, such as Facebook, Twitter, and Instagram. Participate in forums where you can connect with prospective students and fellow instructors. Create videos introducing yourself and your services to share on hosts, such as YouTube, and share links to these videos on social media.

GROUND SCHOOL COURSE ORGANIZATION

We hope you will use ***Pilot Handbook***, as well as ***Private Pilot FAA Knowledge Test Prep***, **FAA Test Prep Online**, and/or **Gleim Online Ground School** for your ground school. Based on that presumption, it is probably easiest to follow our study unit organization, which is the same in both ***Pilot Handbook*** and ***Private Pilot FAA Knowledge Test Prep***.

We recommend that you incorporate a Sport Pilot ground school with your Private Pilot ground school to help you maximize the number of students interested in the course. Sport pilots need to know approximately 70% of the required material for Private Pilot to pass their FAA knowledge test. It is beneficial for them to learn more than what is required for them to pass the FAA knowledge test; therefore, we include additional study units in ***Sport Pilot FAA Knowledge Test Prep***.

Make sure that you are aware of the differences between Sport Pilot and Private Pilot and make it clear to your students which information they may omit for Sport Pilot.

Private Pilot FAA Knowledge Test Prep

Study Unit 1 • Airplanes and Aerodynamics
Study Unit 2 • Airplane Instruments, Engines, and Systems
Study Unit 3 • Airports, Air Traffic Control, and Airspace
Study Unit 4 • Federal Aviation Regulations
Study Unit 5 • Airplane Performance and Weight and Balance
Study Unit 6 • Aeromedical Factors and Aeronautical Decision Making (ADM)
Study Unit 7 • Aviation Weather
Study Unit 8 • Aviation Weather Services
Study Unit 9 • Navigation: Charts and Publications
Study Unit 10 • Navigation Systems
Study Unit 11 • Cross-Country Flight Planning

Sport Pilot FAA Knowledge Test Prep

Study Unit 1 • Airports
Study Unit 2 • Airspace
Study Unit 3 • Federal Aviation Regulations – 14 CFR Parts 1 through 71
Study Unit 4 • Federal Aviation Regulations – 14 CFR Parts 91.3 through 91.131
Study Unit 5 • Federal Aviation Regulations – 14 CFR Parts 91.155 through 91.417 and NTSB Part 830
Study Unit 6 • Aeromedical Factors and Aeronautical Decision Making (ADM)
Study Unit 7 • Aviation Weather
Study Unit 8 • Weather Services
Study Unit 9 • Sectional Charts and Airspace
Study Unit 10 • Navigation and Preflight Preparation
Study Unit 11 • Airplanes and Aerodynamics
Study Unit 12 • Airplane Instruments
Study Unit 13 • Airplane Engines and Systems
Study Unit 14 • Airplane Performance and Weight and Balance

You will probably not have exactly 11 class sessions, which may necessitate combining study units for various classes. Approximately 12 sessions of 2 hours each should be adequate if your course objective is to get your students ready for their pilot knowledge test. Even if you have 11 sessions, you may still want to combine certain study units and spend more time on other units. As an example of how study units might be combined for Private Pilot, if you have a 5-week program that meets for 10 sessions, you might want to combine Study Units 9, 10, and 11. You could easily cover the Introduction in Session 1 and still use a good part of the session to get into Study Unit 1. Then spend another entire meeting to finish Study Unit 1.

If your course objective is to cover all the subjects in the amount of detail needed by proficient pilots (rather than simply to "teach the test"), 16 to 18 2-hour sessions should be adequate. More time is needed for this comprehensive course because the FAA does not test every topic that your students need to know in order to be safe, capable pilots. Having 16 to 18 sessions will allow you to spend more than one session on the largest and most important study units in ***Pilot Handbook*** (Study Units 1 through 4) and will allow you to spend extra time on challenging concepts like airspace and radio navigation. A comprehensive course outline for Private Pilot might entail two sessions for the Introduction and Study Unit 1, two sessions for Study Unit 2, two sessions for Study Unit 3, one to two sessions for Study Unit 4 (depending on how detailed you wish to get), one to two sessions for Study Unit 5, and one session each for Study Units 6 through 11. Any extra time left in the course can be spent reviewing difficult topics and engaging in test-specific preparation.

Regardless of your course objective, you may wish to reserve 5 or 10 minutes at the end of each session for an overview and introduction of the material to be covered in the next session. That will help your students study for the next session and help them understand it. Remember to always assign additional study at home to keep your students engaged and prepared.

COURSE SYLLABUS AND HANDOUTS

1. At the beginning of the course, you should distribute an outline of the material to be covered in the course. It should show the meeting times, quiz schedule, and reading assignments for each session.
2. A suggested syllabus for a 9-week class (whose objective is to prepare students for the test) that meets for 3 hours one night per week is presented on the following page.
    a. Undoubtedly, you will have to change the scheduling of topics. The topics have been overlapped so that you can talk about the same topic during two periods; i.e., you can provide double exposure. Introducing the topic the week before provides 3 weeks' coverage, which may be useful to your students.
3. Of course, the six study units in this book will be helpful to you as general background in preparing and presenting your ground school.

GLEIM PILOT KITS

The Gleim **Private Pilot Kit** and **Sport Pilot Kit** are designed to simplify and facilitate your students' flight and ground training. There are different levels of each kit available. The Pilot Kits may include

- *FAA Knowledge Test Prep*
- *Flight Maneuvers and Practical Test Prep*
- *Pilot Handbook*
- *FAR/AIM*
- *Syllabus*
- *ACS and Oral Exam Guide* (Private Pilot only)
- Logbook (hard cover)
- Training Record
- Online Ground School
- FAA Test Prep Online
- Audio Review (Private Pilot only)
- Online Communication Course
- Security-Related Airspace Course
- Navigational plotter
- Flight computer
- Flight bag

For ground training, your students will need to have at least a textbook ***(Pilot Handbook)***, a ***FAR/AIM***, a means of test preparation (***Private Pilot FAA Knowledge Test Prep*** or ***Sport Pilot FAA Knowledge Test Prep***, **FAA Test Prep Online**, and/or Gleim **Online Ground School**), a navigational plotter, and a flight computer. These items make up most of the Pilot Kits; the remaining items are primarily concerned with flight training. Because most people who take ground school courses intend to undertake flight training, it makes sense for your students to go ahead and obtain everything they will need at one time (at substantial savings) by purchasing the Pilot Kit.

SAMPLE COURSE SYLLABUS

COURSE SYLLABUS

Jonesville Community College
Evening Education Course 1121

Tuesday evenings, 7:00 - 10:00 p.m.
North Campus, Building C, Room 171

PRIVATE PILOT/SPORT PILOT GROUND SCHOOL
Summer Term A, 20XX
June 1 - July 27

INSTRUCTOR: Mr. Harold Gray, AGI
Office: (111) 555-5252
Home: (111) 555-2525

COURSE OBJECTIVE: Learn the material required by the FAA for the private pilot knowledge test (airplane) and sport pilot knowledge test with the objective of each student passing the test.

CLASSROOM PROCEDURE: Lecture and guided discussion.

1. Each class will begin with a review and questions from the last class (approximately 5-15 minutes).
2. Next, there will be a brief overview and core concepts for the current evening's assignment, followed by class discussion and questions.
3. When appropriate, after the class break, an in-class quiz will be administered, self-graded, and analyzed through class discussion.
4. The last 15-30 minutes of each class session will be directed toward an overview and discussion of the next class's assignment.
5. Visual aids and handouts will be used as appropriate.

REQUIRED TEXT: *Private Pilot FAA Knowledge Test Prep*, by Irvin N. Gleim and Garrett W. Gleim, or *Sport Pilot FAA Knowledge Test Prep*, by Irvin N. Gleim and Garrett W. Gleim

RECOMMENDED TEXT: *Pilot Handbook*, by Irvin N. Gleim and Garrett W. Gleim

These texts are available in the College Bookstore on the North Campus, which is open until 8:00 p.m. each Tuesday.

SCHEDULE

Class	Date	PPKT* Study Units	SPKT** Study Units	Topic
1	June 1	Introduction, 1	Introduction, 11	Introduction, Aerodynamic Theory
2	June 8	1, 2	11, 13	Aerodynamics and Airplane Systems
3	June 15	2, 3	1, 2, 13	Airplane Systems, Airports, ATC
4	June 22	3, 4	2-5	Airspace, 14 CFR
5	June 29	4, 5	3-5, 14	14 CFR, Airplane Performance
6	July 6	5, 6	6, 14	Weight and Balance, Aeromedical Factors
7	July 13	7, 8	7, 8	Aviation Weather and Weather Services
8	July 20	9, 10, 11	9, 10	Navigation, Cross-Country Flight
9	July 27			Review for pilot knowledge test

* PPKT = *Private Pilot FAA Knowledge Test Prep*
** SPKT = *Sport Pilot FAA Knowledge Test Prep*

You may photocopy this syllabus and change it in any way you like.

ENROLLMENT PROCEDURES

1. You should make a list of the students and their contact information so you can contact them in the event the classes need to be changed, rescheduled, etc.
   a. Note the form and date of their payment.
2. As each student enrolls, you can sell (or give, if the materials are included in the cost of the ground school course) him or her book(s), software, and/or online course access.
3. If you have a syllabus ready, distribute copies to your students and encourage them to do some study in advance.
4. With respect to requiring or recommending ***Pilot Handbook*** and ***Aviation Weather and Weather Services***, you may proceed as follows:
   a. For each student, put one copy of each title on reserve in the bookstore of your choice.
   b. Get one copy of each book and pass them around to the class; indicate students can purchase another one from you, a local FBO, or the bookstore you are using.
   c. Alternatively, have them order the materials by calling us at (800) 874-5346 or ordering online at www.GleimAviation.com.
5. Note that you may wish to encourage each person who enrolls or even inquires about the program to invite friends to take the course with him or her. The idea is to build enrollment through enthusiasm for and interest in aviation.

THE FIRST CLASS SESSION

1. Preliminaries
   a. Arrive early with a supply of books, handouts, and your lecture notes for the first lecture.
   b. Begin by enrolling any students who show up at the first class without having already enrolled.
   c. Go over the roll and pass out the syllabus.
   d. Introduce yourself.
2. Student-Instructor Interaction
   a. Tell the students about your background, the origin of the course, your reasons for teaching, and any other relevant personal things.
   b. Tell the class that you need to learn more about them in order to teach effectively.
      1) Ask people to introduce themselves.
      2) Unless the class is too large, make notes on your roster to individualize participants and help you learn their names.
      3) Ask them why they are taking the course, if they have any flying experience, if they know anyone else who flies, if they have ever flown before in a small aircraft, etc.
   c. Such interaction is an ice-breaker, allowing you to get to know your students and allowing them to get to know you and one another.

3. Discussion of Course Objective (FAA Pilot Knowledge Test)
    a. Display ***Private Pilot FAA Knowledge Test Prep*** and ***Sport Pilot FAA Knowledge Test Prep***.
    b. Point out that the textbooks have sample FAA questions reorganized by topic with answer explanations next to them.
    c. Indicate that the areas tested on the exams will be the topics specified on your syllabus (course outline), that the test will be only 60 questions for private and 40 questions for sport, and that the students need to get at least 42 questions correct for private and 28 questions correct for sport in order to pass.
        1) This will be very easy because they will have gone over many possible test questions during your course (all of which appear in ***Private Pilot FAA Knowledge Test Prep*** and ***Sport Pilot FAA Knowledge Test Prep***), as well as additional material to help them learn how to fly safely.
    d. Explain the content of ***Private Pilot FAA Knowledge Test Prep*** and/or ***Sport Pilot FAA Knowledge Test Prep***.
        1) Explain that the Introduction is the current topic of discussion.
        2) Show them the organization of Study Units 1 through 11 for Private Pilot and Study Units 1 through 14 for Sport Pilot.
            a) Each study unit begins with an outline, subunit by subunit (topic by topic).
            b) Following the outlines are questions and answer explanations organized in the same subunits and presented in the same order.
            c) Thus, the students are able to study and try to learn the material before they answer the questions. This format provides an extra level of reinforcement as they study the material.
4. Discussion of Course Objective (Comprehensive Coverage)
    a. Display ***Pilot Handbook*** and ***Private Pilot FAA Knowledge Test Prep*** or ***Sport Pilot FAA Knowledge Test Prep***.
    b. Explain that both ***Pilot Handbook*** and ***Private Pilot FAA Knowledge Test Prep*** have the same study unit numbers and titles, which means that the content of each study unit number in both books will correspond (for ***Sport Pilot FAA Knowledge Test Prep***, they will need to refer to the index).
        1) Explain that, because the study units of these books are complementary, Study Units 1 through 4 of ***Pilot Handbook*** are disproportionately larger than their counterparts in ***Private Pilot FAA Knowledge Test Prep*** and ***Sport Pilot FAA Knowledge Test Prep***. Explain that this is because there is a lot of material that the FAA does not test, but with which a pilot must be familiar in order to fly safely (much of this untested material happens to fit into the first four study units).
        2) Explain that more time will therefore be spent on Study Units 1 through 4 of ***Pilot Handbook***.
    c. Explain that, while your students will be well prepared for their pilot knowledge test at the completion of this course, it is not your goal to simply "teach the test" and that you plan to give them a solid background in aviation topics.
        1) Explain that they will be expected to follow the progress of the course in ***Private Pilot FAA Knowledge Test Prep*** or ***Sport Pilot FAA Knowledge Test Prep*** on their own and that you will primarily be teaching out of ***Pilot Handbook***.
        2) Provide additional background about how to use ***Private Pilot FAA Knowledge Test Prep*** or ***Sport Pilot FAA Knowledge Test Prep*** based on item 3. of this list.

LECTURE PRESENTATION

1. There are many ways to present a lecture, and you should use the method with which you feel most comfortable. The best method for you will be the best method for your students because you will perform better.
2. One approach to keep in mind is the idea of hitting the high points or key concepts.
   a. What are the basic or major concepts within any topic? These are generally outlined at the opening of each study unit in ***Private Pilot FAA Knowledge Test Prep*** and ***Sport Pilot FAA Knowledge Test Prep***.
   b. To amplify these concepts and provide additional discussion, consult ***Pilot Handbook***, after which you can use additional examples from other textbooks, including the FAA/ government textbooks.
3. A major objective of your lecture presentation is to make it interactive: The students must respond to you and participate.
   a. Learning is **not** a one-way communication from you to your students.
   b. You need to ask questions of individual students and of the class as a whole so that they can react and commit to an answer (silently or orally), and then get immediate feedback about the accuracy of their responses.
4. Have them work examples, e.g., provide them with a calculation and ask them to determine the answer.
   a. You could present a series of sample questions, take away the alternative answers, and have them work through a couple of exercises.
   b. You might also put these on overhead projectors.
5. Your preparation before class is very important. You should consult the lesson plan discussed in Study Unit 5, Subunit 3, "Lesson Plan," beginning on page 104 and review Study Unit 4, "Teaching Methods," beginning on page 81.

VISUAL AIDS

1. Visual aids include small model airplanes, videos, slides, blackboard presentations, overhead projector pictures, etc.
2. Visual aids are most helpful in explaining ideas that are abstract when presented verbally (e.g., airspace).
3. You can bring items to class and pass them around, such as navigation tools/charts and operating manuals from airplanes.
4. Experiment with visual aids. Use them as attention-getters or to break the pace of the normal presentation.
5. If using presentation software (such as Microsoft PowerPoint), avoid reading from slides. Use this tool to present important (i.e., tested) concepts as well as images, animations, and/or video.

COURSE EVALUATIONS

1. At the end of the course, but before the session set aside for the FAA knowledge test, you should administer a course evaluation.
   a. Your objective is to obtain feedback from your students about how the course can be improved in several aspects, including
      1) Course organization
      2) Textbook(s)
      3) Lecture presentation
      4) Physical facilities

   b. Let the students know that you are seeking constructive criticism across many areas.
   c. Tell them that you do not want to make them ill at ease, so you are going to ask one member (tell them who) to hold the evaluations until the course is over.
   d. If the course is for grade credit, the evaluations should be held until after you have turned in the grades.
2. Please feel free to photocopy and modify the course evaluation illustrated below. Note that you should leave the back blank for additional written comments.
3. Remember that, at the conclusion of the last class session prior to your students taking the FAA pilot knowledge test, you need to complete the Instructor Certification Form at the back of ***Private Pilot FAA Knowledge Test Prep*** or ***Sport Pilot FAA Knowledge Test Prep*** for each student.

Date ____________

(NAME OF COURSE)
GROUND SCHOOL EVALUATION FORM

This Ground School is being presented to aid you in your preparation for the FAA knowledge test. Please help us by answering the following questions, keeping in mind our objective: to help you prepare for the FAA knowledge test. Please check one response for each line. Return the completed form to the person designated to hold the evaluations until the completion of the last class (or after grades have been turned in).

Instructor	**Excellent**	**Good**	**Adequate**	**Poor**
1. Instructor presentation of material	___	___	___	___
2. Instructor knowledge of subject	___	___	___	___
3. Allocation of time to topics	___	___	___	___
4. Use of slides, boards, visual aids, etc.	___	___	___	___
5. Use of handouts, problems, etc.	___	___	___	___
Other questions				
6. Overall rating of instructor	___	___	___	___
7. Classroom comfort	___	___	___	___
8. Progress of class as a whole	___	___	___	___
9. Outlines in *FAA Knowledge Test Prep*	___	___	___	___
10. Answer explanations in *FAA Knowledge Test Prep*	___	___	___	___
11. Overall rating of *FAA Knowledge Test Prep*	___	___	___	___

12. **Other comments.** Please explain poor responses and make any other suggestions you feel may be relevant in the space provided below and on the back of this sheet. **Thank you.**

HELPING YOUR STUDENTS SELECT A COMPUTER TESTING CENTER

1. Since most computer testing centers have limited seating, it is unlikely that you will be able to have all of your students take the test at the same time and place.
   a. Thus, you will need to help your students in the selection of a computer testing center.
2. Call each testing service to determine if any discounts are being offered and the payment policy. Explain your class situation (number of students, etc.).
   a. Some students may not have a credit card, so they need to select a computer testing center that will accept a check or cash at the time of the test.
      1) Some computer testing services may require that a check or money order be sent before the student can take the test.
   b. Make yourself available to assist your students as necessary.

3. Provide your students with the contact information for the following PSI computer testing service and the results of your inquiries.

   PSI (800) 211-2754 or www.psiexams.com

4. Discuss the examination process and demonstrate testing procedures by using Gleim **FAA Test Prep Online**.
5. You, as a flight instructor, are required to maintain a record of each person for whom you sign a certification for a pilot knowledge test, including the kind of test, date of test, and the test result (14 CFR 61.189).
   a. An efficient way of obtaining test results is to pre-address and stamp one postcard for each student (include the student's name on the card) and explain why you need these returned.
      1) Hand them out on the exam day.
      2) Ask students to mail their numerical scores to you.
      3) List the student scores on your roster as they come in the mail.
      4) Call any individuals who have not submitted cards.
   b. Email is another simple method for obtaining this information.
   c. You can use these pass rates in future advertising.

AN ALTERNATIVE APPROACH: EXPANDING YOUR MARKET

1. You may wish to broaden your ground school course so that it appeals to aviation enthusiasts interested in doing more than passing the FAA private pilot (airplane) or sport pilot knowledge test. If so, you need to
   a. Diversify your marketing plan and advertisements.
   b. Edit the suggested syllabus (make it more general).
   c. Prepare fewer class assignments focused on the FAA pilot knowledge test.
2. Can you prepare student pilots for the FAA pilot knowledge test **and** provide a general-interest aviation course?
   a. Many ground schools are so directed, especially at community colleges where a considerable number of enrollees do not take the FAA pilot knowledge test.
   b. One approach is to emphasize discussion of sample FAA test questions at the end (optional part) of each class, e.g., in a 100-minute class.
      1) The last 30 minutes might be restricted to discussion of sample FAA questions in ***Private Pilot FAA Knowledge Test Prep*** and/or ***Sport Pilot FAA Knowledge Test Prep***.
      2) The first 70 minutes would involve lecture discussion.
   c. Occasional questions might be discussed, but the emphasis would be on learning about airplanes, weather, and navigation rather than passing the FAA pilot knowledge test.
   d. In such a course, ***Pilot Handbook*** would be the required text instead of ***Private Pilot FAA Knowledge Test Prep*** or ***Sport Pilot FAA Knowledge Test Prep***, which can be optional.
3. With these general guidelines, we trust you will take the plunge and **start your class** (or at least begin to prepare for it) **right now**! It is fun, and it provides a valuable service -- teaching new aviation enthusiasts to **ENJOY FLYING -- SAFELY!**

CROSS-REFERENCES TO THE FAA LEARNING STATEMENT CODES

Pages 319 through 322 contain a listing of all of the questions from our fundamentals of instructing knowledge test bank. The questions are in FAA Learning Statement Code (LSC) sequence. (Refer to page 12 in the Introduction for a complete listing and description of each.) To the right of each LSC, we present our study unit/question number and our answer. For example, look below and note that PLT022 is cross-referenced to 3-17, which represents our Study Unit 3, question 17; the correct answer is B.

The first line of each of our answer explanations in Study Units 1 through 6 contains the correct answer and a reference for the answer explanation, e.g., *FAA-H-8083-9A Chap 1.* If this reference is not useful, use the following chart to identify the learning statement code to determine the specific reference appropriate for the question.

FAA Learning Code	Gleim SU/ Q. No.	Gleim Answer
PLT022	3–17	B
PLT022	3–20	C
PLT022	3–24	A
PLT103	3–21	B
PLT103	3–23	A
PLT103	3–30	A
PLT103	3–32	B
PLT204	3–36	B
PLT204	3–37	B
PLT204	3–38	A
PLT204	3–39	C
PLT204	3–40	C
PLT204	3–41	B
PLT204	3–42	A
PLT204	3–43	B
PLT204	3–44	C
PLT204	3–45	C
PLT204	3–46	C
PLT204	3–47	C
PLT204	3–51	B
PLT204	3–52	B
PLT204	3–53	C
PLT204	3–54	A
PLT204	3–55	C
PLT204	3–56	A
PLT204	3–57	B
PLT211	6–11	A
PLT211	6–15	B
PLT211	6–19	C

FAA Learning Code	Gleim SU/ Q. No.	Gleim Answer
PLT211	6–59	C
PLT211	6–60	B
PLT227	4–46	A
PLT227	4–47	A
PLT227	4–48	C
PLT227	4–49	B
PLT227	4–50	A
PLT227	4–51	B
PLT227	4–52	A
PLT228	5–22	C
PLT228	5–24	C
PLT228	5–26	C
PLT228	5–29	B
PLT228	5–30	A
PLT228	5–31	A
PLT228	5–32	B
PLT228	5–33	C
PLT228	5–34	C
PLT228	5–35	C
PLT228	5–36	B
PLT228	5–37	C
PLT228	5–43	C
PLT228	5–44	A
PLT229	3–72	A
PLT229	3–73	B
PLT229	3–74	A
PLT229	3–75	C
PLT229	3–76	A
PLT229	3–77	C

FAA Learning Code	Gleim SU/ Q. No.	Gleim Answer
PLT229	3–78	B
PLT229	3–79	B
PLT229	6–7	C
PLT230	2–38	A
PLT230	3–18	B
PLT230	3–63	C
PLT230	3–64	B
PLT230	3–65	B
PLT230	3–67	B
PLT230	3–68	C
PLT230	3–69	A
PLT230	3–70	B
PLT230	4–54	B
PLT231	1–16	A
PLT231	1–17	A
PLT231	1–21	A
PLT231	2–17	B
PLT231	2–18	C
PLT231	2–19	B
PLT231	2–20	B
PLT231	2–21	A
PLT231	2–22	A
PLT231	2–23	C
PLT231	2–25	A
PLT231	2–27	A
PLT231	2–29	C
PLT231	2–30	A
PLT231	2–31	C
PLT231	2–32	C

FAA Learning Code	Gleim SU/ Q. No.	Gleim Answer
PLT231	3–7	A
PLT232	2–26	C
PLT232	2–28	B
PLT232	2–34	B
PLT232	2–35	B
PLT232	2–37	B
PLT232	3–31	B
PLT232	3–34	A
PLT232	4–37	A
PLT233	2–5	C
PLT233	2–6	C
PLT233	2–7	B
PLT233	2–8	C
PLT233	2–9	A
PLT233	2–10	B
PLT233	2–11	B
PLT233	2–12	B
PLT233	2–13	B
PLT233	2–14	B
PLT233	2–15	B
PLT233	2–16	B
PLT270	3–1	B
PLT270	3–2	C
PLT270	3–3	C
PLT270	3–4	C
PLT270	3–22	B
PLT271	3–19	C
PLT271	3–26	C
PLT271	3–27	A
PLT271	3–28	A
PLT271	3–29	C
PLT272	2–24	A
PLT272	3–25	C
PLT272	3–33	C
PLT272	3–35	C
PLT295	1–69	B
PLT295	1–70	C
PLT295	1–76	A
PLT295	1–77	B
PLT295	2–33	B
PLT295	2–36	C
PLT295	3–49	C

FAA Learning Code	Gleim SU/ Q. No.	Gleim Answer
PLT295	3–50	C
PLT295	4–55	B
PLT295	5–1	A
PLT295	5–6	A
PLT295	5–12	A
PLT295	5–25	A
PLT295	5–28	C
PLT295	5–38	A
PLT295	5–45	A
PLT306	1–3	C
PLT306	1–19	B
PLT306	1–27	B
PLT306	1–31	B
PLT306	1–39	B
PLT306	1–40	C
PLT306	1–41	A
PLT306	1–42	A
PLT306	1–43	A
PLT306	1–46	B
PLT306	1–47	A
PLT306	1–48	C
PLT306	1–55	A
PLT306	1–57	A
PLT306	1–67	A
PLT306	1–71	A
PLT306	1–72	C
PLT306	1–73	B
PLT307	1–2	C
PLT307	1–22	B
PLT307	1–23	C
PLT307	1–25	A
PLT307	1–26	A
PLT307	1–29	C
PLT307	1–30	C
PLT307	1–32	A
PLT307	1–33	B
PLT307	1–34	C
PLT307	1–35	C
PLT307	1–36	B
PLT307	1–37	B
PLT307	1–38	C
PLT307	5–39	B

FAA Learning Code	Gleim SU/ Q. No.	Gleim Answer
PLT307	5–40	A
PLT308	1–1	A
PLT308	1–4	B
PLT308	1–5	C
PLT308	1–6	A
PLT308	1–7	A
PLT308	1–8	A
PLT308	1–9	C
PLT308	1–10	B
PLT308	1–11	A
PLT308	1–12	A
PLT308	1–15	B
PLT308	1–18	A
PLT308	1–24	B
PLT308	1–28	A
PLT308	1–50	B
PLT308	1–51	C
PLT308	1–52	C
PLT308	1–53	A
PLT308	1–54	B
PLT308	1–56	C
PLT308	1–58	A
PLT308	1–59	B
PLT308	1–60	C
PLT308	1–61	A
PLT308	1–62	C
PLT308	1–63	B
PLT308	1–64	A
PLT308	1–65	B
PLT308	1–74	A
PLT308	1–75	B
PLT308	2–1	C
PLT308	2–2	A
PLT481	1–20	C
PLT481	1–66	B
PLT481	1–68	B
PLT481	1–78	A
PLT481	1–79	B
PLT481	3–58	C
PLT481	3–59	C
PLT481	3–61	B
PLT481	3–62	A

FAA Learning Code	Gleim SU/ Q. No.	Gleim Answer
PLT481	6–13	B
PLT481	6–42	C
PLT481	6–64	C
PLT482	1–44	C
PLT482	1–45	C
PLT482	4–56	C
PLT482	6–1	C
PLT482	6–2	C
PLT482	6–3	B
PLT482	6–4	C
PLT482	6–5	B
PLT482	6–6	A
PLT482	6–8	B
PLT482	6–10	C
PLT482	6–12	A
PLT482	6–17	C
PLT482	6–18	A
PLT482	6–20	B
PLT482	6–21	C
PLT482	6–22	B
PLT482	6–23	B
PLT482	6–24	A
PLT482	6–25	C
PLT482	6–26	A
PLT482	6–27	B
PLT482	6–28	A
PLT482	6–29	B
PLT482	6–30	A
PLT482	6–31	A
PLT482	6–32	B
PLT482	6–33	A
PLT482	6–34	B
PLT482	6–35	A
PLT482	6–36	C
PLT482	6–37	C
PLT482	6–38	B
PLT482	6–39	A
PLT482	6–40	C
PLT482	6–41	A
PLT482	6–43	C
PLT482	6–44	A
PLT482	6–45	B
PLT482	6–46	B
PLT482	6–47	B
PLT482	6–48	C
PLT482	6–49	A
PLT482	6–50	C
PLT482	6–51	B
PLT482	6–52	C
PLT482	6–53	A
PLT482	6–54	C
PLT482	6–55	A
PLT482	6–56	B
PLT482	6–57	C
PLT482	6–58	B
PLT482	6–61	A
PLT482	6–62	B
PLT482	6–63	B
PLT487	3–71	B
PLT487	4–22	C
PLT487	4–23	C
PLT487	4–24	C
PLT487	4–25	B
PLT487	4–26	C
PLT487	4–27	C
PLT487	4–28	B
PLT487	4–29	B
PLT487	4–30	B
PLT488	3–48	A
PLT488	4–1	A
PLT488	4–2	A
PLT488	4–3	B
PLT488	4–4	B
PLT488	4–5	B
PLT488	4–6	C
PLT488	4–7	C
PLT488	4–8	B
PLT488	4–9	A
PLT488	4–10	C
PLT488	4–11	A
PLT488	4–12	B
PLT488	4–13	B
PLT488	4–14	B
PLT488	4–15	A
PLT488	4–16	B
PLT488	4–17	A
PLT488	4–18	C
PLT488	4–19	B
PLT488	4–20	C
PLT488	4–21	C
PLT489	5–18	B
PLT489	5–19	B
PLT490	1–13	A
PLT490	1–14	A
PLT490	2–3	A
PLT490	2–4	C
PLT490	2–39	A
PLT490	2–40	B
PLT490	3–5	B
PLT490	3–6	B
PLT490	3–8	A
PLT490	3–9	A
PLT490	3–10	B
PLT490	3–11	B
PLT490	3–12	C
PLT490	3–13	A
PLT490	3–14	C
PLT490	3–15	B
PLT490	3–16	A
PLT490	3–60	A
PLT490	3–66	A
PLT490	4–53	B
PLT490	5–23	A
PLT491	4–31	B
PLT491	4–32	A
PLT491	4–33	A
PLT491	4–34	A
PLT491	4–35	A
PLT491	4–36	C
PLT491	4–38	C
PLT491	4–39	B
PLT491	4–43	B
PLT491	4–44	C
PLT491	4–45	B
PLT491	5–2	B
PLT491	5–3	C

FAA Learning Code	Gleim SU/ Q. No.	Gleim Answer
PLT491	5–4	C
PLT491	5–5	C
PLT491	5–7	B
PLT491	5–8	C
PLT491	5–9	C
PLT491	5–10	C
PLT491	5–11	B
PLT491	5–13	B
PLT491	5–14	C
PLT491	5–15	A
PLT491	5–16	A
PLT491	5–17	A
PLT491	5–20	A
PLT491	5–21	C
PLT491	5–27	A
PLT491	5–41	A
PLT491	5–42	C
PLT504	5–46	B
PLT504	5–49	A
PLT504	5–50	B
PLT504	6–9	A
PLT504	6–14	A
PLT504	6–16	C
PLT505	1–49	A
PLT505	4–40	A
PLT505	4–41	C
PLT505	4–42	C
PLT505	5–47	C
PLT505	5–48	B
PLT505	5–51	A

LESSON:

STUDENT: ______________________________ **DATE:** ______________

OBJECTIVE

CONTENT

SCHEDULE

EQUIPMENT

INSTRUCTOR'S ACTIONS

STUDENT'S ACTIONS

COMPLETION STANDARDS

INSTRUCTOR CERTIFICATION FORM
FUNDAMENTALS OF INSTRUCTING KNOWLEDGE TEST
FOR SPORT PILOT INSTRUCTORS

Name: ____

I certify that I have reviewed the above individual's preparation for the FAA Fundamentals of Instructing knowledge test [covering the topics specified in 14 CFR 61.407(a)(1) through (6)] using the *Fundamentals of Instructing FAA Knowledge Test Prep* book, software, and/or online course by Irvin N. Gleim and Garrett W. Gleim and find him/her competent to pass the knowledge test.

____________________	__________	____________________	__________	__________
Signed	Date	Name	CFI or CGI Number	Expiration Date N/A if CGI

GLEIM®

Aviation

ABBREVIATIONS AND ACRONYMS IN *FUNDAMENTALS OF INSTRUCTING FAA KNOWLEDGE TEST PREP*

14 CFR	Code of Federal Regulations
AC	Advisory Circular
ACS	Airman Certification Standards
AD	Airworthiness Directive
ADM	aeronautical decision making
AFSS	Automated Flight Service Station
AGL	above ground level
AIM	*Aeronautical Information Manual*
AIRMET	Airman's Meteorological Information
AME	aviation medical examiner
ANDS	accelerate north, decelerate south
AOE	airport of entry
ARTS	Automated Radar Terminal System
ASEL	airplane single-engine land
ATA	actual time of arrival
ATC	Air Traffic Control
ATIS	Automatic Terminal Information Service
AWOS	Automated Weather Observing System
CAL	computer-assisted learning
CDI	course deviation indicator
CDT	central daylight time
CFI	certificated flight instructor
CG	center of gravity
CH	compass heading
CT	control tower
CTAF	Common Traffic Advisory Frequency
DME	distance measuring equipment
DT	daylight time
DVFR	defense VFR
ELT	emergency locator transmitter
ETA	estimated time of arrival
ETD	estimated time of departure
FAA	Federal Aviation Administration
FAA-H-8083-9A	*Aviation Instructor's Handbook*
FAR	Federal Aviation Regulation
FBO	fixed-base operator
FCC	Federal Communications Commission
FD	winds and temperatures aloft forecast
FL	flight level
FSS	Flight Service Station
GPH	gallons per hour
Hg	mercury
HOTS	higher order thinking skills
HP	horsepower
IAS	indicated airspeed
ICAO	International Civil Aviation Organization
IFR	instrument flight rules
IMC	instrument meteorological conditions
IR	instrument route
ISA	International Standard Atmosphere
LLWAS	low-level wind-shear alert system
mb	millibar
MB	magnetic bearing
MC	magnetic course
MEF	maximum elevation figure
METAR	aviation routine weather report
MH	magnetic heading
MOA	Military Operations Area
MSL	mean sea level
MTR	military training route
MVFR	marginal VFR
NFCT	nonfederal control tower
NM	nautical mile
NPRM	Notice of Proposed Rulemaking
NTSB	National Transportation Safety Board
OAT	outside air temperature
OBS	omnibearing selector
PAPI	precision approach path indicator
PBL	problem-based learning
PCL	pilot-controlled lighting
PIC	pilot in command
PIREP	pilot weather report
POH	Pilot's Operating Handbook
PTS	Practical Test Standards
RB	relative bearing
SBT	scenario-based training
SFC	surface
SIGMET	Significant Meteorological Information
SM	statute mile
SRM	single-pilot resource management
STC	supplemental type certificate
SVFR	special VFR
TACAN	Tactical Air Navigation
TAF	terminal aerodrome forecast
TAS	true airspeed
TC	true course
TH	true heading
UHF	ultra high frequency
UTC	Coordinated Universal Time
V_A	maneuvering speed
VASI	visual approach slope indicator
V_{FE}	maximum flap extended speed
VFR	visual flight rules
VHF	very high frequency
VHF/DF	VHF direction finder
VIP	video integrated processor
V_{LE}	maximum landing gear extended speed
V_{NE}	never-exceed speed
V_{NO}	maximum structural cruising speed
VOR	VHF omnidirectional range
VORTAC	collocated VOR and TACAN
VOT	VOR test facility
VR	visual route
V_{S0}	stalling speed or the minimum steady flight speed in the landing configuration
V_{S1}	stalling speed or the minimum steady flight speed obtained in a specific configuration
V_Y	speed for best angle of climb
V_Y	speed for best rate of climb
WCA	wind correction angle
Z	Zulu or UTC time

AUTHORS' RECOMMENDATIONS

Gleim cooperates with and supports all aspects of the flight training industry, particularly organizations that focus on aviation recruitment and flight training. Below are some of the top organizations for anyone interested in aviation.

EXPERIMENTAL AIRCRAFT ASSOCIATION: YOUNG EAGLES PROGRAM

The Experimental Aircraft Association's (EAA) Young Eagles Program has provided free introductory flights to over 1 million young people ages 8 to 17. This program helps young people understand the important role aviation plays in our daily lives and provides insight into how an airplane flies, what it takes to become a pilot, and the high standards flying demands in terms of safety and quality.

NOTE: The Gleim *Learn to Fly* booklet (available for free at www.GleimAviation.com/learn-to-fly) is used as "ground school" training for Young Eagles programs. For more information about the Young Eagles Program, visit www.youngeagles.org or call 1-800-564-6322.

AIRCRAFT OWNERS AND PILOTS ASSOCIATION

The Aircraft Owners and Pilots Association (AOPA) hosts an informational web page on getting started in aviation for those still dreaming about flying, those who are ready to begin, and those who are already making the journey. Interested individuals can order a FREE subscription to Flight Training Magazine, which explains how amazing it is to be a pilot. Other resources are available, such as a flight school finder, a guide on what to expect throughout training, an explanation of pilot certification options, a FREE flight training newsletter, and much more. To learn more, visit www.aopa.org.

CIVIL AIR PATROL: CADET ORIENTATION FLIGHT PROGRAM

The Civil Air Patrol (CAP) Cadet Orientation Flight Program is designed to introduce CAP cadets to flying. The program is voluntary and primarily motivational, and it is designed to stimulate cadets' interest in and knowledge of aviation.

Each orientation flight is approximately 1 hour, follows a prescribed syllabus, and is usually in the local area of the airport. Except for takeoff, landing, and a few other portions of the flight, cadets are encouraged to handle the controls. For information about the CAP cadet program nearest you, visit www.gocivilairpatrol.com.

WOMEN IN AVIATION INTERNATIONAL

Women in Aviation International (WAI) is a nonprofit organization dedicated to the encouragement and advancement of women in all aviation career fields and interests. Its diverse membership includes astronauts, corporate pilots, maintenance technicians, air traffic controllers, business owners, educators and students, journalists, flight attendants, air show performers, airport managers, and many others.

WAI provides year-round resources to assist women in aviation and encourage young women to consider aviation as a career. WAI also offers educational outreach programs to educators, aviation industry members, and young people nationally and internationally. An annual Girls in Aviation Day was recently initiated for girls ages 8 to 17. Learn more at www.wai.org.

NINETY-NINES

The Ninety-Nines (99s) is an international organization of women pilots with thousands of members from over 40 countries. Its goal is to promote advancement of aviation through education, scholarships, and mutual support. The 99s have co-sponsored over 75% of FAA pilot safety programs in the U.S. and annually sponsor hundreds of educational programs, such as aerospace workshops for teachers, airport tours for school children, fear-of-flying clinics for airline passengers, and flight instructor revalidation seminars. Learn more at www.ninety-nines.org.

INDEX